ALBERT E. HARTUNG
GENERAL EDITOR

A Manual of the Writings in Middle English

1050-1500

ALBERT E. HARTUNG
GENERAL EDITOR

A Manual of the Writings in Middle English

1050-1500

*By Members of the Middle English Group of the
Modern Language Association
of America*

Based upon
A Manual of the Writings in Middle English 1050–1400
by John Edwin Wells, New Haven, 1916
and Supplements 1–9, 1919–1951

THE CONNECTICUT ACADEMY OF ARTS AND SCIENCES, NEW HAVEN, CONNECTICUT
MDCCCCLXXV

Library of Congress Cataloging in Publication Data

Main entry under title:

A Manual of the writings in Middle English, 1050–1500.

"Based upon A manual of the writings in Middle English 1050–1400, by John Edwin Wells, New Haven, 1916, and supplements 1–9, 1919–1951."
Includes bibliographies.
CONTENTS: v. 1 Romances, by M. J. Donovan, and others.—v. 2 The Pearl poet, by M. P. Hamilton. Wyclyf and his followers, by E. W. Talbert and S. H. Thomson. Translations and paraphrases of the Bible, and commentaries, by L. Muir. Saints' legends by C. D'Evelyn and F. A. Foster. Instruction for religious, by C. D'Evelyn. v. 3. Dialogues, Debates, and Catechisms, by F. L. Utley. Thomas Hoccleve, by W. Matthews. Malory and Caxton, by R. H. Wilson. v. 4. Middle Scots Writers by Florence H. Ridley. The Chaucerian Apocrypha by Rossell Hope Robbins. [etc.]
    1. English literature—Middle English (1100–1500)—History and criticism. 2. English literature—Middle English (1100–1500)—Bibliography. I. Severs, Jonathan Burke, ed. II. Wells, John Edwin, 1875–1913. A manual of the writings in Middle English, 1050–1400. III. Hartung, Albert E., 1923–   ed. IV. Modern Language Association of America. Middle English Group.
PR255.M3   016.82′09′001   67–7687
ISBN 0–208–01459–4 (v. 5)

© 1975 by The Connecticut Academy of Arts and Sciences
Published for The Connecticut Academy of Arts and Sciences by Archon Books / The Shoe String Press, Inc., Hamden, Connecticut 06514

Printed in the United States of America

Volume 5

XII. DRAMATIC PIECES

by

Anna J. Mill, Sheila Lindenbaum,
and Francis Lee Utley and Barry Ward

XIII. POEMS DEALING WITH CONTEMPORARY CONDITIONS

by

Rossell Hope Robbins

PREFACE

This manual of Middle English literature is a collaborative project of the Middle English Group of the Modern Language Association of America. Printed in parts as the various chapters of the work are completed, the *Manual* already comprises four volumes: Volume 1 on the Romances; Volume 2 on the *Pearl* Poet, Wyclyf and His Followers, Translations and Paraphrases of the Bible, Saints' Legends, and Instructions for Religious; Volume 3 on Dialogues, Debates, and Catechisms, Thomas Hoccleve, and Malory and Caxton; Volume 4 on Middle Scots Writers and The Chaucerian Apocrypha. The present Volume 5 includes chapters on Dramatic Pieces and Poems Dealing with Contemporary Conditions. Chapter XII, Dramatic Pieces, which has had a complex editorial history, is intended to be complete for all serious studies to 1970 for the section on the Miracle Plays and Mysteries, to 1973 for the section on the Moralities, and to Spring 1972 for the section on Folk Drama. Chapter XIII, Poems Dealing with Contemporary Conditions, is intended to be complete to 1973. Occasional later studies are included to the time of going to press (January 30, 1975). A full account of the principles followed by the editors of the work will be found in the Preface to Volume 1.

On behalf of the Middle English Group and on his own behalf, the General Editor is deeply grateful to the Connecticut Academy of Arts and Sciences for continuing to undertake the publication of this revised *Manual*, as it had undertaken publication of the original. With the completion of the editorial work on this fifth volume, he wishes to express appreciation for the considerable and capable help of his editorial assistant, Mrs. Marilyn C. Dunlap, who has now assisted in the editing of the last three volumes of the *Manual*. Her indispensable contribution to the project has been made possible by financial support from the National Endowment for the Humanities.

The General Editor wishes also to note with regret the death of Francis Lee Utley. Professor Utley had been with the project since its beginning and served first as a member and later as chairman of the *Manual's* editorial and advisory committee. He contributed a chapter to the third volume and coedited a section in the present volume. His vast knowledge of scholarship and scholars, and the friendly cooperation with which he made this knowledge available in the affairs of the *Manual* must be numbered among the most cherished rewards of the present writer's editorial activities. With his passing the *Manual,* in common with the whole scholarly community, has suffered a severe loss.

Albert E. Hartung
General Editor

CONTENTS

XII. DRAMATIC PIECES

by

*Anna J. Mill, Sheila Lindenbaum,
and Francis Lee Utley and Barry Ward*

1. THE MIRACLE PLAYS AND MYSTERIES

by

Anna J. Mill

The chronology of the dramatic pieces presents its own peculiar problems. From municipal and other sources, we know that the surviving manuscripts of certain plays are considerably later than the earliest recorded performances of those plays. It is the aim of this chapter to include, regardless of date, all the extant pieces wholly, or partially, in the English vernacular that definitely belong to the medieval tradition. *Caiphas* and the *Shrewsbury Fragments* show traces of church presentation and use Latin along with the vernacular not only in the rubrics but in the body of the text. The later Bodley *Burial and Resurrection*, using Latin sparingly, is clearly in the same liturgical tradition. In the *Rickinghall Fragment* and more recently discovered *Cambridge Fragment*, French alternates with English. *The Interludium de Clerico et Puella* is a unique specimen of early secular drama. Of miracle plays proper, the only survivals are the *Croxton Sacrament* and, possibly, *Dux Moraud*; of saints' plays, the Digby *Conversion of St. Paul* and the composite *Mary Magdalene*. The great bulk of early English religious drama is contained in the cycles of Chester, York, Wakefield and in the *Ludus Coventriae*; in parts of cycles from Coventry, Newcastle, Norwich; or in scriptural plays like the Brome and Dublin *Abraham and Isaac*, which have either broken away from or never belonged to any cycle. The *Resurrection of Our Lord* and *Stonyhurst Pageants* testify to a late continuing mystery tradition. To complete the chapter, the earlier group of moralities has been included; that is, the morality has been carried to the point where the genre is fully established but has not yet adopted characteristic Renaissance features.

For background material the reader is referred to the introductory sections, necessarily selective, of the Bibliography. (See under GENERAL TREATMENTS, LITURGICAL DRAMA, ANGLO-NORMAN TRANSITION PLAYS, ENGLISH VERNACULAR PLAYS, ENGLISH MIRACLE PLAYS, and ENGLISH MYSTERIES.) The cardinal importance of church ritual in this connection has long been a commonplace of scholarly comment. Within the framework of the liturgy, the argument runs, were created two main groups of liturgical plays, those centering in the *Visitatio*, deriving ultimately from the Easter *Quem quaeritis in sepulchro* trope (represented in the British Isles by Winchester, Barking and Dublin texts) and those centering in the Nativity, deriving mainly from the Christmas *Officium stellae*. Part of a pseudo-Augustinian sermon, convicting the Jews of error through the utterances of their own prophets and used as a *lectio* in the matins of the Christmas season, was shown by Sepet to be the source of the liturgical play of the *Prophetae*, which links the Old and New Testament stories. Sepet's further suggestion, however, of the genesis of the Old Testament cyclical plays in the expansion of the *Processus prophetarum* proved more controversial and eventually was to lead to Craig's alternative hypothesis of origin in additions to the Passion play from *lectiones* and accompanying ritual of the days after Epiphany. Cargill's plea for replacing ecclesiastics by professional entertainers as the real creators of the mysteries made little impact. The publication in 1933 of Young's great corpus of church drama gave formidable support, despite lacunae in the evidence, to the orthodox theory of liturgical origins. And if Stumpfl and his disciples, in their postulation of Germanic cult rites as the primary sources of Christian drama, have gone far beyond Chambers's concession to non-Christian elements, they have not seriously undermined the position of the Latin liturgy as the main, if not exclusive, agent in the moulding of the English vernacular mystery plays.

No clear chronology can be established for any migration of the liturgical plays from the church interior to some exterior locale, whether precincts or street or playfield, for the substitution of the vernacular for the Latin language, the incorporation of lay actors, or for the transfer of the administration of the performance, if never of the ultimate control, to secular authorities. But there has been general acceptance of the fact that the confirmation of the festival of Corpus Christi by Pope Clement in 1311 led to the compilation of great cosmic cycles dealing with the implicit theme of that day, the Fall and Redemption of Man. Though the earliest English records give 1376 (not 1378, as constantly stated) for the York and 1377 for the (lost) Beverley plays, a common assumption has been that the English cycles were initiated within some twenty years of the papal decree. Salter's rebuttal (see under *Chester Plays* [9] below), which would delay such inception until his period of "firm references" in the last quarter of the fourteenth century, cannot be refuted but may well give too little weight both to the paucity of municipal and guild documents earlier in that century and to the actual nature and wording of random allusions, with their implications of established craft plays under municipal aegis. Moreover, by 1390, when 39 crafts are enjoined to have ready their pageants and pageant cars ("suos ludos et pagentes"), the Beverley Corpus Christi play is professedly "antiqua consuetudo"; and by 1394 the York stations along the pageant route are determined by "locis antiquitus assignatis."

There was no uniform pattern for the staging of the Corpus Christi cycle. The text of the *Ludus Coventriae* has been widely accepted as that of a stationary play with multiple setting, though with possible traces of an older processional play envisaged by the Proclamation. Relevant Wakefield town records are scanty and late, but again on textual grounds, if at times on a too literal interpretation of the text, there has been considerable pressure for the relegation of the Towneley (Wakefield) plays also to the stationary category. On the other hand, the ("true") Coventry, the (lost) Beverley, and the Chester cycles—for all of these sufficient municipal records are extant, and for Chester, in addition, the perhaps too readily discounted Rogers evidence—would seem to have been performed processionally. Because, however, of its length combined with the number of stations en route and the fact that it was not spread, as at Chester, possibly at Wakefield, over several days, the York cycle has presented scholars with undoubted problems. On the basis of elaborately constructed timetables, Nelson has insisted that the traditional conception of processional representation of the complete cycle in a single day must be ruled out. His critics, on the other hand, would point out that he ignores important evidence in the very full York records and would hold out for some form of essentially processional production of the plays even if this should not conform to his (Nelson's) rigid definition of a "true"-processional set-up.

As to the relationship of the Corpus Christi plays generally with the Corpus Christi religious processions, there has been much speculation. The frequent references in records to participation of the craft guilds with their "pageants" are inconclusive by themselves; the term was used indifferently for the moveable stages carrying dumbshows, as in continental practice, and for the spoken plays. What can be stated with some degree of certainty is that in the heyday of the cycles, when records are relatively abundant, there is no clear evidence for the incorporation of the Corpus Christi plays in the ecclesiastical procession, and in one or two cases the reverse is implied. In 1426 the Franciscan friar William Melton was able to induce the Corporation and commons to vote in favour of transferring the York plays to the previous day, so as to avoid interference with the religious ceremony. A later record testifies to the transference of the procession to the following day and the reestablishment of the plays on the day of the festival, if, indeed, they had ever been moved from that day. From an ordinance of the Saddlers' Company at Newcastle, 1552–53, we know that the plays followed immediately *after* the Corpus Christi procession. In Chester, at least by 1521, the cycle was spread over three days at Whitsuntide, though the name Corpus Christi Plays survives to confuse the issue.

As some guilds expanded and others decayed, the burden of production had to be equalized and new assignments made. To meet changing needs and tastes, plays or portions of plays were written, revised, borrowed, recopied, discarded. Revisions in the play registers have been a constant challenge to scholarship. Through close textual and bibliographical studies an older generation of scholars sought to identify different layers of composition, to reconcile the preliminary banns and official lists of the pageants with the extant texts, to establish relationships among the cycles or among the several manuscripts, as in Chester, of one cycle. It was as an attempt to find a scientific method for determining such manuscript relationships that Greg constructed his *Calculus of Variants.*

During the last three decades in particular, there has been a marked reaction against the Chambers-Young-Greg hegemony; nor has Craig always escaped unscathed. In this field, as elsewhere, a newer generation of scholars has tended to view with suspicion the historical teleological approach of Cargill's "outmoded evolutionists." There has been a disposition to accept the plays as they stand, regardless of "layers," to be evaluated independently and in relation to their milieu rather than as links in a chain of organic growth from simple to complex. Individual plays, groups of plays, whole cycles have been subjected to scrutiny from the angles of thematic patterns, structural unity, doctrinal exegesis and dramatic effectiveness. Ritualists, folklorists, theologians, metaphysicians, typologists and musicologists have swelled the ranks of the more traditional literary critics. A proportion of their output may have been too narrowly selective, too thesis-ridden, too much divorced from sound textual disciplines, too cavalier, on occasion, in their dismissal of past scholarship to be finally convincing. But the mere focusing of critical attention on the plays themselves, their audiences and their staging, has in general been regarded as salutary and often illuminating. Nor has solid textual work been at a standstill. Monographs stemming from the re-examination of manuscripts have yielded important results. Davis's recent edition of the *Non-Cycle Plays and Fragments,* based on fresh collations with the original manuscripts and involving detailed linguistic study of the texts, is specially welcome. New editions, long overdue, of the Chester, York and Towneley Cycles, and, though less urgently needed, of the *Ludus Coventriae*, as also of the *Bodley Burial and Resurrection* and the *Digby Plays*, are in the course of preparation.

CAIPHAS [1]. MS Sloane 2478, ff. 43ª–44ᵇ. Early fourteenth century. Latin and English (Southwest). 28 six-line tail-rime stanzas, of which one in Latin.

Designated by its first editor "Ceremonial Verses for Palm-Sunday," this piece is the second item in a manuscript comprising Latin saints' lives, extracts from the church fathers and other ecclesiastical items, and written in the same hand. The last stanza, pronounced nearly illegible by Wright, has since been brought out by reagents. The single character, Caiphas, not only sings his prophecy but, now in liturgical Latin prose, now, for the laity, in more relaxed vernacular verse, expounds the significance of the festival and exhorts his hearers to shrive themselves and make amends. Brown sees evidence in the invocation of the Dean ("O decane reuerende") for association with a secular church; on the basis of the dialect of the vernacular portions, narrows the choice down to Salisbury and Wells; and, finally, on the basis of liturgical usage, favours Wells. Young finds no direct connection with the *Ordo prophetarum*.

SHREWSBURY FRAGMENTS [2]. MS Shrewsbury School Mus.iii.42, ff. 38ª–42ᵇ. Early fifteenth century. 175 lines. Latin-English (Northwest Midland).

The text consists in the main of a single actor's part with cues in each of three plays: the first, clearly the *Officium pastorum* but lacking heading and possibly some of the initial lines; the second headed "Hic incipit Officium Resurreccionis in die Pasche" and containing three Latin couplets almost identical with three in the Dublin dramatic office for Easter; and the third headed "Feria ijª in ebdomada Pasche Discipuli insimul cantent." The rôles are those of the third shepherd in a *Pastores*; of the third Mary in a *Quem quaeritis*; and, probably, of Cleophas in a *Peregrini*. The speeches are mainly in the vernacular, Latin being, for the most part, reserved for headings and stage directions and for parts to be said or sung by more than one actor. Music is provided for some of the Latin passages. The final Latin couplet may have led into the scene of the Incredulity of Thomas, occasionally included in the *Peregrini*.

Skeat's original suggestion that the fragments might be part of the lost Beverley cycle is now out of favour. The fact that a processional for the commemoration of St. Chad, in the same hand as the Latin portion of the *Fragments*, is found elsewhere in the manuscript miscellany would seem to connect the plays with one of the many churches dedicated to that saint. Litchfield, the centre of the cult, can produce evidence in her cathedral statutes, as revised in the thirteenth or fourteenth century, for the provision of a *Pastores*, a *Resurrectio* and a *Peregrini* at the appropriate seasons, but, on the basis of the text as preserved, may be unacceptable dialectically. Skeat's theory of a close textual link with the York cycle has been reinforced by later scholarship. The final stanza of the *Pastores*, in particular, is nearly identical with that of the corresponding York Play no. 15, lines 120–29, though representing there, as elsewhere, an earlier stage than that surviving in the York Register. Davis finds no corresponding similarities between the second and third Shrewsbury fragments and the corresponding York plays but has no doubt that the *Pastores* and York Play no. 15 derive from a common original.

BODLEY BURIAL AND RESURRECTION [3]. MS Bodleian 3692 (e Museo 160), ff. 140ᵃ–172ᵃ. Mid-fifteenth century. 864 lines (Burial), 767 lines (Resurrection). Northern with Midland forms. Irregular stanzas, with ababbcbc sequence for the Virgin's Lament. Its inclusion in the Furnivall edition of the *Digby Plays* in the belief that it had originally formed part of MS Digby 133, see item [19], has long been suspect. Evidence based on a recent close examination of both manuscripts by Baker and Murphy indicates that MS e Museo 160 was from the beginning a distinct separate book.

The piece is headed, "The prologe of this treyte or meditatione off the buryalle of Criste & mowrnynge therat" and begins with an appeal to the Christian soul to "Rede this treyte." But on the back of the first leaf (folio 140ᵇ) at the foot in the mutilated margin a change of purpose is indicated: "This is a play to be playede on part on gudfriday after-none & þe other part opon Esterday after the resurrectione, In the morowe, but at [the] begynnynge ar certene lynes which [must] not be saide if it be plaiede which . . . ." Many narrative tags such as "saide mawdleyne," "The secund Mary began to saye," "Than saide Josephe right peteoslee" are crossed out, and, after line 419, disappear completely, each speech being set off only by the speaker's name. At the foot of folio 171ᵇ (after "Now is Ioy . . . plentee," line 1624 in Furnivall) is "wretten by me," but the page is torn and any name is lost.

The Good Friday section includes the lament of the three Marys with Joseph of Arimathea; the Deposition, with Nicodemus added to the group; the lament of the Virgin Mary, with John offering consolation; the Burial. It is an extended *planctus* with little action and has close affinity with the *planctus* of the *Cursor Mundi* (lines 23945–24658). The Easter scene includes an amplified *Quem quaeritis*; a lamentation of the remorseful Peter, with Andrew and John offering consolation; a *Hortulanus*; a second appearance of Christ to the three Marys and a singing of *Victimae paschali* with participation by the three Apostles in the *Dic nobis*; the announcement of the Resurrection; the visit of the Apostles to the sepulchre, and the singing of the *Scimus Christum*.

Town records indicate the performance of Resurrection plays independently of the regular cycles and perhaps of the Passion itself. Our text has obvious affinities with liturgical sources. It is deeply reverent in tone, highly charged with emotion, and makes no concession to humour or realism. Recently it has been claimed as the primary source for Grimald's *Christus Redivivus*.

CAMBRIDGE FRAGMENT [4]. MS Cambridge University Mm.1.18, f. 62ᵃ (formerly 58ᵃ). 1275–1300. 44 lines, octosyllabic riming couplets. French-English (Southwest and North Midlands).

Preserved on a fly-leaf of a miscellany of Latin tracts, this piece has 22 lines in French, followed by the same number in the English vernacular, in which the substance of a proclamation is repeated. The audience is warned to sit firm so that men, possibly the actors, may pass freely among them, and not to talk too loud, for, by Mahoun, those who "lette hure game" will be subject to dire penalties decreed by the emperor. From the mode of address to the audience, Robbins, the first editor, accepted the dramatic nature of the lines and cited evidence for the use of "game" in this sense, thus presenting the earliest known scrap of English vernacular drama in England. Salter has questioned the genre, has roundly declared that it is a French, not an English, document (but see *Rickinghall Fragment* [5] below) and is sceptical in any case as to the probability of an English mystery before 1300. Davis, however, sees no reason to challenge Robbins's finding.

RICKINGHALL (BURY ST. EDMUNDS) FRAGMENT [5]. MS British Museum Roll 63481B. Early fourteenth century. 24 lines, six-line tail-rime stanzas. French-English (East Midland).

The piece is preserved on a scrap of vellum (with a note of manorial dues on the back) found attached to a Rickinghall Manor court roll which was at one time in the possession of the Abbey of Bury St. Edmunds and was bought at the Redgrave Hall sale in 1921 by the British Museum. The heading is a pious invocation in Latin followed by an irrelevant hexameter. Then follows the twelve-line speech in French of a king who would summon his lieges to hear a proclamation, the gist being repeated in nine lines of English. A stage direction in the margin, "Tunc dicet nuncio," introduces three more lines of French in which the king briefs his messenger; after which the fragment breaks off. Remarking that the first English stanza was defective, lacking three lines corresponding to the opening lines of the French version, Greg suggested that the scribe may have discovered his omission and begun afresh. The discarded folio would then become "scrivener's waste" until utilized for the 1370 manor roll—an explanation which might account for certain puzzling features of the scrap of vellum.

Like the preceding *Cambridge Fragment*, this piece is of much interest linguistically and raises the question as to whether the two languages were alternatives for different performances, or, as seems more likely, were used in turn at the same performance to meet the needs of a mixed audience. Gilson's theory, on the analogy of the Octavian and the Sybil episode introduced by Nuntius in the Chester cycle, was that the speaker is Octavian, about to announce his decree for all the world to be taxed. Davis suggests "conceivably" Herod. Studer's query, based on certain similarities with the *Mystère d'Adam*, as to whether the fragment might belong to a later adaptation of that play remains a query.

INTERLUDIUM DE CLERICO ET PUELLA [6]. MS British Museum Additional 23986, vellum roll, verso. Early fourteenth century. 84 lines, couplets, Northeast Midland.

This piece consisting wholly of dialogue, with speakers indicated in the margin, is clearly the beginning of an early specimen of secular dramatic writing. Two scenes only remain: the first, where the clerk unsuccessfully tries to seduce the maiden; the second, where he tries to enlist the help of a bawd, who is still protesting her godliness when the fragment breaks off. The gaps, however, can be filled in from the English *Dame Siriz*, a representative of the Weeping Bitch Tale (see under Tales). The two works have verbal parallels, even identical lines; the rôles are similar, the curious clerk, the procuress (Mome Elwis or Dame Siriz) and the victim, though in the interlude Malkyn is, uniquely, a maiden, and in the tale Margeri is a married woman. Heuser's theory, in general currency, that neither piece derives from the other but from a common source, a thirteenth century interlude preserved through recollection, has been seriously challenged by Schröder. For him the author of the *Interludium* was inspired to rework the lively dialogue of the composite English version of the tale in more definitely dramatic form, though the lack of stage directions may point to reading aloud or declamation rather than representation. *De Clerico et Puella* (see VII [54]), sometimes confused with the *Interludium*, is a simple debate, involving capitulation without intervention of a third party.

DURHAM PROLOGUE [7]. Discovered on the dorse of a composite volume, MS Archid Dunelm 60 (Durham Dean and Chapter). Probably early fifteenth-century copy of somewhat earlier piece. 36 lines of six-line stanzas, riming aaabab. Northeast.

This fragment, first published in 1959 by Cooling and now re-edited by Davis, is probably in a monastic hand. The heading "W Willm," apparently in the same hand, may have been a pen trial, as may also the "Fuit homo" written vertically downwards to the right of the fourth stanza (not noticed by the first editor). From internal evidence there seems to be no doubt that this is the prologue to a play, apparently a unique English miracle play drawn from the legend of St. Theophilus. The speaker, after calling on the audience for peace, gives the gist of the action. A virtuous knight, reduced to poverty, falls into the power of the devil and is rescued miraculously by the Virgin Mary.

DUX MORAUD [8]. MS Bodleian 30519 (Eng poet f.2.R). 1425–50? 268 lines. East Anglian.

This fragment, written on a strip of parchment attached to a roll of earlier date, consists not of a sequence of single pieces, as was at one time believed, but of a single player's part (incomplete). An audience is implied in the opening lines. Strokes and gaps in the manuscript indicate the omission of other rôles. The name Dux Moraud appears both as heading and in the text ("Duk Moraud I hot be name").

The theme is that of an incestuous relationship between father and daughter leading to the murder of the wife and mother, of the child of the unnatural union, and, finally, of the repentant father himself at the hands of his mistress. As the text stands, the interest centers in the father's sin and redemption. But widespread analogues of the tale of the incestuous daughter lend support to the theory that the piece originally concluded with the miraculous conversion of the daughter.

On both internal and external grounds, Heuser, the original editor, was convinced that his text was no part of either a mystery play or a morality, but rather of a miracle play of the order of the French Miracles of the Virgin. As his view is fully endorsed by Hieatt's recent intensive study of the fragment and its background, there would seem to be no reason for following Davis in his new edition and classing it as a morality.

CHESTER PLAYS [9]. The full cycle is preserved in five manuscripts of late date, all probably postdating the last performance of the plays.

These manuscripts with their customary designations are: D (Huntington HM 2), 1591, imperfect at beginning, Banns and first play supplied from R; W (British Museum Additional 10305), 1592; R, sometimes cited as h or K (Harley 2013), 1600; B (Bodleian 175), 1604; H (Harley 2124), 1607. (See Bibliography. CHESTER PLAYS, MSS, nos. 12, 7, 4, 1, 5.) These may have been ultimately derived from a late fifteenth-century official register. They fall into two groups, H and DWRB. H and W lack the (late) Banns of the plays, an additional copy of which is, however, found in MS Harley 1944, an antiquarian miscellany dated 1609(?) with tag end verses, possibly spurious, not in any other manuscript. An earlier set of Banns, which may date in its original form from 1467, was entered in MS Harley 2150 in 1540. There are also two additional manuscripts of single plays and a fragment of a third. The 41-line Manchester fragment of the Resurrection is written, probably in a late sixteenth-century hand, on the upper portion of a leaf of vellum which originally formed part of a bookbinding, perhaps of MS Harley 1950. The National Library of Wales, Peniarth 399, with a separate text of *Antichrist* dated about 1500 (hence the oldest manuscript of a Chester play) is folded down the middle and may have been a prompt copy. The play of the Trial and Flagellation in the Chester Coopers' Enrolment Book is in the hand of George Bellin, the scribe of WR.

In his edition of *Antichrist*, Greg adopted the procedure of his own *Calculus of Variants* to determine the relationship of the manuscripts of the Antichrist play, with the idea that this relationship might be provisionally assumed to hold throughout the cycle. When this assumption was challenged by Salter on the basis of his study of the variants in the Coopers' Play, Greg conceded the need for individual treatment of certain plays but maintained that no evidence had by then been produced which seriously affected his tentative *stemma* for the cycle.

The extant cycle as given in H, the youngest manuscript but that chosen by the EETS editor as preserving some original traces, has 24 plays. The subjects are:

1. Tanners: Fall of Lucifer; 2. Drapers: Creation and Fall; 3. Waterleaders & Drawers of Dee: Noah's Flood; 4. Barbers: Abraham and Isaac; 5. Cappers: Balaam and Balaak; 6. Wrights: Christ's Nativity; 7. Painters & Glasiers: Adoration of Shepherds; 8. Vint-

ners: Adoration of Magi; 9. Mercers: Gifts of Magi; 10. Goldsmiths: Slaughter of Innocents; 11. Smiths: Purification; 12. Butchers: Christ's Temptation; 13. Glovers: Healing
of Blind Man, Raising of Lazarus; 14. Corvisers: Visit to House of Simon the Leper;
15. Bakers: Last Supper and Betrayal; 16. Bowers, Fletchers & Ironmongers: Christ's
Passion; 17. Cooks & Innkeepers: Descent into Hell; 18. Skinners: Resurrection; 19.
[Saddlers]: Journey to Emmaus; 20. Tailors: Christ's Ascension; 21. Fishmongers: Pentecost; 22. Shearmen: Prophets and Antichrist; 23. Dyers: Coming of Antichrist; 24. Web-
sters: Doomsday.

Here, as in the Late Banns, the Trial and Flagellation are combined, a
fact which can no longer be used in support of H's representing an older
tradition than DWRB, where they are separate. From a new document,
Salter has established those plays as distinct at least as early as the earliest known reference to the cycle, 1422, and thinks they may have remained so as late as 1574. The Assumption, listed in the Early Banns as
presented by the "wurshipfful wyffis of this towne," and mentioned also
in a document of about 1500, is not included in any of the play manuscripts. It is known to have been performed independently on occasion
and probably had only a loose and sporadic connection with the cycle.

The "tradition" stems from a proclamation of Newhall, common clerk
of Chester, written in 1532. As cited by Morris, the plays are said to be
"devised and made" by Henry Francis, monk of St. Werburgh (who obtained an indulgence from Pope Clement for people resorting peacefully
and devoutly to the plays) and "devised" by John Arneway, then mayor.
The preservation of the obscure name of Francis in an official proclamation was not lightly dismissed by Chambers; but he could not ignore
either Arneway, a name constant in the tradition, or the gap between
Arneway's mayoralty (1268–77) and the documented *floruit* of Henry
Francis a century later. During 1327–29, however, one Richard Erneis or
Herneys was mayor and the name of Erneis might well have been confused with that of the more famous Arneway. This would be a suitable
date not only for the inception of the cycle but for the persistent later
tradition linking Randulf Higden, author of the *Polychronicon*, with
that inception. With support from an early seventeenth-century authority, Francis was relegated to the single rôle of obtaining the pardon.

This Chambers version of the tradition, with occasional dissent, has
been diffused through more than 50 years of commentary. Salter's recent

frontal attack is based on an independent examination of the manuscript sources. He has exposed the garbled nature of the Morris text of New-hall's proclamation and has probed the growth of the "legend," dismissing out of hand the Chambers Erneis-Arneway solution. His reinstatement of the monk Francis (whom, however, he cites incorrectly as abbot, and indifferently as Abbot of the Benedictine Abbey of St. Werburgh's and Carmelite monk) would, of chronological necessity, invalidate any argument for the formation of the cycle before the late fourteenth century; a date which he feels is in any case more consonant with the earliest "firm references" to such cycles as York and Beverley. (But see introductory comment on chronology above.)

A stationary play of more primitive character may have preceded the establishment of a processional cycle. But at least by 1422 the play is apportioned among the craft guilds, and, some seven years later, a city treasurer's account itemizes a rental of 4d. for ground for the Fish-mongers' pageant house; after which, references to guild participation accumulate. The route was from the Abbey gates to the Roodee with stops at intermediate stations, the maximum recorded number of pageants, in the Early Banns, rising to twenty-six. The plays were spread over three days at Whitsuntide, and, though the term "Whitsun plays" has not been traced before 1521, the transference from Corpus Christi day may have been earlier. Surviving accounts of the Smiths (1547–74) and Coopers (1570–1616) record heavy expenditure on players, play gear and pageant cars; but the oft-cited description of the cars from Archdeacon Rogers's Breviary must be used with caution. The latest date for the cycle's performance is probably 1575. Evidence for a final performance in 1600 in the mayoralty of Henry Hardware is tenuous, though by 1601, under a less puritanical mayor, a truncated revival of the plays may have been contemplated; in which case the lines added, probably by David Rogers, son of the Archdeacon, to the Harley 1944 version of the Banns, indicating an indoor performance, may conceivably have some authority.

Certain *prima facie* resemblances of the cycle to the French mysteries have intrigued scholars, whose positions have ranged from frank scepticism as to Chester's indebtedness, through acceptance of a hypothetical common (Latin) source, to endorsement of deliberate use of French originals; this last alternative falling in with the tradition of Higden's having "englished" the plays. Ungemach (who included also in his study of sources Petrus Comestor's *Historia scholastica* and the *Cursor Mundi*) compared corresponding portions of the Chester cycle with the *Viel Testament* and Greban's *Mystère de la Passion,* and his awareness of dealing mainly with late redactions did not prevent his concluding in favour of Chester's direct borrowings. Baugh accepts much of the commonly cited evidence of French elements with considerable reservation and finds the strongest argument for French influence in apparent similarities in plan and structure. Foster's advocacy of the *Stanzaic Life of Christ* as a major vernacular source for the New Testament plays (which led to her pushing forward the date of the cycle's origin, independently of Salter) was not acceptable to Wilson, for whom the *Life* was used as later embellishment of pre-existent plays rather than source, except possibly in the case of the Harrowing of Hell.

The versification of the Chester cycle is more homogeneous than that of the other cycles, a fact which has suggested the possibility (not accepted by Chambers) of extensive rewriting at some stage. The predominating *rime couée* eight-line stanzas (aaa⁴b³ccc⁴b³, aaa⁴b³aaa⁴b³, with variants) which gives way at times to revisions and borrowings in couplets, quatrains, and other stanzaic patterns, is a lyrical rather than dramatic form of versification, suggesting liturgical influence. In general, the language is bare and the scenes follow the scriptures with little attempt at elaboration or probing of motives. Yet the very simplicity can be strangely moving. Ugly naturalism characterizes the speeches of the women and soldiers in the Slaughter of the Innocents, but the Passion scenes are on the whole less violent than those of York and Towneley. Though not so fully developed as in other cycles, the comic element has invaded such plays as Noah's Flood with the recalcitrance of Vxor Noe, muted at first but culminating in the boxing (*alapam*) of Noah's ears, and the Shepherds' Play with the grumblings of henpecked Tud, the wrestling match with Trowle the Boy, and the efforts of the rustics to recapture the *Gloria in excelsis* of the angelic choir. There are realistic details of building materials for the Ark, of food for the shepherds and herbal cures for the sheep.

For the episode of Christ and the Doctors, see below under *York Plays* [10].

YORK PLAYS [10]. MS British Museum Additional 35290. Fifteenth century. Northern, modified by East Midland. Many different stanza forms.

In this official register of the York Corporation were entered the texts of the originals belonging to the individual craft guilds. The date given by its first editor, Lucy Toulmin Smith, as 1430–40, roughly a century later than her conjectural date for the cycle's formation, was not accepted either by Greg or, latterly, by Chambers, both of whom would place it as late as about 1475. The earliest actual record of the Register, given by Smith as 1554, can now be pushed back considerably, and her statement that at one stage it was in the care of the priory of Holy Trinity may be questioned. A recently published list of leases of scaffolds for the Corpus Christi play in 1538 shows that no rent is paid for the first place at "Trenytie yaitis" where the common clerk "kepys the Registre" (that is, presumably, checks on the order and accuracy of the plays as presented)— an entry repeated almost verbatim in 1542. In 1568, when the Corporation is endeavouring to placate the puritanical Dean Hutton by inspection and revision of the cycle, and again, in 1579, the Register seems to have been passed backwards and forwards between the civic and ecclesiastical authorities. No answer is on record in the city archives to the commons who did "earnestly request" in 1580 that Corpus Christi play might be played this year; and evidence cited from the Bakers' Book for a 1580 (or later) performance probably rests on a misplaced account. The next links in the history of the Register are provided by a note on a fly-leaf, "H. Fairfax's Book, 1695" and a record of its presentation by Henry Fairfax to Ralph Thoresby. At the Thoresby sale it was bought by Horace Walpole, whose bookplate it bears. Through intermediate owners it came into the possession of Lord Ashburnham, from whose library it was acquired in 1899 by the British Museum.

The first two plays of the cycle, together with a second copy of the third, are written apparently in a somewhat later hand on a quire inserted at the beginning of the Register. The scribe leaves four blank pages after Play 22 for the Vintners' Marriage at Cana, of which only two lines are given, and after Play 23 for the Ironmongers' Visit to the House of Simon the Leper. The writing of the Fullers' Adam and Eve "never before registred" is recorded in the chamberlain's account for 1558, and two other pieces in the same hand are thought to have been added to the Register at that time: the Brewbarret addition to the Glovers' Cain and Abel and the Hatmakers', Masons' and Labourers' Purification. This last may conceivably have eluded official inspection (as it did originally its first editor), being badly misplaced in the Register; hence its inclusion in the directive to John Clerk in 1567 to enter certain plays "not enregistered." At the end, in still another later hand, is a fragment of a new play for the Innholders. Emendations and annotations throughout testify not only to normal revisions and reassignments but to rewriting of matter to meet the demands of external censorship.

The Sykes manuscript, now in the possession of the York Philosophical Society, consists of four leaves on which is written in a hand of about the second quarter of the sixteenth century the Scriveners' Play of the Incredulity of Thomas, with one line and several important words wanting in the text in the Register. The fact that this manuscript has a cover with a flap and has been folded lengthwise down the middle has suggested its use as a prompt book.

In the York civic records are two lists of the Corpus Christi pageants and the guilds responsible for their production. The first, dated 1415 and compiled by the common clerk, Roger Burton, lists 51 plays with a Latin summary of each. The second, tentatively dated a few years later and customarily ascribed to Burton (an ascription undermined by Frampton), lists 57 plays with the bare titles. The Register itself contains only 48 plays, untitled save for three Latin titles but with the names of the guilds concerned:

1. Barkers: Creation, Fall of Lucifer; 2. Plasterers: Creation to Fifth Day; 3. Cardmakers: Creation of Adam and Eve; 4. Fullers: Adam and Eve in the Garden; 5. Coop-

ers: Fall of Man; 6. Armourers: Expulsion from Eden; 7. Glovers: *Sacrificium Cayme et Abell*; 8. Shipwrights: Noah's Ark; 9. Fishers & Mariners: The Flood; 10. Parchmenters and Bookbinders: Abraham's Sacrifice; 11. Hosiers: Exodus from Egypt; 12. Spicers: Annunciation and Visitation; 13. Pewterers & Founders: Joseph's Trouble; 14. Tilethatchers: Birth of Christ; 15. Chandlers: Angels and Shepherds; 16. Masons: Herod and the Three Kings; 17. Goldsmiths: Adoration of Three Kings; 18. Marshalls: Flight into Egypt; 19. Girdlers & Nailers: Massacre of Innocents; 20; Spurriers & Lorimers: Christ with the Doctors; 21. Barbers: Baptism of Christ; 22. Smiths: Temptation of Christ; 23. Curriers: Transfiguration; 24. Capmakers: Woman Taken in Adultery, Raising of Lazarus; 25. Skinners: Entry into Jerusalem; 26. Cutlers: Conspiracy of Jews; 27. Bakers: Last Supper; 28. Cordwainers: Agony and Betrayal; 29. Bowers & Fletchers: Peter's Denial, Christ before Caiphas; 30. Tapissers & Couchers: Dream of Pilate's Wife, Christ before Pilate; 31. Litster's: Trial before Herod; 32. Cooks & Waterleaders: Trial before Pilate, Remorse of Judas; 33. Tilemakers: Second Trial before Pilate, continued; 34. Shearmen: Christ Led up to Calvary; 35. Pinners & Painters: *Crucifixio Cristi*; 36. Butchers: *Mortificacio Cristi*; 37. Saddlers: Harrowing of Hell; 38. Carpenters: Resurrection; 39. Winedrawers: Appearance to Mary Magdalene; 40. Sledmen: Journey to Emmaus; 41. Hatmakers, Masons & Labourers: Purification; 42. Scriveners: Incredulity of Thomas; 43. Tailors: Ascension; 44. Potters: Descent of Holy Spirit; 45. Drapers: Death of Mary; 46. Weavers: Appearance of Our Lady to Thomas; 47. Ostlers: Assumption and Coronation of the Virgin; 48. Mercers: Judgment Day. Innholders: Coronation of Our Lady (fragment).

Much scholarship has been devoted to the relationship of the two lists with the Register. The city records support generally the testimony of the Register, but there are discrepancies. A 1485 decree seems to indicate that the pageant of Fergus (*Portacio Corporis Mariae*) had been "laid apart"; but as late as 1518, though unrecorded in the Register, it still figures in the city ordinances as the linenweavers' play. The Dying, Assumption and Coronation of Our Lady, expressly prohibited in 1548–49, reinstated in the reign of Mary Tudor, and finally suppressed in 1561, remain undeleted in the Register.

The *York Plays* share the general indebtedness of medieval mysteries to liturgical, scriptural, lyrical, hagiographical and other sources. Of special interest to scholars have been the contributions of the *Northern Passion* and the strophic *Gospel of Nicodemus*. For relationship with other cycles, see especially under *Towneley (Wakefield) Plays* [11]. The complex relationship of the texts of Christ and the Doctors in the cycles of York and Towneley, of Coventry (where it is only an episode in the Weavers' Play) and of Chester (where it is amalgamated with the Purification, though not conforming to the regular Chester stanza) is puzzling. Greg concluded that the York text with its regular metrical pattern (mainly the twelve-line $ababab ab^4 cdcd^3$ stanza) preserves the play in its earliest form; that Towneley, apart from a mutilated opening and two important rewritten passages, is practically identical; that Coventry has been virtually rewritten in an irregular metre; and that the Chester redactor, working in simple quatrains, was less tempted to rewrite what he preserved but took liberties with the order. Further, the extant York and Towneley texts might derive independently, in the case of Towneley perhaps through an intermediate source, from a copy in the hands of the York guild of Spurriers and Lorimers; and this intermediate source or a derivative (possibly the Beverley play) may have come into the hands of the Chester playwright, who then passed it on to Coventry.

For the cycle as a whole, Greg accepted in theory Davidson's and Gayley's three stages of development and argued for: (1), a simple, rather dull didactic cycle, carefully composed in elaborate stanzas by a single author or small school; (2), an elaboration by more than one hand, including that of a great metrist, with an introduction of humour in such plays as those of Cain, Noah, and the Shepherds; (3), a revision, mainly of the Passion, by a single writer whose work is marked by dramatic realism and the use of a powerful but loose alliterative metre. Chambers, in his later work, detects the outline of the original cycle in survivals of the so-called Northern Septenar together with simple quatrains or octaves or cross-rime; notes in the versatile metrist of the second period a distinct tendency to concatenation of stanzas; and differentiates the tumultuous stress alliteration of the realist of the third period from the alliteration of the first and second periods. Reese feels that the intricate techniques of alliterative metre and its rich potential in the hands of an artist have been barely appreciated; he is sceptical about "levels."

While the cardinal importance of the York cycle from the angle of comprehensiveness and historical influence has never been underestimated, its achievement as drama has received more grudging recognition. Individual scenes of genuine feeling, especially in the Nativity group, have not outweighed the high proportion of insipid mechanical writing credited to the cycle as a whole. The presence of humour has served mainly as a text to expound the superiority of that element in other cycles. If the stanzaic patterns of the "York metrist" were acclaimed, the tumbling verse of the "York realist" was excused by virtue of his rôle as precursor of the Wakefield master. Coffman's suggestion of the need for reappraisal of the York cycle, in particular, has borne fruit. Single plays have emerged not as closed units in a loose episodic cycle but as essential structural links in the larger drama. Studies of the Passion group from the angle of scene-manipulation and rhetorical style and of the metrical contribution to dramatic effectiveness have induced a truer understanding of the Passion playwright. The postwar revival of the *York Plays*, albeit in modified form, has finally vindicated the claims of the cycle as a whole to be taken seriously as drama.

For the York *Pater Noster* and *Creed Play*, see [24–25] below.

TOWNELEY (WAKEFIELD) PLAYS [11]. MS Huntington HM 1. Mid or late fifteenth century (except last play in sixteenth-century hand). East Midland with Northern traces. Mixed verse forms.

The pressmark suggests the manuscript's link with the Towneley family as early as the time of the great collector Christopher Towneley (d. 1674). In 1814, it was sold, but returned to the Towneley Hall Library five years later, there to remain until purchased by Quaritch in 1883. Some fifteen years later it became the property of Edward Coates, from whose library it was bought, in 1922, on behalf of Henry E. Huntington. There has been much conjecture as to its original locale. According to Douce in his note to the 1814 Towneley sale catalogue, it was supposed previously to have "belonged to the Abbey of Widkirk, near Wakefield, in the County of York" (later, in the Roxburghe edition of the *Judicium*, he substituted the Abbey of Whalley). The Surtees Society editor of the cycle, 1822, challenged the non-existent Abbey of Widkirk and credited the original ownership to a cell of Augustinian or Black Canons at Woodkirk (equated later by Skeat with Widkirk) and possible authorship to a member or members of the cell or of the larger fraternity at Nostel. He did not ignore either the name of Wakefield, actually an integral part of the original title in the manuscript both at the beginning of the cycle and at the head of the third play, or the ascription, though in a later hand, of pageants 1, 2, 8, and 27 to the Barkers, Glovers, Litsters and Fishers, respectively; but he turned his back on his own clues and, in the interest of Woodkirk, pursued certain local allusions to "Horbery Shroges" and to the "crokyd thorne." Peacock's appropriation of those same local allusions for Wakefield, reinforced by his own significant addition of "gudeboure" (Goodybower) failed, in the absence of evidence for a Wakefield municipal cycle, to shake the Woodkirk-Whalley tradition; but when, some quarter of a century later, he was able to cite certain items in the fragmentary Burgess Court records of Wakefield concerning regulations for the Corpus Christi play, his claim for Wakefield was generally accepted (with Wann still hankering after Whalley). A 1576 prohibition in the records of the York Diocesan Court of High Commission of matter "to the derogation of the Majestie and glorie of God" in the Wakefield Corpus Christi play serves merely to strengthen that claim. The Towneley manuscript, like that of the York Plays, was apparently an official compilation of the craft guild pageants, which, after their cessation, passed from the municipality into private hands.

With the manuscript now more accessible to scholars, the textual study of the cycle has been put on a sounder basis. Wann's examination of the original document revealed certain points that had escaped previous investigators. Frampton's review of the EETS edition, with details of errors in transcription and in the notes and of weakness in metrical organization, has made possible a more accurate assessment of the shortcomings of the edition. A recent study by Stevens seems to vindicate the accuracy of the main Towneley scribe, and, in turn, to invalidate certain linguistic findings of Trusler.

The titles of the plays (from headings or *incipits* and *explicits*) are:

1. [The Creation], (incomplete); 2. *Mactacio abel*; 3. *Processus Noe cum filiis*; 4. *Abraham* (end missing); 5. *Isaac* (last 35 couplets); 6. *iacob*; 7. *Processus Prophetarum* (end missing); 8. *Pharao*; 9. *Cesar Augustus*; 10. *Annunciacio*; 11. *Salutacio Elezabeth*; 12. *Pagina pastorum*; 13. *Alia eorundem*; 14. *oblacio magorum*; 15. *fugacio Iosep & Marie in egiptum*; 16. *magnus Herodes*; 17. *Purificacio marie*; 18. *Pagina Doctorum* (beginning missing); 19. *Iohannes baptista*; 20. *Conspiracio, Capcio Ihesu*; 21. *Coliphizacio*; 22. *Fflagellacio*; 23. *Processus crucis, crucifixio Christi*; 24. *Processus talentorum;* 25. *extraccio animarum (ab inferno)*; 26. *Resurreccio domini*; 27. *Peregrini*; 28. *Thomas Indie*; 29. *Ascencio Domini, et cetera* (end missing); 30. *Iudicium* (beginning missing); 31. *Lazarus*; 32. *Suspencio Iude* (end missing).

Lazarus should follow Play 19; and *Suspencio Iude*, in an early sixteenth century hand, should follow Play 22. Earlier in the cycle the order of *Processus Prophetarum* and *Pharao* should be reversed. Unlike his York opposite number, the Towneley scribe does not leave blanks for the insertion of plays not to hand but carries straight on.

From the time that Lucy Toulmin Smith called attention to correspondences between five York plays and their Towneley counterparts, the genesis and relationship of the two cycles has engaged the interest of scholars. Other correspondences have been noted, and in Towneley, as in York, several layers of composition detected. Pollard, endorsed generally by Greg and others, argued for three stages: the first characterized by a simple religious tone and leaning heavily on the $aa^4b^3cc^4b^3$ ($aa^4b^3aa^4b^3$) stanza; the second, a period of borrowing from or composition under the influence of York; the third, a period of later additions and revision by a single remarkable writer using an intricate nine-line stanza with bob ($aaaa^4b^1cccb^2$), with internal rimes in the first four lines (sometimes given as $abababab^2c^1dddc^2$). Cady on the other hand, argued for a common liturgical source for the two cycles and would place the borrowings from York in the final stage of evolution. Lyle in her detailed study of textual parallels, metrics, structure and sources, rejected Davidson's "parent cycle" theory, based on use of the Northern Septenar, and brought forward her own case, not presupposing a uniform versification, for the original identity of the two cycles, with Towneley borrowing from York outright sometime before 1390; after which each evolved in its own way to form the extant cycles. Her opponents, somewhat less liberal in their acceptance of parallels, were more inclined to account for such as did clearly exist as due to borrowings backwards and forwards of individual plays or to the independent use of common sources such as the liturgy, the *Vulgate*, the *Northern Passion* and the vernacular *Gospel of Nicodemus*, and queried some of her metrical assumptions; with Frank striving to find a "tenable compromise." Frampton would date the whole Towneley cycle after 1415, and Chambers, finally, not earlier than 1425; before which time Wakefield could scarcely have sustained a civic cycle. Craig, while conceding some points to the opposing forces, has been faithful to the end to the Lyle theory, which, indeed, he sponsored in the first place.

It was Gayley who christened as the "Wakefield Master" that man of genius whose humour and realism and vitality of language declared themselves so plainly in certain parts of the cycle. The Master's "canon" was subsequently formulated by Carey. Applying her test of the complex nine-line stanza peculiar to Towneley as the best single criterion for the Wakefield Master, though not ignoring other metrical and stylistic considerations, she brought into the group nine plays or parts of plays in addition to those four with which her study was mainly concerned: the *Mactacio Abel*, the *Processus Noe* and the *Prima* and *Secunda Pastorum*. The urge to identify a writer of the Master's calibre was natural; but Cargill's suggestion of Dominus Gilbertus Pilkington, whose name appears in the colophon of the *Northern Passion*, and his arguments for the common authorship of the *Northern Passion*, the *Turnament of Totenham* and the Wakefield Group did not find general acceptance. On the basis of costume allusions, local conditions and bibliographical evidence, Frampton would place the date of the flourishing of the Master about 1425–50, a date which he finds confirmed through his close study of such individual plays as the *Conspiracio et Capcio* and the *Processus Talentorum*. Insofar, however, as his argument hangs on deriving the latter play from the lost York Millers' *Particio vestimentorum Christi*, discarded by 1422, it was rejected by Stevens on linguistic grounds.

The Towneley text, with special emphasis on the "canon," was used by Speirs to explicate his thesis of the mystery cycles as ritual drama, compounded of pagan folk plays and Christian liturgy in the process of becoming art drama. From this and other studies the First Shepherds' Play emerges more clearly as no mere rough sketch for its more famous successor. But it is the Second Shepherds' Play which has continued to absorb the lion's share of scholarly investigation. As will be seen from the bibliography, the main preoccupation of recent years has been not with analogues, which still turn up for the Mac episode, but with the episode's dramatic function not only in the play as a whole but in the complete cycle. The now popular symbolic or figural approach serves as an argument for considering the realistic dialogue of the shepherds and the parody of the Nativity not as an excrescence to be welcomed as a forerunner of later comedy, still less as an unwelcome intrusion on the biblical scene, but as an integral part of a highly complex drama in which even anachronisms express the typological concept of time in relation to eternity.

As a corrective to what has sometimes been felt to be disproportionate concern with the Second Shepherds' Play and with comedy elements in general, to the neglect of other aspects of the cycle and its design, such a study as that of Williams gave an important lead. Here the writer focused attention on the dramatic artistry of the Passion and Resurrection group, dominated by the brilliantly conceived character of Pilate, the chief antagonist in the tragedy, and in so doing did not hesitate when necessary to range outside of the time-honoured confines of the "canon." The whole complex problem of the canon itself, together with the rôle of the Wakefield Master, whether as assembler or reviser or original playwright, or, as recently suggested, as actor-playwright, would seem to be due for fuller reappraisal and restatement.

Following up the theory propounded by Rose that the Wakefield plays were not enacted processionally, as at York, but in one fixed locality on a multiple stage setting, Stevens considers the necessary adjustment to be made by the literary critic to the idea of this cycle's presenting a sustained and unified theatrical effect; a possibility not contemplated by Prosser in her stand against the "one-drama" thesis.

LUDUS COVENTRIAE (HEGGE PLAYS) [12]. MS British Museum Cotton Vespasian D.viii, ff. 1ª–225ᵇ. Third quarter fifteenth century. East Anglian. Variety of stanza forms.

The manuscript was probably acquired by Sir Robert Cotton's librarian, Richard James, in 1629 on the death of its owner Robert Hegge, after whom the plays are sometimes named. James's own note on the flyleaf runs: "Elenchus contentorum in hoc codice. Contenta novi testamenti scenicè expressa et actitata olim per monachos sive fratres mendicantes • vulgò dicitur hic liber Ludus Coventriae • sive ludus corporis

Christi • scribitur metris Anglicanis." This note is responsible for much
of the loose scholarship by which discussion of the cycle has been be-
devilled from the seventeenth century until comparatively recently. The
erroneous limitation of the contents to the New Testament was accepted
originally by Dugdale, and, notwithstanding Smith's "historiae veteris et
N. Testamenti" in his catalogue of the Cotton collection, passed into
general currency. A recent theory that the Old Testament plays were
later accretions has no manuscript validity.

Dugdale further enriched the legend by his conversion of "actitata
olim per monachos sive fratres mendicantes" into "acted with mighty
state and reverence by the [Grey] friers" of Coventry, a statement accepted by Sharp, with reservation, and by Halliwell, and not completely
ruled out by Block. But the reading of "by" as agent rather than place
has been rightly questioned, independently of Wanley's "at the grey-
friars" in his MS Annals (Harley 6388). Sharp's distinction between the
Ludus Coventriae and the Corpus Christi Coventry cycle was mainly ignored. The consensus of later opinion, however, rejects Coventry as the
place either of origin or of performance of the *Ludus Coventriae*. James's
alternative title, "ludus corporis Christi," is explained away as popular
nomenclature (*vulgò dicitur*), a generic term for a cycle of religious plays
not necessarily confined to Corpus Christi day. Attempts have been made
to locate the cycle in Durham (Hegge was a Durham man, "Dunelmensis") or in Bury St. Edmunds, with or without Lydgate as author. The
announcement in the banns of a performance to begin at 6 a.m. on Sunday at "N. towne" has suggested Northampton or Norwich; though "N"
may stand, as in the marriage service, for *Nomen*, with the name to be
supplied by a touring company—a theory to which Chambers finally
subscribed.

If he did not initiate the theory of Lincoln provenance, Craig has been
its main protagonist. Not only does the dialect of the manuscript "point
straight to Lincoln," but, from the angle of content and emphasis, he
argues, there is a general appropriateness in assigning this very learned
cycle to a place of high intellectual culture with a great cathedral dedicated to the cult of the Blessed Virgin Mary and of St. Anne. Nelson,

however, disagrees with Craig on several counts: Lincoln probably never had so extensive a cycle; its St. Anne's Day procession was purely processional; the language of the *Ludus Coventriae* is not northeast midland but the east-Anglian dialect of Norfolk (as indeed seems now to be confirmed in detail by Eccles). While making no claim for Norwich as its original home, he finds sufficient cause to justify his hypothesis of a much more complete cycle at Norwich than has hitherto been conceded and suggests the "tantalizing possibility" that the *Ludus Coventriae* may represent some form of the lost Norwich plays. (See below, *Norwich Grocers' Play* [15].)

The text of the cycle bristles with problems.

A series of Old Testament plays beginning with the Creation and the Fall of Lucifer is followed by a prophets' Root of Jesse play, which prepares for the Anne-Mary series: The Conception of Mary, Mary in the Temple, The Betrothal of Mary; the Parliament of Heaven, with the Four Daughters of God, leading into the Salutation and Conception; Joseph's Return, the Visit to Elizabeth. This latter series is preceded by a prologue spoken by Contemplacio, who reappears to introduce and conclude Mary in the Temple and as an epilogue to the Visit to Elizabeth. The Trial of Joseph and Mary, preceded by the Prologue of Summoner (Den), is not mentioned in the Contemplacio prologue. Next come three Nativity plays, followed by the Purification, the Massacre of the Innocents, the Death of Herod, Christ and the Doctors, the Baptism, the Temptation, the Woman Taken in Adultery, the Raising of Lazarus. Demon's prologue and a prophecy by John the Baptist lead into a first Passion group, dealing with the Entry into Jerusalem, the Machinations of the Jews and the Betrayal of Christ. Two doctors interpret a procession of the Apostles, after which Contemplacio speaks the prologue to the second Passion group, dealing with the Trial and Condemnation of Christ and his Crucifixion and including Pilate's Wife's Dream. Then come the Harrowing of Hell, the Resurrection, Christ's appearances, the Ascension, Pentecost, Assumption of the Virgin, Doomsday.

One cannot catalogue in detail the plays without running into difficulties regarding enumeration and division. What are clearly new plays according to subject matter sometimes begin in the middle of a stanza. Halliwell's enumeration of 42 plays would seem to tally with the number assigned by the scribe to the final play in the manuscript, but depends on manipulation of divisions to make up for the scribe's omission of the numbers 17 and 22. Block retains the manuscript numbers with its omissions and gives still another division of the material in a tabulation in her edition, to which the reader is referred.

The cycle is preceded in the manuscript by a Proclamation or Banns spoken by three Vexillatores who announce in turn the contents of the cycle, pageant by pageant, generally with one stanza to each. The variation in number and subject matter of the plays as between proclamation and cycle is only one of the perplexing discrepancies. Through the Old Testament series the Proclamation summaries keep close to the cycle, a notable omission being the Death of Lamech, which is inserted in the text of the Noah play. Both summary and play of the *Prophetae* stress the Radix Jesse theme and prepare for the birth of the Virgin rather than directly for the birth of Christ. In the Anne-Mary sequence, however, the Proclamation ignores the Conception of Mary, Mary in the Temple, the Visit to Elizabeth, as also the Parliament of Heaven, and, in a later group, the Purification. In the Passion sequence there is not only additional material in the text of the cycle but a reordering into two groups (Block's Passion Plays I and II) with separate prologues. The omission of various episodes and details should not be pressed too far, though the fact that the Assumption of the Virgin is unannounced is noteworthy.

Further, notwithstanding the allusion to a "pleyn place" (sometimes interpreted as *platea*) and the lack of any allusion to craft guilds or stations, the Proclamation would seem to contemplate the familiar English processional cycle. For most scholars, however, the textual evidence of the cycle itself is definitely in favour of a polyscenic stage, the movable Ark and "hic intrabit page[n]tum de purgacione Marie et joseph" in the stage directions of the Noah and Trial plays being explained on the theory that either, on occasion, such pageant cars were drawn into the *platea* or that they were vestigial remains of an older version of the text, closer to the Proclamation. Again, the Proclamation gives the impression of the performance on one day of a complete cycle. But the extant cycle, with additional episodes and links and much scholastic and theological matter of which there is no hint in the Proclamation, was clearly unplayable on a single day. In his prologue to Passion Play II, Contemplacio announces, not without ambiguity: "We intendyn to procede þe matere þat we lefte þe last ȝere/ . . . [when] we shewyd here how oure lord for

love of man/ Cam to the cety of jherusalem • mekely his deth to take/
. . . Now wold we procede how he was browth þan/ befortn Annas and
cayphas . . ."

The question of priority as between the texts of Proclamation and
cycle is closely bound up with the complicated problem of the chronology and organization of the cycle It has been argued, on the one hand,
that the Proclamation was later and omitted material already discarded
in the cycle, and, on the other hand, that it represented an earlier and
more primitive form of the cycle. Block's intensive study of watermarks,
interpolated quires and folios, handwriting, rubrication and pointing not
only confirmed Greg's surmise of a more complex relationship but yielded
important new evidence. Her main findings are that the *Ludus Coventriae* is the book of a compiler who had command of other versions of
plays or groups of plays and whose plan for the collection shifted as he
worked; who made use of certain plays (notably the Purification, bearing the date 1468, the Passion sequence and the Assumption) which had
had a separate existence; and who at times incorporated in his compilation actual portions of independent manuscripts. The Proclamation
neither antedated nor postdated the cycle, but was composed in its present form in close connection with the cycle's compilation. Evidence of
its correspondence with certain unique interpolated matter in the cycle
points to the compiler as responsible for both.

The *Ludus Coventriae* stands apart by virtue of certain plays and episodes peculiar to itself, or, as in the case of Christ and the Doctors, independent in treatment; by virtue also of its conspicuous Marian trend
and marked theological emphasis. As with the other cycles, there is constant indebtedness to the Bible and Apocrypha, the liturgy, legendaries
and patristic writings. The Lamech episode, unique in English medieval
drama though found in the *Mistère du Viel Testament*, would seem to
derive directly from Petrus Comestor; and the Parliament of Heaven
episode, unique in the cycles though found in the *Castle of Perseverance*,
links with the literature of the Court of Sapience. Bonaventura's *Meditationes vitae Christi*, the apocryphal gospels, the thirteenth-century
Harrowing of Hell, the Dance of Death theme, all have left their imprint
on the New Testament plays. Particularly significant for the Passion

group is the *Northern Passion* and for the Assumption the *Legenda aurea*. (See also under *Croxton Sacrament* [18] and *Digby Plays: Killing of the Children* [19]).

Block refused to accept the usual evaluation of the *Ludus Coventriae* as inferior in literary merit to the other cycles, pointing out certain "compensations for deficiencies" in more singing, more processions, more considered exploitation of stage business; and, less negatively, the artistic skill with which certain dramatic situations are developed. Several recent studies, all more theologically conscious, have sought to establish the essential unity of the extant cycle. The Prologue of Demon has been selected as the unifying factor in a heterogeneous group of plays. The somewhat vague concessions of previous scholarship to the basic underlying doctrine of Redemption have been superseded by more precise and systematic formulations of the doctrine and its function in the cycle. In particular, Fry sees the abuse-of-power, a special patristic theory of the Redemption, as a dominant dramatic motive in the final redaction, with each manifestation of the theme taking its place naturally in the architectonic structure of the cycle.

COVENTRY PLAYS [13], sometimes called TRUE-COVENTRY to prevent confusion with the *Ludus Coventriae*, consisting of the Shearmen and Tailors' Nativity (900 lines) and the Weavers' Presentation in the Temple and Christ with the Doctors (1192 lines). No trace exists of an official register of the Corpus Christi cycle and the surviving plays have come down through the redactions of Robert Croo, "nevly correcte [translate] be Robart Croo" March 1534–35, based apparently on individual guild copies. The Croo manuscript of the Shearmen's play, accessible to the first editor, Thomas Sharp, perished, together with other valuable Coventry material, in the Birmingham Free Reference Library fire in 1879. That of the Weavers remained in the hands of the original guild, now the Clothiers and Broad Weavers of Coventry, to be rediscovered by Craig; along with two loose leaves, corresponding to lines 1–58 and 182–243 of the play, torn, sometimes illegible, probably in a fifteenth century hand (hence predating the Croo version).

A cartulary of St. Mary's citing "domum pro le page(a)nt pannarum"

(1392) provides the earliest evidence for the Coventry cycle. From at least the early fifteenth century, Leet Book bills and ordinances confirm the control exercised by the civic authorities so that the plays would be forthcoming, the burden of expenses for pageants and pageant cars distributed, the citizens satisfied with the allocations of stations, and so that the players "bene et sufficienter ludant." Sharp's excerpts from guild accounts now lost date from the mid-fifteenth century and preserve many details regarding payments for actors, playbooks, costumes, stage properties and machinery (including three worlds to burn), rehearsals, music, refreshments. The unusual scaffolds with wheels of the Smiths' accounts, stored in the pageant house and driven along with the pageant cars, may have been supplementary stages for the multi-episodic Coventry plays. According to Wanley's MS Annals (Harley 6388), the Corpus Christi cycle was "laid down" in 1579–80. In 1584, Mr. Smythe of Oxford was subsidized for writing a new play called the Destruction of Jerusalem, which was produced through the concerted efforts of the craft guilds. Songs in a late hand appended to the two Croo manuscripts under the name of Thomas Mawdycke, and, in the case of the Shearmen and Tailors' play, with the date May 13, 1591, may point to a contemplated revival of the cycle; but any such revival was ruled out by the authorities' decision in favour of the Destruction of Jerusalem and other matter.

In addition to the Nativity and Presentation plays, guild accounts testify to the Smiths' Passion, the Cappers' Harrowing of Hell and Resurrection, the Drapers' Doomsday; and the Mercers may have played the Assumption of the Virgin. Craig, who sees evidence for ten pageants in all, originally suggested that the three remaining pageants, of the tanners, whittawers and girdlers, might have covered such missing New Testament themes as John the Baptist, the Last Supper, the Ascension, with a *Processus Prophetarum* broken up and distributed through the cycle. But, uneasy over his exclusion of Old Testament episodes from a Corpus Christi cycle, he later rejected separate identity for the Burial in the developed cycle and found a residue of four unidentified plays; of which he would retain one for Christ's Ministry and tentatively assign the remainder to the Creation and Fall (not the only scholar to be tempted by Sharp's "apeltrie," an obvious misreading for "axeltrie"), to Noah, and to Abraham and Isaac, with the *Processus Prophetarum* distributed as before.

The Shearmen and Tailors Pageant opens with a prologue by Isaiah, followed by the Annunciation, Joseph's Trouble, the Journey to Bethlehem, the Nativity, the Shepherds, an interpolation (lines 332–485) by two unnamed prophets; after which a long speech by Herod leads into a second series consisting of the Magi, the Flight into Egypt, the Slaughter of the Innocents. *The Weavers' Pageant*, introduced by a dialogue between two unnamed prophets, consists of the Presentation in the Temple linked, as at Chester, with Christ and the Doctors.

Through the activities of Robert Croo, or perhaps of earlier revisers or copyists, the texts are very corrupt. In the metrical chaos three main stanzas have been detected: (1) four-stress quatrains, representing possibly the oldest stratum; (2) the eight-line Chester stanza (aaabaaab, aaabcccb), used in so-called excrescent scenes, including that of the Shepherds, as well as in parts of the Magi and in the dove episode in the Presentation; (3), and not necessarily later, rime royal, both in regular five-stressed and in four-stressed verses, often continuing the rime of the final couplet in the first and third lines of the following stanza.

The fragmentary state of the cycle has not deterred scholars from attempting to work out its relationship with the other cycles. For Cady, the Coventry Christmas sequence was linked with the parallel sequences of York and Towneley through a common liturgical source (possibly the Use of York), its primitive structure being due to retarded growth. For Lyle, True-Coventry originated in the York "parent cycle," from which it broke away earlier than Towneley and preserved its archaic form.

For the relationship of the Coventry Christ and the Doctors with the corresponding episode in the Chester, York and Towneley cycles, see under *York Plays* [10].

NEWCASTLE NOAH'S ARK [14]. Shipwrights' play. 206 lines. Mainly quatrains with some six-line stanzas, much irregularity. Preserved in the eighteenth-century *editio princeps* of Bourne, perhaps from a sixteenth-century copy of a fifteenth-century manuscript in the Northern dialect. A restored text was constructed by Brotanek, based textually on English mystery literature and phonologically and orthographically on a manuscript of the *Wars of Alexander* (Ashmole 44) of Northumbrian provenance. Davis reproduces Bourne's text along with his own edited edition.

There seems no reason to question the play's connection with the lost Newcastle Corpus Christi cycle, of which there are records of performance and craft participation, together with both Old and New Testament titles, from 1426–27. A 1569 deposition regarding the will of Sir Robert Brandling, not without obscurity originally and garbled in later citation, has figured prominently, with contradictory results, in discussions as to the time of performance of the cycle. The only scrap of clear testimony comes from an ordinary of the Saddlers (1532–33) for the setting forth and playing of the "pagions" on Corpus Christi day immediately after the religious procession. The argument for a stationary *mise-en-scène* with the pageant cars drawn up in a playfield rests mainly on the slight and ambiguous reference of the Devil in the Noah play to any unbelievers "gathered in this stead"; the guild and corporation records, if they give any lead, suggest rather a processional cycle.

The piece has interesting divergences from the Biblical story. In no other cycle does Noah's wife appear so early in the action; and her temptation by the Devil and use of a potion whereby Noah reveals his secret building of the Ark are unique in medieval drama. Similar motives were noted in medieval iconography (especially in the English *Queen Mary's Psalter* and in Swedish church wall-paintings) and their ramifications in apocryphal and folk literature have been confirmed and extended by subsequent investigations. Hence the Newcastle Devil-Uxor conspiracy is no local excrescence, but, however transmitted, linked closely with a widely disseminated legend.

NORWICH GROCERS' PLAY [15] of the Fall of Man has been preserved only in an eighteenth-century transcript of sixteenth-century items from a lost Grocers' Book. This transcript, first edited by Fitch in the nineteenth century and then used by Waterhouse for his edition, was never officially in the muniment room at Norwich Castle and cannot now be traced. Davis's new edition, involving a re-examination of the Norwich City records, is based on the Fitch-Waterhouse texts.

There are two versions of the play. The A version, dated by Waterhouse as 1533, is a fragment of 90 lines with a gap just before the expulsion from Paradise, after which the concluding lines are a song of lamentation sung by Adam and Eve and taken up by a chorus of four parts. The B version (153 lines), "newly renvied and according unto the Skripture" and begun in 1565, departs radically from A. Alternative prologues are assigned to a Prolocutor, the first (28 lines) if the pageant is played "withowte eny other goenge befor yt," the second (21 lines) "yf ther goeth eny other pageantes before yt." After God's curse Adam and Eve go to the "nether parte" of the pageant, the allegorical characters, Dolor and Misery, take over and the Holy Ghost speaks words of comfort. An appended short hymn of praise replaces the earlier song of lamentation.

A May 1534 account in the transcript of the Grocers' Book details various expenses for the play, including grease for the wheels of the pageant-wagon and fees to the individually named players of the different rôles, not forgetting the serpent. But, as regards the general staging of the cycle to which the play belongs and the festival for which it was produced, certain doubts remain. Much has been made of a 1527 petition of the hard-pressed Guild of St. Luke to be relieved from the burden of the long established Whitsuntide pageants, responsibility for which on Whit Monday, the Corporation conceded, should be distributed among the individual "occupations." Two lists of craft guilds, one marked "new orderyd," and a list of twelve pageants including, third in order, the Grocers' "Paradyse," all those items undated but in the same hand as the petition, were cited by Harrod. Hence scholars have assumed that what the petition demands is the inclusion of the Norwich cycle of plays; with which assumption Davis would seem to concur.

In a recent article, however, Nelson has challenged the name Whitsun Plays under which the Norwich cycle has "masqueraded" for over a century. He argues (and surely not without reason, for the triple possibilities of the term "pageant" cannot be ignored): that the "diuers disgisings and pageants" of the St. Luke's Guild, the nature of which is indicated in their petition, bear little resemblance to the surviving list of craft guild pageants; that the Whit Monday "procession" for which the pageants were to be required was processional, not dramatic; and indeed that those pageants were probably pageant-*wagons* used by the crafts in the Corpus Christi Day religious procession rather than the plays themselves which may not necessarily have been confined to the twelve-pageant list. (See above, *Ludus Coventriae* [12].) The first and only clear evidence of a link between the cycle and Whitsuntide comes in the first (older) prologue to the revised B text of the Grocers' Play, where the "Wittsun dayes," Nelson believes, may signify a post-Reformation shift to a festival less distasteful to the Protestants than Corpus Christi Day.

Whether the later version of the play was ever produced is not known, though a 1565 inventory of stage properties belonging to the Grocers shows that provision has been made for one of the new rôles, Dolor. A last record, sometime after 1570, tells of the ousting of the elaborate pageant-wagon from its rented house in default of payment, its rotting in the street, and its final demolition.

BROME ABRAHAM AND ISAAC [16]. Mid-fifteenth century. 465 lines with some five-line stanzas and quatrains, otherwise much metrical irregularity. East Anglian. Preserved in a commonplace book (ff. 15ᵃ–22ᵃ) at one time in the muniment room at Brome Hall, Suffolk. Since Smith's original edition the manuscript has passed through the hands of several owners, temporarily disappearing from scholarly ken. The final private owner, Mr. Denis Hill-Wood, deposited it for some years on loan at the Ipswich and East Suffolk Record Office. In 1966 it was sold and acquired by Yale University.

This is probably one of the various independent Abraham plays of which texts or records exist in England and elsewhere, rather than a cyclical play. A close resemblance of its central portions to those of the Chester play on the same subject inevitably suggested a common French source. Hohlfeld, however, argued, mainly on metrical grounds, that Chester derived from an earlier version of Brome and that the comparatively regular stanzaic pattern of the Chester Abraham, in conformity with that of the Chester cycle and in strong contrast to the highly irregular Brome metre, would otherwise be inexplicable. Harper felt that the more primitive Chester play would precede rather than follow the technically advanced Brome play and, though working from another angle, Fort was in general agreement. In his detailed textual study Severs reverted to Brome priority on the grounds that the greater regularity of the stanzaic forms in Chester has obscured the fact that its text, with clear deviations from sense and continuity, is much more seriously corrupt than Brome and that the very irregularity of the Brome versification may in itself achieve certain literary effects. The Chester text, he concluded, whether through faulty scribal copyings or memorial reconstruction, is a degenerate version of the original Brome play; which conclusion made no impact on Craig but has been tentatively endorsed by Davis.

Whether as source or derivative, the Brome Abraham and Isaac is generally conceded to outrank all other English versions. With its successive movements of the divine command, the preparation for the sacrifice, the release, and its rigorous exclusion of irrelevancies, the play is structurally firm. The tragedy of the immediate situation is conveyed through the father's heartrending conflict, its pathos and charm through the natural behaviour of his young son (no mature man as in the divergent tradition of York and the *Ludus Coventriae*). The patristic theme of prefiguration of the Crucifixion, familiar to medieval audiences through sermons and iconography, if not stressed is clearly implicit and serves to give another dimension to a work of fine artistry.

DUBLIN ABRAHAM AND ISAAC [17]. Mid-fifteenth century. 369 lines. South Midland. Mainly eight-line Chester stanza. Like [16], preserved in a commonplace book, now Trinity College Dublin 432 (refoliated), ff. 74b, 76a, 77b–81a.

On insufficient evidence this play was originally assigned to a lost Dublin Corpus Christi cycle, but closer study of the language established Midland origin. As the commonplace book contains in the same handwriting a list of Northampton dignitaries, the play is now generally associated with that town or its vicinity, although almost the only evidence for Northampton mysteries is the controversial "N-towne" of the *Ludus Coventriae* (see under [12] above). A list of English rulers, also in the same hand, with regnal years incomplete for the last king, Henry VI, would seem to place the play in that reign (1422–61). For reasons of metre and locale, Patch suggested that it was once part of the *Ludus Coventriae*.

This is the only English version where Sara appears in person, showing a motherly concern for Isaac's safety on the journey and reproaching Abraham for consenting to the sacrifice. In such emphasis on the active rôle of Sara, who is likewise more present to the minds of Abraham and Isaac than in either Brome or Chester, as also in the arrangement of the scenes, the Dublin play diverges from English tradition and links with the corresponding play in the *Mistère du Viel Testament* or with a closely related separate play, *Le sacrifice de Abraham a huyt personnages*. Waterhouse and Davis give general endorsement to Brotanek's theory of French influence.

CROXTON SACRAMENT [18]. Preserved in a miscellany, MS Trinity College Dublin 652, Art 6, ff. 338ᵃ–356ᵃ. Late fifteenth or early sixteenth century. 1007 lines, of which the preliminary Banns account for 80 lines. East Midland. Mainly four-stressed quatrains or double quatrains linked by rime, otherwise much metrical variety.

Two Vexillatores recount briefly in the Banns the story of the miracle of the Holy Sacrament in the forest of Aragon, presented in Rome in 1461, and announce that "At Croxston on Monday yt shall be sen." Then "foloweth the Play of þe Conuersyon of Ser Jonathas þe Jewe by Myracle of þe Blyssed Sacrament." By a bribe Jonathas secures from Aristorius, the Christian merchant, a consecrated wafer that he may torture it, but his hand withers. Through a miraculous image of Christ with bleeding wounds, he repents, has his hand restored, is baptised; and the play ends with the singing of the *Te Deum*. A colophon repeats the location in 1461 in Aragon, adding "in the famous cité of Eraclea" and omitting the reference to Rome.

The *Croxton Sacrament* is the only complete English miracle play proper, as distinct from such saints' plays as the Digby *Conversion of St. Paul (Saul)* and *Mary Magdalene* [19]. The episode of the quack doctor,

Master Brundyche of Brabant and his boy Colle, which provides low, boisterous humour, is clearly an importation from the seasonal folk play; and possibly a later addition, though its use of the eight-line tail-rime stanza, which Craig finds significant, is found elsewhere in the play.

Continental Jew-Host analogues, in both narrative and dramatic form, have been cited from France, the Netherlands and Italy, in particular the French *Le mistére de la saincte hostie*, but the *Croxton Sacrament* is markedly different not only in content, but, lacking anti-semitism, in tone. From its doctrinal teaching, Cutts interprets it as deliberate anti-Lollard propaganda at a time when Lollardry in certain areas was far from a spent force, and stresses English antecedents rather than foreign sources. Mainly on metrical grounds, Patch would associate the play with a group including the *Digby Plays* [19] and the *Dublin Abraham and Isaac* that was drawn on by a scribe or compiler of the *Ludus Coventriae*.

Of various Croxtons, those in Cambridgeshire and Norfolk have been favoured. The proximity of the doctor's lodging at the "colkote" beside Babwell Mill (lines 620–21) to Bury St. Edmund's may point to a Bury origin for that episode, at least. The doubling of parts envisaged at the end of the play gives no more than dubious support to the theory of wandering players. The stage directions are unrevealing, but "Jonathas [shall] goo don of his stage" (line 148) should be noted.

DIGBY PLAYS [19]. A group of plays, probably copies of somewhat earlier texts, assembled fortuitously in MS Digby 133 (Bodley 1734), ca. 1510–20. East Midland. The manuscript was apparently at one time in the possession of Miles Blomefylde, alchemist, physician and book collector, born at Bury St. Edmunds in 1525, whose name (or initials M B) appears on three of the plays and who is not to be confused with William Blomefylde, monk of Bury. The statement after the "Namys of the Pleyers" of the *Killing of the Children* that "Jhon Parfre ded wryte thys booke," generally assumed to indicate the scribe, may, as the result of fresh evidence deriving from a recent study of the manuscript by Baker and Murphy, turn out to refer to the actual author of this particular play, at least. How the manuscript was acquired for Sir Kenelm Digby's library, and, subsequently, through an intermediary for the Bodleian is not altogether clear.

Conversion of St. Paul (Saul) (ff. 37ª–50ᵇ). 663 lines. East Midland with Southern forms. Basically rime royal, irregular. Written except for an interpolated episode (ff. 45ª–47ª) in one main hand.

The play divides into three parts, each with prologue and epilogue spoken by Poeta: (1) Saul as "aunterous knyth" and boastful persecutor, commissioned by Cayphas and Annas to bring all Christians bound to Jerusalem; (2) his vision, conversion, and baptism at Damascus; (3) his sermon, the plot against his life, the angelic warning and his plan of escape. Comic relief is provided in (1) by the crude dialogue between Servus and Stabilarious, and in (2) by the later interpolated scene of the Council in Hell.

The *Conversion* links closely in subject matter with a Latin liturgical play in the Fleury play book, and, like it, makes use of a *platea* or "place" (for Saul to ride "abowt" and "owt of") and three "stacions"; the latter term, however, being used indifferently, as is "pagent," either for the particular episode or for the "loca" or "sedes" ("ffinis istius stacionis et altera sequitur," "ffinis istius secunde stacionis et sequitur tarcia," "to vnderstond thys pagent at thys lytyll stacion"). At the end of (1) the audience is invited by Poeta to follow the general procession and is then addressed by him from the second "pagent."

Mary Magdalene (ff. 95ª–145ª). 2144 lines. West Midland with Kentish forms. Written in still another main hand. Schmidt suggested that lines 2137–40 of the priest's epilogue may have been a later scribal addition, as also the last four lines, 2141–44; hence the shift between audience and readers in the course of the epilogue. Whether the "oreginale" in the explicit after line 2140 refers to the poet's source or the copyist's text is left unresolved.

The main plot deals with the legendary life of Mary Magdalene, daughter of Syrus, and sister of Martha and Lazarus, her seduction, repentance, forgiveness, her mission to the heathen King of Marseilles with the miracle that effects his conversion, her renunciation of worldly goods and withdrawal to the wilderness, where she is fed by angels and finally received into heaven. Dispersed through the saint's life are various

scenes, familiar in the mystery cycles, of biblical and liturgical origin and such significant morality features as allegorical characters (the World, the Flesh and the Devil,
the Seven Deadly Sins); the siege of the Castle of Maudleyn; the activities of the Good
and Bad Angels.

The play is thus a combination of miracle, mystery and morality. In
main outline it runs parallel to the versions in the *Legenda aurea* and
South English Legendary, but its source, Craig suggests, is a liturgical
play in the Fleury-Benedictbeuern tradition, where the death and resurrection of Lazarus are combined with the Mary Magdalene story. In time
the popular saint's legend with its sensational episodes and expansive
possibilities would seem to have outgrown and absorbed the simpler biblical episode.

The loose ranging play, with enormous cast, metrically crude and textually corrupt is of historic rather than literary value. Coarse comic relief
is provided by the horseplay in hell, by the dialogue between Presbyter
and his irreverent clerk Hawkyn, and by the altercation ending in blows
between the shipman and his boy. The *mise-en-scène* is clearly that of an
elaborate stationary play with separate "loca" for the localized action in
Rome, Bethany, Jerusalem, Marseilles, the wilderness, Heaven and Hell,
and with the "platea" for unlocalized action. A moveable ship plies to and
from Marseilles, as indicated by such stage directions as: "Here xall
entyre a shyp with a mery song" (line 1395); "Ett tunc navis venit in
placeam" (line 1716); "et tunc remigant a monte" (line 1915).

Killing of the Children or *Massacre of the Innocents* (ff. 146ᵃ–157ᵃ).
566 lines. Midland with Southern forms. Mainly double quatrains. Written in one main hand, not that of the *Conversion of St. Paul (Saul)*. In a
later hand is the heading "candelmes day & the kyllynge of the children
of Israell" with the date 1512. Another hand (John Stow's?) adds "the
vij booke." Prologue and Epilogue confirm a series in honour of St. Anne
and the Virgin Mary, with different episodes in different years. A *Pastores*
and *Magi* having been given last year, the Purification and Massacre this
year, the audience may expect a Disputation in the Temple next year.
The date 1512 is repeated at the end of the play.

Similarities between the Digby *Killing of the Children* and the *Ludus
Coventriae* have been noted: their unusual combination of tumbling

metre with double quatrains; the parallel rôles of Poeta and Contemplacio and their review of last year's and preview of next year's matter; the
unique placing of the Purification before the Massacre in the Digby Prologue (not in the play itself) and in the *Ludus Coventriae* (where, however, it is a later interpolation not mentioned in the Proclamation).

At times the piece degenerates into low farce, as in the comic intrusion
of the would-be knight Watkyn who is bullied by Herod and capitulates
to the women's distaffs in the massacre scene. There is a dance of virgins
at the end of the prologue, and Anna the Prophetess joins in the dance
at the conclusion of the scene in the temple. The scanty references in the
stage directions to the "place" and to going towards and from the temple
would seem again to point to a stationary play with multiple stage setting.

For the *Wisdom* fragment in the Digby manuscript, see [28] below. See
also *Bodley Burial and Resurrection*, [3] above.

CAESAR AUGUSTUS (ASHMOLE) FRAGMENT [20]. MS Bodleian
6621 (Ashmole 750), f. 168ᵃ. Late fifteenth century. Twelve lines, tail-
rime.

This fragment of one and a half stanzas, written on the lower part of a
page in a volume of miscellaneous matter, is a speech for Secundus Miles
whose name heads the complete stanza, with catch words from the previous rôle. The knight pledges loyalty to "Sure Emperoure," in all probability Caesar Augustus. Certain verbal parallels with those of corresponding speeches in the cycles occur but the lines are not identical.

EPILOGUE (REYNES EXTRACT) [21]. MS Tanner 407, f. 44ᵇ. East
Anglian. Late fifteenth century.

The piece consists of two irregular stressed and riming thirteen-line
stanzas, followed by a four-stressed quatrain riming abab, written in a
commonplace book compiled by Robert Reynes of Acle, Norfolk, sometime churchwarden. The speaker thanks the audience of "wursheppful
souereyns" for their "soferyng sylens" during the play, apologizes for any
shortcomings, invites them to an ale before leaving, and assures them
that all profits will go to the church. A certain similarity has been ob-

served to the prologue and epilogue of Poeta in the Digby *Killing of the Children*; but there is no indication as to the nature of the play itself, whether secular, or, as seems more probable, religious.

For the *Speech of Delight* which precedes this item in the manuscript, see [32] below.

THE RESURRECTION OF OUR LORD [22]. MS Folger Shakespeare Library 1828.1. Fragments in late sixteenth century(?) hand of play written ca. 1530. 1321 lines.

Two of the fragments belong to the "first dayes playe," the other two to the "Seconde dayes playe." There is a cast of thirty persons, including the "Appendix." The writer is saturated with the doctrines of Wyclif and gives evidence of reading in Tindale's New Testament and in the works of the Continental Reformers. But even with some readjustment of dates, the restrained and unpolemical tone of the fragments would seem to rule out any ascription to the militant John Bale, for which the editors would fain have discovered positive documentation. The *Resurrection*, still dramatically in the medieval tradition, forms a link between the mystery cycles and the later Bible plays of Bale and his followers.

STONYHURST PAGEANTS [23]. MS Stonyhurst College A.VI.33. First quarter of seventeenth century. Old Testament cycle of 8,740 lines. Northern. Irregular septenary couplets.

The manuscript lacks the first 55 folios, beginning on folio 56 with an imperfect sixth pageant, and five folios containing the thirteenth pageant. The eighteenth (and last) pageant is incomplete at the end and only a narrow stub remains of folio 186 in the middle. When complete, the cycle must have extended to at least 13,000 lines. The *terminus a quo* is established by proof of indebtedness to the English translation of the Vulgate (1609–10). Lancashire vocabulary and the names of Lancashire owners scribbled on the pages suggest both the genesis and retention of the manuscript in that area.

The surviving pageants deal mainly, and at inordinate length, with material new to the mysteries. No typological scheme of selection has been detected in the dogged dramatizing of the sacred story. A Roman Catholic playwright is indicated, but whether priest or layman, whether Englishman or foreigner using an acquired language has not been finally determined. Craig's discovery of the translation of the eighteenth pageant (Naaman) from the *Terentius Christianus* of Cornelius Schonaeus not only renders obsolete certain conjectures regarding this particular pageant but calls for further study of the authorship of the cycle as a whole. The use (except in Naaman) of the Chorus or Nuntius and traces of a three-day division of the material, combined with some (dubious) evidence for the late survival of Corpus Christi plays in northwest England, have suggested composition for an audience rather than deliberate closet drama.

For the CORNISH PLAYS and RECORDS OF LOST PLAYS see the Bibliography.

2. THE MORALITY PLAYS

by

Sheila Lindenbaum

Though the English morality can be traced back to the fourteenth century, it flourished and attained variety of expression in the fifteenth century to which most of the texts in this section may be safely assigned. Traditionally the genre has been held to begin with the lost Pater Noster plays mentioned in late fourteenth-century records shortly after the earliest recorded performances of the mystery cycles; however, it is difficult to say to what extent these or the lost Creed play of York resembled the later moralities except that they evidently had a similar concern for instructing their audiences in the essentials of the Christian faith. Firmer evidence for the early history of vernacular moral drama is found in *The Pride of Life*, believed to originate in Ireland, which may according to the most recent dating go back as far as the mid-fourteenth century. This play shows a mixture of elements, combining stern homiletic counsel with a dramatic combat resembling that of the mummers' plays. Of the later East Midland Macro Plays, *The Castle of Perseverance* has cosmic scope, comprehending the totality of man's life ending in the final judgment; *Wisdom* analyzes the faculties of the human soul and their workings; *Mankind* with its peasant hero and farcical villains has been called "highly sophisticated folk-drama." In the early Tudor period, *Everyman*, probably a translation of the Dutch *Elckerlijc*, shows remarkable sobriety and unity of action; Medwall's *Nature* reflects the ambience of Cardinal Morton's household for which it was presumably written. The evidence of these texts provides scant basis for any theory about the "evolution" of the early morality play. Nevertheless, for all their differences, these plays have a common subject and purpose: all treat the sin and repentance of a representative Christian soul and dramatize the Church's doctrine of salvation.

Various literary sources have been proposed to account for the origins of the morality plays. The most important of these in many studies is the *Psychomachia* of Prudentius, to which Creizenach traced the plays' allegorical conflict between good and evil powers of the soul. It was Creizenach's theory which inspired scholars to create a hypothetical chain of development leading from the *Psychomachia* through its literary off-spring to the Pater Noster plays and fifteenth-century moralities; the Coming of Death, the Debate of the Four Daughters of God, and the Debate of the Body and Soul were seen as "contributory" allegories to the basic Conflict of Virtues and Vices. Chambers, like many earlier scholars, saw the morality as an offshoot of the mystery cycles; but he too sought out the origins of the familiar allegorical themes. Thompson, while accepting the *Psychomachia* as the ultimate source of the basic conflict and allegorical method, concluded that the morality derived immediately from the popular sermon, just as the mystery cycles were thought to have developed out of the liturgy. This view gained widespread acceptance through the influence of Owst's study which held the sermon to be the direct source of the plays' allegorical themes, satiric portraits, and somber treatment of everyman's life and death.

Recent scholars have been less inclined to see the plays in the light of direct lines of development and have viewed them instead as a natural outgrowth of the late medieval concern with moral and religious education. They have pointed to two types of works that reveal analogous structural and thematic patterns. One is the allegorical poetry and prose on moral themes (including semi-dramatic dialogues)—works like de Guileville's *Pelerinage de la vie humaine*—that present man's life in serial or cyclical patterns: the Ages of Man, the Pilgrimage of Life, Sin-Repentance-Salvation. The other is the great body of vernacular didactic literature that grows up in the fourteenth and fifteenth centuries—moral tracts, manuals of instruction, and sermons. Fundamental to both kinds of literature is the theme of repentance that is central to the plays.

Early historians of the English drama were concerned with the moralities primarily as a stage in the evolution of Elizabethan tragedy and comedy. They pictured a process in which the crude religious morality, degenerating amid the intellectual currents of humanism and the Reformation, broke down completely and furnished the new secular drama arising from classical and Italian models with little more than some of its satiric and realistic elements. Their object was to discover transitional points where doctrinal emphasis shifted to historical and humanistic concerns and where the allegorical battle of vices and virtues turned into a drama of actual human characters and events. More recent studies have stressed the continuity of the morality tradition through its sixteenth-century stages of development. Farnham showed the medieval moralities paving the way for Elizabethan tragedy; following his lead, others have shown how the structure, characterization, and stage conventions of the morality helped shape other Elizabethan dramatic kinds, especially the history play and Jonsonian comedy. In addition to a more sympathetic evaluation of the contributions made by the medieval moralities to later drama, there has been a greater appreciation of these plays as dramatic art in their own right. As with the mystery cycles, closer attention has been paid to their principles of dramatic structure. Where earlier critics saw a collection of allegorical episodes loosely unified by a battle between virtues and vices, recent writers have observed greater method and direction governing the events of mankind's moral life.

The appreciation of the plays as drama has coincided with a number of studies of the way in which they were actually staged. Southern, Craik, Wickham, and Bevington in particular have added greatly to our knowledge about the many aspects of performance. Still we cannot always be positive whether a particular play was designed for indoor or outdoor performance, for amateur or professional actors, for a popular or limited audience; indeed a single play may have been performed in more than one set of circumstances. The staging plan of *The Castle of Perseverance* suggests that the morality may have begun as theatre in the round, outdoors with place-and-scaffold staging. It is not clear, however, at what point more portable moralities began to be acted by itinerant troupes of professionals on greens, in innyards (or inside the tavern), and in manorial halls—under conditions, that is, like those now usually inferred from the text of *Mankind*. Early Tudor "interludes" like *Nature* are commonly thought to have been played indoors before a hall screen, although interludes acted by professionals may have employed other methods of staging. Unfortunately the early history of strolling troupes (one of which may have performed *The Pride of Life*) remains obscure, and there is a lack of evidence in the medieval period for the use of the booth stage with which such troupes are frequently associated. Other matters of conjecture or controversy are the relative importance of inn-yard or hall for the design of the Elizabethan public playhouses and the degree to which strolling players adopted the conventions of courtly entertainments when they performed for more sophisticated audiences in halls. Even though some of these questions remain open, the studies of staging, of the conventions of playing, of actor-audience relationships, and of the use of costume and spectacle for symbolic effect have revealed new dimensions in the plays discussed below.

THE PATER NOSTER PLAY [24]. Although no text of a Pater Noster play has survived, records verify that plays of this name were per-formed in York, Lincoln, and Beverley during the late medieval period.

The most extensive evidence concerning these productions comes from York, where the Pater Noster play became established, along with the Creed and Corpus Christi plays, as one of the great religious dramas of the city. What may be the earliest reference to the York play occurs in the Wyclyfite *De Officio Pastorali* (1382–95): "& herfore freris han tauʒt in englond the paternoster in engliʒsch tunge, as men seyen in the pley of ʒork, & in many othere cuntreys." It is not known, however, whether the play actually originated with or was promoted by the friars. By 1389, as the earliest documentary evidence shows, it had become the responsibility of a religious fraternity: a return made by the Pater Nos-ter guild to the King's council in that year states that the guild had been founded for the sole purpose of perpetuating the play. By the 1440's, responsibility for the play had passed to the religious guild of St. An-thony, which had absorbed the Pater Noster guild, and which retained a connection with the play until its suppression by the ecclesiastical authorities. Exactly how and to what extent St. Anthony's cooperated with the civic authorities in producing the play remains unclear. In her examination of the relevant guild and civic documents, Johnston concludes that beginning in the late fifteenth century the play came under at first the partial and finally the complete control of the city council. From the late fifteenth century until the final production of 1572, it appears that the play was performed about once in every decade, usually on or about Lammas, and usually not in the same year as the Creed or Corpus Christi plays. Only three performances of the York Pater Noster play are actually recorded—in 1536, 1558, and 1572, the last two replacing the Corpus Christi play on its appointed day.

Because the 1389 return of the Pater Noster guild indicates that members accompanied the players "per certas principales stratas ciuitatis," most scholars have concluded that the York play was performed processionally at stations throughout the city. Recently Johnston has supplied detailed support for this position, emphasizing the crying of banns in 1558, when the production was financed by the craft guilds, and the appointment of the usual stations of the Corpus Christi play for the 1572 performance. Using the same evidence, but arguing against the feasibility of true-processional performance, Nelson concludes that the play consisted of a processional spectacle followed by a separate dramatic play in the chamber at Common Hall gates.

Productions of the Lincoln Pater Noster play receive brief mention in records of civic activity and in the Account Books of the cathedral, whose canons saw the play twice in the late fifteenth century. Kahrl finds eight productions recorded, the earliest in 1397–98, the latest in 1521–22; but there is little to indicate the play's usual mode of performance. The Beverley Pater Noster play is known from evidence in the Governors' Minute Book concerning productions on Midsummer Eve in 1441 and on the Sunday after Lammas in 1467. In both years, town worthies and craft guilds were assigned to eight pageants—one for "Viciouse" and the others for the seven deadly sins. The record for 1467 specifies stations for what is generally considered to be a processional play.

The subject matter of these lost plays is usually inferred from the medieval teaching that each of the seven deadly sins had a corresponding remedy in one of the petitions of the Pater Noster. Since the petitions also corresponded to virtues, most critics have assumed that the plays dramatized a conflict between vices and virtues. The York return of 1389, which describes the York play as one in which "plura vicia et peccata reprobantur et virtutes commendantur," seems to support this theory, as do the documents appointing the Beverley pageants to "Viciouse"—usually taken to be a chief vice or representative of frail humanity—and the seven deadly sins. Yet an actual conflict between vices and virtues, a dramatized *psychomachia*, is nowhere indicated in the surviving evidence. Alternative theories have been proposed by Craig, who argues for a cycle of plays on saints known for resisting the various sins; and by Johnston, who suggests that the petitions were dramatized, along with exposition of the matching vices, by scenes borrowed from the Corpus Christi play. In evaluating these theories, one might also consider Owst's hypothesis that the plays resembled recitations of religious tracts more closely than they did the extant morality drama. Doyle has suggested that the York play had some direct relationship to the *Speculum Vitae*, an English poem on the Pater Noster attributed to William Nassington.

THE CREED PLAY [25]. The Creed play of York is first mentioned in 1446 in the will of William Revetour, a chantry priest, deputy town clerk, and warden of the Guild of Corpus Christi. It was to this guild that Revetour deeded the play's register, described as ancient and worn when a new copy was made in 1455. No text has survived, but guild and civic documents indicate that the play was normally produced once every ten years, usually in late summer, as long as it remained in the custody of the Corpus Christi guild. The play was mounted for a visit of Richard III in 1483, and again in 1495 when the Guild of St. Anthony failed to bring forth its Pater Noster play. In 1495 the city officially agreed to a production every ten years, at the same time recording a stipulation to this effect by Revetour's executor. The play was subsequently mounted in 1505, 1525, and 1535; a production contemplated in 1545 apparently did not take place.

After the Corpus Christi guild was dissolved in 1547, the Hospital of
St. Thomas, which had been associated with the guild, remained active
under the control of the city council. This Hospital preserved the register of the Creed play. The city council briefly considered mounting the
play in 1562, and planned a production for 1568, when the craft guilds
were to contribute their pageant money towards expenses. But under
pressure by Dean Matthew Hutton, the elaborate arrangements of 1568
were abandoned and the play effectively suppressed.

Johnston has recently amplified the case for processional performance
of the Creed play at stations throughout the city. Emphasizing fifteenth-
century instructions that the play be performed "palam et publice" and
"in varijs locis," she draws attention also to the crying of banns in 1495
and "the pageantes playeng geare and neccssarics" specified in 1568.
According to Johnston's argument, records of 1525 and 1535 indicate that
the mayor and council saw the play from the Common Hall station.
These same records were interpreted differently by Chambers, who proposed a stationary play acted at the Common Hall. Also stressing these
records, Nelson has argued for a dramatic play in the chamber at Common Hall gates following a procession viewed from outside the Hall.

Whatever the Creed play's mode of performance, we know that it was
a drama of considerable scope. A guild inventory of 1465 describes one
copy as "continens xxij quaternos," probably at least 176 leaves. In the
same record are listed "xij rotule nuper scripte cum articulis fidei catho-
lice" and diadems for Christ and the apostles. On the basis of these items,
nineteenth-century scholars supposed that the play consisted of twelve
episodes on the subject of the apostles (each of whom according to medieval teaching contributed one article to the Apostle's Creed). But there
has since been wide-ranging speculation about the specific form and content of the play. Chambers suggested an expanded version of the scene
dramatized in the Chester Pentecost play; Craig a cyclic miracle play on
the lives of the apostles, perhaps including the lost play of St. James also
owned by William Revetour or the York "interlude" of St. Thomas the
Apostle mentioned in a letter of Henry VIII. More recently, Anderson has
offered still a third suggestion, a play of twelve scenes on subjects used
to illustrate the articles of the Creed in pictorial art. Since nine of the

twelve scenes correspond to events dramatized in the York mystery cycle, she proposes that they could have been adapted from that play. Johnston conjectures further that ten of the scenes were mounted from the wagons and properties of the crafts, the other two from properties owned by the Corpus Christi guild. It can be seen from these increasingly elaborate speculations that scholars have generally ceased to consider the Creed play a morality. Rather the tendency has been to seek other dramatic analogues, such as the Innsbruck *Fronleichnamsspiel* compared by Woolf or the York Corpus Christi play.

THE PRIDE OF LIFE [26]. Middle to late fourteenth century; Anglo-Irish; 502 lines in quatrains riming abab; incomplete.

The manuscript of *The Pride of Life*, so called by its first editor, James Mills, was lost in 1922 when the Public Record Office in Dublin was destroyed. Part of a collection of documents preserved by the canons of Christ Church, Dublin, the play was written on the back of a parchment roll of accounts pertaining to the Priory of the Holy Trinity during the years 1337–1346. Of the two scribes who copied the play, apparently in the first half of the fifteenth century, one has been distinguished from the other by his irregular hand and eccentric spelling. References to Berwick-on-Tweed and "Gailispire on the Hil" led Heuser and the early editors to conclude that the play was composed in England, but Davis argues for an Irish origin, pointing out linguistic affinities with the Kildare poems not only in scribal practice but also in features confirmed by rime. On the same linguistic grounds, Davis argues for an earlier date than that of previous editors and critics, one as early as the middle of the fourteenth century. Previously the play had been dated by a reference to the earldom of Kent, which the King of Life bestows upon his messenger: the earldom became vacant in 1408.

Despite the imperfect state of the manuscript brought to light by Mills, the play emerges as a vigorous example of morality drama:

Following a prologue which commands the audience's attention, the King of Life boasts of his power and enjoys the homage of his Queen and his two knights, Strength and Health. When the Queen advises him that he should prepare for death through

a godly life, he scorns her, declaring that he will live forever. He is supported in this
folly by his knights and his messenger, Mirth. The Queen then sends Mirth to summon the Bishop, who preaches a sermon on the abuses of the age and the terrors in
store for those who forfeit grace by refusing to think of death. But the King rudely
banishes the Bishop and sends Mirth to challenge Death to a combat. Although the
text breaks off at this point, the prologue indicates that Death appeared and conquered the King of Life. The prologue also suggests that the King's soul, after parting
from his body, was saved from the fiends by the intercession of Our Lady; but it is
not clear whether the Virgin or the soul and body actually appeared as characters in
the play.

The play's allusions to death as the universal conqueror, together with
the grim warnings given the heedless King, have suggested links with the
Dance of Death and pulpit treatments of the *memento mori* theme. However, except for a homiletic poem on the Twelve Abuses of the Age
(Brown-Robbins, Robbins-Cutler, no. 906), the source of the Bishop's
lament, no specific source has been discovered. The most frequently
cited dramatic analogue is *Everyman* (see [30] below). Both plays are
traditionally classified as moralities of "restricted" scope on the Coming
of Death; both open with the doomed protagonist at the height of
worldly folly and therefore lack any dramatization of his seduction into
sin. But *The Pride of Life* differs markedly from the more somber
Everyman in its spirited portrayal of the braggart King and his lively
messenger. Axton explains this element of the play in terms of the
tendency of pre-cycle, clerical drama to conjoin sermon with game and
to employ popular modes of playing, such as the vaunt and combat,
intimidation of the audience, and running about the "place." Performance was out of doors, to judge from the prologue's reference to the
weather, with the action taking place in a *platea* and in relation to at
least two thrones—one for the Bishop and another with curtains for the
King.

THE MACRO PLAYS (THE CASTLE OF PERSEVERANCE, WIS-
DOM, MANKIND). A group of morality plays, all written in an East
Midland dialect, and associated with the name of their eighteenth-
century owner, the Reverend Cox Macro (1683–1767). In the late fifteenth century, the manuscripts of *Wisdom* and *Mankind* belonged to a
monk named Hyngham, possibly of Bury St. Edmunds; later both passed

into the hands of a Robert Oliver. These manuscripts and that of *The Castle of Perseverance* were acquired by Macro, who was a native of Bury and noted collector of literary manuscripts and historical documents. At some point before 1820, when the plays were bought by Hudson Gurney of Keswick Hall, Norfolk, they were bound in a single volume also containing other manuscripts. The three plays were rebound for Gurney in a separate volume, in which form they were bought by the Folger Shakespeare Library in 1936. The Folger Library disbound the plays in 1971.

Eccles' 1969 edition for the Early English Text Society corrects many errors in the Furnivall texts of 1904 and supplies an extensive scholarly apparatus, including new discussion of each play's language. Bevington's 1972 facsimile edition includes useful transcriptions of the marginalia as well as of the texts. The dialect and indications of ownership point to an East Anglian origin for all three plays, and thus encourage comparison with the dramatic conventions and staging of other late medieval plays from the same area.

THE CASTLE OF PERSEVERANCE [27]. Ca. 1400–25; East Midland with Northern influence; 3649 lines (including 156 lines of banns); mainly thirteen-line tail-rime stanzas, usually riming ababababcdddc, with a number of nine-line stanzas, and other stanzaic forms.

The recent editors have clarified and in some cases formed new conclusions on issues that have long occupied scholars of the play. Bevington explains that both of the obvious imperfections in the manuscript—two lacunae resulting from the loss of a single sheet and the interchange of four extant sheets—occurred after rather than before the manuscript was copied. On the question of language, Eccles concludes that the play could have been written by a scribe from Norfolk but not one from Lincolnshire. This conclusion has been favorably received, despite the long-standing acceptance of Smart's theory that both dialect and a reference to the gallows of Canwick point to Lincoln or its vicinity. Eccles' response to Bennett's theory of revision is also likely to become the prevailing view. Bennett argued that, soon after the original play was composed, different authors added first the banns at the beginning and then the Debate of the Four Daughters in place of the original ending. Bennett considered stanza form, meter, alliterative technique, and other stylistic matters, as well as the fact that the banns allude to the intervention of "oure lofly Ladi" after Mankind's death and do not mention the Four Daughters. Eccles judges that a second author probably wrote the banns, while one author could have written the rest of the play.

The Castle of Perseverance embodies a number of common morality themes in a highly symmetrical form. The large cast is evenly divided between the forces of good and evil, and Mankind moves through two cycles of temptation, sin, and repentance in the main body of the play.

The action begins as man's enemies—the World, the Devil, and the Flesh—declare the nature and scope of their power. Against this background, Mankind appears flanked by his Good and Bad Angels: he is a newborn child about to begin his progress through the ages of man. He sins first by becoming a servant of the World, who sends him to Avarice and the other Deadly Sins (the Three Enemies' retainers). When Penance pierces him with a lance, he confesses to Shrift, receives absolution, and enters the Castle of Perseverance. But Mankind's enemies, alerted by Backbiter, summon the Sins to a siege against the Castle. Although six of the Sins are repelled by their opposing Virtues, Avarice succeeds in enticing the aging Mankind back to worldly goods. This time, only the coming of Death causes Mankind to repent. He realizes that his treasure will go to an unknown heir, and he dies calling on God for mercy. The Soul reproaches the body and cries again for mercy until it is carried off to hell by the Bad Angel. The Four Daughters then debate Mankind's case, after which God rescues him from the fiend but issues a stern warning to sinners.

The *Psychomachia* of Prudentius, once regarded as an immediate influence, is now seen as a distant ancestor of the play. Its series of combats between personified virtues and vices has traditionally been compared to the Virtues' encounters with the Deadly Sins. Cornelius has pointed to an affinity between the play and a passage in Grosseteste's *Chasteau d'amour*, where a sinful man seeking entrance to the Castle of the Virgin describes himself as assailed by the Three Enemies in command of the Seven Deadly Sins. The playwright may have been influenced by this suggestion as it appeared in Grosseteste's poem, one of its English translations, or a related work such as the *Cursor Mundi*. Traver proposed that the Debate of the Four Daughters in *The Castle of Perseverance, The Charter of the Abbey of the Holy Ghost*, and the

Ludus Coventriae all derived from a lost version of the debate similar to that in the *Meditationes vitae Christi*. But while the other versions of the debate mentioned in Traver's argument take place at the traditional time, preceding the Incarnation, the debate in *The Castle of Perseverance* occurs when the individual soul is judged after death. In this it resembles the version in de Guileville's *Pelerinage de l'ame*. Analogues to the attack of the Deadly Sins, the Address of the Soul to the Body, and the Coming of Death have also been noted. Nelson has compared *Of the Seven Ages* (VII [14]), a short verse dialogue with illustrations, in which a progressively aging mankind figure stands between a good and a bad angel.

From the time of Creizenach, literary critics have viewed the play as a dramatized version of the *psychomachia*, a conflict between good and evil forces for the soul of Mankind. Recently, however, Schell has shifted emphasis to the stages in Mankind's progress to salvation, and has defined the play as a pilgrimage of life, analogous in the action imitated to de Guileville's *Pelerinage de la vie humaine*. As Wenzel points out, the play does not share the emphasis of de Guileville's poem on the hero's active quest for bliss. Nevertheless, Schell's analysis of the play's shape and rhythm usefully complements the attention given by earlier critics to its episodes of debate.

Southern's study of the play's manner of performance has led to an appreciation of its spectacle and patterns of stage movement. At the same time, his interpretation of the well-known staging diagram at the end of the manuscript has aroused considerable controversy. In the diagram, the ring surrounding the castle is labelled: "this is the watyr abowte the place, if any dyche may be mad ther it schal be pleyed, or ellys that it be strongely barryd al abowt." In Southern's reconstruction, this ring is a huge ditch surrounding the entire area occupied by spectators and actors; just inside the ring is a mound formed by the dirt removed from the ditch, and on the mound sit the five scaffolds and some of the spectators. Southern's critics have questioned whether the diagram represents an entire theatre in which both spectators and actors occupy the "place." In an important article, Schmitt argues that the diagram is merely a stage design, with the ring indicating a small moat around the castle at the center of the playing area. Whether or not scholars accept Schmitt's alternative theory, they often agree that the scaffolds should remain outside the ring as shown in the diagram. They have also tended to question Southern's use of the Cornish rounds as supporting evidence for the huge mound and ditch. It is generally accepted that a travelling company performed the play, though Bevington suggests that amateurs may have been recruited to take some of the thirty-five roles.

WISDOM [28]. Ca. 1460–70; East Midland; 1163 lines; eight-line stanzas riming ababbcbc or aaabaaab, with few variations.

The play was entitled *Mind, Will, and Understanding* by Thomas Sharp in 1835; Furnivall retitled it *A Morality of Wisdom, Who is Christ* in 1882. It exists complete in the Macro manuscript and in incomplete form (lines 1–752) in MS Digby 133. (For other plays in MS Digby 133, see [19] above.) It is unlikely that either manuscript was copied from the other. The Digby manuscript, usually considered to be in a hand of later date, supplies several lines missing in the Macro text and contains a number of superior readings. The two manuscripts also differ in dialect: Eccles points out that the Macro scribe's representation of certain consonants, particularly *x* for *sh-* in *xall* and *xulde,* shows him to have been an East Anglian. Both manuscripts have been connected with Bury St. Edmunds, the Macro through tentative identification of the monk Hyngham and other persons whose names are written in the heavily annotated margins, the Digby through its sixteenth-century owner Miles Blomefylde, a native of Bury. Though Furnivall and others assigned the play to London from references to the Holborn Quest and legal quarters in the city, an East Midland origin is now generally accepted.

In a highly schematic action, the play dramatizes the progress of the soul as it seeks to attain Wisdom, becomes deformed by sin, and is restored by grace to the condition of perfection.

Wisdom, who appears as Christ the King, begins by defining himself as the spouse of the Church and of each chosen soul. After declaring the power of divine love, he teaches Anima the significance of her black and white garments: the soul is the image of God but has been disfigured by Adam's offence; it has reason but also a potentially corrupting sensuality. Anima is then joined by the Five Wits of the Soul and by the Three Mights—Mind, Understanding, and Will. Wisdom explains that the Mights enable the soul to know the three persons of God and to have faith, hope, and charity; he also warns that these faculties can become perverted if temptation is not withstood. Despite Wisdom's warning, Lucifer is able to suggest sin to Mind, bring Understanding to delight in sin, and gain the consent of Will. Disguised as a gallant, Lucifer purports to recommend the *vita mixta*; however, his specious arguments actually lead Mind to pride, Understanding to covetousness, and Will to lust. Newly attired as "curtely personys," the Mights and their retainers delight in maintenance, perjury, and lechery—vices associated both with the devil, world, and flesh, and with appropriate London locales. But Wisdom inspires contrition by bringing forth Anima dressed "fowlere than a fende" with the seven devils of deadly sin under her mantle. While Wisdom preaches the nine points of virtue, Anima and her Mights retire to receive the sacrament of penance, finally reappearing to celebrate their reformation through grace.

Particularly in the sections involving Wisdom's teaching ,the playwright drew upon religious treatises in English and Latin. These have been identified by Smart in his important study of sources and works containing parallel ideas. Wisdom's initial speech and most of the first part of the dialogue with Anima (lines 1–90) are based on passages in the English version of Henry Suso's *Orologium sapientiae*. The anonymous *Novem virtutes* is the source of Wisdom's instruction on that subject towards the end of the play. For the analysis of the soul, the playwright drew significantly on Hilton's *Scale of Perfection*; and he may have based his treatment of the *vita mixta* on the same author's *Epistle on Mixed Life*. Other sources of specific passages include the *Soliloquium* of St. Bonaventure and the *Meditationes de cognitione humanae conditionis* and *Tractatus de interiori domo* formerly attributed to St. Bernard. The playwright seems to have drawn most heavily upon English works of contemplative doctrine, which would have been current among devout laymen as well as secular and regular clergy. This choice of sources and their use have been interpreted in diverse ways. Smart concludes in his study of sources and parallels that the playwright was both a mystic and a monk, and that he adapted the mystical teachings drawn upon in the temptation scene to make them exclusively relevant to monastic life. Molloy places greater emphasis on the relevance of the sources to the devout layman. He reasons that the playwright chose sources which stressed his general theme, the necessity of striving after perfection in charity. Bevington proposes that the playwright followed his sources in teaching a balanced life of contemplation and fulfillment in social action. In the play, Bevington argues, this program of self-reform also becomes a solution for church abuses.

Implied in all these views are interpretations of the playwright's purpose and intended audience. Smart concludes from references in the temptation scene that the Three Mights are monks ("fonnyde fathers") whom Lucifer lures from a life of contemplation. He maintains that the play was written for an exclusively monastic audience to counteract the spirit of apostasy prevalent at the time. Bevington agrees with Smart that the Mights are monks, but shifts the emphasis to the play's political satire. For Bevington, the play primarily aims at reforming secular abuses among the monastic orders, while offering general advice to a popular audience. Against these topical interpretations, both Molloy and Eccles argue for a widely applicable play on Christian living, Molloy suggesting a Lenten performance at an Inn of Court, Eccles a town or guild production for a general audience.

It seems more likely that the play satirizes contemporary abuses in general than specific abuses among the religious orders. As in *Mankind,* [29] below, and *Nature,* [31] below, social satire is a vehicle for moral doctrine rather than the dramatist's primary emphasis. At the same time, the play's devotional tone and mystical psychology, unusual in a morality, may indicate a special audience. Also unusual are the full stage directions in English for processions, dances, and other visual effects. Among these are the optional dances performed by the Three Mights' retainers, the procession of the Five Wits of the Soul, and the spectacular exit of the devils from under the skirts of Anima. The text specifies elaborate costumes, including the magnificently regal garb and appurtenances of Wisdom. Various doubling patterns have been suggested, but the conditions of performance remain unclear.

MANKIND [29]. Ca. 1465–70; East Midland; 914 lines, mainly four-line stanzas riming abab (or abab bcbc) and eight-line tail-rime stanzas riming aaabcccb.

Two scribes copied the manuscript. The first, who wrote all but the last four pages, Eccles identifies as the same scribe who wrote the Macro manuscript of *Wisdom*. Lacking are a single leaf within the manuscript and probably two or more leaves before the present beginning of the text. Pollard conjectures that the text originally may have included banns or have been preceded by some other piece in a miscellany book. According to Eccles, the language suggests Norfolk speech about 1465–70. This conclusion is consistent with a number of place names suggesting that the play was acted in Cambridgeshire and Norfolk, and with a reference to the "rede reyallys" first coined in 1465. Smart proposed a precise date of February, 1471, on the supposition that this was a Shrovetide play written during the time when Edward IV was temporarily deposed (hence the allusions "Edwardi nullateni" and "regis nulli"). However, Baker dates the play within a year or two of 1466, after the term "reyallys" had time to become popular, and before the minting of the angel (1468–70), the only late fifteenth-century coin not mentioned in the play.

The play opens with a sermon by Mercy, Mankind's spiritual adviser, who beseeches the audience to incline to Christ. Man must be stable in good works and resist corruption by the devil: his salvation depends upon the mercy exemplified in Christ's sacrifice. Intruding on this sermon, Mischief mocks Mercy's preaching, and is joined by New Guise, Nowadays, and Nought, who revel in the "ydyll language" of the world. After the worldlings go out, Mankind approaches Mercy and learns that he must resist his three enemies—his own flesh, the worldlings, and most of all the devil Titivillus. Mankind accordingly sets to work tilling the soil, and succeeds in driving off the worldlings when they attempt to mock his labor. But he is unable to resist Titivillus, whom Mischief and the worldlings call in to their aid. Unseen by Mankind, Titivillus uses tricks to make him grow tired of labor and prayer and shift his allegiance from Mercy to the worldlings. Mischief and the worldlings then hold a mock court at which Mankind swears to follow their example of thievery, lechery, and murder. Urged on by his tempters, Mankind is about to hang himself in despair, when Mercy intervenes and persuades him to seek forgiveness through confession.

Taking Mankind's tilling of the plot of ground as the central motif, Keiller suggested that the playwright was influenced by the half-acre episode in *Piers Plowman*. Mackenzie argued instead for the verse dialogue, *Merci Passith Riȝtwisnes* (see VII [27]), in which a priest called Mercy counsels a sinner tempted by the devil to despair, and leads him to seek grace through penance. Both of these works are now considered analogues rather than sources. The anonymous playwright, thought by different commentators to have been a Dominican friar, a country clergyman, or a lawyer apparently drew on traditional teachings. He was closely acquainted with the penitential doctrine and observances discussed in Coogan's important study; and his treatment of Mankind's descent into sin, as Wenzel has shown, combines a scholastic interest in the psychology of sloth with the image of the sin developed in popular catechetical literature. Coogan proposes that *Mankind* is a Shrovetide play intended to encourage confession and continuing penance during Lent, but the play's moral themes also have the wide relevance of the penitential doctrine in other morality plays.

Until recent years, *Mankind* was considered a crude and unintegrated play in which the villains' exuberant humor overwhelmed the sententious doctrine. It is now generally accepted that the comic routines effectively serve the play's moral purpose. Coogan shows that the comic scenes illustrate the homiletic passages through parody and negative example; Heiserman and Bevington that they satirize contemporary abuses. Even the villains' "ydyll language" has been shown to serve the moral aim in that it grows increasingly tedious and so leads the audience to welcome Mercy's intervention. Elements of the mummers' plays appear in the comic routines, particularly in Mischief's mock beheading and "cure" of Nowadays and the elaborate presenting of Titivillus. Yet the play's learned elements—Mercy's eloquence and the villains' English Latin—balance the popular aspects of the presentation.

Mankind is often cited as the earliest indisputable example of English professional drama. Pollard noted evidence of commercial production for rural audiences by a troupe of itinerant players: the portable properties and small cast, the references to places around Cambridge and King's Lynn indicating the route of the tour, and the collection of money from the audience before Titivillus' appearance. Since the collection begins with "the goodeman of this house" and New Guise later calls for an "hostlere," Pollard assumed that the play was performed in an innyard. Bevington came to similar conclusions in his authoritative study of the early popular theatre, where he discussed along with much other evidence the close contact between the players and a diversified audience ("ʒe souerens that sytt and ʒe brothern that stonde ryght wppe"). Craik and others have suggested that the play may have been performed in a room inside the inn rather than in the yard, for Mankind says "I wyll into thi ʒerde," and references to winter and a fire suggest an indoor performance. Bevington has recently revised his argument to allow for this possibility. The evidence behind all of these judgments continues to be re-evaluated.

EVERYMAN [30]. Late fifteenth to early sixteenth century; London; 921 lines in a variety of verse forms.

Called the *Somonynge of Eueryman* in the Messenger's prologue, the play is titled in the Skot editions: *Here begynneth a treatyse how the hye fader of heuen sendeth dethe to somon euery creature to come and gyue a-counte of theyr lyues in this worlde/and is in maner of a morall playe*. There is a single copy of each of the two editions printed by John Skot; Richard Pynson's two editions survive in a fragment and an imperfect copy. None of the four editions is dated, and none was printed from any of the others. Greg concludes, after comparing the readings of *Elckerlijc*, that the two Pynson editions are sometimes united in error and therefore had a common original. He also finds some slight evidence for a common original of the two Skot editions. Cawley cites instances in which three or four of the editions are united in error, and infers that the two Pynson and Skot originals themselves had a common ancestor.

Much of the commentary on *Everyman* has been devoted to its relationship with the Dutch *Elckerlijc*. The two plays parallel each other very closely, the most obvious difference being *Everyman's* added prologue. There is a possible distinction in meaning, much discussed, between such corresponding words as *rodde-roeyken, good dedes-duecht*, and *knowlege-kennisse*. The verse of *Everyman* is less regular than that of *Elckerlijc*, which has often been associated with *Rederijker* practice. The major issue in *Everyman-Elckerlijc* scholarship, however, has been the question of priority. Although all commentators have agreed that one of the plays was translated from the other, only recently has it been generally accepted that *Everyman* is the translation and *Elckerlijc* the original play. Most scholars have now discounted the numerous attempts to show that one play is prior to the other because it is superior in meter, theology, or the sense conveyed by certain passages. The decisive arguments are those based on systematic analysis of the rimes. Tigg shows that a pair of rime words from *Elckerlijc* is sometimes found inside the corresponding lines of *Everyman*, with added tags making the new rimes. Since a Dutch translator was not likely to have found his rime words ready-made within the lines of an English original, Tigg concludes that the English play must be the translation. This conclusion is supported by Manly's earlier argument that the English translator was occasionally influenced by a wrong line division in the Dutch play. Recently several authorities, including Cawley, have accepted van Mierlo's thesis that the English play was translated specifically from the Vorsterman print of *Elckerlijc* (ca. 1518–25). But van Mierlo's rather slender evidence does not rule out the possibility that the translator used a text now lost. The date of *Everyman* therefore remains uncertain, as do the identities of the Dutch author (traditionally Peter Dorlandus) and the English translator. Whoever the English translator was, he has gained recognition in his own right for the clear and natural English in which he realized the Dutch text.

A number of studies have related *Everyman* to the literary and pictorial traditions of the Dance of Death. Death's summoning of Everyman from a life of riches and worldly pleasure has invited comparison with the similar encounters in Lydgate's *Dance of Death*, as has the Doctor's epilogue with the speech of "Machabre the Doctoure" at the end of Lydgate's poem. The woodcuts brought together on the title page of the Skot editions may reflect pictorial illustrations of Death and the Gallant, a motif suggested in the text itself when Death refers to his victim's gay dress.

Perhaps closer to the play's central concerns are treatises on the *ars moriendi*. Two English dialogues in this tradition—the *Ars Sciendi Mori* of Hoccleve (see VIII [6]) and "a lytel treatyse of the dyenge creature" (STC, no. 6034)—strongly suggest the dramatic situation in *Everyman*.

Both center on a frightened man who learns by good counsel not to depend on friends or temporal goods but to prepare himself for death by doing penance. To these treatises can be added the many analogues to Everyman's desertion by his first set of friends. The ultimate source of this story is the Testing of Friends tale, an oriental fable found in *Barlaam and Josaphat* and in later collections such as the *Legenda aurea* and *Gesta Romanorum*. The names of Everyman's faithless companions (Fellowship, Kindred, and Goods) and his only faithful friend (Good Deeds) derive from the Christian applications of the tale. It is not known what version the author of *Elckerlijc* followed, but he may not have been the first to combine the Summons of Death with the Testing of Friends. The two themes are found together in another analogue, the third of *The Thrie Tailes of the Thrie Priests of Peblis*. For the episode in which Everyman receives the last sacraments, and for his desertion by his second group of friends (Beauty, Strength, Discretion, and Five Wits), some parallels in the *ars moriendi* treatises have been noted. Recently Kolve has proposed that the dramatist expanded the Testing of Friends tale in the light of the parable of the talents and patristic commentary upon it. Kolve argues that the parable explains the figure of Everyman as one summoned to render accounts, offers a comprehensive rationale for all the *dramatis personae*, and helps define Everyman's pilgrimage as a soul-journey.

Comparatists have shown how the themes and structural motifs of *Elckerlijc-Everyman* were adapted in later literature. Through *Elckerlijc*, *Everyman* is related first to two Latin plays, Ischyrius' *Homulus* (1536) and Macropedius' *Hekastus* (1539), and then to a series of Dutch and German reworkings which served both sides of the Reformation controversy on faith and good works. A number of twentieth-century plays, most importantly Hofmannsthal's *Jedermann*, draw on *Everyman* itself in their treatment of modern alienation and materialism.

From the time of Percy, critics have remarked on the play's emotional power, its unity of action, and its consequent closeness to tragedy. Like its Dutch model, *Everyman* sustains a somber tone throughout. Though there are touches of humor in Everyman's encounters with his worldly friends, the play lacks the lively comedy of evil that one expects in the early English moralities. Also unusual in an English morality is the stress placed on Everyman's increasing loneliness and extended spiritual suffering. In most of these respects, *Everyman* differs from *The Pride of Life* ([26] above), the only other medieval play in English to concentrate so exclusively on its protagonist's approaching death. Yet, although *Everyman* approaches tragedy more closely than the other English moralities of the period, it shares their emphasis on the doctrine of salvation. Recent studies, in particular, have focused on the effective dramatic expression of this doctrine. As Everyman comes to understand the remedies offered by Knowledge and Good Deeds, his progress clarifies, step by step, the complexities of Church teaching on what a man must do to be saved. His fall into despair is balanced by a rising action carrying him to spiritual rebirth; and, in the process of parting with his gifts of fortune and nature, he is illumined within by his gifts of grace.

Because the early prints lack stage directions, some scholars have doubted that *Everyman* was intended for acting. The text does refer to properties, including Everyman's account book; his change of costume when he assumes the garment of contrition; and certain *sedes*: the "hous of saluacyon" at which Everyman meets Confession, the grave, and a place "Here aboue" where Cawley suggests that God speaks at the beginning and the Angel receives Everyman at the end. While these references may indicate that *Elckerlijc* was acted, they do not prove that the English play was performed in its own time. Nevertheless, many of the host of modern productions initiated by Poel's revival in 1901 have testified to the play's effectiveness in performance.

NATURE [31]. Ca. 1490–1500; London; in two parts of 1439 and 1421 lines; mainly in rime royal and six- or eight-line tail-rime stanzas, with two sentences in prose.

The play is described on the title page as *A goodly interlude of Nature compylyd by mayster Henry Medwall chapleyn to the ryght reuerent father in god Johan Morton somtyme Cardynall and arche byshop of Canterbury*. It survives in two full copies and four fragments, all of a single edition probably printed by William Rastell. The modern editors, Brandl

and Farmer, were unaware of the Cambridge copy, which is better preserved than that in the British Museum.

Born in 1462, Medwall was admitted to Eton as a King's Scholar about
1475 and to Cambridge as a scholar of King's College in 1480. A University of Cambridge record lists him as B.Civ.L. He was ordained in 1490
and in later years presented with two livings in the gift of the Crown.
From a Chancery suit unsuccessfully brought against him after Morton's
death, it appears that, in addition to serving as Morton's chaplain, he
also held office in the ecclesiastical courts over which his patron had
authority. His acquaintance with the More circle is assumed from his
connection with Morton, the printing of his plays by the Rastells, and
records showing that both he and John Rastell repaid obligations to the
Treasurer of the King's Household during the same year. Nothing is
known of Medwall after 1501.

Like *Fulgens and Lucres*, the only other work known to have been
written by Medwall, *Nature* is a play in two parts apparently intended for
performance before Morton and his household and so dated before the
Cardinal's death in 1500. It resembles *The Castle of Perseverance*, [27]
above, in dramatizing the central character's progress through the Ages
of Man, in taking him through two cycles of sin and repentance, and in
conceiving his struggle in terms of a siege against a castle. The play's
image of Man as lord of the world and its progression from infancy to
old age link it with *Mundus et Infans*, printed by de Worde in 1522 but
perhaps written not much later than *Nature* itself. The initial situation
may have been derived from Lydgate's *Reson and Sensuallyte* and has a
close analogue in Thomas Chaundler's *Liber apologeticus de omni statu
humanae naturae* (ca. 1460).

I. Nature begins by defining herself as God's minister—the agent who sustains His
creatures, reconciles the elements, and influences all activity in the created world.
She then sends Man, the chief of God's creatures, on a journey through the world,
with the warning that he must subdue his Sensuality to his Reason. When Reason and
Sensuality debate, Man chooses Reason as his guide. After the World installs him as
lord of the earth, however, he dismisses Innocency and, counseled by Worldly Af-
fection, allows Sensuality to engage the corrupt courtier Pride as his servant. Soon
Sensuality reports that Man has quarreled with Reason at a tavern and has taken
into his service Pride's kinsmen—the other deadly sins disguised as respectable worldly

types. But man repents his folly, accepts the service of Shamefacedness, and becomes reconciled to Reason.

II. Despite Reason's warning that man is like a castle besieged by three enemies, Man succumbs to the blandishments of Sensuality and goes off to the stews with Bodily Lust. When he attempts to assemble his servants for a fray against Reason, all the Sins except Covetise eventually appear; but they quarrel, refuse to fight, or outwit one another. The battle is never fought, for Man in old age has had to forgo his pleasures, even Covetise, and again seek Reason's good advice. This advice is to discover the seven Virtues, who appear in a series to offer Man remedies for the deadly sins. After Man goes out briefly to receive the sacrament of penance, Reason extols God's great patience with sinners and finally proclaims Man the child of salvation.

In histories of the drama, *Nature* has occupied an uneasy position between the early moralities and moral plays of the sixteenth century. It is frequently stated that the play resembles its predecessors in form but anticipates later drama in its secular and intellectual emphasis on man's life in the world. Commentators have noted as evidence of secularization the important roles given to Nature and Reason, the comparatively indulgent view of Man's sensuality, the comic *psychomachia*, and the lively presentation of the vices as contemporary types. It has been suggested that Medwall's treatment of Man's youthful folly looks forward to educational moralities like *Wit and Science*, and that his sense of a material world inhabited by good and bad counselors anticipates the court settings of later political plays. Although Bevington does not argue for a secularized play, he emphasizes the specific political advice—against extravagant dress, reckless spending, and maintenance—given along with the play's general moral instruction.

The innovations in *Nature* have at times been overstressed. Neither the topic of Reason and Sensuality, the contemporary portrayal of the vices, nor the sense of a court setting is unique in fifteenth-century religious drama. The play's association with John Rastell's *Interlude of the Four Elements* (ca. 1517–18) has perhaps been misleading. Medwall's *Nature* is a medieval goddess whose primary role is to provide Man with spiritual guidance; only in Rastell's play does Nature's counterpart, a masculine deity, encourage the study of natural philosophy. It is Rastell who shifts the emphasis to the material world by presenting instruction in the four elements, the roundness of the earth, and other scientific phenomena. Medwall's play is probably best regarded as a product of his devout humanism. It is a basically conservative morality adapted in tone and language to the demands of a sophisticated audience.

References in the text to a household, doors, and evening indicate performance in a hall, the second half of the play to follow the first "Whan my lord shall so deuyse." Southern envisions the seats specified for Nature and the World at opposite ends of the hall. Most scholars have assumed that the actors were adult professionals who employed doubling, but servants under Medwall's direction and boy actors have also been suggested. The vices' wit and play-acting within the play seem particularly suited to boys.

A SPEECH OF DELIGHT (REYNES EXTRACT) [32]. Late fifteenth century; East Anglian with Northern influence; ten six-line tail-rime stanzas riming aabaab.

The speech is written in a commonplace book compiled by Robert Reynes of Acle in Norfolk, who is known from other entries in the book to have been a churchwarden in the 1470's. A lively character named Delight introduces himself to the audience as one who loves "sporte, myrthe, and play." A word of reproof, apparently from a virtuous female character, gives impetus to a vivid catalogue of his pleasures. He rejoices first in the wonders of the natural world and then in worldly vanities, including stately houses, splendid clothes, and beautiful women. His opening lines have suggested a comparison with those of Lust-and-Liking in *Mundus et Infans*, and it seems probable that the speech is an extract from a morality play.

For the *Epilogue* which follows this item in the manuscript, see [21] above.

PROCESSUS SATANAE [33] is known only from a manuscript containing a single actor's part for God, with brief cues from the parts of other speakers. Greg dates the manuscript about 1570–80 on the evidence of hand and spelling. From an inscription in a later hand, "old verses/From limebrook," he traces its origin to the vicinity of Limebrook in north Herefordshire.

As Greg's title indicates, the *Processus Satanae* is a treatment of the suit brought by Satan against God for having unjustly redeemed mankind. Though far less complex than the *Processus Belial* of Jacobus Palladinus de Theramo, the play contains some of the same motifs: the opening allusion to the harrowing of hell; the preliminary challenge in which God is accused of cheating Satan of his prey; the attempt to employ Biblical personages as advocates; and the decisive debate of God's Daughters. (The text shows that the Debate of the Four Daughters occupied "an houre space" in the play.) A relationship has been suggested with the lost *ludus de Bellyale* given at Aberdeen in 1471. The play's date of composition is uncertain, as is its relationship to the known English dramatic genres. Greg calls it a "late miracle play," and Bawcutt sees a resemblance to the style and manner of John Bale's religious drama; but Chambers proposes that it may be an earlier work preserved in an antiquarian copy. God's judgment in this play differs from that in the mystery cycles, since he does not separate the saved from the damned. Neither does the Debate of the Four Daughters preface the Incarnation as it does in the *Ludus Coventriae*, [12] above. The surviving portion of the play more closely resembles the ending of *The Castle of Perseverance*, [27] above, where the Debate of the Four Daughters also concludes with God's rescue of mankind from the fiend.

3. THE FOLK DRAMA

by

Francis Lee Utley and Barry Ward

The problem of the medieval folk play is very much like that of the ballad and the folktale; most of the recorded items are later than the Middle Ages, and therefore can always be claimed by skeptics as later compositions, which in some part at least they must be. Yet there is a sense of continuity in the study of each of these genres: plot, form and even words greatly resemble the few medieval documents or literary versions, and there is as much likelihood that the modern versions, with modifications, are derived from the medieval versions, the bulk of them now lost, as that they are wholly new creations of a later age. For the English medieval folk play the classic reference appears in a letter of April 16, 1473, by Sir John Paston to John Paston: "No mor, but I have ben, and ame troblyd with myn over large and curteys delyng with my servants, and now with ther onkynd nesse." Several have deserted him, above all, "Dawbeney, God have hys sowle, at Castre, that iff ye wolde take hym in to be ageyn with me that then he wold never goo ffro me, and ther uppon I have kepyd hym thys iij. yer to pleye Seynt Jorge and Robyn Hod and the Shryff of Nottyngham, and now when I wolde have good horse he is goon into Bernysdale, and I without a keeper."

Though there are no St. George plays extant in England from before 1500, this reference assures us that the many ritual plays discovered in the nineteenth century and later which include St. George as a character may well have fifteenth-century antecedents. In the case of ROBIN HOOD AND THE SHERIFF OF NOTTINGHAM [34] there is no doubt, since we have a fifteenth-century Robin Hood play, closely related in plot to Child ballad 118, "Robin Hood and Guy of Gisbourne," extant in a Trinity College Cambridge manuscript formerly owned by Le Neve (Norroy) and W. Aldis Wright. It is the upper half of a leaf once pasted at the end·of some folio volume, with accounts on the verso of house rent extending from May 1475 to August 1476, perhaps once owned by William Paston, second earl of Yarmouth, and hence sound documentary witness to the play mentioned by Sir John Paston:

Sir Guy promises to take Robin Hood for gold and fee. In Scene II (as marked by Adams) Sir Guy and Robin contest in archery, casting the stone, and wrestling, and Robin wins each bout. Sir Guy attempts to blow his horn to call his allies, but Robin appeals to his chivalry, and they then duel with swords. Robin kills the knight and dresses in his clothing. In Scene III the Sheriff overcomes Robin's men, including Little John, Will Scarlet, and Friar Tuck, whereupon Robin appears disguised as Sir Guy, looses the bonds of his men, and puts the Sheriff to death and his men to flight.

Now this early version (beginning "Syr sheryffe for thy sake") is straight outlaw theatrics, with little evidence of ritual (unless we wish to push the evidence of the normal ballad combats); there has been much dispute about the fertility ritual or *hieros gamos* aspect of the later Robin Hood and Maid Marian dramas and ballads. Probably the Frazerian element in the tradition has been overemphasized, just as it was in Jessie Weston's account of the derivation of Arthurian romance from the ritual drama of the East. Yet there is no doubt that some elements of the dying and resurrected god play a part in the extant St. George and related plays. These have now been extensively collected and ordered, and Cawte, Helm, and Peacock locate over a thousand occurrences, many closely related, in England, Scotland, Ireland and the Isle of Man. These dramas have likewise found their way to the West Indies, Canada (notably Newfoundland), the Leeward Islands, and the United States (Kentucky, Massachusetts, and Pennsylvania). The Cawte classifications include the Sword Dance, the Bridal Play of the East Midlands, and the Hero-Combat Play. Modern studies by Halpert, Ward and Abrahams have emphasized the functional shift of the modern plays from seasonal rituals to entertainment; there is an extensive literature for the Continent as well as the British Isles, and the British migration to the New World is paralleled by that from Spain to Latin America, where there are undeniable links (*Los Pastores*) with medieval *autos* of a very early vintage as well as remarkable adaptations to New World custom and belief. There are many problems to solve, including that of the mutual texts and their history (a computer collation of the English texts is promised), their relationship to balladry and medieval drama in general, and the complex development in oral and in printed versions. Many modern representations, for instance, go back to one nineteenth-century Cheshire chapbook.

St. George's role in England undoubtedly increased in the seventeenth century, with Richard Johnson's *Seven Champions of Christendom*. But there are evidences that the saint also appealed to medieval folk: there is the ST. GEORGE CAROL [35] in MS Egerton 3307, "Worschip of vertu ys the mede" (Robbins-Cutler, no. 4229.5) and the nine-line ST. GEORGE CHARM [36] in MS Bodleian 15353 (Brown-Robbins, Robbins-Cutler, no. 2903), "Seynt Iorge our Lady knyȝth/ He walked day he walked noyȝth" which explains how Our Lady's Knight walked day and night until he found the Night Goblin, beat her and bound her, until she promised she would not come at night within seven rods of land when St. George was named, so long as a natural-holed flint stone were hung over the stable door or over the horse itself (compare our modern horse-shoe over the barn door), and the charm written and hung in the horse's mane.

As for the Robin Hood tradition, it is a maze of conjecture and con-tradictory evidence, but there is no doubt that there was a live dramatic tradition after the Paston occurrences. Adams prints a *Robin Hood and the Friar* from the Copland *Gest of Robin Hood* (1553–69) to be used in May Games, and cites a fragmentary *Robin Hood and the Potter* of the same nature. (See ROBIN HOOD AND THE FRIAR: ROBIN HOOD AND THE POTTER [37] in Bibliography.) Maid Marian, perhaps not originally connected with Robin, appears in the *Friar* specimen. Adams also prints as relevant to medieval-early renaissance drama a Shetland Sword-Dance (ca. 1788, with St. George and his fellow six champions of Christendom, studied by Sir Walter Scott), an Oxfordshire St. George Play (1853), a Leicestershire St. George Play (1863), and a Revesby Sword Play (1779).

XIII. POEMS DEALING WITH CONTEMPORARY CONDITIONS

by

Rossell Hope Robbins

The more than 300 poems [1] discussed in this chapter are grouped together on the basis of their predominating concern with contemporary political, social, ecclesiastical, or moral conditions, or with several or all of these themes [2].

Their subject matter is intensely circumscribed to events in the British Isles or affecting England. If the Duke of Burgundy is discussed, it is only for his perfidy against the English (see [77] below). One possible exception might be the dubious reference to the Council of Basle in an obscure prophecy (see [303] below). Throughout, these poems are all intensely provincial, home-town, nationalistic.

They range in scope from two- or three-line tags preserved in chronicles to formal, intricate art lyrics. Between these extremes of crude phrases of illiterate soldiers and fashionable conventions of experienced poets of the court circle, they encompass minstrel rimes jubilant at an English victory or the course of a famous battle, upper-class commentary on Parliamentary deliberations, bills exhorting to action in a public-cause, and versified dispatches and releases on the civil wars. Prose items dealing with contemporary conditions and chronicles, in prose and verse, are described elsewhere.

With few exceptions, these poems were designed for immediate ends: conveying a limited idea or feeling, stimulating admiration or support, inciting to action. Perhaps inevitably they form a public poetry, written to order, technically competent and immediately useful. These pieces are but the native vernacular products of a great activity that also found its voice in a host of similar compositions in Latin or in French [3].

The best known poets of political verse are Lydgate, Gower, and Hoccleve. Lydgate's shorter poems in this genre are more "official" than poetical; the commemoration of *The Entry of Henry VI into London* (Brown-Robbins, no. 3799), for example, found in six manuscripts, occurs also in three prose paraphrases as a kind of semi-official program of the ceremonies, and numerous stanzas were incorporated into Fabyan's *Chronicle* (see [21] below). Five other poems (Brown-Robbins, nos. 928, 1929, 2211, 2218, 2445) are similar commissions carried out by Lydgate for the Coronation. Gower wrote in Latin and French as well as English; he composed an attractive *Praise of Peace* (Brown-Robbins, no. 2587). The third famous name in political writing, because of his *De Regimine Principum* (VIII [2]), ca. 1412, is Thomas Hoccleve. Hoccleve also penned pedestrian ballades to Henry V, pleas for gratuities, and a vicious 512-line attack on Sir John Oldcastle (VIII [19]).

The vast majority of the poems on contemporary conditions, however, are anonymous, and only a few other names are recorded, like Ashby (see [251] below) or Page (see [74] below). Even names mean little: for example, nothing certain is known of one Laurence Minot ([43] below), probably a professional minstrel. Two of the prolific writers of religious lyrics may be counted political by virtue of a single poem each: Audelay, by his recollection of Henry V (Brown-Robbins, no. 822), written about 1429; and James Ryman, by a comparable poem on Henry VI ([186] below), a retrospective review composed in 1492, thirty years after the deposition.

In general, all writers of political poems were employed like other craftsmen or technicians to serve and promote the special interests of those classes with power or money; sometimes they came from those classes.

The poems on contemporary conditions occur in all kinds of manuscripts [4], partly because the boundaries between political and religious, historical and didactic verse were vague. Many categories, now clearly defined, overlapped in Middle English, particularly the poems on the Evils of the Age or the commemorations of kings, where a religious attitude prevails; on the other hand, poems attacking the friars or Lollards are perhaps more political than theological. Consequently, poems which some might consider "political" are sometimes subsumed in other chapters with an overriding unity (e.g., works by Lydgate) or generic unity (gnomic and proverbial pieces).

For the most part, the political pieces exist in unique texts, but some —generally the most dreary—had extensive circulation. As is to be expected, Lydgate's productions and the prophecies rank highest:

53 MSS   Lydgate's *Verses on the Kings of England* (Brown-Robbins, Robbins-Cutler, nos. 444, 882, 3632, 4173.3)

21 MSS   *When Rome is Removed* [285]

20 MSS   *The Abuses of the Age* (Brown-Robbins, Robbins-Cutler, no. 906)

17 MSS   *Chaucer's Prophecy*, XI [11]
         The Cock in the North [281]

16 MSS   *The Libel of English Policy* [249]
         Page's *Siege of Rouen* [74]

15 MSS   Chaucer's *Lak of Stedfastnesse* (Brown-Robbins, Robbins-Cutler, no. 3190)

14 MSS   *The Abuses of the Age* (Brown-Robbins, Robbins-Cutler, no. 1820)

11 MSS   *Tomas of Ersseldoune* [290]
         Lydgate's *Prayer to St. Edmund for Henry VI* (Brown-Robbins, Robbins-Cutler, no. 2445)
         A Prophecy by the Dice [297]

10 MSS   Lydgate's *Verses Against Women's Headdresses* (Brown-Robbins, Robbins-Cutler, no. 2625)

 6 MSS   Lydgate's *Entry of Henry VI into London* (Brown-Robbins, Robbins-Cutler, no. 3799)
         The Evils of the Times (Brown-Robbins, Robbins-Cutler, no. 2364)

 5 MSS   Lydgate's *Prayer for England* (Brown-Robbins, Robbins-Cutler, no. 2218)
         The Evils of the Times (Brown-Robbins, Robbins-Cutler, no. 2787)

Of the Middle English poems on contemporary conditions, less than fifty antedate 1400; they become more numerous later, and the propaganda of the Wars of the Roses heralds the Tudor and Elizabethan political broadsheet.

For convenience of treatment, the poems are discussed in the following divisions:

1.   Verses Inserted into Chronicles
      I. Miscellaneous Scraps
     II. Tags in Langtoft and Mannyng

2.   Political Poems in MS Harley 2253

3.   Political Poems in the Kildare MS

4.   War Poems by Laurence Minot

5.   Political Poems in MS Digby 102

6.   Historical Ballads and Poems in Chronicles

7.   Politics in Song

8.   The Wicked Age: Satires and Complaints
      I. General Evils: Summaries
     II. General Evils: Expansions of the Abuses of the Age
    III. The Clergy
    IV. Women
     V. Contemporary Life: Vignettes

9.   The Wars of the Roses
      I. The Lancastrians
     II. The Yorkists

10.   The Estates
      I. The Rulers
         1. Commemoration of Rulers
         2. Advice to Rulers
         3. Longer Discussions on National Policy
     II. The Ruled

11.   Political Prophecies
      I. The Merlin Prophecies
     II. The John of Bridlington Prophecies
    III. The Thomas of Erceldoune Prophecies

IV. The Thomas à Becket Prophecies

V. Other Prophecies

1. Verses Inserted into Chronicles

I. Miscellaneous Scraps

MISCELLANEOUS SCRAPS [5]. Of the political and satirical pieces composed in the twelfth, thirteenth, and fourteenth centuries, a few fragments (in forms sometimes modified in transmission) have been preserved in several of the chronicles. No complete specimens of political poems in Middle English antedating 1300 are known to survive. Longer (and later) poems included in chronicles are generally entered with the Historical Ballads and Poems in Section 6 below or The Estates in Section 10, I, 1 below. Few of the earlier scraps exhibit more than limited antiquarian interest.

THE OLD ENGLISH CHRONICLE FRAGMENTS [6] comprise several passages conjectured to represent songs. The later passages occur in three of the original seven manuscripts of the Chronicle continued after the Conquest: at Winchester and Abingdon (now MS Cotton Tiberius B.i) to 1070, at Worcester (now MS Cotton Tiberius B.iv) to 1079, and at Peterborough (now MS Laud Miscellany 636) to 1154. The following pieces date after 1050: (a) Death of Edward the Prince or the Son of Ironside, ca. 1057; (b) Dirge of King Edward the Confessor, ca. 1065; (c) The Wooing of Margaret, ca. 1067; (d) Baleful Bridal, ca. 1076; (e) The Highhanded Conqueror, ca. 1086; and (f) Couplet for the year 1104.

PEMBROKE CAMBRIDGE SCRAPS [7] consist of a few twelfth-century lines: (a) "Ynguar and Vbbe. Beorn was the thriddle. Lothebrokes sunes. Lothe weren criste"; and (b) "In clenche qu becche under ane thorne liet kenelm kinebern heued bereued." The first scrap refers to famous Vikings of the ninth century.

LIBER ELIENSIS [8] quotes four lines, which Thomas of Ely at the end of the twelfth century ascribes to King Canute. These and other scraps, he says, were sung at dances.

> Merie sungen the munaches binnen Ely,
> Tha Cnut king reu ther by ;
> Roweth cnites noer the land
> And here we thes munaches saeng.

DESCRIPTION OF DURHAM [9] in Simeon of Durham's *Chronicle* consists of 21 alliterative lines written about 1100. It is noteworthy as a rhetorical *tour de force*: "Every phrase of the poem is a stereotype illustrating what Greek and Roman text-books had prescribed as fitting ingredients for an *encomium urbis*" (Schlauch).

TAGS IN MATTHEW OF PARIS [10], in his *Historia Anglorum*, include: (a) a scrap on the Battle of the Standard, ca. 1138, "Yry, yry, standard"; (b) an account of a dream of Bartholomew, Bishop of Exeter, ca. 1161, "Riseth op, alle Cristes icorne / Levenoth ure fader of þis wrold fundeth"; and two fragments of soldiers' songs, which may, however, perhaps be much later dance burdens; (c) Song of the Flemish Soldiers under the Duke of Leicester in 1173, "Hoppe hoppe Wilekin, hoppe Wilekin / Engelond is min"; and (d) Song of the Soldiers of Geoffrey de Mandeville, Earl of Essex, "I ne mai aliue / For Benoit ne for Ive," which Friedman interprets as an ironical allusion to the manner of the Earl's death in 1216.

HUGH BIGOD'S DEFIANCE OF KING HENRY [11], a popular scrap, written at a later date, associated by the chroniclers William Harrison and William Camden in the sixteenth century with the First Earl of Norfolk's defiance of King Henry II in 1174.

If I were in my castell of Bungeie,
Vpon the watere of Waueneie,
I wold not set a button
By the king of Cockneie.

A WELL-ORDERED KINGDOM [12] describes its characteristics in irregular riming lines:

Kyneriche wel idist nudliche habbe mot   strengthe of miste
                                            wisedom of riste
                                            plente of heite
miste wid ricste wodnesse of uuele
ricste wit hute micste
micste and ricste wit hute helste sorful wicste

WALTER OF GUISBOROUGH'S FRAGMENT [13], a stanza in the *Chronicon* formerly attributed to Walter of Hemingsburgh or Walter of Hemingsford, apparently from some contemporary popular song about 1279. Four of the ten complete manuscripts preserve this scrap. Edward I asked the sons of some of his chief lords what they discussed while their fathers were deliberating in the parliament. The sons expressed their dislike of the statute, Quo warranto:

Le roy cuuayte nos deneres
E la rayne nos beau maners
E le Quo voranco
Sale mak wus al at do.

A LAMENT AFTER THE DEATH OF ROBERT DE NEVILLE [14], a fragment of four lines from a thirteenth-century narrative ballad (post 1282), quoted in a lawsuit of 1331 between Lord Ralph [Dandulphus] de Neville of Raby and the Prior of Durham. To counter Lord Neville's claim that the family retainers every September 4th had offered a stag as quit rent, all the time blowing their horns in the cathedral, the

Prior introduced this stanza to show that the presentation of the stag took place on September 14th (Holy Rood Day)—a legalistic quibble to sidetrack the main issue, that Ralph's grandfather Lord Robert had indeed presented his stag ceremonially at St. Cuthbert's shrine in Durham Cathedral. The suit is recorded by Robertus de Graystanes in chapter 178 of his history of Durham.

> Wel and wa sal ys hornes blawe
> > Holy Rod the day;
> Nou es he ded and lies lawe,
> > Was wont to blaw tham ay.

This historical quatrain may be compared with similar fragments, like [8] above and Robbins-Cutler, no. 2830.5, two couplets of a Robin Hood ballad found on a flyleaf.

EVIL TIMES OF EDWARD II [15], in the so-called *Short English Metrical Chronicle* (Brown-Robbins, no. 1105), consists of two English couplets, preceded by three French lines, supposedly criticizing the government of Edward II by listing three evil things. However, the idea is at least biblical (Ecclesiastes 10:16): "Vae tibi, terra, cujus rex puer est." This scrap follows a French poem on the death of Edward I (see [29] below).

For other pieces against Edward II see [37] and [82] below, and Brown-Robbins, no. 1787.

WYNTOUN'S CHRONICLE FRAGMENTS [16]. (a) One eight-line stanza, a popular lament (or "Cantus") at the end of Book 7 (lines 3619–26) on the times following the death of Alexander III of Scotland in 1286. Though the extant lines date ca. 1420, they probably represent a piece at the end of the thirteenth century, and (if so) thereby become the earliest extant Scottish poetry. Elsewhere in Wyntoun are: (b) two couplets (Book 8, lines 4997–5000) representing a song of the English against the Black Agnes, Countess of March, at the siege of Dunbar in 1337; (c) two popular couplets on the marriage of Robert II to Elizabeth Moor in 1370 (Book 9, lines 21–24); and (d) the Duke of Orleans' defense of the Scots in 1391, in 44 lines (Book 9, lines 1472–1526), copied separately in the Pepys Maitland Folio MS (1570–90).

Wyntoun's *Orygynale Cronykil* itself, in couplets, is listed elsewhere (Brown-Robbins, no. 399).

NEVILLE'S CROSS FRAGMENT [17] is a single line of a presumably popular song preserved in a detailed Latin poem on this battle (1346), extant in three manuscripts:

Clamabant 'In a day go we to the tyrie with hay,'
Ipsis sit Waleway, meschef tristissima woday.

See [52] below for a poem on this battle by Minot.

TREVISA'S POLYCHRONICON FRAGMENTS [18]. About 1387 John Trevisa translated the Latin *Polychronicon* of Ralph Higden, a monk of Chester, who wrote early in the first half of the fourteenth century. The translation was initiated by Lord Thomas of Berkeley, whom Trevisa served as chaplain, to be rendered in easy-to-understand English prose; the mandate, *Dialogue on Translation*, is described elsewhere. Several short verse pieces are scattered throughout the long work, half of them concentrated in Book I, Chapter 24; in addition, there is a long description of Wales in Book I, Chapter 38. Trevisa's translation was first published complete by Caxton in 1482, although sections on the "descripcion of Britayne and also Irlonde" had been printed in 1480. A full account of Trevisa's translation will be found in the chapter on Chronicles. The fragments are:

(a) In Praise of Rome, two couplets (Book I, Chapter 24).

(b) Epitaph for the Giant Pallas, three monoriming lines (Book I, Chapter 24).

(c) A riddling couplet inscribed on a pillar (Book I, Chapter 24).

(d) Verses on a table of brass, five cross-rimed quatrains (Book I, Chapter 24).

(e) Couplet from Ovid's *Ars amatoria,* i.114 (Book I, Chapter 24).

(f) Of the Land of Wales, 460 lines in doggerel couplets (Book I, Chapter 38).

(g) Peaceful England, thirteen couplets (Book II, Chapter 41).

(h) Translation of lines in Virgil, one quatrain (Book II, Chapter 44).

(i) Verses on Chester Castle, thirteen doggerel couplets (Book I, Chapter 48).

(j) The Chair of a Judge, four couplets, advocating honesty in law suits (Book III, Chapter 8). The following somewhat garbled text occurs separately in Lansdowne MS 210:

> [Sittynge on this see,]
> Iustyce loke thu stedfast be.
> Kepe hand and erys
> From yeftys and mennys prayers.
> Take and do strew law—
> Lest thy skyn be of-drow.
> Thir settyst in place yett
> Wher thy father ded sett.

(k) An Introduction extolling virtues of the book, printed by de Worde, five stanzas rime royal, added in 1495.

SCOTICHRONICON FRAGMENTS [19]. The *Scotichronicon,* a popular history of Scotland to the death of James I (1437), in sixteen books, was compiled by Abbot Walter Bower, ca. 1440; Books 1–5, however, were written by John Fordun (died ca. 1384), who gave the work his name, and Books 6–16 were put together by Bower partly from Fordun's notes. It went into several recensions.

Inserted into the original Latin are several English passages: (a) Against young men's counsel, two couplets ("sic vulgariter"), based on I Kings 12:8 (Bk. 14, chap. 14); (b) Against fashionable ladies with trailing gowns, three couplets (Bk. 14, chap. 30); (c) "Indisciplinata mulier," five couplets comparing the faults of women to those of animals, translating seven short Latin distiches from a Latin comedia, *Babio,* "Cornuta capite, ut hoedus" (Bk. 14, chap. 31); (d) an English couplet translating an aphorism from *Babio*: Trust neither the horse's foot, the hound's tooth, nor woman's faith (Bk. 14, chap. 32); (e) four macaronic lines, actually lines 13–16 of a longer macaronic poem (Brown-Robbins, no. 2787) on the Evils of the Times (Bk. 16, chap. 1).

In addition, several lines, possibly verse, occur: (f) Warning to Sir John Montague, Earl of Salisbury, by "Blak Annas," Countess of March, at the Siege of Dunbar in 1337 (Bk. 13, chap. 11): "O Montagow! Montagow! be war, for ferry sall thi sow." See also Wyntoun's fragment on this episode, [16](b) above; (g) "Now row we merely, quoth John Birley" (Bk. 14, chap. 21).

An English prose passage (Bk. 15, chap. 9) gives the traditional form of challenge by Henry IV for the crown of England; Richard's abdication speech, which immediately precedes, is in Latin.

In a Scottish version (manuscript not established) of the *Scotichronicon* is: (h) seven couplets translating seven Latin lines ("Scotia sit guerra pedibus" in Bk. 12, chap. 10), on King Robert the Bruce's advice to the Scots on the conduct of the war, ca. 1306.

Treated elsewhere is *Ane Ballet of the Nine Nobles* (Brown-Robbins, no. 1181), added to MS Brechin Castle and MS Edinburgh University 186 of the *Scotichronicon*; the poem equates Robert the Bruce as equal with "les neuf preux"; it is paralleled in the *Buik of Alexander*, both texts being translated from *Les voeux du paon*.

JOHN CAPGRAVE'S VERSE FRAGMENTS [20]. In John Capgrave's prose *Chronicle*, about 1450, are inserted six short verses, presumably written or translated by Capgrave himself.

(a) Terence (B.C. 146) on "what gile in women is"—five lines, Latin and English.

(b) Simon of Norwich (A.D. 1259), elected bishop because he gave the monks three hundred marks as a bribe (recalling Simon Magus in Acts 8:18–19)—a Latin couplet followed by an English translation.

(c) On Pope Benedict (A.D. 1299)—a Latin couplet followed by an English translation:

Oro, nomen habe—Benedic, Benefac, Benedice:

Aut rem perverte—Malefic, Maledic, Maledice.

I pray ye have this name—Say wel, Do wel, and Be Good;

Or ellis turn thi fame—Say evel, Do evel, Be cursed and wood.

(d) The great hurricane (A.D. 1362)—a Latin couplet followed by an English translation.

(e) Bridlington's Prophecy (A.D. 1404)—one Latin couplet, four short lines in English:

Pes schul thei tretyn,

Gile under that schul thei betyn;

For no maner mark

Schal be saved that blessed Ierark.

For other Bridlington prophecies see [279] below.

(f) The Emperor's farewell to England (A.D. 1416). "And in his goyng he mad his servauntis for to throwe billis be the way, in which was writyn swech sentens"—three English couplets:

Farewel, with glorious victory

Blessed Inglond, ful of melody,

Thou may be cleped of Angel nature;

Thou servist God so with bysy cure.

We leve with the this praising,

Whech we schul evir sey and sing.

THE FABYAN CHRONICLE VERSES [21]. (a) Over sixty verse compositions are inserted into Robert Fabyan's prose *New Chronicles of England and France* (1516); one or two poems are found in earlier chronicles (e.g., Caxton's *Chronicles of England*, 1480), and some later (e.g., Rastell's revision of Fabyan, 1533). Although Fabyan industriously relied on earlier chronicles, most of the poems are late formal compositions, like: (b) the stilted Prologue of 28 stanzas rime royal to the entire chronicle, which opens with the same first line as Burgh's *Parvus Cato* (Brown-Robbins, no. 3955); (c) the three stanzas on King John, clearly very late; or (d) the four lines on the death in 1272 of Henry III, "King Henry is dede bewtye of the worlde for whom grete dole."

On the other hand, two groups of poems are surely contemporary with the events they commemorate. One group consists of the popular rimes current in the English-Scottish wars in the early fourteenth century, resembling in a general way the verses in Langtoft, and to some extent the later diatribes of Minot during the wars of Edward III:

(e) Song of the Scots, "What wenys Kynge Edwarde with his longe shankes," against Edward I at Berwick in 1302. Earlier versions are contained in Langtoft ([23](d) below).

(f) Song of the English, "These scaterande Scottes holde y for sottes," one six-line tail-rime stanza, "in reproche of ye Scottes," whom the English had defeated at Berwick in their attempt to relieve Dunbar. A similar piece occurs in the fifteenth-century *Brut* variants. Langtoft includes a tail-rime stanza on this subject ([23](g) below).

(g) Song of the Scots, "cnflamyd with pryde," after their victory at Bannockburn in 1314, "Maydens of Englande sare may ye morne," one six-line tail-rime stanza with a refrain similar to that sung by the mariners in *Richard Coer de Lyon*, I [106], "with a heue a lowe . . . with rumbylowe," and in the *Squyer of Lowe Degre*, I [104]. The clerk of the Tolsey Court Book, now in the City of Bristol archives, at the end of the fifteenth century scribbled a few doggerel rimes in his record, including the mariners' refrain and a reprise from [182] below:

Hail and howe! Rumbylowe!
Steer well the good ship and let the wind blow.

This Fabyan scrap appeared also in Caxton's *Chronicle* (1480), and later chronicles; and it is very common in various forms of the *Brut*.

(h) Song of the Scots in derision of the marriage of Robert the Bruce with "Jane Make Peace," sister of Edward III, in 1328, four short lines, "Longe beerdys hartless." Numerous other chronicles contain a similar tag.

The second and longer series of contemporary verses commemorates the Entry and Coronation in 1432 of Henry VI in London. For this event, John Lydgate wrote a long poem in 76 stanzas rime royal with an eight-line Envoy to serve as a sort of program note for the entire celebration (Brown-Robbins, no. 3799). Lydgate's poem was copied in full in several manuscripts of historical or chronicle material (like the *Chronicle of*

London or the *Great Chronicle*), and it even appeared in a prose redaction in at least three manuscripts. From Lydgate's longer text, Fabyan extrapolated and partly rewrote the Sotelties and eight selections, but he omitted Lydgate's Coronation Ballade (Brown-Robbins, no. 2211). The following items are the Lydgate extracts:

(i) The Sotelties at the Coronation Banquet, three eight-line stanzas, a variant of Lydgate's text, also found in several fifteenth-century chronicles, like the *Great Chronicle*, the *London Chronicle*, and *Gregory's Chronicle*. Attention might be directed to other examples of sotelties, including Robbins-Cutler, nos. 461.5, 1270.8, 1331.5, 1386.5, 3563.5.

(j) Confound the King's enemies, one stanza rime royal.

(k) Pageant verses by Nature, Grace, and Fortune, three stanzas rime royal.

(l) Roundel sung by the Fourteen Virgins, "Soveraygne lorde welcome to your citie."

(m) Pageant verses by Dame Sapience, one stanza rime royal.

(n) Pageant verses by Cleanness, two stanzas rime royal.

(o) Pageant verses by Enok and Eli, two stanzas rime royal.

(p) Pageant verses by the Tree of Jesse, two stanzas rime royal.

(q) At the Conduit at Paul's Gate, two stanzas rime royal.

Finally, one other scrap, probably contemporary, is the famous couplet (r) against the advisers of Richard III, posted by William Colingbourne in 1485 on the doors of St. Paul's Cathedral. The couplet was taken from Fabyan by later chroniclers like Hall and Holinshed:

> The catte, the ratte, and Louell our dogge
> Rulyth all England vnder a hogge.

At this point, attention might be drawn to the huge and still unpublished rimed chronicle in MS Pepys 2163, with occasional stanzaic passages inserted, continuing to the reign of Henry VIII. It draws heavily on Fabyan and Harding (Brown-Robbins, no. 710); it is described elsewhere (Robbins-Cutler, no. 4174.5).

Another series of pageant verses for the marriage of Prince Arthur and Princess Catharine occurs in MS Cotton Vitellius A.xvi; these are listed elsewhere.

A proverbial couplet (Robbins-Cutler, no. 4198.8) inserted into a London chronicle is listed elsewhere.

LATER MISCELLANEOUS INDIVIDUAL FRAGMENTS [22] of political poems are found in various other manuscripts, some of them chronicles. None has much literary importance, and additional scraps may be expected to be found with further research on the manuscripts of chronicles.

For the curse on Urse d'Abitot, quoted in William of Malmesbury's *Gesta Pontificum*, see [294] below.

For the Canute Song, quoted in the *Historia Eliensis* of Thomas of Ely (ca. 1175), see [8] above.

For a couplet ("Wille Gris") in the *Lanercost Chronicle* (Brown-Robbins, no. 4174), see the chapter on Proverbs, Precepts, and Monitory Pieces.

(a) Four lines on Henry Hotspur.

(b) Approach of Earl of March on London, a couplet in *Gregory's Chronicle*.

(c) A scripture for a London pageant, a couplet in *Gregory's Chronicle*.

(d) Profits from fishing for Bristol merchants, four irregular lines written as prose:

>Heryng of Slegothe
>And salmon of Bame
>Heis made in Brystowe
>Many a ryche man.

(e) The Hawleys of Dartmouth, one couplet:

>Blow the wind high, blow the wind low,
>It bloweth good to Hauleys hoe.

(f) John Barton the Wool Merchant, one couplet:

>I thank God and ever shall
>It is the sheep hath payed for all.

(g) A Warning to John Howard, Duke of Norfolk, in 1485, found in various early chronicles:

Jacke of Norffolke be not to bolde,

For Dykon thy maister is bought and solde.

A few other verses in prose chronicles are listed elsewhere in this chapter in more appropriate positions, e.g., [66] below.

II. Tags in Langtoft and Mannyng

TAGS IN LANGTOFT AND MANNYNG [23]. It has been claimed that the first important group of Middle English political songs survives in the Anglo-Norman *Chronicle* of Pierre de Langtoft, who was (according to his translator, Robert Mannyng de Brunne) an Augustinian canon of Bridlington. Some time after the death of Edward I (1307), presumably under upper-class patronage, Langtoft wrote a history of England in corrupt Anglo-Norman. The first part derives from Geoffrey of Monmouth's *Historia Regum Britanniae,* and the second from various Latin chronicles such as those by William of Malmesbury, Henry of Huntington, and Florence of Worcester. On the other hand, the third part, justifying Edward's Scottish Wars, is first-hand, written by a contemporary, a native of the north of England, and a partisan; it is therefore historically the most valuable. Here, Langtoft frequently interrupts his hexameter couplets and turns to six-line tail-rime stanzas, generally in English or in French which breaks into English.

There are twelve such interpolations. Significantly, all except one deal with the events of 1296.

All eleven manuscripts of Langtoft, most of them early fourteenth-century, show some variants, and not all manuscripts contain all the English scraps. Representative of the standard text, receiving the widest currency in the fourteenth century and retaining many features of the presumed North Midland original, is MS Royal 20.A.xi. Similar are the slightly earlier and more readily understood MS Cotton Julius A.v (printed by Wright), and MS Royal 20.A.ii and MS College of Arms Arundel 61. Three manuscripts contain only the history of Edward I. MS College of Arms Arundel 14, a recension of the time of Edward III, modernizes certain lines to remove archaisms; it resembles the fragmentary MS Fairfax 24. MS Cambridge University Gg.1.1, an important variant, has more lines of verse than the other manuscripts, and its language, while obscure, is more racy and idiomatic.

In the fourteenth century (1338), Langtoft's *Chronicle* was englished by Robert Mannyng de Brunne. When he came to Langtoft's tail-rime stanzas, Mannyng neither transliterated the Anglo-Norman nor reproduced the Middle English, but substituted his own versions. Thus, for most of these little pieces, there are two forms: the French and English of Langtoft, and the English of Mannyng.

This paralleling of versions, as well as the multiplicity of variants in Langtoft, has given rise to a theory that these tail-rime stanzas are "fragments of popular songs interwoven into the *Chronicle* by its writer" (Wright, and so Wells and Wilson). However, it is more probable that Langtoft's scraps are the work of a professional minstrel seeking to improve the morale of the English army. There was indeed a tradition: Henry II had commissioned Jordan Fantosme to write an eye-witness account of the defeat of William the Lion, the Scottish leader, in 1174. Edward II employed a Carmelite monk, Robert Baston, prior of the monastery at Scarborough and famous as a minstrel, to celebrate the anticipated victories of his expedition into Scotland for the relief of Stirling. When the English were defeated at Bannockburn, Baston was captured. The Scots exacted poetic justice: as his ransom Baston had to compose praises of the English defeat. Minot himself could be cast in this role of self-appointed laureate for Edward III. And so Langtoft for Edward I.

The sub-verse of men like Langtoft made possible the political lyrics of the following centuries.

(a) *The Battle of Ellendune*, A.D. 825, a couplet in Langtoft, dubiously recalling a twelfth-century English heroic poem on this early battle, or more likely a rendering of Henry of Huntingdon:

>   Ellendune rivus cruore rubuit,
>   Ruinae restitit, foetore tabuit.

Robert de Brunne turned it into English:

>   Under Elendoune the bataile was smyten.
>   Men syng in that cuntre, fele yit it witen,
>   Elendoune, Elendoune, thi lond is fulle rede
>   Of the blode of Bernewolf, ther he toke his dede.

(b) *Against Balliol,* one six-line tail-rime stanza in Anglo-Norman; in Langtoft only:

> Dount li rays Eduuard
> Du ray Jon musard
>   Est rewerdoné,
> De Escoce sait cum pot;
> Parfurnyr nus estot
>   La geste avaunt parlé.

This item is included here for sake of completing the series of inserted verses.

(c) *Against the Scots I,* three English lines in two manuscripts (Fairfax and College of Arms Arundel 14); in Langtoft only:

> Trput Scot riueling
> With mikel mistiming
>   Crop thu ut of kage.

Langtoft's abusive word *riueling* was picked up in a Harley MS 2253 poem (Brown-Robbins, no. 1889) and by Minot in [44] below.

(d) *Jeering of the Scots at Edward's Earthworks,* two stanzas in Langtoft, an additional stanza in Mannyng. This is the only tag paralleled in other chronicles, such as Rishanger, *Brut,* and Fabyan [21](e), and the only certain example where external evidence supports a "popular" base for Langtoft's minstrelsy.

(e) *The Messenger's Speech to Balliol,* from Sir Robert Siward besieged in Berwick in 1296; in Langtoft two Anglo-Norman and one English stanzas; and three Middle English stanzas in Mannyng.

(f) *Diatribe at Defeat of Scots at Dunbar.* Mannyng adds an introductory stanza to the two stanzas in Langtoft. Langtoft's text has all the hallmarks of minstrel composition addressed to his audience. His use of *nages* (buttocks), misunderstood by some transcribers as *wages* (to retain the rime), is curious, for it is a French word preserved in English only in this tag.

(g) *Against the Scots II,* one stanza in Langtoft and Mannyng:

> For Scottes
> Telle I for sottes

> and wirches unwarre,
> Unsele
> Dintes to dele
>   Thaim drohg to Dunbarre.

For the versions in the *Brut,* Caxton's, and Fabyan's *Chronicles,* see [21](f) above.

(h) *Admonition to Edward for Vengeance Against Balliol,* eight Anglo-Norman stanzas and one Middle English stanza in Langtoft; seven English stanzas in Mannyng (an additional stanza in the Cambridge MS).

(i) *Against the Scots III,* deriding their poverty, five Anglo-Norman and two Middle English stanzas in Langtoft; seven variant stanzas in Mannyng.

(j) *Merlin's Prophecies Fulfilled in Edward,* six Anglo-Norman stanzas in Langtoft; Mannyng has an English variant with two added stanzas. For the Merlin prophecies see [272] below.

(k) *Against the Scots after Dunbar,* nine Middle English lines in one manuscript only (Cambridge) of Langtoft; not in Mannyng.

> for thar wer tha bal brend
> he kauged ham thidre kend
>   ant dreued to dote
> for scottes at dunbar
> Hauld at thayre gan char
>   Schame of thar note
> war neuer dogges there
> hurled out of herre
>   fro coylthe ne cotte

(l) *Exultation over the Execution of Wallace,* one Anglo-Norman stanza and one Middle English stanza in Langtoft; three stanzas in Mannyng.

2. POLITICAL POEMS IN MS HARLEY 2253

MS HARLEY 2253: POLITICAL POEMS [24]. The main body of the religious and secular lyrics of MS Harley 2253 is treated in the chapter on Lyrics. In the present chapter are described the poems from this manuscript on contemporary conditions and political events: seven of the early fourteenth century and one on the earlier Battle of Lewes. The short prophecy in the Harley MS linked to Thomas of Erceldoune is discussed in [288] below.

A SONG OF LEWES [25], sometimes called *The Song Against the King of Almaigne*, composed in the South some time between the Battle of Lewes on May 14, 1264, and the fall of Simon de Montfort on August 9, 1265, comprises eight stanzas, aaaabcb, the fifth line having three and the others four stresses. The last two lines form a swinging mocking refrain: "Richard, though thou be a tricker, trick shalt thou never more."

A partisan of the barons and Simon de Montfort exults over the defeat and capture of Henry III, his son, and Richard, Earl of Cornwall (King of Germany since 1258). He mocks their importing foreign troops, jeers at Richard's valiant defense of himself in the mill at the conclusion of the Battle of Lewes, voices Simon de Montfort's threats against the Earl of Warren and Sir Hugh de Bigot, and promises that Prince Edward shall ride spurless on his hack to Dover and to banishment.

SONG OF THE HUSBANDMAN [26], 72 four-stress alliterative lines in stanzas alternately abababab and abab, generally with stanza-linking; dialect Southern, composed ca. 1300. The wars of Edward I imposed such crushing taxes that many peasants and workers could scarce exist. In passionate bitterness, the poet raises a powerful plaint of despairing misery.

Men on the earth make lamentation; the good years and the corn are both gone— now must we work without hope. I can no longer live by my gleanings, yet ever the fourth penny must go to the King. Hayward and woodward and bailiff oppress us— there remain to us neither riches nor repose. The poor are robbed and picked full clean; barons and bondmen and clerks and knights and clergy are borne down; many who once wore robes now wear rags. More than ten times I paid tax, yet must I give feasts for the beadles when they come to collect. What I used to save, I must spend on them. The master-beadle declares he will make my house bare; I must bribe him with a mark. They hunt us as hounds do hares. I sold my seed to get silver for the King, so my land lies fallow. Since they took away my fair cattle from the fold, I well nigh weep when I think on my weal. Thus breed they bold beggars. Our rye is rotted ere we reap, because of the evil weather. Consternation and woe are awake—it were as well to perish at once, as so to labor.

THE FLEMISH INSURRECTION [27], in Southern dialect, seventeen eight-line tail-rime stanzas normally aaabaaab. It voices the national hostility to France in exultation over the slaughter of the army of the Comte d'Artois by the Flemish burghers under Peter Conyng, at the Battle of Courtrai in July 1302. The poem must have been written soon after that date; but the final stanza, which speaks of the Prince of Wales as the avenger who shall punish France, is probably an addition of about 1305.

With rude mockery and almost brutal jests, the poet jeers at the proud French as "bought and sold" by Peter Conyng and his weavers and fullers; at Sir Jacques de St. Paul and his sixteen hundred knights, whose "basins of brass" the burghers "began to clink" and "broke all to pieces as a stone breaks glass," until the French "lay in the streets stuck like swine"; at the proud boasts of King Philip and his officers; and at the slaughter of the sixty thousand French, whose heads were "dabbed" and "dodded off" without ransom, and heaped into pits—all this by a few fullers!

THE EXECUTION OF SIR SIMON FRASER [28], 233 lines in stanzas normally aaabccb, the second half of the stanza forming a wheel and bob. The dialect is Southern. The poem was composed between September 7, 1306, when Fraser was executed, and November 7, 1306, the day of execution of the Earl of Athole, who in line 218 is still uncaptured; and possibly before September 27, when Fraser's body was burned.

The song expresses the English feeling toward the Scots, all of whom are traitors to the realm. It presents vividly the trial of Fraser and his fellows, their execution, the hanging and the beheading, the burning of the bowels, and the drawing and the quartering; and it points its hearers to the parts of the bodies hanging on London Bridge close guarded, a warning to all other traitors. The treacherous Scots planned to bring the English barons to death, and Charles of France would willingly have given them aid.

THE DEATH OF EDWARD I [29], composed soon after the King's death on July 7, 1307, consists of 91 four-stress lines normally in stanzas ababbcbc, in Southern dialect with some West Midland forms. Unlike the other political pieces in this manuscript, it is a translation, sometimes close, of a French poem of the same date, and is much more finished than are most of the other English political poems. It is also notable as the only Harley political poem duplicated in another manuscript. It stresses less Edward's martial and political achievement than his religious attitude and purpose. Most lines are occupied with the lament of the Pope of Poitiers, with dramatic narrative presentation of Edward's dying bequest and directions for a crusade, and with the thwarting of his purpose, which the writer ascribes to the machinations of the King of France. The song rings throughout with sincere emotion in face of the passing of the great personality that had been so potent. "Though my tongue were made of steel, and my heart wrought out of brass, never might I tell the goodness that was with King Edward. King, as thou art called conqueror, in every battle hadst thou glory!"

In the Cambridge MS which contains fragments of this elegy, is another fragment on the Evils of the Times ([81] below).

SATIRE ON THE CONSISTORY COURTS [30] consists of five stanzas each of eighteen lines, essentially twelve-line tail-rime stanzas, aabccbddbeeb, with a six-line bob, ffgggf, similar in form to the *Notbrowne Mayde* (VII [61]). The poem belongs to the reign of Edward I, and is a Southwest Midland reworking of an original in mixed Northumbrian and East Midland.

The poem is a coarse and abusive attack on the minor ecclesiastical courts by a poor peasant summoned for trial, apparently for illicit behavior with a woman whom he is ordered to marry. Very realistically are presented the "old churl in a black robe" presiding like a lord, "laying his leg along," with his forty clerks that "pink with their pens on their parchment"—all ready to take bribes; the half-dozen summoners who reach forth their rolls—the bane of the peasantry; the court crier in yellow, who jigs with his rod and calls in Mag or Mall, who enters covered with mold like a moor-hen, ashamed in face of the assembly of men, but screeching out that the culprit must marry her; the black thralls, who order the marriage; the priest proud as a peacock, who, after the man has been driven like a dog through the market, weds the pair.

The poem is one of the earliest of a continuing series of attacks and satires on the venality of those concerned with administering the law. See also [92], [93], and [158] below, and two carols, *Money, Money* (Brown-Robbins, no. 113; Greene E E Carols, no. 393) and *Truth Is Unpopular* (Brown-Robbins, no. 72; Greene E E Carols, no. 385).

SATIRE ON THE RETINUES OF THE GREAT [31], ten long alliterative monoriming quatrains, a Southwestern reworking of an original
Western dialect, was written perhaps before the death of Edward I (1307).

In galloping rhythm the minstrel vents his wrath against the swarm of horse-boys
and pages and hangers-on that accompany those who "ride on horses." Bitterly he inveighs against the ribald, impudent knaves, who rise early, scraping their scabs, and
cramming their impudent crops before cockcrow; who ape the fashions, going about
with buttons as if they were brides, wearing low-laced shoes, and content with only
the pick of fine food. Christ walked; he would have no snarling, jawing gadelings
attend him. "Hearken this way, horsemen . . . ye shall hang and lodge in hell."

THE FOLLIES OF FASHION [32], sometimes entitled *Against the
Pride of Ladies,* five stanzas consisting of four alliterative monoriming
lines and an expanding bob of three monoriming lines, in Southwest
Midland dialect, is an intense outburst against the vanity of women of
the lower and middle classes who bedeck themselves in the elaborate
mode fashionable about 1300. Driven by intense moral feeling, and filled
with disgust, the author attacks the offenders with bitter, passionate invective, expressive of the attitude of the clergy toward the excesses of
fashion.

For other poems satirizing extravagance in dress, see [136–138], [140–
141], and [160–161] below.

3. POLITICAL POEMS IN THE KILDARE MS

THE KILDARE MS [33]. MS Harley 913 was compiled in the first
decades of the fourteenth century (whole manuscript completed post
1329, according to Hardy) by emigrants from Southern or Southwestern
England at the Franciscan Abbey of Kildare, Ireland; it is therefore often
called the Kildare manuscript. Opposing this traditional view, Garbáty
suggests compilation at Athlone, and a date (at least for [34]) before 1327.
Its contents, in Latin and English with some French, are contemporary
and range from a Latin parody (The Drinkers' Mass), through a Lollai
song in English (Brown-Robbins, no. 2025) with a Latin translation, to
various indulgences. Many of the English poems seem designed for popu-

lar preaching purposes. The political entries are discussed below; most of the other poems are distributed through the chapters on Homilies, on Proverbs, Precepts, and Monitory Pieces, or on Lyrics.

The Land of Cokaygne, [34] below

Five Evil Things (Brown-Robbins, no. 1820)

Satire on the People of Kildare, [35] below

Homily by Friar Michael Kildare, [36] below

A Sarmun (Brown-Robbins, no. 3365)

Fifteen Signs before the Judgment (Brown-Robbins, no. 3367)

Appeal of Christ (Brown-Robbins, nos. 1943 and 2047)

The Fall and Passion, IV [29]

Homily on the Ten Commandments (Brown-Robbins, no. 2344)

Lullaby Warning Song (Brown-Robbins, no. 2025)

Song on the Times of Edward II, [37] below.

Homily on the Seven Deadly Sins (Brown-Robbins, no. 3400)

Sir Pers of Birmingham, [38] below

Old Age (Brown-Robbins, no. 718)

A Fragment (Brown-Robbins, no. 2003)

Song of Nego, [39] below

Erthe Upon Erthe (Brown-Robbins, no. 3939)

THE LAND OF COKAYGNE [34] lies in the main tradition of Coquaigne or the Land of Fair Ease. In spite of the fact that 70 of its 95 short couplets ridicule the monks and nuns (an aspect not general in this type), the comparable French poem in MS Harley 2253, *Qui vodra a moi entendre*, is far more a clerical satire. The stories of the abbot's ruse to round up his wandering novices and the mixed bathing episode justify the poem's description as a fabliau.

"Bi weste Spaygne" lies the Land of Cokaygne, compared to which Paradise is naught. There is every joy, free from strife and all ill. The rivers are oil and milk and wine and honey. There is a fine abbey of white and gray monks, with a cloister and a church, whose walls and roofs are meat and pastry and pudding. In the cloister a tree bears all kinds of pleasant spices. There are wells of balm and wine. Birds sing sweetly. Geese fly roasted to the abbey, crying, "Geese all hot! All hot!" Larks fly down to one's

mouth all ready to be eaten. The glass windows turn to crystal when more light is
needed for Mass. The abbot knows how to beat a drum roll on a neighboring nun so
that his erring novices rush home to join the fun. Great games these monks have
bathing with the nuns. A virile monk will be well looked after, and the laziest will be
made abbot. To gain this paradise, a penance of seven years wading in swine's ordure
is demanded.

The poem may owe as much to a folk background of social discontent
as to the overtly Franciscan animosity against the Cistercians. Morton
sees in the last lines a limitation of this happy pie-in-the-sky earthly
paradise to despised manual workers now doing the most menial tasks.
On the other hand, the writer, possibly a Goliardic clerk of specially
lively imagination, is not hostile toward these clerical pranks. High
praise has been lavished on the poem; Furnivall, for example, called it
"the airiest and cleverest piece of satire in the whole range of Early English, if not of English, poetry."

SATIRE ON THE PEOPLE OF KILDARE [35], twenty stanzas,
aabcdd, in a very loose galloping metre, almost doggerel. In each stanza,
the first line addresses an individual or group, and the last two lines give
the author's commentary on his own writing. The rest of the lines expose
with bold impudence the personal flaws of the individual or the general
vices of the group: Michael, Christopher, Mary, Dominic, Francis (the
remarks to the saints are very free), the friars, monks, nuns of St. Mary's,
the priests, the merchants, tailors, cobblers, skinners, potters, bakers,
brewers, hucksters, and wool-combers. The poem concludes with bidding
its hearers drink and make merry. The satire could, of course, be directed
against any locality, not necessarily Kildare.

A similar but longer satire in Anglo-Norman, *Rithmus facture ville de
Ross*, or *The Entrenchment of Ross*, in 1265, occurs at ff. 64, 61, 55, 56.

HOMILY BY FRIAR MICHAEL KILDARE [36], fifteen complicated
but skillfully handled stanzas, aaabababab (b of three stresses with feminine ending, the rest of four stresses), with internal rime in the last two
"a" lines. Stanza 15 ascribes the poem to Michael Kildare, a Franciscan.
The piece chides the rich for devotion to vanities and urges amendment.

SONG ON THE TIMES OF EDWARD II [37], 198 four-stress lines, the first two stanzas ababcbcb, the last stanza ababc, and the rest ababcdcd.

The poem complains against the prevalent lawlessness, and the oppression of the poor by the powerful and ruthless rich. The world is full of sorrow and strife; hate and wrath are dominant; true love is rare; and the highest are most charged with sin. Covetousness controls the law, pride and contention rule. Holy Church and Law should exert themselves against the oppressors of the poor, who should not be buried in church but cast out like dogs. The King's ministers favor whoever bribes them; the upright man loses his possessions and is borne to death. Next follows an animal fable (taken from Bozon): The Lion, king of beasts, summoned the Wolf and the Fox to answer charges of evil-doing. The simple innocent Ass was also charged. The Fox and the Wolf sent fowls as presents to the Lion and, though guilty, were pardoned. The Ass sent nothing and was, though innocent, condemned. God and the Trinity preserve us; one can live only through covetousness and contention, and pride is master. As a man comes, so shall he go—alone and with nothing. Yet the beggar scorns his crust and curses the giver. Trust no one, not even sister or brother. Honor God and the Church; give to the poor—thus do God's will and win Heaven.

The expression is direct and crisp. Sermonizing goes side by side with satire. The poem reflects the proverb literature of the period, and stanza 20 recalls *Erthe Upon Erthe* in this same manuscript (Brown-Robbins, no. 3939).

For similar satires see *The Sayings of the Four Philosophers* [80], *The Evil Times of Edward II* [15], and *A Satire of Edward II's England* [82]. Another similar piece is a short macaronic fragment, [19](e) above, of the longer poem on the Evils of the Times (Brown-Robbins, no. 2787).

SIR PERS OF BIRMINGHAM [38], 132 three-stress lines in stanzas, aabccb, rude and without artistic merit, laments the death on April 20, 1308, of Peter of Birmingham, Baron Tethmoy, the really ruthless champion of the English settlers in Ireland, and extols his suppression of thieves and his relentless and treacherous pursuit of the Irish. Nearly half of this exultation narrates Peter's outwitting and destroying of some Irish who plotted against the English; the conclusion praises the benefits of pilgrimages.

SONG OF NEGO [39], a fragment of twelve short couplets of no poetical worth, is directed against the trickery of dialecticians. "Nego" is taken as the most representative and objectionable of the terms (among others, Dubito, Concedo, Obligo, Verum Falsum) employed by the clerical hair-splitters, as, knowing nothing, they conceal their ignorance, and, pretending search for truth, distort the truth. Truth draweth to the bliss of Heaven; "Nego" surely doth not so.

WARNING TO THE YOUNG MEN OF WATERFORD [40], a fragment in tail-rime, aaaabcccb, probably the first stanza of a longer poem, copied into MS Lansdowne from a now missing part of the Kildare manuscript. The copyist states that the original was "a long discourse in meter" warning the youth of Waterford against the Anglo-Norman family of le Poers or Powers who had settled in the district of Decies.

Two other items may be included here:

ON THE DECAY OF THE ENGLISH LANGUAGE IN IRELAND [41], a single stanza, aabccb, beginning "By granting charters of peace," added probably about the middle of the fourteenth century to *The Book of Howth*. The lines lament the undoing of the land through unwise grants, improper practices regarding children, and the adoption of Irish for the English language.

THE MAYOR OF WATERFORD'S METRICAL EPISTLE [42], 44 rime royal stanzas of dignified doggerel, a letter sent to the Archbishop of Dublin in 1487, with concluding ascription of eleven lines in three tail-rime stanzas, signed by John Butler (Mayor of Waterford), James Rice, and William Lyncolle. The poem has been transcribed from some lost original by some unknown antiquary about 1600.

In 1487, Lambert Simnel was crowned in Dublin. His backer, the Earl of Kildare (Governor of Ireland), wrote to John Butler (Mayor of Waterford) ordering him to proclaim the new king and to aid him in every way. The Mayor not only refused to do this, calling Simnel a traitor, but summoned the Butlers, the Walshes, and the towns of Carrick, Clonmel, etc., to come to Waterford in defense of the rights of Henry VII. After English troops had landed in Ireland and captured the rebels, the Mayor and City of Waterford wrote a versified epistle to Walter FitzSimmons, Archbishop of Dublin, "most noble pastour, chosen by God," regretting that the incident had severed the old friendship that had always existed between the two cities, and proving Henry's rights through his wife to the crown of England. They rebuked the Archbishop for the part he had taken in the rebellion and exhorted him and the people of Dublin to repent their wrongdoing.

4. War Poems by Laurence Minot

LAURENCE MINOT [43]. The only set of political poems in the fourteenth century consists of eleven poems (mid-Lincolnshire dialect), associated with Laurence Minot, so named in two poems ([48] and [50] below). The subject matter deals with the military exploits of Edward III in the Scottish and French Wars from 1332 to 1352. The manuscript containing these pieces, Cotton Galba E.ix, later than the events by almost a century, is a careful copy of these and other major English poems. Determined efforts have been made to identify Minot, but the evidence is illusory. Several documents, however, have been printed by Moore relating to the purchase of land in Cressy Forest, France, by a Laurence Minot in 1320, and a remission of the mortgage by Edward III in 1331. It seems best to follow the *Cambridge History of English Literature* and regard Minot as "a professional gleeman, who earned his living by following the camp and entertaining soldiers with the recitation of their own heroic deeds."

Of Minot's eleven poems, comprising in all some 923 lines, eight deal with the French Wars and three with the Scottish, each written shortly after the event it describes. Minot's presence at all the battles he describes is doubtful; some poems seem eyewitness accounts, others fictions. At the time of writing his last poem, Minot added rubrics to provide continuity and apparently revised the whole series. The poem on *The Sea Fight at Sluys*

[48], for example, refers to the "Duke" of Lancaster—Henry, created Earl of Lancaster only in 1345, was not titled Duke until seven years later.

Perhaps because of his long alliterative lines or the pattern of poetical commonplaces, Minot's verse is at times routine, dull, and filled with padding. Yet what is remarkable is not the plethora of clichés, but his power of evoking striking images in simple words—the plight of the burghers of Calais [51], or the bloody slaughter at Southampton [46], or the man without a country, pounding the pavements of an alien city [45], or his vituperation of the Scots [44].

From the literary view, Minot is furthermore important because at an early date he expressed a fervid nationalism, and an unswerving devotion to "gude king Edward." The omission of English defeats or English trickery, the rancor against the Scots and French, and the spirit of "my country right or wrong," assured his poems their popularity. From the historical view, the date of the manuscript is important: by the early fifteenth century the need for the unity of England behind the crown had crystallized, and the fifteenth-century scribe realized the political significance of these earlier (and by then historical) accounts. The myth which Froissart constructed for the rich and highborn was duplicated for the humble by Laurence Minot.

There is no basis for Hall's claim of *A Prayer to the Trinity* (Brown-Robbins, no. 775) for Minot.

THE BATTLE OF HALIDON HILL I [44], 92 alliterative lines in eight-line stanzas, abababab, with stanza linking, commemorates Edward III's victory on July 19, 1333, over a larger Scottish army attempting to raise the siege of Berwick. Minot gives utterance to the militant joy which the English felt at their first success for several decades. Besides gloating over the cracked crowns of the wild Scots, Minot exults over the defeat at Dundee of ten French ships sent to assist them.

For a verse extract in a prose chronicle, see [66] below.

BANNOCKBURN AVENGED [45], six virile alliterative stanzas, aaabb, in four-stress lines with stanza linking, continues the theme of [44], but is less narrative and more lyrical. The theme of the treachery of the Scots is emphasized by the refrain word "gile"—they are taunted for their defeat, and the English minstrel mocks their flight to Bruges, painting vivid pictures of the man without a country.

THE EXPEDITION TO BRABANT [46], 63 short couplets, tells how King Philip of France, to assist his allies the Scots, in 1328 attacked Agen in Gascony (claimed by the English). Edward III was forced to declare war (lines 1–10) and went to Antwerp to negotiate with his allies in the Low Countries and with the Emperor, Louis IV of Bavaria (lines 11–40). Philip then sent a fleet to ravage Southampton (October 4, 1338); having done considerable damage, it was driven off (lines 41–74). Some time previously, the French had captured the ship called the Christopher (lines 75–116). The French will pay for this (lines 117–26).

THE FIRST INVASION OF FRANCE [47], sixteen six-line tail-rime stanzas, describes the first weeks of Edward's invasion of France on September 20, 1339, continuing the narrative from the preceding poem [46]. Edward drew up his troops near La Flamengerie on October 23, but King Philip refused to give battle. Minot spends most of his lines scoffing at the cowardice of the French.

THE SEA FIGHT AT SLUYS [48], 88 lines in varying stanzas formed basically of groups of four or six long monoriming alliterative lines, tells of the great English naval victory at Sluys on June 24, 1340. Lord Morley, the English Admiral, and other English notables are commemorated in short stanzas, culminating in Minot's customary adulation of King Edward III.

THE SIEGE OF TOURNAY [49], six short alliterative eight-line stanzas, abababab, followed by three eleven-line stanzas, ababababcab (the c line being a bob), with stanza linking, is a flyting against the citizens of Tournay, abusing them and mocking them for King Philip's inability to raise the English siege. A truce on September 25, 1340, prevented the capture of the town.

THE BATTLE OF CRECY [50], nineteen short alliterative eight-line stanzas, abababab, with stanza linking, describes the invasion of France in July 1346, an exaggerated account of the sack of Caen, and the Battle of Crecy in the following month (stanzas 8–19). An introduction of ten short couplets relates Merlin's prophecies to Edward III. Minot avoids detailed description of the battle, naming no commanders (in contrast to his practice in [48]).

THE SIEGE OF CALAIS [51], twelve short alliterative eight-line stanzas, abababab, with stanza linking (compare [50]), commemorates the year-long siege, from September 4, 1346, to August 4, 1347, when Calais surrendered. Minot gives some details of the siege, and some striking vignettes of the misery of the citizens, who had eaten up not only their horses but their cats and dogs.

THE BATTLE OF NEVILLE'S CROSS [52], 66 lines in varying stanzas formed basically of groups of four or six monoriming alliterative lines (like [48]), gives, for Minot, a relatively detailed account of the battle fought on October 17, 1346. After his victory at Halidon Hill (see [44]), Edward set harsh terms of submission, so the Scots maintained a state of resistance. After the English victories over the French, described by Minot in [48], [50], and [51], the French King appealed to David Bruce for a diversionary attack. After some initial successes, Bruce's Scottish army and French mercenaries were defeated by an army of Northern lords not serving in France with Edward. Edward Balliol then replaced Bruce as the Scottish king. This poem is less vituperative than many of Minot's works; like [48], it briefly enumerates and lauds the battle leaders.

For a fragment of a contemporary English ballad on this battle, see [17] above. For a later ballad, see [55] below.

THE DEFEAT OF THE SPANIARDS [53], five six-line alliterative stanzas, aaaabb, with internal line linking, tells of the defeat of the Spanish fleet off Winchelsea on August 29, 1350. This victory removed a threatened invasion by Pedro of Castile. Minot very lightly sketches the military events and, as in [49], concentrates on abuse of Edward's enemies.

THE TAKING OF GUINES [54], 40 long alliterative lines in six-line stanzas, aaaabb, with internal line linking, on how Edward with his great engines won the castle of Guines in 1352. The "hero" of this attack was "gentle" John of Doncaster, an English adventurer who betrayed the town to the highest bidder, who happened to be Edward III. Minot describes John's exploits and warns the French, especially the men of St. Omer, to beware. A concluding quatrain forms an isolable prayer for the King.

DURHAM FIELD [55], a later popular and typical ballad in 66 quatrains, probably composed at the end of the fifteenth century, commemorates the Battle of Neville's Cross. It is similar to other later ballads on the English-Scottish wars, like *The Battle of Otterburn* [67], *The Hunting of the Cheviot* [68], *The Battle of Harlow* [70], and *Flodden Field*, [220] below.

5. POLITICAL POEMS IN MS DIGBY 102

MS DIGBY 102 [56]. The 24 poems in Bodleian MS Digby 102 can be dated about the first quarter of the fifteenth century; while their syntax is sometimes forced to conform to the needs of scansion, they show competency according to the formal use of the time. The manuscript is a fair copy, neatly rubricated in red and blue, with relatively few calligraphic errors. The basic dialect is East Midland (*not* Western, or Southwestern, as Kail says), perhaps round Derbyshire; but there are occasional Northern forms, along with a few Southern, probably acquired in London. It points to a man from the provinces residing in London, a conclusion suggested by the texts.

The poems are a closet production and the work of one author. Not only is their approach consistent—throughout deeply moral, church-supporting, gentry-favoring, monarchy-loving—but phrases and echoes recur throughout the series. Clues about the social class of the man who composed the Digby series arise only from internal evidence. First are indications of potential audience. The poems offer advice to a king, address a "kyngis counselere," and "lordis." Twice they speak to those "that ouer puple hav gouernaunce." They severely admonish the justices and warn the clergy against neglect of duty. Kail observed certain specific evils behind the generalized moral laments on the wickedness of the world. Prompted by this and other allusions to Parliament, he saw a relation to the deliberations of the Commons, as given in the *Rolls of Parliament* in the early fifteenth century. In this way, Kail dated some of the poems. For example, in *Evils in the State* [61], a seemingly apolitical piece, appear three stanzas condemning those who clip money, use false weights, and pervert the law. Parliament, meeting just before Easter, 1410 ("this holy tyme" of the first line), had broached these very topics. Their appearance in the poem, in this sequence of the Commons' debates, is strong evidence for Kail's identification.

This circumstantial evidence may not suffice to prove Kail's inspired guess that the author was "most probably an abbot or prior," who, "as such, occupied a seat in parliament, and voted with the Commons," but the proposal is possible. At any rate, the author spoke to those found in the Commons—the knights of the shires, the minor gentry whose lot was to be thrown with the growing strength of the merchants of London, and the lesser clergy.

This conglomerate grouping, not yet dominant in the life of the country, was fighting on many fronts: it opposed the great feudal magnates who set themselves outside the law and turned the King's power to their own advantages; it had to contend with the discontent of laborers and apprentices; and it resented the political activities of the bishops. Its logical ally was the crown; and the Digby series mirrors the growing nationalism focused in the person of the King. In so strengthening the King, the Commons were attacking the cosmopolitanism of the feudal system, and *What Profits a Kingdom* [58] perspicaciously notes the changing economic conditions starting to shackle the nobility. Such candor and insight are unusual at so early a date.

The poems are bound with a copy of *Piers Plowman*, and it is curious that many of the sentiments can be paralleled in this work. The Digby author shares Langland's views that the King and the Commons have mutual responsibilities, that they should seek the common profit and punish wrong, and that the Commons form the King's treasure.

The Digby poems, therefore, may best be regarded as occasional closet verse, written by some lesser religious dignitary in one of the orders, for circulation among sober-minded laity and clergy who had a special interest in practical politics. It seems likely that the "prior" (if such he were) wrote the series over a period of years, one or two a year; for the poems successively deal with events ranging from 1401 to 1421. No doubt, apart from the wish to entertain, the poet hoped, by recalling recent events and commenting on them, to influence those in a position to legislate and so indirectly to influence the King.

In their religious-political subject matter and their form (refrain, wheel and bob), the Digby series suggests the more numerous and better-known Vernon-Simeon poems (such as *The Insurrection and Earthquake of 1382*, [85] below).

The complete list of the 24 poems follows; nine are considered here.

Love God and Redress Abuses, 1400, [57] below
Meed and Much Thanks, VII [41]
What Profits a Kingdom, 1401, [58] below
Learn to Say Well, Little or Nothing, 1404 (Brown-Robbins, no. 411)
Wit and Will (Brown-Robbins, no. 2048)
Do Evil and Be Feared—A Satire, [59] below
Learn to Die (Brown-Robbins, no. 2088)
Evils in the Church, 1408, [60] below
Evils in the State, 1410, [61] below
A Good Stirring Heavenward, 1410 (Brown-Robbins, no. 2091)
God and Man Made at One, 1412 (Brown-Robbins, no. 911)
God Save King Henry V, 1413, [62] below

Maintain Law and Henry's Foreign Policy, 1414, [63] below

Precepts for Successful Living (Brown-Robbins, no. 3381)

The State Compared to Man's Body, [64] below

The Follies of the Duke of Burgundy, 1419, [65] below

Love What God Loves (Brown-Robbins, no. 3279)

The Declaring of Religion, 1421 (Brown-Robbins, no. 4109)

God's Appeal to Man (Brown-Robbins, no. 1508)

How Man's Flesh Complained to God Against Christ (Brown-Robbins, no. 3484)

Learning to Good Living (Brown-Robbins, no. 2763)

Know Thyself and God (Brown-Robbins, no. 3564)

The Sacrament of the Altar (Brown-Robbins, no. 1389)

The Lessons of the Dirige II, IV [7]

LOVE GOD AND REDRESS ABUSES [57], 21 eight-line stanzas, ababbcbc, with refrain, "Man, know thyself, love God, and dread," combines pious clichés threatening hell fire to thieves with practical advice how to avoid rebellion. It may be dated about 1400.

All office holders should beware of bad counsel, oppression, and injustice, and govern according to God's commandments, for a reckoning will be demanded. If the law be kept, the people will not rebel. Do as you would be done by: men with ill-gotten goods will not prosper, but those who benefit the poor will be rewarded; judges should hear both parties and take no bribes; men should reconcile their quarreling neighbors.

WHAT PROFITS A KINGDOM [58], about 1401, states how a kingdom is greatly harmed by talebearers, changes in government, and civil wars. What profits it are truth, permanence, and peace. As in [57], the warning is given that if the laws are violated, the Commons will revolt; but a kingdom consists of wise clergy, valiant knights, a just king, and rich commoners. This last estate is what makes a kingdom thrive, and therefore king and knights must govern the people with justice. The 21 eight-line stanzas, ababbcbc (with a refrain word, "peace"), conclude with a warning on the transitoriness of the world, comparing it to a cherry fair.

DO EVIL AND BE FEARED—A SATIRE [59], nine eight-line stanzas, ababbcbc (with a refrain based on the rubric, "To lyf bodyly is perylous"), gives a series of satirical injunctions on the evil life:

Give nobody his due, but take from everybody. Maintain wrong, rob the poor, never say a prayer. Frequent taverns and promote disputes. Despise those who teach you good; never pass a just sentence. Do nobody a benefit, calumniate your faithful servant and cause him to be imprisoned. Get a maid with child but marry her not. Speak good of no one, do harm to every man—then all will dread you.

EVILS IN THE CHURCH [60], about 1408, a companion piece to [61], opens with an exhortation to reflect on one's sins, but quickly passes to a list of the specific sins of parish priests. In thirteen eight-line stanzas, ababbcbc, it warns priests to teach as well as take tithes, not to neglect their parishioners in their eagerness for wealth, and to give more than verbal observance to Creed and Commandments. Priests will be damned if they are faithless, and death may strike them at any moment. Therefore learn to die.

EVILS IN THE STATE [61], probably referring to events of 1410, in 24 eight-line stanzas, ababbcbc, laments the moral and political troubles of England. Following a general exhortation to confession come three specific stanzas (7–9) rebuking those who use false weights and measures or accept bribes in the law courts. In a country where God's law is ignored come all sorts of miseries; therefore pay your debts to man and God. Several classes are next admonished: warriors not to be covetous, bishops to look after their dioceses, priests to be models for their parishioners. The poem concludes by returning to the general motif of confession, and urges shriving and communion.

GOD SAVE KING HENRY V [62], nineteen eight-line stanzas, ababbcbc, condemns the recent conspiracy against Henry V in 1413, and discusses the symbolism of a king's crown. Those who interfere with the administration of justice strip that crown of its jewels. "God save the king and keep the crown," as the poem is rubricated, continues with a plea for the Commons' support of the king's foreign policy and the avoidance of civil wars at home. England's renown has spread throughout the world—may everybody keep England safe.

MAINTAIN LAW AND HENRY'S FOREIGN POLICY [63], written ca. 1414, deplores (in the first thirteen of its 21 eight-line stanzas, ababb-cbc) the arbitrary interpretation of the law. Only in England is justice not inviolate, but bought and sold as a beast. The poem suggests remedies: listen to your tenants' complaints, suppress treason, help the guiltless to avoid suffering, banish the wicked from court. The second part (stanzas 14–21) demands full support for Henry V, who is urged to emulate King Edward in his relations with France. Kail sees in this poem (as in [61] above) detailed allusions to contemporary problems, similar to those discussed in Parliament and described in the *Rotuli Parliamentorum*.

THE STATE COMPARED TO MAN'S BODY [64], or *The Descryvyng of Mannes Membres*, in nineteen eight-line stanzas, ababababab, provides an extended allegory of a man and the state. It likens a man's head to the king, his neck to a just judge, his breast to a good priest, his shoulders to lords, his arms to knights, his fingers to yeomen, his ribs to men of law, his thighs to merchants, his legs to handicraftsmen, his feet to plowmen, and his toes to faithful servants. A kingdom in good condition is like a healthy man who eats in moderation. All the limbs stand in need of one another; if some enemy is permitted to hurt your finger, he will end by taking your arm. God saves the man—and kingdom—whose limbs are in full harmony and support one another.

THE FOLLIES OF THE DUKE OF BURGUNDY [65], nine fourteen-line stanzas, abababab with a bobbed tail-rime ccdddc, describes the follies of John, Duke of Burgundy, leading up to his assassination in 1419. The list of 52 follies is a catena of generalized moral and political ineptitudes and stupidities, e.g., he is a fool who trusts his enemies or goes to war without money. The poem concludes that of all people, only four take no bribes: illness, sorrow, death, and fear.

6. HISTORICAL BALLADS AND POEMS IN CHRONICLES

A comparison of historical ballads with the prose chronicles shows a general uniformity of presentation and material. The various English chronicles often went to popular songs and ballads for their information, sometimes copying out the verse as if prose (e.g., the MS Harley 753 text of *The Siege of Rouen* [74]). At other times they transformed the verse into prose—a process seen in *The Battle of Agincourt I* [71], where rime slowly intrudes until at last the compiler discards pretense and copies out his source in the stanzas in which it was composed. Elsewhere, as in *Mockery of the Flemings* [76], the chronicler records the actual song, "here sette for a remembraunce." Other poetry incorporated into chronicles includes *The Life of King Arthur* (see I [15]), *The Battle of Halidon Hill II* [66], and *The Siege of Rouen* [74]. Some poems, of course, are also preserved independently, such as *The Siege of Calais* [75] and the *Ballade Set on the Gates of Canterbury* [197]. The trustworthiness of the poems for historical information is seen in such a piece, for example, as *The Death of the Duke of Suffolk* [193], or in *The Rose of Rouen* (Brown-Robbins, no. 1380).

For other historical ballads praising a particular noble family, see [55] above and [213–225] below. The short rimes included as illustrative material in chronicles are listed above under Section 1, Verses Inserted into Chronicles. Some other historical ballads are described elsewhere. Complete chronicles in verse are also listed elsewhere.

THE BATTLE OF HALIDON HILL II [66], an extract from a fifteenth-century prose chronicle about the defeat of the Scots by Edward III in 1333. The short couplets—32 in MS Harley and twelve in MS Arundel—relate incoherently and redundantly the pursuit and plunder.

Minot's poem ([44] above) shows how a professional poet could treat the same theme.

For a ballad in the Percy Folio manuscript on the Battle of Neville's Cross, see above under [52].

THE BATTLE OF OTTERBURN [67] is the earliest of several poems commemorating this outstanding event of August 1388. Although not contemporary, the poem is much earlier than its copying in the mid-sixteenth century; Percy thought the piece composed after 1449, when Alexander, Lord of Gordon and Huntley, was created Earl (line 103). The 70 cross-rimed quatrains (heptameter ballad couplets, in fact), in two fits of 28 and 42 stanzas respectively, tell of the ravaging raid by a Scottish army as far south as Durham and the spirited resistance of the northern English lords.

James, Earl of Douglas, and Robert Stewart, Earl of Fife, raid Northumberland and push on to Newcastle to attack Sir Henry Percy (Hotspur). Taunted by the Earl of Douglas, Hotspur agrees to give battle at Otterburn, where, finding himself outnumbered 44,000 to 9,000, he and his men slay their horses and prepare to fight to the death on foot. For fear of being held a coward, the Percy refuses to wait for reinforcements from his father. The battle is joined, "tyll the bloode from ther bassonetts ranne." Hotspur slays the Douglas, but is himself taken captive, and later exchanged for Sir Hugh Montgomery. Only eighteen Scots survive, but—"with the allowable partiality of an English poet" (Percy)—five hundred Englishmen live on.

Froissart called the fight "the hardest and most obstinate battle that was ever fought," and this feeling of gallantry pervades the whole poem.

THE HUNTING OF THE CHEVIOT [68], although found in a late sixteenth-century manuscript belonging to Richard Sheale, a well-known ballad singer of Tamworth, is surely of the fifteenth century (but not earlier than 1424). It is in two parts, the first of 25 cross-rimed quatrains (or internal riming heptameter couplets), the second of 45. Like its later variant, *Chevy Chase* [69], this ballad treats of the defiant hunt. The description of the resulting conflict, say Hales and Furnivall, is "historically highly valuable for the picture it gives of Border warfare in its more chivalrous days, when ennobled by generosity and honor." Historically, this incident may possibly refer to the Battle of Pepperden in 1436, a private feud between William Douglas, Earl of Angus, and the second

Earl of Northumberland, the son of Percy Hotspur, each with an army of about 4,000 men.

The defiant hunt theme, however, was confused and jumbled with the border raid described in *The Battle of Otterburn* [67], several stanzas in fact being borrowed from this earlier poem, and the affair transferred to the reign of Henry IV (lines 90, 244), who immediately avenges the death of Percy with an English victory at Homildon Hill in 1402:

> This was the hontynge off the Cheviat,
> > That ear begane this spurn.
> Old men that knowen the grownde well yenoughe
> > Call it the Battell of Otterburn.

"The Perse owt of Northombarlande" vows to hunt in the Cheviot forest and carry off its fattest harts, without first seeking permission from the Earl Douglas, who swears to prevent him. One Monday morning, Percy comes into Cheviot with 1,500 archers, who kill one hundred harts. The Douglas intervenes with 2,000 spearmen and commands the hunters to desist, asking who they are that hunt without his leave. The good Lord Percy refuses to tell and persists in his whim to hunt where he chooses. To avoid the purposeless slaughter of their followers, Douglas challenges Percy to single combat. To his shame, Richard Wytharrington, a squire of Northumberland, refuses to let his lord fight alone. All join battle. The English archers kill 120 Scots spearmen. Earl Douglas, dividing his spearmen into three groups, attacks the English, who now fight hand-to-hand. At last, the Douglas and the Percy meet in mortal combat and tauntingly admire the other's prowess. An arrow, however, kills Earl Douglas, who exhorts his men to fight on. While Percy is lamenting his foe's death, a Scottish knight, Sir Hugh Montgomery, rides through the English archers, and pierces Lord Percy. In revenge, an English archer shoots Sir Hugh. The battle which began an hour before noon still continues at evensong. Only 53 English and 55 Scots survive. The list of the dead follows, including Wytharrington, who "when both his leggis wear hewyne in to, he knyled and fought on hys kne." The widows bear away the dead. King James of Scotland mourns his fallen men, but King Henry IV of England decides to avenge Percy's death, which he accomplishes at the Battle of Homildon Hill. Men call this hunting of the Cheviot the Battle of Otterburn. Christ bring us all to good ending.

The ballad continued very popular, being quoted in *The Complaint of Scotland* (ca. 1548) and in Sir Philip Sidney's *Defense of Poetry*: "I never heard the old song of Percy and Douglas, that I found not my heart moved more than with a trumpet."

CHEVY CHASE [69] is a broadside version in 64 ballad quatrains of *The Hunting of the Cheviot* [68], composed in the sixteenth century. In this late form, it stirred the admiration of Addison in *The Spectator* (nos. 70 and 71), and led Bishop Thomas Percy to write: "These genuine strokes of nature and artless passion, which have endeared it to the most simple readers, have recommended it to the most refined." It appears in many late collections of ballads, e.g., Percy Folio, Pepys, Douce, Roxburghe, Wood, Bagford, etc.

"God prosper long our noble king!" A woeful hunt was held in Chevy Chase. Earl Percy vows to kill Scottish deer for three days, despite the Douglas, and with 1,500 archers one Monday began his hunt. By noon a hundred bucks are slain. After dinner, the hills echo the cries of the continuing hunt. While wondering whether his adversary will appear, he sees Douglas with 2,000 men. Douglas asks whose men they are that hunt his deer. Percy will not tell, but will fight for his right to hunt. Declaring it would be wrong to kill their guiltless followers, Lord Douglas challenges Percy to single combat. Percy accepts. A squire, Witherington, protests: he will fight, too. The English archers shoot, killing 80 Scots. The foes close, and many are slain. Christ! it was sad to see. Percy and Douglas fight till their blood drops like rain. Douglas calls on Percy to yield. Percy will never yield to a Scot. An English arrow kills Douglas as he exhorts his men to continue fighting. Percy laments over his dead foe—a braver knight never died. A Scots knight, Sir Hugh Montgomery, vowing revenge, runs Percy right through the body. Thereupon an English archer shoots Montgomery through the heart. The fight lasts all day. The English knights slain are listed—Witherington fights on his stumps when his legs are cut off; then come the names of the fallen Scots knights. Of 2,000 Scots, scarce 55 were left; of 1,500 English, only 53. Next day the widows come and weep and bear away the corpses. King James laments the loss of Douglas: no such captain has he left. King Henry I laments Percy's loss, but he has five hundred equally good captains still alive; he will take vengeance for Percy's death —which he does right away at Homildon Hill (fourteen years later, in 1402!), killing lords, and hundreds of less account. God grant that strife between noble men may cease!

THE BATTLE OF HARLAW [70], 31 eight-line stanzas, usually four-stress lines riming ababbcbc, of little merit, was written soon after the event (July 24, 1411), but is not known in any copy earlier than Ramsay's *Ever Green* of 1724—although an edition of 1668 has been noted by Laing. *The Complaynt of Scotland* (ca. 1549) lists a Battle of Harlaw among the popular songs of Scotland. The ballad is founded on Boece's *History of Scotland*.

As the storyteller comes down by the hill of Banochie, he sees mourning on all sides. At Inverury, a man tells him what has happened at Harlaw. Great Donald of the Isles claimed the earldom of Ross, and getting no satisfaction from Duke Robert, gathered his weir-men to surprise the north, subdue Aberdeen, Mearns, Angus, and all

Fyfe to Forth. The countrymen yielded without opposition until he reached the Bruch of Aberdeen. Here the stout and mighty Alexander Stewart (Earl of Marr), accompanied by Lord Ogilvy (the Sheriff of Angus), Sir James Scrimgeor (the Constable of Dundee), Lord Salton, Sir Alexander Irving (Laird of Drum), Laird of Lauristone, Sir Robert Davidson (the Provost of Aberdeen), all with their men in armor, waited to suppress the tyranny of Donald of the Isles. They fought at Harlaw: there was slaughter of thousands of both Lowland and Highland men, including many of the above and Malcomtosh and Macklean, leaders of their clans. Each of these leaders is praised in a verse. Many will surely remember the brim battle of the Harlaw when men know the truth about it.

Several later versions have been preserved from the nineteenth century.

THE BATTLE OF AGINCOURT I [71] is, according to Kingsford, "the best and most spirited of the Agincourt poems." Unfortunately, the beginning of what was once a complete ballad has been paraphrased in prose and included as part of the narrative of the chronicle, so that only eight eight-line stanzas, ababbcbc, remain. The poem is mainly an account of the great nobles who fought with so much heroism, leading up to the prayer that the "fals flemynges" shall "neuer wayt Inglond good." The dialect is London. The poem adheres to the prose chronicles very closely.

THE BATTLE OF AGINCOURT II [72] is a long composite describing the whole campaign (even including the Dauphin and the tennis balls story) in three passus: The Siege of Harfleur, the Battle, and the Triumph at London (following the official program of ceremonies). In the fullest version (Harley), sometimes erroneously ascribed to Lydgate, it has 69 eight-line stanzas with additional refrain lines: "Wot ye right well that thus it was, Gloria Tibi Trinitas." MacCracken commented: "It seems to contain the fragments of earlier half-popular ballads on the subject. It is written in the style of the street, with the rhyme equipment of a poor minstrel." A second variant version occurred in a Cotton manuscript (burned in the fire of 1731, but previously recorded); it lacks Passus III (variants: Passus I, 221 lines; Passus II, 251 lines; lacks refrains). It is older and somewhat rougher than the Harley text. A third version, somewhat later, occurs in a Rawlinson manuscript.

THE BATAYLL OF EGYNGSCOURTE [73] is the early sixteenth-
century form of the account, a short metrical narrative of 380 lines in
four-stress cross-rimed quatrains.

Henry V sent to the Dauphin of France for his heritage of "Gascoyne and Gyen
and Normandye," all that belonged to the first Edward. But the Dauphin mocked
Henry's youth and sent back a ton of tennis balls for his play. The angry Henry declares to his lords that he shall send back such a tennis ball as shall bear down the
roof of the Dauphin's hall. Great ordnance of guns, bows and arrows, spears, daggers,
swords, bucklers, and bright harness are brought to Southampton, where fifteen fair
ships waited the king's arrival. The English reached Normandy after a day and a night
and sent forth a fleet of a thousand boats filled with men of arms. The king took up
his position at "Harfflete" [Harfleur] and bade his brother Clarence be ready for the
game of tennis with balls from their great guns. Finally, the French captain "Gorgeaunt"
asked for a respite until Sunday and, leaving hostages, rode to Rouen to seek the
Dauphin, where the lords advised him to yield. With Harfleur in his possession, Henry,
accompanied by his brother, the Duke of Gloucester, and many other notables, all
mentioned by name, devastated the land on his way to Calais. There the Dukes of
Orleans and Bourbon swore to defeat the lords of England at this tennis game and
take them prisoners. Meanwhile Henry knelt with his men and blessed the ground as
the archers took their position. Eleven thousand Frenchmen were slain in the rout.
King Henry V fought with his own hands and spared neither high nor low until the
field was conquered. He returned to London after stopping at the shrine at Canterbury. The French prisoners were ransomed. Henry made ready for the greatest battle
of all, called "ye sege of Rone."

For other poems on the battle, see the famous Agincourt carol and
The Rose of Ryse (Brown-Robbins, nos. 2716 and 3457; Greene E E
Carols, nos. 426 and 427). Other songs and ballads continued to be writ-
ten throughout the sixteenth century.

THE SIEGE OF ROUEN [74], ascribed to John Page, is often inserted
into the prose *Brut*. The prose chronicles which stop at 1419 give only a
prose paraphrase, but others which continue to 1430 give the first part
in a fuller prose paraphrase and the last part in verse. The only complete
text is that in MS Egerton 1995. All seventeen manuscripts show considerable variations and many are incomplete. The original dialect was
Northern or North Midland, and the poem was probably composed soon
after the siege (July 30, 1418, to January 16, 1419).

This long text has received high praise: "For all its rude versification
it is the most authentic account which we possess," wrote Kingsford; and

Gairdner believed: "No other contemporary writer states the facts with so much clearness, precision, minuteness and graphic power." This account, though simple and unpretentious yet possessed of a vivid narrative and genuine pathos, colored all later chronicles, including, for example, Titus Livius, the pseudo-Elmham, and Hall, Stow, and Holinshed.

The starving men of Rouen ask the English nobles to beg Henry V to grant safe conduct for twelve of them to negotiate. Umfraville agrees and gets support from the Dukes of Clarence, Exeter, and Gloucester, and other nobles. Henry V agrees to see the twelve representatives the next day. How manful and merciful he is, truly a child of God. As Henry comes from Mass, the Roueners kneel to him, hand him a petition, and beg him to pity them. Their poor are starving, many are dead. Henry replies that they have kept his city from him. They plead they are lieges of the French king. In turn, Henry tells them he will not go without his city; their French king and the Duke of Burgundy have known of this siege and it's no use to send them messages. He'll win Rouen, and if they oppose him they will suffer. But on the pleading of a clerk, Henry grants them time for a parley. Two tents are pitched for the negotiations. The English are represented by the Lords Warwick, Salisbury, Fitzhugh, and Hungerford. It is a solemn sight: the heralds are dressed like lords, adorned with gold, but the poor French have hardly a clout. A child of two begs for bread, its parents lie dead. Mothers hold up their children, ten or twelve dead to one living. We discuss with them for a fortnight in vain, then break off. They pray for delay until midnight—this is granted. In Rouen, the poor abuse the rich, call them murderers, and appeal to God against them. If the delegates will not yield to Henry V, the poor will kill them. The people of Rouen say they must either give up their city or die, and therefore they send their submission to the English. Negotiations are resumed for four days, but end when the men of Rouen ask for a truce of eight days to communicate with the French King. The agreement is this: if no rescue comes in eight days, Rouen will surrender to Henry, pay fifty thousand pounds, build the English a new castle on the Seine. Word arrives that Rouen will not be rescued. On the eighth day, Henry receives the keys of the city and hands them to the Duke of Exeter, who enters the city with a brilliant suite and is welcomed by acclamation. Yet many are dying and hundreds crying for bread. Next day Henry enters and is greeted by the bishops and abbots and sprinkled with holy water. The inhabitants of Rouen cheer the King on his brown steed. He alights at the Minster, hears Mass, and goes to the castle, where he lodges in his city, which is soon plentifully fed. So the siege is ended.

THE SIEGE OF CALAIS [75] is one of several poems expressing the popular feelings against Philip the Good, Duke of Burgundy, and his subjects in the Netherlands, the Flemings. Four such poems treat this same incident, the raising of the siege of Calais in 1436, but vary in the stress and details, although all follow the traditional interpretation of the prose chronicles.

After a July nature gambit, the poem (28 tail-rime stanzas, aabccb) tells how the Duke of Burgundy assembled his forces, beseiged Calais, and was beaten off with heavy losses. The narrative is vigorous, with close details that show that the writer's heart and eye were on the work, and that give an excellent picture in action of the various features of a fifteenth-century siege. The accounts of the Irishman who did such scathe to the French, and of the hound belonging to the water-bailey that rushed out and attacked the besiegers, horse and man, are more specific examples of the picturesque narrative that carries one right into the midst of the scene.

In the Cotton manuscript is added a four-line tag, paraphrased in *The Libel of English Policy* [249], lines 826–27:

Lytelle wote the fool
Who mygth chcs
What harm yt wer
Good Caleys to lese.

MOCKERY OF THE FLEMINGS [76] is the second attack on the Flemings. The poem is in fact a rough paraphrase and elaboration of the preceding prose narrative in a *Brut* chronicle about the behavior of the besiegers around Calais. Kingsford called it "the best and most spirited of all the fifteenth-century ballads." Its 33 semi-alliterative long couplets are divided into eight irregular stanzas by "Remembres how ye" anaphora, all going to show that "flemmynges is but a flemed [i.e., outlawed] man." Like the preceding item, this poem too makes mention of "Goby, the watir-bailiffes dog, How he scarmysshed with you twyes vpon the day, And among you on the sandes made many a fray."

SCORN OF THE DUKE OF BURGUNDY [77] in one manuscript (Rome) immediately precedes another poem against the Flemings [75]. The fourteen eight-line stanzas, ababbcbc, fall into two sections: (1) Stanzas 1 and 9–14 refer to the siege of Calais, and cover the same ground as the two preceding pieces [75–76]; (2) Stanzas 2–8 refer to the earlier history of Duke Philip from 1419 to 1435, so as to emphasize his perfidy in going against the English, a subject touched on in the Digby poem, *The Follies of the Duke of Burgundy* [65].

The scorn and venom are somewhat reminiscent of Minot (e.g., [45], [52], [54]), and link this poem to others of personal abuse (e.g., [102], [103], [105], [161], [182], [192], [193], and Brown-Robbins, nos. 551, 892, 2524, 2580).

The fourth English song against the Flemings (Brown-Robbins, no. 2657), also inserted in a chronicle, is generally ascribed to Lydgate and is accordingly entered under his name.

7. POLITICS IN SONG

Poems specifically lyric in content or in form are discussed in their appropriate chapter.

For carols and songs with political interest, see:

The Death of Archbishop Scrope, 1405 (Brown-Robbins, no. 3308; Greene E E Carols, no. 425)

The Agincourt Carol, 1415 (Brown-Robbins, no. 2716; Greene E E Carols, no. 426)

The Rose of Ryse, 1415 (Brown-Robbins, no. 3457; Green E E Carols, no. 427)

A Recollection of Henry V, by Audelay, 1429 (Brown-Robbins, no. 822; Greene E E Carols, no. 428)

In Honor of King Edward IV, ca. 1461 (Brown-Robbins, no. 3127; Greene E E Carols, no. 429)

The Rose of Rouen, ca. 1461 (Brown-Robbins, no. 1380; Greene E E Carols, no. 431)

Willikin's Return, ca. 1470 (Brown-Robbins, no. 3742; Greene E E Carols, no. 430)

A Carol for the King, ca. 1485 (Robbins-Cutler, no. 3206.5; Greene E E Carols, no. 436)

The Lily White Rose, ca. 1486 (Brown-Robbins, no. 1450; Greene E E Carols, no. 432)

The Roses Entwined, ca. 1486 (Brown-Robbins, no. 1327; Greene E E Carols, no. 433)

For Victory in France, ca. 1492 (Robbins-Cutler, no. 306.8)

A Prayer for Peace, ca. 1499 (Brown-Robbins, no. 1710; Greene E E Carols, no. 435)

The Ostrich Feather, ca. 1500 (Robbins-Cutler, no. 2394.5; Greene E E Carols, no. 434)

Marriage of Princess Margaret and James IV, ca. 1503 (Robbins-Cutler, no. *2797.5)

For Victory in France, ca. 1513 (Robbins-Cutler, no. 2766.8)

In Praise of Henry VIII (Robbins-Cutler, no. 558.5)

For carols which include moral, didactic, and religious elements with the political, see:

Truth Is Unpopular (Brown-Robbins, no. 72; Greene E E Carols, no. 385)

The Evils of the Age (Brown-Robbins, no. 320; Greene E E Carols, no. 121)

A Carol of Money (Brown-Robbins, no. 113; Greene E E Carols, no. 393)

Of Covetous Guile (Brown-Robbins, no. 1020; Greene E E Carols, no. 383)

Against False Executors (Brown-Robbins, no. 2050; Greene E E Carols, no. 382)

Sir Penny (Brown-Robbins, no. 2747; Greene E E Carols, no. 392)

Against Pride (Brown-Robbins, no. 2771; Greene E E Carols, no. 355)

God Speed the Plough (Brown-Robbins, no. 3434)

Abuses of the Age (Brown-Robbins, no. 3852; Greene E E Carols, no. 386)

Man, Make Amends (Brown-Robbins, no. 3707; Greene E E Carols, no. 356)

The State of the World (Brown-Robbins, no. 356)

8. The Wicked Age: Satires and Complaints

I. General Evils: Summaries

Of what may be called satire in the limited sense of the term, there is little in English before the sixteenth century. Yet extant from the fourteenth century are a number of English writings that deal with contemporary distresses, abuses, or ill conduct with an ultimate objective of correction.

For purposes of organization, the generally short lists complaining about current abuses or evils of the times are entered in the chapter on Proverbs, Precepts, and Monitory Pieces. Consequently only cursory reference is made to such items in this present chapter.

Although hewing to their original Latin sources, often these little summations passed beyond stereotyped moralizations on degeneracy to imply specific and contemporary wrongs.

The catalogue of abuses entered English literature through a Latin tract, ascribed variously to Cyprian, Augustine, and Origen, first translated in Aelfric's *Homilies*. Although there is much variation and interplay between them, two main versions are distinguishable.

One version spread through being incorporated into the Sexta Tabula of the *Speculum Christiani* (in 46 manuscripts), which describes how his four wise men told an unfortunate king the reasons for the sorry plight of the nation. This Latin is the immediate source of the twelve riming English phrases (Brown-Robbins, no. 2167):

Duodecim abusiua sunt saeculi, hoc est: sapiens sine
operibus, senex sine religione, adulescens sine
obedientia, diues sine eleemosyna, femina sine pudicitia,

dominus sine virtute, christianus contentiosus, pauper
superbus, rex iniquus, episcopus neglegens, plebs sine
disciplina, populus sine lege, sic suffocatur iustitia.

A variant fragment ("Word is best") in six lines occurs in a Latin sermon (MS Cambridge University Ii.3.8), and is followed by another list of evils in three long riming lines.

Other pieces repeat all or some of these abuses:

King conseilles (Brown-Robbins, no. 1820), short monoriming lines ending in -les, in fourteen manuscripts. Another version (Robbins-Cutler, no. 86.6) exists in a collection of Rolle tracts.

Wisman wranglere / Richeman robbere (Brown-Robbins, no. 4180) six riming phrases in a collection of sermons, which also includes short lists on *Falseness* (Brown-Robbins, nos. 759 and 760) and *Unrighteous Judgments* (Brown-Robbins, no. 2829).

A Song on the Times (Brown-Robbins, no. 2787) with reference to the first years of Edward II, has 36 macaronic lines (Latin, French, and English) in its longest form, but several of its seven manuscripts preserve only fragments. Similar fragments include *Lex ys leyd adoun* (Brown-Robbins, nos. 1870–1871); a sophisticated punctuation poem (Brown-Robbins, no. 2364) in six manuscripts, using similar phrases to the preceding items: *Truth Is Dead* (Brown-Robbins, nos. 2145–2146), and *Degeneracy of the Times* (Brown-Robbins, no. 3650).

The second major version (Brown-Robbins, no. 906), sixteen riming phrases, was translated from a version in the *Gesta Romanorum*. Like the *Speculum Christiani*, it sets the lines in the same story framework. The Latin original, heading some manuscripts, reads:

Munus fit iudex, fraus est mercator in urbe;
Non est lex dominus, nec timor est pueris.
Ingenium dolus est, amor omnis ceca voluptas,
Ludus rusticitas, et gula festa dies.
Senex ridetur, sapiens mendosus habetur,
Dives laudatur, pauper ubique iacet.
Prudentes ceci, cognati degeneres sunt;
Mortuus inmemor est, nullus amicus erit.

This version, occurring in twenty manuscripts, was soon divorced from the story, acquired an independent existence, and appeared in many guises.

One variant of Brown-Robbins, no. 906, was utilized in the play, *The Pride of Life*. Abbreviated lists of the Evils are found as tags in sermon collections. MS Harley 7322 has: Brown-Robbins, no. 4273, six lines; Brown-Robbins, no. 2008, seven lines; and Brown-Robbins, no. 592, twelve lines. The *Fasciculus Morum* has Brown-Robbins, no. 3282, four lines, and Brown-Robbins, no. 3133, five lines. John Grimestone's Commonplace Book contains Brown-Robbins, no. 873, four lines with four of the Twelve Abuses. Two other sermon manuscripts contain Brown-Robbins, no. 2319, four lines.

Simple and direct catalogues of these abuses, following the pattern of *Munus fit iudex*, include:

Brown-Robbins, no. 2356, eight lines.

Brown-Robbins, no. 4006, five lines.

Brown-Robbins, no. 4051, fourteen lines, an early version of the Abuses, here ascribed to Bede and approximating a prophecy.

Brown-Robbins, no. 2085, three lines.

Brown-Robbins, no. 1138, four or six lines.

Brown-Robbins, no. 3851, 31 irregular lines, a long but still simple catalogue derived from the preceding item, ending with a prayer to forsake sin.

All these texts are discussed elsewhere.

Occasionally, in the shorter versions, some literary embellishment was attempted. Thus the Abuses or Evils of the Age appear in two carols, *Gyle and Gold Togedere Arn Met* (Brown-Robbins, no. 1020; Greene E E Carols, no. 383) and *Vycyce Be Wyld and Vertues Lame* (Brown-Robbins, no. 3852; Greene E E Carols, no. 386), and in a song without burden in the same manuscript, English poet e.1 (Brown-Robbins, no. 2056). The evils of the world are listed in a lullaby song in the Kildare MS (Brown-Robbins, no. 2025). And the listing turns up again in two of the formal stanzaic forms in the fifteenth century: *On the Times* (Brown-

Robbins, no. 1580), in eight-line stanzas, and *Signa seculi degenerantis* (Brown-Robbins, no. 4131), in two rime-royal stanzas.

The shorter versions of the Abuses of the Age were also incorporated either as or into pieces of essentially different character. Thus [256](a) below, based on Brown-Robbins, no. 2356, was used by John Ball, and [256](e) below was also adapted for use by John Ball or Jack Trueman in the Peasants' Revolt. Brown-Robbins, no. 4006, was incorporated into the Second Scottish Prophecy, *When Rome Is Removed* ([285] below); other lists become part of the so-called *Chaucer's* or *Merlin's Prophecy*, XI [11]. Similar is Brown-Robbins, no. 3987, but it lacks the vaticinal purpose. Finally, Lydgate's *Advice to the Estates* (Brown-Robbins, no. 920) paraphrases the Latin and includes a shortened version of the Abuses.

For further references see in the chapter on Proverbs, Precepts, and Monitory Pieces the following items: Brown-Robbins, nos. 592, 759, 760, 873, 906, 1138, 1580, 1820, 1870, 1871, 2008, 2085, 2145, 2146, 2167, 2319, 2356, 2364, 2787, 2829, 3282, 3650, 3851, 3987, 4006, 4051, 4131, 4180, and 4273.

II. General Evils: Expansions of the Abuses of the Age

SATIRES AND COMPLAINTS [78]. In addition to these relatively unadorned catalogues of the foregoing section, many poems elaborated on these cancers and blemishes of society. However, because medieval England viewed in terms of religion what today would be considered basically political or economic wrongs, those items predominantly descriptive of the Evils or Abuses of the Age are relatively few. Many of the moral and religious poems take on added significance when regarded as half-formed expressions of hope for a better world order.

WORCESTER CATHEDRAL FRAGMENT [79], eighteen alliterative lines, written near Winchester ca. 1170, in Southern dialect, a fragment preserved in a manuscript in Winchester Cathedral. The first ten

lines tell how Bede and Alcuin turned books into English for the education of the people. Then follows a list of bishops. Eight final lines declare
these taught the people in English, their light shone; but now their lore
is lost, and the folk are forlorn—others teach our folk, and many of the
teachers perish and the folk likewise.

For another fragment from the same manuscript see *The Address of
the Soul to the Body*, VII [18](c) (Robbins-Cutler, no. *2684.5).

A Lutel Soth Sermon (Brown-Robbins, no. 1091), of the first half of
the thirteenth century, fulminates against various types of evil doers; it
is discussed in the chapter on Lyrics. It may be compared with the more
overtly political *Against Simony*, [96] below, likewise in MS Jesus College Oxford 29.

THE SAYINGS OF THE FOUR PHILOSOPHERS [80] exists in two
distinct variants, both given additional point by their criticism of two
reigning monarchs. The earliest, about 1300, in twelve macaronic Anglo-
Norman and English lines, links the Abuses of the Age to Edward I,
recalling the Provisions of Oxford which tried to curb Henry III in 1258.
The longer text, in the Auchinlech MS (1330–40), in 98 lines including
five cross-rimed macaronic quatrains as introduction, criticizes Edward II
for breaking the Ordinances he had signed on October 11, 1311, and similarly refers back to 1258.

At a great parliament at Westminster, the King made a charter of wax, which was
held too near the fire and is now melted away—and all goes the Devil's road (lines
1–20, macaronic Anglo-Norman and English). Then follow the Sayings of the Four
Philosophers on the Abuses of the Age, each in one six-line tail-rime stanza and two
monoriming triplets (lines 21–68). The poem ends with five six-line tail-rime stanzas of
Christian exhortations to do good.

For another macaronic poem in Latin, French, and English on the
Evils of the Time see Brown-Robbins, no. 2787.

THE WICKEDNESS OF THE TIMES [81]. In the same tiny pages
that contain fragments of the elegy on Edward I, [29] above, are 24 lines

(in eight-line stanzas) on the evils of the age, which probably refer to the earlier fourteenth century.

A SATIRE OF EDWARD II'S ENGLAND [82], in three versions all composed about the second quarter of the fourteenth century: Advocates MS (sometimes called *The Simonie*), 476 lines in 79 six-line stanzas, the last two lines a wheel and bob, East Midland; Peterhouse MS, in a folio volume of homilies by Radulphus Acton (ca. 1320), 468 lines, probably Kentish; and a redaction, Bodley MS (*Symonye and Covetise*), 414 lines in tail-rime stanzas, including 114 lines not found in the other versions, East Midland. In all manuscripts, the poem is incomplete; the expanded form in Peterhouse MS terminates with a stanza corresponding to lines 391–92 of Advocates MS. Ross gives a critical composite text of 660 lines.

The piece is interesting for its presentation of the conditions of the early fourteenth century, for its reflection of the attitude of many persons of the time toward those conditions, and for its anticipation, by perhaps fifty years, of much of the motive and the spirit that animated Langland (a topic emphasized by Salter). Specific accusations, however, are cautiously passed over. Yet the poem remains a powerful invective by an ardent, patriotic, devout nature indignant at the disgrace of the Church, the higher classes, and his fellow men.

Why the land is full of violence, why hunger and dearth have laid low the poor, why beasts perish, why corn is dear—this the satirist will truly tell. All the clergy and all the laity are vicious. Covetousness and simony and pride and lewdness possess all churchmen. Pope, archbishops, bishops, archdeacons, abbots, priors, Minorites, Jacobins, Carmelites, Augustinians, deans and officers of chapters—all are selfish oppressors and false livers. Earls and barons and knights and squires are untrue to their professions and base in conduct. Justices, sheriffs, mayors, bailiffs, beadles, all the civil officials, are rogues and self-seekers. Merchants are cheats; the members of the crafts are thieves. For this God has cursed the land with vexation and sorrow, has inflicted dearth and pestilence and strife and slaughter. Pride and falseness are the cause of it all. Each man knows the cause, but each blames others; did each but examine himself, all were well done.

For other poems on the evil times of Edward II, see [15] and [37] above; also Brown-Robbins, no. 2787. For an attack on simony, see [96] below.

DE VERITATE ET CONSCIENCIA [83], thirteen twelve-line stanzas, ababbcbccdcd, including refrain ("Can tell where Conscyens ys become"), with the fourth stanza having an additional four lines (dede), in all 160 lines, of the mid-fifteenth century. The poem falls in the general tradition of the allegorical and macaronic poems on the Evils of the Times (e.g., Brown-Robbins, nos. 1870, 1871, 2364, 2787), but structurally it is organized into a unity, possibly by the poet's acquaintance (suggests Kane) with *Piers Plowman*, associating Truth and Conscience. The single stanza on f. 8^b seems added as an afterthought for the sake of inclusiveness.

The speaker hesitates to inquire about Truth and Conscience from the clerks or lords, and will seek information from "the pore Comyns." Once Right reigned, but now robbing and stealing are dominant. I heard a palmer complaining he had found no one who could tell him where Truth and Conscience had gone. This palmer received the King's permission to search the law courts and the lords' council chambers, but he found there Pride and Covetice had replaced Truth and Conscience. It was the same story with the sheriffs, the mayors, the merchants (who falsified their weights and measures), and even with the farmers and laborers. "And now ther ys none in this countre/kann tell where Conscyens ys be come." The Pope and cardinals are taken with simony, as are bishops and priests down to the lowest vicar, and all four orders of religious. We can only hope that, since Truth and Conscience are found among no estate, Christ will show us mercy. The added stanza, which follows after some interpolated Latin verses, attacks prelates who wear "scarlet, beige and gryse."

ON HAMDEN OF HAMDEN [84], three lines, probably later than the incident commemorated:

Hamden of Hamden did forgoe
The manors of Tring, Wing, and Ivinghoe,
For striking the Black Prince a blow.

THE INSURRECTION AND EARTHQUAKE OF 1382 [85], eleven four-stress eight-line stanzas, ababbcbc, is one of the Vernon-Simeon series of refrain poems, discussed in the chapter on Lyrics. It warns that "the rysing of the comuynes in londe, the pestilens, and the eorthequake" are signs of God's displeasure, thereby stressing a political moral to its account of the sins of the period.

God is a courteous lord, who shows his might meekly; he would lead men all in accord to live rightly. Many warnings has he given. First was the outbreak of the commons, when no lord however great was not afraid. Had they had grace, the lords might have crushed the insurrection at once, but God showed them the slightness of their power. Then he sent the earthquake, when all forgot worldly goods, and, completely terrified, burst out of their abodes as chambers and chimneys were hurled asunder, and churches and castles, steeples and pinnacles, toppled to the ground. Yet men went back to doing evil. The pestilence and these other two great curses were enough to warn all to beware, but they had no lasting effect. Apparently, nothing can avail; men are so lost that they would betray father and mother and all their kindred for money. "Vr bagge hongeth on a sliper pyn, bote we of this warnyng be ware."

Like almost all the other contemporary pieces of the class, these verses are little poetical. But they ring with intense sincerity and are permeated with the awful darkness and foreboding that encompassed many a serious thinker on the social and religious conditions of the day.

For other poems on the Peasants' Revolt, see [255–257]. For a macaronic couplet on the 1381 Rebellion, see [254].

ON THE TIMES OF RICHARD II [86], a satire on manners and costume, and on the state of the nation at large, 236 irregular three-stress lines alternately English and Latin, in cross-rimed quatrains, the Latin lines with feminine ending, exists in three manuscripts. It was written probably about 1388, the retreat of Jack and Jack Noble mentioned in it no doubt referring to the flight to the Continent of the King's favorite, Robert de Vere, Duke of Dublin, and Michael de la Pole, Earl of Suffolk.

England and the English have lost all their former glory. Lechery and pride reign. The land is full of violence; those who feared us, now press upon us. The fear of God is departed; the speaker of truth is punished; whisperers and flatterers have their way. The rich make merry; worn out, the people grieve. Spiritual forces decay; God's holy days are not observed. The laws are perverted; the evil go unpunished. Jack and Jack Noble are gone; but plenty of the evil remain. Penniless gallants roam the cities. The people assume ridiculous fashions—they pad out their shoulders to make them seem broad; they have wide and high collars, as if making their necks ready for the ax; they wear spurs and long pointed shoes; their hose has a straight band, as if their thighs were fastened to their bodies. They dare not try to bend, for fear of hurting their hose; for this and their long toes, they pray standing. The women are as bad as the men, or worse than they. Drinking and cursing prevail everywhere. Simony is loose; the Church is vicious, not a clear light. May God rule and grant that as the King grows in years, he shall learn the grief of England. "Oh King, if thou art King, rule thyself, or thou shalt be a king without a realm."

ON KING RICHARD'S MINISTERS [87], fifteen tail-rime stanzas, aabccb, composed in 1399, is an allegory about the ministers of King Richard II. The writer's intense expression of the bitter hatred and the ardent hope for vengeance against the agents of oppression, that he felt with the people, are only superficially veiled.

By punning on "a busch that is forgrowe," "the long gras that is so grene," and "the grete bagge that is so mykille," the writer utters his feeling against the King's three most objectionable ministers, Bushey, Greene, and Bagot. Designating the persons by the features of their arms, he declares that Bushey caused the death of the swan (the Duke of Gloucester, murdered in 1397); that Greene slew the horse (the Earl of Arundel); that a bearward (the Earl of Warwick) found a rag, and made a bag through which he is undone (i.e., he aided to raise up Bagot, who became instrumental in his banishment). The swan's mate is grief-stricken, her eldest bird (Humphrey Plantagenet) is taken from her; the steed's colt (Thomas of Arundel) has escaped, and has joined the heron (the Duke of Lancaster); and the bearward's son (Richard Beauchamp) has been married off, but is watching to join the heron. The heron and the colt are up in the North in company with the geese and the peacocks (the Percys and the Nevilles). The heron will alight on the bush, and will fall upon the green. The bag is full of rotten corn; the geese and peacocks and many other birds will be fed. The bush is bare and waxes sere, it puts forth no new leaves—there's no remedy but to hew it down. The long grass, though green, must be beaten down if it is to become nourishing. The great bag is so torn that it will hold naught; when it is hung up to dry, it may be improved enough to buy a beggar. May God grant us to see that sight, and give peace to our lean beasts that were like to be ruined.

THE DANGERS OF PRIDE [88], twelve long macaronic lines, in English and Latin, written early in the fifteenth century, in a Central or North Midland dialect, is a satire against pride, "mater visyorum," and flaunting manners.

NOW IS ENGLAND PERISHED [89], seven tetrameter quatrains, generally monoriming, about 1450, listing the Evils of the Age, both serious and trivial, including a condemnation of short gowns and slit sleeves.

For satires on dress, see [136–138] below on women's headdresses and trains, and [160–161] below on the attire of "galaunts."

THIS WORLD IS VARIABLE [90], five tail-rime stanzas, aabaab, deploring the falsity and sham prevalent in the world. Nothing is stable; may God help us. The fourth stanza refers to two "impossibilities"

("Whane brome wyll appolles bere / and humlok hony in feere") reminiscent of Brown-Robbins, no. 3999. Compare [93] below.

ALAS THAT KYNDEMAN WANTYS GODE [91], seven stanzas,
ababbcbc, partly alliterative, introduced by a chanson d'aventure gambit
wherein the poet, hidden under a holly tree, hears a "gome" moaning
the refrain, "Allas, that kyndeman wantys goode." The theme is the common reversal of fortune, of a nobleman who once had men in attendance
and a rich house—now all is gone. The piece concludes with a prayer
that God bring the writer to heaven.

Similar contrasts in fortune occur in the elegies on kings ([208], [210–
211] below).

THE BISSON LEADS THE BLIND [92], a typical catalogue of conventional corrupt practices, in ten Monk's Tale stanzas, ababbcbc, gives
a vivid picture of life in the mid-fifteenth century. The poem is localized
in London and to the year 1456 by a reference to a thief turned state in-
former who secured his own life by falsely accusing of treason men with
whom he had at some time been acquainted. The incident is related in
Gregory's Chronicle. The poem may be compared to *London Lickpenny*
[158].

THE WORLD UPSIDE DOWN I [93], seven rime royal stanzas, an
Evils of the Age poem in reverse: by listing what should be, it points out,
by the use of a "destroying" refrain ("Stablenesse foundon, and spesialli
in attire"), what is not. From the traditional viewpoint, the refrain is so
obviously impossible that by implication the other statements of the preceding six lines are likewise improbable. The last stanza clinches the
ironic approach: If it were not for their wisdom, and for the perfect
stability of those women who wear fashionable apparel, we should all be
in the mire.

The impossibilities formula also occurs in Brown-Robbins, nos. 1116,
3435, 3943, and 3999; the destroying refrain also in Brown-Robbins, no.
1485. See also [90] above.

For a comparable direct attack, mentioning similar ills, see [92]; and compare the carol *Vycyce Be Wyld and Vertues Lame* (Brown-Robbins, no. 3852; Greene E E Carols, no. 386) and *Hoccleve's Complaint*, VIII [3].

THE WORLD UPSIDE DOWN II [94], preserves only the first four lines of a fragmentary song, headed "This werlde es tournede vpso downe." Mutability is the cause of the poet's confusion. Compare line 45 of [92] above: "Ther werld is turnyd up so down among."

THE KINDS OF USURY [95], 158 lines in twelve irregular stanzas in short couplets, of the mid-fifteenth century. The piece is simply a mnemonic device, similar to several prose accounts, such as that in *Jacob's Well*, of the traditional objections to money lending. In other versions, notably that in the *Ayenbite of Inwyt* (which derives from *La Somme des Vices et Vertues*), there are only seven dangers. Here there are twelve.

All usury is to be condemned, but especially (1) lending against collateral; (2) lending without collateral, but nevertheless expecting and receiving interest; (3) using inherited money originally acquired by usury; (4) lending at interest through agents or servants; (5) lending another's goods supposedly to be kept in safety; (6) speculation by buying cheap and selling dear; (7) taking advantage of the urgent needs of the poor; (8) buying on speculation before the proper time for selling; (9) retention of profit on money originally taken for surety; (10) retaining a deposit even after the full sum has been paid; (11) demanding full security with half the profits that may accrue to the borrower; (12) accepting excessive work in payment of a bad debt.

III. The Clergy

Two subjects attracted special attention from the moralists: the wickedness of clergy and the wickedness of women. With these condemnations of priests, monks, and friars are included here invectives against Lollards, and the Jack Upland series of pieces.

AGAINST SIMONY [96], eighteen pentameter couplets, composed in the Southwest of England about 1225–50, is directed against the prevalent simony, and is one of the many very early outbursts against abuses by the clergy. Unfortunately, the earnestness of its author does not atone for its absence of poetic merit.

> Christ called Peter a stone and upon him set the Church. Now those who should be her protectors are almost gone. For Simon, Simony rules. After Peter, came Clement and Gregory, who suffered much but preserved the Church aright; for some time after them, she stood firm. Now with silver and gold men seek to fell her to earth. None will suffer for her as did Stephen and Thomas, or honor her as did Edmund. High and low, clerks and laymen, hold her in hatred. The Pope takes gifts. May God send her salvation, that we in this life may see it!

For a condemnation of simony see also *A Satire of Edward II's England* [82].

AGAINST WORLDLY CLERICS [97], 63 couplets, of which the first 41 are incorporated (in one manuscript) into *The Pricke of Conscience* (Brown-Robbins, no. 3428). The other manuscript has 108 couplets.

ABC POEM AGAINST PRIDE OF CLERGY [98], three stanzas rime royal, attributed to William Thorpe, ca. 1407.

AGAINST LAZY CLERICS [99], a five-line tag in the Franciscan sermon collection, the *Fasciculus Morum*, in fifteen manuscripts, and found separately in two other manuscripts.

For a biting satire against worldly clerics, composed by Franciscans to ridicule the Cistercians, see *The Land of Cokaygne*, [34] above. *Satire on the People of Kildare*, [35] above, includes various orders of friars as well as citizens in its attack. For a complaint written ca. 1408, see *Evils in the Church*, [60] above.

AGAINST THE FRIARS I [100], fifteen twelve-line stanzas, aaabcccb-dede, of the later fourteenth century, is full of intense passion against the "orders of Cain." The almost light tone of irony in the first six stanzas describing the contrast between precept and practice gives way to direct abuse, with sledgehammer blows against the friars' lechery (cf. [107] below) and greed. In the manuscript the poem is preceded by a similar Latin diatribe with an "O and I" refrain, somewhat more specific in its allegations against the various orders.

The friars surpass all other religious in devotion, for they apply themselves to chivalry, riot, and ribaldry, to great standing, and to long prayers. Who keeps their rule shall have Heaven's bliss. Their appearance shows their great penances and simple sustenance; in my forty years I never saw men fatter about the arse; they are so meager that each is a horse-load. Their founder was a man of simple ordinance; they have to wander, alas! from town to town in pairs selling purses, pins, knives, gloves, and the like, to wenches and wives (cf. Brown-Robbins, no. 3864). The husband fares ill if he's away from home, for the friar does his will wherever he comes; with fine dress finishings and spices he catches women's fancy. They are masters of tricks beyond all pedlars. Let each man who has a wife or daughter watch them, for they can win them away. Were I a householder, no friar should come near. They declare they destroy sin; but they foster it, for if a man has slain his kin, they will shrive him for a pair of shoes. What men in many lands say of them seems true, that Caym (Cain) founded them—Carmelites come of K, Augustinians of A, Jacobins of I, Minorites of M. There's not room in hell, it's so full of friars. They labor to bring down the clergy and abuse them. But soon they will be made low as were the Templars. They cheat in chantries. No possessioners can equal their array. They were to live by begging, and to pray for those who gave them alms; but they have supplanted the secular priests. They preach wisely, but do not practice. I was long a friar and I know. When I saw that they did not follow their teachings, I cast off the habit and went my way, commending prior and convent to the devil. I am no apostate, for I lacked a month and nine or ten odd days of my twelve month novitiate. Lord God, who with bitter pain redeemed men, let never a man desire to become a friar.

AGAINST THE FRIARS II [101], seven stanzas, aabbcc, with an "O and I" refrain, is a biting attack on the Franciscans. Heuser suggested an Irish background for this attack, from the reference to Richard Fitz-Ralph, Archbishop of Armagh. Wright and Halliwell considered the whole piece directed against the Franciscans' use of "pageants and theatrical shows," but Robbins suggests the descriptions of their offenses more suitable to the wall paintings in their large churches.

The friars hang one of their number on a green cross with bright leaves and blossoms—men judge them to be mad! They fasten on him wings as if here to fly—may Armachan destroy them! Another fellow comes down out of the sky in a gray gown, as if he were a hogherd hieing to town—why should they not be burned? There wants but a fire! I saw another representing Christ bleeding at his side, and with great wounds in the hands. Another Franciscan represented Elijah in a cart of fire—just as he ought to be! Well ought they all to be burned! May God grant me grace to see it. They preach wholly of poverty, but like it not themselves; the town is ransacked for victuals for them; their dwellings are spacious and wondrously wrought—murder and whoredom have paid for them—slay thy father and betray thy mother, and they will assoil thee for sixpence!'

The problems of the "O and I" refrain are discussed in the chapter on Lyrics.

THE LAYMAN'S COMPLAINT AGAINST THE FRIARS [102], three tail-rime stanzas, aabccb, added in a fifteenth-century hand by a Wycliffite (as Utley suggested) to a copy of a fourteenth-century orthodox *Poor Caitiff*. The poem emphasizes simony, and some lines resemble *Pierce the Ploughman's Crede*, [109] below. The companion piece, *The Friars' Answer* [103], follows in the manuscript without break.

THE FRIARS' ANSWER [103], nine short quatrains, is an ironic defense of the friars to the charges of the preceding piece [102].

All our troubles started when ignorant men learned to read. The devil was responsible for englishing the Bible. People quote St. Paul that priests should work, and dare to argue with us. If things proceed at this pace, there won't be a friar left in England.

CARMINA IOCOSA [104], "flen flyys and freris populum domini male caedunt," is a pig-Latin and English macaronic satire, 33 lines sometimes in couplets, especially directed against the Carmelites of Cambridge (whose morals, noted in cyphers in lines 8 and 10, are, says Wright, "rather gross"). Wright also comments that some lines were still known to English schoolboys of the mid nineteenth century:

Tres fratres coeli navigabant roundabout Ely,

Omnes drounderunt qui swimaway non potuerunt.

FRIARS, MINISTRI MALORUM [105], 21 macaronic English and Latin couplets of the late fifteenth century, accuses the friars of spreading many pernicious practices. They will do anything for money. They rape women, girls, and boys. Ill may they thrive.

LAMPOONS ON THE FRIARS [106]: (a) two scurrilous couplets, early sixteenth century, attacking the friars; (b) another sixteenth-century flyleaf addition, one six-line tail-rime stanza, "Quod the Devill to the Frier."

LYARDE [107], 130 discursive lines in couplets, indirectly satirizes friars for their licentious ways, and directly husbands for their laziness.

When an old horse, Lyarde, is past work, it has its shoes pulled off, and is put out to pasture in a huge park. This is the sort of park to which impotent husbands should be sent, to live with the old horses. The last man to come to this park was a Franciscan. The friars were angry at this disgrace to their prowess, and explained he must have been untonsured—for "a crowne schorne" induces great virility. Now the friars admit no one into their order "bot if he may wele swyfe . . . twyse or thrise at the leste on a schorte somer nyghte." The laymen in the park challenge the friars to battle, but are defeated; these "sory swyvers" troop back to their homes, to the displeasure of their wives.

Lines 73–96 resemble *Against the Friars I*, [100] above.

ALLITERATIVE PIECES [108]. Apparently, from the date of the B-Text up into the sixteenth century, *Piers Plowman* was very popular and either begat or greatly influenced many alliterative pieces. The letters of the rebels of 1381 used the names of Piers Plowman and Dowel and Dobet for the designation and concealment of their intent (cf. [256]). About 1394 appeared *Pierce the Ploughman's Crede* [109]; perhaps before 1400, the Lollard poem that was later expanded in the sixteenth century to the *Complaint of the Plowman* or *The Plowman's Tale* [110], in stanzas, printed about 1532 with Chaucer's works. In 1401 or 1402 was composed *Jack Upland* [113], a Wycliffite attack on the friars, possibly originally in alliterative verse. This was followed by the alliterative *Friar Daw's Reply* [114], to which was made *Jack Upland's Rejoinder* [115], similar in form to [113]. At about 1403 came *Mum and the Sothsegger* [246]. Of the many other alliterative pieces listed by Skeat, and included in this chapter, are to be mentioned the *Crowned King* [247], *Scottish Feilde* [217], chiefly an account of the Battle of Flodden, written soon after the event, and perhaps rewritten later, and *Death and Liffe* [245].

PIERCE THE PLOUGHMAN'S CREDE [109], 850 long lines, South-west Midland dialect, is a major poem in the alliterative tradition attacking the friars, the first and the best imitation of *Piers Plowman*. Reference to the persecution of Walter Brut at the end of 1393, and an allusion to flattering kings (lines 364–65) suggest a date about 1394 (Wright, accepted by Skeat). Several lines (528–30) refer admiringly to Wyclif. The general plan of the poem seems derived from *Piers Plowman*—particularly from the prologue to *Vita de Dowel*, where the dreamer sets out on his quest and falls in first with two Minorites, whom he questions as to the whereabouts of Dowel.

The poet knew his *Pater noster* and *Ave*, but was ignorant of the Creed. In great distress he set out in search of one who would teach him. Successively from representatives of the Minorites, the Dominicans, the Augustinians, and the Carmelites, he obtained extended abuse of each other's order, and direct evidence of the mercenary and carnal ends of all—but no knowledge of the Creed. As he proceeded hopelessly, he caught sight of Piers at the plow, all in tatters, urging his emaciated nags through the muddy field. With a goad walked his wife miserably clad, her bare feet leaving bloodtracks on the ice. The youngest child was sheltered in a bowl, and the two others lay beside it in bits of garments, all moaning sorrowfully. Yet Piers comforted the traveler, and offered him sustenance from his poor scraps. He exposed at length the viciousness of the friars, showing in detail their lack of all that Christ commended and enjoined. Finally, he taught the poet his Creed.

Direct discourse prevails. Particularly to be noted are the descriptive passages, especially the detailed account of the building and luxury of the Dominicans (lines 155–215), the portrait of the fat friar with a double chin big as a goose egg (lines 220–30), and the picture of Piers and his family (lines 421–42). R. W. Chambers wrote that this poem is "a most important document for the history of English social life, and shows powers of no mean order in the writer."

THE COMPLAINT OF THE PLOWMAN or THE PLOWMAN'S TALE [110], 1380 alliterative lines in eight-line stanzas, ababbcbc, forms an allegorical debate between the Griffin, representing the prelates and

monks, and the Pelican, who represents Christianity in Wyclif's sense.
Each side accuses the other of falseness. The author clearly sides with
the Lollards, but masks his feeling by the allegory of the birds. The most
recent commentator (Wawn) views the poem as an early-fifteenth-century
Lollard tract consisting originally of lines 53–205 and 229–716, with lines
717–1268 (the debate) revised by another contemporary Lollard, along
with lines 1269–1380. In the sixteenth century, a Henrician propagandist
added the Prologue (lines 1–52) and lines 505–28.

The Prologue (52 lines in rime royal stanzas): The Plowman joins Chaucer's Canterbury pilgrims and starts his tale.

Part I (53 stanzas, each with refrain, "But falsehed foul mote it befall" or "such
false faytours, foul hem fall"): Debate between the Griffin and the Pelican, who upbraids priests for seeking wealth and honors, and in so doing oppressing the poor,
kneeling to kings, living in lechery, and waging war.

Part II (28 stanzas, each with refrain, "And all this God may well amend," or "God
for his mercy it amend"): Priests live contrary to Christ's life and teachings; they curse
men to hell and betray Christ for money. They have purchased more power in England than the King and all his laws. The lords must beware and defend the realm of
England from the pope.

Part III (85 stanzas, without refrain): The Griffin asks what he can preach against
secular canons. The Pelican answers that the parish clergy neglect their parishes and
only collect their rents and dress like dandies. The Pelican tells the Griffin about the
sins of the monks, who serve the devil of hell. The Griffin tries to defend the Church,
saying it needs a head to govern it, strength to protect itself from enemies. The Pelican
interrupts, saying defense of the Church should lie in humility, righteousness, true
living. The Griffin accuses the Pelican of stirring up contention, of preaching heresy,
and of serving the devil. Fiends have put these ideas in his mind to speak against the
sacraments and the pope. Why meddle in other people's affairs? The Pelican says he
speaks against only those who betray Christ by selling the sacraments; he believes in
transubstantiation, and if pope and cardinals lived decently he would not preach
against them. The Griffin replies that the Pelican and all his sect should be burned,
hanged, and drawn as heretics. The Pelican says he is ready to suffer, and he fears
nothing. As the Griffin flies away, the Pelican asks the poet to write down what was
said, as he wishes only to amend men's trespasses. The Griffin returns with the birds
of prey (ravens, rooks, crows, and magpies) to destroy his rival, but the Phoenix rescues the Pelican and destroys the robbers. The poet insists that these words are not
his but the Pelican's and are to be taken as a fable. He too bows to Holy Church. May
Christ send space to each man to amend himself.

This pseudo-Chaucerian poem should not be confused with Hoccleve's
miracle tale of the Virgin, VIII [14], which in one manuscript of *The
Canterbury Tales* is linked with a spurious "Prologe of the Ploughman."

GOD SPEED THE PLOW I [111], twelve eight-line stanzas, ababbcbc, with refrain, "I praye to God, spede wel the plough," testifies to the vitality of the alliterative tradition about 1500. It is a lamentation by a plowman on the extortionate tithes demanded by the Church.

GOD SPEED THE PLOW II [112] is a couplet caption for a picture of a man ploughing in one manuscript of *Piers Plowman*.

For a carol on the theme, "God spede the plowe alle way" (line 21), see Robbins-Cutler, no. 1405.5.

JACK UPLAND [113] in its present form is more prose than poetry. Since *Friar Daw's Reply* [114] is in very rough alliterative verse, Wright suggested that *Jack Upland* was originally written in a similar form (which the *Reply* in fact imitated). Opposing Wright, Skeat maintained both *Jack Upland* and *Jack Upland's Rejoinder* [115] were prose. Heyworth considers *Jack Upland* prose, and the other two pieces debased alliterative verse. The surviving printed text of *Jack Upland* is probably the later of three versions, for the *Reply* quotes lines verbatim, not the same as those in the manuscripts or early prints, which must come from a now lost (third) manuscript.

I, Jack Upland, make my complaint to all true believers of Christ, that Antichrist and his followers have been brought into the Church and transposed virtues into vices. These orders of friars obey neither bishops nor the King; they neither till, sow, nor reap to sustain themselves. They say they have the power of God to sell heaven or hell. Since they claim to be the greatest clerks of the Church, men should ask them some questions and tell them to ground their answers in reason and holy writ. Then follows a series of questions, divided into 64 clauses, about the orders, rules, habits, sects, dispensations, begging, and so forth. Jack assails the "golden trentall" to bring souls from purgatory, the friars' greediness for confessing and burying the rich, the selling of the Mass for money, the gathering of goods and jewels yet refusal of coined money, the letters of fraternity. The series concludes with questions beginning, "Frere what charite is this?"—to overcharge the people by begging, to beguile children into their orders, to make so many friars in every country a charge on the people, to lie that friars practice poverty, to collect precious books and lock them in a treasury, to entice rich men by letters of fraternity, to act as confessors to lords and ladies yet not try to amend them? Friar, why name ye the patron of your order more than any other saint? Was St. Francis a fool and a liar since ye claim he made the rule so hard that ye cannot keep it and seek dispensation from the pope? Which of the four orders is best? Or is there any more perfect rule than that which Christ gave to his brethren?

Can ye find any fault in Christ's rule, by which he taught all men how to be saved?
Go now and answer these questions by the law of God. If ye cannot answer them, it is
right that such orders be destroyed.

FRIAR DAW'S REPLY [114], "among the most remarkable of the
popular records of the history of the religious movement during the
period" (Wright), is the reply to Jack Upland by a self-styled John
Walsingham, who facetiously calls himself Friar Daw Topias (seemingly
indicative of a comparatively unlearned man). This poem appears in a
contemporary manuscript and can be dated early fifteenth century. "John
Walsingham" may have been a Dominican (possibly from the London
Blackfriars), for he states that the preaching of the friars wrought much
good—and Dominicans were especially proud of their teaching—and re-
fuces one charge by countering that Austin friars or Dominicans were
guiltless.

Among other defenses, Friar Daw makes the following points: friars obey bishops
"although not so far as secular priests"; friars belong to the order of Christ and practice the contemplative life; the golden trental delivers no soul that is unworthy; friars
do not sell the Mass but give freely to those who give freely to them; it is no robbery
to win souls by enticing children to the orders (as Christ did the disciples). He explains the habit as denoting the order, the wide cope signifying charity, the hood patience in adversity, and the scapulary obedience to superiors. Finally he attacks the
Lollards, saying that Wycliffites are heretics who ought to be burned.

JACK UPLAND'S REJOINDER [115] is added in the margins of the
manuscript containing the *Reply of Friar Daw Topias*, to which it forms,
item by item, a coarse rebuttal about one third the length of the *Reply*.
For example, on the alleged loyalty of friars to the crown, the *Rejoinder*
points out that some prior is always at hand to free friars accused of any
crime from the hands of royal justice. The friars, says the *Rejoinder*, are
like foxes—even worse; they do not labor, but lie and fornicate. All the
remarks are directed personally to Friar Daw, whose name often opens
the various irregular sections of the piece. The level of the debate is indicated by such lines as "Thou argust, Topias, wonderly / as if thou
were an asse."

In his edition Heyworth advances a new theory of dating, not the 1402 of Wright and Skeat, but 1450—backdating *Friar Daw's Reply* to ca. 1420 and *Jack Upland* to ca. 1390.

The first and third of these related poems have been briefly noted among the Wyclyffite writings in Chapter III [95–96].

For other attacks on the friars, see Audelay's *Against the Friars* (Brown-Robbins, no. 947), *Satire on the People of Kildare* ([35] above), including friars, monks, nuns, and priests, *Wynnere and Wastoure* ([243] below), and a later sixteenth-century poem in BM Royal Appendix 58, FRERE GASTKYN WO YE BE [116].

Another late satirical poem, in forty short couplets, against the friars, THE EPISTILL OF THE HERMIT OF ALAREIT TO THE GRAY FREIRS [117], was preserved by John Knox about 1566 in his *History of the Reformation*. Knox attributed it to Alexander, Earl of Glencairne, an early reformer. Thomas the hermit with great irony warns the friars against the attacks of the Lutherans, and advises them to work by crafty ways, such as miracles and the laying of ghosts. He will reward them.

Similar is Sir David Lyndsay's *Ane Plesant Satyre of the Thrie Estates*, ca. 1540.

THE PAPELARD PRIEST [118], a mid-fourteenth-century complaint of a priest in nine vigorous stanzas in ten long alliterative lines, ababababbb, including a refrain phrase, "Wyth an O and an I" at line 9. The dialect is West Midland. Some of the phrasing comes within the common alliterative tradition, but there is much originality and richness of vocabulary. Many sentiments are paralleled in *Piers Plowman* (e.g., III, 307, and XV, 122–B version).

The "ʒeddingus de Prust papelard" is the satirical advice of a parish priest to others to covet no church, for he has got one and, compared with the time when he wore "robes of ray," he is now so distracted by his office and his duties, by the management of his farm, his implements and tools, his property and all the cares of husbandry, that he has no time for company, and his former friends shun him as "a papelard priest, plucked as a pye." Even now if he seeks solace with his peers, a boy "bustling on a bellrope as though the town were on fire" calls him to his offices. Even if he exchanges his church for a chapel, he will still have his troubles; it were wise to give up somewhat to God and His service, and fear neither the devil nor his power.

For other poems with "O and I" refrains, see discussion in the chapter on Lyrics.

WHY I CAN'T BE A NUN [119], an acephelous satire of the early fifteenth century in 392 lines in eight-line stanzas, ababbcbc, exposing the vices and shortcomings of nuns and nunneries.

The poem is an elaborate development of a *chanson de nonne*, progressing from the confessions of a girl, Katherine, who is learning from her father and the commissioners about the actual state of the nunneries. From this point, a May morning dream vision is introduced with the usual furnishings: a garden with flowers and an allegorical Lady Experience, who takes Katherine on a tour of a house of nuns, a fair building without but unclean within. Here Katherine meets various nuns, such as Dames Pride, Hypocrisy, Sloth, Vainglory, Envy, Love Unordinate, Lust, Wantonness. Dames Patience and Charity dwell outside the convent. Lady Experience tells Katherine she showed her this revelation to reconcile the young girl to her father's opposition. Most nuns are "feeble, ignorant, and froward." Yet they should be what their habit indicates. "A fair garland of ivy green which hangeth at a tavern door is a false token, as I ween, but if there be good wine and sure." Nuns should follow the example of holy virgin saints.

On this poem, scholars have seen various influences working: the *Pearl* (Schofield) and Gower, Erasmus, and Lyndsay (Power).

The Difficulty of Choosing a Profession in Religion (Brown-Robbins, no. 655) is listed elsewhere.

DEFEND US FROM ALL LOLLARDRY [120], nineteen eight-line stanzas, ababbcbc, although written about forty years later, refers to conditions in England between 1414 and 1417, the year of Oldcastle's execution.

The author warns against meddling in heresy and to beware the "lewde lust of lollardie," in view of the severe measures being taken against it—"yut is a moch folie for fals beleue to ben brent." Especially foolish is the Lollard leader, Sir John Oldcastle, who ought to be behaving like any decent knight, instead of "to babel the bibel day and night." In fact, many people are going to suffer with him. There is some word play and political imagery on the figure of the "old castel" and several stanzas of general vilification. Heresy is bad, but insurrection is worse, and the Bible tells us that traitors will come to "shamful deth."

This is the only poem dealing exclusively with the Lollards, though [58] notes the statute, *De haeretico comburendo*, and [62] refers to Oldcastle's relations with Henry V. Hoccleve's poem *On Richard II's Burial at Westminster* (VIII [25]) praises Henry V for attacking the Lollards, and *Address to Sir John Oldcastle* (VIII [19]) is his appeal to Oldcastle to repent.

IV. Women

ATTACKS ON WOMEN [121], varying from short scraps in sermons to involved and lengthy art compositions, penetrated into almost every type of Middle English prose and poetry from the thirteenth century to way beyond the close of the medieval period, possibly becoming more numerous and abusive in the sixteenth century. Poems critical of a specific woman or women generally which are inverse counterparts of love poems—a group of "un-love" lyrics, in fact—are described elsewhere. Such pieces include, as well as the Holly and Ivy poems, poems of impossibilities, punctuation verses, ironic defenses of women, discussions of true love, straightforward invective, poems of the rebellious lover, and poems critical of or satirizing courtly love. Debates on the *querelle des dames* appear in Chapter VII and poems by the Middle Scots Writers in Chapter X. The chapters on Proverbs, Precepts, and Monitory Pieces and on Carols will include short proverbial pieces and all carols.

This section is concerned only with attacks on women in which the social conditions of the age are involved: for example, the scrutiny of an institution (e.g., marriage), ridicule of a social misdemeanor or vice (e.g., extravagance in dress or fashion), or realistic portraits of ale-wives and others who dissect love and marriage.

ADVICE ON MARRIAGE I [122], two couplets in a collection of Latin sermons, satirizes marriage: It is hard to choose between marriage and hanging, but, since woman is the worse, "drive forthe the carte!"

This theme is developed in a poem in the Bannatyne Manuscript, ff. 263b–264a (ca. 1568), six eight-line stanzas, *Aganis Mariage of Evill Wyvis*, which concludes "for sykerly thair is no difference betuix the gallowis and the spowsing claith."

A carol in the mid-sixteenth-century play, *Tom Tyler and His Wife*, also uses the proverbial "wedding and hanging is destiny" for its burden. See also a carol on *The Tyranny of Women* (Brown-Robbins, no. 667).

ADVICE ON MARRIAGE II [123], in the early sixteenth-century MS Harley 2252, consists of five four-line stanzas of warning: Marry a rich wife while you are young, for when you are old the wealthy women won't have you.

On the other hand, two semi-proverbial couplets against matrimony advise that if you have avoided marriage when young, you will be too wise to marry when you are old (Brown-Robbins, no. 1427).

ADVICE ON MARRIAGE III [124], five long lines abbaa, counsels against hasty marriage and favors a careful choice "er thou the knot knytte." Compare lines 11–12 of a series of six related couplets on the *Fickleness of Women* (Brown-Robbins, no. 4137).

For a carol on the same theme, its first quatrain almost duplicating the above, see Brown-Robbins, no. 1938, and Greene E E Carols, no. 403; one of its lines occurs as the refrain of VII [63] and of Brown-Robbins, no. 1338: "Turn up her halter and let her go."

The imagery continued in use until the later sixteenth century, as in the four eight-line stanzas, "I will not knit before I knowe," part of *The Dispraise of Women* (STC, no. 20523).

Knitting the knot is the subject of a moral couplet in MS Laud Misc. 77:

þat knotte þat is knytte scholde not be brokone.
Trw loue in hertus to-gydur scholde be lokone.

Lydgate's *Mumming at Hertford* (Brown-Robbins, no. 2213) deals with a dispute between husbands and wives, adjudicated by the King, who advises men to "beware therfore or they be bounde" in marriage.

ADVICE ON MARRIAGE IV [125], two long couplets, gives a semi-proverbial warning on the need for caution in selecting a mate, because "poverty parteth company." It is followed by [126], and a third similar warning [127].

ADVICE ON MARRIAGE V [126], two long couplets, advises a man to keep his eyes wide open when he marries: Wink when you take a wife, and you will stare afterward!

ADVICE ON MARRIAGE VI [127], two long couplets following [125] and [126], brackets "rekeles" wives with unnatural children and covetous executors. This couplet crops up in a series of proverbial but diverse couplets signed "Wyllughby" in a Hunterian manuscript:

> . . . A welde best a man may meyke
> A womans answere is never for to seyke
> A lordes purpose and a ladyes thoghtt
> In a yer schonyth full offtt . . .
> Man on the molde haue this in mynde
> That thow doyth here that sall thou fynd
> Wemen ben laches and chyldren onkynd
> Seckurs euer aftur and tak qwat they fynd

ADVICE ON MARRIAGE VII [128], a three-line tag in a collection of Latin, English, and macaronic verses, verbally parallels a foregoing item [126]—this writer did indeed "wink" when he married. A Latin distich immediately following warns against marriage to widows; and a Latin line preceding compares virginity to wax.

A series of gnomic lines on "a fox, a fryyr, and a woman" with what may be a burden or heading is listed elsewhere (Brown-Robbins, no. 3552).

A Scottish prose text, *The Spektakle of Luf*, translated from Latin by "M G Myll" in 1492, while inveighing against lecherous women, advises a young man to marry a chaste wife of good family and govern her well. This text has no connection with an English prose text of similar nature, *The Spectacle of Louers* (STC, no. 25008).

VIRTUOUS MAIDENS BUT WICKED WIVES [129], seven stanzas rime royal, incorrectly ascribed to Chaucer in both manuscripts, complains that maidens are virtuous but become vicious when they are married. Eve, a wife, brought the world to confusion; wives destroyed Solomon, Samson, David. But the Blessed Virgin, the poet interjects, redressed Eve's sin.

Chaucer's *Envoy to Bukton* (Brown-Robbins, no. 2262) forms "The Counceyll of Chaucer Touchyng Maryag": better to marry than to burn, but the husband becomes his wife's thrall. A long Chaucerian apocryphon is *The Remedy of Love* (XI [34]).

Peter Idley's Instructions (Brown-Robbins, no. 1540) has two isolable rime royal stanzas (Part II, A. 2197–2210) satirizing marriage and mentioning the Dunmow flitch of bacon.

THE SNARES OF WOMEN [130], two couplets added in a sixteenth-century hand on a manuscript of Chartier's *Quadrilogue*, warns against women, possibly cautioning against loveless marriage:

He that to women hys credens gyffe,
Ordeynith snares hymselfe to mysscheffe.
Better yt is for loue good seruise to do,
Than thankeles to be compelled thero.

THE TRIALS OF MARRYING A YOUNG WIFE I [131], one Monk's Tale stanza, ababbcbc, is a lament of an old man married to a young wife, recalling [132] below. The poem concludes with the proverbial "The blind eateth many a fly," included in the pseudo-Chaucerian poems, *Balade Against Hypocritical Women*, described in Chapter XI [32], and *Beware of Deceitful Women* (Brown-Robbins, no. 1944; also see under XI [31]) as a refrain.

THE TRIALS OF MARRYING A YOUNG WIFE II [132], two cross-rimed quatrains on the tribulations of marriage: there is no peace either for a man with a young wife or for a harvest goose.

For a long poem, attributed to Lydgate but perhaps by Gower, counselling an old gentleman who wished to marry a young wife, using the Chaucerian imagery of December marrying July, see Brown-Robbins, no. 86.

For a warning to beware a false mistress, see Robbins-Cutler, no. 79.5.

A short poem by Sir Richard Maitland on the same topic, *The Folye of ane Auld Man*, occurs in three sixteenth-century Scottish manuscripts (Maitland Folio and Quarto, Reidpath), similarly borrowing its metaphor from Chaucer's *Merchant's Tale*—fresh May and cold January do not agree upon a song in June.

Impingham's Proverbs (Brown-Robbins, no. 2290), attacking the traditional faults of women, also contains an allusion to Chaucer's *Merchant's Tale*: a man must marry his equal, for May and January are always at war.

SORROWS OF MARRIAGE [133] consists of four couplets:

Quhat aylt ye man to ved a vyf
Cowd ȝou nocht find in al þi lyf
A viddy or a raip of nycht
A helter for to hang ye vitht
Or at a vindow to fal downe
Or our a brig to lowpe and drowne
Quhat vengeance ves in thyne Entente
To tak sic sorow and torment

Many a Man Blamys his Wyffe Perde (Brown-Robbins, no. 2090; Greene E E Carols, no. 410) is a carol extant in two manuscripts. Stanzas 10–14 are extrapolated in a third manuscript (Robbins-Cutler, nos. 994.5 and 2090) which satirically advises husbands to yield to their wives' desire for mastery.

For two carols satirizing women's shrewishness see *Strife in the House* (Brown-Robbins, no. 65; Greene E E Carols, no. 408) and *A Henpecked Husband's Complaint* (Brown-Robbins, no. 210; Greene E E Carols, no. 406).

Bycorne and Chychevache, a series of tapestry verses satirizing women's shrewishness, is treated with Lydgate's poems (Brown-Robbins, no. 2541). See also *The Payne and Sorow of Evyll Maryage*, Lydgate's translation of *Golias De Coniuge Non Ducenda*: the author is saved from marriage by the exposé by three angels about woman's evil nature (Brown-Robbins, no. 919).

For a pseudo-Chaucerian poem attacking woman and marriage, see *The Remedy of Love*, XI [34].

Audelay's *On the Decadence of Marriage* (Brown-Robbins, no. 1630; Greene E E Carols, no. 411) is a carol warning against the adultery of courtly love.

IRONIC PRAISE OF WOMEN [134], ten twelve-line stanzas, ababab-abcdcd, with considerable artificial literary flourish, including a modified chanson d'aventure gambit, praises women with considerable ambiguity. The refrain might almost pass as "destroying" (as in [93] above and Brown-Robbins, no. 1485):

For all the falsehede in this worde
Fyrst sprange owt of a womans trewthe.

In stanzas 8 and 9 are several unusual allusions to "Cocke Lorrels bote," "Sknoballys chyldren," and "The viij chapter of Isopes fables." The manuscript may be dated after 1560, but Seaton considers the poem before 1440.

Many other poems critical or satirical of womankind are catalogued elsewhere, many in the chapters on Lyrics and Carols. These poems include, *inter alia*, Brown-Robbins, Robbins-Cutler, nos. 37.3, 79.5, 81.5, 232, 3174.5, 3701.5, 3909.6, 3911.5, 3914.5, 3919.5, 4056.5, 4090, 4166.5.

LATER POEMS ATTACKING WOMEN [135] include the following: Two sixteenth-century broadsides, *Women Will Have Their Will,* ironic like [132], and *The Discontented Husband,* argue that wives always have the mastery.

Doctrina et Consilium Galiensis is a prose text in the mid-fifteenth-century manuscript, Harley 78, giving semi-satirical counsel on how to rule one's wife.

The Curste Wyfe Lapped in Morrelles Skin is a sixteenth-century jest of some 1120 lines, mainly in eight-line stanzas, which tells how to charm or cure a shrewish wife.

Two companion pieces in the sixteenth-century Maitland Folio manuscript present the problems of a bridegroom and of a faithless wife. *God Gif I Were Wedow Now* expresses the wish of a twelve-month old husband that he were a widower, so that he could find another wife who would not nag or beat him. *Wo Worth Maryage,* by "Clappertoun," is the plaint of a wanton maid who laments her marriage to a churl: she dare neither dress well, nor "scantlie gif Sir Iohne ane kis." This poem is in fact a parody of a *chanson de mal mariée,* a rare form in English (for others, see Brown-Robbins, no. 1265).

Other sixteenth-century poems on the problems of marriage include: *A Complaynt of Them That Be To Soone Maryed* (STC, no. 5729), 50 eight-line stanzas, by Robert Copland (whose name appears in an acrostic in the Envoy), printed ca. 1535, attacks shrewish wives, poverty in marriage (cf. [125] above), and mothers-in-law. This piece is based on the French *Complainte du trop tot mariée* of Pierre Gringoire.

A companion piece is *The Complaynte of Them That Ben To Late Maryed* (STC, no. 5728), 53 stanzas rime royal, also based on the French of Pierre Gringoire, wherein an old husband, now impotent because of his riotous youth, laments the fact that he did not marry earlier in life. The poem satirizes the aging lover rather than the woman, however.

Two early sixteenth-century carols on an old forester present a similar theme; a third describes an old forester who is still able to make love (Robbins-Cutler, nos. 1303.3, 1303.5, 4068.6).

To be given passing mention here are *Gyl of Braintford's Testament* (STC, no. 5730), and *The Seuen Sorowes That Women Haue When Theyr Husbandes Be Dead* (STC, no. 5734), both translated by Robert Copland.

The XV Joyes of Maryage (STC, no. 15258), a verse translation in 41 stanzas rime royal of *Les quinze joyes de mariage*, is also attributed to Copland.

Further late items are listed under [139] below.

Discussion of the uxorial life, including goodwives' tales, are treated in [146–151] below.

Extreme fashions in feminine apparel were targets of a group of satires, some of which extended to male costumes. Especially singled out were women's high headdresses or "horns."

AGAINST WOMEN'S HORNS I [136], four lines "contra mulieres ornantes" in a thirteenth-century Latin sermon, one of the earliest of such attacks, ridicules also ladies' long trains.

> Who haues hornes als ha ram
> and ha nech als a swan
> and a midel als ha brock
> ha tayl als ha pacock.

For another thirteenth-century tag on the vanity of fashions, which likewise includes trailing dresses with horns, see Brown-Robbins, no. 2285. The late thirteenth-century *The Follies of Fashion* ([32] above) is included with the poems of MS Harley 2253. In the same manuscript is a general condemnation of extravagant dress, *Satire on the Retinues of the Great* ([31] above).

AGAINST WOMEN'S HORNS II [137], late fourteenth or early fifteenth century, exists in three versions, one (Corpus) of eight lines and the other (Armagh) of two six-line stanzas: "Destroy the pryde of womens hornes!" The first stanza alone occurs in a Bodleian manuscript. The Corpus version attacks courtly fashions and hypocrisy, without regard to sex, and resembles another scrap in the Corpus manuscript, *Epigram on Extravagance* II [141].

AGAINST WOMEN'S HORNS III [138], eight octosyllabic lines, aabbbbcc, invokes Christ's wrath to destory the pride of women's horns and long tails and hoods like "carrake saylis." Men also have their vanity in dress. A couplet immediately following may possibly be related to the piece:

And never the hyer that thowe erte
So moche lower beo thyne herte.

The first four lines are similar to the second stanza in the Armagh text of [137].

For John Lydgate's *Dyte of Womenhis Hornys* (Brown-Robbins, no. 2625), see the chapter on Lydgate. For Hoccleve's poem against extravagant dress (Brown-Robbins, no. 1398), see VIII [2].

FURTHER LATER POEMS ATTACKING WOMEN [139] include the following items:

(a) Sir David Lyndsay's *In Contemptioun of Syde Taillis* (ca. 1540), satirizing women who wear long trains to their dresses.

(b) Sir Richard Maitland's *Satire on the Town Ladies*, in the Maitland Folio and Quarto manuscripts, which condemns women's vanity in clothes and cosmetics, with especial reference to the bourgeois wives who ape the nobility and who waste their husbands' money.

(c) Robert Crowley's *Of Nyce Wyues*, also mid-sixteenth century, an attack on the high fashions of women as indications of wantonness.

(d) George Turbervile's *To an Olde Gentlewoman That Painted Hir Face*, slightly later, a satire on an ugly woman who still adorns herself as though she were young.

(e) Charles Bansley's *Treatyse* (STC, no. 1374), a mid-sixteenth-century prose attack on exaggerated fashions.

Two short comments on extravagance may be included here:

EPIGRAM ON EXTRAVAGANCE I [140], two couplets signed "Quod More," predicting disaster to wasters, is retained here since it is found separately:

He that louyth welle to fare
eur to spend and neuer spare
But he haue the more good
His here wol grow throw his hood.

The lines occur with four other proverbial stanzas in another manuscript copied from texts on the wall of the Aula at Launceston Priory.

EPIGRAM ON EXTRAVAGANCE II [141], a six-line stanza, aabaab, which links the downfall of England to Envy and Felony—and overlong beards! Followed in the manuscript by [137].

One quatrain from the *Poema Morale* (Brown-Robbins, no. 3246), lines 149–50, occurring separately, warns on the cost of luxuries.

Satires on overdressed braggarts, or "galaunts," are discussed under [160–163] below. Men's slit sleeves are condemned in [89] above.

Another small group of anti-feminist poems centers round women's wantonness, ranging from short tags against "clattering" to full-length pictures of gossips at the alehouse, comparable to the realistic glimpses of medieval life listed in the following section. Further attacks on women's inconstancy are described in the chapter on Lyrics.

TUTIVILLUS: AGAINST GOSSIPING WOMEN [142], six maca-ronic English and Latin stanzas, consisting of a four-stress English cou-plet with a three-stress Latin line (riming throughout), warns women against gossiping in church, for the devil Tutivillus records everything they have said. Better be quiet and so win Heaven's bliss. Tutivillus is the well-known noonday devil who appears (line 447) as a character in the morality play, *Mankind*.

For a proverbial saw on women disagreeing with each other, like two dogs over a bone, see Brown-Robbins, no. 3818, in the chapter on Prov-erbs, Precepts, and Monitory Pieces.

Lines (Part II, A. 1028–55) in Peter Idley's *Instructions* (Brown-Rob-bins, no. 1540) refer to jangling in church.

AGAINST INDISCREET WOMEN [143], two long couplets in a col-lection of sermons, discusses women's lack of discretion.

Say Me, Viit in the Brome (VII [62]) gives the amusing answer to a wife's inquiry how to retain her husband's love—Be quiet.

Several proverbial pieces against women are described elsewhere: *Beware of Deceitful Women* (Brown-Robbins, no. 1944), *Three Things Causing Trouble* (Brown-Robbins, no. 861), and Lydgate's *Four Things Make Man a Fool* (Brown-Robbins, no. 4230).

THE HART LOVETH THE WOOD [144] is a series of satirical proverbs against the sovereignty of women in four monoriming lines: The hart loves the wood, the hare the hill, the churl his "byll," the fool his folly, the wise man his skill, and "the properte of a shrod qwen ys to have hyr wyll."

Another proverbial couplet in the fifteenth-century MS Sloane 1210, *The Smallere Pese the Mo to the Pott*, suggests the fairer the women, the more "gyglott " (i.e., harlot).

ADVICE ON CONDUCT [145], a scrap of four doggerel couplets added on the margin of a fourteenth-century psalter, warns ladies to avoid unchaste conduct.

For a song of impossibilities against faithlessness in women, see Robbins-Cutler, no. 1355.5, similar in scope to Brown-Robbins, no. 3999. A retroverted extract from *The Remedy of Love* (XI [34]) turns the impossibilities topos to a praise of women (Robbins-Cutler, no. 1409.3).

The majority of the anti-feminist poems are described in the chapter on Lyrics.

THE ALE-WIFE GROUP [146] includes several late poems.

Lydgate's *Ballade on an Ale Seller* (Brown-Robbins, nos. 2809, 3823) satirizes a beautiful ale-wife whose wantonness and kisses and false oaths are only to obtain money. The same thought is used to warn men in *Warning Against Lechery* (Brown-Robbins, no. 551). *If I Be Wanton I Wotte Well Why* is a sixteenth-century carol of a wench enticing to wantonness. *Take iij Clateras* is a late fifteenth-century riddle comparing a woman to a magpie, wasp, weasel, and shrew. An early sixteenth-century prose satire on women's lasciviousness, *A Harlatt, a Hunter and a Hore*, occurs in MS Rawlinson C.813; the same manuscript has another prose text satirizing women in more general terms, *A Woman Most Haue iij Propretes*. A late sixteenth-century broadside ballad in thirteen stanzas rime royal by John Wallys lampoons the desires of lascivious women.

Brilliant studies of lascivious women are drawn by William Dunbar: *The Tretis of the Tua Mariit Wemen and the Wedo* (X [68]), a discussion, as the three women sit drinking, how they deal with their husbands; *The Ballad of Kynd Kyttok* (X [106]), an amusing but gentle satire of the ale-wife's adventures in heaven; *The Twa Cummeris* (X [67]), or the two gossips drinking wine the first day of Lent; and *Ballate Against Evil Women* (X [107]), generally ascribed to Dunbar, forming "one of the most violent satires against women's lasciviousness" (Utley).

The best known of the ale-wife poems is the very early sixteenth-century *Tunnyng of Elynour Rummyng*, by Skelton (Robbins-Cutler, no. 3265.5).

THE GOSSIPS' MEETING [147] or *The Ten Wives' Tale*, twenty six-line stanzas of the mid-fifteenth century, opens with a chanson d'aventure gambit, which links the poem to the *chanson de mal mariée* tradition. The author then describes the conversation of ten wives who lament their husbands' inadequacies in love-making.

The song *Old Hogyn* (Brown-Robbins, no. 1222) might be the story of such a husband seeking to prove himself in extra-marital relations.

GOOD GOSSIPS [148], a less outspoken piece, exists in carol form in a Balliol MS (Brown-Robbins, no. 1362; Greene E E Carols, no. 419), but what is probably its original non-carol form occurs in eight-line tail-rime stanzas, each broken by two refrain tags, "Good gosyp." It describes the dialogue of several gossips at the tavern poking fun and derision at their husbands. The carol variant is described elsewhere.

The Good Gossippes Songe occurs in the Chester Play of the *Deluge*, and a similar piece, *Four Wittie Gossips*, is found in Pepys' collection of ballads.

THE GOSSIPS' ROYAL FEAST [149] is a poem in couplets with the title, "How the gosyps made a royal feest."

JOHN CROPHILL'S ALE POTS [150], an unusually curious poem, in nine rough eight-line tail-rime stanzas, with three concluding couplets, inasmuch as it was written by John Crophill, a leech of Wix, Essex, about 1457–58 to celebrate a brewing party. A certain Friar Thomas Stanfield had made a gift of a drinking cup; Crophill proffers the cup to five important female guests (some addressed as Dame), and makes mock dedications. Crophill joins in the toasts, advises the guests to be of good cheer, prays for long life for Friar Thomas, and gives his own name.

THE FRATERNITY OF DRINKERS [151], a satirical burlesque in 30 six-line tail-rime stanzas, aabccb, describes the founding of an imaginary "order" of tipplers.

The narrator proposes to establish a "hospital" and set its rules; initiation fees and yearly dues ("a potell of good ale" and a quart "onys yn the yer"), trinitarian methods of drinking ("iij sypys"), and dress ("toryn gowne," "a pach at the kne"). The almshouse will receive drunken debtors, habitual drunkards ("so drunke that they canot speke"), and those with troublesome wives! These brethren—and sisters, too—will drink to loosen their tongues and "tell a mery tale."

The piece recalls the French *Order of Fair Ease* ("Qui vodra a moi entendre") and *The Land of Cokaygne* ([34] above), several poems on drinking (Brown-Robbins, no. 2675; Robbins-Cutler, nos. 2358.5, 4256.8), and the various "merry tales" popular in the fifteenth century.

PROSE PIECES AGAINST WOMEN [152]. Reference may be made here to the prose pieces against women wherein gossips advise how to rule their husbands, somewhat resembling the spirit of several carols (Brown-Robbins, no. 1362; Robbins-Cutler, no. 2358.5; Greene E E Carols, no. 419): *The Gospelles of Dystaues* (STC, no. 12091), a late fifteenth-century translation by Henry Watson of *Les Evangiles des*

Quenouilles, and *The Proude Wyues Pater Noster* (STC, no. 25938), about 1560, which includes, among many reflections on women's fashions and a wife's need for money, the advice of one gossip to another how to rule a husband.

LATER POEMS AGAINST WOMEN WITH DOUBLE ENTENDRE

[153]. Attention should be drawn to several poems against women with double entendre:

Piers of Fulham's Conceytis in Love (Brown-Robbins, no. 71), against woman's inconstancy and dominance "under covert termes off fysshyng and fowlyng."

Pulle Of Her Bellys (Brown-Robbins, no. 4090), a satire on the fickleness of paramours, using terms of falconry.

To a Fickle and Unconstaunt Dame, by George Turbervile (about 1567), also employing terms of falconry to satirize woman's inconstancy.

Sore This Dere Strykyn Ys, a carol type of poem by William Cornysh, in two mid-sixteenth-century manuscripts, describing an encounter with an amorous wench in terms of hunting.

The Auncient Acquaintance, Madam, Betwen Vs Twayn, by John Skelton, satirizing woman's lust under the guise of horsemanship (Robbins-Cutler, no. 3302.5).

The Plowman's Song (XI [36]) using the terminology of ploughing land to describe love-making.

In the mid-sixteenth-century Bannatyne manuscript are several satires employing a play on words:

I Haiff a Littill Fleming Berge, in eight eight-line stanzas, describing a noted harlot, Margaret Fleming, who is compared to a ship that all may board.

Now Gossop I Must Neidis Begon, a satire on the insatiability of his wanton mistress in nautical terms.

My Mistress Is in Musik Passing Skilfull, similar, but using musical terminology.

Off Cullouris Cleir, appraising three harlots in clothmaking metaphors.

V. Contemporary Life: Vignettes

This section includes a diverse cross section of poems notable for their graphic portrayal of various facets of medieval life, generally critical. They include satires on the power of money, vivid pictures of city life and its overdressed braggarts, and schoolboys' laments.

Several poems, from the time of Walter Mapes to the sixteenth century, decry the influence of money; some are in Latin, some in French, and some in English. Early are the Latin *De cruce denarii* and *De nummo*; of the thirteenth century are the Latin *Versus de nummo* and the French *De Dan Denier*.

NARRACIO DE DOMINO DENARII [154], 123 lines in tail-rime stanzas, aabccb, occurs in a mid-fifteenth-century manuscript, although probably composed earlier. A similar but shortened text of 93 lines, aabaab, is found in a Caius manuscript.

> Sir Penny rules wherever he goes, and clergy and laymen, rulers and people, serve him. He changes men's spirits, he influences the court, he wins women, he buys heaven and hell, he looses and binds. Sir Penny makes bold the meek, blinds jurors to the truth, makes peace from strife and friends of foes, buys judgments by perjury, may lend and give, may slay and grant life. He is a jovial fellow, welcomed and served as a guest, however often he comes. He serves every need, and gives his owner his way when others are set aside. He goes in rich clothes and makes merry; he is ever pre-eminent. No one can approach him. Delight not in money, but spend it in charity. God grant us wisely to spend our goods, that we may have the bliss hereafter.

A similar piece, [159] below, seven stanzas, ababbcbc, occurs in two sixteenth-century manuscripts (Pepys 2253 and Advocates 1.1.6).

THE POWER OF THE PURSE [155], nine quatrains aaab (with refrain, "But thou haue the peny redy to tak to"), shows how money is essential for advancement in all walks of life—the church, law, court, and business.

ON PENNY [156], a fourteenth-century scribble of five lines, on saving and spending, recalling *Go Peni Go* (Brown-Robbins, no. 2747; Greene E E Carols, no. 292).

GRAMERCY MYN OWN PURSE [157], five four-stress eight-line stanzas, ababbcbc, with the refrain "Ever, gramercy, myn owne purse," occurs in Dame Juliana Berner's *Boke of Hawkynge and Huntynge* (STC, no. 3308), printed by de Worde about 1486.

The author claims that friendship is now so fallen that the only faithful friend is his own purse. When he rides with gold and silver, men seek his company. But when it happened that he lost his horse, cattle, and goods, his friends refused to help him. Therefore, test your friends before you have a fall and may the Lord send us spending in our own purse.

Two carols on the same theme use the refrain of this poem for their burdens (Brown-Robbins, nos. 1484, 3959; Greene E E Carols, nos. 390–391).

LONDON LICKPENNY [158] exists in two versions, in eight-line stanzas in MS Harley 542 and in rime royal in MS Harley 367, the latter formed (Hammond suggested) by dropping or telescoping a line of the original version. The poem paints a vivid word picture of the busy life in the first half of the fifteenth century in London—"a lick-penny (as Paris is called by some, a *pick-purse*) because of feastings" (Skeat).

A countryman comes to the capital to institute a law suit. But he finds everything costs money: none of the lawyers or judges in the various courts (st. 1–7) will listen to him, so "for lack of mony, I cold not spede." He leaves the courts to return home, and here commences the series of vignettes of London street life, where vendors offer ribs of beef at Westminster Gate (st. 8), fresh fruits (st. 9), fine cloth in Westcheep (st. 10) or on Candlewick Street (st. 11). He tours the lively streets of Eastcheep and sees his stolen hood on sale in Cornhill—"to by my own hood I thought it wronge—I knew it well as I did my crede." He can afford only a penny for a pint of ale (st. 14), and has no money to pay for crossing the Thames. Finally (st. 16) he resolves that "of the law wold I meddle no more."

In MS Harley 367 the poem is attributed without any foundation to Lydgate. Compare [92] above.

Other poems giving intimate portrayals of the power of money come in carol form: *Gramercy Mine Own Purse* (Brown-Robbins, nos. 1484, 3959; Greene E E Carols, nos. 390–391), *Money, Money* (Brown-Robbins, no. 113; Greene E E Carols, no. 393), and *Sir Penny* (Brown-Robbins, no. 2747; Greene E E Carols, no. 392).

SIR PENNY [159] is a late Scottish poem, in seven eight-line stanzas, on the same subject.

Several poems describe the man of fashion, whose corrupt dress and manners are alleged to be destroying England. Such a dandy was epitomized by an anagram of the seven deadly sins—"Galaunt."

A SONG OF GALAUNT [160], 32 stanzas rime royal—31 in Astor MS and only twenty in Trinity MS—is the most detailed of these pieces.

England may wail over the fraud, pride, and deceit of this new dissimulation that blinds and consumes the nation as it takes the place of the old prosperity, chivalry, manhood, and rich merchandise that shone through "the world so clear." The new array of men as women and women as men disfigures nature. Guile was the father and Jealousy the dame of these gallants who spend the days in getting and jangling. Why did they not remain in France? Scorn is cast upon their garments: the rolled hoods, the new brooched doublets open at the breast, the gowns, coats, tippets, as they labor in their wits to find fantasies. Pray God England may again rejoice in its old felicity.

The piece includes an acrostic on the name "Galaunt" built on the Seven Deadly Sins:

For in thys name Galaunt ye may se expresse
Seuyn lettres for som cause in especiall,
Aftyr the seuyn dedly synnes full of cursydnesse,
That maketh mankynde vnto the deuyll thrall.
Was nat pryde cause of lucyferes fall?
Pryde ys now in hell, and Galaunt nygheth nere.
All England shall wayle that eure came he here.

G   for glotony that began in paradyse.
A   for Auaryce that regneth the world thorough.
L   for luxury that noryssheth euery vyce.
A   for Accydy that dwelleth in towne and borough.
V   for Wrathe that seketh both land and forough.
N   for noying Enuy that dwelleth euery-where.
T   for toylous pryde. these myscheuen oure land here.

Following these stanzas comes a series of stanzas each describing the sins in the above order.

AGAINST PROUD GALAUNTS [161] consists of two parts: (1) two monoriming stanzas blaming galaunts with their high caps, short gowns, long piked shoes and long hair, for having "brought this lond to gret pyne," (2) four monoriming stanzas giving the galaunts' reply to these charges of "poopeholy prestis fulle of presomcioun." Priests also follow the fashions in dress—short stuffed doublets and pleated gowns—and are as lewd as the galaunts they condemn. First let them amend themselves, so they can the better reprove others and so "bryng pese to londe."

A MACARONIC COUPLET ON GALAUNT [162] attacks their spendthrift ways.

AN EPITAPH WITH WARNING TO GALAUNTS [163], two stanzas rime royal, is found in Hungerford Chapel, Salisbury.

This theme is continued in several related pieces. A carol, *Huff a Galaunt* (Brown-Robbins, no. 892), condemning the extremes of male fashion as leading to the discomfiture of England, is listed in the chapter on Carols. Also entered in the chapter on Lyrics is an acephalous attack on extreme fashions with an appeal to Christ "vpon the rode" (Robbins-Cutler, no. *1585.8).

A song in sixteen irregular riming lines, "Hof hof hof a frysche new galavnt," occurs in Part I, Scene 9, of the Digby Play of *Mary Magdalene* (XII [19]). In the Towneley Play of the *Judgment*, Tutivillus attacks fashions in male dress, but the stanzas (31, 33, 38) are not extrapolable (XII [11]).

Jolly Rutterkin (Robbins-Cutler, no. 2832.2), a satire on penniless foreigners, is often ascribed to Skelton. For a satirical picture of a good-for-nothing drunkard, see Lydgate's *Jack Hare* (Brown-Robbins, no. 36). A very realistic depiction of a drunken man, a monologue, is found on a small parchment slip (Robbins-Cutler, no. 4256.8).

THE SCHOOLBOY'S WISH [164], four six-line tail-rime stanzas, aabccb, expresses considerable venom against the usher, or assistant to the teacher, who administers "strokes gret." A Latin rendering follows. The stanzas are added to a textbook of the *Accentuarius* and the *Dictionarius* of John de Garlandia.

FULGENS SCOLA DISCOLUS EST MERCATOR PESSIMUS [165], five macaronic English and Latin long couplets with this heading describe the rigorous but carefree life of the schoolboy who pays little attention to his teacher.

THE SCHOOLBOY'S PLEA [166], "ante finem termini baculus portamus," fourteen macaronic lines, Latin and (last half of line) English, is the plea of the schoolboy to close the school in good time for Christmas.

The Schoolboy's Lament (Brown-Robbins, no. 1399; Greene E E Carols, no. 413) about his cruel teacher is listed in the chapter on Carols. *A Lesson To Be Kept in Mind By a Virtuous Child* (Brown-Robbins, no. 1416) appears with the instructional pieces.

SCHOOLBOY EXERCISES [167] are occasionally found as specific examples of passages for translation or exercises in simple rhetoric. Among many examples of a few words, a single sentence, or pen trials, the following may be noted. The five fragments listed below occur on the same leaf of a child's textbook in Latin:

(a) Names of birds. Irregular monoriming lines continuing as prose catalogues, followed by Latin with gloss ("Today in the dawnyng").

(b) Animal noises. English and Latin original, twelve lines in couplets, followed by the Latin ("At my house I have a Jaye").

(c) Aphorisms, in Latin and English.

(d) In the spring, five riming lines with Latin:

When the clot klyngueth
and the cucko synguth
and the brome spryngyth
Then his tyme a yongelyng
for to go a wowyng

(e) An aphorism, English and Latin: What for ryght / What for wrong / mony men be made ryche.

THE CHORISTERS' LAMENT [168], or *The Monks' Complaint on the Difficulty of Learning Church Music*, 52 riming alliterative lines of the later fourteenth century, dialect Northeast Midland, presents Dan Walter bemoaning his inability to read music, remember it, or carry a tune. Dan William has his troubles, too. Their choir master scolds them "que wos ren ne vaut."

For a warning to older scholars, see Robbins-Cutler, no. 407.5.

Two early references to children's games may be listed here:

HOW MANY MILES TO BEVERLEY [169] is a little tag used in a children's game, described in an early Latin sermon:

> Christians who at one moment make haste to Heaven and at another relapse are compared "pueris qui ludunt 'Quot leucas habeo ad Beverleyham?' Alius dicut 'viij.' Primus dicit 'Possum venire per lucem?' Alius dicit iuramento 'ita potes,' et ille incipit bonum cursum ac si festinanter ire vellet, et tunc retro saltat et est in pristino statu et dicit 'Ha ha petipas ʒuot ich am þer ich was.' " (Mynors)

BLINDMAN'S BUFF [170], another tag for a children's game, quoted in a fifteenth-century sermon:

> A bobbid a bobbid a bilirred
> Smyte not her bot thu smyte a gode.

THE BLACKSMITHS [171], 22 long alliterative lines of the later fourteenth century, Southeast Midland dialect, is a magnificent example of realism in verse, and the onomatopoeic effect of the lines is outstanding.

> The "swarte smekyd smethes" drive men mad with their hammering and blowing their bellows. Their huffing and puffing, spitting and cursing, their shouts blend in a fiendish symphony.

Alliteration is used to mimic the crash of the hammers. The onomatopoeic representation of the rattle and clatter of the smaller hammers, the clang of the sledges, the roaring of the bellows, the shouts of the men, is admirable. The scene, with its hurry and noise, and its gaunt leathery-skinned actors, is strikingly real, and gives an excellent picture of the activity of smiths before an expedition, in the days when armor was worn generally.

Another prime instance of medieval realism occurs in this same manuscript, preceding this piece, *The Choristers' Lament* [168].

For another realistic piece, see *The Debate of the Carpenter's Tools* (VII [31]).

PILGRIMS' SONG [172], nine eight-line stanzas, aaabcccb, describes the difficulties of travelling by sea, from Sandwich, Winchelsea, or Bristol, on a pilgrims' boat to Saint James of Compostella. The bustling of the sailors as they respond to the officers' orders, reported in vigorous colloquial dialogue, and the plight of the passengers give a graphic realization of life on shipboard.

For accounts of the itineraries to Jerusalem, see Brown-Robbins, nos. 883, 986. A long poem on the different places of pilgrimage occurs in Purchas' *Pilgrimes*, ca. 1625 (Robbins-Cutler, no. 1557.5). For *The Stations of Rome*, see Brown-Robbins, nos. 1172, 1962.

Prose texts of similar information include *The Itineraries of William Wey to Saint James of Compostella*, 1456, and *To Jerusalem*, 1458 and 1462, and the *Informacion for Pilgrymes vnto the Holy Lande*, printed by de Worde in 1498.

THE SHIRES [173], a jocular mnemonic catalogue of the characteristics of the English counties, the land and the inhabitants, twenty-one couplets, is found in a manuscript ca. 1500.

9. THE WARS OF THE ROSES

Some two dozen poems are preserved dealing with the Wars of the Roses; considering the potential use of lampoons, rimed reports, tags, and personal paeans or invectives as war propaganda, more should have survived. The poems are largely found in four manuscripts, three presenting the Yorkist point of view. Lancanstrian-oriented verse is therefore rare, but it is possible to garner six or seven poems whose authors were loyal to Henry.

COTTON ROLLS ii.23 [174] is a small roll containing various political items, written about 1450 or 1451, including articles against the Duke of Suffolk, the Duke of York's declaration to the King, lists of persons indicted at Rochester, and the demands of Jack Cade; in addition there are political prophecies [281], [299], and a series of six poems favorable to the Yorkists [189–192], [194–195], and Brown-Robbins, no. 1138, an Evils of the Age tag with political overtones. They are contemporary pieces, written amid the excitement of the halfway mark of the century, when the protagonists were jockeying for position and lining up allies. Venom and plain speaking mark all these productions. The author cannot be identified; but the poems hint at the group to which he might have belonged, and mention with approbation "the comyns." *Advice to the Court I* ([194] below) instructs the confidants of the king, "Duke, Iwge, Baron, Archebisshop," not, for fear or favor of the Duke of Suffolk, to lose "the loue of alle the commynalte," a factor often stressed in poems opposing the dominant court circle. While leading noblemen themselves were much aware of the need of support of the commons—the rich London merchants who were daily gaining in political power—these poems reflect the attitude of the Commons themselves. The list of commercial grievances (Article 12 in the manuscript) and the notes on taxes (Article 11) suggest a London citizen, rather than a cleric (as Brotanek suggested).

Another Yorkist manuscript is LAMBETH 306 [175], containing many religious and secular lyrics, poems, and romances, along with domestic, medical, and historical notes, including the Proclamation of the Kentish Rebels (f. 49[a]), the christening of Prince Arthur (f. 53[a]), the retinue of Edward III at Calais (f. 139[a]), a pro-Yorkist *Short English Chronicle* (f. 1[a]), and several historical poems [193], [199], and Brown-Robbins, nos. 3632 and 3880. Often these latter add to historical knowledge: *The Death of the Duke of Suffolk* [193], for example, confirms much in the chronicles and implicates many high clerics not noted elsewhere for their friendship to Suffolk.

The third Yorkist collection, TRINITY DUBLIN 432 [176], includes four poems dealing with the events of 1460 and 1461: [196], [198], [199], and *The Rose of Rouen* (Brown-Robbins, no. 1380; Greene E E Carols, no. 431). Like the preceding manuscripts, it is also a miscellany; written in two hands, it çomprises folios 59–87 of the complete volume, bound with various Latin, French, and English items of the thirteenth century. Brotanek, who has made a comprehensive study of this manuscript, believes that the poems were composed by a partisan of some Yorkist lord, presumably living in the Warwick-Coventry-Northampton triangle. Kingsford also suggested that the poems "may be the work of one writer." As with the Cotton text of *Prelude to the Wars* ([189] below), so the account of *The Rose of Rouen* (see above) could have been written only by an intimate, familiar with the chief personages involved: the casual allusions to 27 ensigns would no doubt have been recognized by contemporaries similarly informed, but modern research has yet to identify all of them. The dominant aim of the Dublin poet was to influence people, whether it were the lords set high on Fortune's wheel (in [196] below), or "the trewe comynerys of Kent" and the upper-class citizens of "London that fayre cyte" (in [198] below).

The fourth manuscript is the pro-Lancastrian TRINITY DUBLIN 516 [177]. It is a typical mid-fifteenth-century commonplace book, written by a Londoner and contains items [181–182], [279], and [297].

These poems of the later years of the fifteenth century do not reveal any profound truths about that period beyond that it was an age of turmoil following an earlier period of hope (reflected in *The Land of Cokaygne*, [34] above). Men could see no more than the bleak loss of the French possessions and nobles killing each other. The greater hope forming, leading directly into the Tudor and Elizabethan periods and on to the Civil War, was underground.

I. The Lancastrians

THE CORONATION OF HENRY VI [178], 59 lines in couplets, describes the coronation of Henry VI in 1429, from the procession to Westminster, the anointing, the banquet, and the challenge by the King's champion, including details of the protocol and the names of the chief participants. The account is framed by prayers for the peace of England. Preceding the poem is the official "manner and form" of the coronation.

Extracts of Lydgate's "program" for the Coronation (Brown-Robbins, no. 3799) are included in most of the Caxton and Fabyan chronicles, [21] above.

For related poems see *A Recollection of Henry V and the Coronation of Henry VI* (Brown-Robbins, no. 822) by John Audelay, Lydgate's poem (Brown-Robbins, no. 2211) and roundel (Brown-Robbins, no. 2804) on the coronation; also three prayers for England and King Henry VI by Lydgate (Brown-Robbins, nos. 2156, 2218, 2445). For a prayer supposedly composed for Henry VI on his expedition to France, March 25, 1430, for his coronation in Paris, see *This Dread Voyage* (Brown-Robbins, no. 2154), and for the same occasion *Salvum Fac Regem Domine* (Brown-Robbins, no. 1830). For Henry's ensuing triumphal entry into London, with a roundel, see Brown-Robbins, no. 3799, by Lydgate. For Lydgate's translation of Calot's French poem on the claims of Henry VI to the French crown, see Brown-Robbins, no. 3808.

THAT PEACE MAY STAND [179], eight twelve-line stanzas, ababab-abbcbc, with refrain, "And lene hus grace that pes may stand." Contemporary chronicles show that the years which best fit the description in the poem are 1437–40. The manuscript is about fifty years later.

May Jesus save us and help the people who everywhere throughout this land have been robbed and slain. Yet some people want this misery and disturbance to continue —may they be damned! For three years there have been floods and other bad weathers, destruction of grain, great poverty, rioting in north and south, robbery and murder everywhere; soldiers holding back in combat only to rob the men of their own side, and many good warriors slain. During this time, negotiations for a truce have been undermined by men who profited from the confusion. At last, a truce has been arranged, and things look better: there is good weather and more grain, and although England is weak it should still be able to fend off invaders if everybody supports the king.

A similar poem is *A Prayer for England*, [205] below. For a poem attributed to Lydgate, *On the Truce of 1444*, see Brown-Robbins, no. 3173.

VICTORY AT WHITBY [180] describes the English naval victory over the French at Whitby Haven in November, 1451, recalled to encourage the English with hopes of regaining some of their former territories in France. It consists of fifteen eight-line stanzas. Documents in French possession were discovered showing the joint plans of French and Scots to invade England, against which threat the poet advises assembling of a naval force and appeals for national unity. "It is curious that chroniclers paid so little attention to this rare English success, and omitted any mention of the disposition and ransom of the prisoners, the diplomatic and military leaders of France." (Robbins) The writer (probably not the author) of the bulk of the manuscript containing this poem was John Benet, priest at Harlington, Bedford.

THE FIVE DOGS OF LONDON [181] is a Lancastrian attack on Richard Duke of York. Following riots in London, which Yorkist supporters used to embarrass the government, on September 19, 1456, five dogs were slain and hung before the Duke's lodgings in London (described in Bale's *Chronicle*). To each dog a notice was attached, stating how it had been sacrificed to the ambitions of the Duke. In the poem, the five quatrains are each headed by a proverbial saying, and conclude with a summarizing couplet.

The dogs have been punished for their master; it is he who should be hanged. Not only is the offense his, but he even refused help when they were apprehended.

The moral is implied: such is the reward of those who support the treacherous Yorkists—how much better to uphold Henry VI.

THE SHIP OF STATE [182], about 1458, ten eight-line tail-rime stanzas with a two-line heading, is a popular catalogue of the chief figures on the Lancastrian side, compared to the several parts of a warship, namely, Henry VI. In form, style, and even phraseology, this poem closely resembles *The Death of Edward III*, [209] below; other poems employing the ship allegory include *Mum and the Sothsegger* [246], and *Willikin's Return* (Brown-Robbins, no. 3742; Greene E E Carols, no. 430). *Prelude to the Wars* [189] and *The Rose of Rouen* (Brown-Robbins, no. 1380; Greene E E Carols, no. 431) give comparable lists of the Yorkist nobles.

RECONCILIATION OF HENRY VI AND THE YORKISTS [183] commemorates the visit to St. Paul's Cathedral on March 25, 1458, by the King and Queen and the rival Yorkist lords, which concluded the meeting of the Great Council. The gathering was expected to be tumultuous, but the Mayor of London kept the peace by force of arms. The eight eight-line stanzas, ababbcbc, rejoice that the danger of civil war was apparently removed, and that the Lancastrian lords (Somerset, Northumberland, Clifford, and Egremont) were reconciled to the Yorkists (York, Warwick, and Salisbury). The poem closely duplicates the accounts in contemporary chronicles. *Take Good Heed* ([196] below) is a Yorkist interpretation of this same event.

A PRAYER FOR VICTORY [184] is actually the first five lines of the *Secrees of Old Philisoffres* (Brown-Robbins, Robbins-Cutler, no. 935), by Lydgate and Burgh, appearing separately in one manuscript, and used here as a prayer for victory by Henry VI.

Similarly, the last two lines of stanza 1 of Lydgate's *Prayer for England* (Brown-Robbins, Robbins-Cutler, no. 2218) had an existence independent of the complete poem in at least four manuscripts (Robbins-Cutler, no. 1955.5):

Lord God preserve under thy mighty hande
The kynge the qwene the people and this land.

For further political prayers see [187–188] below.

A Defense of the Proscription of the Yorkists, in prose, mostly English with some Latin and French, about 1459–60, is described elsewhere. For a carol on the Battle of Towton, 1461, see *The Rose of Rouen* (Brown-Robbins, Robbins-Cutler, no. 1380; Greene E E Carols, no. 431).

GOD AMEND WICKED COUNSEL [185], 53 lines in cross-rimed quatrains, ending imperfectly, written about 1464 but added in an early sixteenth-century hand on a flyleaf, presents the popular view of Henry VI that his troubles dated from his marriage in 1445 to Margaret of Anjou.

The poet in a chanson d'aventure gambit hears the complaint of Henry VI beside a hall underneath a hill. Henry's power is now clean overthrown; formerly he was wont to ride through England in his cloth of gold so red, yet now he dare not show himself. In the wars, many had been slain; the commons opposed him; his mind failing, his lords refused to obey him. All these troubles were due to his wife; she "was the cause of all my mon." Henry accepted her dictates; she was responsible for the exile of the Duke of York into Ireland and for the murder of the Duke of Gloucester.

The repetition of a refrain, "God amende wykkyd cownscell," irregularly throughout the poem, turns it in fact into a moralizing lament on the uncertainty of worldly greatness, a stock theme of Middle English didactic verse, and provokes comparison with a Latin elegy of 1461 quoted by Abbot Whethamstede.

English literary parallels come in *Summer Sunday* [208], *The Death of Edward III* [209], *The Death of Edward IV* [211], and especially in *The Lamentation of the Soul of Edward IV* (Brown-Robbins, no. 2192).

For a carol on the restoration of Henry VI in 1460 see *Willikin's Return* (Brown-Robbins, no. 3742; Greene E E Carols, no. 430).

A REMEMBRANCE OF HENRY VI [186], by James Ryman, eight jogging rime royal stanzas, filled with commonplaces, praises Henry VI as the saintly king, devout, merciful, patient, and steadfast. Miracles happen at his tomb at Windsor. His incompetence and insanity, as well as the usurpation of his throne by Edward IV, are forgotten. Since there is here no hint of murder, accepted by later Lancastrians, Chambers suggests a date of composition as early as 1471, but the design of the poem permits the later date about 1492, when the manuscript was written.

A PRAYER TO HENRY THE SIXTH I [187], two rime royal stanzas with interlocking rime, asks for Henry's prayers for the petitioner:

As far as hope will yn lengthe
On the, Kyng Henry, I fix my mynde,

That be thy prayour I may have strenkith
In vertuous lyfe my warks to bynde. . . .

A PRAYER TO HENRY THE SIXTH II [188], six eight-line stanzas beginning "O blyssed king so full of vertu," was added to the flyleaf of a very early fifteenth-century primer.

In spite of the dearth of vernacular material favorable to Henry VI, there was considerable official propaganda, such as John Capgrave's *Liber de Illustribus Henriciis*, ante 1446, where Henry is included in Part II.

II. The Yorkists

PRELUDE TO THE WARS [189], nine irregular cross-rimed quatrains, discussing the popular discontent at the disasters in France in 1449, "paved the way for the popularity of the house of York" (Wright). Rather than direct propaganda for the Yorkists, the poem seems to reflect the dismay and uncertainty of the fluid political situation in 1448 and 1449, just prior to the outbreak of the civil war. The poem refers to the political leaders by their traditional cognizances (e.g., the White Lion of Norfolk), a technique also employed in the Galfridian symbols of [196–198], [220], and *The Rose of Rouen* (Brown-Robbins, no. 1380; Greene E E Carols, no. 431), and the earlier sarcastic verses *On King Richard's Ministers* [87].

ON BISHOP BOOTH [190], seventeen rime royal stanzas, attacks Bishop William Booth of Chester (Lichfield), for simony, usury, and neglect of clerical duties. He had been promoted through the Duke of Suffolk, who is also attacked in these poems of the Cotton Rolls ii.23. With Booth are also condemned Trevilian for his falsehood and Suffolk for his ambition. The poem includes an appeal to God that King Henry VI be better advised. The venom of the piece gives it a certain literary vigor.

BILL AGAINST THE DUKE OF SUFFOLK [191], a seven-line tag, is preserved on a page of John Piggot's memoranda (ca. 1450) in one of Stow's manuscripts, "set on the gate of powles writen to this effecte":

. . . But Suthfolke, Salesbury and Say
Be don to deathe by May
England may synge well-away.

THE ARREST OF THE DUKE OF SUFFOLK [192], fifteen lively couplets, gloats over the arrest of the unpopular "fox," William de la Pole, Duke of Suffolk, by the gentle hunting dog, Lord Beaumont, the Lord Constable of England. The hunting metaphor is held throughout the poem, which must have been composed soon after Suffolk's indictment on February 7, 1450, but before his restoration to favor by Easter, 1450. The main charge of these verses is Suffolk's responsibility for the disasters in France by withholding supplies from Talbot, the English commander there.

For a popular rime protesting the acquittal of the Duke of Suffolk, see [261] below.

THE DEATH OF THE DUKE OF SUFFOLK [193], a dramatic satire on the death of William de la Pole, Duke of Suffolk, forming a "hideous parody" of a Requiem Mass built round phrases from the Office of the Dead, which are distributed among the Lancastrian leaders (priests and peers). These eight-line stanzas, ababbcbc, with an irregular refrain, "For Iac Napes soule, Placebo and Dirige," result in "an extraordinary demonstration of the depth of political hatred" (Kingsford)—72 lines in Cotton and 116 in Lambeth. The verses must have been written between May 3, 1450, the date of the murder of Suffolk, and June 29, 1450, the date of the murder of the Bishop of Salisbury. Stow headed the poem "a dyrge made by the Comons of Kent in the tyme of ther rysynge, when Jake Cade was theyr cappitayn."

ADVICE TO THE COURT I [194], about 1450, one fifteen-line stanza, ababbabaababbcc, obliquely attacks the Duke of Suffolk and his friends by admonishing the advisers of King Henry VI to respect the "loue of alle the cominalte." In the manuscript it follows a copy of the articles of impeachment against Suffolk, and may have been an attempt to force the King to such action. Ritson (following Warton) suggested the poem was affixed to the gates of the royal palace. The simple phrases, bereft of ornament, reflect an almost rabble-rousing incisiveness.

ADVICE TO THE COURT II [195], also written in 1450, ten six-line tail-rime stanzas, forms a companion piece to the preceding, and includes in the attack other unpopular court favorites such as Daniel and Saye. The King is excused of any complicity. The poem deplores government corruption and determines to set matters to right. The use of the word "bill" suggests its use as a public proclamation, perhaps for distribution in London.

TAKE GOOD HEED [196], 24 octosyllabic couplets, warns the Yorkist leaders to beware of treachery by the Lancastrians, especially their promises to keep the expected decrees of the Grand Council. The most likely date is not 1457 (Brotanek) or 1460 (Madden and Kingsford), but the period from the end of 1457 to March 1458. The poem thus becomes a counterpart to the Lancastrian poem ([183] above). Like the *Prelude to the Wars* [189], this piece identifies military leaders by their badges. Although its opening lines address "lordes," the simple diction and homely proverbs seem more suited to the foot soldiers doing the Yorkist fighting.

BALLADE SET ON THE GATES OF CANTERBURY [197], ten eight-line stanzas, ababbcbc, and a concluding six-line tail-rime stanza, attempts to assess popular feeling for the proposed Yorkist invasion of Kent (on June 28, 1460). Preserved in a pro-Yorkist *Brut* Chronicle, the verses may have been copied directly from the handbill itself. Strangely, the poem contains Latin quotations, as do other poems designed for popular appeal (e.g., [202] below). That the poem had some circulation is seen from the incorporation of lines in *The Battle of Northampton* [198] and *Twelve Letters Save England* [199].

England is sore beset and divided against itself, and the traditional Evils of the Age have become an actuality. Henry VI was born out of wedlock; he is impoverished and his throne is tottering. It is time to act. May God send home the Duke of York, and the Earls of March, Salisbury, and Warwick to settle the score.

For other "bills" attached to gates or doors of churches, public buildings, etc., see [21](h), [21](r), [191], [194–195], [259], [264], [266], and [267].

THE BATTLE OF NORTHAMPTON [198], twenty eight-line stanzas, ababbcbc (twice abababab), with interlocking rime, was written within two months after the battle (July 10, 1460). Its close descriptions of events confirms the accounts in contemporary prose chronicles. The leaders are identified by their badges; cf. [189], [196].

The framework is allegorical: The Bearward (Edward, Earl of March) and the Bear (Warwick) went to chase the Dogs (Shrewsbury, Beaumont, and Egremont) and the Buck (Buckingham). The Bear and the Bearward save the Hunt (King Henry) and beg him not to take their act unkindly. The Hunt replies that the Buck and the Dogs had brought him into distress. Then the Hunt is reverently brought into London, over which the Eagle (Salisbury) had meantime watchfully hovered.

A French poem lamenting the death of Richard Duke of York in 1460 at the Battle of Wakefield was composed by the Chester Herald.

The Rose of Rouen (Brown-Robbins, no. 1380; Greene E E Carols, no. 431) gives a careful eyewitness account of the Battle of Towton (1461), but since it is technically in carol form it is described in the chapter on Carols.

TWELVE LETTERS SAVE ENGLAND [199], in quatrains (eighteen in Trinity Dublin, seventeen in Lambeth, much inferior), is a Yorkist celebration (about July 1461) of Edward and his reigning as King, with a commemoration of the three other leaders responsible for this success— Richard of York and Richard of Salisbury, both now dead, and Richard of Warwick. Employing a chanson d'aventure gambit, the poet tells how walking down Cheapside he saw a woman embroidering letters, which he expounds to reveal anagrams of the names of the Yorkists. Like *The Battle of Northampton* [198], this poem incorporates lines from the Canterbury proclamation [197].

Edward Dei Gratia (Brown-Robbins, no. 3127; Greene E E Carols, no. 429), a commemoration of the accession of Edward IV in carol form, is described in the chapter on Carols.

THE VIRTUES OF THE EARL OF WARWICK [200] is a macaronic tristich acrostic on Warwik, also in the Trinity Dublin MS.

A POLITICAL RETROSPECT [201], ca. 1462, fourteen eight-line stanzas, ababcbc, with refrain word (langoure), commemorates the triumph of Edward IV and gives a review of recent history as seen through the eyes of a Yorkist.

The reign of Richard II was "habundaunce with plentee." Henry IV usurped the throne, was responsible for Richard's death in prison and the martyrdom of Archbishop Scrope: leprosy was God's judgment on him. Henry V upheld England's honor, though he reigned unrightfully. Henry VI by great folly brought "huge langoure." For example, the Duke of Gloucester was murdered. Again, Queen Margaret sought to impose her domination, even bringing in foreign troops. But now Edward IV is mowing down the weeds in the garden of England, with his victories at Northampton, Mortimer's Cross, and Towton, signs of God's favors, with the help of Richard, Earl of Warwick. May Edward bring peace and joy to England.

For *The Receiving of King Edward IV at Bristol* see Brown-Robbins, no. 3880. Prose accounts of the marriage of Edward IV (1464), an affray under Edward IV in the same year, and the burial of Edward IV, are described elsewhere. *The Arrival of King Edward IV*, in prose, is treated in the chapter on Chronicles.

THE BATTLE OF BARNET [202], a short poem in four eight-line stanzas, ababcbc, with refrain, "Conuertimini ye comons and drede your kyng," on the return of Edward IV (1471), represents the popular London view of the king.

CONDITIONS IN ENGLAND 1460–1480 [203] are described in 66 obscure lines (beginning "The lyon sens thre days as ded had bestylt").

THE RECOVERY OF THE THRONE BY EDWARD IV [204], or *The Balet of the Kynge*, is a long narrative poem in 46 rime royal stanzas (with the same C rimes throughout) detailing the return of Edward IV and his victory at the Battle of Barnet. The poem ends with a close account of the defeat of the Bastard of Fauconberg's attack on London.

The prose *Boke of Noblesse* was addressed to Edward IV on his invasion of France in 1475.

For a couplet attacking the government of Richard III, see [21](r).

For two carols, probably composed about 1486, on the establishment of
the Yorkists, see *The Lily White Rose* (Brown-Robbins, no. 1450; Greene
E E Carols, no. 432) and *The Roses Entwined* (Brown-Robbins, no. 1327;
Greene E E Carols, no. 433) in the chapter on Carols.

A Prayer for Peace (Brown-Robbins, no. 1710; Greene E E Carols, no.
435) may be about 1499, but more probably about 1479–83, with reference to Edward's negotiations with Scotland. For laments on the Death
of Edward IV, see [211–212] below, and a poem probably by Skelton, *The
Lamentation of the Soul of Edward IV* (Brown-Robbins, no. 2192). For
pageant verses in 1474 to Prince Edward at Coventry, see Brown-Robbins,
no. 3881.

A PRAYER FOR ENGLAND [205] is a generalized complaint on the
corruptions of the times turned into a litany that "Of alle oure synnys
God made a delyveraunce," which forms the refrain for the nineteen
eight-line stanzas, ababbcbc. The poem might have been written at almost
any time during the second half of the fifteenth century.

May God help England in its great need and restore "good governaunce." Graft is
prevalent everywhere and is destroying the Church and the Commons. Murder, usury,
and rapine, idleness and theft grieve us all. Justice is thwarted, so that white is black,
and vengeance brings more confusion. Let everyone pray for deliverance.

Other political prayers include *That Peace May Stand* [179], *A Prayer
for Victory* [184], and a carol, *A Prayer for Peace* (Brown-Robbins, no.
1710; Greene E E Carols, no. 435), in the chapter on Carols.

ANTHEM FOR MARRIAGE OF HENRY VII AND ELIZABETH
[206], five lines beginning "God save King Henry wheresoe'er he be,"
with music composed in 1486 by Thomas Ashwell, later Master of the
Choristers at Lincoln Cathedral, to be sung at a Mass, symbolizes the
termination of the Wars of the Roses by the union of the two recognized
representatives of Lancaster and York. Ashwell also composed music for
a processional carol to the Virgin (Robbins-Cutler, no. 66.5).

Other songs commemorate this event; see Brown-Robbins, nos. 1327, 1450.

ON THE UNION OF THE LANCASTRIANS AND YORKISTS [207] in 1486 is the topic of a single couplet added to the cover of a *Pricke of Conscience*:

The red rose and the wythe
Be knyght togeder with grett delyghte

For an acrostic on Elizabeth, see Robbins-Cutler, no. 735.5; for an epitaph see [235] below.

For two songs in praise of Henry VIII, see Robbins-Cutler, no. 558.3, and its political variant, Robbins-Cutler, no. 588.5.

10. THE ESTATES

The poems in this section fall into two groups: those describing the rulers and, of less literary merit, those describing the ruled.

The first group includes commemoration of rulers and famous noble houses and individuals; a small body of poems in the *De Regimine Principum* tradition; and finally the longer poems discussing national policy, among the outstanding items of this chapter.

I. The Rulers

1. Commemoration of Rulers

The poem preserved in the most manuscripts, at least 53, is a catalogue of *The Kings of England*, traditionally ascribed to Lydgate (Brown-Robbins, Robbins-Cutler, nos. 444, 882, 3632, 4174.3).

The Death of Edward I ([29] above) is listed with the MS Harley 2253 poems, and *Adam Davy's Five Dreams About Edward II* ([296] below) with the Political Prophecies.

For a fifteenth-century poem on the origin and description of heraldry, see Brown-Robbins, no. 800.

Three of the major fifteenth-century poets wrote many commemorative verses of kings and nobles; these are discussed in their appropriate chapters. For poems by Hoccleve, see balades to Henry V (VIII [15] and [22]), virelais to Henry V (VIII [21] and [32]), *Balade au tres Honourable Compaignie du Garter* (VIII [23]), and *On Richard II's Burial at Westminster* (VIII [25]). For poems by Lydgate, see *On the English Title of Henry VI to the Crown of France* (Brown-Robbins, no. 3808), *Roundel on Henry VI* (Brown-Robbins, no. 2804), *King Henry's Triumphal Entry into London* (Brown-Robbins, no. 3799), *Gloucester's Marriage to Jacqueline of Hainault* (Brown-Robbins, no. 3718), *Complaint for My Lady of Gloucester* (Brown-Robbins, no. 92), *Verses on The Kings of England* (Brown-Robbins, Robbins-Cutler, nos. 444, 882, 3632, 4174.3), and the *Rimed Charters of the English Kings* (Brown-Robbins, no. 1513). For poems by Skelton, see *Lamentation of the Soul of Edward IV* (Brown-Robbins, no. 2192), *Verses to Henry VII* (Brown-Robbins, no. 2526), *Death of the Earl of Northumberland* (Brown-Robbins, no. 1378), and *Epitaph on Jaspar Tudor, Duke of Bedford* (Brown-Robbins, no. 520).

Reference should be made also to Pageants and Mummings celebrating royalty, described elsewhere.

SUMMER SUNDAY [208] is a very skillfully constructed poem in 133 alliterative lines in eight thirteen-line stanzas of the *Pistill-of-Susan* type, two inserted versus of eight short lines each, and a final thirteen-line stanza with the groups of long and short lines reversed. The dialect is West Midland. In a chanson d'aventure hunting scene setting, the singer of the piece sees Fortune and her wheel, and a splendid king who has come to a lamented evil fate. Madden (in *Reliquiae Antiquae*) identified the king as Richard II, dating the poem about 1400. Brown, however, on paleographical and linguistic grounds, suggested (less conclusively) Edward II.

THE DEATH OF EDWARD III [209], in the Vernon-Simeon series, has fourteen eight-line stanzas ababbcbc with refrain, "Selden seȝe sone forȝete." The piece is permeated with the gloom that marks all the verse dealing with the social and political events of the date (1377).

> All wears and wastes away. Formerly we had a noble English ship, strong against storms, a defense of the land, feared through all Christendom. A rudder governed the ship. While rudder and ship held together, they feared naught, and sailed all seas in all weathers; but now they are flitted asunder, and all is ill. The ship had a sure mast and a strong, large sail, and to it belonged a barge that set all France at naught, and was a shield to all of us. The rudder was the noble King Edward III; the helm was borne up by the Prince of Wales, never discomfited in fight; the barge was Duke Henry of Lancaster, who ever chastised his enemies; the mast was the Commons; the wind that bore the vessel on, good prayers. But all these are gone. A promising imp (Richard II) of the stock of these lords, is beginning to grow. I hope he will prove to be a conqueror. Meanwhile, let both high and low aid and maintain him. The French are bragging and are scorning us. Take heed of your doughty King who died in his age, and of his son Edward; two lords of such worth know I not—and they are being forgotten.

For *On Richard II's Burial at Westminster* by Hoccleve, see VIII [25]. For *Praise of Peace* (to Henry IV) (Brown-Robbins, no. 2587), see the chapter on Gower.

THE FALL OF RICHARD II [210], an acephalous poem of eight cross-rimed quatrains on Fortune's wheel, warns "kynges and other of hye estate" to think on the death of King Richard. The last two quatrains form a prayer for "oure kynge [Henry VI ?] that regnythe nowe in his regalite" requesting God to "saue this lond from all myschance."

For an aphoristic warning on the Wheel of Fortune, see Robbins-Cutler, no. 3647.5.

For a short lyric in three quatrains on the troubles of high estate, spuriously attributed to Henry VI, see Robbins-Cutler, no. 1824.2.

THE DEATH OF EDWARD IV [211], ten rime royal stanzas with refrain, "All men of Englond ar bound for hym to pray," is the adulation of a devoted Yorkist. It draws a contrast between the bustling prosperity of the years of the King's life and the desolation and inactivity following the death of "the well of knyghthode, withouten any pere." The last stanza, a general lament on the world's transitoriness, suggests the poem might have served as an epitaph on the tomb (like [230] below).

THE LAMENTATION OF LADIES FOR EDWARD IV [212], a contemporary lament "of ladyes that were clothed in blake," exists as a fragment (the left half of the lines torn), originally five rime royal stanzas with refrain, introduced by a chanson d'aventure opening.

The Lamentation of the Soul of Edward IV, a review of the main events of his life linked to an Ubi-sunt motif, is dubiously attributed to Skelton (Brown-Robbins, no. 2192).

For *Edward Dei Gratia*, a carol (Brown-Robbins, no. 3127; Greene E E Carols, no. 429), see the chapter on Carols.

The Receyvyng of Kyng Edward the IIIJth at Brystowe (Brown-Robbins, no. 3880) is more appropriately classed with the Pageants.

A political chanson on the birth of Prince Arthur in 1486 is found in the series of songs in MS BM Additional 5465 (Robbins-Cutler, no. 1866.8).

THE HOUSE OF STAFFORD [213] is a riming history, "the coppie of the table that was hanging in the priorie of Stone at the time of the suppression." Its 162 generally four-stressed lines in rough couplets describe the foundation by Earl Robert of a priory of canons at Stone, at the time of the Conquest. Then follows a list of the succeeding earls who patronized the priory. Although one was buried in a Franciscan monastery, because of a friar who was his confessor, the other earls were buried near the high altar of the priory.

THE FOUNDING OF WORKSOP ABBEY [214] may be noted here: 26 rime royal stanzas transcribed in 1587 from an old copy of John Piggot's *Chronicle*, otherwise only known from a reference to some memoranda in Stow's MS Harley 543 (cf. [191] above). The Augustinian Worksop Priory was founded in 1291 with provision for a prior and eighteen canons.

THE HOUSE OF VERE [215] has attracted more than customary notice since its attribution in 1810 to Chaucer. The verses appear in the Ellesmere Chaucer manuscript, which attributes them to "Rotheley," perhaps a scribe. From an allusion in *The Testament of Love*, then mistakenly thought Chaucer's, Todd separated the introduction ("Halfe in dede sclepe not fully revyved") and the poem ("All thyng ys ordaynyd by Goddys provysyon") into two poems "written by Chaucer during his imprisonment." Actually, the introduction (nine eight-line stanzas) and the poem (eighteen rime royal stanzas) form a tribute to the House of Vere, probably addressed to the twelfth Earl, executed by the Yorkists, February 1462. Since internal evidence can fix the terminal dates only as 1445 and 1472, it is possible that the thirteenth Earl, John de Vere, might be the recipient; but, unlike his father, he cannot fill the description: "His progenie neuer distayned with falsenesse" (since he had no children and since he was guilty of treachery). Piper's suggestion that the poem praises Richard III and accompanied the thirteenth Earl's gift of the Chaucer manuscript is untenable, confusing the White Boar crest of the King with the Blue Boar of the Veres. The poem is typical formal verse, passing from the figure of Vere as spring to Vere as a boar, full of all the noble virtues, who fulfills old prophecies of aiding his king, and including an account of the significance of the Vere arms. The first line echoes *La Belle Dame Sans Mercy* (XI [46]).

The House of Clare (Brown-Robbins, no. 3910), a "dialogue betwix a secular asking and a friar answering . . . showeth the lineal descent of the lords of the honor of Clare . . . until 1456," is described under *Dialogue between a Secular and a Friar* (VII [38]).

The following six poems [216–221] laud the House of Stanley.

THE ROSE OF ENGLAND [216], an allegorical ballad of 32 quatrains, abab, in praise of Sir William Stanley (ca. 1435–95), probably composed by a minstrel in his service some time after the Battle of Bosworth (1485), when Sir William's forces decided the day for the future King Henry VII.

England is described as a fair garden with a beautiful red rose tree. There came a beast called a (White) Boar (Richard III) who 'rooted this garden up and down,' and tore the rose tree asunder. But a sprig of the rose (Henry Tudor, Earl of Richmond) was preserved, and returning to England (in 1485) with the Blue Boar (John de Vere, thirteenth Earl of Oxford), sent for help to his stepfather, the old Eagle (Lord Stanley). Together they won the victory. (Kingsford)

For later and expanded variants see [218–219].

An acrostic on Sir Thomas Stanley (1406–59), created Baron Stanley in 1456, forms the concluding seventh stanza of William Huchen's *Prayer to the Virgin*, ca. 1460 (Brown-Robbins, Robbins-Cutler, no. 3228):

> Saue hem fro syn and worldly shame
> That the worship with humble herte,
> And to thi son, Iesus by name,
> Not sece to pray that we not smert.
> Lord, thi iugement we may not sterte;
> Euere therfor thi grace we hight,
> In worship of thi modere bright.

Sir Thomas Stanley was the father of Sir William, the hero of Bosworth, and the grandfather of Sir Edward, the hero of Flodden. Huchen's hymn is described in the chapter on Lyrics.

SCOTTISH FEILDE [217], 422 alliterative long lines (Lyme MS imperfect), the latest of the alliterative poems, was composed about 1515 somewhere in Lancashire or Cheshire to extol the glories of the House of Stanley and its achievements at Bosworth Field (1485) under Sir William Stanley, who placed the crown on Henry Richmond, and at Flodden Field (1513), when Sir William's nephew, Sir Edward Stanley (First Baron Monteagle, ca. 1460–1523) killed with his own hand James IV of Scotland. There is no evidence of common authorship with the much earlier dialogue, *Death and Liffe* [245]. "It forms a fitting epilogue to the Alliterative Revival in England," says Oakden. "It is marred throughout by the constant repetition of stock phrases and tags, and leaves the impression of a mosaic derived from earlier works, for quite half the poem consists of phrases of all types, which can easily be paralleled in other alliterative poems." The text in the Percy Folio MS begins: "Now let vss talk of Mount of Flodden."

Three later poems continue praise of the Stanley family, especially for its part in the two decisive battles of Bosworth and Flodden; and a fourth poem, by Thomas Stanley, Bishop of Sodor and Man, gives a riming chronicle. Though in their present form all four are considerably later ([220] is in the seventeenth-century Percy Folio MS), they probably preserve earlier elements, and are included here to round off a group of related poems, which thematically should not be divided. In addition, two further late poems, based on Flodden, are included, though they are not pro-Stanley effusions.

THE MOST PLEASANT SONG OF LADY BESSY [218], beginning "God that is most of myghte," is a much longer retelling—1082 lines in quatrains—of *The Rose of England* [216], probably composed by Humphrey Brereton early in the sixteenth century.

The story concerns the alleged offer of marriage by Richard III to Elizabeth of York after Bosworth Field, when Richard had already murdered her two brothers. Elizabeth wishes to marry Henry Tudor, Earl of Richmond, and appeals to Lord Stanley for help. Brereton, the supposed author, becomes the go-between in a series of intrigues involving Henry Tudor. Eventually, Richard III is killed, and Sir William Stanley sets the crown on the heads of Elizabeth and Henry, uniting the Yorkist and Lancastrian parties.

There are variations between the Harley and Percy Folio (BM Addit) manuscripts.

For a later variant see [219].

BOSWORTH FIELD [219], beginning "God that shope both sea and land / and ffor all creatures dyed," 656 lines in quatrains, derives from *The Rose of England* [216] and *Lady Bessy* [218]. Child notes how Henry VII, kneeling and desiring the vanguard, is subordinated to old Sir William Stanley, who grants his request.

A later account, ca. 1600, prose sometimes breaking into verse, is apparently a reworking of an old ballad, entitled "Richard the Third his deathe, by the Lord Stanley, borowyd of Henry Savylle."

FLODDEN FIELD [220], beginning "O Rex Regum in thy realme celestialle," 26 stanzas rime royal, with refrain, "By the helpe of God and in theyr Princes right," was included in the 1587 version of the *Mirror for Magistrates*, there introduced as describing "the names of the noble men, Knights and gentlemen, which serued at the same fielde" (Flodden or Brampton). The verses are expected to encourage their countrymen "to the like loyall seruice of their Prince," as well as to the praise of "their parents or auncestors." The chief commanders are referred to (lines 120–50) by their cognizances, as in other political poems like [170], [176], [177], [178], and Brown-Robbins, no. 1380. Although a late composition, the style is typically fifteenth-century.

THE CHRONICLE OF STANLEY [221], beginning "I intend with true report to praise" in the Bodleian manuscript; "Amonge all delyghtes and most warldie comfort" in the Harley manuscript. Thomas Stanley (died 1570), the second son of Sir Edward Stanley, First Baron Monteagle, who had played a conspicuous part at Flodden in 1513, became Bishop of Sodor and Man, and in about 1562 wrote a long poem in praise of his family.

Related poems on Flodden include the following, [222] and [223].

LAMENT ON MISFORTUNES FOLLOWING FLODDEN [222], beginning "O Schotland thow was flowryng / in prosperus welthe," is a short poem in six stanzas rime royal.

LAMENTATION OF KING OF SCOTS [223], beginning "As I lay musyng myself alone," the lamentation of King James IV of Scotland after his defeat of Flodden, in fifteen eight-line stanzas, is introduced in a classic two-stanza dream vision. The refrain, "Miserere mei Deus et salua mee," is continued throughout the whole poem. Stanzas 3–15 form a piece similar to other laments of dead kings, like [208–212], and include a justification of his reign, moral admonitions to beware false friends, an acknowledgment of his misdeeds, an upbraiding of the false King Louis of France, and a farewell anaphora. It was incorporated into the 1587 version of the *Mirror for Magistrates*, as was [220], and introduced: "Thinke then (quoth I) that you see him [King James] standing all

wounded, with a shafte in his body, and emongst other woundes, one
geuen by a byll, both deadly, to say in his rude and faithlesse maner as
followeth." The poem mentions that "one valiaunt earle our power ouer-
came," which probably refers to the Earl of Surrey; the poem is pro-
English rather than specifically pro-Stanley.

For two poems attacking James IV and "the prowde Scottes," attributed
to John Skelton, see Robbins-Cutler, nos. 1822.5 and 1931.3.

In addition, other famous families were commemorated in ballads:

THE HOUSE OF PERCY [224], beginning "Cronykillis and annuall
bookis of kingis," is celebrated in an early sixteenth-century *Metrical
Chronicle* in 97 stanzas generally rime royal by William Peeris (died
1527), priest-secretary to Henry, Fifth Earl of Northumberland. It was
written between 1516 and 1523.

Also extant is a prose chronicle by Thomas Pickering (died 1475),
Abbot of Whitby from 1462, of the Percy Family down to 1454, derived
from a Latin work of 1458. The genealogy continues to 1485, and the roll
includes some very fine but small drawings of medieval towns (London
on membrane 3; Colchester on membrane 4). Pickering also compiled
accounts of the Tyson and Eure families.

The Percy Family features prominently in the ballads on the hunting
of the Cheviot, [68] and [69].

THE HOUSE OF WILLOUGHBY [225], beginning "O holy St.
George o very champion oundefyled," by James Packe, has eight stanzas
rime royal, "out of an old roll of parchemin," in a late sixteenth-century
Harley manuscript.

The Talbot Hours contain a brief prayer for John Talbot, Earl of
Salisbury (Robbins-Cutler, no. 1786.5).

SIR ROGER BELERS [226], five derogatory couplets, in Latin and
English, on Sir Roger Belers, a prominent Leicestershire politician, murdered in 1326.

MEMORIAL VERSES FOR THE TOMB OF THE EARL OF DUN-
BAR [227], who governed his estates for 48 years and died in 1416—three
couplets added to a flyleaf of a Fordun's *Chronicle*.

THE LAMENTATION OF THE DAUPHIN FOR HIS WIFE [228],
in two parts, both highly artificial and aureate, Scottish dialect, inserted
in the Latin *Liber Pluscardensis* (Book XI, *Chronicon Jacobi Primi Regis
Scottorum*) compiled in 1461 by Maurice de Buchanan: (1) *Lamentatio
domini Dalphini Francie pro morte uxoris sue dicte Margarete*, 23 ten-
line stanzas, aabaabbcbc, beginning "Thee mychti Makar of the major
monde." The poem invokes Nature to mourn with the Dauphin, Louis
(XI), in grief for the death (in 1445) of his wife, Margaret, eldest daughter of James I of Scotland. (2) *Consolatio rationis ad lamentationem*, 18
ten-line stanzas, beginning "Thow man that is of power and smal
valoue." Buchanan, in an early attempt at literary criticism, commented:
"Bot nocht withstandyng thaire is mare of this lamentacioune xviii
coupill, and in the ansuere of Resoune alse mekill, this may suffyce, for
the Complant is bot fenȝeit thing; bot be cause the tothir part, quhilk is
the ansuere of Resoune, is verray suthfastnesse, me think it gud to put
mare of it, quhilk followis thus efterwarte."
   Another poem in the *Liber Pluscardensis* comparing the Scottish kingdom to a harp is described in [248] below.

EPITAPH FOR THE DUKE OF GLOUCESTER [229] is a dreary
piece of some thirteen eight-line stanzas, ababbcbc, with refrain, "Have
mercy on hym buryed in this sepulture," at one time attributed to Lyd-
gate. It may have been placed on the tomb of Humphrey, Duke of
Gloucester (who died in 1447), in the same way as [211], [230], and Dun-
bar's *To The King—Off Benefice Schir* (X [34]).
   Seven stanzas on the death of the Duke appear in Lydgate's *Fall of
Princes* (Brown-Robbins, no. 1168). Lydgate's shorter poem, *The Sudden
Fall of Princes* (Brown-Robbins, no. 500) includes Gloucester with other
English and continental rulers, mostly murdered. Gloucester, his second

wife, and John Beaufort are listed in an elegy, *Examples of Mutability*, [236] below.

ELEGY FOR THE TOMB OF LORD CROMWELL [230] or *The Mirror of Mortality*, eight eight-line stanzas, ababbaba, using only two rimes throughout the whole poem, meditates on Death, "that mover arte of moornynge and of moon." Death comes to men of all estates: worldly joy is transitory. Those in prosperity especially must remember this lesson, "for odir warnyng in this world is none." Stanza 7 (omitted in Cotton MS) asks for devout prayers, when looking on this tomb, for Ralph, Lord Cromwell, Lord Treasurer of England, and for his wife. Lord Cromwell, who founded Tattershall College, died in 1454, and this poem was no doubt written during his lifetime by one of the chaplains as a tombstone epitaph, "to hang by the tomb until the inscription should be needed to record the demise of its builders" (as MacCracken suggested).

The Epitaffe of the Moste Noble and Valyaunt Iasper, Late Duke of Beddeford (Brown-Robbins, no. 520; Robbins-Cutler, no. 2818.6), ca. 1496, is listed with Skelton's poems.

COMMEMORATION OF GEOFFREY BARBER [231] is almost a parody of the preceding tomb verses (such as [229] or [230]). "Richard Fannande, ironmonger, in the year 1457, composed a description, or account, in rude and barbarous verse of the building of Culhambridge, near Abingdon, in Berkshire, which he caused to be hung up, on a table, in the hall of St. Helen's Hospital there, to the memory and honor of Geoffrey Barber, a principal founder of that bridge." (Ritson) The piece shows a curious survival of alliterative phrases (23 quatrains abab, and two couplets). It describes the blessings accruing from the bridge, which, though paid for by Barber, was constructed by hardworking men, whose wives refreshed them with cheese and chickens. At one point the poem cautions: "And be not to covetous of youre owne purse / For peril of the peynes in the pit of Helle."

OTHER EPITAPHS [232] are known from before 1500, but for the most part they have not received much attention from literary historians.

THE LAMENT OF THE DUCHESS OF GLOUCESTER [233], a dramatic monologue by Eleanor Cobham, the second Duchess, in eight-line stanzas, ababbcbc, with refrain, "All women may be ware by me," and Wheel of Fortune imagery and concluding "Farewell" anaphora— 104 lines in Balliol and 136 lines in Cambridge. The poem was probably written soon after her degradation in 1441 for her alleged attempt to kill the young king by witchcraft, and is not unsympathetic.

"Thorowowt a palys as I gan passe, I herd a lady make gret mone" that all worldly joy and friends have fled. In a dramatic monologue, the Duchess says all women may take her as an example. Chosen by a prince as his mate, she was high upon the Wheel of Fortune, Duchess of Gloucester, magnified among all women and surrounded by worldly joy and dignity. Suddenly she fell from this wheel, as she stood before the council at Westminster and no man dared speak for her, except her sovereign lord King Henry VI, who took pity and changed the sentence of death. She was led before two cardinals, five bishops, and other men of high degree who questioned her of all the deeds of her life. As a penance she walked barefoot through the streets where she had ridden royally. Father of Heaven, so must it be. The sin of pride will have a fall. Farewell all the good things of this life, "all worldly joy" put aside for prayers.

The same subject was treated in a later ballad in quatrains, which stresses Eleanor's sins, her spells, and magic. Laments of Dame Eleanor Cobham, Duchess of Gloucester (47 stanzas rime royal) and of Hvmfrey Plantagenet, Duke of Gloucester (63 stanzas rime royal) were added to the 1578 edition of the *Mirror for Magistrates*.

THE LAMYTACION OF QUENE ELIZABETH [234], ascribed to Sir Thomas More, is a soliloquy in twelve stanzas rime royal by Henry VII's Queen, as if spoken to a viewer of her tomb. The Queen died in childbed in 1503. The piece includes Ubi-sunt themes, farewell anaphora, and the customary injunction to pray for her soul. In the Balliol MS it is followed by Latin and English epitaphs.

EPITAPH ON QUEEN ELISABETH [235], nine couplets, the first eight with "Here lith" anaphora, has a modest touching simplicity.

EXAMPLES OF MUTABILITY [236] is an elegy in eight eight-line stanzas on the sudden falls from fortune of Eleanor Cobham, Duchess of

Gloucester (who is less sympathetically portrayed than in [233]), John Beaufort (killed by a bull), and Humphrey, Duke of Gloucester. Kingsford considered this poem and the foregoing lament [233] "rather literary exercises than political poems or ballads." The piece was written probably about 1466.

The Lamentatyon of Edward Late Duke of Buckyngham (Robbins-Cutler, no. 2409.5) is treated with the other lyrics of MS Rawlinson C.813 elsewhere. Also in this manuscript are The Lamentatyon of the Lady Gryffythe (Robbins-Cutler, no. 2552.5) and its companion poem, The Epytaphye of Sir Gryffyth ap Ryse (Robbins-Cutler, no. 3962.5).

The virelai composed by Earl Rivers on the eve of his execution in 1483 is described in XI [22].

Attention may be directed here to the numerous poems in praise of the Golden Mean, some of which have contemporary political overtones. These pieces are discussed elsewhere, predominantly in the chapter on Lyrics: Brown-Robbins, Robbins-Cutler, nos. 474, 512.5, 512.8, 513, 584 (Lydgate), 1218, 1295.5, 1386, 1456, 1824.2, 2064, 2152 (Lydgate), 3382, 3768.2.

2. Advice to Rulers

Several of the major productions in Middle English were designed as handbooks for good governance, and circulated in many manuscripts far beyond the limited scope of their original audience. Such are Hoccleve's De Regimine Principum (VIII [2]) and the Secrees of Philisoffres (Brown-Robbins, no. 935), as well as Lydgate's short Advice to the Estates (Brown-Robbins, no. 920). All the items in Section 3 below (Longer Discussions on National Policy) are also in effect propaganda poems urging a specific course of action upon the ruling clique surrounding the monarch. Even Chaucer wrote his Lak of Stedfastnesse (Brown-Robbins, no. 3190) and his Prologue to The Legend of Good Women (Brown-Robbins, no. 100) in this vein. Thus the ground was being prepared for the Renaissance guides to princes and governors. Less politically-oriented works of instruction are listed in the chapter on Works of Religious Instruction. Here are included a few items not easily grouped elsewhere.

See also Brown-Robbins, nos. 411 and 1824.

RULERS' TITLES [237] consists of four lines of the technical terms for rulers' titles, found in a book of heraldry with blazons:

A pope in hys solempnyte
An emperor in his mayeste
A kyng in hys royalte
A duc in hys estat

A CHARGE TO JUDGES [238], three couplets admonishing judges to dispense justice righteously, one of many English tags in a collection of Latin treatises. The English is presumably a translation of three Latin leonines:

Sede sedens ista judex inflexibilis sta
Set tibi lucerna lex lux pellisque paterna
A manibus reuoces munus ab aure preces.

ON GOOD RULE [239], in six couplets, opens with "The Gouernowre that gydethe with vertue and grace."
See also an admonition to judges in Trevisa's translation of *Polychronicon*, [18](j) above.

ADMONITION ON LOVEDAYS [240], 196 lines in quatrains and couplets, with a few interspersed passages in Latin, is addressed to officers of justice, and deals with the ignominy of persons who forswear themselves on lovedays. Pontius Pilate is cited as an example of an incompetent judge, and the poem adds some rules on how not to conduct lovedays (or days of peacemaking between litigants). The admonition to judges (at line 131) recalls [238–239] above.

ADVICE TO PRELATES [241], six Monk's Tale stanzas; after a routine chanson d'aventure gambit, the poet hears shepherds complaining of wicked bishops, ending each stanza with the refrain, "Kepe well the shepe of Crystis fold." The present pope is not like Peter, who "our lordis lawe he kepte truly," nor are bishops who prick to parliament like the original disciples.

ADVICE TO THE ESTATES [242], ten rime royal stanzas, added to a copy of Lydgate's *Fall of Princes*, is largely a collection of typical aphorisms explaining and inculcating the medieval theory of estates or degrees. It is, however, not an original poem, but an extract from Barclay's *Lyfe of St. George*, lines 1261–1330.

For Lydgate's *Advice to the Estates*, see Brown-Robbins, no. 920.

A single stanza (Robbins-Cutler, no. 856.5), extrapolated from Walton's translation of Boethius (Brown-Robbins, no. 1597), praises the bliss "yff onely wyse men shold haue [comyn gouernaunce] on hand." From Walton another stanza on the evils of prosperity had an independent existence in seven manuscripts (see XI [12]).

3. Longer Discussions on National Policy

WYNNERE AND WASTOURE [243]—its full title is *A Tretys and God Schorte Refreyte Bytwixe Wynnere and Wastoure*—consists of 503 unriming alliterative long lines. The date is indicated at about 1350 by two allusions in lines 206 and 317; Steadman has confirmed Gollancz's more precise year of 1353; and Bestull, who has written a complete monograph on this poem, accepts 1352–53. Like the following poem [244], the dialect of the present text is North Central Midlands.

In a short prologue the author complains of the decay of the times and of the prevalent neglect of the true poet for the mere prattler of the words of others. Then he tells at length that he wandered in the West. He lay down by a burn's side under a hawthorn. The birds sang so loud and the stream made such a rushing noise, that he fell asleep only as night was coming on. He dreamed that he was in a fair green land shut in by a hill a mile long. On each of two sides was an army ready for battle. All prayed for a truce until the Prince should come to pacify them. On a cliff was a cabin, its roof railed with red, and its sides decked with English besants (gold coins), each tied round with garters made of gold and inscribed "Honi soit qui mal y pense." There was also a man garbed like a satyr, with a golden leopard on his helmet, which was adorned with the arms of England and of France. A King appeared bearing the blue belt of the Garter. He summoned a Knight (the Black Prince) to bid the armies withhold from fighting. The Knight harangued the hosts at length, with many allusions to social and political and ecclesiastical conditions. A representative of each party followed him to the King: one was Wynnere (gainer, hoarder), the other was Wastoure (spendthrift). They argued the merits of their respective natures and activities. The King ordered Wynnere to the Pope at Rome; Wastoure he sent to London until the King should return from his wars in France. Here the work breaks off unfinished. (Wells)

The poem is an interesting composite of dream vision, allegory, debate, occasional poem, and satire or complaint. In view of the incompleteness of the manuscript, the confusion of the matter, and the obscurity of many of what evidently were meant to be significant allusions, the primary object of the poem is difficult to perceive. Stillwell believes that the poet tries to mediate between the two alternatives of Winner and Waster, and that Winner may be identified at times with the middle classes and at times with the wealthy friars, and that one basic point in the poem is associated with the need for money for military purposes on the part of Edward III, the King.

The connection with the Order of the Garter is of great interest, because of the contention that *Sir Gawayne and the Grene Knight* is a Garter poem (see I [25]), and because of the connection with the Order of the Bath declared in *The Grene Knight* (see under I [26]). The descriptive passages are composed carefully and effectively. The prologue twice mentions the "West" from the point of view of a man of that district; but, like the poet of *Piers Plowman*, the author knew London and its conditions. The poem is full of satire much after the manner of *Piers Plowman* —on questions of labor, prices, wages, food, dress, on the friars and the power of the Pope, on the moneyed classes, etc.

THE PARLEMENT OF THE THRE AGES [244] and *Wynnere and Wastoure* [243] are perhaps the earliest extant representatives of the Alliterative Revival of the fourteenth century (see [108] above). Although preserved in the same fifteenth-century manuscript, and showing similarity of form, style, and language, they are not by the same author. The *Parlement* was probably written about 1370, some twenty years after *Wynnere and Wastoure*, perhaps even in the last quarter of the century. The dialect is North Central Midlands: either Nottinghamshire (Serjeantson), Ribble Valley (Oakden), or central or southern West Riding (Offord). The poem consists of 665 alliterative long lines.

At dawn of a beautiful day in May, on the bank of a stream, the poet lay in wait for deer, enjoying the loveliness of the flowers, the song of the birds, and the movements of foxes and hares and other wild creatures. A most stately deer appeared, accompanied by a buck that watched to protect it from hunters. The poet slew the deer, brittled it, and concealed the parts that the forester might not be aware. Then, as he watched his spoils, he fell asleep and had a vision of three men. One was a young knight on horseback, most elaborately decked with jewels and embroidery; the second, of middle age and clad in ill-shaped russet and gray, sat meditating on his possessions; the third, clothed in black, with a white beard, bald, blind, and crippled, lay on his side mumbling his beads and crying to God for mercy. The youth exclaimed long of the joys of the hunt, of ladies' love, of reading the romances, of revel in hall. The man in russet chid his folly. Old Age in black warned both: the pleasures of Youth and the thrift of Middle Age fail; all must come to his condition, and all must die. This lesson he enforced with short accounts of each of the Nine Worthies, and with a list of the most famous heroes of Romance. "Vanity of vanities!" he cried. "Death takes all! Go shrive you, Youth and Middle Age." A bugle call awakened the poet. The sun was setting. He made his way toward town. (Wells)

The poem ranks high because of its elaborate and effective descriptions of Nature, of hawking and hunting, and of the outer appearance of the personages, and because of its interesting summaries of the stories of the heroes (the longest list in Middle English). But these passages are out of proportion, and are over-stressed as compared with the treatment of the main theme of the poem. Like the reader, the poet is more interested in them than in the doctrine that the verses were meant to bring home. The descriptions of deer-stalking and of hawking, the detailed account of the brittling of the deer, and the author's susceptibility to the charm of material things, connect the piece with *Sir Gawayne and the Grene Knight*. The only other pieces with any close connection to the *Parlement* are *Morte Arthure* (I [16]) and *The Siege of Jerusalem* (I [107]).

The theme of the Nine Worthies was widely popular in medieval literature from a period antedating Longueyon's *Voeux du paon*, ca. 1312, translated ca. 1438 as *The Avowis of Alexander* (see under I [68]). The Worthies are listed in the prologue of the *Cursor Mundi* (Brown-Robbins, no. 2153); the first six are mentioned in *Golagrus and Gawain*, line 1253 (I [31]). They are dealt with in Arthur's dream in *Morte Arthure*, line 3220 (I [16]); referred to by Caxton in his preface to *Morte Arthure*; in Arbuthnot's and Hay's *Buiks* (I [69]); the Scottish version of the *Voeux* (I [68]); *Ane Ballet of the Nine Nobles* (Brown-Robbins, no. 1181); and other poems (Brown-Robbins, no. 4247; Robbins-Cutler, no. 1181.5). They were the subject of a fifteenth-century mumming (Brown-Robbins, no.

3666), whose popularity is attested in *Love's Labor's Lost* (V.i). The subject is included in a Coventry pageant to Queen Margaret (Brown-Robbins, no. 2781), and in another to Prince Edward (Brown-Robbins, no. 3881). In addition, there is an early sixteenth-century poem in the hand of Richard Kaye (Robbins-Cutler, no. 1270.1), and two other poems each describe three—Julius Caesar, Alexander, and Hector (Robbins-Cutler, no. 1322.5), and King Arthur, Charlemagne, and David (Robbins-Cutler, no. 1929.5).

DEATH AND LIFFE [245], a poem in the tradition of the Alliterative Revival, combining love vision, allegory, and debate, is listed here mainly for convenience of reference. It is known only from the late and careless copy in the seventeenth century Percy Folio MS, some 200 years after its probable date of composition (before 1450), but preserving words and phrases common to other alliterative poems, especially *Piers Plowman* (C Text xxi), *The Parlement of the Thre Ages* [244], and *Winnere and Wastoure* [243]. For its Lady Nature theme, it is indebted to *De planctu nature* of Alanus de Insulis. Hanford and Steadman judged the dialect to be North Midland with Northern modifications, but Oakden considered it Midland. There is no evidence to link this poem with the later *Scottish Feilde* [217].

The debate is "fundamentally one of relative power and right. Liffe complains that Death is wantonly trampling down her children. Death boasts of her superior might, and also defends her utility in the scheme of things. Finally Liffe proclaims her eternal victory over the enemy through Christ. There is also in our poem the customary appeal to a judge (God), who sends Countenance to restrain the ravages of death." (Hanford and Steadman).

Fit 1: After an invocation to Christ, Christian King that "on the crosse tholed to bringe vs into blisse," (1–21) comes the chanson d'aventure gambit: the poet meditates under a hawthorn tree in a flower-bedecked river valley, and falls asleep. (22–38) In a dream, the poet finds himself walking on a great mountain, from which he can see "all the world full of welth," with a Lady, to whom kings and princes do honor, "all profereth her to please, the pore and the riche," along with a noble company of lords and ladies. The Lady was beautiful to gaze on and sumptuously attired. Who might she be? (82–117) Sir Comfort tells him "this is my Lady Dame Liffe that leadeth vs all." (118–35) About two in the afternoon, the happiness and revelry of the whole company is interrupted by "the burlyest blast that ever blowne was," from a man "so grislye and great and grim to behold," and his ugly consort (vividly described), whom no man could look on and live. Sir Comfort tells the poet he is watching Lady Death and her soldiers, Envy, Anger, Mourning and Moan, Sorrow and Sickness. (136–90) Nature quails before Death, who kills hundreds of the most beautiful kings and queens in Lady Liffe's train "att the first flappe." (191–209) Dame Liffe implores God's aid, and Countenance is sent to the rescue to get rid of Lady Death. (210–28) Lady Liffe thanks Countenance, and upbraids Death, who kills without reason and destroys Earth's beauty. (229–55) Lady Death answers that the sin of Adam and Eve gives her this power. (256–85)

Fit 2: Lady Liffe inⁱsts Death does the work of the devil (286–303), but Death replies that fear of her leads men to obey God, and that no one can escape her, listing her conquests from Biblical celebrities to Arthurian heroes. Even Christ himself was vanquished. (304–47) Lady Liffe falls to her knees at the name of Christ, and answers that Christ did not die, although she paints a vivid picture of the Crucifixion. In fact, Christ sent Death to hell hole and told its inhabitants "how he had beaten thee on thy bent and thy brand taken." "Boste this neuer of thy red deeds, thou ravished bitche." (348–400) Christ opened hell's doors, bound Lucifer, and freed all from their chains, Liffe continues, rallying her company. Death has no might against Everlasting Liffe. (401–44) Liffe restores to life those of her company just slain by Death, more beautiful now than before, and continues her way. The poet would follow her; although this was a dream, yet Christ did save us from death. (445–59)

Oakden, while admitting the poem's power, considers Steadman's praise too fulsome: "There are few finer things in the whole range of Middle English poetry. The author has brought to his didactic theme a lofty imagination and a sense of poetic phrase which make *Death and Liffe* rank high even among the most powerful productions of the alliterative school."

MUM AND THE SOTHSEGGER [246] was known, before the discovery of the longer fragment of 1751 alliterative long lines in MS BM Additional 41666, as *Richard the Redeless* or *Poem on the Deposition of Richard II* (857 different lines in a Cambridge University MS). The date of the latter lies between 1403 and 1406, and the poem "is directly connected with the events which had occurred in 1399 with the removal of Richard II from the throne on charges of tyrannical rule" (Schlauch).

The fragment in the Cambridge University MS has a Prologue and four Passus:

The poet dedicates the poem to the King, and assumes the role of devoted and anxious counselor of Richard. Yet the work is certainly strongly partial to Henry. It is not strictly a vision, but purports to have originated from strange news of Henry's invasion that the poet heard at Christ Church as he was passing through Bristol. Passus I discourses to the King on the ill-doings of his favorites. Passus II inveighs against the King's servants (styled the White Harts, from their badges) as plagues of the people; it reproves the King for failing to favor the good Greyhound (Westmoreland), who would have preserved to him a multitude of retainers. Meanwhile, the Eagle (Bolingbroke) was cherishing his own nestlings. In puns similar to those in *On King Richard's Ministers* ([87] above), the poem tells of the punishment of Bushey, Greene, Scrope, and Bagot. Passus III holds forth on the unnatural attacks of the White Harts on the Colt (FitzAlan), the Horse (Earl of Arundel), the Swan (Gloucester), and the Bear (Earl of Warwick), and how they came to grief. It then deals at length with the luxurious and wasteful lives and practices of Richard's courtiers and favorites. Passus IV continues the reprehension of Richard's enormous expenditures, and violently abuses the Parliament of 1397 for its cowardly subservience. Here the piece breaks off. (Wells)

The fragment in the BM Additional MS is not divided into passus, and is a long extract referring to events after 1402. Day and Steele, its editors, give the following summary:

The opening lines continue the poet's remarks on the authorities in Henry's household: I think that a professional truth-teller would be the most valuable of them all (99). But where is such a one to be found? No one dares to tell the truth about his people to the King or to his Council (205). I have drawn up a perfect scheme for the service of our King (231). "You had better be silent," says Mum. "I get on well with everybody. Do as I do." I reply, "You are self-seeking and allow the King to shame himself," and so we parted. I wondered at Mum's success, and set out to learn the truth about it from books (322), the Universities (327), the Seven Sciences (391), the friars (with a digression on their faults) (535), the monks (552), and the secular clergy. Mum advised me to let the clergy alone—tithes are a ticklish question (701)—"I will not till I know more," said I. "I can trust the clergy" (713). "You are making a mistake," said Mum. "The clergy have failed in their duty of exhorting princes not to quarrel" (766). "Now you are talking sense," said I. "Tell them of it" (774). "I will have no more to do with you," said Mum. "Keep out of the way of the clergy, and try the citizens and lords" (787). So I did, and found they all followed Mum. Everywhere Mum was master, so I sat down wearied, and slept for seven hours (870). In a fair country I dreamed of a gardener (954) who was killing drones from his bee-hives, and expounded the philosophy of bee-keeping (1086). I asked his advice about Mum and the truth-teller. He said, "All the evil of the land comes from Mum" (1217). "Where am I to find the truth-teller?" said I (1221). He described the truth-teller's abode (1275). "I must leave you and return whence I came," said the gardener; "write your book and send it to the King" (1287). On waking I reflected that dreams are sometimes true, so I set myself to my task, and here I lay open my bag (1343) full of complaints of the wrongdoing and folly of all classes: prelates, archdeacons, monks, women, spreaders of rumors (introducing the story of Jenghis Khan), jurors, suitors at law, maintainers, unlucky defendants, lords who detain the king's revenues, misers and their executors, believers in false prophecies, and of lamentation for the decline of clergy and knighthood from the ways of their forefathers.

The author (or authors), under the influence of such democratic theorists as William of Ockman, Marsilius of Padua, and Nicholas of Cusa, reflects the conditions of his own day. He favors the monarchy above feudalism, popular sovereignty and law above lawless absolutism, resistance and deposition of the faulty kings above passive obedience; like any medieval writer he recognizes the great force of Natural Law, but at the same time inveighs against the violations of Positive or man-made Law by kings, lords, and clergy. Above all he senses "the importance to monarchy, if it was to survive, of a lawful rule through recognition of the powers of Parliament."(Mohl) Similarly Helen Cam notes the "vivid recognition of the obligations a member owed the electors . . . unique at this date . . . within a few months of the deposition of Richard II."

The verbal similarities of the Additional fragment with *Piers Plowman* indicate a familiarity with an A-text of that poem and a knowledge of a B-text.

Since 1936, with the publication of both fragments by the Early English Text Society, scholars have generally accepted the two fragments as parts of one longer poem. This view has been forcibly disputed by Dan Embree: "But if we are to believe that these are fragments of the same poem, we must believe that the poet began with a definite plan for a poem organized around Richard and, in fact, addressed to him, stuck to that plan for 857 lines, and then, without nearly exhausting the potential of that plan, abandoned it so completely that 247 lines later Richard has disappeared without a trace and the poem has become a treatise on Henry's household." Shifts of focus in audience and time, unusual repetition of episode, confusion between historical and allegorical modes, and differing conceptions of self on the part of the author are additional considerations advanced by Embree in support of his conclusion.

In addition to the three foregoing poems, other long-line alliterative poems on contemporary conditions before ca. 1400 include *The Blacksmiths* ([171] above), *Pierce the Ploughman's Crede* ([109] above), and, of course, *The Vision Concerning Piers the Plowman*.

THE CROWNED KING: ON THE ART OF GOVERNING [247], recalling both *Mum and the Sothsegger* [246] and *Piers Plowman*, is a short political allegory of 144 alliterative long lines, localized at Southampton on Corpus Christi Eve, May 29, 1415, just prior to King Henry's embarkation for the wars in France. The poet refers to the sizable grant Henry had obtained from the Commons the previous year, and the possible capture of castles abroad. Straight in the *De Regimine Principum* tradition, the poem proceeds to advise Henry in his governing:

After the dream introduction, a cleric receives permission to speak "sum sawes of salomon." This advice covers the need to rule righteously, remembering the value of the "pouere peple" who provide the real riches of the kingdom; giving leadership for the nobility, avoiding wicked advisers, promoting the worthiest fighters, and acquiring knowledge and ability to exercise personal leadership.

Advice to Henry's successor on the throne, Henry VI, is contained in passages in Hardyng's *Metrical Chronicle* (Brown-Robbins, no. 710).

For a late carol on the clergy's place in the three estates, see Robbins-Cutler, no. 1494.5.

THE SCOTTISH KINGDOM LIKE A HARP [248], 44 rime royal stanzas, "Sic Figurata per Citheram Statum Regni Designans Quaedam Moralitas," inserted in the Latin *Liber Pluscardensis* (Book XI, *Chronicon Jacobi Primi Regis Scottorum*, chap. 2), compiled in 1461 by Maurice de Buchanan.

The poem presumes to inform and censure the King, James I of Scotland, using the imagery of a well-tuned harp, the strings being the various estates, to denote a well-ordered kingdom ("De regimine principum bonum consilium"). The King must take responsibility for his deputies, for example, seeing that young lords study the law so as to give adequate counsel, and take "the commoun profyt" to heed; above all, the king must maintain justice. Now Scotland is barren of treasure: women and children are "suowand for falt of bred"; judges sell their verdicts. Saint David praised righteous judges, yet our King countermands his orders for justice.

In the Fairfax MS the poem ends imperfectly in the 41st stanza; the version in the Chepman and Myllar print has 224 lines.

Another Scottish insert in the *Liber Pluscardensis* concerns the Dauphin's lament on the death of his Scottish bride [228].

For advice to James III of Scotland, see *Lancelot of the Laik* (I [21]).

THE LIBEL OF ENGLISH POLICY [249] is one of the longest and most important political poems in Middle English, preserved in some sixteen manuscripts, in several recensions. It consists of a Prologue of seven rime royal stanzas and 1092 lines in couplets, and an Envoy of two eight-line stanzas, summarizing its theme: "exhortynge all Englande to keep the see environ and namely the Narowesee, shewynge whate worshipe, profite and salvacione commeth thereof to the reigne of Englonde, etc." Its terminus a quo is fixed by references to the Duke of Burgundy's siege of Calais in July, 1436, and the counterattack by Humphrey, Duke of Gloucester, the following August. The terminus ad quem is established by a reference to the Emperor Sigismund (who died in December, 1437) "whyche yet regneth." In its initial form, therefore, the *Libel* must have been composed between 1436 and 1437.

Another version refers to Sigismund "which late regned" (possibly a routine scribal correction), but in the Envoy, substituting for the earlier "wyse lorde baron of Hungerforde," appeals for approval to "my lordes" of the Privy Council. Two of these lords may be identified as William de la Pole, Earl of Suffolk, the Steward of the Household, along with Ralph, Lord Cromwell, the Lord Treasurer of England. The third lord is described as a "grete prelate, the highest confessour"; Wright suggested Cardinal Beaufort, and Warner suggested Bishop John Stafford, then Chancellor. This second version was probably written sometime between 1437 and 1441.

A third recension (in Harley 78 and Rylands) names Archbishop Chichele as one of the three members of the Council, thereby establishing a date after 1441.

The *Libel*, provoked by the 1436 attack on Calais to review England's maritime policy, summed the situation up in the lines:

Cheryshe marchandyse, keepe th'amyralte
That we bee maysteres of the narowe see.

The author naturally turned to address those magnates whose opinions carried most weight, and who had the power "to kepe thys regne in rest." As author, Warner suggested the clerk of the Council, Adam Moleyns, later Bishop of Chichester, but Taylor disputed this proposal, and also dismissed other attributions to Lydgate.

The Prologue emphasizes the vital importance of Dover and Calais as controlling the Channel and consequently European trade. Nowadays, English shipping is attacked, and England loses the value of this commerce. In ten successive chapters, the *Libel* expands the benefits and nature of the sea-borne trade between various countries: Flanders and Spain, Portugal, Brittany, Flanders and Scotland, Prussia and the Hanse League, Italy, the Low Countries, Ireland, and Iceland. Much detailed information on current commodities and recent political events is included in these accounts. Chapter 11 includes a discussion on England's navy, and the twelfth and final chapter contends that a strong navy will ensure prosperity and keep the peace.

There is no evidence, in spite of the later versions, that the poem succeeded in influencing the national policy.

ENGLAND'S TRADE POLICY [250] is not merely a redaction of *The Libel of English Policy* [249], but, while using the opening four lines of the *Libel* and paralleling a few others, actually a different poem, omitting the illustrations and digressions and introducing many new concepts. It aimed at drawing public attention to certain commercial grievances, and also, more significantly, at sparking legislation to prevent victimization of clothing workers. It speaks to the manufacturers of cloth and wool, almost as if a merchant were providing his fellow guildsmen with an economic review: sell to foreigners only that wool which English factors cannot use, for it costs just as much to weave poor wool as the finest, yet what a difference in the selling price of the cloth. Most of the poem, however, argues not from the position of the upper-class "comynalte," but from that of "the pore pepyll" or "poreyll." It declaims against the dishonest tricks by which unscrupulous capitalist clothiers fleeced their employees: wages paid in over-evaluated merchandise rather than in cash; false weighing practices. This change of audience (and author) from the national administrators interested in the *Libel* is confirmed by the other contents of the manuscript, which includes lists of "syses" for varying occupations (regulations governing weight, size, etc., of bread, cloth, wine) useful to members of the guilds. What is curious is that these specific demands for regulation of the woolen trade and for protection of the workers put forward in the poem were accepted into law. In 1463, and again in 1464, Parliament was petitioned to forbid the export of wool (inasmuch as English weavers were short of raw materials), the importing of foreign woolens, and payment in kind to cloth workers.

ACTIVE POLICY OF A PRINCE [251], by George Ashby, 131 rime royal stanzas, was written about 1470 for Edward, Prince of Wales, the son of Henry VI. It attempts to instruct the Prince on his bearing toward his subjects, and how to profit by bad examples of recent history—falsehood, misrule, and extortion. The Prince should practice moderation, live within his income, see that his laws are kept, and suppress "maintenance." The author was George Ashby, who died in 1475, a clerk of the signet to Henry VI, and later to Queen Margaret of Anjou. Of this piece Saintsbury commented: "The sense is sound and often shrewd enough, showing the rather Philistine and hard but canny temper of the later Middle Ages; and the verse is not so irregular as in some of Ashby's contemporaries. But it is not illumined by one spark of the divine fire."

For other works by Ashby see his translation of *Dicta Philosophorum* (Brown-Robbins, no 738), which may perhaps be regarded as an extension of his *Active Policy*; and his *Prisoner's Reflections* (Brown-Robbins, no. 437).

II. The Ruled

MEDIEVAL LIBERTY POEMS [252]. The complaints and protests against the wicked age are generally those of the middle and upper classes. The recurring theme is the corruption of the law courts, the venality of judges and jurors—a preoccupation of those with land, money, and property. The legitimate complaints of serfs and peasants were seldom discussed, simply because these men were illiterate and without spokesmen. However, some of the sentiments of the rising middle classes filtered down to lower groups and were taken over as slogans in the Revolt of 1381 (see [256] below); these scraps, says Trevelyan, breathe "the deep and gallant feeling that led the noblest among the rebels to defy gallows and quartering block in the cause of freedom." The remaining poems in this section show the continuation and extension of this spirit.

THE EVIL STATE OF ENGLAND [253], a quatrain added on a blank leaf to a Cambridge MS that includes a *Short Metrical Chronicle*

(Brown-Robbins, no. 1105), is a grim reminder of conditions in 1381, when "the stool [block] was hard, the ax was scharp." A shortened version, a distich in St. John's Oxford MS refers to 1391. Another couplet in a Cotton manuscript retains 1381.

For a short piece, in English and in French, criticizing the government of Edward II, see [15] above.

THE GREAT REBELLION [254] is noted in a macaronic couplet on a flyleaf of Gower's *Vox Clamantis*:

In Kent alle care bygan
Ibi pauci sunt sapientes.

JOHN BALL'S PROVERBIAL COUPLET [255], the opening text of the preacher's famous sermon at Blackheath that sparked the Peasants' Revolt, has become one of the most quoted texts of Middle English verse:

When Adam delved and Eve span,
Who was then a gentleman?

The couplet became one of the famous battle cries of English radicalism, and inspired much later compositions by Southey and William Morris.

LETTERS OF THE REBELS [256]. What was purportedly the organizational communiqués of leaders of the Great Rebellion or Peasants' Revolt have been preserved by monastic chroniclers, notably Thomas of Walsingham in his *Historia Anglicana*, the only authority for all texts, and by Henry Knighton of Leicester in his *Chronicon*, and in the St. Albans based *Chronicon Angliae* (which gives two variants). Later English chroniclers, for example Stow and Holinshed, used these sources to provide their English verse illustrations. The texts appear in varying order (some being omitted) and in variant texts in several Latin manuscripts, on which further study is needed.

(a) *John Ball Saint Mary Priest* opens with a rhythmical prose salutation beginning "John Balle seynt Marye prist greetes wele alle maner men . . . [to] stonde manlyche togedyr in trewthe." Then come six lines on the Degeneracy of the Age, which exist separately (Brown-Robbins, no. 2356), and a final line, "God doe bote for nowe is tyme amen."

(b) *John the Miller Hath Ground Small*, beginning "John the Miller hath ygrounde smal smal," is addressed to "Iohan nameles and Iohn the mullere and Iohn cartere," peasants of Essex, as in (g) below. It gives political advice how to know "your friend fro your foo." The missive contains some eight irregular riming lines amidst prose.

(c) *John Ball Greeteth You Well*, beginning "Jon Balle greetyth you wele alle," resembles (a), and also mentions that "nowe is tyme." Some lines might be considered to form a quatrain, with a concluding prose prayer.

(d) *Jack Miller*, seventeen irregular lines, supposedly a subversive address to the rebels by Jack Miller, who "asketh help to turn hys mylne aright." There is considerable aphoristic play on words—mill, will, might, right. This text resembles the Walsingham version of (b).

(e) *Jack Trueman*, irregular lines on the Abuses of the Age, in the name of Jack Trueman, used to encourage the rebels in 1381: "Jakke Trewman doth yow to understande that falsnes and gyle havith regned to long."

(f) *Jack Carter* is a rhythmical prose appeal from Jack Carter to make a good end of what has been begun. Stow observes, "I leaue out John Carters Epistle, a libell, so named."

(g) *John Sheep*. "Iohan Schep som tyme Seynte Marie prest of York," is the version in Walsingham and the *Chronicon Angliae* that to some extent parallels (a). He urges Iohan Nameless, Iohan the Mullere, and Iohon Cartere to stand together in God's name. It is followed immediately in all chronicles by (b).

THE COURSE OF REVOLT [257], or *The Rebellion of Jack Straw*, in seven six- or eight-line macaronic stanzas in English and Latin, was composed probably by a clerk, and apparently soon after the crushing of the rebellion in 1381.

In a few rapid lines (the Latin form a sort of chorus or comment), the writer out-lines the rebellion, from the beginnings in Kent to the death of Straw [i.e., Wat Tyler] in Smithfield. The author has no sympathy with the uprising and the violent behavior of the churls. He feels ardently with the King; he regards him not at all responsible for the distresses of the land but as in the grasp of evil—like the rest of the realm. May God ever defend and guide him!

For *The Insurrection and Earthquake of 1382*, see [85] above.

THE YORKSHIRE PARTISANS [258], five tail-rime stanzas, aabccb, on the riots at Beverly, Hull, and at other places in Yorkshire, in the summer of 1392. In the Coram Rege roll, the poem forms part of an indictment, which explains that the stanzas were publicly sung by John Berwald, Jr., of Cotyngham, and others, in explanation and celebration of their outbreak. The poem expresses a fine spirit of yeoman independ-ence to "mayntayn our neighbour with all our might."

STUDENT ABUSE OF THE MAYOR OF CAMBRIDGE [259], thirty irregular lines in Harley MS, comprising four couplets, three six-line tail-rime stanzas, aabccb, and a cross-rimed quatrain, in the form of "a scrowe set on this gate," warns the Mayor that the Cambridge students will mete out severe punishment to him and his adherents one of these winter nights of 1418.

Other "bills" posted on doors or gates include [21](h), probably the earliest, [21](r), and [191], [194], [195], [197], [264], [266], and [267]. Ap-parently the custom was common. William Rolleston in 1408 had English translations of a royal pardon "placed on the doors of most of the Inns of the town of Beverley"; and Walter Aslak in 1424 posted "Englische billes rymed in partye" on the city gates of Norwich.

A SONG OF FREEDOM [260], three quatrains, aabb, in a Latin ser-mon by Friar Nicholas Philipps, separated from one another by short commentaries. After explaining the fatherhood of God, the poem appar-ently incorporates a stanza of some popular song of protest—"Euery beste that leuyth now is of more fredam than thow"—but in the context im-poses a spiritual interpretation. The third quatrain reverses the foregoing subversive comment, and points out the dangers of owning money! The year 1434 seems a suitable date.

For a carol expressing popular feelings of protest about 1445, see *The Day Will Dawn* (Brown-Robbins, no. 320; Greene E E Carols, no. 121).

THE KENTISH INSURRECTION [261] is the subject of a single tail-rime stanza, aabccb, forming a brief manifesto to encourage the rebels in Kent, who mustered under Jack Cade to protest the acquittal of the Duke of Suffolk for alleged murder of the Duke of Gloucester in 1450. In the Magdalen charter, the verses form part of a popular proclamation which sets forth twelve causes of England's economic distress. In the Harley MS of Stow's *Chronicle*, the verses are linked to the rising of Robin of Redesdale.

In the Cotton Rolls MS is a poem similarly attacking the Duke of Suffolk ([192] above).

ROBIN OF REDESDALE [262], a couplet referring to the loosely organized support of Richard Neville, Earl of Warwick, in Lancashire, which later helped Warwick defeat Edward IV at the Battle of Edgecote (1469). Robin may possibly be associated with an experienced captain, Sir John Conyers, but the name had the effect of a rallying cry:

Yf any man askyth ho made this crye,
Say Robyn Rydesdale, Jac Nag, and I.

ON JUSTICE IN NORWICH [263], a piece of doggerel consisting of seven irregular riming lines, apparently written about 1433, against five men charged with attempting to overthrow the court.

INJUSTICES AT COVENTRY I [264], seven couplets on injustices in Coventry in 1494 by the supporters of Laurence Saunders, imprisoned for causing a riot. A "bill" was attached to the door of St. Michael's Church, in the same way as [266] and [267] below.

The city is bond! Once Godiva made it free, but now apprentices have to pay fees. Curses on Robert Green for this. Watch out for trouble after harvest. Saunders has been put to ransom. Beware.

LADY GODIVA [265]. Attention might be directed here to a couplet in a stained glass window in Trinity Church in Coventry commemorating the ride (cf. lines 3–4 of [264]) of Lady Godiva:

I Luriche for the love of thee
Doe make Coventre tol free.

INJUSTICES AT COVENTRY II [266], four six-line tail-rime stanzas, aabccb, forming a bill of protest attached to the minster door at Coventry in 1496, by the friends of Laurence Saunders, an active member of the Dyers Guild, who had been removed from the Common Council of Coventry on charges of fomenting a riot. The hare [i.e., Saunders] is in prison; small bees sting, beware of wasps!

INJUSTICES AT COVENTRY III [267], twelve rough couplets forming a second bill attached to Coventry minster in 1496 in support of Laurence Saunders (cf. [264] and [266]).

The city is bond. The common's champion is a prisoner. Pick away our thrift and make us all blind. The commons are estranged. Mend that is amiss.

SEVEN NAMES OF A PRISON [268], eight rime royal stanzas, the first line and the last two words in each stanza in Latin, movingly describes the plight of a prisoner. Seven stanzas give various names, e.g., carcer, "a place to ponyshe man for his trespas," or a place to get rid of one's possessions in order to keep alive, "for lake of mony straytly kepte here under quorum." The last stanza asks for pity and mercy for those kept in Ludgate jail.

Compare also [91] above.

THE PRISONER'S PRAYER [269], 22 English lines in stanzas of varying length with the French equivalent, with music, is one of the earliest poems in Middle English (not later than 1250). Brown concluded the English was a translation, but Wager has his reservations. Wager further suggests that this poem is one of the very rare examples of an early monodic song in England showing troubadour or trouvère influence. The prisoner prays help from God, for he has been wrongfully imprisoned for another's theft. He prays for forgiveness of those who wronged him, and concludes with an appeal to the Virgin.

For similar pieces, see *The Prisoner's Lament* (Brown-Robbins, no. 1277), George Ashby's *A Prisoner's Reflections* (Brown-Robbins, no. 437), and, in the Chaucerian apocrypha, *Earl Rivers' Virelai on Fickle Fortune*, XI [22].

JOHN MY LORD'S HYNE [270] is a curious addition to a manuscript of the homilies of Haymo, in six stanzas (st. 1, 3–6, abab; st. 2, aabccb) with a heading or burden: "Synge and blow blow wel blow. synge wen sey blow." Apparently it is a cynical statement that a whole village is dominated by its lord, and that John will continue doing the menial tasks all his life. The hand is early fifteenth century, probably that of John Morton, Rector of Berwick St. John, South Wiltshire, who also wrote a sophisticated religious lullaby (Robbins-Cutler, no. 4242.5).

11. Political Prophecies

POLITICAL PROPHECIES [271]. Of all the political poems, the prophecies are at once the most political and the least poetic, and the closest to propaganda. Unfortunately, many of them, including the un-published items, are such doggerel that they lack interest even as *literaria curiosa*.

The obvious function of all the political prophecies was to influence some future course of action or policy, recommended by the writer, to the king or royal advisers or (less often) to some nobleman. Generally past events were included in the prophecy, suitably veiled, to give credence to the hoped-for events prophesied. In this sense, for practical purposes, it mattered little whether a Galfridian (using animal cognizances) or the less common Sybilline techniques (with initial letters) were used. All English monarchs regarded these prophecies with much concern, and strict laws were passed and enforced, becoming especially severe in the latter years of the reign of Queen Elizabeth I, owing to the uncertainty about the succession.

The two dozen or so published Middle English prophecies, including variants, are generally fathered on famous figures of British prophecy—Merlin (from Geoffrey of Monmouth's *Historia Regum Britanniae*), John of Bridlington, Thomas of Erceldoune, and St. Thomas à Becket. To these names are linked four major groups of prophecies. But the indiscriminate attribution to one of these names of any trivia, cliché, or nonsense, would immediately ensure its high prestige.

It became customary to quote such authorities throughout the prophecy. *When Rome is Removed* [285] gives one such omnibus list:

This Bridlyngton, bede, bokis and Banaster tellis,
Thomas, and merlyon, the same withouten lese,
They recorden and other that with prophecy mellis.

Elsewhere there is an appeal to "Blase"—"li premier mestre" or most important of the *notatores* who, in the romances, recorded Merlin's prophecies.

The twenty manuscripts of *The Cock in the North* [281] show how indiscriminately the authorities were used. In MS Lansdowne 762 the poem is headed "Brydlyngton." In MS Peniarth 26 it is "the last saying of Thomas of Arsedon." In MS Caius Cambridge 249 the rubric reads "Quod Herryson." Part of the Lansdowne, as well as the Sloan 2578 version, is found incorporated into *Tomas of Erselldoune* [290]. Part of the Cambridge University Kk.1.5 text occurs in the "Prophecy of Bertlington" in the Waldegrave collection of 1603. Here, *The Cock in the North* has its first fourteen lines ascribed to Merlin, and the rest given as "The Prophecie of Bede." Another prophecy [278](d) uses Bridelyngton, Banistor, Merlyn, and Thomas Assheldon!

Throughout all the centuries of their popularity, the Middle English prophecies followed the pattern of Geoffrey of Monmouth's Book of Merlin (see [272] below), wherein animals personify humans or wherein the animal cognizances represent their bearers. In earlier prophecies there is no animal symbolism. When the symbol remains constant, recognition of the prophecy is not too difficult; however, in order to provide an escape clause should the veracity of the prophecy be questioned, or on the other hand should it be held too pointed, symbols were purposely confused; two animals would represent one man, and one animal two or more men. Thus the lynx is sometimes King John, Henry II, Henry III, or Edward III. This type of prophecy is commonly called "Galfridian" after Geoffrey of Monmouth. There are a few examples in Middle English verse of the other form, the "Sybilline" (called after the early Latin prophecies), where initial letters of a name or numbers in a dynasty are used to represent people. *Twelve Letters Save England* [199] is an example.

The art of obfuscation by multiple interpretation was discussed at length in the Commentary to John of Bridlington's Latin poem, where he classified the various devices of symbolism under ten heads, most of which are to be found in the English poems (e.g., arbitrary names, accidental designation, metaphor, etymologized translation, enigma, abbreviation, etc.).

Sometimes prophecies were linked with two groups of poems: prognostications according to the weather, e.g., Brown-Robbins, nos. 1423, 1545, 4053; and the Evils of the Age, e.g., [86], [90], [286], and Brown-Robbins, nos. 906, 1820, 2356, 3851, which are all closely related to *Merlin's* or *Chaucer's Prophecy*, XI [11]. For a version of the Twelve Abuses, ascribed to Bede, approximating a prophecy, see Brown-Robbins, no. 4051, in the chapter on Proverbs, Precepts, and Monitory Pieces.

Students proposing study on prophecies should heed the caution advocated by Meyvaert: "Much work would be needed to sort out the whole 'prophecy' literature of the fourteenth and fifteenth centuries and identify the various additions and interpolations."

The prophecies are grouped in the following five sections: I, The Merlin Prophecies; II, The John of Bridlington Prophecies; III, The Thomas of Erceldoune Prophecies; IV, The Thomas à Becket Prophecies; V, Other Prophecies.

I. The Merlin Prophecies

MERLIN PROPHECIES [272]. The Book of Merlin appeared as the Seventh Book of the *Historia Regum Britanniae*, originally dedicated to Alexander, Bishop of Lincoln, about 1139, by Geoffrey of Monmouth. The *Vita Merlini* was dedicated to Robert, Bishop of Lincoln, about 1149. It is generally supposed to be an interpolation, included because of its oral popularity, into the later written history. The Merlin prophecies became well known over the whole continent, both in more or less faithful as well as in derivative forms.

THE PROPHECY OF THE SIX KINGS TO FOLLOW KING JOHN [273], the *Prophecia de Merlyn*, contains much material from The Book of Merlin, and its development can be followed in successive versions in Latin, Anglo-French, and in English prose and verse. Its 139 short couplets translate a French version. Although originally composed in the early fourteenth century, the prophecy as it exists now is an attack on Henry IV by the Percy-Glendower-Mortimer faction (cf. Shakespeare's *I Henry IV*, III.ii). The prophecies begin with the Lamb of Winchester (Henry III), who is to be succeeded by his heir, the Dragon (Edward I), who is to be followed by a Goat (Edward II), after whom shall come a Lion (Edward III), who shall be followed by an Ass (Richard II), to whom shall succeed a Mole (Henry IV). Taylor refers to this text by its title in MS Hatton, "John the Hermit's Prophecy."

A closely-related English prose version of the *Six Kings* occurs in the fifteenth-century *Brut* (see the chapter on Chronicles).

GEOFFREY OF MONMOUTH'S PROPHECY [274] is the only direct translation of the Book of Merlin, and uses similar framework and symbols to the *Six Kings*. Its eleven quatrains come from the "Lynx" or "Great Prophecy," which was frequently copied and had an independent existence. The English were continually afraid of the combination of the Scots and Welsh. The threat was especially immediate in the time of Edward III (the Lynx).

A PROPHECY OF THE CONQUEST OF FRANCE [275], 26 couplets, seen by Scattergood as a poor modification of an older prophecy (tempus Edward III) or pieces of prophecies in order to relate to 1424 ("When a m cccc togyther be knett / and xxiiij with them be mett"). "The result . . . is confused and unsatisfactory," says Scattergood, who speculates on a possible interpretation: The English defeated the French and Scots at the Battle of Verneuil in 1424, and the prophecy looks forward to the war between the King of France ("the lylie that faire flowre") and the Duke of Burgundy, in which the King of England will intervene and gain the French throne. The first line in the manuscript, however, reads 1500, and line 6 reads the Duke of Flanders & (not p = Philip) Burgundy, so that an entirely different interpretation is conceivable (especially since the manuscript is as late as 1540). The incomplete text in Harley refers to the year 1536. Preceding the prophecy is a *Declaracio signorum*, similar to others occasionally found in collections of prophecies. The only positive statement from this prophecy is the victory of England over France—a presumption popular in any year.

THE STREETS OF LONDON [276], "The prophecy of Merlyon," probably referring to the reign of Richard III, in 134 irregular riming lines, combines two styles of identification, the Sybilline (initial letters of characters) and the Galfridian (animal symbols deriving from crests). A reasonably certain reference to the death of Edward IV in 1483 is followed by very veiled allusions, perhaps to the future Henry VII. The prophecy foresees great woe for England from the rival factions, so "that the streets of London shall ron all on blod."

MS Lansdowne 762 has numerous other English prophecies, but most of them probably relate to the second quarter of the sixteenth century. For *An Animal Prophecy* from this manuscript, see [301] below.

A MERLIN STANZA [277]. The prophetic character of *Chaucer's Prophecy*, XI [11], also called *Merlin's Prophecy*, is emphasized by this eight-line stanza which follows it in one manuscript.

UNPUBLISHED MERLIN PROPHECIES [278]. Because of their dog-gerel and obscurity, many English Merlin prophecies are still unpub-lished and even uncatalogued. Typical items are noted here.

(a) An English prophecy with Latin interpolations, including *A Proph-ecy by the Dice* [297] on p. 135; 85 lines in cross-rimed quatrains, begin-ning:

A dragoun with a rede rose that ys of grete fame
A bastard in wedloc boryn schall he be
The croun to optayne he wyll chalenge by name
but ij yeres and mor the blew bor schall haue degree

and including such lines as (p. 131):

A bysschop the crown schall haue in gouernance
And neuer boryn to that astate
The comyns on hym schall aske a vengance
ffor he schal be the caws of grete debate

(b) Merlin's Prophecy in 49 lines, beginning:

A king out of the North shull come
King borne crowned bak his breast upon
A lion rampant strange to se
And C I S his name shal be

(c) A political prophecy, 45 irregular riming lines, beginning:

An Egyll shall ryse with a bore bold

(d) Prophecia Bridelyngton, Banestor, Merlyn, and Thomas Assheldon. The first sixteen lines are illegible because of reagent stains. Line 17 reads:

He that is ded and buried in syght

and the last line reads:

And in the vale of Josaphath men shall hym bor

(e) A late Merlin prophecy, beginning:

How a lyon shall be banished and to Berwyke gone

(f) A late prophecy, 76 lines using only four rimes in irregular stanzas, the majority of which start abab or aabc, beginning:

O myghty mars that marrith many a wight

Lines 28, 31–35 occur separately as a political prophecy according to the throw of the dice [297]. Another unpublished prophecy with number prognostics (not from dice) is noted later [304](d).

(g) An animal prophecy attributed to Merlin in twelve alliterative quatrains, beginning:

> Of al the merueile of merlyn how he makys his mone
>
> Take tent to his tulkyng in tales that he tellys
>
> how a lyon shal be bansched and to barwik gone
>
> The rose and the ragged staf in frithes and by feldes

and ending:

> Bede merlyon and Assheldon with saint Th of Caunterby
>
> and bridlyngton in ther prophecie acord . . .
>
> When the child smytes the moder the fader shal hym destroye . . .

(h) Metrical prophecies in English and Latin on English history, ten couplets beginning:

> Thare is a boke men calles merlyns Bulbrane

II. The John of Bridlington Prophecies

JOHN OF BRIDLINGTON'S LATIN PROPHECY [279]. John Thwenge, Prior of Bridlington, became associated even before his death in 1379 with an earlier long Latin prophecy, "Febribus infectus," "one of the most popular prophecies in the fourteenth century." But he did not write it. This vaticinium was followed by a commentary written about 1361 by John Erghome, Prior of the Austin Friars in York, who dedicated it to Humphrey de Bohun, Earl of Hereford (who died in 1372). The Commentary is a literary and political discussion on those who favored the Black Prince. The Prophecy was not translated into English, but exists in parallel forms in *The Cock in the North* [281] and *When Rome is Removed* [285].

For a so-called Bridlington's prophecy in John Capgrave's *Chronicle*, see [20](e) above.

A EULOGY OF JOHN THWENGE [280], Prior of Bridlington, in 239 lines in rough couplets, was written after his death in 1379 and before his canonization in 1401. The author, probably a cleric, was no doubt laying popular support for his candidate; incidentally he refers to John as "ful prophetable."

THE COCK IN THE NORTH [281], sometimes called *The First Scottish Prophecy*, absorbs material from John of Bridlington's Latin poem or from some common source for both, and, on the other hand, has close parallels with the vaticinations of Thomas of Erceldoune. The seventeen variants vary from 75 to 139 lines, and exist in manuscripts from the mid-fifteenth century to the end of the sixteenth century; consequently it is impossible to give one single interpretation for all the variants. Inevitably there will be a different meaning to every text, for a prophecy's only value lies in its topicality—the many variations are proof that each writer was trying to allude to his own current situation. Parts of the original (not susceptible of contemporary orientation) might be left undisturbed, and other parts (suited to the times) altered or added.

In one manuscript (Trinity Dublin), the prophecy is preceded by a couplet on wonders in England (Robbins-Cutler, no. 4030.5):

When the ded arysen and comen hom,
Than yn ynglond schal falle wondres many on.

AN ALLITERATIVE POLITICAL PROPHECY [282], 45 non-riming alliterative lines generally in four-line strophes; some of the lines appear in *The Cock in the North* [281], perhaps directly from this piece. The lion is free and, after gaining victories over his opponents, rules his kingdom in prosperity. If the prophecy is Scottish, the lion may refer to James I who in 1424 married Joan Beaufort (= ? "the mightful meiden"). In 1425 James overcame the Duke of Albany and two of his sons. The poem may be dated ca. 1431, though the manuscript is later.

A SECOND ALLITERATIVE POLITICAL PROPHECY [283] is found in two manuscripts of the mid-fifteenth century: it begins: "S mysed in myndes and merke ther a P."

A PROPHECY FOR 1560 [284]. This is a curious prophecy for the year 1560 in two five-line stanzas, retained here as a literary curiosity because, though the hand is clearly sixteenth-century, the scribe seems to be imitating an earlier fourteenth-century hand, even including the obsolete wen. It is followed immediately by one eight-line stanza on "Alle olde things ar not ill" (Brown-Robbins, no. 1146).

WHEN ROME IS REMOVED [285], or *The Second Scottish Prophecy*, tells what will happen "when Rome is removed into England." Its seventeen manuscripts and the fragments show tremendous variations, in length and attitude, but are all probably derived from an original short prophecy, apparently Scottish in sympathy, developing some of the symbols used by Geoffrey of Monmouth. The texts group themselves into three versions: the first consists of as many as 98 lines; the second version omits the first sixteen lines; the third version takes the first four lines and ten other separate lines from the first version. The texts show how a short general prophecy could be applied to almost any historical period. Later, according to Haferkorn, it acquired other sets of prophecies concerned with social and ecclesiastical troubles. Some manuscripts include four lines from the *Abuses of the Age* (Brown-Robbins, no. 4006), expanded to a fifteen-line *Another Old Prophecie*.

SCOTLAND'S FUTURE PROSPERITY [286], a political prophecy in seven couplets looking forward to Scotland's prosperity in A. D. 1581, is found in two Scottish manuscripts. It incorporates a version of the *Abuses of the Age*.

III. The Thomas of Erceldoune Prophecies

THOMAS RYMOUR OF ERCELDOUNE [287]. Thomas Rymour of Erceldoune, the reputed composer or singer of an earlier version of the English *Sir Tristrem* (I [43]), was made the hero of a romantic narrative, and was famed from the thirteenth to the seventeenth century as author of various prophecies concerning England and Scotland. That an actual Thomas dwelt at Erceldoune in Berwickshire is attested by contemporary legal documents, and by tradition known to Barbour, Fordun, Mannyng, Henry the Minstrel, and Andrew of Wyntoun. His fame as a poet is shown perhaps by the name "Rymour," possibly by Mannyng's reference to "Thomas" as author of *Sir Tristrem*, certainly by the *Tristrem* writer's declaration that he had heard him recite the story of Tristrem, and by the same writer's reference to him as authority. Before his death, which must have occurred earlier than 1294, Thomas had great celebrity for prophecy, his supposed prediction of the death of Alexander III in 1286 being perhaps the most notable exhibition of his gift.

With Thomas were associated utterances of contemporary origin, and about him clustered vague and mysterious predictions of greatly later date—as similar matter clustered about the name of Merlin, and proverbial utterance about that of Alfred. To these predictions the English and the Scots for three centuries looked for light. In *King Lear*, Shakespeare (or an interpolator) parodies these obscure and confused declarations.

The prophecies fathered on Thomas were held in high esteem all through the fifteenth and sixteenth centuries, and even in the uprisings of 1715 and 1745. Thomas' name was associated with those of Merlin and Bede and Gildas, and in many cases his authority supplanted that of the other sages. Collections were made. Notable is the *Whole Prophesie of Scotland*, printed in Edinburgh in 1603, containing the "Prophecie of Thomas Rymour." Interesting, too, are the prophecies of Rymour, Reid, and Marlyng, [291] below, associated with Sir David Lyndesay and the young James V. Ballads seem to have been composed on the romantic story of Thomas; two of them of somewhat questionable authenticity were published by Jamieson and Sir Walter Scott.

THOMAS OF ERCELDOUNE'S PROPHECY [288], in MS Harley 2253, is the earliest (though not the most important) prophecy associated with his name. In eighteen alliterative lines it replies to the Countess of Dunbar's question when the Scottish War will end—an answer open to interpretations for 1286 or 1306.

TONIGHT IS BORN A BAIRN [289], about 1340, is a prophecy of ten lines by Thomas to Alexander concerning the "birth of the King Edward that now is."

TOMAS OF ERSSELDOUNE [290] is the most important of all the Middle English prophecies. It is in three "fyttes," and was probably originally Northern English, being preserved in six full texts and in five scattered fragments. Though the manuscripts agree in general as to their matter, they supplement each other in a number of cases. The total number of unrepeated lines culled from the various texts is 700. The Thornton manuscript (Lincoln Cathedral 91), the best and the oldest, has 636 lines in four-stress cross-rimed quatrains.

A Prologue (only in Thornton) begs attention to the difficulty of telling of fighting, and promises to recount battles of the past and prophecies of battles in the future. The first fit opens after the fashion of *Piers Plowman* and the *Parlement of the Three Ages*: One glad May morning, I wandered out by Huntley banks [on the Eildon Hills near Melrose] listening to the birds. As I lay under a tree, I saw riding on a dapple-gray steed, a lovely lady most richly clad, with hounds and arrows and a hunting horn. Thomas [the text shifts to the third person] took her for Mary, and hastened to her and knelt in prayer for mercy. The lady declared she was not the Virgin. Thereupon, Thomas, enamored, asked her love. Sin, she declared, would destroy her beauty. Thomas persisted; the lady became a hideous hag. She bore him with her down to middle earth, where she showed him a vision of the roads to Heaven, Paradise, Purgatory, and Hell, and of the fair country over which she was queen. Then she took him to the palace. Thomas lived there most joyously for three years that seemed but three days. Then, that he might not be taken by a fiend who was coming for his annual tribute, the lady brought him up again to earth. As she was taking farewell, Thomas begged a token of her. She predicted to him various events of 1332–45, and the principal events between 1298 and 1388. Thereafter follows a confused passage with allusions to Black Agnes of Dunbar. Thomas and the lady parted with great grief, the lady promising to meet him at some time hereafter. She disappeared on the way to Helmsdale.

The nature of the prophecies and the switching from first to third person (lines 73, 274, 317, 672 in the parallel-text edition) suggest cumulative authorship. Line 83 implies former existence of an earlier version in which was designated the place where Thomas and the lady met. The latest identifiable reference is to the Battle of Otterburn (1388), at line 469—or possibly to Henry IV's invasion of Scotland in 1400, at line 505.

As the first group of prophecies covers 1325–45 in chronological order, it was composed after 1345, and probably before the next group. As the second group disregards the first and covers 1298–1388 in chronological order, it was composed probably after 1388, and after the first group. The possible allusion to 1400 would put the piece in its present form after that date. The Thornton manuscript is about 1430–40. However, it has also been argued that the poem dates between 1388 and 1400. Lines 521 ff. consist of a mixture of stock traditional prophecies. Apparently the piece as it appears in the various manuscripts is the result of a choice from earlier materials by various persons, with additions made at will without regard to unity. This hypothesis is borne out by the appearance of the prologue only in MS Thornton, inclusion of some passages in only one or two of the manuscripts, and omission of the first fit in MS Sloane. The earlier matter would appear to be represented by lines 1–356 and lines 521 to end. Child urged that the first fit, dealing with Thomas and the lady, was originally an independent poem. This fit seems too long and too detailed to have been written merely as an introduction to the prophecies, and may well have existed long before they were composed.

The wonder story of fairy visitation and transfer to the underworld makes *Tomas of Ersseldoune* a remarkable poem of fancy and mystery that throws about us today an atmosphere of mystic glamour. But to the fifteenth century and later periods the prophecies were more than this— the writer of MS Sloane, for example, copied only fits 2 and 3.

Two texts of *The Cock in the North* [281] are included in *Tomas of Ersseldoune* (Lansdowne 762 and Sloane 2578). Most of the sixteenth-century prophecies bearing this or a similar title bear no relation to this text.

THE PROPHISIES OF RYMOUR, REED, AND MARLYNG [291] is a later version of *Tomas of Ersseldoune* [290], 628 lines in eight-line stanzas. The Lansdowne manuscript carries the prophecies forward to 1531. In the seventeenth century, *The Whole Prophesie of Scotland* contains a later shortened version in a seventeenth-century print. *The Prophesie of Sir Thomas of Astledowne* is another seventeenth-century adaptation of *Tomas of Ersseldoune* [290].

A BALLAD ON THE SCOTTISH WARS [292], as Ritson styled it, beginning "As y yod on ay mounday" and composed in Northumberland about 1300, consists of 63 four-stress cross-rimed quatrains. The general setting of the poem has some similarity to that of *Tomas of Ersseldoune* [290]. The speaker tells of meeting a strangely dressed little man who, despite him, leads him into a garden where are lords and ladies at pleasure. His inquiry of what shall be the outcome of "this war" between the Northern folk and "ours," brings him prophetic declarations as to the Mole, the Tup, the Bear, the Lion, and the Leopard.

IV. The Thomas à Becket Prophecies

MIRACLES AND PROPHECIES OF ST. THOMAS OF CANTERBURY [293] occurs in two mid-fifteenth-century manuscripts, both defective, one with about 100 alliterative lines (London dialect) and the other with some 256 lines (Northern or possibly Scottish). The two versions agree generally in content, and one complements the other. The piece apparently referred to the wars of Edward III in France—the latest event mentioned is the Battle of Poitiers, 1356—and may have been written to arouse confidence in the King and encourage the English expedition of 1360. However, the prophecy was also used in the time of Henry V, about 1420. Close relationship of features here to *The Prophecy of the Six Kings to Follow King John* [273] has been noted. This poem occurs in the manuscripts with two Scottish prophecies, and together all three are sometimes called *The Scottish Prophecies*.

V. Other Prophecies

ALDRED'S CURSE ON URSE [294] is a fragment ("Hattest thu Urs, haue thu Godes kurs") of a metrical prophetic curse ascribed by William of Malmesbury to Aldred, last Saxon Archbishop of York (died 1069), against Urse d'Abitot, the Sheriff of Worcester, who had built his castle too close to a monastery.

THE HERE PROPHECY [295], five riming lines, composed probably near the beginning of 1191 in a Northeast Midland dialect, is preserved by Benedict of Peterborough and by Roger of Hoveden. It prophesies the division of England into three parts with ensuing misery when a hart is seen in the village of Here (not as yet conclusively identified). In 1189 Ralph FitzStephen raised the image of a hart on a dwelling given him by Henry II.

ADAM DAVY'S FIVE DREAMS ABOUT EDWARD II [296], 83 octosyllabic couplets devoid of literary merit, probably written soon after 1308, are complimentary prophetic verses to the king, no doubt composed to persuade him to adopt certain political positions. Nothing is positively known of the author, although an Adam le Mareschall of the Cirencester region was prominent in the early fourteenth century.

In the first dream, Davy has a vision of King Edward before the shrine of St. Edward the Confessor, with red and white rainbows issuing from his ears covering all the country. The second depicts the King riding as a pilgrim to Rome to be chosen Emperor. The third envisions the coronation of Edward as Emperor by the Pope. The fourth shows the Virgin replying to Christ that the King has served her well both day and night. The fifth has the King "at Caunterbury, bifore the heighe autere." Finally, an angel tells Adam [Davy] the Marshall, in Stratford-atte-Bowe, to reveal these previous dreams.

Scattergood suggests Davy's *Dreams* "are a loose and individualistic treatment of a well known and popular political philosophy."

A PROPHECY BY THE DICE [297], in at least eleven manuscripts, identifies the various estates with the numbers on the dice (six = vulgus, ace = rex), and by the cast of the dice prophesying the victory of the people. There are numerous variants, but the common form has five couplets, as in the text from Cambridge University MS:

Euery syse ys bed of the dise
When ase bereth upp syse
Then ys England paradise
When synk and Cater ys sett asyde

Then the word of syse springeth full wyde
When dewsse putteth owght tree then ys all schentt
Then must we haue a new perlament
The sysse schall vp the ase schall downe
The lyon the red roose and the flower de lyse
The cock schall vndoo and the sys zall bere the price

In three manuscripts (Trinity Cambridge, Sloane, and Trinity Dublin), sketches of the dice are given.

A PROPHECY BY THE STARS [298]. In four manuscripts, *A Prophecy by the Dice* [297] is immediately followed (or in one manuscript preceded) by a short *Prophecy by the Stars*, in long lines promising political changes, as in this text from MS Cotton Cleopatra:

The Blake shall blede The Blewe shall haue his hed
The sone shall shyn The ster that stydly stode
That called is fixe Shall mevabull be anonne
The sun and the mone on the sterre shall gone
That after shall it neuer shyn ne couer
And Iubiter shall doo that dede atte douer.

Actually this prophecy is an extrapolation (lines 28, 31, 33, 34, and 35) of [278](f).

A PROPHECY BY THE DOMINICAL LETTERS [299]. In three manuscripts, *A Prophecy by the Dice* [297] is preceded by *A Prophecy by the Dominical Letters*, which is also found separately in a fourth manuscript (Peniarth). Again, all forms show variations, but Peniarth gives a corrupt basic version in two couplets:

chwen sonday goth by E d and C
and prime by one and too
A ster selcouth shall men see
That semys not to be soo

This manuscript is dated approximately 1456, and the dominical letters refer to the years 1449, 1450, and 1451. A version combined with *A Prophecy by the Dice* occurs in the Cambridge MS:

When sonday gothe by D and C
And the prime by i and ii
After schall cumme this may men see
That semes nat to be soo

The confusion of texts, the transfer of lines from one prophecy to another, the continuation of medieval prophecies into manuscripts as late as mid-seventeenth century, all confound an already confounded situation.

The Preface to Thomas More's *Book of Fortune* (Robbins-Cutler, no. 2183.5) contains an allusion (line 218) to rolling the dice. For a long poem on divination by means of the dice, see Robbins-Cutler, no. 3694.3; for eleven irregular lines on casting the dice according to the signs of the zodiac, see Robbins-Cutler, no. 752.5, in Harley 671, a whole manuscript apparently devoted to prognostics by casting the dice. A set of "fortunes," mainly satirical attacks against women, exists on an ancient set of ten fortune cards (Robbins-Cutler, no. 108.7).

A PROPHECY ON THE STATES OF EUROPE [300], 48 irregular riming lines, forewarns of disaster for all Europe—France, Burgundy, Rome, Savoy—but a "breton" shall ultimately "ryde into Rom with renkes ynow." In the meanwhile, "the werre schal be wakned in this wyde landes." Scattergood sees a possible allusion to the Council of Basle in 1433. For other prophecies from this manuscript, which contains many Welsh, Latin, and English prophecies, in prose and in verse, see [281] and [285] above.

AN ANIMAL PROPHECY [301], 141 irregular riming lines, divided into irregular stanzas often of eleven or twelve lines, including a refrain line, "When cuckowe tyme cometh oft so sone." The saucy cuckoo enjoys his reputation as prophet and harbinger of spring, but many dangers attend the time of the cuckoo's song. The inclusion of the wolf, swan, fox, fulmart, and greyhound among the animals awakened by spring suggests a political interpretation of this more than usually literary prophecy. The poem concludes with a prayer for peace.

ROSS OF WARWICK'S PROPHECY [302] consists of four lines in *Joannis Rossi Warwicensis Historia*, beginning "Water shall wex and wod shall wane."

For nonsense verses, possibly parodying a prophecy, see Brown-Robbins, no. 3435.

A PROPHECY OF THE END OF THE WORLD [303], two long couplets: When the hills smoke, then Babilon shall end; but when they burn as a fire, then will be the end of the world, and all men will die.

MISCELLANEOUS UNPUBLISHED PROPHECIES [304]. In addition to the foregoing prophecies, a number of prophecies are found in books of special collections, like, for example, Bodley 4062 (Hatton 26), Bodley 13184 (Rawl D.1062), Lansdowne 262, National Library of Wales Peniarth 26, National Library of Wales Peniarth 50, or else added to flyleaves or inserted into various non-prophetic works. Perhaps a hundred or more texts might be garnered from a thorough reexamination of Middle English and Latin manuscripts. The majority of the prophecies are badly written and garbled, often the lines are gibberish, and numerous lines are transferred from one prophecy to another. Often the political message of the prophecy is confused in a welter of unnecessarily obscure references.

For the convenience of any scholar who has the fortitude to pursue this genre, the following miscellaneous unpublished prophecies are provided as a sampling of its complexity.

(a) When England shall be Britain, one cross-rimed quatrain, beginning:

A Bastar schall come owt of the west

(b) A political prophecy, 152 lines generally in couplets, beginning:

As I mused in my dys mekyll towart

(c) A political prophecy using emblems or devices, fourteen cross-rimed quatrains, beginning:

Burnys ne batelles brytten ut schall be
And barnes on hillys bloo

and ending:

The fourth branche of the tree schall dee
That lost hath bowes moo   Explicit

(d) A sixteenth-century prophecy, 96 lines generally in quatrains, beginning:

Crist hathe made hys complainte
for losyng of hys possession

(e) A political prophecy using numbers (not of the dice), twenty lines in all, most of them illegible because of reagent stains, beginning:

Fals love when VI setteth ayenst VIIJ

(f) A political prophecy in one cross-rimed quatrain:

ffrance and fflaunders than shall ryse
Spane shall supporte them in all their myght
The danes will com to take enterpryse
nowght shall they do but all abowght lyght

(g) A political prophecy in six irregular lines:

In may when myrth moves vpon lofte
And the kelandes of Iune bene knytt all togeder
And euery sede opon erthe sawne in ther kynde
And euery bogh with his blomes blossome so fayre
And M M off thro yeres ben com to an ende
And CCCC off a sewter be cesset for ever

(h) A metrical prophecy about England, in couplets, beginning:

O Albeon of all landes to behold
To thinke of thy sorow it maketh me could

(i) Doggerel prognostics and prophecies, ten lines tailing off into general weather prognostics and tags (e.g., fer well love I take my leve) in prose, beginning:

R shall rech and the p shall prech

and the T shall trymbyll for his rest

The original prophecy on f. 97ᵃ may be fifteenth century, written on a larger sheet added to the manuscript, and then copied in a sixteenth-century hand on ff. 96ᵃ–96ᵇ.

(j) Concluding ten quatrains of a prophecy beginning:

Schall come trewly as y ow say

and ending:

That all this worll is come to ryght

That many a day so darke hath be

(k) A political prophecy, seven quatrains, beginning:

The beme schall bynde that berys the assise

(l) A prophecy in 300 lines with possible reference to the year 1450, beginning:

Primo die

The prophecy professed and j-pight

Of maiden Sibille and many mo

Merlion a man of mykell myght

That in his thadam was full throo

(m) An English prophecy, originally in about 300 lines, in nine-line stanzas ababbcbbc, beginning:

The sone shalle the fadre slo

A wounder diuision than es tweyne

On the grounde aganes the fadre to

hym to tray and also to teyne

Both in batle and be full fayne (?)

his sone to assail and fell in seight

Then oon shall come with myght and mayne

Apon a beste of blode and bayne

An hewy asse howeth on hight

(n) A political prophecy in three quatrains beginning:

Then a ded mon shall aryse and agrement make

(o) A long collection of Latin prophecies with some English verse scattered throughout, beginning:

Then all bestis and fowles shall maike thaym gaie

(p) The Fall of London, a political prophecy in two stanzas rime royal, in a miscellaneous commonplace book of pro-Lancastrian poetry:

This is the propheci that thai have in wales
When Walsh Scotes and Irish flittith thair fane
and cum vn to london by dovnes eke and dales
wyth cros baner pendent and thair pavilane
tovres cast dovn and castels and many a man
Than schall thar ther a post oute of Wales rise
that euer schall last an equite iustice

Old Edfrikke lawse that kyng excellent
he schall certes vp takc and thaym wele maynten
for ryghtwysnes and peass with hym hath merdent (?)
oued and made frends as yt schall be seen
that way schall be trod a fore that was grene
by twyx man and man for gode peass and rest
and sir lyonil the Mortimer schall have the best
                    the prise

(q) A fragment of an allegory or prophecy, perhaps with religious over-tones, in five lines:

Thre flourys in a nyght can spryng
From euery floure in a streme rennyng
A clerk among the flowrys bryng
Hem fond but noght durst say nor syng
For drede of the more

(r) A prophecy in two couplets, beginning:

Quhen sharpe and fair field are maried in fere

(s) A political prophecy, ending imperfectly after eleven quatrains, beginning:

When the pellican begynnyth to fle

(t) Bede's prophecy, 58 lines, occurs in a number of English prose and verse prophecies, all badly written; for example, in this text of [273] there are gaps as if the scribe could not even read his copy. This prophecy begins:

Who so wyll the cronycles grathely loke

Pageants and mummings, because they were composed for specific occasions, certainly form part of the corpus of Poems Dealing with Contemporary Conditions. However, they are more appropriately listed elsewhere.

Bibliography

TABLE OF ABBREVIATIONS

For abbreviations and shortened forms not appearing in this table consult the list of background books at the beginning of the appropriate chapter of the Bibliography.

AAGRP	Ausgaben und Abhandlungen aus dem Gebiete der romanischen Philologie
AC	Archaeologica Cantiana
Acad	Academy
AEB	Kölbing E, Altenglische Bibliothek, Heilbronn 1883–
AELeg 1875	Horstmann C, Altenglische Legenden, Paderborn 1875
AELeg 1878	Horstmann C, Sammlung altenglischer Legenden, Heilbronn 1878
AELeg 1881	Horstmann C, Altenglische Lekenden (Neue Fogle), Heilbronn 1881
AESpr	Mätzner E, Altenglische Sprachproben, Berlin 1867–
AF	Anglistische Forschungen
AfDA	Anzeiger für deutsches Alterthum
AHR	American Historical Review
AJ	Ampleforth Journal
AJA	American Journal of Archaeology
AJP	American Journal of Philology
ALb	Allgemeines Literaturblatt
ALg	Archivum linguisticum
Allen WAR	Allen H E, Writings Ascribed to Richard Rolle

	Hermit of Hampole and Materials for His Biography, MLA Monograph Series 3, N Y 1927
Angl	Anglia, Zeitschrift für englische Philologie
AnglA	Anglia Anzeiger
AnglB	Beiblatt zur Anglia
AN&Q	American Notes and Queries
Antiq	Antiquity
APS	Acta philologica scandinavica
AQ	American Quarterly
AR	Antioch Review
Arch	Archiv für das Studium der neueren Sprachen und Literaturen
Archaeol	Archaeologia
Ashton	Ashton J, Romances of Chivalry, London 1890
ASp	American Speech
ASR	American Scandinavian Review
ASt	Aberystwyth Studies
Athen	Athenaeum
BA	Books Abroad
BARB	Bulletin de l'Académie royale de Belgique
Baugh LHE	Baugh A C, The Middle English Period, in A Literary History of England, N Y 1948; 2nd edn 1967
BB	Bulletin of Bibliography
BBA	Bonner Beiträge zur Anglistik
BBCS	Bulletin of the Board of Celtic Studies (Univ of Wales)
BBGRP	Berliner Beiträge zur germanischen und romanischen Philologie
BBSIA	Bulletin bibliographique de la Société internationale arthurienne
Bennett OHEL	Bennett H S, Chaucer and the Fifteenth Century, Oxford 1947
Best BIP	Best R I, Bibliography of Irish Philology, 2 vols, Dublin 1913

BGDSL	Beiträge zur Geschichte der deutschen Sprache und Literatur
BHR	Bibliothèque d'humanisme et renaissance
BIHR	Bulletin of the Institute of Historical Research
Billings	Billings A H, A Guide to the Middle English Metrical Romances, N Y 1901
Blackf	Blackfriars
Bloomfield SDS	Bloomfield M W, The Seven Deadly Sins, Michigan State College of Agriculture and Applied Science Studies in Language and Literature, 1952
BNYPL	Bulletin of the New York Public Library
Böddeker AED	Böddeker K, Altenglische Dichtungen des MS Harl 2253, Berlin 1878
Bossuat MBLF	Bossuat R, Manuel bibliographique de la littérature française du moyen âge, Paris 1951; supplément Paris 1955; deuxième supplément Paris 1961 [the item numbers run consecutively through the supplement]
BPLQ	Boston Public Library Quarterly
BQR	Bodleian Quarterly Record (sometimes Review)
Brandl	Brandl A, Mittelenglische Literatur, in Paul's Grundriss der germanische Philologie, 1st edn, Strassburg 1893, $2^1.609$ ff, Index $2^2.345$
Brown ELxiiiC	Brown C F, English Lyrics of the 13th Century, Oxford 1932
Brown Reg	Brown C, A Register of Middle English Religious and Didactic Verse, parts 1 and 2, Oxford (for the Bibliographical Society) 1916, 1920
Brown RLxivC	Brown C F, Religious Lyrics of the 14th Century, Oxford 1924
Brown RLxvC	Brown C F, Religious Lyrics of the 15th Century, Oxford 1939
Brown-Robbins	Brown C and R H Robbins, The Index of Middle English Verse, N Y 1943; see also Robbins-Cutler
Bryan-Dempster	Bryan W F and G Dempster, Sources and Ana-

	logues of Chaucer's Canterbury Tales, Chicago 1941
BrynMawrMon	Bryn Mawr College Monographs, Bryn Mawr 1905–
BSEP	Bonner Studien zur englischen Philologie
BUSE	Boston University Studies in English
CASP	Cambridge Antiquarian Society Publication
CBEL	Bateson F W, Cambridge Bibliography of English Literature, 5 vols, London and N Y 1941, 1957
CE	College English
CFMA	Les classiques français du moyen âge; collection de textes française et provençaux antérieurs a 1500, Paris 1910–
Chambers	Chambers E K, The Mediaeval Stage, 2 vols, Oxford 1903; rptd from corrected sheets 1925, 1948, 1954
Chambers OHEL	Chambers E K, English Literature at the Close of the Middle Ages, Oxford 1945
CHEL	Ward A W and A R Waller, The Cambridge History of English Literature, vols 1 and 2, Cambridge 1907, 1908
CHR	Catholic Historical Review
ChS	Publications of the Chaucer Society, London 1869–1924
Ch&Sidg	Chambers E K and F Sidgwick, Early English Lyrics, London 1907; numerous reprints
CJ	Classic Journal
CL	Comparative Literature
CMLR	Canadian Modern Language Review
Comper Spir Songs	Comper F M M, Spiritual Songs from English Manuscripts of Fourteenth to Sixteenth Centuries, London and N Y 1936
Conviv	Convivium
Courthope	Courthope W J, History of English Poetry, vol 1, London 1895
CP	Classical Philology
Craig HEL	Craig H, G K Anderson, L I Bredvold, J W Beach, History of English Literature, N Y 1950

Cross Mot Ind	Cross T P, Motif Index of Early Irish Literature, Bloomington Ind 1951
Crotch PEWC	Crotch W J B, The Prologues and Epilogues of William Caxton, EETS 176, London 1928
CUS	Columbia University Studies in English and in Comparative Literature, N Y 1899–
DA, DAI	Dissertation Abstracts, Dissertation Abstracts International
DANHSJ	Derbyshire Archaeological and Natural History Society Journal
de Julleville Hist	de Julleville L Petit, Histoire de la langue et de la littérature française, vols 1 and 2, Paris 1896–99
de Ricci Census	de Ricci S and W J Wilson, Census of Medieval and Renaissance Manuscripts in the United States of America and Canada, vols 1–3, N Y 1935, 1937, 1940
Dickins and Wilson	Dickins B and R M Wilson, Early Middle English Texts, Cambridge 1950
DLz	Deutsche Literaturzeitung
DNB	Stephen L and S Lee, Dictionary of National Biography, N Y and London 1885–1900, and supplements
DomS	Dominican Studies: An Annual Review, Blackfriars Publications, London
DUJ	Durham University Journal
EA	Études anglaises
EBEP	Erlanger Beiträge zur englischen Philologie
EC	Essays in Criticism
EETS	Publications of the Early English Text Society (Original Series), 1864–
EETSES	Publications of the Early English Text Society (Extra Series), 1867–
EG	Études germaniques
EGS	English and Germanic Studies
EHR	English Historical Review
EIE, EIA	English Institute Essays (Annual), N Y 1939–

EJ	English Journal
ELH	Journal of English Literary History
Ellis EEP	Ellis G, Specimens of Early English Poetry, 3 vols, London 1811
Ellis Spec	Ellis G, Specimens of Early English Metrical Romances, 3 vols, London 1805; rvsd Halliwell, 1 vol, Bohn edn 1848 (latter edn referred to, unless otherwise indicated)
Enc Brit	Encyclopaedia Britannica, 11th edn
Engl	English: The Magazine of the English Association
E&S	Essays and Studies by Members of the English Association, Oxford 1910–
E&S Brown	Essays and Studies in Honor of Carleton Brown, N Y 1940
Esdaile ETPR	Esdaile A, A List of English Tales and Prose Romances Printed before 1740, London 1912
EStn	Englische Studien
ESts	English Studies
ETB	Hoops J, Englische Textbibliothek, 21 vols, Heidelberg 1898–1935?
Expl	Explicator
Farrar-Evans	Farrar C P and A P Evans, Bibliography of English Translations from Medieval Sources, N Y 1946
FFC	Folklore Fellows Communications
FFK	Forschungen und Fortschritte: Korrespondenzblatt der deutschen Wissenschaft und Technik
Flügel NL	Flügel E, Neuenglisches Lesebuch, Halle 1895
FQ	French Quarterly
FR	French Review
FS	French Studies
Furnivall EEP	Furnivall F J, Early English Poems and Lives of Saints, Berlin 1862 (Transactions of Philological Society of London 1858)
Gautier Bibl	Gautier L, Bibliographie des chansons de geste, Paris 1897

Gayley	Gayley C M, Plays of Our Forefathers, N Y 1907
GdW	Gesamtkatalog der Wiegendrucke, Leipzig 1925–
Germ	Germania
Gerould S Leg	Gerould G H, Saints' Legends, Boston 1916
GGA	Göttingische gelehrte Anzeiger
GJ	Gutenberg Jahrbuch
GQ	German Quarterly
GR	Germanic Review
Greene E E Carols	Greene R L, The Early English Carols, Oxford 1935
GRM	Germanisch-Romanische Monatsschrift
Gröber	Gröber G, Grundriss der romanischen Philologie, Strassburg 1888–1902, new issue 1897–1906, 2nd edn 1904– (vol 2^1 1902 referred to, unless otherwise indicated)
Gröber-Hofer	Hofer S, Geschichte der mittelfranzösischen Literatur, 2 vols, 2nd edn, Berlin and Leipzig 1933–37
Hall Selections	Hall J, Selections from Early Middle English 1130–1250, 2 parts, Oxford 1920
Hammond	Hammond E P, Chaucer: A Bibliographical Manual, N Y 1908
Hartshorne AMT	Hartshorne C H, Ancient Metrical Tales, London 1829
Hazlitt Rem	Hazlitt W C, Remains of the Early Popular Poetry of England, 4 vols, London 1864–66
Herbert	Herbert J A, Catalogue of Romances in the Department of MSS of the British Museum, London 1910 (vol 3 of Ward's Catalogue)
Hermes	Hermes
Hibbard Med Rom	Hibbard L, Medieval Romance in England, N Y 1924
HINL	History of Ideas News Letter
Hisp	Hispania
HispR	Hispanic Review
HJ	Hibbert Journal

HLB	Harvard Library Bulletin
HLF	Histoire littéraire de la France, Paris 1733–; new edn 1865–
HLQ	Huntington Library Quarterly
Holmes CBFL	Cabeen D C, Critical Bibliography of French Literature, vol 1 (the Medieval Period), ed U T Holmes jr, Syracuse N Y 1949
HSCL	Harvard Studies in Comparative Literature
HSNPL	Harvard Studies and Notes in Philology and Literature, Boston 1892–
HudR	Hudson Review
IER	Irish Ecclesiastical Review
IS	Italian Studies
Isis	Isis
Ital	Italica
JAAC	Journal of Aesthetics and Art Criticism
JBL	Journal of Biblical Literature
JCS	Journal of Celtic Studies
JEGGP	Jahresbericht über die Erscheinungen auf dem Gebiete der germanischen Philologie
JEGP	Journal of English and Germanic Philology
JEH	Journal of Ecclesiastical History
JfRESL	Jahrbuch für romanische und englische Sprache und Literatur
JGP	Journal of Germanic Philology
JHI	Journal of the History of Ideas
JPhilol	Journal of Philology
JPhilos	Journal of Philosophy
JRLB	Bulletin of the John Rylands Library, Manchester
Kane	Kane G, Middle English Literature: A Critical Study of the Romances, the Religious Lyrics, Piers Plowman, London 1951
Kennedy BWEL	Kennedy A G, A Bibliography of Writings on the English Language from the Beginning of Printing to the End of 1922, Cambridge Mass and New Haven 1927

Kild Ged	Heuser W, Die Kildare-Gedichte, Bonn 1904 (BBA 14)
Körting	Körting G, Grundriss der Geschichte der englischen Literatur von ihren Anfängen bis zur Gegenwart, 5th edn, Münster 1910
KR	Kenyon Review
Krit Jahresber	Vollmüller K, Kritischer Jahresbericht über die Fortschritte der romanischen Philologie, München und Leipzig 1892–1915 (Zweiter Teil, 13 vols in 12)
KSEP	Kieler Studien zur englischen Philologie
Lang	Language
LB	Leuvensche Bijdragen, Periodical for Modern Philology
LC	Library Chronicle
Leeds SE	Leeds Studies in English and Kindred Languages, School of English Literature in the University of Leeds
Legouis	Legouis E, Chaucer, Engl trans by Lailvoix, London 1913
Legouis HEL	Legouis E and L Cazamian, trans H D Irvine and W D MacInnes, A History of English Literature, new edn, N Y 1929
LfGRP	Literaturblatt für germanische und romanische Philologie
Libr	The Library
Litteris	Litteris: An International Critical Review of the Humanities, New Society of Letters
LMS	London Medieval Studies
Loomis ALMA	Loomis R S, Arthurian Literature in the Middle Ages, A Collaborative History, Oxford 1959
LP	Literature and Psychology
LQ	Library Quarterly
Lund SE	Lund Studies in English
LZ	Literarisches Zentralblatt
MÆ	Medium ævum
Manly CT	Manly J M, Canterbury Tales by Geoffrey Chaucer,

	with an Introduction, Notes, and a Glossary, N Y 1928
Manly Spec	Manly J M, Specimens of the Pre-Shakespearean Drama, vol 1, 2nd edn, Boston 1900
Manly & Rickert	Manly J M and E Rickert, The Text of the Canterbury Tales Studied on the Basis of All Known Manuscripts, 8 vols, Chicago 1940
Manual	A Manual of the Writings in Middle English 1050–1500, New Haven 1967– (vols 1 and 2, ed J B Severs; vols 3–5, ed A E Hartung)
MBREP	Münchener Beiträge zur romanischen und englischen Philologie
MED	Kurath H and S M Kuhn, Middle English Dictionary, Ann Arbor 1952– (M S Ogden, C E Palmer, and R L McKelvey, Bibliography [of ME texts], 1954, p 15)
MH	Medievalia et humanistica
MHRA	MHRA, Bulletin of the Modern Humanities Research Association
Migne PL	Migne, Pastrologiae Latinae cursus completus
Minor Poems	Skeat W W, Chaucer: The Minor Poems, 2nd edn, Oxford 1896
MKAW	Mededeelingen van de Koninklijke akademie van wetenschappen, afdeling letterkunde
ML	Music and Letters
MLF	Modern Language Forum
MLJ	Modern Language Journal
MLN	Modern Language Notes
MLQ (Lon)	Modern Language Quarterly (London)
MLQ (Wash)	Modern Language Quarterly (Seattle, Washington)
MLR	Modern Language Review
Monat	Monatschefte
Moore Meech and Whitehall	Moore S, S B Meech and H Whitehall, Middle English Dialect Characteristics and Dialect Boundaries, University of Michigan Essays and Studies in Language and Literature 13, Ann Arbor 1935

Morley	Morley H, English Writers, vols 3–6, London 1890
Morris Spec	Morris R (ed part 1), R Morris and W W Skeat (ed part 2), Specimens of Early English, part 1, 2nd edn, Oxford 1887; part 2, 4th edn, Oxford 1898
MP	Modern Philology
MS	Mediaeval Studies
MSEP	Marburger Studien zur englischen Philologie, 13 vols, Marburg 1901–11
MUPES	Manchester University Publications, English Series
NA	Neuer Anzeiger
Neophil	Neophilologus, A Modern Language Quarterly
NEQ	New England Quarterly
NLB	Newberry Library Bulletin
NM	Neuphilologische Mitteilungen: Bulletin de la Société neophilologique de Helsinki
NMQ	New Mexico Quarterly
NNAC	Norfolk and Norwich Archaeological Society
N&Q	Notes and Queries
NRFH	Nueva revista de filologia hispánica
NS	Die neueren Sprachen, Zeitschrift für de neusprachlichen Unterrecht
O'Dell CLPF	O'Dell S, A Chronological List of Prose Fiction in English Printed in England and Other Countries, Cambridge Mass 1954
OMETexts	Morsbach L and F Holthausen, Old and Middle English Texts, 11 vols, Heidelberg 1901–26
Oxf Ch	Skeat W W, The Works of Geoffrey Chaucer, Oxford 1894–1900 (6 vols; extra 7th vol of Chaucerian Poems)
Palaes	Palaestra, Untersuchungen und Texte
PAPS	Proceedings of the American Philosophical Society
Paris Litt Franç	Paris G P B, La littérature française au moyen âge, 4th edn, Paris 1909
Patterson	Patterson F A, The Middle English Penitential Lyric, N Y 1911
Paul Grundriss	Paul H, Grundriss der germanischen Philologie,

	3 vols, 1st edn, Strassburg 1891–1900; 2nd edn 1900–
PBBeitr	Paul H and W Braune, Beiträge zur Geschichte der deutschen Sprache und Literatur, Halle 1874–
PBSA	Papers of the Bibliographical Society of America
PBSUV	Papers of the Bibliographical Society, Univ of Virginia
PFMS	Furnivall F J and J W Hales, The Percy Folio MS, 4 vols, London 1867–69; re-ed I Gollancz, 4 vols, London 1905–10 (the earlier edn is referred to, unless otherwise indicated)
Philo	Philologus
PMLA	Publications of the Modern Language Association of America
PMRS	Progress of Medieval and Renaissance Studies in the United States and Canada
Pollard 15CPV	Pollard A W, Fifteenth Century Prose and Verse, Westminster 1903
PP	Past and Present
PPR	Philosophy and Phenomenological Research
PPS	Publications of the Percy Society
PQ	Philological Quarterly
PR	Partisan Review
PS	Pacific Spectator
PSTS	Publications of the Scottish Text Society, Edinburgh 1884–
PULC	Princeton University Library Chronicle
QF	Quellen und Forschungen zur Sprach- und Culturgeschichte der germanischen Völker
QQ	Queen's Quarterly
RAA	Revue anglo-américaine
RadMon	Radcliffe College Monographs, Boston 1891–
RB	Revue britannique
RC	Revue celtique
RCHL	Revue critique d'histoire et de littérature
REH	The Review of Ecclesiastical History

Rel Ant	Wright T and J O Halliwell, Reliquiae antiquae, 2 vols, London 1845
Ren	Renascence
Renwick-Orton	Renwick W L and H Orton, The Beginnings of English Literature to Skelton 1509, London 1939; rvsd edn 1952
RES	Review of English Studies
RevP	Revue de philologie
RF	Romanische Forschungen
RFE	Revista de filología espanola
RFH	Revista de filología hispánica
RG	Revue germanique
RHL	Revue d'histoire littéraire de la France
Rickert RofFr, RofL	Rickert E, Early English Romances in Verse: Romances of Friendship (vol 1), Romances of Love (vol 2), London 1908
Ringler BEV	Ringler W, A Bibliography and First-Line Index of English Verse Printed through 1500, PBSA 49.153
Ritson AEMR	Ritson J, Ancient English Metrical Romances, 3 vols, London 1802, rvsd E Goldsmid, Edinburg 1884 (earlier edn referred to, unless otherwise indicated)
Ritson APP	Ritson J, Ancient Popular Poetry, 2nd edn, London 1833.
Ritson AS	Ritson J, Ancient Songs from the Time of Henry III, 2 vols, London 1790, new edn 1829; rvsd W C Hazlitt, Ancient Songs and Ballads, 1 vol, London 1877 (last edn referred to, unless otherwise indicated)
RLC	Revue de littérature comparée
RLR	Revue des langues romanes
RN	Renaissance News
Robbins-Cutler	Supplement to Brown-Robbins, Lexington Ky 1965
Robbins-HP	Robbins R H, Secular Lyrics of the 14th and 15th Centuries, Oxford 1959

Robbins SL	Robbins R H, Secular Lyrics of the 14th and 15th Centuries, 2nd edn, Oxford 1955
Robson	Robson J, Three Early English Metrical Romances, London (Camden Society) 1842
Rolls Series	Rerum Britannicarum medii aevi scriptores, Published by Authority of the Lords Commissioners of Her Majesty's Treasury, under the Direction of the Master of the Rolls, London 1857–91
Rom	Romania
RomP	Romance Philology
RomR	Romanic Review
Root	Root R K, The Poetry of Chaucer, Boston 1906
Rot	Rotulus, A Bulletin for MS Collectors
Roxb Club	Publications of the Roxburghe Club, London 1814–
RSLC	Record Society of Lancashire and Cheshire
RUL	Revue de l'Université laval
SA	The Scottish Antiquary, or Northern Notes and Queries
SAQ	South Atlantic Quarterly
SATF	Publications de la Société des anciens textes français, Paris 1875–
SB	Studies in Bibliography: Papers of the Bibliographical Society of the University of Virginia
SBB	Studies in Bibliography and Booklore
ScanSt	Scandinavian Studies
Schipper	Schipper J, Englische Metrik, 2 vols, Bonn 1881–88
Schofield	Schofield W H, English Literature from the Norman Conquest to Chaucer, N Y 1906
SciS	Science and Society
Scrut	Scrutiny
SE	Studies in English
SEER	Slavonic and East European Review
SEP	Studien zur englischen Philologie
ShJ	Jahrbuch der deutschen Shakespeare-Gesellschaft
SHR	Scottish Historical Review

Skeat Spec	Skeat W W, Specimens of English Literature 1394–1579, 6th edn, Oxford
SL	Studies in Linguistics
SN	Studia neophilologica: A Journal of Germanic and Romanic Philology
SP	Studies in Philology
Spec	Speculum: A Journal of Mediaeval Studies
SR	Sewanee Review
SRL	Saturday Review of Literature
SSL	Studies in Scottish Literature
STC	Pollard A W and G R Redgrave, A Short-Title Catalogue of Books Printed in England, Scotland, and Ireland and of English Books Printed Abroad 1475–1640, London 1926
StVL	Studien zur vergleichenden Literaturgeschichte
Summary Cat	Madan F and H H E Craster, A Summary Catalogue of Western Manuscripts Which Have Not Hitherto Been Catalogued in the Quarto Series, Oxford 1895–1953
SUVSL	Skriften utgivna av Vetenskaps-societeten i Lund
SWR	Southwest Review
Sym	Symposium
Ten Brink	Ten Brink B A K, Early English Literature, English Literature, trans Kennedy et al, vol 1, vol 2 (parts 1–2), London and N Y 1887–92 (referred to as vols 1–3)
Texas SE	Texas Studies in English
Thompson Mot Ind	Thompson S, Motif Index of Folk-Literature, 6 vols, Helsinki 1932–36
Thoms	Thomas W J, A Collection of Early Prose Romances, London 1828; part ed Morley, Carlsbrooke Library, whole rvsd edn, London (Routledge); new edn, Edinburgh 1904
TLCAS	Transactions of Lancashire and Cheshire Antiquarian Society

TLS	[London] Times Literary Supplement
TNTL	Tijdschrift voor nederlandse taal- en letterkunde
TPSL	Transactions of the Philological Society of London
Trad	Traditio, Studies in Ancient and Medieval History, Thought, and Religion
TRSL	Transactions of the Royal Society of Literature
TTL	Tijdschrift voor taal en letteren
Tucker-Benham	Tucker L L and A R Benham, A Bibliography of Fifteenth-Century Literature, Seattle 1928
UKCR	University of Kansas City Review
UQ	Ukrainian Quarterly
Utley CR	Utley F L, The Crooked Rib: An Analytical Index to the Argument about Women in English and Scots Literature to the End of the Year 1568, Columbus O 1944
UTM	University of Toronto Monthly
UTQ	University of Toronto Quarterly
VMKVA	Verslagen en mededeelingen der Koninklijke vlaamsche academie
VQR	Virginia Quarterly Review
Ward	Ward H L D, Catalogue of Romances in the Department of MSS of the British Museum, 2 vols, London 1883–93 (see Herbert for vol 3)
Ward Hist	Ward A W, A History of English Dramatic Literature to the Death of Queen Anne, 3 vols, new edn, London 1899
Wehrle	Wehrle W O, The Macaronic Hymn Tradition in Medieval English Literature, Washington 1933
WBEP	Wiener Beiträge zur englischen Philologie
Weber MR	Weber H W, Metrical Romances of the 13th, 14th, and 15th Centuries, 3 vols, Edinburgh 1810
Wells	Wells J E, A Manual of the Writings in Middle English 1050–1400, New Haven 1916 (Supplements 1–9, 1919–1951)
Wessex	Wessex

WHR	Western Humanities Review
Wilson EMEL	Wilson R M, Early Middle English Literature, London 1939
WMQ	William and Mary Quarterly
WR	Western Review
Wright AnecLit	Wright T, Anecdota literaria, London 1844
Wright PPS	Wright T, Political Poems and Songs from the Accession of Edward III to That of Richard III, 2 vols, London (Rolls Series) 1859–61
Wright PS	Wright T, Political Songs of England from the Reign of John to That of Edward III, Camden Society, London 1839 (this edn referred to, unless otherwise indicated); 4 vols, rvsd, privately printed, Goldsmid, Edinburgh 1884
Wright SLP	Wright T, Specimens of Lyric Poetry Composed in England in the Reign of Edward I, Percy Society, 2 vols, London 1896
Wülcker	Wülcker R P, Geschichte der englischen Literatur, 2 vols, Leipzig 1896
YCGL	Yearbook of Comparative and General Literature
YFS	Yale French Studies, New Haven 1948–
Yksh Wr	Horstmann C, Yorkshire Writers, Library of Early English Writers, 2 vols, London 1895–96
YR	Yale Review
YSCS	Yorkshire Society for Celtic Studies
YSE	Yale Studies in English, N Y 1898–
YWES	Year's Work in English Studies
YWMLS	Year's Work in Modern Language Studies
ZfCP	Zeitschrift für celtische Philologie (Tübingen)
ZfDA	Zeitschrift für deutsches Alterthum und deutsche Litteratur
ZfDP	Zeitschrift für deutsche Philologie
ZfFSL	Zeitschrift für französische Sprache und Literatur
ZföG	Zeitschrift für die österreichischen Gymnasien
ZfRP	Zeitschrift für romanische Philologie

ZfVL   Zeitschrift für vergleichende Litteraturgeschichte,
                        Berlin

Other Commonly Used Abbreviations

ae	altenglische	AN	Anglo-Norman	OF	Old French
af	altfranzösische	c	copyright	ON	Old Norse
engl	englische	ca	circa	pt	part
f	für	crit	criticized by	re-ed	re-edited by
me	mittelenglische	f, ff	folio, folios	rptd	reprinted
u	und	ME	Middle English	rvsd	revised
z	zu	n d	no date	unptd	unprinted

XII. DRAMATIC PIECES

by

Anna J. Mill, Sheila Lindenbaum,
and Francis Lee Utley and Barry Ward

1. THE MIRACLE PLAYS AND MYSTERIES

by

Anna J. Mill

BACKGROUND BOOKS: The following important, frequently listed entries, here given full statement, are referred to in abbreviated form in the pages that follow. For abbreviations not appearing in this list, consult the general Table of Abbreviations.

Adams CPSD	Adams J Q, Chief Pre-Shakespearean Dramas, Cambridge Mass 1924
Baldwin EED	Baldwin T W, Earlier English Drama from Robin Hood to Everyman, N Y 1929 (American edn of Tickner EED, with additions)
Bates	Bates K L, The English Religious Drama, N Y and London 1893
Craig ERD	Craig H, English Religious Drama, Oxford 1955
Creizenach	Creizenach W M, Geschichte des neueren Dramas. Mittelalter und Frührenaissance. 2nd edn rvsd, Halle a S 1911
Davis N-CP	Davis N, Non-Cycle Plays and Fragments, EETS Suppl 1, London 1970
Eccles MP	Eccles M, The Macro Plays, EETS 262, London N Y and Toronto 1969

Greg	Greg W W, Bibliographical and Textual Problems of the English Miracle Cycles, rptd from The Library 3s 5, London 1914
Hardison CR&CD	Hardison O B, Christian Rite and Christian Drama in the Middle Ages, Baltimore 1965
Hemingway	Hemingway S B, English Nativity Plays, Edited with Introd and Notes, and Glossary, in YSE 38, N Y 1909
Klein	Klein J L, Geschichte des engl Drama's, 2 vols, Leipzig 1876 (vols 12, 13 of Geschichte des Drama's)
Kolve	Kolve V A, The Play Called Corpus Christi, London 1966
Pollard EMP	Pollard A W, English Miracle Plays, Moralities and Interludes, Oxford 1890; 8th rvsd edn 1927
Prosser	Prosser E, Drama and Religion in the English Mystery Plays: A Re-evaluation, Stanford Studies in Language and Literature 23
Stratman	Stratman C J, Bibliography of Medieval Drama, Berkeley and Los Angeles 1954
Tickner EED	Tickner F J, Earlier English Drama from Robin Hood to Everyman, London and Edinburgh 1926 etc.

GENERAL TREATMENTS OF MEDIEVAL DRAMA.

Alt H, Theater und Kirche, Berlin 1846.

Mone F J, Schauspiele des Mittelalters aus Handschriften herausgeben und erklärt, 2 vols, Karlsruhe 1846.

du Méril E, Origines latines du théâtre moderne, Paris 1849; reproduced in facsimile, Paris and Leipzig 1897.

Hase C A, Das geistliche Schauspiel des Mittelalters, Leipzig 1858; trans A W Jackson, Miracle Plays and Sacred Dramas, London 1880.

Klein J L, Geschichte des Drama's, Leipzig 1867–76, vols 4–13.

Petit de Julleville L, Les mystères, 2 vols, Paris 1880.

Prölss R, Geschichte des neueren Dramas, Leipzig 1880–83, 1.10.

D'Ancona A, Origini del teatro italiano, 2nd edn, Torina 1891.

Cloetta W, Beiträge zur Litteraturgeschichte des Mittelalters und der Renaissance, Halle 1890–92.

Pearson K, The Chances of Death, London and N Y 1897, 2.246 (The German Passion Play).

Heinzel R, Beschreibung des geistlichen Schauspiele im deutschen Mittelalter, Beiträge zur Ästhetik 4, Hamburg 1898.

Mantzius K, Skuespilkunstens historie middelalder og renaissance, København 1899; trans L von Cossel, A History of Theatrical Art, London 1903, vol 2.

Hastings C, Le théâtre français et anglais ses origines grecques et latines, Paris 1900; authorized trans F A Welby, The Theatre Its Development in France and England, London 1901.

Sepet M, Origines catholiques du théâtre moderne, Paris 1881–1901.

Chambers (crit P M[eyer], Rom 33.316; W L Phelps, MLN 19.207; G Sarrazin, AnglB 17.353; R C Bald, EStn 66.416).

Sepet M, Le drame religieux au moyen âge, Paris 1903.

Matthews B, The Mediaeval Drama, MP 1.71.

Manly J M, Literary Forms and the New Theory of the Origin of Species, MP 4.577.

Tunison J S, Dramatic Traditions of the Dark Ages, Chicago and London 1907 (crit H C Lancaster, MLN 23.254).

Creizenach.

Duriez G, Les apocryphes dans le drame religieux en Allemagne au moyen age, Mémoires et trauvaux publiés par des professeurs des facultés catholiques de Lille 10, 1914.

Whitmore C E, The Supernatural in Tragedy, Cambridge Mass 1915, p 113.

Rudwin M J, A Historical and Bibliographical Survey of the German Religious Drama, Pittsb 1924.

Coffman G R, A New Approach to Medieval Latin Drama, MP 22.239.

Cohen G, Le théatre en France au moyen âge, 2 vols, Paris 1928, 1931; rvsd 1948.

Cargill O, Drama and Liturgy, N Y 1930 (crit G Frank, MLN 46.62; G R Coffman, Spec 6.610; N C Brooks, JEGP 30.433; E Fischer, AnglB 43.293).

Nicoll A, Masks Mimes and Miracles Studies in the Popular Theatre, London and N Y 1931, p 135.

Kennard J S, The Italian Theatre from Its Beginnings to the Close of the Seventeenth Century, N Y 1932, vol 1, chaps 1, 2.

Dubech L, Histoire générale illustrée du théatre, Paris 1931–34, vols 2, 3¹.

Borcherdt H H, Das europäische Theater im Mittelalter und in der Renaissance, Leipzig 1935.

Hess H, Studien zum Mistere du Viel Testament, Frankfurt am Main 1936.

Stumpfl R, Kultspiele der Germanen als Ursprung des mittelalterlichen Dramas, Berlin 1936 (crit F E Sandbach, MLR 32.317; E Scheunemann, ZfDP 61.432; 62.95 [Stumpfl reply to Scheunemann, ZfDP 61.432]; N C Brooks, JEGP 37.300).

Hartl E, Das Drama des Mittelalters sein Wesen und sein Werden, Leipzig 1937, Introd.

Toschi P, Dal dramma liturgico alla rappresentazione sacra, Bibliotheca del Leonardo 17, Firenze 1940.

Thiry P, Le théâtre français au moyen âge, Bruxelles 1942.

Apollonio M, Storia del teatro italiano, 1 La drammaturgia medievale dramma sacro e mimo, 2nd edn, Firenze 1943.

Dürrer A, Forschungswende des mittelalterlichen Schauspiels, ZfDP 68.24.

Kernodle G R, From Art to Theatre Form and Convention in the Renaissance, Chicago 1944 (crit G F Reynolds, JEGP 44.299).

Gardiner H C, Mysteries' End An Investigation of the Last Days of the Medieval Religious Stage, YSE 103 (crit below under ENGLISH MYSTERIES, General Treatments).

Nicoll A, The Development of the Theatre A Study of Theatrical Art from the Beginnings to the Present Day, 3rd edn rvsd, N Y [1946] and London 1948, p 60.

Rossiter A P, English Drama from Early Times to the Elizabethans Its Background Origins and Developments, London N Y etc 1950.

D'Amico S, Storia del teatro drammatico, 4 vols, Milan 1950, 1.219.

Cohen G, Melanges d'histoire du théâtre du moyen-âge et de la renaissance, Offerts à Gustave Cohen . . . par ses collègues ses élèves et ses amis, Paris 1950.

Nagler A M, Sources of Theatrical History, N Y 1952.

Frank G, The Medieval French Drama, Oxford 1954 (crit J H Watkins, MÆ 24.62).

Hunningher B, The Origin of the Theater, The Hague 1955 (crit A Williams, Spec 32.564).

Craig H, English Religious Drama of the Middle Ages, Oxford 1955 (crit YWES 36.75; R R Rylands, Church Quarterly Rev 156.432; TLS Jan 20 1956, p 36; A Williams, Spec 31.348; M W Bloomfield, MP 54.129; A P Berthet, EA 9.344; A C Baugh, MLN 72.207; T Fry, American Benedictine Rev 8.74; F M Salter, JEGP 56.253; A Brown, RES ns 8.426; A C Cawley, ESts 39.76; D Hoenigher, UTQ 27.226).

Hardison CR&CD (crit G Frank, RomR 57.285; C Gauvin, EA 19.70; A Holaday, JEGP 65.712; A S Downer, SN 38.363; M Schlauch, Zeitschr f Anglistik u Amerikanistik 15.81; J Stevens, MÆ 36.289; G W G Wickham, RES ns 18.300).

Mimes. Reich H, Der Mimus, Berlin 1903, 2.744.

Allen P S, The Medieval Mimes, MP 7.329; 8.1.

Allen P S and H M Jones, The Romanesque

Lyric, Chapel Hill N C 1928, p 250.

Nicoll A, Masks Mimes and Miracles, pp 135, 150.

Ogilvy J D A, Mimi Scurrae Histriones Entertainers of the Early Middle Ages, Spec 38.603.

Theatres. Loomis R S, Some Evidences for Secular Theatres in the Twelfth and Thirteenth Centuries, Theatre Annual 1945, p 33; Were there Theatres in the Twelfth and Thirteenth Centuries? Spec 20.92 (with commentary by G Cohen).

Bigongiari D, Were there Theaters in the Twelfth and Thirteenth Centuries? RomR 37.201.

Marshall M, Theatre in the Middle Ages Evidence from Dictionaries and Glosses, Sym 4.1, 366.

Nelson A H, Early Pictorial Analogues of Medieval Theatre-in-the-Round, Research Opportunities in Renaissance Drama (medieval suppl) 12.93.

Staging, etc. Brandstetter R, Die Technik der luzerner Heiligenspiele, Arch 75.383.

Endepols H J E, Het decoratief en de opvoering van het middelnederlandsche toneelstukken, Amsterdam 1903.

Cohen G, Histoire de la mise en scène dans le théâtre religieux français du moyen âge, Paris 1906; rvsd edn 1951; Le livre de conduite du régisseur et compte des dépenses pour le Mystère de la Passion joué à Mons en 1501, Publications de la Faculté des Lettres de l'Université de Strasbourg 23, Paris 1925.

Müller W, Der schauspielerische Stil im Passionspiel des Mittelalters, Leipzig 1927.

Nicoll A, Masks Mimes and Miracles, p 187; The Development of the Theatre, p 64.

Frank G, Popular Iconography of the Passion, PMLA 46.333 (from Vatican Codex Reg 473).

Galante Garrone V, L'apparato scenico del dramma sacro in Italia, Torino 1935.

Fischel O, Art and the Theatre, Burlington Magazine 66.4, 54.

Hildburgh W L, English Alabaster Carvings as Records of the Medieval Religious Drama, Archaeol 93.51; rptd for Soc of Antiquaries of London, Oxford 1949 (crit A S Tavender, Spec 25.571).

Michael W F, The Staging of the Bozen Passion Play, GR 25.178.

Sadron P, Notes sur l'organistation des représentations théâtrales en France au moyen âge, in Mélanges d'histoire . . . offerts à Gustave Cohen, Paris 1950, p 205.

Anderson M D, Drama and Imagery in English Medieval Churches, Cambridge 1963 (crit TLS Feb 27 1964, p 176; W O Hassall, MÆ 33.241).

Schmitt N C, Was There a Medieval Theatre in the Round? Theatre Notebook 23.130; 24.18.

Other Problems. Haslinghuis E J, De Duivel in het Drama der Middeleeuwen, Leyden 1912.

Henshaw M, The Attitude of the Church toward the Stage to the End of the Middle Ages, MH 7.3.

Boughner D C, The Braggart in Renaissance Comedy A Study in Comparative Drama from Aristophanes to Shakespeare, Minneapolis and London 1954.

Michael W F, Problems in Editing Medieval Drama, GR 24.108.

Wolff E, Die Terminologie des mittelalterlichen Dramas in bedeutungsgeschichtlicher Sicht, Angl 78.1.

General Bibliographies. Stoddard F H, References for Students of Miracle Plays and Mysteries, Univ of Calif Libr Bulletin 8, Berkeley 1887.

Chambers, 1.xiii; 2.1, 68.

Klein D, A Contribution to a Bibliography of the Medieval Drama, MLN 20.202 (additions to Stoddard and Chambers).

Gamble W B, The Development of Scenic Art and Stage Machinery, A List of References in the N Y Public Libr, N Y 1920, p 12.

CBEL, 1.274; 5.156.

Farrar-Evans, index under Mystery.

Holmes CBFL, 1.179.

Baldensperger F and W P Friedrich, Bibliography of Comparative Literature, Chapel Hill N C 1950, p 189.

Henshaw M, A Survey of Studies in Medieval Drama, 1933–50, PMRS 21.7; rptd privately 1951.

Bossuat MBLF (and 2nd suppl), pt 1, chap 9; pt 2, chap 12.

Mummendey R, Language and Literature of the Anglo-Saxon Nations as Presented in German Doctoral Dissertations 1885–1950, Biblio Soc of Virginia, 1954.

Stratman C J, Bibliography of Medieval Drama, Berkeley and Los Angeles 1954 (crit M R L de Malkiel, RomP 9.470; T W Baldwin, JEGP 54.405; E Francheschini, Aevum 29.286; M H Marshall, Spec 34.140).

Craig ERD, p 390.

LITURGICAL DRAMA.

General Treatments. Magnin C, Les origines du théâtre moderne ou histoire du génie dramatique depuis le 1er jusqu'au XVIe siècle, Paris 1838, l.iii, xxiii (see Chambers, l.xxx, under Magnin).

du Méril E, Origines latines du théâtre moderne, Paris 1849, 1897.

Schönbach A, Über die Marienklagen ein Beitrag zur Geschichte der geistlichen Dichtung in Deutschland, Graz 1874.

Sepet M, Les prophètes du Christ étude sur les origines du théâtre au moyen âge, Paris 1878 (rptd from Bibl de L'Ecole des Chartes 28, 29, 38); Le drame chrétien au moyen âge, Paris 1878; Origines catholiques du théâtre moderne Les drames liturgiques, Paris 1881, p 3.

Hartmann K A M, Über das altspanische Dreikönigsspiel, Bautzen 1879.

Milchsack G, Die Oster-und Passionsspiele Literarische Untersuchengen ueber den Ursprung und die Entwickelung derselben bis zum siebenzehnten Jahrhundert vornemlich in Deutschland . . . 1 Die Lateinischen Oesterfeiern, Wolfenbüttel 1880.

Maskell W, The Ancient Liturgy of the Church of England According to the Uses of Sarum York Hereford and Bangor and the Roman Liturgy Arranged in Parallel Columns with Pref and Notes, 3rd edn, Oxford 1882.

Reiners A, Die Tropen-Prosen-und Präfations-Gesänge des feierlichen Hochamtes im Mittelalter, Luxembourg 1884, Introd.

Gautier L, Histoire de la poésie liturgique au moyen âge les tropes, Paris 1886.

Lange C, Die lateinischen Osterfeiern Untersuchengen über den Ursprung und die Entwickelung der liturgisch-dramatischen Auferstehungsfeier . . . , München 1887.

Froning R, Das Drama des Mittelalters, Stuttgart [1891].

Davidson C, Studies in the English Mystery Plays, New Haven Conn 1892 (also in Trans of the Connecticut Acad of Arts and Sciences 9.130).

Köppen W, Beiträge zur Geschichte der deutschen Weihnachtsspiele, Paderborn 1893, p 9.

Feasey H J, Ancient English Holy Week Ceremonial, London 1897, p 129.

Frere W H, The Use of Sarum, 2 vols, Cambridge 1898–1901.

Hastings C, Le théâtre français, 1900, p 103 (see above under GENERAL TREATMENTS OF MEDIEVAL DRAMA).

Butler P, A Note on the Origin of the Liturgical Drama, in An English Miscellany Presented to Dr Furnivall, Oxford 1901, p 46.

Brooks N C, The Lamentations of Mary in the Frankfurt Group of Passion Plays, JEGP 3.415.

Wagner P, Origine et développement du chant liturgique jusqu'à la fin du moyen âge, Tournai 1904 (trans from German by l'Abbé Bour).

Anz H, Die lateinischen Magierspiele Untersuchengen und Texte zur Vorgeschichte des deutschen Weihnachtsspiele, Leipzig 1905.

Young K, The Harrowing of Hell in Liturgical Drama, Trans Wisconsin Acad of Sciences Arts and Letters 16².889; Observations on the Origin of the Mediaeval Passion-Play, PMLA 25.309; Officium Pastorum A Study of the Dramatic Developments within the Liturgy of Christmas, Trans Wisconsin Acad of Sciences Arts and Letters 17¹.299; La procession des Trois Rois at Besançon, RomR 4.76; The Origin of the Easter Play, PMLA 29.1; The Poema Biblicum of Onulphus, PMLA 30.25 (rejects du Méril's claim for liturgical drama status); Ordo Rachelis, Univ of Wisconsin Stud in Lang and Lit 4; The Dramatic Associations of the Easter Sepulchre, Univ of Wisconsin Stud in Lang and Lit 10 (crit A Greebe, Museum 33.214); Ordo Prophetarum, Trans Wisconsin Acad of Sciences Arts and Letters 20.1; The Home of the Easter Play, Spec 1.71; Dramatic Ceremonies of the Feast of the Purification, Spec 5.97. (See also Young, The Drama of the Medieval Church, below.)

Sondheimer I, Die Herodes-Partien im lateinischen liturgischen Drama und in den französischen Mysterien, Halle a S 1912.

Craig H, The Origin of the Old Testament Plays, MP 10.473; The Origin of the Passion Play Matters of Theory as Well as Fact, Univ of Missouri Stud 21.83; Craig ERD, p 48.

Kretzmann P E, A Few Notes on The Harrowing of Hell, MP 13.49; The Liturgical Element in the Earliest Forms of the Medieval Drama, Univ of Minneapolis Stud in Lang and Lit 4 (crit N C Brooks, JEGP 16.609; B W Downs, MLR 13.491).

Jenney A M, A Further Word as to the Origin of the Old Testament Plays, MP 13.59.

Flood W H Grattan, Irish Origin of the Officium Pastorum, Month 138.545; The Irish Origin of the Easter Play, Month 141.349.

Klapper J, Der Ursprung der lateinischen Osterfeiern, ZfDP 50.46 (Jerusalem origin; challenged by K Young, Spec 1.71).

Bartholomaeis V de, Le origini della poesia drammatica italiana, Bologna 1924.

Muller H F, Pre-history of the Mediaeval Drama The Antecedents of the Tropes and the Conditions of Their Appearance, ZfRP 44.544.

Schwietering J, Über den liturgischen Ursprung des mittelalterlichen geistlichen Spiels, ZfDA 62.1.

Mâle E, L'Art religieux du XIIe siècle en France, 3rd edn, Paris 1928, p 121.

Cohen G, Le théâtre en France au moyen âge, Paris 1928, 1.9.

Brinkmann H, Zum Ursprung des liturgischen Spieles, Bonn 1929.

Cargill O, Drama and Liturgy, N Y 1930 (crit G Frank, MLN 46.62; G R Coffman, Spec 6.610; N C Brooks, JEGP 30.433; E Fischer, AnglB 43.293).

Young K, The Drama of the Medieval Church, 2 vols, Oxford 1933 (crit TLS July 20 1933, p 485; K Hammerle, DLz 54.2330; E K Chambers, EHR 49.108; H S Bennett, RES 10.460; N C Brooks, JEGP 33.286; G R Coffman, Spec 9.109; G Frank, MLN 49.112; J M Manly, MP 31.307; A W Reed, MLR 30.222; W H Shewring, Dublin Rev 195.280). See Young, above, for separate studies antedating 1933.

Knoll F O, Die Rolle der Maria Magdalena im geistlichen Spiel des Mittelalters, Berlin and Leipzig 1934.

Wright J G, A Study of the Themes of the Resurrection in the Mediaeval French drama, Bryn Mawr Pa 1935.

Wright E A, The Dissemination of the Liturgical Drama in France, Bryn Mawr Pa 1936 (crit G R Coffman, MLN 53.233; L Cons, RomR 28.67).

Shull V, Clerical Drama in Lincoln Cathedral 1318–1561, PMLA 52.946.

Vito M S de, L'Origine del dramma liturgico, Bibliotheca della Rassegna 21, Milan 1938 (crit G Frank, RomR 30.69; K Young, MLN 54.299).

Toschi P, Dal dramma liturgico alla rappresentazione sacra, Bibliotheca del Leonardo 17, Firenze 1940, pp 45, 67.

Pascal R, On the Origins of the Liturgical Drama of the Middle Ages, MLR 36.369.

Marshall M, The Dramatic Tradition Established by the Liturgical Plays, PMLA 56.962; Aesthetic Values of the Liturgical Drama, EIE 1950, p 89.

Mahr A C, Relations of Passion Plays to St Ephrem the Syrian, Columbus Ohio 1942; The Cyprus Passion Cycle, Notre Dame Ind 1947, Introd.

Woerdeman J, The Source of the Easter Play, Orate Fratres 20.262.

Coucke A, Van liturgisch tot geestlijk drama. Bijdragen tot de kennis van het mideleeuws toneel, in Miscellanea J Gessler, Deurne Anvers 1948, 1.317.

Marichal R, Les drames liturgiques du Livre de la Trésorie d'Origny-Sainte-Benoîte, in Mélanges d'histoire . . . offerts à Gustave Cohen, Paris 1950, p 37.

Hunningher B, De liturgische oorsprong van het theater, MKAW ns 17.51; The Origin of the Theater, The Hague 1955, Introd, p 48.

Dunn E C, Lyrical Form and the Prophetic Principle in the Towneley Plays, MS 23.82 (defense of Sepet against Craig).

Hardison CR&CD, p 178.

Music. Liuzzi F, L'espressione musicale nel dramma liturgico, Studi Medievali 2¹.74.

Adler G, Handbuch der Musikgeschichte, Berlin 1930, 2.173 (Winchester Troper).

Waesberghe J S van, Muziek en drama in de middeleeuwen, Amsterdam [1942].

Smoldon W L, The Easter Sepulchre Music-Drama, Music and Letters 27.1; Liturgical Drama, in New Oxford Hist of Music, ed Dom Anselm Hughes, London N Y Toronto 1954, 2.175; The Music of the Medieval Church Drama, Musical Quart 48.476.

Staging, etc. Shull, PMLA 52.946.

Galante Garrone V, L'apparato scenico del dramma sacro in Italia, Torino 1935, p 3.

Rava A, Teatro medievale L'apparato scenico nella visita delle Marie al sepolchro, Roma 1939; Teatro medievale Lapparato scenico negli offici drammatici del tempo di Natale, Roma 1940.

Cohen G, Nativités et moralités liégeoises du moyen-âge, Mémoires de L'Académie Royale de Belgique 2s 12¹.129.

Easter Sepulchre. Heales A, Easter Sepulchres Their Origin Nature and History, Archaeol 42.263.

Feasey H P, The Easter Sepulchre, American Ecclesiastical Review 32.337, 468.

Gaaf W van der, Miracles and Mysteries in

South-East Yorkshire, EStn 36.228 (reply E Sorg, EStn 37.172; counterreply EStn 37.461).

Bonnell J K, The Easter sepulchrum in Its Relation to the Architecture of the High Altar, PMLA 31.664 (crit Brooks, The Sepulchre of Christ, p 26, see below; Young, JEGP 21.694).

Young K, The Dramatic Associations of the Easter Sepulchre, Univ of Wisconsin Stud in Lang and Lit 10 (crit Brooks, The Sepulchre of Christ, p 30, see below; G. Frank, MLN 37.62); The Drama of the Medieval Church, 2.507.

Brooks N C, The Sepulchre of Christ in Art and Liturgy with Special Reference to the Liturgic Drama, Univ of Illinois Stud in Lang and Lit 8² (crit Young, JEGP 21.692; G Frank, MLN 37.367; A Greebe, Museum 33.214); The Sepulchrum Christi and Its Ceremonies in Late Mediaeval and Modern Times, JEGP 27.147.

Corbin S, La déposition liturgique du Christ au Vendredi saint, Paris 1960, pp 94, 251 (crit I Pope, Spec 39.130).

Hardison CR&CD, p 178.

Liturgical Origins of Miracle Plays. Manly J M, Literary Forms and the New Theory of the Origin of Species, MP 4.577.

Coffman G R, A New Theory Concerning the Origin of the Miracle Play, Menasha Wisconsin 1914 (reply K Young, Concerning the Origin of the Miracle Play, in Manly Anniversary Stud in Lang and Lit, Chicago 1923, p 254); A Note Concerning the Cult of St Nicholas at Hildesheim, in Manly Anniversary Stud in Lang and Lit, p 269; A New Approach to Medieval Latin Drama, MP 22.239; The Miracle Play Notes and Queries, PQ 20.204; 21.249.

Young K, The Drama of the Medieval Church, 2.307, 487 (biblio).

Foulon C, La représentation et les sources du Jeu de Saint-Nicolas, in Mélanges d'histoire . . . offerts à Gustave Cohen, Paris 1950, p 55.

Liturgical Texts. Wright T, Early Mysteries and Other Latin Poems of the Twelfth and Thirteenth Centuries, London Paris Leipzig 1838.

Schmeller J A, Carmina Burana lateinische und deutsche . . . , Stuttgart 1847; rptd Breslau 1883 etc, pp 80 (Nativity), 95 (Passion).

du Méril E, Origines latines du théatre moderne, p 89.

Coussemaker E de, Drames liturgiques du moyen âge (texte et musique), Rennes 1860.

Milschsack G, Die Oster-und Passionsspiele. 1 Die lateinischen Osterferien, Wolfenbuettel 1880.

Reiners A, Die Tropen-Prosen-und Präfations-Gesänge des feierlichen Hochamtes im Mittelalter, Luxembourg 1884.

Lange C, Die lateinischen Osterferien, München 1887, p 38 (Quem quaeritis).

Logeman W S, De Consuetudine Monachorum [Cod.Cotton.Tib.A.III], Angl 13.426 (Quem quaeritis with Anglo-Saxon gloss).

Migne PL, 78.678, 769 (Quem quaeritis).

Gasté A, Les drames liturgiques de la Cathédrale de Rouen (contribution à l'histoire des origines du théâtre en France), Evreux 1893.

Frere W H, The Winchester Troper from MSS of the 10th and 11th Centuries, Henry Bradshaw Soc 8, London 1894 (crit C Blume, Analecta Hymnica 47.31).

Manly Spec, l.xix, xxii (Winchester and Dublin Quem quaeritis).

Linder A, Plainte de La Vierge en vieux vénitien texte critique précédé d'une introduction linguistique et littéraire, Upsala 1898.

Meyer W, Fragmenta Burana, Berlin 1901, pp 123, 126, 136.

Chambers, 2.306 (Regularis Concordia), 310 (Durham Sepulci.rum), 312 (Sarum Sepulchrum), 315 (Dublin Quem quaeritis).

Meyer P, Les trois Maries mystère liturgique de Reims, Rom 33.239.

Anz H, Die lateinischen Magierspiele, Leipzig 1905, p 140.

Blume C and G M Dreves, Analecta Hymnica 49.9 (Limoges Quem quaeritis).

Young K, A Contribution to the History of Liturgical Drama at Rouen, MP 6.201; Some Texts of Liturgical Plays, PMLA 24.294; Observations on the Origin of the Mediaeval Passion-Play, PMLA 25.344 (Depositio Dublin and Barking); A Liturgical Play of Joseph and His Brethren, MLN 26.33; A New Text of the Officium Stellae, MLN 27.68; A New Version of the Peregrinus, PMLA 34.114; Ordo Rachelis, Univ of Wisconsin Stud in Lang and Lit 4; The Dramatic Associations of the Easter Sepulchre, Univ of Wisconsin Stud in Lang and Lit 10.

Brooks N C, Neue lateinische Osterfeiern, ZfDA 50.297; Some New Texts of Liturgical Easter Plays, JEGP 8.463; Liturgical Easter Plays from Rheinau MS, JEGP 10.191; Osterfeiern aus bamberger und wolfenbüttler

Handschriften, ZfDA 55.52; Eine liturgisch-dramatische Himmelfahrtsfeier, ZfDA 62.91; A Rheinau Easter Play of the Late Sixteenth Century, JEGP 26.226.

Adams CPSD, p 1 (texts with trans).

Jeanroy A, Le théâtre religieux en France du xiᵉ au xiiiᵉ siècles, Paris 1924.

Pollard EMP 1927, pp 157, 162.

Hilka A and O Schumann, Carmina Burana, Heidelberg 1930, 2.54* (see below Young, 1.686 for notes on dramatic texts in MSS lat 4660 and 4660a).

Young K, The Drama of the Medieval Church, passim; and see Young above under LITURGICAL DRAMA, General Treatments.

Albrecht O E, Four Latin Plays of St Nicholas from the 12th Century Fleury Playbook, Phila 1935 (crit G R Coffman, Spec 11.521).

Rauhut F, Der Sponsus, RF 50.21.

Inguanez Dom Mauro, Un dramma della Passione del secolo xii, Miscellanea Cassinese 12 (1936).21; Il Quem quaeritis pasquale nei codici Cassinesi, Studi Medievali 14.142.

Hartl E, Das Drama des Mittelalters, Leipzig 1937; Das Benediktbeurer Passionsspiel Das St Galler Passionsspiel, Halle/Salle 1952.

Zucker A E, The Redentin Easter Play, N Y 1941 (trans from Low German; crit J M Clark, MLR 37.398; E H Sehrt, MLN 58.149; B R and G R Coffman, Journal of American Folk-Lore 56.228).

Bühler C F and C Selmer, The Melk Salbenkrämerspiel An Unpublished Middle High German Mercator Play, PMLA 63.21.

Jones C W, Medieval Literature in Translation, N Y London Toronto 1950, p 929 (Barking).

Stammler W, Kleine Schriften zur Literaturgeschichte des Mittelalters, Berlin 1953, p 260 (Marienklage).

Chambers, 2.1; Gayley, p 14; Creizenach, 1.43; Craig ERD, pp 19, 48.

For additional items see bibliographies in Chambers, 2.1; Young, 2.544; CBEL, 1.274; 5.156; Henshaw, PMRS, 21.7; Bossuat MBLF (and 2nd suppl), pt 1, chap 9; Stratman, pp 92, 326 (crit above under General Bibliographies). See also above under GENERAL TREATMENTS OF MEDIEVAL DRAMA and General Bibliographies.

ANGLO-NORMAN TRANSITION PLAYS.

a. Le Mystère D'Adam.
MS. Bibl de Tours 927 (late 12 cent).

Editions. Grass K, Das Adamsspiel Anglo-normannisches mysterium des XII Jahrhunderts, 3rd edn rvsd Halle a S 1928 (Romanische Bibliothek 6).

Studer P, Le Mystère d'Adam An Anglo-Norman Drama of the Twelfth Century, Manchester and London 1918; rptd 1928 (critical edn; crit T A Jenkins, MP 17.415).

Chamard H, Le Mystère d'Adam Drame religieux du XIIᵉ siècle, Paris 1925 (new text from Tours MS of first 590 lines, with modern French trans).

Aebischer P, Le Mystère d'Adam (Ordo representacionis Ade), Genève and Paris 1963.

Translations. Stone E N, Adam A Religious Play of the Twelfth Century Translated from the Norman French and Latin into English Verse, Univ of Wash Publ in Lang and Lit 4.159 (crit G R Coffman, Spec 2.351).

Barrow S F and W H Hulme, Antichrist and Adam Two Mediaeval Religious Dramas Translated into English, Western Reserve Univ Bull 28⁸ (crit Coffman, MLN 42.129).

Clark B H, World Drama . . . An Anthology, N Y and London 1933, 1.304 (based on Stone).

Kreymborg A, Poetic Drama, N Y 1941, p 180 (based on Stone).

Jones C W, Medieval Literature in Translation, N Y London and Toronto 1950, p 937.

Textual Problems, Staging, Literary Criticism. Axelsen A, Studie til en literær og sproglig vurdering af Jeu D'Adam, København 1920.

Monteverdi A, Sul testo del Mistero d'Adamo, Archivum romanicum 9.446.

Breuer H, Untersuchungen zum lateinisch-altfranzösischen Adamsspiel, ZfRP 51.625; 52.1.

Walberg E, Quelques aspects de la littérature anglo-normande, Paris 1936, p 75.

Urwin K, The Mystère d'Adam Two Problems, MLR 34.70.

Frank G, The Genesis and Staging of the Jeu D'Adam, PMLA 59.7; The Medieval French Drama, Oxford 1954, p 76.

Auerbach E, Mimesis The Representation of Reality in Western Literature, trans W R Trask, Princeton N J 1953, p 143.

Calin W C, Structural and Doctrinal Unity in the Jeu d'Adam, Neophil 46.249.

Legge M D, Anglo-Norman Literature and its Background, Oxford 1963, p 312.

Hardison CR&CD, Essay 7.

Stevens J, Dramatic Function of Music in Some Early Medieval Plays, in Studies in the Arts, Oxford 1968, p 32.

Chambers, 2.70, 80; Creizenach, 1.127; Craig ERD, pp 64, 67, 98.

For additional items see Holmes CBFL, p 181; Bossuat MBLF, p 363; Henshaw, PMRS, 21.24; Stratman, pp 144, 277.

b. Resurrection Play.

MSS. 1, BM Addit 45103, ff 214ᵃ–220ᵃ (late 13 cent); 2, Bibl Nat fr 902, ff 97ᵃ–98ᵈ (late 13 cent).

Descriptions of Canterbury (Penrose) MS. Flower R, A Canterbury Manuscript the Play of the Resurrection from a 13th Century Library, The London Times Dec 28 1937, p 13; Brit Mus Quart 12.40.

Manly J M, The Penrose MS of La Resurrection, MP 37.1.

Trethewey W H, La Petite Philosophe, ANTS 1.vi.

Editions. Jubinal A, La Résurrection du Sauveur, Paris 1834.

Schneegans F E, La Résurrection du Sauveur fragment d'un mystère anglo-normand du XIIIᵉ siècle, Strasbourg 1925.

Wright J G, La Résurrection du Sauveur, in Les Classiques français du moyen âge 69, Paris 1931.

Jenkins T A, J M Manly, M K Pope and J G Wright, La Seinte Resureccion from the Paris and Canterbury MSS, ANTS 4 (full critical apparatus).

Sources, etc. Wright J G, A Study of the Themes of the Resurrection in the Mediaeval French Drama, Bryn Mawr Pa 1935, passim.

Chambers, 2.82.

Walberg E, Quelques aspects de la littérature anglo-normande, Paris 1936, p 82.

Frank G, The Medieval French Drama, Oxford 1954, p 86.

Craig ERD, p 116.

Legge M D, AN Lit and its Background, p 321.

Hardison CR&CD, Essay 7.

For additional items see Jenkins et al, p ix; Holmes CBFL, p 182; Bossuat MBLF, p 363; Henshaw, PMRS, 21.24; Stratman, p 281.

ENGLISH VERNACULAR PLAYS.

General Treatments. Hone W, Ancient Mysteries Described Especially the English Miracle Plays Founded on Apocryphal New Testament Story Extant among the Unpublished Manuscripts in the British Museum

. . . , London 1823, p 199.

Collier J P, The History of English Dramatic Poetry, London 1831; new edn 1879; 1.1; 2.123.

Herrig L, Die Entwicklung des engl Drama's, Arch 1.28.

Ahn F H, English Mysteries and Miracle Plays, Trier 1867, p vi.

Klein J L, Geschichte des engl Drama's, vols 12 and 13, Leipzig 1876.

Genée R, Die engl Mirakelspiele und Moralitäten als Vorläufer des engl Dramas, Berlin 1878, p 629 (Sammlung gemeinverständlicher wissenschaftlicher Vorträge herausg v R Virchow und Fr v Holkendorff, no 305).

Jusserand J J, Le théatre en Angleterre depuis La Conquête jusqu'aux prédécesseurs immédiats de Shakespeare, 2nd edn, Paris 1881, chaps 1–3.

Bates.

Ward Hist, vol 1, chaps 1, 2.

Symonds J A, Shakespere's Predecessors in the English Drama, London 1884; rvsd edn 1900.

Chambers, 2.106.

Gayley, p 83.

Moore E H, English Miracle Plays and Moralities, London 1907 (crit W W Greg, MLR 3.396).

Brooke C F Tucker, The Tudor Drama, Boston 1911, chaps 1, 2.

Creizenach, 1.155, 289, 457, 468.

Schelling F E, English Drama, London and N Y 1914, p 17.

Pennington J, Mystery and Miracle Plays, International Studio 80.207 (illustrations).

Pollard EMP 1927, Introd, p xxi.

Eckhardt E, Das englischen Drama im Zeitalter der Reformation und der Hochrenaissance, Berlin 1928.

Nicoll A, British Dramas An Historical Survey from the Beginnings to the Present Time, 3rd rvsd edn, London Bombay and Sydney 1932, pp 24, 41.

Chambers OHEL, p 12.

Rossiter A P, English Drama from Early Times to the Elizabethans Its Background Origins and Developments, London N Y etc 1950, pp 62, 79, 95 (crit TLS Feb 10 1950, p 90; F S Boas, Fortnightly 173.196; A Brown, MLR 45.369; D Traversi, Scrut 17.181; D Everett, YWES 31.88).

Craig ERD, p 151.

Lombardo A, Il dramma pre-Shakespeariano, Studi sul teatro inglese dal medioevo al rinascimento, Venezia 1957 (crit T Silverstein, MP 55.202; H Craig, MLN 73.612).

Williams A, The Drama of Medieval England, East Lansing Mich 1961 (crit H Craig, Spec 36.695; E Wolff, Angl 79.477; M G Jones, MLR 57.238; A Brown, RES ns 14.72; A Holaday, JEGP 62.214; K S Rothwell, MP 60.286).

Staging. Albright V E, The Shakespearian Stage, N Y 1909, chap 1.

Nicoll A, The Development of the Theatre, 3rd rvsd edn, N Y [1946] and London 1948, pp 69, 74, 76.

Stamm R, Geschichte des engl Theaters, Bern 1951, chaps 1–3 (crit H Oppel, DLz 73.245; H H Borcherdt, Angl 71.367).

Southern R, The Medieval Theatre in the Round A Study of the Staging of the Castle of Perseverance and Related Matters, London 1957 (crit TLS Dec 6 1957, p 742; P Hartnoll, N&Q 203.453; R Hosley, MLR 53.557; G Wickham, MÆ 28.138).

Wickham G, Early English Stages 1300–1600, Vol One 1300 to 1576, London and N Y 1959, pp 112, 229, 291 (crit TLS May 15 1959, p 291; H Craig, Spec 34.702).

Rôles and Themes. Graf H, Der Miles Gloriosus im engl Drama bis zur Zeit des Bürgerkrieges, Schwerin [1891], p 9 (crit O Glöde, LfGRP 14.243).

Cushman L W, The Devil and the Vice in the English Dramatic Literature before Shakespeare, in SEP 6, Halle a S 1900 (crit H Logeman, EStn 29.427; W Dibelius, Arch 112.199).

Eckhardt E, Die lustige Person im älteren englischen Drama (bis 1642), Palaes 17 (crit W Keller, ShJ 39.316; W Dibelius, Arch 112.200).

Gothein M, Die Frau im englischen Drama vor Shakespeare, ShJ 40.1.

Röhmer R A, Priestergestalten im englischen Drama bis zu Shakespeare, Berlin 1909.

Zandvoort R W, The Messenger in the Early Church Drama, ESts 3.100.

Moore J R, The Tradition of Angelic Singing in English Drama, JEGP 22.89.

Roszbach J, Das erste Auftreten der Personen im älteren englischen Drama, Giessen 1928.

Tergau D, Die sozialen Typen im Dramen des englischen Mittelalters, Göttingen 1932.

Tomlinson W E, Der Herodes-Charakter im englischen Drama, Palaes 195.

Boughner D C, Retribution in English Medieval Drama, N&Q 198.506; The Braggart in Renaissance Comedy A Study in Comparative Drama, Minneapolis and London 1954, p 119.

Weimann R, Die Furchtbare Komik des Herodes Dramaturgie und Figurenaufbau des vorshakespearischen Schurken, Archiv 204.113.

Other Scholarly Problems. Symmes H S, Les débuts de la critique dramatique en Angleterre jusqu'à la mort de Shakespeare, Paris 1903, p 1.

Crowley T, Character-Treatment in the Mediaeval Drama, Notre Dame Ind 1907, p 64.

Lott B, Der Monolog im englischen Drama vor Shakespeare, Greifswald 1909, p 10.

Oelrich W, Die Personennamen im mittelalterlichen Drama Englands, Kiel 1911 (crit M Förster, ShJ 52.253).

Crawford M, English Interjections in the Fifteenth Century, Univ of Nebraska Studies 13.361 (draws on vernacular drama).

Spaar O, Prolog und Epilog im mittelalterlichen engl Drama, Grünberg 1913.

Wieland G, Lustspieleelemente in me Drama (bis 1500), Bühl (Baden) 1913.

Campbell E M, Satire in the Early English Drama, Columbus Ohio 1914, p 16.

Haller J, Die Technik des Dialogs im mittelalterlichen Drama Englands, Worms a Rh 1916 (crit W Keller, ShJ 55.167).

Weiner K, Die Verwendung des Parallelismus als Kunstmittel im englischen Drama vor Shakespeare, Hamburg 1916.

Owst G R, Literature and Pulpit in Medieval England, Cambridge 1933, p 471 (influence of sermons).

Young K, An Interludium for a Gild of Corpus Christi, MLN 48.84 (discussion of term interlude).

Whiting B J, Proverbs in the Earlier English Drama, HSCL 14.

Bland D S, Interludes in Fifteenth-Century Revels at Furnivall's Inn, RES ns 3.263, 266 (discussion of term interlude).

A Tretise of Miraclis Pleyinge (MS. BM Addit 24.202, f 14 [late 14 cent]).

Rel Ant, 2.42 (text).

Mätzner E, AESpr, 2.222 (text).

Cook A S, A Literary Middle English Reader, Boston etc 1915, p 278 (selection).

Kaiser R, Alt-und me Anthologie, Berlin 1954, p 216 (selection).

Loomis R S and R Willard, Medieval English Verse and Prose in Modernized Versions, N Y 1948, p 289 (selection).

Craddock L G, Franciscan Influences on Early English Drama, Franciscan Stud 10.397.

Chambers 1.84; 2.102.

Young K, The Drama of the Medieval

Church, 2.414.

Chambers OHEL, p 14; Craig ERD, p 92.

Editions of Selected Plays. Collier J P, Five Miracle Plays or Scriptural Dramas, London 1836.

Marriott W, A Collection of English Miracle-Plays or Mysteries, Basel 1838.

Manly Spec.

Hemingway.

Adams CPSD.

Pollard EMP.

Modernizations. R[hys] E, Everyman with Other Interludes Including Eight Miracle Plays, London 1909 and many reprints.

Child C G, The Second Shepherds' Play, Everyman and Other Early Plays, Boston etc 1910.

Matthews B and P R Lieder, The Chief British Dramatists, London and N Y 1924.

Tickner EED.

Schweikert H C, Early English Plays, N Y 1928.

Rubinstein H F, Great English Plays, London and N Y 1928.

Baldwin T W, Earlier English Drama from Robin Hood to Everyman, N Y 1929 (American edn of Tickner EED, with additions).

Hubbell J B and J O Beaty, An Introduction to Drama, N Y 1927.

Parks E W and R C Beatty, The English Drama an Anthology 900–1642, N Y 1935.

Tatlock J S P and R G Martin, Representative English Plays from the Miracle Plays to Pinero, 2nd rvsd edn, N Y and London 1938.

Loomis R S and H W Wells, Representative Medieval and Tudor Plays, N Y 1942.

Bentley G E, The Development of English Drama An Anthology, N Y 1950.

Crump G H, Selections from English Dramatists, 2nd edn, London 1950.

Cawley A C, Everyman and Medieval Miracle Plays, London and N Y 1956.

Thomas R G, Ten Miracle Plays, York Medieval Texts, London 1966.

For other edns see Stratman, p 23.

General References. Ten Brink, 2.234; Körting, § 133; Courthope, 1.393; CHEL, 5.1.

Wilson EMEL, p 282.

Baugh LHE, p 277; Renwick-Orton (1952), p 334.

Bibliographies. Halliwell J O, A Dictionary of Old English Plays Existing either in Print or in Manuscript from the Earliest Times . . . , London 1860.

Chambers, 2.106, 149, 407; CHEL, 5.432; Tucker and Benham, 2.195.

Coleman E D, The Bible in English Drama, N Y 1931.

CBEL, 1.275; 5.156.

Harbage A, Annals of English Drama, Phila and London 1940; rvsd S Schoenbaum 1964.

Chambers OHEL, p 210; Henshaw, PMRS, 21.14; Stratman, p 75 (crit above under *General Bibliographies*); Craig ERD, p 390 and ftnts to chaps 4–10. And see above under *General Bibliographies*.

ENGLISH MIRACLE (SAINTS') PLAYS.

General Treatments. Coffman G R, The Miracle Play in England—Nomenclature, PMLA 31.448; The Miracle Play in England Some Records of Presentation and Notes on Preserved Plays, SP 16.56.

Gerould G H, Saints' Legends, Boston and N Y 1916, pp 294, 374 (crit G L Hamilton, MLN 36.240).

Manly J M, The Miracle Play in Mediaeval England, in Essays by Divers Hands, TRSL ns 7.133.

See also above under LITURGICAL DRAMA, *Liturgical Origins of Miracle Plays.*

St Hugh of Lincoln. Leach A F, Proc of the Brit Acad 1913–14, p 444.

Manly J M, Sir Thopas a Satire, E&S 13.53.

Loomis R S, Lincoln as a Dramatic Centre, in Mélanges d'histoire . . . offerts à Gustave Cohen, Paris 1950, p 245; Was there a Play on the Martyrdom of Hugh of Lincoln? MLN 69.31.

Spitzer L, Istos ympnos ludendo composuit, MLN 69.383 (challenges Loomis, MLN 69.34).

Timmer B J, YWES 35.53.

Other Plays. Harris M D, St Christian Miracle Play—Was there ever a Miracle Play entitled St Christian? N&Q 10s 11.230.

Thomas C B, The Miracle Play at Dunstable, MLN 32.337.

Brown C, An Early Mention of a St Nicholas Play in England, SP 28.594.

Anderson M D, Drama and Imagery in English Medieval Churches, Cambridge 1963, pp 181, 193 (crit above under GENERAL TREATMENTS OF MEDIEVAL DRAMA).

General References. Ward Hist, 1.41; Chambers, 2.132; Creizenach, 1.155, 159, 301; Pollard EMP 1927, p xix; Young, The Drama of the Medieval Church, 2.503; Chambers OHEL, p 15; Gardiner, YSE 103.54; Craig ERD, pp 81, 320.

For Pater Noster and Creed Plays, see [24–25] below.

ENGLISH MYSTERIES (BIBLICAL PLAYS).

General Treatments. Ebert A, Die englischen Mysterien mit besonderer Berücksichtigung der Towneley-Sammlung, JfRESL 1.44, 131.

Hohlfeld A, Die altenglischen Kollektivmisterien unter besonderer Berücksichtigung des Verhältnisses der York-und Towneley Spiele, Angl 11.219.

Davidson C, Studies in the English Mystery Plays, New Haven Conn 1892, p 91 (also in Trans of the Connecticut Acad of Arts and Sciences 9.215).

Clarke S W, The Miracle Play in England, London [1897].

Gayley C M, The Earlier Miracle Plays of England, International Quart 10.108.

Spencer M L, Corpus Christi Pageants in England, N Y 1911 (crit M Förster, ShJ 48.337; H Craig, JEGP 13.589).

Cron B, Zur Entwicklungsgeschichte der englischen Misterien Alten Testaments, Marburg 1913.

Cargill O, Drama and Liturgy, N Y 1930, p 105 (theories of development).

Melchers P, Kulturgeschichtliche Studien zu den mittelenglischen Misterienspielen, Würzburg 1938.

Gaffney H, The Early Drama and Corpus Christi, Irish Ecclesiastical Record 5s 63.155.

Gardiner H C, Mysteries' End An Investigation of the Last Days of the Medieval Religious Stage, YSE 103 (crit H W Wells, MLQ 7.502; W W Greg, MLR 42.260; A Gwynn, Studies, An Irish Quarterly Review of Letters Philosophy and Science 36.283).

Swart J, The Insubstantial Pageant, Neophil 41.127.

Williams A, The Drama of Medieval England, East Lansing Mich 1961, p 55.

Prosser (crit H Craig, Spec 37.295; P Kean, MÆ 32.77; M Stevens, BA 37.203; P Janelle, Moyen Age 70.141).

Kolve (crit A Williams, JEGP 66.443; O B Hardison, MLQ 29.94; R G Thomas, RES ns 20.76; F L Utley, Manuscripts 13.47; E C Dunn, CHR 55.70).

Methods of Representation, Staging. Pierson M, The Relation of the Corpus Christi Procession to the Corpus Christi Play in England, Trans Wisconsin Acad of Science and Letters 18.110.

Craig H, The Corpus Christi Procession and the Corpus Christi Play, JEGP 13.589.

Blair L, A Note on the Relation of the Corpus Christi Procession to the Corpus Christi Play in England, MLN 55.83.

Adrian G, Die Bühnenanweisungen in den englischen Mysterien, Bochum-Langendreer 1931.

Spitzer L, Pageant = Latin Pagina, AJP 64.327.

Kernodle G R, The Medieval Pageant Wagons of Louvain, Theatre Annual 1943, p 58.

Nicoll A, The Development of the Theatre, pp 69, 74, 76 (see above under GENERAL TREATMENTS OF MEDIEVAL DRAMA).

Stamm R, Geschichte des englischen Theater, Bern 1951, p 21 (crit above under ENGLISH VERNACULAR PLAYS, *Staging*).

Prosser, p 43.

Frank G, Revisions in the English Mystery Plays, MP 15.565 (Playbook).

Beuscher E, Die Gesangseinlagen in den englischen Mysterien, Münster i Westf 1930.

Collins F, Music in the Craft Cycles, PMLA 47.613.

Moore J R, Miracle Plays Minstrels and Jigs, PMLA 48.943.

Ingram R W, The Use of Music in English Miracle Plays, Angl 75.55.

Stevens J, Music in Mediaeval Drama, Proc of the Royal Musical Association 84.81.

Carpenter N C, Music in the English Mystery Plays, in J H Long, Music in Renaissance Drama, Lexington Ky 1968, pp 1, 161 (notes).

Prior E S, The Sculpture of Alabaster Tables, in Illustrated Catalogue of the Exhibition of English Medieval Alabaster Work, Soc of Antiquaries, London 1913, pp 21, 42 (relation to stage costumes).

Hildburgh W L, English Alabaster Carvings as Records of the Medieval Religious Drama, Archaeol 93.51.

Anderson M D, Drama and Imagery in English Medieval Churches, Cambridge 1963, pp 87, 105 (crit above under GENERAL TREATMENTS OF MEDIEVAL DRAMA).

Robinson J W, The Late Medieval Cult of Jesus and the Mystery Plays, PMLA 80.508 (relationship of play and audience).

Sources and Literary Relations. Cook A S, A Remote Analogue to the Miracle Plays, JEGP 4.421 (Greek fathers).

Tisdel F M, The Influence of Popular Customs on the Mystery Plays, JEGP 5.323.

Hulme W H, The ME Harrowing of Hell and Gospel of Nicodemus, EETSES 100.lxvi (influence on medieval drama).

Taylor G C, The English Planctus Mariae, MP 4.605; The Relation of the English Corpus Christi Play to the ME Religious

Lyric, MP 5.1; Relations of Lyric and Drama in Medieval England, Chicago 1907 (reprinting of two previous items).

Craig H, The Origin of the Old Testament Plays, MP 10.473.

Kretzmann P E, The Liturgical Element in the Earliest Forms of the Medieval Drama, Minneapolis 1916 (Univ of Minnesota Stud in Lang and Lit 4).

Miller F H, The Northern Passion and the Mysteries, MLN 34.88.

Frank G, Vernacular Sources and an Old French Passion Play, MLN 35.257; The Palatine Passion and the Development of the Passion Play, PMLA 35.464.

Gilbert A H, Milton and the Mysteries, SP 17.147.

Dustoor P E, The Origin of the Play of Moses and the Tables of the Law, MLR 19.459.

Bald R C, The Development of Greek and Mediaeval English Drama A Comparison, EStn 66.6.

Owst G R, Literature and Pulpit in Medieval England, Cambridge 1933, p 471 (influence of sermons on drama).

Brown C, Sermons and Miracle Plays, MLN 49.394 (Merton MS sermons suggest early tradition of religious plays).

Melchers P, Kulturgeschichtliche Studien zu den me Misterienspielen, Würzburg 1938.

Whiting B J, Proverbs in the Earlier English Drama, HSCL 14.3.

Marshall M H, The Dramatic Tradition Established by the Liturgical Plays, PMLA 56.962.

Weir E G, The Vernacular Sources of the ME Plays of the Blessed Virgin Mary A Study of the Marian Elements in the Homilies and Other Works of Religious Instruction from 1200–1500 in Relation to the Mary Plays, diss Stanford 1942, Stanford Univ Abstracts of Diss 17.45.

Aquin Sister Mary, The Vulgate and the Eve-Concept in the English Cycles, Catholic Biblical Quarterly 9.409.

Craddock L G, Franciscan Influence on Early English Drama, Franciscan Stud 10.383.

Campbell A P, The Mediaeval Mystery Cycle Liturgical in Impulse, Revue de l'Univ d'Ottawa 33.23.

Fry T, The Antiquity of the Tradition of the Triads in the English Cycle Plays, American Benedictine Rev 18.465.

Leigh D J, The Doomsday Mystery Plays An Eschatological Morality, MP 67.211 (argues for close relationship with early moralities).

Rôles.

(See above under ENGLISH VERNACULAR PLAYS, Rôles and Themes, for abbreviated items).

Cushman L W, The Devil and the Vice, p 16.

Eckhardt E, Die lustige Person, Palaes 17.56.

Haslinghuis E J, De Duivel in het Drama der Middeleeuwen, Leiden 1912, p 25.

Bonnell J K, The Serpent with a Human Head in Art and in Mystery Plays, AJA 21.255.

Carstensen C, Kvindetyper i middelalderens religiøse skuespil saerlig de engelske, København 1901 (Studier fra sprog- og oldtidsforskning udgivne af det Philologisk-historiske Samfund 50).

Emerson O F, Legends of Cain Especially in Old and ME, PMLA 21.831.

Dürrschmidt H, Die Sage von Kain in der mittelalterlichen Literatur Englands, Bayreuth 1919 (crit H Jantzen, Zeitschrift für französischen u englischen Unterricht 21.56).

Bonnell J K, Cain's Jaw-bone, PMLA 39.140.

Thien H, Über die englischen Marienklagen, Kiel 1906.

Royster J F, Richard III, iv.4 and the Three Marys of the Mediaeval Drama, MLN 25.173.

Grosch W, Bote und Botenbericht im englischen Drama bis Shakespeare, Mainz 1911, p 5.

Blass J, Die Entwickelung der Figur des gedungenen Mörders im älteren englischen Drama bis Shakespeare, Mainz 1913, p 7.

Lindblom A, Den apokryfa Noahsagan i medeltidens konst och litteratur, Nordisk Tidskrift 1917, p 358.

Mill A J, Noah's Wife Again, PMLA 56.613.

Utley F L, The One Hundred and Three Names of Noah's Wife, Spec 16.426.

Vriend J, The Blessed Virgin Mary in the Medieval Drama of England, Purmerend-Holland 1928 (crit P E T Widdrington, RES 6.90; F Wild, LfGRP 52.428).

Luke Brother Cornelius, The Rôle of the Virgin Mary in the Coventry York Chester and Towneley Cycles, Washington D C 1933.

Parker R E, The Reputation of Herod in Early English Literature, Spec 8.59.

Tomlinson W E, Der Herodes-Charakter im englischen Drama, Palaes 195.

Valency M J, The Tragedies of Herod and Mariamne, CUS 145.26.

Hussey S S, How many Herods in the ME Drama? Neophil 48.252.

Deasy C P, St Joseph in the English Mystery Plays, Washington D C 1937.

Parker R E, Pilates Voys, Spec 25.237.

Williams A, The Characterization of Pilate in the Towneley Plays, East Lansing Mich 1950.

Griffin J R, The Hegge Pilate A Tragic Hero? ESts 51.234.

Garth H M, Saint Mary Magdalene in Mediaeval Literature, Baltimore 1950 (Johns Hopkins Univ Stud in Historical and Political Science 67³).

Boughner D C, The Braggart in Ren Comedy, p 119.

Prosser, pp 67 (Cain), 89 (Joseph), 103 (Woman taken in Adultery), 110 (Magdalene), 147 (Thomas).

Other Problems. Greene A, An Index to the Non-Biblical Names in the English Mystery Plays, in Stud in Lang and Lit in Celebration of the 70th Birthday of James Morgan Hart, N Y 1910, p 313.

Greg.

Brown A, The Study of English Medieval Drama, Franciplegius (F P Macgoun Festschrift, ed J B Bessinger and R P Creed) N Y and London 1965, p 265 (the scholar's problems and needs).

Mills D, Approaches to Medieval Drama, Leeds SE ns 3.47.

Literary Criticism. Wieland G, Lustspielelemente iι. me Drama (bis 1500), Bühl (Baden) 1913.

Wood F T, The Comic Elements in the English Mystery Plays, Neophil 25.39, 194.

Mackenzie W R, The English Moralities from the Point of View of Allegory, Boston and London 1914, p 24 (allegorical elements in mystery plays).

Coffman G R, A Plea for the Study of the Corpus Christi Plays as Drama, SP 26.411; correction SP 27.688.

Withington R, The Corpus Christi Plays as Drama, SP 27.573 (reply to Coffman).

Everett D, YWES 11.109.

McNeir W F, The Corpus Christi Passion Plays as Dramatic Art, SP 48.601.

Taylor J, The Dramatic Structure of the ME Corpus Christi or Cycle Plays, in Literature and Society, ed B Slote, Lincoln Nebraska 1964, p 175.

Pearson L E, Isolable Lyrics of the Mystery Plays, ELH 3.228.

Wells H W, Style in the English Mystery Plays, JEGP 38.360 (repeated with minor variants 38.496).

Eichhorn T, Prosa und Vers im vorshakespeareschen Drama, ShJ 84–86.140.

Lombardo A, The Sacrifice of Isaac e il Miracle Play, English Miscellany 4.1 (ed M Praz for the British Council, Rome 1953).

Woolf R, The Effect of Typology on the English Medieval Plays of Abraham and Isaac, Spec 32.805.

Prosser, p 181 (pitfalls for dramatic critic) and passim.

Hurrell J D, The Figural Approach to Medieval Drama, CE 26.598.

Kolve, p 145 and passim.

Macaulay P S, The Play of the Harrowing of Hell as a Climax in the English Mystery Cycles, Studia Germanica Gandensia 8.115.

Williams A, Typology and the Cycle Plays Some Criteria, Spec 43.677.

Walsh M M, The Judgment Plays of the English Cycles, American Benedictine Rev 20.378.

Elliot J R, The Sacrifice of Isaac as Comedy and Tragedy, SP 66.36.

Randall T, Liberation from Bondage in the Corpus Christi Plays, NM 71.659.

General References. Ten Brink, 2.245; Bates, p 35; Ward Hist, 1.54; Chambers, 2.107, 124, 321; Gayley, p 83; Creizenach, 1.161, 208, 289; Pollard EMP 1927, p xxi; Chambers OHEL, p 17; Baugh LHE, p 277; Renwick-Orton (1952), p 334; Craig ERD, p 115.

Bibliography. CBEL, 1.275; 5.156; Stratman, p 98; and see above under ENGLISH VERNACULAR PLAYS, *Bibliographies.*

[1] CAIPHAS.

MS. Sloane 2478, ff 43ᵃ–44ᵇ (early 14 cent).

Brown-Robbins, Robbins-Cutler, no 180.

Herbert, 3.512.

Brown, edn, p 105.

Editions. Rel Ant, 2.241.

Brown C, Caiphas as a Palm-Sunday Prophet, Kittredge Anniversary Papers, Boston 1913, p 105 (adds some lines to Rel Ant).

Kaiser R, Alt- und me Anthologie, 2nd edn Berlin 1955, p 211; Medieval English (3rd edn of preceding in English, rvsd and enlarged), Berlin 1958, p 249 (lines 1–120 only).

Textual Matters. Brown C, A Textual Correction, MLN 29.60 (three final lines).

Brown, edn, pp 110 (date), 111 (language), 114 (locale; argues for Wells Cathedral).

Brandl, § 27.

Young K, The Drama of the Medieval Church, Oxford 1933, 1.94, 549.

[2] SHREWSBURY FRAGMENTS.

MS. Shrewsbury School VI (formerly Mus. iii.42), ff 38ᵃ–42ᵇ (early 15 cent).

Brown-Robbins, no *73.

Skeat, edn, p 10.

Waterhouse, edn, p xv.

Davis N-CP, frntspc and p xiv.

Editions. Skeat W W, Fragments of Yorkshire Mysteries, Acad 37.27.

Manly Spec, p xxvii (based on Skeat edn).

Waterhouse O, The Non-Cycle Mystery Plays, EETSES 104, London 1909 (based on Skeat edn and Manly Spec edn).

Witty J R, The Beverley Plays, Trans of the Yorkshire Dialect Soc 4²³.36, Appendix (based on Skeat edn).

Adams CPSD, p 73 (based on Waterhouse edn).

Young K, The Drama of the Medieval Church, 2 vols, Oxford 1933, 2.514, Appendix B.

Davis N-CP, p 1.

Language. Skeat, edn, p 11; Waterhouse, edn, p xvi; Witty, edn, p 37; Davis N-CP, p xix.

Versification. Miller F H, Metrical Affinities of the Shrewsbury Officium Pastorum and Its York Correspondent, MLN 33.91.

Davis N-CP, p xix.

Sources and Literary Relations. Skeat, edn, p 11 (relations with York cycle).

Waterhouse, edn, pp xix (relations with York cycle), xvii (relations with Liturgical Drama).

Miller, MLN 33.91 (relations with York cycle).

Craig ERD, pp 210, 219, 222 (relations with York cycle).

Davis N-CP, p xvii (relations with York cycle).

Young, edn, 2.522 (relations with Lit Drama).

Marshall M H, The Dramatic Tradition Established by the Liturgical Plays, PMLA 56.965, 975, 980, 984, 988 (relations with Lit Drama).

Chambers, 2.90, 108; Craig ERD, p 97.

Sisam K, Fourteenth Century Verse and Prose, Oxford 1921, p xxvi.

Stratman, p 154 (omits item 1451).

Music. Davis N-CP, Appendix, p 124 (Notes on the Music in the Shrewsbury Liturgical Plays by F Ll Harrison).

[3] BODLEY BURIAL AND RESURRECTION.

MS. Bodl 3692 (e Museo 160), ff 140ᵃ–172ᵃ (mid 15 cent).

Brown-Robbins, Robbins-Cutler, no 95.

Chambers, 2.431.

Craig ERD, p 310.

Baker D C and J L Murphy, The Bodleian MS E Mus. 160 Burial and Resurrection and the Digby Plays, RES 19.290.

Editions. Rel Ant, 2.124, 144.

Furnivall F J, The Digby Plays, New Shakespeare Soc 7; reissued EETSES 70, London 1896, p 171.

Language. Furnivall, edn, p 170 (note by Morris).

Schmidt K, Die Digby-Spiele, Angl 8.400.

Versification. Schmidt, Angl 8.402.

Craig ERD, p 319.

Date. Chambers, 2.129, 431; Chambers OHEL, p 44.

Sources and Literary Relations. Thien H, Über die englischen Marienklagen, Kiel 1906, p 57 (influences of Planctus and Quem quaeritis).

Taylor G C, The English Planctus Mariae, MP 4.613, 628, 636 (infl of Planctus and Quem quaeritis).

Kretzmann P E, The Liturgical Element in the Earliest Forms of the Medieval Drama, Univ of Minnesota Stud in Lang and Lit 4.153 (infl of Planctus and Quem quaeritis).

Young K, The Drama of the Medieval Church, Oxford 1933, 1.201 (infl of Planctus and Quem quaeritis).

Abel P, Grimald's Christus Redivivus and the Digby Resurrection Play, MLN 70.328.

Hildburgh W L, English Alabaster Carvings as Records of the Medieval Religious Drama, Archaeol 93.87, 94.

General References. Ten Brink, 2.287; Brandl, § 131; Chambers, 2.129, 431; Craig ERD, p 317; Kolve, pp 81, 188.

See also [19] below.

[4] CAMBRIDGE FRAGMENT.

MS. Camb Univ Mm.1.18, f 62ᵃ (formerly 58ᵃ) (1275–1300).

Brown-Robbins, Robbins-Cutler, no 2360.

Robbins, edn, p 30.

Davis N-CP, p cxi.

Editions. Robbins R H, An English Mystery Play Fragment ante 1300, MLN 65.30 (text), 31 (language), 34 (relations with Dux Moraud and Towneley Plays).

Salter F M, Medieval Drama in Chester, Toronto 1955, p 120 (challenges dramatic character).

Legge M D, Anglo-Norman Literature and its Background, Oxford 1963, p 328.

Davis N-CP, pp 114 (text), cxii (verse and language).

[5] RICKINGHALL (BURY ST. EDMUNDS) FRAGMENT.

MS. BM Addit Roll 63481B (formerly Redgrave Hall) (early 14 cent).
Brown-Robbins, Robbins-Cutler, no 1997.
Gilson, edn, p 340.
Greg W W, TLS June 2 1921, p 356.
Davis N-CP, p cxiv.
Editions. Gilson J P, A Fourteenth Century Fragment, TLS May 26 1921, p 340.
Brandl A, Das Bibelstück-Fragment von Rickinghall Manor, Arch 144.255 (based on Gilson edn).
Davis N-CP, pp 116 (text), cxiv (verse), cxv (language).
Textual Problems. Greg, TLS June 2 1921, p 356.
Davis N-CP, p cxv.
Literary Relations. Gilson, edn, p 340 (relation to Chester Nativity Play).
Studer P, TLS June 9 1921, p 373 (relation to Adam Play).
Zandvoort R W, The Messenger in the Early English Drama, ESts 3.103; rptd Collected Papers, Groningen 1954, p 25.
Wilson EMEL, p 285; The Lost Literature of Medieval England, London 1952, p 218.
Legge M D, Anglo-Norman Literature and its Background, Oxford 1963, p 328.
CBEL, 1.277.

[6] INTERLUDIUM DE CLERICO ET PUELLA.

MS. BM Addit 23986, vellum roll, verso, 84 lines (early 14 cent).
Brown-Robbins, Robbins-Cutler, no 668.
Heuser, edn, p 306.
Editions. Rel Ant, 1.145.
Chambers, 2.324.
Heuser W, Das Interludium de Clerico et Puella und das Fabliau von Dame Siris, Angl 30.306.
McKnight G H, ME Humorous Tales in Verse, Boston and London 1913 (printed as Appendix to Dame Siriz).
Cook A S, A Literary ME Reader, Boston etc 1915, p 476.
Brandl A and O Zippel, Me Sprach-und Literaturproben, Berlin 1917, p 203; 2nd edn entitled ME Literature, N Y 1949.
Dickins and Wilson, p 132.
Kaiser R, Alt-und Me Anthologie, Berlin 1954; 2nd edn 1955, p 304; Medieval English (3rd edn of preceding in English, rvsd and enlarged), Berlin 1958, p 486.

Textual Matters. Dickins and Wilson, p 241.
Richardson F E, Notes on the text and language of Interludium de Clerico et Puella, N&Q 207.133.
Miller B D H, Further Notes on Interludium de Clerico et Puella, N&Q 208.248.
Language. Heuser, edn, p 310; Dickins and Wilson, p 240; Richardson, N&Q 207.133.
Relations with Dame Siriz. Heuser, edn, p 312; McKnight, edn, p xxv; Cook, edn, p 476.
Schröder E, Dame Sirith, Nachrichten von der Gesellschaft der Wissenschaften zu Göttingen, Göttingen 1936, p 179.
Gayley C M, Representative English Comedies, N Y 1903, 1.xvii.
General References. Brandl, § 56; Ten Brink, 2.295; Chambers, 2.181, 202; Creizenach, 1.179; Craig ERD, p 329.
See DAME SIRIZ in the chapter on Tales; DE CLERICO ET PUELLA, VII [54].

[7] DURHAM PROLOGUE.

MS. Archid Dunelm 60 (Durham Dean and Chapter), dorse (late 14 or early 15 cent).
Editions. Cooling J, An Unpublished ME Prologue, RES ns 10.172 (text).
Davis N-CP, pp 118 (text), cxv (manuscript), cxvi (textual), cxvii (language, versification).
Literary Relations. Bennett J A W, MÆ 36.94 (relations with Theophilus legend).
Davis N-CP, p cxvi (relations with Theophilus legend).

[8] DUX MORAUD.

MS. Bodl 30519 (Eng poet f.2.R), buckram strip attached to parchment roll, recto (1425–50?).
Heuser, edn, p 180.
Davis N-CP, p c; facsimile lines 26–61 Plate IV facing p 107.
Editions. Heuser W, Dux Moraud Einselrolle aus einem verlorenen Drama des 14 Jahrhunderts, Angl 30.181 (text), 197 (language), 195 (versification).
Adams CPSD, p 207 (based on Heuser edn, with stage directions and scene divisions added).
Davis N-CP, pp 106 (text), cvi (language), cv (versification).
Sources and Literary Relations. Heuser, edn, p 198; Angl 31.24.
Cargill O, Drama and Liturgy, N Y 1930, p 122 (links with author of Secunda Pastorum).
Boughner D C, Retribution in English Medieval Drama, N&Q 198.507.

Davis N-CP, p ciii.
Hieatt C B, A Case for Duk Moraud as a
Play of the Miracles of the Virgin, MS
32.345.

[9] CHESTER PLAYS.

MSS. 1, Bodl 27631 (Bodley 175), 176 folios
(1604; with Banns); 2, Harley 1944, ff 22ᵃ–
25ᵃ (formerly ff 20ᵃ–23ᵃ) (1609?; Breviarye
and Banns only); 3, Harley 1948 (early 17
cent; Breviarye and List only); 4, Harley
2013, ff 1ᵃ–205ᵃ, (formerly 200ᵃ) (1600; with
Banns); 5, Harley 2124, ff 1ᵃ–141ᵃ (formerly
143ᵃ) (1607); 5a, Bodl 20552 (Malone 4; 18
cent transcript of seven plays from MSS 4
and 5); 6, Harley 2150, ff 86ᵃ–88ᵇ (formerly
ff 259ᵃ–261ᵇ) (first half 16 cent; List and
Banns only); 7, BM Addit 10305, ff 1ᵃ–168ᵇ
(1592); 8, BM Addit 27945 (18 cent transcript); 9, Chester, Company of Coopers En-
rollment Book, ff 1ᵃ–9ᵇ (1599; Trial and
Flagellation); 10, Manchester Free Libr (late
16 cent; Resurrection Fragment); 11, Nat
Libr Wales, Peniarth 399 (formerly Heng-
wrt 229), ff 1ᵃ–10ᵇ (late 15 cent; Antichrist);
12, Huntington HM 2 (formerly Devon-
shire), 150 folios, imperfect at beginning
(1591).
Brown-Robbins, Robbins-Cutler, no 716.
A Catalogue of the Harleian Manuscripts,
London 1808, 2.398, 512 (descriptions of
MSS 4 and 5).
Deimling and Matthews, edn, p vii.
Greg, p 34.
Greg W W, The Play of Antichrist from the
Chester Cycle, edn, pp xv (description of
all MSS of the cycle; corrigendum insert to
D), xx (description of MS 11 with account
of modern restoration); The Lists and
Banns of the Plays, edn, pp 123, 140, 164
(descriptions of MSS 6, 2, 3); The Man-
chester Fragment of the Resurrection, edn,
p 85 (MS 10).
de Ricci Census, 1.37 (description of MS 12).
Craig ERD, p 178.
Salter F M, The Banns of the Chester Plays,
RES 15.432 (MSS of Late Banns), 450 (MS
of Early Banns); The Trial and Flagellation
A New Manuscript, edn, p 3 (MS 9).
Charles B G, The Chester Play of Antichrist,
Nat Libr Wales Journ 1.34 (MS 11).
Acad 23, no 574, p 309 (discovery of MS 10).
Matthews G W, The Chester Mystery Plays,
Liverpool 1925 (rptd from Trans Historical
Soc of Lancashire and Cheshire 76.147), p
73 (description of MS 10).

Lumiansky and Mills, edn, p ix.
For MS relations see below under *Textual
Matters.*
Editions. Wright T, The Chester Plays A Col-
lection of Mysteries founded upon Scrip-
tural Subjects and formerly represented by
the Trades of Chester at Whitsuntide, 2
vols, Shakespeare Soc, London 1843–47 (in-
cludes Latin text of Antichrist); rptd as
Suppl to Dodsley's Old Plays 1, 1853.
Deimling H and G W Matthews, The Chester
Plays, EETSES 62 and 115, London 1893,
1916 (based on MS 5); reissued 1926.
Lumiansky R M and D Mills, The Chester
Mystery Cycle, EETS Suppl 3, London 1974
(based on MS 12; text and textural notes).
Editions of The Banns. Ormerod G, The His-
tory of the County Palatine and City of
Chester, 3 vols, 2nd rvsd edn London 1882,
1.385 (MS 4).
Furnivall F J, The Digby Plays, EETSES 70,
London 1896, p xx (additional lines from
MS 2).
Morris R H, Chester in the Plantagenet and
Tudor Reigns, Chester 1894(?), p 307 (MS 6).
Greg W W, The List and Banns of the Plays,
in Chester Play Studies, Malone Soc 76.133
(White Book Banns, MS 6), 147 (Breviary
Banns, MS 2).
Salter F M, The Banns of the Chester Plays,
RES 16.137 (Early Banns), 142 (Late Banns
from MS 12).
Editions of Selected Plays. Markland J H,
Chester Mysteries De Deluvio Noe De Oc-
cisione Innocentium, Roxburghe Club,
London 1818 (MS 4, including Banns, with
variants from MS 5 and MS 1); Introd rptd
in E Malone, Shakespeare 3.525.
Collier J P, Five Miracle Plays or Scriptural
Dramas, London 1836 (Coming of Anti-
christ, Play 23/24 from MS 12).
Marriott W, A Collection of English Miracle-
Plays or Mysteries . . . , Basel 1838 (Plays
3, 23/24).
Wülcker R P, Altenglisches Lesebuch, Halle
a S 1874–80, 2.136, 286 (Play 17).
Manly Spec, p 66 (Play 5 based on Deimling
and Matthews edn), 170 (Play 23 from MS
11).
Hemingway, pp 5, 36 (Plays 6 and 7 from MS
12 with variants).
Cook A S, A Literary ME Reader, Boston N Y
London etc 1915, p 481 (Play 3).
Adams CPSD, pp 111, 132, 167, 187 (Plays 3,
5, 13, 17, based on Deimling and Matthews
edn, with editing).
Pollard EMP 1927, pp 8, 21 (Play 3 and part

of Play 4).

Isaacs J, The Chester Play of the Deluge, London 1927 (based on Pollard EMP edn).

Dustoor P E, The Chester Fall of Lucifer, Allahabad Univ Studies 6[1], Allahabad 1930 (crit D Everett, YWES 11.110).

Salter F M, The Trial and Flagellation A New Manuscript, in Chester Play Studies, Malone Soc 76.46.

Greg W W, The Play of Antichrist from the Chester Cycle, Oxford 1935 (parallel texts from MSS 11 and 12; crit M S Serjeantson, YWES 16.151; H Marcus, DLz 57.886; K Brunner, AnglB 47.264; F M Salter, RES 13.341 [reply by Greg, RES 13.352; 14.79]; H Craig, JEGP 37.97).

Editions of the Manchester Fragment of Resurrection. Manchester Guardian, May 19 1883.

Axon W E A, Cheshire Gleanings, Manchester and London 1884, p 210.

Greg W W, The Manchester Fragment of the Resurrection, in Chester Play Studies, Malone Soc 76.89.

Modernizations. King I and O Bolton, The Chester Miracle Plays Done into Modern English and Arranged for Acting, London N Y and Toronto 1930 (abridged).

Bridge J C, The Chester Whitsun Plays, Chester 1906 (Plays 6, 7 based on Wright edn, abridged); rptd Journ of Chester and North Wales Architectural Archaeolical and Historic Soc 14.269.

Barne H H, The Shepherds' Offering, London 1906 (mainly from MS 5, abridged).

R[hys] E, Everyman with Other Interludes, London 1909 etc, pp 29, 41 (Plays 3, 4).

Tickner EED, pp 104, 118, 138, 171, 179 (Plays 7, 10, 15, 17, 18, abridged); rvsd Baldwin EED, pp 134, 171, 191, 224, 232.

Parry W D, Old Plays for Modern Players Selected and Modernized, London 1930, p 13 (Play 3).

Kreymborg A, Poetic Drama, N Y 1941, p 194 (Play 4).

Bentley G E, The Development of English Drama An Anthology, N Y 1950, p 4 (Play 3).

Crump G H, Selections from English Dramatists, 2nd edn London 1950, p 31 (Play 4).

Textual Matters. Wright, edn, 1.232; 2.202 (notes).

Deimling H, Text-Gestalt und Text-Kritik der Chester Plays, Berlin 1890; edn, EETSES 62.x (MS relations).

Pollard A W, The Chester Plays, EETSES

62.xxxi; 115.xxxv (collation of MS 5 with MS 12 for first 13 plays).

Kölbing E, EStn 16.279; 21.163 (textual emendations for Plays 3 and 4 begun as crit of Pollard EMP 1890).

Craig H, Two Coventry Corpus Christi Plays, EETSES 87.xxviii (the four parallel versions of the Doctors' Play).

Hemingway, pp iv (MS relations), 215, 234 (notes to plays).

Greg, pp 32 (MS relations), 86 (Christ and the Doctors); The Calculus of Variants An Essay on Textual Criticism, Oxford 1927; edn, Malone Soc 76.74 (MS relations; Appendix to Salter's edn of The Trial and Flagellation), 91 (Manchester Fragment notes and MS relations), 101 (Christ and the Doctors and the York Play); The Play of Antichrist, edn, pp xxv (analysis of variants), xli (MS relations), 73 (notes).

Dustoor P E, Textual Notes on the Chester Old Testament Plays, Angl 52.97; edn, pp 38 (notes to the Fall of Lucifer), 59 (relations of Chester MSS with Brome Play).

Salter, edn, Malone Soc 76.4, 28.

Brownstein O L, Revision in the Deluge of the Chester Cycle (based on Harley 2124), Speech Monographs 36.55 (MS 5).

Language. Oakden J P, Alliterative Poetry in ME, 2 vols, Univ of Manchester Publ 205, English Series 18, 1.chap 1 passim.

Versification. Schipper, 1.289, 362, 417.

Fort M D, The Metres of the Brome and Chester Abraham and Isaac Plays, PMLA 41.832 (finds no metrical evidence for deriving Chester from Brome).

Oakden, Allit Poetry in ME, 1.109, 201.

Dustoor, edn, p 38 (Cycle generally, and Fall of Lucifer).

Kiho Y, The Stanza-Division in the Chester Play XVII, Stud in Eng Lit, Imperial Univ of Tokyo, 1932, p 139.

Chambers OHEL, p 25.

Date (The Tradition). Markland, edn, p ii.

Chambers, 2.348; Gayley, p 128; Hemingway, p xx; Chambers OHEL, p 24.

Brown A, A Tradition of the Chester Plays, LMS 2.68, 72.

Salter F M, Mediaeval Drama in Chester, Toronto and London 1955, pp 33, 116, 117 (crit H Gneuss, Angl 73.525; TLS July 27 1956, p 450; C J Stratman, MP 54.131; E Colledge, RES ns 8.183; W A Armstrong, ESts 39.79).

Craig ERD, p 168.

Date (Other Views). Cook A S, The Chester

Plays, N Y Nation 100.599 (argues for dating cycle ca 1350).

Craig H, The Doomsday Play in England, PMLA 32.lv (abstract; finds dating evidence in its relation with Antichrist in Chester cycle).

Deanesley M, The Lollard Bible, Cambridge 1920, pp 210n, 329n (date of composition of Late Banns).

Salter, RES 15.444 (date of composition of Late Banns), 450; 16.1 (date of composition of Early Banns); 16.16 (conjectural dates for entry of plays into Cycle); 16.13 (date of MS 11).

Jones E D, The Date of the Peniarth Antichrist Manuscript, Nat Libr Wales Journ 1.145.

Authorship. Markland, edn, p v.

Leach A F, Some English Plays and Players, in An English Miscellany presented to Dr Furnivall, Oxford 1901, p 230.

Chambers, 2.147, 351.

Bridge J C, The Chester Miracle Plays Some Facts Concerning Them and the Supposed Authorship of Ralph Higden, Journ of Chester and North Wales Architectural Archaeological and Historic Soc ns 9.59.

Gayley, p 128; Hemingway, p xx; Chambers OHEL, pp 24, 26.

Brown, LMS 2.68; Salter, Med Drama in Chester, pp 37, 117n; Craig ERD, p 168.

Sources and Literary Relations. Ungemach H, Die Quellen der fünf ersten Chester Plays, MBREP 1 (crit H Deimling, Arch 86.428; H Suchier, LfGRP 12.86).

Gayley, pp 129, 323.

Utesch H, Die Quellen der Chester-Plays, Kiel 1909 (examines separate sources of all 25 plays).

Cron B, Zur Entwicklungsgeschichte der englischen Misterien Alten Testaments, Marburg 1913.

Melchers P, Kulturgeschichtliche Studien zu den Me Misterienspiele, Würzburg 1938, passim.

Liturgical and Lyrical Backgrounds. Thien H, Über die englischen Marienklagen, Kiel 1906, p 53.

Taylor G C, The English Planctus Mariae, MP 4.613, 623; The Relation of the English Corpus Christi Play to the ME Religious Lyric, MP 5.5 and passim.

Kretzmann P E, The Liturgical Element in the Earliest Forms of the Medieval Drama, Univ of Minnesota Stud in Lang and Lit 4.21 and passim.

Cargill O, Drama and Liturgy, N Y 1930, p 56 (uses Resurrection Play to disprove liturgical origin).

Relations with Stanzaic Life of Christ. Foster F A, A Stanzaic Life of Christ, EETS, London 1926, 166.xxviii.

Wilson R H, The Stanzaic Life of Christ and the Chester Plays, SP 28.413 (crit D Everett, YWES 12.113).

Craig ERD, p 196.

Owst G R, Literature and Pulpit in Medieval England, Cambridge 1933, p 475 and passim.

French Source. Ebert A, Die englischen Mysterien mit besonderer Berücksichtigung der Towneley-Sammlung, JfRESL 1.158.

Hohlfeld A, Die ae Kollektivmisterien unter besonderer Berücksichtigung des Verhältnisses der York-und-Towneley-Spiele, Angl 11.224.

Davidson C, Studies in the English Mystery Plays, Trans of the Connecticut Acad of Arts and Sciences 9.254 (counters Hohlfeld with plea for Anglo-Norman origin).

Hemingway, p xxiv (discounts French influence).

Baugh A C, The Chester Plays and French Influence, in Schelling Anniv Papers, N Y 1923, p 35.

Craig ERD, pp 171, 182 (review of controversy).

Dustoor P E, The Origin of the Play of Moses and the Table of the Law, MLR 19.460.

Chester-Brome Priority. Hohlfeld A R, Two Old English Mystery Plays on the Subject of Abraham's Sacrifice, MLN 5.111.

Waterhouse O, The Non-Cycle Mystery Plays, EETSES 104.lii.

Harper C, A Comparison between the Brome and Chester Plays of Abraham and Isaac, RadMon 15.

Fort M D, The Metres of the Brome and Chester Abraham and Isaac Plays, PMLA 41.832.

Dustoor, The Chester MSS and the Brome Play, Allahabad Univ Studies 6^1.59 (crit D Everett, YWES 11.110).

Severs J B, The Relationship between the Brome and Chester Plays of Abraham and Isaac, MP 42.137 (Chester a corrupt form of Brome).

Bryant J A, Chester's Sermon for Catechumens, JEGP 53.399 (considers Abraham and Isaac Play in relation to preceding episodes in Cycle).

The Dramatic Tradition of Antichrist. Michaelis E A F, Zum Ludus de Antichristo,

ZfDA 54.61.

Barrow S F and W H Hulme, Antichrist and Adam Two Medieval Religious Dramas, Western Reserve Univ Bull 28[8] (trans of the Tegernsee Antichrist Play).

Kamlah W, Der Ludus de Antichristo, Historische Vierteljahrschaft 28.53.

Young K, The Drama of the Medieval Church, Oxford 1933, 2.369.

Levi E, La leggenda dell' Anticristo nel teatro medievale, Studi Medievali ns 7.52.

Steigleder P, Das Spiel vom Antichrist, Bonner Beiträge zur deutschen Philologie 6.

Lucken L U, Antichrist and the Prophets of Antichrist in the Chester Cycle, Washington D C 1940.

Pfleuger J H L, On the English Translation of the Ludus de Antichristo, JEGP 44.24 (emendations to Hulme's trans).

Greg W W, Christ and the Doctors and the York Play, Malone Soc 76.101 (discussion of relations of York 20 and Chester 11, with parallel portions of text). See also below under *Christ and the Doctors* in [10].

For special rôles see above under ENGLISH VERNACULAR PLAYS, *Rôles and Themes*; ENGLISH MYSTERIES (BIBLICAL PLAYS), *Rôles*. For relations with other cycles, see under separate cycles.

Literary Criticism. Haller J, Die Technik des Dialogs im mittelalterlichen Drama Englands, Worms a Rh 1916, p 1.

Wells H W, Style in the English Mystery Plays, JEGP 38.360 (duplicated with minor variations, JEGP 38.496).

Chambers OHEL, p 27.

Rossiter A P, English Drama from Early Times to the Elizabethans, London N Y etc 1950, p 66.

McNeir W F, The Corpus Christi Passion Plays as Dramatic Art, SP 48.601.

Salter F M, Medieval Drama in Chester, Toronto and London 1955, p 81.

Lumiansky R M, Comedy and Theme in the Chester Harrowing of Hell, Tulane Stud Eng 10.5.

Prosser, p 81 and passim.

Bland D S, The Chester Nativity One Play or Two? N&Q 208.134.

Morgan M M, High Fraud Paradox and Double-Plot in the English Shepherds' Plays, Spec 39.682.

See above under ENGLISH VERNACULAR PLAYS, *Literary Criticism*; ENGLISH MYSTERIES (BIBLICAL PLAYS), *Literary Criticism*.

Records of Performances, Staging, etc. Markland, edn, p vii.

Morris, edn, p 309 (Rogers list of plays).

Furnivall, edn, p xviii.

Chambers, 2.138, 348, 408.

Bridge J C, The Chester Miracle Plays, p 93 (Music; for full bibliographical entry, see above under *Authorship*).

Spencer M L, Corpus Christi Pageants in England, N Y 1911, see index under Chester.

Hildburgh W L, Iconographical Peculiarities in English Medieval Alabaster Carvings, Folklore 44.40 (Chester Resurrection stage directions); Note on Medieval English Representations of the Resurrection of Our Lord, Folklore 48.97 (corrects 44.40).

Salter, Trial and Flagellation, edn, p 6 (correction by J Butt, RES 15.92); Mediaeval Drama in Chester, pp 29, 54.

Greg, The Lists and Banns, edn, pp 130, 146, 165, 170.

Crocker S F, The Production of the Chester Plays, West Virginia Univ Stud, Philological Papers 1.62.

Gardiner H C, Mysteries' End, YSE 103, see index under Chester.

Brown, LMS 2.70 (record of performances from MS BM Addit 29777 with re-datings).

Beresford J R, The Churchwardens Accounts of Holy Trinity Chester 1532 to 1633, Journ of the Chester and North Wales Architural Archaeological and Historic Soc 38.100, 125 (players' garments, possibly for Corpus Christi Play).

Carpenter N C, Music in the Chester Plays, Papers on Lang and Lit 1.195.

Mill A J, Medieval Stage Decoration That Apple Tree Again, Theatre Notebook 24.122 (correction of Morris reading).

General References. Klein, 1.711, 741; Körting, § 135.iii; Ten Brink, 2.274; 3.275; Bates, p 105; Brandl, § 47; Ward Hist, 1.76; Chambers, 2.407; CHEL, 5.53, 433; Creizenach, 1.296; Chambers OHEL, p 22; Baugh LHE, p 281; Craig ERD, chap 5 and passim; Prosser, see index under Chester cycle; Kolve, see index under Chester cycle.

Bibliography. CBEL, 1.277; 5.157; Henshaw, PMRS, 21.14; Stratman, p 117.

[10] YORK PLAYS.

MSS. 1, BM Addit 35290 (formerly Ashburnham 137), ff 4[a]–252[b] (formerly 2[a]–248[b]) (1425–75); 2, Yorkshire Philos Soc (formerly Sykes), ff 1[a]–4[b] (1525–50; Scriveners' Play

only).
Brown-Robbins, Robbins-Cutler, no 1273.
Acad 22, no 530, p 9 (description of MS 1 and announcement of editing).
Smith, edn, p xi.
Chambers, 2.409.
Frampton M G, The Brewbarret Interpolation in the York Play the Sacrificium Cayme and Abell, PMLA 52.895 (excised pages in Register).
Cawley, edn, p 45.
Craig ERD, p 200.
Editions. Smith L T, York Plays The Plays Performed by the Crafts or Mysteries of York on the Day of Corpus Christi in the 14th 15th and 16th Centuries, Oxford 1885 (from MS 1; crit J Zupitza, DLz 6.1304; L Proescholdt, AnglA 8.159; LfGRP 7.178; J Hall, EStn 9.448; F H Stoddard, MLN 2.344).
Croft J, Excerpta Antiqua or A Collection of Original Manuscripts, York 1797, p 105 (Scriveners' Play from MS 2).
Halliwell J O, The Yorkshire Anthology, London 1851, p 198 (Scriveners' Play, based on Croft edn).
Turner J H, Yorkshire Anthology, Bingley 1901, p 39 (Scriveners' Play, based on Croft edn).
Collier J P, The Skryveners' Play The Incredulity of St Thomas from a Manuscript in the Possession of John Sykes Esq of Doncaster, Camden Soc 73 (Miscellany 4).
Cawley A C, The Sykes MS of the York Scriveners' Play, Leeds SE 7 and 8, p 45.
Editions of Selected Plays. Manly Spec, 1.153, 198 (Plays 38, 48, based on Smith edn, with variants).
Hemingway, pp 121, 130, 141, 147 (Plays 12, 13, 14, 15, with variants).
Cook A S, A Literary ME Reader, Boston N Y etc 1915, p 518 (Play 14 from MS 1).
Brandl A and O Zippel, Me Sprach- und Literaturproben, Berlin 1917; 2nd edn entitled ME Literature, N Y 1949, pp 204, 205 (Plays 14, 15).
Sisam K, Fourteenth Century Verse and Prose, Oxford 1921, p 171 (Play 37).
Adams CPSD, pp 142, 199 (Plays 14, 48, based on Smith edn, with editing).
Pollard EMP 1927, p 1 (Play 1).
Dustoor P E, The York Creation of Adam and Eve, Allahabad Univ Stud 13.25 (Play 3 from MS 1).
Ford B, The Age of Chaucer, London 1954, p 458 (Play 35).

Kaiser R, Alt- und me Anthologie, 2nd edn Berlin 1955, pp 219, 222 (Play 1; selections from Plays 8, 26).
Modernizations. Purvis J S, The York Cycle of Mystery Plays A Shorter Version of the Ancient Cycle with a Note on the Production Staged at the York Festival of 1951 by E Martin Browne, London 1951; complete version, London 1957 (crit A Brown, RES ns 10.80).
Browne E M, The York Nativity Play Adapted from the York Mystery Cycle (XIV Century), 2nd rvsd edn, York 1952 (abridged and dovetailed).
Schweikert H C, Early English Plays, N Y 1928, p 128 (Play 48).
Baldwin EED, p 73 (selection from Play 10).
Purvis J S, The Fishers' and Mariners' Play, York 1954 (Play 9).
Textual Matters. See above under *Editions*, Zupitza and Hall crit of Smith edn.
Holthausen F, Beiträge zur Erklärung und Textkritik der York Plays, Arch 85.411; Zur Textkritik der York Plays, in Philologische Studien Festgabe für Eduard Sievers, Halle a S 1896, p 30; Zu alt- und me Dichtungen 10 No 57 York Plays, Angl 21.443; Zur Erklärung und Textkritik der York Plays, EStn 41.380.
Kölbing E, EStn 16.278 (crit of Pollard EMP 1890); Beiträge zur Erklärung und Textkritik der York Plays, EStn 20.179.
Coblentz H E, A Rime-Index to the Parent Cycle of the York Mystery Plays and of a Portion of the Woodkirk Conspiracio et Capito, PMLA 10.487; Some Suggested Rime Emendations to the York Mystery Plays, MLN 10.39.
Luick K, Zur Textkritik der Spiele von York, Angl 22.384.
Zippel O, Zwei angebliche me Interjektionen, Arch 134.131 (Play 15, lines 39, 54, colle; lines 37, 47, hudde).
Wallis J P R, The Miracle Play of Crucifixio Christi in the York Cycle, MLR 12.494 (assignment of parts, lines 97–108).
Sisam, edn, p 259 (notes to Play 37).
Dustoor, Some Textual Notes on the English Mystery Plays, MLR 21.427 (Play 5, lines 1–7; Play 10, line 369; Play 11, line 219); Textual Notes on the York Old Testament Plays, Angl 52.26; edn, p 23 (notes to Play 3).
Pollard EMP 1927, p 177 (notes to Play 1).
Sundén K F, A Grammatical Miscellany Offered to Otto Jespersen on his Seventieth

Birthday, Copenhagen and London 1930, p 109 (Play 17, line 122, roþe).

Freeman E, A Note on Play XXX of the York Cycle, MLN 45.392 (sees evidence of gild advertising in lines 127–40, 152–58).

Philip C, A Further Note on Old Age in Chaucer's Day, MLN 53.181 (Play 10, lines 5–8, 80–82, 221–22).

Wells M E, The Age of Isaac at the Time of the Sacrifice, MLN 54.579 (Play 10, lines 81–82).

Whitehall H, The Etymology of ME myse, PQ 18.314 (Play 11, line 273).

Cawley, edn, pp 51 (corrections of Collier edn and Smith edn readings), 58 (variant readings of MSS 1 and 2).

Brown A, Some Notes on Medieval Drama in York, in Early English and Norse Studies (Hugh Smith Festschrift), London 1963, p 2 (Who were the Consules?).

Language. Smith, edn, pp liii, lxix.

Herttrich O, Studien zu den York Plays, Breslau 1886, p 1.

Kamann P J G, Über Quellen und Sprache der York Plays, Leipzig 1887, p 39.

Coblentz, Some Suggested Rime Emendations to the York Mystery Plays, MLN 10.39.

Oakden J P, Alliterative Poetry in ME, Univ of Manchester Publ 205, English Series 18, 1.chap 1 passim.

Trusler M, The Language of the Wakefield Playwright, SP 33.23 (comparison with the language of York).

Dustoor, edn, p 23 (dialectal differences between A and B versions of Play 3).

Cawley, edn, p 52.

Versification. Smith, edn, p 1.

Davidson C, Studies in the English Mystery Plays, [New Haven] 1892, p 116 (also in Trans of the Connecticut Acad of Arts and Sciences 9.240).

Amours F J, Scottish Alliterative Poems in Riming Stanzas, PSTS 27.lxxxvii (Play 46).

Saintsbury G, A History of English Prosody, London and N Y 1906, 1.204.

Medary M P, Stanza-Linking in ME Verse, RomR 7.262 (Play 46).

Miller F H, Metrical Affinities of the Shrewsbury Officium Pastorum and its York Correspondent, MLN 33.91; Stanzaic Division in York Play XXXIX, MLN 35.379.

Lyle M C, The Original Identity of the York and Towneley Cycles, Univ of Minnesota Stud in Lang and Lit 6.47 (interrelation of York and Towneley metres).

Chambers OHEL, p 29.

Reese J B, Alliterative Verse in the York Cycle, SP 48.639.

Cawley, edn, p 56.

Craig ERD, p 219.

Date. Smith, edn, pp xlv, xlvi (authorship). Greg, p 28.

Lyle, The Orig Identity of the York and Towneley Cycles, p 102 (date of separation of York and Towneley cycles).

Frampton M G, The Date of the Wakefield Master Bibliographical Evidence, PMLA 53.86 (York dating); The York Play of Christ Led up to Calvary, PQ 20.198 (date of revised play).

Craig ERD, p 200.

Sources and Literary Relations. Smith, edn, pp xliv (Cursor Mundi), xlvii.

Kamann P J G, Über Quellen und Sprache der York Plays, Leipzig 1887.

Holthausen F, Arch 85.425; Nachtrag zu den Quellen der York Plays, Arch 86.280.

Gayley, p 327.

Cron B, Zur Entwicklungsgeschichte der englischen Misterien Alten Testaments, Marburg 1913.

Melchers P, Kulturgeschichtliche Studien zu den me Mysterienspielen, Würzburg 1938, passim.

Liturgical and Lyrical Backgrounds. Thien H, Über die englischen Marienklagen, Kiel 1906, p 47.

Taylor G C, The English Planctus Mariae, MP 4.612, 623, 635; The Relation of the English Corpus Christi Play to the ME Religious Lyric, MP 5.5 and passim.

Kretzmann P E, The Liturgical Element in the Earliest Forms of the Medieval Drama, Univ of Minnesota Stud in Lang and Lit 4.22 and passim.

Relations with Gospel of Nicodemus. Craigie W A, The Gospel of Nicodemus and the York Mystery Plays, in An English Miscellany Presented to Dr Furnivall, Oxford 1901, p 52.

Hulme W H, The ME Harrowing of Hell and Gospel of Nicodemus, EETSES 100. xviii, xix.

Greg, p 71n.

Lyle, The Orig Identity of the York and Towneley Cycles, p 30.

Clark E G, The York Plays and the Gospel of Nichodemus, PMLA 43.153.

Relations with the Northern Passion. Foster F, The Mystery Plays and the Northern Passion, MLN 26.171; The Northern Passion, EETS 147.81.

Miller F H, The Northern Passion and the Mysteries, MLN 34.88.

Lyle, The Orig Identity of the York and Towneley Cycles, p 4.

Frank G, St Martial of Limoges in the York Plays, MLN 44.233 (Play 27).

Hoffman C H, The Source of the Words to the Music in York 46, MLN 65.236 (Legenda aurea).

Relations with Other Cycles. Smith, edn, p lxii (comparative tables of cycles).

Hohlfeld A, Die altenenglischen Kollektivmisterien unter besonderer Berücksichtigung des Verhältnisses der York- und Towneley- Spiele, Angl 11.241 (comparative tables).

Chambers, 2.321 (comparative tables).

Davidson C, Stud in the Eng Myst Plays, pp 128, 137 (parent cycle), 157 (also in Trans of Connecticut Acad of Arts and Sciences 9.252, 261, 281).

York-Towneley Relations. Smith, edn, pp 68, 156, 372, 396, 497 (parallel texts).

Herttrich O, Studien zu den York Plays, Breslau 1886, p 3 (relationship based on textual and metrical comparisons with Towneley).

Hohlfeld, Angl 11.219.

Davidson, Stud in the Eng Myst Plays, p 168 (correspondences of York-Towneley outside parent cycle; also in Trans of Connecticut Acad of Arts and Sciences 9.292).

Lyle, The Orig Identity of the York and Towneley Cycles (crit G Frank, MLN 35.45).

Foster F, Was Gilbert Pilkington Author of the Secunda Pastorum? PMLA 43.131 (reply to Lyle).

Clark E G, PMLA 43.159 (reply to Lyle).

Lyle, A Rejoinder, PMLA 44.319 (reply to Clark and Foster).

Cady F W, Towneley York and True-Coventry, SP 26.386 (reply to Lyle; urges liturgical source for the three cycles).

Frank G, On the Relation between the York and Towneley Plays, PMLA 44.313.

Everett D, YWES 9.106; 10.134 (summarizes controversy).

Cargill O, Drama and Liturgy, N Y 1930, pp 105 (discounts Cady), 141 (argues against Lyle's theory of parent cycle).

Carey M, The Wakefield Group in the Towneley Cycle, Hesperia 11, Göttingen and Baltimore 1930, p 215 (initiates Brewbarret controversy).

Trusler M, The York Sacrificium Cayme and Abell, PMLA 49.956 (disagrees with Carey as to Towneley priority).

Frampton M G, The Brewbarret Interpolation in the York Play The Sacrificium Cayme and Abell, PMLA 52.895 (supplements Trusler).

Curtiss C G, The York and Towneley Plays on the Harrowing of Hell, SP 30.24 (Towneley Play 25 based on early version of York Play 37).

Frampton, The Towneley Harrowing of Hell, PMLA 56.105 (challenges findings of Curtiss).

Smith J H, The Date of Some Wakefield Borrowings from York, PMLA 53.595.

Cawley, edn, p 66 (York and Towneley Incredulity of Thomas Plays).

Craig ERD, p 210.

And see below under *Towneley-York Relations* in [11].

Christ and the Doctors. Davidson, Stud in the Eng Myst Plays, p 164 (also in Trans of the Connecticut Acad of Arts and Sciences 9.288); The Play of the Weavers of Coventry, MLN 7.92 (inter-relations of York, Towneley, Chester and True-Coventry).

Hohlfeld A, The Play of the Weavers of Coventry, MLN 7.154 (reply to Davidson).

French J C, A Note on the Miracle Plays, MLN 19.31 (reply to Davidson and Hohlfeld).

Craig H, Two Coventry Corpus Christi Plays, EETSES 87.xxviii (inter-relations of York, Towneley, Chester and True-Coventry).

Greg, p 69.

Greg W W, Christ and the Doctors and the York Play, in Chester Play Studies, Malone Soc 76.101 (inter-relations of York, Towneley, Chester and True-Coventry).

York-Shrewsbury Relations. Miller F H, Metrical Affinities of the Shrewsbury Officium Pastorum and its York Correspondent, MLN 33.91.

Craig ERD, p 210.

Davis N-CP, p xvii.

Wall C, The Apocryphal and Historical Background of the Appearance of Our Lady to Thomas (Play 46), MS 32.172.

For special rôles, see above under ENGLISH VERNACULAR PLAYS, *Rôles and Themes*; ENGLISH MYSTERIES (BIBLICAL PLAYS), *Rôles.* For relations with other cycles, see under separate cycles.

Literary Criticism. Smith, edn, p lv.

Gayley C M, The Later Miracle Plays of England: 1 The Wakefield Master of Comedy, International Quarterly 12.67 (York comic and realistic school).

Gayley, p 146 and passim.

Crowley T J, Character Treatment in the Mediaeval Drama, Notre Dame Ind 1907, p 71.

Haller J, Die Technik des Dialogs im mittelalterlichen Drama Englands, Worms a Rh 1916, p 29.

Weiner K, Die Verwendung des Parallelismus als Kunstmittel im englischen Drama vor Shakespeare, Hamburg 1916.

MacKinnon E, Notes on the Dramatic Structure of the York Cycle, SP 28.433, 444 (comparison of York Abraham and Isaac with Brome).

Wells H W, Style in the English Mystery Plays, JEGP 38.360 (duplicated with minor variations in JEGP 38.496).

Frampton M G, The York Play of Christ Led up to Calvary, PQ 20.200 (work of the York realist).

Williams A, The Characterization of Pilate in the Towneley Plays, East Lansing Mich 1950, p 17 (comparison of York Pilate with Towneley from angle of dramatic structure).

McNeir W F, The Corpus Christi Passion Plays as Dramatic Art, SP 48.601.

Cawley, edn, p 68.

Robinson J W, The Art of the York Realist, MP 60.241.

Leiter L H, Typology Paradigm Metaphor and Image in the York Creation of Adam and Eve, Drama Survey 7.113.

And see above under ENGLISH VERNACULAR PLAYS, *Literary Criticism*; ENGLISH MYSTERIES (BIBLICAL PLAYS), *Literary Criticism*.

Records of Performances, Staging, etc. Drake F, Eboracum or The History and Antiquities of the City of York from its Original to the Present Times . . . , London 1736, Appendix, p xxix.

Davies R, Extracts from the Municipal Records of the City of York during the Reigns of Edward IV Edward V and Richard III, London 1843, p 227.

Smith, edn, pp xviii, 517 and plates (music).

Chambers, 2.138, 399, 409.

Spencer M L, Corpus Christi Pageants in England, N Y 1911, see index under York.

Sellers M, York Memorandum Book Lettered A/Y in the Guildhall Muniment Room, Surtees Soc 120; 125.xxxvii (see also subject index in both vols under Corpus Christi, expenses, pageant, etc); The York Mercers and Merchant Adventurers 1356–1917, Surtees Soc 129.xxiii (see also subject index

under pageant; includes details of production of Doomsday Play).

Frank, Revisions in the English Mystery Plays, MP 15.568 (control of Register).

Westlake H F, The Parish Gilds of Mediaeval England, London 1919, p 55.

Pollard EMP 1927, p xxxi.

Mill A J, The York Bakers' Play of the Last Supper, MLR 30.145 (from BM Addit 33852); The York Plays of the Dying Assumption and Coronation of Our Lady, PMLA 65.866; The Stations of the York Corpus Christi Play, Yorkshire Archaeological Journ Pt 148.492.

Frampton, The Date of the Wakefield Master Bibliographical Evidence, PMLA 53.101, n 79 (new text of Burton's second list); The York Play of Christ Led up to Calvary, PQ 20.198.

Raine A, York Civic Records, Yorkshire Archaeological Soc, Record Series, nos 98, 103, 106, 108, 110, 112, 115, 119 (see index under Corpus Christi, pageants, etc).

Gardiner H C, Mysteries' End, YSE 103, see index under York.

Young M J, The York Pageant Wagon, Speech Monographs 34.1.

Nelson A H, Principles of Processional Staging York Cycle, MP 67.303.

General References. Klein, 1.352 (Scriveners' Play); Körting, § 133; Ten Brink, 2.266; 3.275; Bates, p 90; Brandl, § 63; Ward Hist, 1.65; Chambers, 2.409; CHEL, 5.51, 434; Creizenach, 1.291; Chambers OHEL, p 28; Baugh LHE, p 279; for Prosser, Craig ERD, and Kolve, see indexes under York cycle (plays).

Bibliography. CBEL, 1.278; 5.158; Henshaw, PMRS, 21.15; Stratman, p 137. For Pater Noster and Creed Plays, see [24–25] below.

[11] TOWNELEY (WAKEFIELD) PLAYS.

MS. Huntington HM 1 (formerly Towneley Hall), ff 1ª–131ᵇ (1450–1500).

Brown-Robbins, Robbins-Cutler, no 715.

Gordon and Hunter, edn, pp vii, xvii.

England and Pollard, edn, p x (from Gordon and Hunter edn).

Wann L, A New Examination of the Manuscript of the Towneley Plays, PMLA 43.137.

Frampton M G, The Date of the Flourishing of the Wakefield Master, PMLA 50.646.

de Ricci Census, 1.37.

Craig ERD, p 205.

Cawley, edn, p xi.

Stevens M, The Accuracy of the Towneley

Scribe, HLQ 22.1.

Editions. Gordon J and J Hunter, The Towneley Mysteries, Surtees Soc, London 1836 (formerly attributed to J Raine).

England G and A W Pollard, The Towneley Plays, EETSES 71, London 1897; reissued 1907, 1925, 1952 (crit M G Frampton, AnglB 48.330, 366; 49.3).

Editions of Selected Plays. Douce F J, Judicium A Pageant Extracted from the Towneley Manuscript of Ancient Mysteries, Roxb Club, London 1822 (Play 30).

Collier J P, Five Miracle Plays, London 1836 (Play 13).

Marriott W, A Collection of English Miracle Plays or Mysteries . . . , Basel 1838 (Plays 8, 13, 23, 25, 30).

AESpr, 1.360 (Play 3).

Manly Spec, pp 13, 58, 60, 94 (Plays 6, 5, 3, 13).

Hemingway, pp 155, 167, 170, 188 (Plays 10, 11, 12, 13; based on England and Pollard edn, with emendations by Kölbing).

Zupitza J, Alt- und me Übungsbuch, 10th edn, Vienna and Leipzig 1912, p 183 (Play 3; based on England and Pollard edn).

Cook A S, A Literary ME Reader, Boston etc 1915, p 524 (Play 13).

Brandl A and O Zippel, Me Sprach- und Literaturproben, Berlin 1917; 2nd edn entitled ME Literature, N Y 1949, p 207 (Play 13, with parallel Latin 12 cent play).

Sisam K, Fourteenth Century Verse and Prose, Oxford 1921, p 185 (Play 3; based on England and Pollard edn).

Adams CPSD, pp 94, 101, 125, 145, 191 (Plays 2, 3, 8, 12, 26).

Pollard EMP 1927 p 31 (Play 13, abridged).

Auden W H and N H Pearson, Poets of the English Language, N Y 1950 and London 1952, 1.243 (Play 13 with emendations and glosses by E T Donaldson).

Ford B, The Age of Chaucer, London 1954, p 439 (Play 12).

Kaiser R, Alt- und me Anthologie, 2nd edn Berlin 1955, pp 226, 224, 236 (Play 13 and selections from Plays 3, 30).

Cawley A C, The Wakefield Pageants in the Towneley Cycle (Old and ME Texts), Manchester and N Y 1958 (crit M Stevens, Spec 34.453; A Brown, MÆ 29.207; M C Bradbrook, MLR 54.583; K S Guthke, Angl 77.231; E Colledge, RES ns 11.69; R G Thomas, ALg 12.124).

Modernizations. R[hys] E, Everyman with Other Interludes including Eight Miracle Plays, London 1909 etc, pp 52, 99, 137 (Plays 13, 23, 25).

Child C G, The Second Shepherds' Play Everyman and Other Early Plays, Boston etc 1910, p 27 (Play 13).

Kirtlan E J B, A Little Drama of the Crucifixion Being a Modernization of the Crucifixion in the Townley Mystery Plays circa 1400 AD, London [1920] (Play 23).

Kirwan P, The Dawn of English Drama, London 1920, p 39 (Play 26).

Matthews B and P R Lieder, The Chief British Dramatists, London and N Y 1924, p 13 (Play 13).

Everyman and Other Plays Decorated by John Austen, London 1925 (Play 13; based on Rhys, Everyman with Other Interludes).

Tickner EED, pp 55, 128, 131 (Plays 3, 11, 31); Baldwin EED, pp 59, 148 (adds Play 13), 181, 184.

Schweikert H C, Early English Plays, N Y 1928, pp 74, 104 (Plays 3, 13).

Rubinstein H F, Great English Plays, London and N Y 1928, p 9 (Play 13; based on Rhys, Everyman with Other Interludes).

Lieder P R, R M Lovett and R K Root, British Drama Ten Plays, Boston 1929, p 11 (Play 13).

Parry W D, Old Plays for Modern Players, London 1930, p 37 (Play 13).

Clark B H, World Drama . . . An Anthology, N Y and London 1933, 1.325 (Play 13).

Hubbell J B and J O Beaty, An Introd to Drama, N Y 1933, p 86 (Play 13).

Tatlock J S P and R G Martin, Representative English Plays, 2nd rvsd edn, N Y 1938, pp 5, 19 (Plays 3, 13).

Kreymborg A, Poetic Drama, N Y 1941, p 199 (Play 13).

Loomis R S and H W Wells, Representative Medieval and Tudor Plays, N Y 1942, pp 61, 67 (Play 10 abridged, Play 13).

Loomis R S and R Willard, Medieval English Verse and Prose in Modernized Versions, N Y 1948, p 439 (Play 13; based on Cook edn).

Cawley A C, A Modernized Version of the Wakefield Second Shepherds' Play, Trans of the Yorkshire Dialect Soc 8, pt 50, p 8.

Bentley G E, The Development of English Drama An Anthology, N Y 1950, p 21 (Play 13).

Crump G H, Selections from English Dramatists, 2nd edn London 1950, p 36 (selection from Play 13).

Rose M, The Wakefield Mystery Plays, Lon-

don 1961 (complete acting version).
German Translations. Vatke T, Der Tod des Abel, Arch 54.39 (Play 2).
Holthausen F, Das Wakefielder Spiel von Kain und Abel, EStn 62.132; Das zweite Hirtenspiel der Wakefielder Spiele, EStn 63.193.
Textual Matters. Sharpe L, Remarks on the Towneley Mysteries, Archaeol 27.255.
Kölbing E, EStn 16.281; 21.165 (textual emendations for Play 13, begun as crit of Pollard EMP 1890).
Coblentz H E, A Rime-Index to the Parent Cycle of the York Mystery Plays and of a Portion of the Woodkirk Conspiracio et Capito, PMLA 10.487.
England and Pollard, edn, p xvi; Pollard EMP 1927, pp 188, 224a (notes to Play 13).
Hooper E S, Processus Tortorum A Suggested Emendation, Athen Aug 27 1904, p 284 (title of Play 24).
Geldart W M, Processus Talentorum Towneley XXIX, Athen Sept 3 1904, p 321 (reply to Hooper suggesting talorum or allatorum).
Hemingway, pp 273, 278, 279, 284 (notes to Plays 10–13).
Sisam, edn, p 261 (notes to Play 3).
Holthausen F, Studien zu den Towneley Plays, EStn 58.161 (crit E V Gordon, YWES 5.97).
Bonnell J K, Cain's Jaw Bone, PMLA 39.143 (Play 2, lines 323–27).
Malone K, A Note on the Towneley Secunda Pastorum, MLN 40.35 (lines 136–40).
Vriend J, That alle myghtys may in the Towneley Secunda Pastorum, ESts 8.185 (lines 683–84).
Dustoor P E, Some Textual Notes on the English Mystery Plays, MLR 21.428; Textual Notes on the Towneley Old Testament Plays, EStn 63.220.
Strunk W, Two Notes on the Towneley Second Shepherds' Play, MLN 45.151 (line 352, water; line 391, tharmes).
Rogers G, Reduction of Speakers' Parts in the Towneley Pharao, PQ 9.216 (Play 8).
Onions C T, Middle English alod, olod, MÆ 1.206; 2.73 (Play 3, line 56).
Oxley J E, Sam, TLS July 5 1934, p 476 (Play 3, line 320).
Withington R, Water Fastand, MLN 50.95 (addendum to Strunk, MLN 45.151); Thre Brefes to a Long, MLN 58.115 (Play 13, line 657).
Trusler M, Some Textual Notes Based on Examination of the Towneley Manuscript, PQ 14.301.

Frampton M G, PMLA 50.63 (costume allusions); The Early English Text Soc Edition of the Towneley Plays, AnglB 48.330, 366; 49.3.
Smith J H, Another Allusion to Costume in the Work of the Wakefield Master, PMLA 52.901 (Play 13, line 396).
Clark E M, A Restored Reading in the Towneley Purification Play, MLN 56.358 (Play 17, rubric after line 132).
Spencer H, The Lost Lines of Secunda Pastorum, MLN 58.49.
Kökeritz H, Some Marginal Notes to the Towneley Resurrection, MLN 61.529.
Jean Marie Sister, The Cross in the Towneley Plays, Trad 5.331 (Play 23, lines 89–112).
Williams A, ME Questmonger, MS 10.200 (Play 20, line 25).
Cawley A C, Iak Garcio of the Prima Pastorum, MLN 68.169 (lines 179–87); edn, p 91 (Notes).
Rynell A, On the Meaning of foyn and fo in the Towneley Plays, ESts 40.379.
Maltman Sister Nicolas, Pilate—Os Malleatoris, Spec 36.308.
Sisam C, Notes on ME Texts, RES ns 13.387 (Play 3).
Steinberg C, Kempe Towne in the Towneley Herod Play, National Magazine 71.253.
Stevens M, The Missing Parts of the Towneley Cycle, Spec 45.254 (full set of banns; lacunae due to Reformation censorship).
Language. Gordon and Hunter, edn, p xi.
Oakden J P, Alliterative Poetry in ME, 2 vols, Univ of Manchester Publ 205, English series 18, 1.chap 1 passim.
Trusler M, A Study of the Language of the Wakefield Group in Towneley on the Basis of Significant Rime-Words with Comparison of Forms within the Line in Both the Towneley and the York Plays, Chapel Hill N C 1936; The Language of the Wakefield Playwright, SP 33.15.
Cawley, edn, pp xxvii, xxxi, 130, 131.
Stevens M, HLQ 22.5; The Composition of the Towneley Talents Play A Linguistic Examination, JEGP 58.423.
Versification. Schipper J, Altenglische Metrik, Bonn 1881, p 227 and passim.
Davidson C, Studies in the English Mystery Plays, [New Haven] 1892, p 122 and passim (also in Trans of Connecticut Acad of Arts and Sciences 9.246 and passim).
England and Pollard, edn, pp xvi, xxii.
Bunzen A, Ein Beitrag zur Kritik der Wakefielder Mysterien, Kiel 1903, p 20 (crit K

Luick, AnglB 17.161).

Gayley C M, The Wakefield Master of Comedy, International Quarterly 12.67 (repeated with little change in Gayley, p 161).

Saintsbury G, A History of English Prosody, London and N Y 1906, 1.210.

Cady F W, The Couplets and Quatrains in the Towneley Mystery Plays, JEGP 10.572; The Wakefield Group in Towneley, JEGP 11.244.

Lyle M C, The Original Identity of the York and Towneley Cycles, Univ of Minnesota Stud in Lang and Lit 6.45.

Cargill O, The Authorship of the Secunda Pastorum, PMLA 41.813.

Carey M, The Wakefield Group in the Towneley Cycle, pp 217, 237 (full bibliographical entry below under *Sources and Literary Relations*).

Frampton M G, AnglB 49.3; The Processus Talentorum (Towneley XXIV), PMLA 59.646.

Chambers OHEL, p 36.

Craig ERD, p 219.

Cawley, edn, p 127.

Date. England and Pollard, edn, p xxv.

Traver H, The Relation of Musical Terms in the Woodkirk Shepherds Plays to the Dates of Their Composition, MLN 20.1.

Gayley, p 133.

Hemingway, p xlii.

Greg, p 71n.

Lyle, The Orig Identity of the York and Towneley Cycles, p 102.

Cargill, PMLA 41.812.

Frampton, PMLA 50.631; The Date of the Wakefield Master Bibliographical Evidence, PMLA 53.86; Towneley XX The Conspiracio (et Capcio), PMLA 58.937; PMLA 59.654.

Trusler, SP 33.22.

Smith J H, The Date of Some Wakefield Borrowings from York, PMLA 53.595 (reply to Frampton, PMLA 53.86).

Chambers OHEL, p 40 (date of Wakefield Master).

Cawley, edn, pp xxxi, 130.

Authorship. England and Pollard, edn, pp xv, xxii, xxx.

Cargill, The Authorship of the Secunda Pastorum, PMLA 41.810 (initiates theory of authorship of Gilbert Pilkington); Drama and Liturgy, N Y 1930, p 119.

Foster F, Was Gilbert Pilkington Author of the Secunda Pastorum? PMLA 43.124.

Carey M, The Wakefield Group in the Towneley Cycle, pp 210, 230 (Cargill's theory),

Frampton, Gilbert Pilkington Once More, PMLA 47.624.

Trusler, SP 33.27 (summary of Pilkington controversy).

Cawley, edn, p xxx.

Johnson W H, The Origin of the Second Shepherds' Play A New Theory, Quarterly Journ of Speech 52.56 (multiple authorship).

Sources and Literary Relations. Gayley, p 330.

Cron B, Zur Entwicklungsgeschichte der englischen Misterien Alten Testaments, Marburg 1913.

Wann L, The Influence of French Farce on the Towneley Cycle of Mystery Plays, Trans Wisconsin Acad of Sciences Arts and Letters 19.356.

Schering K, Die Quellen der Towneley Plays, Kiel 1923.

Carey M, The Wakefield Group in the Towneley Cycle A Study to Determine the Conventional and Original Elements in Four Plays Commonly Ascribed to the Wakefield Author, Hesperia Ergänzungreihe 11, Göttingen and Baltimore 1930, p 9 and passim (crit E Fischer, AnglB 42.212; H Patch, MLN 46.478; G R Coffman, PQ 12.94).

Melchers P, Kulturgeschichtliche Studien zu den me Misterienspielen, Würzburg 1938, passim.

Speirs J, The Mystery Cycle Some Towneley Cycle Plays, Scrut 18.86, 246 (ritual origins); Medieval English Poetry The Non-Chaucerian Tradition, London 1957, p 307 (substantially as in Scrut 18).

Liturgical and Lyrical Backgrounds. Thien H, Über die englischen Marienklagen, Kiel 1906, p 50.

Taylor G C, The English Planctus Mariae, MP 4.613, 623, 635; The Relation of the English Corpus Christi Play to the ME Religious Lyric, MP 5.5 and passim.

Cady F W, The Liturgical Basis of the Towneley Mysteries, PMLA 24.419; The Passion Group in Towneley, MP 10.587.

Kretzmann P E, The Liturgical Element in the Earliest Forms of the Medieval Drama, Univ of Minnesota Stud in Lang and Lit 4.21 and passim.

Clark E M, Liturgical Remains and Influence in the Towneley Plays, Univ of Oklahoma Abstracts of Theses (1941–53), p 240; Liturgical Influences in the Towneley Plays, Orate Fratres 16.69; The Towneley Peregrini an Unnoticed Step toward the Vernacular, MLN 61.236.

Owst G R, Literature and Pulpit in Medieval

England, Cambridge 1933, p 486 and passim (influence of sermons).

Relations with Northern Passion. Foster F, The Mystery Plays and the Northern Passion, MLN 26.169; The Northern Passion, EETS 147.86 (influence on Play 20).

Miller F H, The Northern Passion and the Mysteries, MLN 34.88.

Lyle, The Orig Identity of the York and Towneley Cycles, p 4.

Frampton, Towneley XX The Conspiracio (et Capcio), PMLA 58.924.

Individual Plays. Hamelius P, The Character of Cain in the Towneley Plays, Journ of Comparative Literature 1.324.

Garvin K, A Note on Noah's Wife, MLN 49.88 (argues for earlier tradition of shrewish wife than conceded by Carey).

Dustoor, The Origin of the Play of Moses and the Tables of the Law, MLR 19.460 (Plays 7, 9, liturgical and homiletic material of Lent).

Eaton H A, A Source for the Towneley Prima Pastorum, MLN 14.265.

Gerould G F, Moll of the Prima Pastorum, MLN 19.225.

Cawley, The Grotesque Feast in the Prima Pastorum, Spec 30.213.

Brown C, The Towneley Play of the Doctors and the Speculum Christiani, MLN 31.223.

Williams A, The Characterization of Pilate in the Towneley Plays, p 1 (heritage and tradition; full bibliographical entry below under *Literary Criticism*).

Bolte J, Der Teufel in der Kirche, ZfVL 11.264 (Tutivullus, Play 30).

Bernbrook J E, Notes on the Towneley Cycle Slaying of Abel, JEGP 62.317 (debt to St Ambrose's De Cain et Abel).

Fry T, The Antiquity of the Tradition of the Triads in the English Cycle Plays, American Benedictine Rev 18.466, 472.

The Second Shepherds' Play. Banzar A, Die Farce Patelin und ihre Nachahmungen, ZfFSL 10.93.

Kölbing E, The Secunda Pastorum of the Towneley Plays and Archie Armstrong's Aith, EETSES 71.xxxi (trans from ZfVL n f 11.137).

Cook A S, Another Parallel to the Mak Story, MP 14.11.

Wann, The Influence of French Farce, Trans Wisconsin Acad of Sciences Arts and Letters 19.360 (challenges Banzar).

Brandl and Zippel, edn, p 207 (Latin analogue).

Baugh A C, The Mak Story, MP 15.729.

Whiting B J, An Analogue to the Mak Story, Spec 7.552 (Macrobius' Saturnalia).

Smyser H M and T B Stroup, Analogues to the Mak Story, Journ American Folklore 47.378, 380.

Parrott T M, Mak and Archie Armstrong, MLN 59.297.

Cosbey R C, The Mak Story and its Folklore Analogues, Spec 20.310.

Johnson, The Origin of the Second Shepherds' Play, Quarterly Journ of Speech 52.47 (saturnalian).

Relations with Other Cycles. Smith L T, York Plays, Oxford 1885, p lxii (comparative tables of cycles).

Hohlfeld A, Die altenenglischen Kollektivmisterien unter besonderer Berücksichtigung des Verhältnisses der York- und Towneley-Spiele, Angl 11.241 (comparative tables of cycles).

Davidson, Stud in the Eng Myst Plays, p 128 (also in Trans of the Connecticut Acad of Arts and Sciences 9.252).

Chambers, 2.321 (comparative tables of cycles).

Towneley-York Relations. England and Pollard, edn, p xiv.

Bunzen A, Ein Beitrag zur Kritik der Wakefielder Mysterien, Kiel 1903, p 10.

Gayley C M, International Quarterly 12.67.

Gayley, pp 161, 330.

Cady, The Liturgical Basis of the Towneley Mysteries, PMLA 24.419 (relations also with True-Coventry); The Couplets and Quatrains in the Towneley Mystery Plays, JEGP 10.572; The Wakefield Group in Towneley, JEGP 11.251; The Passion Group in Towneley, MP 10.587.

Frank G, Revisions in the English Mystery Plays, MP 15.565 (reply to Cady, JEGP 10.572).

Lyle, The Orig Identity of the York and Towneley Cycles (for controversy see above under *York-Towneley Relations* in [10]).

Rogers G, Reduction of Speakers' Parts in the Towneley Pharao, PQ 9.216.

Frampton, The Date of the Wakefield Master Bibliographical Evidence, PMLA 53.86 (reply J H Smith, PMLA 53.595); PMLA 58.920; PMLA 59.646.

Williams A, The Characterization of Pilate in the Towneley Plays, p 53.

Craig ERD, p 210.

And see above under *York-Towneley Relations* in [10].

Towneley-York-Coventry Relations. Brown C, The Towneley Play of the Doctors and the Speculum Christiani, MLN 31.226. And see above under *Christ and the Doctors* in [10].

Dunn E C, The Medieval Cycle as History Play An Approach to the Wakefield Plays, Studies in the Renaissance 7.76.

For special rôles, see above under ENGLISH VERNACULAR PLAYS, *Rôles and Themes*; ENGLISH MYSTERIES (BIBLICAL PLAYS), *Rôles*. For relations with other cycles, see under separate cycles.

Literary Criticism. Ebert A, Die englischen Mysterien mit besonderer Berücksichtigung der Towneley-Sammlung, JfRESL 1.74, 131 (analysis of separate plays).

Hamelius, The Character of Cain in the Towneley Plays, Journ of Comp Lit 1.324.

Gayley, The Wakefield Master of Comedy, International Quarterly 12.72.

Gayley, p 168 (repeated substantially as in International Quarterly 12.72).

Moorman F W, The Wakefield Miracle Plays, Trans of the Yorkshire Dialect Soc 1, pt 7, p 5.

Hemingway, p xlv.

Cady, The Wakefield Group in Towneley, JEGP 11.244, 255.

Haller J, Die Technik des Dialogs im mittelalterlichen Drama Englands, Worms a Rh 1916, p 43.

Carey, The Wakefield Group in the Towneley Cycle, p 32 and passim.

Wells H W, Style in the English Mystery Plays, JEGP 38.360 (duplicated with minor variations in JEGP 38.496).

Watt H A, The Dramatic Unity of the Secunda Pastorum, in E&S Brown, p 158.

Chidamian C, Mak and the Tossing in the Blanket, Spec 22.186.

Thompson F J, Unity in The Second Shepherds' Tale, MLN 64.302.

Williams A, The Characterization of Pilate in the Towneley Plays, East Lansing Mich 1950 (crit G Frank, Spec 26.556; A Brown, MLR 47.60; N Coghill, MÆ 21.53; F A Foster, JEGP 51.247).

Rossiter A P, English Drama from Early Times to the Elizabethans, London etc 1950, p 68.

Carpenter N C, Music in the Secunda Pastorum, Spec 26.696.

McNeir W F, The Corpus Christi Passion Plays as Dramatic Art, SP 48.601.

Speirs, Scrut 18.86, 246.

Cawley, The Wakefield First Shepherds' Play, Proc of Leeds Philos and Lit Soc 7².113; edn, p xxvii.

Zumwalt E E, Irony in the Towneley Shepherds' Plays, Research Stud of the State Coll of Washington 26.37.

Schless H H, The Comic Element in the Wakefield Noah, Stud in Med Lit in Honor of A C Baugh, ed MacEdward Leach, Phila London etc 1961, p 229.

Prosser, p 76 and passim.

Dunn E C, Lyrical Form and the Prophetic Principle in the Towneley Plays, MS 23.80; The Prophetic Principle in the Towneley Prima Pastorum, Linguistic and Lit Stud in Honor of H A Hatzfeld, Washington 1964, p 117; The Literary Style of the Towneley Plays, American Benedictine Rev 20.481.

Manly W M, Shepherds and Prophets Religious Unity in the Towneley Secunda Pastorum, PMLA 78.151.

Morgan M M, High Fraud: Paradox and Double-plot in the English Shepherds' Plays, Spcc 39.676.

Diller H-J, The Craftsmanship of the Wakefield Master, Angl 83.271.

Gardner J, Theme and Irony in the Wakefield Mactacio Abel, PMLA 80.515; Imagery and Allusion in the Wakefield Noah Play, Papers on Lang and Lit 4.3.

Hurrell J D, The Figural Approach to Medieval Drama, CE 26.598 (challenges Watt in E&S Brown, p 158).

Stevens M, The Dramatic Setting of the Wakefield Annunciation, PMLA 81.193.

Cantelupe E B and R Griffith, The Gifts of the Shepherds in the Wakefield Secunda Pastorum An Iconographical Interpretation, MS 28.328.

Davidson C, The Unity in the Wakefield Mactacio Abel, Trad 23.495; An Interpretation of the Wakefield Judicium, Annuale Medievale 10.104.

Ross L J, Symbol and Structure in the Secunda Pastorum, Comparative Drama 1.122.

Weimann R, Realismus und Simultankonvention im Misterien-Drama Mimesis Parodie und Utopie in den Towneley-Hirtenszenen, Shakesp Jahrb (Weimar) 103.108.

Munson W F, Typology and the Towneley Isaac, Research Opportunities in Renaissance Drama (medieval suppl) 11.129 (challenges Woolf's charge of inferiority, Spec 32.816).

Elliott C, Language and Theme in the Towneley Magnus Herodes, MS 30.351.

Altieri J S, The Ironic Structure of the Towneley Fflagellacio, Drama Survey 7.104.

Longo J A, Symmetry and Symbolism in the Secunda Pastorum, Nottingham Med Stud

13.65.

Meyers W E, A Figure Given Typology in the Wakefield Plays, Pittsburgh 1970.

Cutts J P, The Shepherds' Gifts in the Second Shepherds' Play and Bosch's Adoration of the Magi, Comparative Drama 4.120.

Brawer R A, The Dramatic Function of the Ministry in the Towneley Cycle, Comparative Drama 4.166.

Staging, Locale. Spencer M L, Corpus Christi Pageants in England, N Y 1911, see index under Towneley.

Gardiner H C, Mysteries' End An Investigation of the Last Days of the Medieval Religious Stage, YSE 103.77, 115, 121, 122.

Hildburgh W L, English Alabaster Carvings as Records of the Medieval Religious Drama, Archaeol 93.51 and passim.

Rose M, The Wakefield Mystery Plays, London 1961, p 26 (fixed stage theory).

Stevens, The Staging of the Wakefield Plays, Research Opportunities in Renaissance Drama (medieval suppl) 11.115.

Widkirk (Woodkirk)—Wakefield Locale. Skeat W W, The Locality of the Towneley Plays, Athen 102²(Dec 2 1893).779 (identifies Widkirk with Woodkirk).

England and Pollard, edn, pp xii, xxviii (cites Woodkirk tradition from Surtees Soc Pref).

Peacock M H, Towneley Widkirk or Wakefield Plays? Yorkshire Archaeological and Topographical Journ 15.94 (argues for Wakefield); The Wakefield Mysteries The Place of Representation, Angl 24.509.

Leach A F, Some English Plays and Players, in Furnivall Miscellany, London 1901, p 228.

Chambers, 2.415.

Skeat, N&Q 10s 10.37 (again identifies Widkirk with Woodkirk); Peacock, N&Q 10s 10.128 (reply to Skeat); Skeat, N&Q 10s 10.177 (counter-reply).

Hemingway, p xli.

Greg, p 81.

Peacock, AnglB 36.111 (reinforces Wakefield's claim through Burgess Court evidence); TLS March 5 1925, p 156 (reply by R Potter, TLS April 30 1925, p 300; counter-reply by Peacock, TLS May 7 1925, p 316); Yorkshire Archaeol Journ 28.427; TLS June 7 1928, p 431.

Wann L, PMLA 43.150.

Walker J W, The Burges Courts Wakefield, Yorkshire Archaeol Soc, Record Series 74, Pref and pp 20, 21; Wakefield Its History and People, Wakefield 1939, pp 149, 151 (cites Burgess Court records and reaffirms

Wakefield claim).

Frampton, PMLA 50.644.

Gardiner, YSE 103.77, 121 (new record from York Diocesan Registry regarding Wakefield Whitsun play), 122 (Wakefield Burgess Court records).

Dodds M H, A Few Notes on Yorkshire Folk-Drama, N&Q 195.473.

Craig ERD, p 207.

Cawley, edn, pp xiv, 124.

General References. Körting, § 133; Ten Brink, 2.256; Bates, p 48; Brandl, § 63; Ward Hist, 1.71; Chambers, 2.124, 412; CHEL, 5.52, 434; Creizenach, 1.294; Pollard EMP 1927, p xxxv; Chambers OHEL, p 34; Baugh LHE, p 280; Craig ERD, chap 6 and passim; Prosser, see index under Towneley cycle; Kolve, see index under Towneley cycle.

Bibliography. CBEL, 1.277; 5.158; Henshaw, PMRS, 21.16; Stratman, p 129.

[12] LUDUS COVENTRIAE (HEGGE PLAYS).

MS. Cotton Vesp D.viii, ff 1ᵃ–225ᵇ (1450–75).

Brown-Robbins, Robbins-Cutler, no 2321.

Halliwell J O, edn, p vi.

Greg, p 108.

Greg W W, edn, pp 5, 46.

Block K S, Some Notes on the Problem of the Ludus Coventriae, MLR 10.47; edn, p xi.

Craig ERD, p 241.

Editions. Halliwell J O, Ludus Coventriae, Shakespeare Soc, London 1841.

Block K S, Ludus Coventriae or The Plaie Called Corpus Christi Cotton MS Vespasian D.VIII, EETSES 120, London 1922 (crit N&Q 145.319; F Holthausen, AnglB 35.37).

Editions of Selected Plays. Collier J P, Five Miracle Plays or Scriptural Dramas, London 1836 (Play 10).

Marriott W, A Collection of English Miracle Plays, or Mysteries, Basel 1838 (Plays 12, 14).

Dugdale W, Monasticon Anglicanum 6, London 1846, pt 3, p 1534 (Banns and Plays 1–5).

Wülcker R P, Altenglisches Lesebuch, 2 vols, Halle a S 1879, 2.130 (Play 5).

Manly Spec, 1.31, 82 (Play 4, from MS with variants from Halliwell edn; Play 11, from MS with variants from Halliwell edn, Pollard EMP 1890, and E Kölbing, EStn 16.281; 21.166).

Hemingway (Plays 11, 12, 13, 15, 16, with variants from Halliwell edn and E Kölbing,

EStn 16.281; 21.166).

Greg W W, The Assumption of the Virgin A Miracle Play from the N-Town Cycle, Oxford 1915 (Play 41; crit A Brandl, Arch 142.146).

Adams CPSD, pp 81, 139, 175, 179 (Banns abridged; Play 11 omits Prologue; Play 28; selections from Plays 29, 30).

Selections. Hone W, Ancient Mysteries Described . . . , London 1823 (from Plays 8–15; from MS).

Pollard EMP 1927, p 44 (from Play 11).

Modernizations. Tickner EED, pp 69, 82, 147, 159, 191 (Plays 1, 2; selections from Plays 7, 29–31, 31–32, 42); Baldwin EED, pp 99, 110, 200, 212, 245.

Schweikert H C, Early English Plays, N Y 1928, pp 68, 71 (Banns, selections; Play 1).

Browne E M, The Play of the Maid Mary, Religious Plays Series 3, London 1932; The Play of Mary the Mother, Religious Plays Series 4, London 1932.

Loomis R S and H W Wells, Representative Medieval and Tudor Plays, N Y 1942, p 95 (The Mystery of the Redemption, abridged from the Hegge MS).

Textual Matters. Wülcker, edn, p 284 (notes to Play 5).

Kölbing E, EStn 16.281; 21.166 (textual emendations begun as review of Pollard EMP 1890).

Greg, edn, p 64.

Block, edn, p xvii.

Bonnell J K, Cain's Jaw Bone, PMLA 39.143 (Play 3, line 149).

Holthausen F, Das Märchen vom Schneekind, AnglB 35.95 (Play 14, lines 273–80).

Dustoor P E, Some Textual Notes on the English Mystery Plays, MLR 21.428 (Play 4, line 44).

Pollard EMP 1927, p 191 (notes to Play 11).

Wells M E, The Age of Isaac at the Time of the Sacrifice, MLN 54.579 (Play 5, lines 145ff).

Kökeritz H, Outborn in Ludus Coventriae, MLN 64.88 (Play 30, line 326).

Meredith P, Nolo mortem and the Ludus Coventriae, MÆ 38.38 (plea for Nolo mortem peccatoris as integral first line).

Language. Kramer M, Sprache und Heimat des sogen Ludus Coventriae eine Untersuchung zur me Sprachgeschichte, Halle a S 1892.

Greg, edn, p 9.

Craig ERD, p 266.

Versification. Schipper, 1.230 and passim.

Saintsbury G, A History of English Prosody, London 1906, 1.214.

Swenson E L, Univ of Minnesota Stud in Lang and Lit 1.64 (table of distribution of verse forms; full bibliographical entry below under *Development and Organization of the Cycle*).

Greg, edn, p 26.

Patch H R, The Ludus Coventriae and the Digby Massacre, PMLA 35.324 (examines relation on metrical basis).

Craig ERD, pp 247, 257, 259.

Date. Chambers, 2.416.

Hemingway, p xxxvii.

Block, edn, p xv.

Authorship. Chambers, 2.145.

Hemingway, p xxxvii.

Greg, edn, p 36 (argues for separate authorship for Play 41).

Block, edn, p xlvi.

Prosser, Appendix, p 201 (the reviser of Hegge Passion Play, Pt 1).

Sources and Literary Relations. Falke E, Die Quellen des sog Ludus Coventriae, Leipzig 1908 (takes up individual plays).

Gayley, p 325.

Hemingway, p xxxiii.

Mackenzie W R, The English Moralities from the Point of View of Allegory, Boston and London 1914, pp 24, 37.

Patch, *PMLA* 35.324.

Block, edn, pp xliii, lvii, liv (relations with Moralities).

Melchers P, Kulturgeschichtliche Studien zu den me Mysterienspielen, Würzburg 1938, passim.

(The following items are concerned with extra-dramatic sources.)

Thien H, Über die englischen Marienklagen, Kiel 1906, p 54.

Taylor G C, The English Planctus Mariae, MP 4.613, 624, 635.

Kretzmann P E, The Liturgical Element in the Earliest Forms of the Medieval Drama, Univ of Minnesota Stud in Lang and Lit 4.12 and passim.

Foster F, The Northern Passion, EETS 147.89 (parallels with Plays 27–34), 183, vii.

Parker R E, The ME Stanzaic Versions of the Life of Saint Anne, EETS 174.xxxiv (argues for Minnesota version as source of Virgin group of plays).

Owst G R, Literature and Pulpit in Medieval England, Cambridge 1933, p 486 and passim (influence of sermons).

Fry T P, The Unity of the Ludus Coventriae, SP 48.527 (influence of patristic theory).

Craig ERD, pp 254, 258.
Sources and Analogues of Individual Plays.
Hamelius P, De Dood van Kain in de engelsche mysteriespelen van Coventry, Ghent 1903 (Play 3).
Dustoor P E, The Origin of the Play of Moses and the Tables of the Law, MLR 19.461 (Play 6).
Bonnell J K, The Source in Art of the So-called Prophets Play in the Hegge Collection, PMLA 29.327 (Play 7).
Kispaugh Sister Mary Jerome, The Feast of the Presentation of the Virgin Mary in the Temple An Historical and Literary Study, Washington D C 1941 (Play 9).
Traver H, The Four Daughters of God, Bryn Mawr Pa 1907, p 125 and passim (Play 11; allegory of the Four Daughters of God in the Salutation Play).
Bühler C F, The Sources of the Court of Sapience, Beiträge zur englischen Philologie 23.29 (Play 11; relation with Ludus Coventriae; Four Daughters of God).
Brunner K, Der Streit der vier Himmelstöchter, EStn 68.188 (Play 11; Four Daughters of God).
Smith Sister Mary Frances, Wisdom and Personification Occurring in ME Literature before 1500, Washington D C 1935, p 150 (Play 11; Four Daughters of God).
Boughner D C, Retribution in English Medieval Drama, N&Q 198.507 (Plays 18, 20).
Clark J M, The Dance of Death in the Middle Ages and the Renaissance, Glasgow Univ Publ 86, Glasgow 1950, p 93 (Play 20).
Benkovitz M J, Some Notes on the Prologue of Demon of Ludus Coventriae, MLN 60.78 (Play 26).
Taylor G C, The Christus Redivivus of Nicholas Grimald and the Hegge Resurrection Plays, PMLA 41.840 (crit A W Reed, YWES 7.108).
Abel P, Grimald's C R and the Digby Resurrection, MLN 70.330.
Greg, edn, p 39 (Legenda aurea as source of Play 41).
Smith, Wisdom and Personification, p 147 (relation of Play 41 with Court of Sapience).
Forrest M P, Apocryphal Sources of the St Anne's Day Plays in the Hegge Cycle, MH 17.38.
Meredith, MÆ 38.40.
Relations with Other Cycles. Smith L T, York Plays, Oxford 1885, p lxii (comparative tables of cycles).
Hohlfeld A, Die altenenglischen Kollektiv-

misterien unter besonderer Berücksichtigung des Verhältnisses der York- und Towneley- Spiele, Angl 11.241 (comparative tables of cycles).
Chambers, 2.321 (comparative tables of cycles).
Swenson, Univ of Minnesota Stud in Lang and Lit 1.18 (table of prophecies in the four cycles; full bibliographical entry below under *Development and Organization of the Cycle*).
For special rôles, see above under ENGLISH VERNACULAR PLAYS, *Rôles and Themes*; ENGLISH MYSTERIES (BIBLICAL PLAYS), *Rôles*.
Development and Organization of the Cycle. Hemingway, p xxxiii.
Cron B, Zur Entwicklungsgeschichte der englischen Misterien Alten Testaments, Marburg 1913.
Greg, p 108 (The Fabrication of a Cycle).
Dodds M H, The Problem of the Ludus Coventriae, MLR 9.79.
Craig H, An Inquiry into the Composition and Structure of Ludus Coventriae, Univ of Minnesota Stud in Lang and Lit 1.81 (reply to Dodds).
Block, Some Notes on the Problem of the Ludus Coventriae, MLR 10.47 (reply to Dodds).
Swenson E L, An Inquiry into the Composition and Structure of Ludus Coventriae with a Note on the Home of Ludus Coventriae by Hardin Craig, Univ of Minnesota Stud in Lang and Lit 1 (crit W W Greg, Libr 1.182).
Block, edn, pp xii, xxxii.
Clark T B, A Theory Concerning the Identity and History of the Ludus Coventriae Cycle of Mystery Plays, PQ 12.144.
Baugh A C, A Recent Theory of the Ludus Coventriae, PQ 12.403 (reply to Clark).
Salter F M, The Old Testament Plays of Ludus Coventriae, PQ 12.406 (challenges Clark on basis of handwriting).
Bryant J A, The Function of Ludus Coventriae 14, JEGP 52.340.
Literary Criticism. Gayley, p 191.
Haller J, Die Technik des Dialogs im mittelalterlichen Drama Englands, Worms a Rh 1916, p 55.
Block, edn, p lv.
Wells H W, Style in the English Mystery Plays, JEGP 38.360 (duplicated with minor variations, JEGP 38.496).
Fry, SP 48.527 (unity).
McNeir W F, The Corpus Christi Passion Plays as Dramatic Art, SP 48.601.

Craig ERD, p 260.
Forrest M P, The Role of the Expositor Contemplacio in the St Anne's Day Plays of the Hegge Cycle, MS 28.60 (unifying effect). Meredith, MÆ 38.43.
Griffin J R, The Hegge Pilate A Tragic Hero? ESts 51.234.
Records, Staging. Dugdale W, The Antiquities of Coventre . . . , Coventry 1765, p 43.
Chambers, 2.419.
Thompson E N S, The Ludus Coventriae, MLN 21.18.
Gayley, p 135.
Hemingway, p xxviii.
Spencer M L, Corpus Christi Pageants in England, N Y 1911, pp 172, 178.
Block, edn, p xxxvii.
Bryant, JEGP 52.340 (Play 14 as a money-gathering device).
Craig ERD, pp 239, 243.
Cameron K and S J Kahrl, The N-Town Plays at Lincoln, Theatre Notebook 20.68 (argue for stationary semi-circular production on pageant cars); Staging the N-Town Cycle, Theatre Notebook 21.122, 152.
Locale. Kramer M, Sprache und Heimat des sogen Ludus Coventriae, Halle a S 1892.
Craig H, The Coventry Cycle of Plays, Athen Aug 16 1913, p 166 (initiates campaign for Lincoln as home of Ludus Coventriae).
Greg W W, The Coventry Cycle of Plays, Athen Sept 13 1913, p 262 (reply to Craig).
Craig, N Y Nation 97.308 (plea for Lincoln).
Dodds, MLR 9.79 (argues for Bury St Edmunds).
Swenson, Univ of Minnesota Stud in Lang and Lit 1.1.
Craig, Note on the Home of Ludus Coventriae, in Swenson, Univ of Minnesota Stud in Lang and Lit 1.72 (reply to Dodds on the home of the Ludus Coventriae); The Lincoln Cordwainers' Pageant, PMLA 32.615.
Hartman H, The Home of the Ludus Coventriae, MLN 41.530 (supports Craig).
Loomis R S, Lincoln as a Dramatic Centre, in Mélanges d'Histoire . . . offerts à Gustave Cohen, Paris 1950, p 5.
Craig ERD, p 265 (Lincoln).
Cameron and Kahrl, Theatre Notebook 20.61.
Nelson A H, Recovering the Lost Norwich Corpus Christi Cycle, Comparative Drama 4.246.
Eccles M, Ludus Coventriae Lincoln or Norfolk? MÆ 40.135.
General References. Klein, 1.727, 739; Körting, § 133; Ten Brink, 2.283; 3.276; Bates,

p 117; Brandl, § 43; Ward Hist, 1.84; Chambers, 2.124, 126, 416; CHEL, 5.22, 54, 433; Creizenach, 1.298; Pollard EMP 1927, p xxxvii; Chambers OHEL, p 47; Baugh LHE, p 282; Prosser, see index under Hegge Cycle; Craig ERD, chap 7 and passim; Kolve, see index under Ludus Coventriae.
Bibliography. CBEL, 1.277; 5.157; Fry, SP 48.527n; Henshaw, PMRS, 21.19; Stratman, p 126.

[13] COVENTRY (TRUE-COVENTRY) PLAYS.

MSS. 1, Coventry Corporation, 17 folios, one missing (1534–35; Croo transcript of Weavers' Pageant); 2, Two loose leaves along with MS 1 (15 cent); 3, See under Sharp's 1817 edn of Shearmen and Taylors' Play.
Brown-Robbins, Robbins-Cutler, no 3477; Brown-Robbins, no 4248.
Chambers, 2.422.
Craig, edn, p xxxv; reissued The Manuscripts of the Weavers' Pageant of Coventry, Princeton Univ Bull 14.199.
Craig ERD, pp 163, 283, 295.
Flower R, The Coventry Mysteries, Brit Mus Quart 8.98 (description of proof sheets of Sharp's edn of Dissertation from MS BM Addit 43645).
Editions. Sharp T, The Pageant of the Company of Sheremen and Taylors in Coventry as performed by them on the Festival of Corpus Christi, Coventry 1817; rptd 1871 (from MS in possession of Sharp and lost in Shakespeare Memorial Library fire in Birmingham, 1879).
Sharp T, A Dissertation on the Pageants or Dramatic Mysteries anciently performed at Coventry . . . to which are added the Pageant of the Shearmen & Taylors' Company . . . , Coventry 1825, p 83.
[Sharp T], The Presentation in the Temple A Pageant as Originally Represented by the Corporation of Weavers in Coventry, Abbotsford Club, Edinburgh 1836 (ed J B Gracie from Croo transcript 1534–35).
Marriott W, A Collection of English Miracle Plays or Mysteries . . . , Basel 1838, p 59 (Shearmen and Taylors).
Manly Spec, p 120 (Shearmen and Taylors, based on Sharp edn with emendations).
Holthausen F, Das Spiel der Weber von Coventry, Angl 25.209 (based on Sharp edn).
Craig H, Two Coventry Corpus Christi Plays: 1. The Shearmen and Taylors' Pageant re-edited from the edition of Thomas

Sharp 1825; and 2. The Weavers' Pageant re-edited from the manuscript of Robert Croo 1534; with a plan of Coventry and Appendixes containing the chief records of the Coventry Plays, EETSES 87, London 1902 (Play 1 based on Sharp edn with Manly Spec edn emendations; Play 2 based on Sharp edn with Holthausen edn emendations; App IV, fragments of earlier version of Weavers' play); reissued 1931, Princeton Univ Bull 14.200 (fragments rptd from EETSES 87, App IV, with minor variations); 2nd edn 1957 (with minor corrections and supplementary material).

Adams CPSD, p 158 (Shearmen and Taylors, lines 475 to end).

Kaiser R, Alt- und me Anthologie, 2nd edn Berlin 1955, p 239 (Shearmen and Taylors, lines 475–539, based on Craig edn).

Modernizations. Pollard A W, A Miracle Play of the Nativity, in Edward Arber An English Garner, London 1903, p 245 (Shearmen and Taylors).

R[hys] E, Everyman with Other Interludes including Eight Miracle Plays, London 1909 etc, p 74 (Shearmen and Taylors).

Tickner EED, p 84 (Shearmen and Taylors); Baldwin EED, p 112.

Robinson D F, The Harvard Dramatic Club Miracle Plays, N Y 1928, p 5 (Shearmen and Taylors, abridged and adapted).

Allen J, Three Medieval Plays, The Drama Library, London 1953 (Shearmen and Taylors).

Textual Matters. Craig, edn, pp xxviii, xxxv; reissued Princeton Univ Bull 14.203 (notes on fragments of earlier version of Weavers' Play).

Versification. Craig, edn, pp xxiv, xxvi.

Craig ERD, pp 164, 296.

Sources and Literary Relations. Melchers P, Kulturgeschichtliche Studien zu den me Misterienspielen, Würzburg 1938.

Liturgical and Lyrical Elements. Taylor G C, The Relation of the English Corpus Christi Play to the ME Religious Lyric, MP 5.7, 23, 30 (Shearmen and Taylors lyrics).

Munro J, Tyrly Tirlow and the Coventry Play of the Nativity, N&Q 11s 1.125 (connection with carol).

Kretzmann P E, The Liturgical Element in the Earliest Forms of the Medieval Drama, Univ of Minnesota Stud in Lang and Lit 4.23 and passim.

Greene R L, Early English Carols, Oxford 1935, pp 50, 71, 366, 373 (Shearmen and Taylors lyrics).

Relations with Other Cycles. Davidson C, Studies in the English Mystery Plays, [New Haven] 1892, p 164 (Christ with the Doctors; also in Trans of Connecticut Acad of Arts and Sciences 9.288); The Play of the Weavers of Coventry, MLN 7.92 (crit A R Hohlfeld, MLN 7.154; J C French, MLN 19.31).

Craig, An Edition of the Weavers' Play of Coventry, Princeton Univ Bull 13.8; edn, p xxviii (four parallel versions of the Doctors' Play).

Greg, p 86.

Greg W W, Chester Play Studies, Malone Soc 76.101.

Brown C, The Towneley Play of the Doctors and the Speculum Christiani, MLN 31.226 (Weavers' Play, lines 977–1000; relations with Towneley and York).

Cady F W, Towneley York and True-Coventry, SP 26.386.

For special rôles, see above under ENGLISH VERNACULAR PLAYS, *Rôles and Themes;* ENGLISH MYSTERIES (BIBLICAL PLAYS), *Rôles.*

Records, Staging, etc. Sharp, edn, A Dissertation.

Poole B, Coventry Its History & Antiquities, Coventry 1870, p 37; C Nowell (index to Poole), Coventry 1952, see under Mysteries, Pageants.

Halliwell-Phillipps J O, Outlines of the Life of Shakespeare, 2nd edn, London 1882, p 321.

Harris M D, Life in an Old English Town A History of Coventry from the Earliest Times Compiled from Official Records, London and N Y 1898, p 340; The Story of Coventry, London 1911, p 287; The Coventry Leet Book Or Mayor's Register Containing the Records of the City Court Leet or View of Frankpledge A D 1420–1555 with Divers Other Matters, Pt 4, EETS 146.ix and see index under Pageants; The World in the Doomsday Mystery Play, N&Q 149.243 (correction of item in Sharp's reading of Drapers' Accounts).

Craig, edn, pp xi, 72 Appendix I (Extracts from Coventry Leet Book), 82 Appendix II (Trading Company records relating to Corpus Christi Play).

Chambers, 2.357.

Mill A J, Mediaeval Stage Decoration That Apple Tree Again, Theatre Notebook 24.123 (correction of Sharp reading).

General References. Ten Brink, 2.280; Chambers, 2.422; Chambers OHEL, p 41; Craig ERD, see index under Coventry plays;

Kolve, see index under Coventry plays.
Bibliography. CBEL, 1.277; Stratman, p 123.

[14] NEWCASTLE NOAH'S ARK.

MSS. No MS extant.
Brown-Robbins, no 865.
Editions. Bourne H, The History of New-castle upon Tyne, Newcastle upon Tyne 1736, (text of play, pp 139–141, has MS status; but see Davis N-CP, p xli).
Brand J, The History and Antiquities of the Town . . . of Newcastle upon Tyne, London 1789, 2.373 (based on Bourne edn with minor changes).
Sharp T, A Dissertation on the Pageants . . . anciently performed at Coventry . . . , Coventry 1825, p 223 (based on Brand edn).
Holthausen F, Das Noahspiel von Newcastle upon Tyne, Göteborg's Högskolas Årsskrift 3, no 3, Göteborg 1897 and separately (based on Bourne edn; critical text; crit A Brandl, Arch 100.436; E L, Revue Critique 45.511; H Logeman, EStn 28.115).
Brotanek R, Noah's Arche ein misterium aus Newcastle upon Tyne, Angl 21.165 (restored text parallel with Sharp's 1825 text).
Waterhouse O, The Non-Cycle Mystery Plays, EETSES 104.19 (based on Bourne edn with variants).
King R, Noah's Ark The Only Surviving Mystery Play of the Newcastle Cycle, Tyne-mouth 1922 (based on Waterhouse edn without critical apparatus).
Dustoor P E, The Newcastle Noah's Ark, Allahabad Univ Stud 8, Pt 1, Arts Section (crit D Everett, YWES 13.120).
Davis N-CP, pp 19 (Bourne's text), 25 (edited text).
Modernizations. Dodds M H, Noah's Ark The Play of the Shipwrights' Gild of Newcastle-upon-Tyne in the Cycle of Miracle Plays acted by the Gilds of the City at the Feast of Corpus Christi (circa 1450), Newcastle-upon-Tyne 1925.
Tickner EED, p 49; Baldwin EED, p 53.
Textual Matters. Holthausen, edn, p 34; Zur Noah-Legende, AnglB 31.91.
Dustoor, Some Textual Notes on the English Mystery Plays, MLR 21.429; Notes on the EETS Edition of the Newcastle Noah's Ark, MLN 43.252; edn, p 15.
Davis N-CP, p xli.
Language. Holthausen, edn, p 19.
Waterhouse, edn, p xxxvi.
Davis N-CP, p xliv.
Versification. Davidson C, Studies in the English Mystery Plays, [New Haven] 1892, p 136 (also in Trans of Connecticut Acad

of Arts and Sciences 9.260).
Holthausen, edn, p 21.
Waterhouse, edn, p xxxvii.
Dustoor, edn, p 16.
Davis N-CP, p xliii.
Sources and Literary Relations. Cushman L W, The Devil and the Vice in the English Dramatic Literature before Shakespeare, SEP 6.37, 51.
Holthausen, Die Quelle des Noahspiels von Newcastle upon Tyne, ShJ 36.277 (angel messenger from Avitus de Diluvio Mundi); AnglB 31.90.
Waterhouse, edn, p xxxvii (relations with Towneley and York).
Haslinghuis E J, De Duivel in het Drama der Middeleeuwen, Leiden 1912, p 83.
Wieland G, Lustspielelemente im me Drama (bis 1500), Bühl (Baden) 1913, pp 92, 97.
Lindblom A, Den apokryfa Noahsagan i medeltidens konst och litteratur, Nordisk Tidskrift 1917, pp 358, 363.
Carey M, The Wakefield Group in the Towneley Cycle, Hesperia 11, Göttingen and Baltimore 1930, p 69 (English tradition of shrewish wife).
Garvin K, A Note on Noah's Wife, MLN 49.88 (Eng trad of shrewish wife).
Dustoor, edn, p 16.
Mill A J, Noah's Wife Again, PMLA 56.613 (sources of Devil's temptation of Uxor).
Utley F L, The One Hundred and Three Names of Noah's Wife, Spec 16.450; Noah's Ham and Jansen Enikel, GR 16.247 (sources of Devil's temptation of Uxor).
Records, Staging. Brand, edn, 2.311, 369.
Sharp, edn, p 221.
Holthausen, edn, p 12.
Chambers, 2.385.
Waterhouse, edn, p xxxix.
Dodds M H, The Northern Stage, Archaeologia Aeliana 3s 11.40.
Hodgson J C, The Company of Saddlers of Newcastle, Archaeologia Aeliana 3s 19.1, 3.
King, edn, p 27.
Mill, The Hull Noah Play, MLR 33.489.
Davis N-CP, p xlii.
General References. Körting, 135n; Ten Brink, 2.273; 3.275; Bates, p 139; Brandl, § 131; Ward Hist, 1.70, 91; Chambers, 2.138, 424; Gayley, p 140; Chambers OHEL, pp 43, 216; Craig ERD, p 303; Kolve, pp 53, 148.
Bibliography. CBEL, 1.279; Stratman, p 152.

[15] NORWICH GROCERS' PLAY.

MS. Formerly (unofficially) Norwich Castle Record Room, 18 cent transcript of the

lost Grocers' Book.
Brown-Robbins, Robbins-Cutler, no 714.
Waterhouse, edn, p xxvii.
Davis N, TLS Apr 16 1964, p 317 (query as to location).
Editions. Fitch R, Norwich Pageants The Grocers' Play, Norfolk Archaeology 5.11; rptd separately Norwich 1856.
Manly Spec, pp 1, 4 (texts A and B, based on Fitch edn with emendations).
Waterhouse O, The Non-Cycle Mystery Plays, EETSES 104.8, 11 (texts A and B, from 18 cent transcript with collations of Fitch edn and Manly Spec edn).
Adams CPSD, p 88 (text B, based on Waterhouse edn with emendations from Fitch edn and Manly Spec edn).
Davis N-CP, pp 8 (text A), 11 (text B).
Textual Matters. Parsons E S, A Grocer's Play, MLN 21.224 (text B, alternative Prologue, lines 1–14).
Dustoor P E, Textual Notes on Three Non-Cycle Mystery Plays, MLR 23.209.
Davis N-CP, p xxv.
Records, Staging. Harrod H, A Few Particulars Concerning Early Norwich Pageants, Norfolk Archaeology 3.3.
Fitch, edn, p 24.
Bolingbroke L G, Pre-Elizabethan Plays and Players in Norfolk, Norfolk Archaeology 11.341.
Chambers, 2.386.
Hudson W and J C Tingey, The Records of the City of Norwich, 2 vols, Norwich and London 1906, 2.liii, lv, 126, 135, 230.
Spencer M L, Corpus Christi Pageants in England, N Y 1911, pp 87, 131, 176, 254.
Craig ERD, pp 124, 298.
Anderson M D, Drama and Imagery in English Medieval Churches, Cambridge 1963, p 87 (Norwich bosses).
Davis N-CP, p xxvi.
Nelson A H, Recovering the Lost Norwich Corpus Christi Cycle, Comparative Drama 4.241.
General References. Ten Brink, 2.253; Ward Hist, 1.91; Chambers, 2.425; Chambers OHEL, pp 17, 18, 43; Craig ERD, p 298; Kolve, pp 53, 92.
Bibliography. CBEL, 1.279; Stratman, p 153.

[16] BROME ABRAHAM AND ISAAC.

MS. Yale Univ Libr, The Book of Brome, ff 15ᵃ–22ᵃ (mid 15 cent).
Brown-Robbins, Robbins-Cutler, no 786 (Robbins-Cutler gives earlier location).

Smith, edn, Angl 7.316; edn, Norfolk Antiquarian Miscellany 3.115.
Waterhouse, edn, xlviii.
Greene R L, The Brome Manuscript, TLS March 31 1932, p 229 (location of MS).
Davis N, TLS Aug 28 1959, p 495 (location of MS).
Charman D, TLS Dec 25 1959, p 755 (location of MS).
Marston T E, The Book of Brome, Yale Univ Libr Gazette 41.141.
Kahrl S J, The Brome Hall Commonplace Book, Theatre Notebook 22.157.
Davis, The Brome Hall Commonplace Book, Theatre Notebook 24.84.
Davis N-CP, p lviii.
Editions. Smith L T, Abraham and Isaac A Mystery Play from a Private Manuscript of 15th Century, Angl 7.323.
Smith L T, A Commonplace Book of the Fifteenth Century, containing A Religious Play . . . Printed from the Original Manuscript at Brome Hall Suffolk by Lady Caroline Kerrison Edited with Notes by Lucy Toulmin Smith, London and Norwich 1886, p 46.
Smith L T, Notes on A Common-place Book of the Fifteenth Century with a Religious Play of Abraham and Isaac, Norfolk Antiquarian Miscellany 3.127.
Manly Spec, p 41 (based on Smith edn with Holthausen, Angl 13, emendations).
Waterhouse O, The Non-Cycle Mystery Plays, EETSES 104, London 1909, p 36.
Cook A S, A Literary ME Reader, Boston etc 1915, p 497 (based on Smith edn with emendations by Holthausen, Angl 13, and Manly Spec edn).
Adams CPSD, p 117 (based on Waterhouse edn with emendations).
Davis N-CP, p 43.
Selection. Pollard EMP 1927, Appendix IV, p 173 (lines 316–435).
Modernizations. An Old English Miracle Play of Abraham and Isaac, De La More Booklets, London 1905.
Child C G, The Second Shepherds' Play Everyman and Other Early Plays, N Y 1910, p 7.
Matthews B and P R Lieder, The Chief British Dramatists excluding Shakespeare, Boston etc 1924, p 3.
Schweikert H C, Early English Plays, N Y 1928, p 90.
Lieder P R, R M Lovett, and R K Root, British Drama Ten Plays, Boston 1929, p 1.
Baldwin EED, p 82.

Parry W D, Old Plays for Modern Players, London 1930, p 26.

Browne E M, The Sacrifice of Isaac Adapted from the Brome MS, Religious Plays Series, no 2, London 1932.

Hubbell J B and J O Beaty, An Introd to Drama, N Y 1933, p 99.

Tatlock J S P and R G Martin, Representative English Plays, 2nd rvsd edn, N Y 1938, p 13.

Loomis R and R Willard, Medieval English Verse and Prose, N Y 1948, p 250 (prose text).

Bentley G E, The Development of English Drama An Anthology, N Y 1950, p 12.

Textual Matters. Holthausen F, Zu ae und me Dichtungen, Angl 13.361 (emendations to Smith edn).

Dustoor P E, [Textual Notes], MLR 21.429; 23.211; Textual Notes on the Chester MSS and the Brome Play, Allahabad Univ Stud 6, Arts Section, p 59.

Wells M E, The Age of Isaac at the Time of the Sacrifice, MLN 54.582 (line 246).

Kahrl, Theatre Notebook 22.60 (inaccuracies in Smith edn).

Davis, Theatre Notebook 24.85 (reply to Kahrl).

Davis N-CP, p lxiii.

Language. Davis N-CP, p lxvi.

Versification. Varnhagen H, De fabula scenica immolationem Isaac tractante quae sermone medio-anglico conscripta in codice Bromensi asservata est, Erlangen 1899 (analysis of metre).

Waterhouse, edn, p xlix.

Fort M D, The Metres of the Brome and Chester Abraham and Isaac Plays, PMLA 41.832.

Davis N-CP, p lxiv.

Date. Waterhouse, edn, p xlviii.

Davis N-CP, pp lxii, lxx.

Relations with Other Abraham Plays. Smith, edn, Angl 7.317; edn, Norfolk Antiquarian Misc 3.123.

Waterhouse, edn, p *l.*

Craig ERD, p 305.

Woolf R, The Effect of Typology on the English Mediaeval Plays of Abraham and Isaac, Spec 32.805.

And see under *Brome-Chester Relations* below.

Brome-Chester Relations. Ungemach H, Die Quellen der fünf ersten Chester Plays, MBREP 1.127.

Hohlfeld A R, Two Old English Mystery Plays on the Subject of Abraham's Sacrifice, MLN 5.111 (prints parallel passages from Brome and Chester).

Varnhagen, De fabula scenica immolationem Isaac tractante (relationship discussed on basis of versification).

Gayley, pp 126, 132.

Waterhouse, edn, p lii.

Harper C, A Comparison between the Brome and Chester Plays of Abraham and Isaac, RadMon 15.

Cron B, Zur Entwicklungsgeschichte der englischen Misterien Alten Testaments, Marburg 1913, p 87.

Fort, PMLA 41.832.

Dustoor, Allahabad Univ Stud 6, Arts Section, p 59.

Severs J B, The Relationship between the Brome and Chester Plays of Abraham and Isaac, MP 42.137 (Chester a corrupt form of Brome).

Craig ERD, p 309.

Davis N-CP, p lxiii.

Smith A M, The Iconography of the Sacrifice of Isaac in Early Christian Art, AJA 26.159.

Literary Criticism. Crowley T J, Character-Treatment in the Mediaeval Drama, Notre Dame Ind 1907, p 102.

Gayley, pp 198, 201.

Mackinnon E, Notes on the Dramatic Structure of the York Cycle, SP 28.444 (comparison of Brome with York Abraham and Isaac).

Lombardo A, The Sacrifice of Isaac e il Miracle Play, English Miscellany 4.20 (ed by M Praz for the British Council, Rome 1953).

Woolf, Spec 32.805.

Burgess C F, Art and Artistry in the Brome Miracle Play of Abraham and Isaac, Cithara 1².37.

Elliott J R, The Sacrifice of Isaac as Comedy and Tragedy, SP 66.36.

General References. Ten Brink, 2.253; Bates, p 141; Brandl, § 120; Ward Hist, 1.91; Chambers, 2.426; Chambers OHEL, p 43; Craig ERD, p 309; Kolve, p 257.

Bibliography. CBEL, 1.278; Stratman, p 142.

[17] DUBLIN ABRAHAM AND ISAAC.

MS. Trinity Coll Dublin 432 (formerly D.iv. 18), ff 74ᵇ, 76ᵃ, 77ᵇ–81ᵃ (mid 15 cent).

Brown-Robbins, no 2617.

Brotanek, edn, p 21; Me Dichtungen aus der Handschrift 432 des Trinity College in Dublin, Halle/Salle 1940, p 1.

Waterhouse, edn, p xliii.

Greene R L, Early English Carols, Oxford 1935, p 347.

Davis N-CP, p xlvii; facing p 41, Plate I (facsimile).
Editions. Collier J P, Five Miracle Plays, or Scriptural Dramas, London 1836.
Brotanek R, Abraham and Isaak, Angl 21.41.
Waterhouse O, The Non-Cycle Mystery Plays, EETSES 104, London 1909, p 26.
Davis N-CP, p 33.
Textual Matters. Brotanek, edn, p 52 (emendations to Collier edn and notes).
Holthausen F, Zu ae und me Dichtungen, Angl 21.441 (emendations to Brotanek edn).
Dustoor P E, Textual Notes on Three Non-Cycle Mystery Plays, MLR 23.209.
Language. Brotanek, edn, p 24; Me Dichtungen aus der Handschrift 432, p 184.
Waterhouse, edn, p xlvii.
Davis N-CP, p liv.
Versification. Brotanek, edn, p 36.
Waterhouse, edn, p xlviii.
Davis N-CP, p liii.
Date. Brotanek, edn, p 21; Me Dichtungen aus der Handschrift 432, pp 5, 199.
Waterhouse, edn, p xliii.
Davis N-CP, pp li, lvii.
Sources and Literary Relations. Rothschild J de, Le Mistère du Viel Testament, Paris 1878, l.xxviii; 2.i, 1 (relations with French Viel Testament and English Abraham plays).
Davidson C, Concerning English Mystery Plays, MLN 7.171 (rejects connection with Dublin cycle).
Brotanek, edn, pp 24 (rejects connection with Dublin cycle), 27 (relations with French Viel Testament and Eng Abraham plays).
Waterhouse, edn, pp xliv (rejects connection with Dublin cycle), l (relations with French Viel Testament and Eng Abraham plays).
Patch H, The Ludus Coventriae and the Digby Massacre, PMLA 35.336 (relation with Ludus Coventriae).
Seymour St John D, Anglo-Irish Literature 1200–1582, Cambridge 1926, p 126 (rejects connection with Dublin cycle).
Woolf R, The Effect of Typology on the English Medieval Plays of Abraham and Isaac, Spec 32.816, 820.
Davis N-CP, p lii (relations with French Viel Testament and Eng Abraham plays).
General References. Ten Brink, 2.278; Bates, p 138; Brandl, § 120; Ward Hist, 1.92; Chambers, 2.386, 426; Craig ERD, p 308; Kolve, p 257.
Bibliography. CBEL, 1.279; Stratman, p 143 (some confusion).

[18] CROXTON SACRAMENT.

MS. Trinity Coll Dublin 652, Art 6 (formerly F.iv.20), ff 338^a–356^b (late 15 or early 16 cent).
Brown-Robbins, Robbins-Cutler, no 2363.
Stokes, edn, pp 101, 104.
Waterhouse, edn, p lv.
Davis N-CP, p lxx; facing p 68, Plate II (facsimile).
Editions. Stokes W, The Play of the Sacrament, Trans Philological Soc, Berlin 1861, p 105.
Manly Spec, p 239 (based on Stokes edn with MS collations and Holthausen emendations).
Waterhouse O, The Non-Cycle Mystery Plays together with the Croxton Play of the Sacrament and The Pride of Life, EETSES 104, London 1909, p 54 (based on Manly Spec edn, collated with MS and Stokes edn).
Adams CPSD, p 243 (based on Waterhouse edn with collations of Manly Spec edn and Stokes edn).
Davis N-CP, p 58.
Textual Matters. Holthausen F, Beiträge zur Erklärung und Textkritik alt- und mittelenglischer Denkmäler, EStn 16.150; Zu alt- und mittelenglischen Denkmälern, Angl 15.198.
Davis N-CP, p lxxi.
Language. Stokes, edn, p 101.
Davis N-CP, p lxxvi.
Versification. Waterhouse, edn, p lx.
Craig ERD, p 326.
Davis N-CP, p lxxv.
Sources and Literary Relations. Waterhouse, edn, p lvii.
Eckhardt E, Die Dialekt- und Ausländertypen des älteren englischen Dramas, Materialen zur Kunde des älteren englischen Dramas 32.150, 154.
Gerould G H, Saints' Legends, Boston and N Y 1916, p 304 (Croxton Sacrament based on stock exemplum; challenged by G L Hamilton, MLN 36.240).
Barnicle M E, The Exemplum of the Penitent Usurer, PMLA 33.410.
Patch H R, The Ludus Coventriae and the Digby Massacre, PMLA 35.340 (relation of Croxton Sacrament with Ludus Coventriae).
Barns F E, The Background and Sources of the Croxton Play of the Sacrament, Univ of Chicago Abstracts of Theses, Humanities Series 5.443.
Cutts C, The English Background of the

Play of the Sacrament, Univ of Washington Abstracts of Theses 3.369; The Croxton Play An Anti-Lollard Piece, MLQ 5.45.
Davis N-CP, p lxxiii.
Representation, Locale. Chambers, 2.427; Waterhouse, edn, p lxiii.
General References. Brandl, § 120; Bates, p 146; Ward Hist, 1.98; Chambers, 2.427; Creizenach, 1.303; Chambers OHEL, p 45; Craig ERD, p 324.
Bibliography. CBEL, 1.279; Stratman, p 148.

[19] DIGBY PLAYS.

MS. Bodl 1734 (Digby 133), ff 37ᵃ–50ᵇ, 95ᵃ–145ᵃ, 146ᵃ–157ᵃ (ca 1510–20).
Brown-Robbins, Robbins-Cutler, nos 1291 and 2814; Brown-Robbins, no 3642.
Schmidt K, Die Digby-Spiele, Berlin 1884, p 5.
Chambers, 2.428.
Craig ERD, p 310.
Baker D C and J L Murphy, The Late Medieval Plays of MS Digby 133 Scribes Dates and Early History, Research Opportunities in Renaissance Drama 10.153.
Editions. Sharp T, Ancient Mysteries from the Digby Manuscripts, Abbotsford Club, Edinburgh 1835.
Furnivall F J, The Digby Mysteries, New Shakespeare Soc 7; reissued EETSES 70, London 1896 (adds [3] above; crit R Wülcker, AnglA 6.74).
Editions of Selected Plays. Hawkins T, The Origin of the English Drama Illustrated in its Various Species . . . , Oxford 1773, 1.5 (Massacre).
Marriott W, A Collection of English Plays . . . , Basel 1838, p 197 (Massacre).
Candelmas Day A Mystery, The Journ of Sacred Literature, Jan 1867, p 413.
Manly Spec, p 215 (Conversion, based on Furnivall edn).
Adams CPSD, pp 212 (Conversion, based on Furnivall edn with Manly Spec edn emendations), 225 (Mary Magdalen, based on Furnivall edn).
Pollard EMP 1927, p 49 (Mary Magdalen, selections).
Modernizations. Tickner EED, p 195; Baldwin EED, p 248.
Ayliff H K, The Malvern Festival Plays, London 1933, p 3 (abridged).
Textual Matters. Zupitza J, The Digby Mysteries, Acad 22.281 (p 297, Furnivall accepts emendation).
Kölbing E, EStn 21.166 (emendations to Pol-

lard's 1890 text of Mary Magdalen).
Pollard EMP 1927, pp 193, 224c (notes to Mary Magdalen incorporating emendations by Kölbing and Logeman).
Hill B, The Digby Harrowing of Hell Lines 232 [and] 217, N&Q 209.374.
Language. Schmidt, Die Digby-Spiele, pp 18, 28 (Massacre, Conversion); Angl 8.385 (Mary Magdalen).
Baker and Murphy, Research Opportunities in Renaissance Drama 10.163.
Versification. Schmidt, Die Digby-Spiele, pp 19, 29 (Massacre, Conversion); Angl 8.387 (Mary Magdalen).
Patch H R, The Ludus Coventriae and the Digby Massacre, PMLA 35.338 (relation on basis of metre).
Date and Authorship. Schmidt, Die Digby-Spiele, pp 6, 8.
Chambers, 2.145, 428.
Baker and Murphy, Research Opportunities in Renaissance Drama 10.155 (Parfre).
Sources and Literary Relations. Schmidt, Die Digby-Spiele, p 14 (sources of Massacre).
Kretzmann P E, The Liturgical Element in the Earliest Forms of the Medieval Drama, Univ of Minnesota Stud in Lang and Lit 4, pp 64, 70, 72.
Patch, Ludus Coventriae and Digby Massacre, PMLA 35.324.
Cornelius R D, The Figurative Castle, Bryn Mawr Pa 1930, p 65 (use in Mary Magdalen).
Young K, The Drama of the Medieval Church, 2.199 (liturgical plays of Lazarus and Conversion).
Elton W, Paradise Lost and the Digby Mary Magdalene, MLQ 9.412.
Garth H M, Saint Mary Magdalene in Mediaeval Literature, Johns Hopkins Univ Stud in Hist and Polit Science 67³.13 and passim.
Craig ERD, pp 311, 315 (relations of Conversion and Mary Magdalen with Fleury Playbook, also of Mary Magdalen with Benediktbeuern Passion).
For special rôles, see above under ENGLISH VERNACULAR PLAYS, *Rôles and Themes*; ENGLISH MYSTERIES (BIBLICAL PLAYS), *Rôles.*
Literary Criticism. Gayley, p 207.
Emrich W, Paulus im Drama, Berlin and Leipzig 1934, p 20.
Velz J W, Sovereignty in the Digby Mary Magdalene, Comparative Drama 2.32 (unifying effect).
Staging. Chambers, 2.429.

Adams CPSD, p 225n (conjectural stage for Mary Magdalen).
Collins F, Music in the Craft Cycles, PMLA 47.621 (dance at end of Massacre).
Moore J R, Miracle Plays Minstrels and Jigs, PMLA 48.943 (cites parallels from Cornish plays).
Emrich, Paulus im Drama, p 21.
Craig ERD, pp 312, 316 (Conversion, Mary Magdalen).
General References. Collier J P, The History of English Dramatic Poetry, London 1831; new edn 1879, 2.230, 196n.
Klein, 1.750; Körting, § 136; Bates, p 151; Ward Hist, 1.92; Chambers, 2.428; Creizenach, 1.301; Chambers OHEL, p 44; Craig ERD, p 310; Kolve, see index under Digby Plays.
Bibliography. CBEL, 1.279; Henshaw, PMRS, 21.19; Stratman, p 149.
For BODLEY BURIAL AND RESURRECTION see [3] above; for WISDOM fragment see [28] below.

[20] CAESAR AUGUSTUS (ASHMOLE) FRAGMENT.

MS. Bodl 6621 (Ashmole 750), f 168ᵃ (late 15 cent).
Robbins-Cutler, no *3117.2.
Editions. Robbins R H, A Dramatic Fragment from a Caesar Augustus Play, Angl 72.31 (description of MS, text of actor's part, discussion of relation to corresponding plays in Cycles).
Davis N-CP, pp 120 (text), cxviii (MS), cxx (language and versification), cxviii (date).

[21] EPILOGUE (REYNES EXTRACT).

MS. Bodl 10234 (Tanner 407), f 44ᵇ (late 15 cent).
Brown-Robbins, Robbins-Cutler, no 2380.
Calderhead, edn, p 1.
Robbins, edn, p 134.
Davis N-CP, p cxx.
Editions. Calderhead I, Morality Fragments from Norfolk, MP 14.7 (epilogue for 'benefit' for local church).
Robbins R H, A Sixteenth Century English Mystery Fragment, ESts 30.134.
Davis N-CP, p 123.
Language. Calderhead, edn, p 8.
Davis N-CP, p cxxiv.
Literary Relations. Robbins, edn, p 135 (relation to prologue and epilogue of Digby Massacre).
Date. Davis N-CP, p cxx.

[22] THE RESURRECTION OF OUR LORD.

MS. Folger Shakespeare Libr 1828.1 (formerly Bertram Dobell), 17 folios (late 16 cent?).
Wilson and Dobell, edn, pp v, vii.
Scharpff P, Über ein englisches Auferstehungsspiel Ein Beitrag zur Geschichte des Dramas und der Lollarden, Winnenden Württ 1919, p 5.
de Ricci Census, 1.428.
Edition. Wilson J D and B Dobell, The Resurrection of Our Lord, Malone Soc Reprints 28 (1st and 2nd days' plays, both incomplete).
Date and Authorship. Wilson and Dobell, edn, p vi.
Scharpff, Über ein engl Auferstehungsspiel, p 47.
Other Problems. Scharpff, pp 21, 32, 54 (sources and literary relations), 8, 54 (literary criticism).
For PROCESSUS SATANAE see [33] below.

[23] STONYHURST PAGEANTS.

MS. Stonyhurst Coll A.VI.33, ff 56ᵃ–190ᵇ (1600–25).
Brown, edn, p 7*.
Edition. Brown C, The Stonyhurst Pageants, Hesperia Ergänzungsreihe 7, Göttingen and Baltimore 1920 (crit W W Greg, MLR 15.441 [reply by Brown, MLR 16.167]; K Young, MLN 35.492; H Craig, AJP 42.280; H N Hillebrand, JEGP 20.574; F Holthausen, AnglB 33.84).
Other Problems. Brown, edn, pp 13* (language), 24* (versification), 19* (date and authorship), 15* (main source, Douay Bible), 21* (literary criticism), 28* (influence of Plautus on Naaman play).
Craig H, Terentius Christianus and the Stonyhurst Pageants, PQ 2.56 (influence on Naaman play).
Cole H W, The Influence of Plautus and Terence upon the Stonyhurst Pageants, MLN 38.393 (especially on Naaman pageant).
Boas F S, YWES 4.100 (correction to Cole).
Eckhardt E, Das engl Drama im Zeitalter der Reformation und der Hochrenaissance, Berlin und Leipzig 1928, p 9.
Craig ERD, p 371.
Stratman, p 154 (bibliography).

CORNISH PLAYS.

Manuscript Listings. Norris, edn, 2.438.
Chambers, 2.433; Stratman, p 145.

Editions. Gilbert D, Mount Calvary or the History of the Passion Death and Resurrection of . . . Jesus Christ written in Cornish . . . Interpreted in the English Tongue in . . . 1682 by John Keigwin Gent, London 1826.

Gilbert D, The Creation of the World with Noah's Flood Written in Cornish in the Year 1611 by William Jordan with an English Translation by John Keigwin, London 1827.

Norris E, The Ancient Cornish Drama, 2 vols, Oxford 1859 (parallel Cornish and English texts).

Stokes W, The Passion, Trans Philological Soc of Berlin 1860–61, Appendix; separate issue, Berlin 1862 (parallel texts in Cornish and English).

Stokes W, Gwreans an Bys The Creation of the World, Trans Philological Soc of Berlin 1863 (parallel texts in Cornish and English).

Stokes W, Beunans Meriasek The Life of St Meriasek Bishop and Confessor, London 1872 (parallel texts in Cornish and English).

Modernizations. Tickner EED, p 40 (Noah's Flood selections); Baldwin EED, p 44.

Date. Fowler D C, The Date of the Cornish Ordinalia, MS 23.91.

Sources and Literary Relations. Chambers, 2.321 (comparative table of Cycles and Cornish Plays).

Jenner H, The Cornish Drama, Celtic Review 3.374; 4.41 (combined with detailed analysis of plays).

Longsworth R, The Cornish Ordinalia Religion and Dramaturgy, Cambridge Mass 1967 (crit J Helterman, Shakespeare Soc 5.341).

Meyer R T, The Liturgical Background of Medieval Cornish Drama, Trivium 3.48.

Cornish Rounds, Staging. Borlase W, Antiquities Historical and Monumental of the County of Cornwall, London 1769, p 207.

Gilbert D, The Parochial History of Cornwall, London 1838, 3.328.

Peter T C, The Old Cornish Drama, London 1906, facing pp 12, 34, 45 (plates of stage plan, rounds).

Jenner, Celtic Review 3.366.

Moore, J R, Miracle Plays Minstrels and Jigs, PMLA 48.943.

Nance R M, The Plen an gwary or Cornish Playing place, Journ of the Royal Institute of Cornwall 24.190.

Holman T, Cornish Plays and Playing Places,

Theatre Notebook 4³.52 (challenges Borlase on Perran round).

General References. Ten Brink, 2.279; Bates, p 131; Ward Hist, 1.56; Chambers, 2.127, 433; Gayley, p 126; Prosser, see index under Cornish Cycle; Craig ERD, pp 142, 333; Kolve, see index under Cornish Drama.

Bibliography. CBEL, 1.279; Stratman, p 145.

RECORDS OF LOST PLAYS.

Chambers, 2.107, 329.

Spencer M L, Corpus Christi Pageants in England, N Y 1911.

Dodds M H, The Northern Stage, Archaeologia Aeliana 3s 11.36 (Durham, Newcastle).

Pierson M, The Relation of the Corpus Christi Procession to the Corpus Christi Play in England, Trans Wisconsin Acad of Sicence and Letters 18.111.

Craig H, The Lincoln Cordwainers' Pageant, PMLA 32.605.

Witty J R, The Beverley Plays, Trans Yorkshire Dialect Soc 4²³.18.

Mill A J, Mediaeval Plays in Scotland, Edinburgh and London 1927, pp 60, 113; The Edinburgh Hammermen's Corpus Christi Herod Pageant, Innes Review 21.77; The Perth Hammermen's Play A Scottish Garden of Eden, SHR 49.146.

Seymour St J D, Anglo-Irish Literature 1200–1582, Cambridge 1929, pp 121 (Dublin), 130 (Kilkenny).

Shull V, Clerical Drama in Lincoln Cathedral 1318–1561, PMLA 52.946.

Mill, The Hull Noah Play, MLR 33.489.

Hassall W O, Plays at Clerkenwell, MLR 33.564 (correction by ed MLR 34.79).

Blair L, A Note on the Relation of the Corpus Christi Procession to the Corpus Christi Play in England, MLN 55.83.

Harbage A, Annals of English Drama 975–1700, Phila and London 1940; rvsd S Schoenbaum 1964.

Mcpham W A, Essex Review 54.52, 107, 139 (general survey of medieval drama in Essex in 15 and 16 cent); 55.8 (Heybridge and Braintree); 55.57, 129 (Dunmow); 55.169; 56.34 (Maldon); 56.148, 171 (Chelmsford).

Gardiner H C, Mysteries' End An Investigation of the Last Days of the Medieval Religious Stage, YSE 103.122.

Wilson R M, The Lost Literature of Medieval England, London 1952, p 215; 2nd edn rvsd 1970, p 210.

Robertson J and D J Gordon, A Calendar of Dramatic Records in the Books of the Livery Companies of London 1485–1640,

Malone Soc Collections 3.xiii, xx, xlvi.

Stratman, p 155.

Craig ERD, pp 144n (bibliography), 265 (Lincoln).

Clark W S, The Early Irish Stage The Beginnings to 1720, Oxford 1955, pp 11 (Dublin), 21 (Kilkenny).

Wickham G, Early English Stages 1300 to 1660, London 1959, 1.332.

Dawson G E, Records of Plays and Players in Kent 1450–1642, Malone Soc Collections 7.

Kahrl S J, Medieval Drama in Louth, Research Opportunities in Renaissance Drama (medieval suppl) 10.129.

2. THE MORALITY PLAYS

by

Sheila Lindenbaum

GENERAL AND TANGENTIAL STUDIES.

General Treatments. Collier J P, The History of English Dramatic Poetry, London 1831, 1.23; 2.258.

Klein, 2.1; Morley, 7.172; Ten Brink, 2.297.

Bates, p 201; Courthope, 1.416.

Brandl A, Quellen des weltlichen Dramas in England vor Shakespeare, ein Ergänzungsband zu Dodsley's Old English Plays, QF 80, Strassburg 1898, Introd (crit J M Manly, JEGP 2.389; F I Carpenter, MLN 14.134 [268]; O Proescholdt, LfGRP 22.110).

Ward Hist, 1.99.

Chambers, 2.149, 436; Chambers OHEL, pp 49, 217.

Ramsay R L, Magnyfycence, EETSES 98, London 1906, Introd Pt 2.

Gayley, pp 279, 293; CHEL, 5.23, 56.

Thompson E N S, The English Moral Plays, Trans Connecticut Acad of Arts and Sciences 14, New Haven 1910, p 291 (crit M Förster, ShJ 47.355; E K Chambers, MLR 8.121); rptd as separate vol, N Y 1970.

Creizenach, 1.461, 468.

Brooke C F Tucker, The Tudor Drama, Boston 1911, p 47.

Mackenzie W R, The English Moralities from the Point of View of Allegory, Harvard Stud Eng 2, Boston and London 1914; rptd N Y 1966.

Pollard EMP, p xli; Baugh LHE, p 283.

Rossiter A P, English Drama from Early Times to the Elizabethans, N Y etc 1950, pp 79, 95 (crit A Brown, MLR 45.369).

Craig ERD, pp 337, 341, 377.

Wickham G, Early English Stages 1300–1600, Vol One 1300–1576, London 1959, pp 229, 234, 318 (crit H Craig, Spec 34.702; J W Robinson, Theatre Notebook 14 [1959–60] .21; A Brown, RES ns 11.423); Shakespeare's Dramatic Heritage, London 1969, pp 21, 24.

Williams A, The Drama of Medieval England, East Lansing Mich 1961, p 142 (crit M G Jones, MLR 57.238; K S Rothwell,

MP 60.286; A C Cawley, ESts 49.245); portions rvsd in The English Moral Play before 1500, Annuale Mediaevale 4(1963).5.

Potter R A, The Form and Concept of the English Morality Play, diss Claremont 1965; DA 26.7323.

Wilson F P, The English Drama 1485–1585, ed G K Hunter, N Y and Oxford 1969, pp 1, 59, 74, 203 (crit T W Craik, N&Q 214.317; N Sanders, Shakespeare Stud 6 [1970].389; S Schoenbaum, Yearbook of Eng Studies 1[1971].226).

Kahrl S J, Traditions of Medieval English Drama, London 1974, p 99.

And see above, under ENGLISH VERNACULAR PLAYS, *General Treatments.*

Sources and Literary Relations. Chambers, 2.151, 157.

Ramsay, EETSES 98.cl (the Psychomachia); Morality Themes in Milton's Poetry, SP 15.123.

Manly J M, Literary Forms and the New Theory of the Origin of Species, MP 4.586.

Traver H, The Four Daughters of God, BrynMawrMon 6(1907).125 (crit R L Ramsay, MLN 24.91); PMLA 40.44.

Thompson, Trans Connecticut Acad of Arts and Sciences 14.293, 312 (basis in homilies); 320, 333 (the Psychomachia); 341 (contributory allegories).

Creizenach, 1.461 (Dance of Death, the Psychomachia).

Mackenzie, Harvard Stud Eng 2.24; The Origin of the English Morality, Washington Univ Stud 4s 2²(1915).141 (challenges view of morality as outgrowth of mystery play).

Barnicle M E, The Exemplum of the Penitent Usurer, PMLA 33.409 (influence of theme on conflict-morality).

Wharey J B, Bunyan's Holy War and the Conflict-Type of Morality Play, MLN 34.65.

Roberts M, A Note on the Sources of the English Morality Play, Wisconsin Stud Lang and Lit 18(1923).100.

Cornelius R D, The Figurative Castle: A Study in the Mediaeval Allegory of the

Edifice with Especial Reference to Religious Writings, Bryn Mawr Pa 1930, p 58.

Ball L F, The Morality Theme in Book II of the Faerie Queene, MLN 46.371.

Owst G R, Literature and Pulpit in Medieval England, Cambridge 1933 (crit H R Patch, Spec 9.233); 2nd edn N Y 1961, p 526.

Whiting B J, Proverbs in the Earlier English Drama, HSCL 14, Cambridge Mass 1938, p 65.

Brooks N C, A Latin Morality Dialogue of the Fifteenth Century, JEGP 42.471.

Wright N, The Morality Tradition in the Poetry of Edward Taylor, American Lit 18(1946–47).1.

Chew S C, The Virtues Reconciled: An Iconographic Study, Toronto 1947, pp 35, 43.

De Vocht H, Everyman: A Comparative Study of Texts and Sources, Materials for the Study of the Old Eng Drama 20, Louvain 1947, p 179 (moralities as models for Everyman).

Clark J M, The Dance of Death in the Middle Ages and the Renaissance, Glasgow Univ Publ 86(1950); MLR 45.336.

Craig H, Morality Plays and Elizabethan Drama, Shakespeare Quart 1(1950).64 (reconsiders origin of morality plays).

Craig ERD, pp 338, 344.

Rossiter, Eng Drama from Early Times, p 79.

Brown A, Folklore Elements in the Medieval Drama, Folklore 63(1952).65.

Peter J, Complaint and Satire in Early English Literature, Oxford 1956, p 188.

York E C, Dramatic Form in a Late Middle English Narrative, MLN 72.484 (suggests an embryonic morality play).

Spivack B, Shakespeare and the Allegory of Evil, N Y 1958, pp 60, 105 (the Psychomachia; homiletic origin of the morality play).

Anderson M D, Drama and Imagery in English Medieval Churches, Cambridge 1963, pp 51, 60, 72 (crit J W Robinson, Theatre Notebook 19[1964–65].31).

Elliott R W V, The Topography of Wynnere and Wastoure, ESts 48.134 (parallels with the medieval circular theatre).

Davis N, Two Unprinted Dialogues in Late Middle English and Their Language, Revue des Langues Vivantes 35(1969).461 (notes affinities with early morality plays).

Dronke P, Poetic Individuality in the Middle Ages, Oxford 1970, p 169 (discussion and text of Hildegard of Bingen's Latin morality play, the Ordo virtutum).

Leigh D J, The Doomsday Mystery Play: An Eschatological Morality, MP 67.211; rptd in Medieval English Drama, J Taylor and A H Nelson, edd, Chicago and London 1972, p 260.

Wenzel S, The Pilgrimage of Life as a Late Medieval Genre, MS 35.381.

Chaundler T, Liber Apologeticus, ed D Enright-Clark Shoukri, London and N Y 1974 (13 cent morality play in Latin).

Relation to Renaissance Drama. Genée R, Die englischen Mirakelspiele und Moralitäten als Vorläufer des englischen Dramas, Sammlung gemeinverständlicher wissenschaftlicher Vorträge 305, Berlin 1878, p 648.

Chambers, 2.199.

Thompson, Trans Connecticut Acad of Arts and Sciences 14.359, 375, 386.

Moore J R, Ancestors of Autolycus in the English Moralities and Interludes, Washington Univ Studies Humanistic Series 9^2 (1922).157.

Farnham W, The Medieval Heritage of Elizabethan Tragedy, Berkeley 1936, pp 173, 177 (crit W W Lawrence, MLN 52.435; K M Lea, MÆ 27.49).

Adams H H, English Domestic or Homiletic Tragedy, N Y 1943, pp 54, 114, 142.

Craig, Shakespeare Quart 1.64.

Craig ERD, p 377.

Rossiter, Eng Drama from Early Times, pp 79, 102, 113.

Cormican L A, Morality Tradition and the Interludes, The Age of Chaucer, ed B Ford, London 1954, p 188.

Kesler C R, The Importance of the Comic Tradition of English Drama in the Interpretation of Marlowe's Doctor Faustus, diss Missouri 1954; DA 15.1387.

Ribner I, Morality Roots of the Tudor History Play, Tulane Studies in Eng 4(1954) .21; Othello and the Pattern of Shakespearean Tragedy, Tulane Stud Eng 5(1955).69 (pattern derived from the morality play); The English History Play in the Age of Shakespeare, Princeton 1957; rvsd London 1965, p 31 (morality roots) and passim.

Peter, Complaint and Satire, pp 194, 209, 212, 264.

Spivack B, Falstaff and the Psychomachia, Shakespeare Quart 8(1957).449; Shakespeare and the Allegory of Evil, N Y 1958, chaps 7–12 (changes in the morality convention after 1500; crit H Levin, RN 11.279; J A Bryant, SR 67.692; I Ribner, JEGP 58.292).

Wickham, Early English Stages, Vol One 1300–1576, London 1959, pp 156, 235, 322; Vol Two 1576–1660, Pt One, London 1963, pp 13, 35, 196.

Creeth E H, Moral and Tragic Recognition: The Uniqueness of Othello, Macbeth, and King Lear, Papers of the Michigan Acad of Science, Arts, and Letters 45(1960).381 (relation to the structural pattern of the early moralities).

Bevington D M, From Mankind to Marlowe: Growth of Structure in the Popular Drama of Tudor England, Cambridge Mass 1962 (crit G K Hunter, N&Q 208.355; I Ribner, JEGP 62.216; B Spivack, RN 16.133; W Habicht, Arch 201.210; J Tulip, MP 62.66).

Cole D, Suffering and Evil in the Plays of Christopher Marlowe, Princeton 1962, pp 23, 231, 247 and passim.

Pineas R, The English Morality Play as a Weapon of Religious Controversy, Stud in Eng Lit 1500–1900 2(1962).157 (compares techniques of pre- and post-reformation moralities).

Righter A, Shakespeare and the Idea of the Play, London 1962, pp 23, 31 (crit F Kermode, New Statesman Feb 22 1963, p 274; E Jones, RES ns 15.314; E M Waith, Stud in Eng Lit 1500–1900 4[1964].333; D M Bevington, Shakespeare Quart 16[1965].118).

Stroup T B, The Testing Pattern in Elizabethan Tragedy, Stud in Eng Lit 1500–1900 3(1963).175 (pattern derived from the morality play).

Dessen A C, The Estates Morality Play, SP 62.121 (departures from the Humanum Genus structure in the late morality); Jonson's Moral Comedy, Evanston 1971, pp 8, 37 (includes revision of earlier article).

Hunter R G, Shakespeare and the Comedy of Forgiveness, N Y and London 1965, pp 16, 37, 79 and passim.

Margeson J M R, The Origins of English Tragedy, Oxford 1967, pp 29, 67, 130, 184 (crit D Bevington, Shakespeare Stud 5 [1969].343; N W Bawcutt, N&Q 215.229).

Weimann R, Shakespeare und die Tradition des Volkstheaters, Berlin 1967, p 159 (crit W Habicht, Arch 206.49; D Mehl, RES ns 20.220; G Müller-Schwefe, Renaissance Quart 22[1969].408; G K Hunter, N&Q 215. 233).

Habicht W, Studien zur Dramenform vor Shakespeare, AF 96, Heidelberg 1968, p 21 and passim (crit M Mincoff, N&Q 216.469; T Stemmler, Arch 208.51; H-J Diller, ESts

54.169).

Feldman S D, The Morality-Patterned Comedy of the Renaissance, De Proprietatibus Litterarum, Series Practica 12, The Hague and Paris 1970 (crit J A B Somerset, MLR 67.401; J H Kaplan, Renaissance Drama ns 5[1972].229).

Wierum A, Actors and Play Acting in the Morality Tradition, Renaissance Drama ns 3(1970).189.

Bergeron D M, Medieval Drama and Tudor-Stuart Civic Pageantry, Journ of Medieval and Renaissance Stud 2(1972).79.

Braggart, Devil, Vice. Graf H, Der Miles Gloriosus im englischen Drama bis zur Zeit des Bürgerkrieges, Schwerin [1891], p 19.

Cushman L W, The Devil and the Vice in the English Dramatic Literature before Shakespeare, SEP 6, Halle 1900, pp 44, 54 (crit G B Churchill, ShJ 38.272).

Eckhardt E, Die lustige Person im älteren englischen Drama (bis 1642), Palaes 17.53, 98, 110.

Chambers, 2.203.

Gayley C M, Representative English Comedies, N Y 1903, l.xlvi.

Ramsay, EETSES 98.cii, cxc.

Haslinghuis E J, De duivel in het drama der middeleeuwen, London 1912, p 114.

Zandvoort R W, The Messenger in the Early English Drama, ESts 3.100; rptd Collected Papers, Groningen 1954, p 20 (challenges Cushman and Eckhardt as to origin of Vice).

Allison T E, The Paternoster Play and the Origin of the Vices, PMLA 39.789.

Withington R, The Development of the Vice, Essays in Memory of Barrett Wendell, Cambridge Mass 1926, p 155; The Ancestry of the Vice, Spec 7.525 (influence of folk play); Braggart, Devil and Vice: A Note on the Development of Comic Figures in the Early English Drama, Spec 11.124 (influence of homilists' devil on Vice); Excursions in English Drama, N Y and London 1937, pp 42, 61 (Vice ancestry, development), 91 (morality play and melodrama).

Tomlinson W E, Der Herodes-Charakter im englischen Drama, Palaes 195.46.

Boughner D C, Vice, Braggart, and Falstaff, Angl 72.35; The Braggart in Renaissance Comedy, Minneapolis 1954, p 145.

Craik, The Tudor Interlude (see below, under *Records and Staging*), pp 38 (Vice), 49 (distinctive costumes of various rôles).

Mares F H, The Origin of the Figure Called the Vice in Tudor Drama, HLQ 22.11.

Spivack, Shakespeare and the Allegory of Evil, pp 57, 87, 119, 123, 130, 151 and passim (crit L Scragg, Shakespeare Survey 21[1968].53).

Bevington, From Mankind to Marlowe, pp 79, 122 and passim.

Pineas, Stud in Eng Lit 1500–1900 2.160 (the Vice's homiletic task).

Happé P, The Vice and the Folk-Drama, Folklore 75(1964).161 (crit V Alford, Folklore 76[1965].62).

Weimann R, Rede-Konventionen des Vice von Mankind bis Hamlet, Zeitschr f Anglistik und Amerikanistik 15(1967).117; slight revisions in Shakespeare und die Tradition des Volkstheaters, p 176.

Wilson, The English Drama 1485–1585, p 59.

Other Rôles. Röhmer R, Priestergestalten im englischen Drama bis zu Shakespeare, Berlin 1909, p 41.

Swain B, Fools and Folly during the Middle Ages and the Renaissance, N Y 1932, p 157.

Spivack, Shakespeare and the Allegory of Evil, pp 92, 195, 207, 227, 304 (Mankind figure).

Habicht, AF 96.21 and passim (Mankind as hero).

Shuchter J D, Man Redeemable: The Mankind Character in the English Morality Plays, diss Berkeley 1968; DA 29.3156A.

Wertz D, Mankind as a Type-Figure on the Popular Religious Stage, Comp Stud in Soc and Hist 12(1970).83.

Themes. Russell H K, Tudor and Stuart Dramatizations of the Doctrines of Natural and Moral Philosophy, SP 31.1.

Collins Sister M E, The Allegorical Motifs in the Early English Moral Plays, diss Yale 1936; DAI 30.682A.

Koldewey E, Über die Willensfreiheit im älteren englischen Drama, Würzburg 1937, p 21 (crit W Héraucourt, LfGRP 60.479; AnglB 50.44).

Bloomfield SDS, pp 66, 82, 108, 205.

McCutchan J W, Justice and Equity in the English Morality Play, JHI 19.405.

Heiserman A R, Skelton and Satire, Chicago 1961, pp 85, 95 (key satiric ideas, particularly the "now-a-days" theme, in the early moralities).

Chew S C, The Pilgrimage of Life, New Haven and London 1962 (allegorical themes in lit and art).

Wenzel S, The Sin of Sloth: Acedia in Medieval Thought and Literature, Chapel Hill N C 1967, p 147; The Three Enemies of Man, MS 29.65; The Seven Deadly Sins: Some Problems of Research, Spec 43.16.

Bevington D, Tudor Drama and Politics, Cambridge Mass 1968, pp 27, 42 (crit A C Dessen, MLQ [Wash] 30.448; M Eccles, Stud in Eng Lit 1500–1900 9(1969).369).

Wertz D, The Theology of Nominalism in the English Morality Plays, Harvard Theological Rev 62(1969).371.

Literary Criticism. Gayley, Representative English Comedies, 1.lvii.

Ramsay, EETSES 98.cxlvii, clxxiii, cxciv.

Crowley T J, Character-Treatment in the Mediaeval Drama, Notre Dame Ind 1907, p 118.

Mackenzie, Harvard Stud Eng 2.

Haller J, Die Technik des Dialogs im mittelalterlichen Drama Englands, Worms a Rh 1916, p 84.

Weiner K, Die Verwendung des Parallelismus als Kunstmittel im englischen Drama vor Shakespeare, Hamburg 1916, p 12.

Winslow O E, Low Comedy as a Structural Element in English Drama: from the Beginnings to 1642, Menasha Wisc 1926, p 44.

Eckhardt E, Die metrische Unterscheidung von Ernst und Komik in den englischen Moralitäten, EStn 62.152.

Eichhorn T, Prosa und Vers im vorshakespeareschen Drama, ShJ 86.147.

Rossiter, Eng Drama from Early Times, pp 87, 95.

Frank R W, The Art of Reading Medieval Personification-Allegory, ELH 20.237.

Boughner, The Braggart in Renaissance Comedy, p 145.

Spivack, Shakespeare and the Allegory of Evil, pp 63, 96, 151, 238.

Bevington, From Mankind to Marlowe, chaps 1–4, 8–9 (effect of troupe composition upon dramatic structure).

Bloomfield M W, A Grammatical Approach to Personification Allegory, MP 60.161.

Williams, Annuale Mediaevale 4.5.

Habicht, AF 96.21.

Kantrowitz J S, Dramatic Allegory, or, Exploring the Moral Play, Comparative Drama 7(1973–74).68.

Records and Staging. Chambers, 2.156.

Ramsay, EETSES 98.cxxviii (effect of external conditions on staging).

Lauf E, Die Bühnenanweisungen in den englischen Moralitäten und Interludien bis 1570, Emsdetten Westf 1932.

Fischel O, Art and the Theatre, Burlington Magazine 66(1935).13.

Stamm R, Geschichte des englischen Theaters, Bern 1951, p 37.

Southern R, The Medieval Theatre in the Round, London 1957 (crit TLS Dec 6 1957, p 742; P Hartnoll, N&Q 203.453; R Hosley, MLR 53.557; P M Ryan, Quart Journ of Speech 44[1958].444; G Wickham, MÆ 28.138; J F Arnott, RES ns 11.316); The Staging of Plays before Shakespeare, London 1973, chaps 1–7 and passim.

Craik T W, The Tudor Interlude, Leicester 1958 (crit A Brown, MLR 54.412; G Wickham, Theatre Notebook 14[1959–60].30; R J Schoeck, MP 58.121; W A Armstrong, RES ns 12.185; K S Rothwell, RN 14.114).

Wickham, Early English Stages, 1.89, 156, 229, 234.

Arnott P D, The Origins of the Medieval Theatre in the Round, Theatre Notebook 15(1960–61).84 (affinities with the tournament; crit J F Arnott, Theatre Notebook 16[1961–62].32).

Freeman A, A Round outside Cornwall, Theatre Notebook 16.10 (crit N C Schmitt, Theatre Notebook 24.22).

Bevington, From Mankind to Marlowe, chaps 1–6, 8–9 (investigates conditions of popular commercial production, troupe structure).

Nicoll A, The Development of the Theatre, 5th edn rvsd London etc 1966, pp 58, 62, 64.

Fifield M, The Castle in the Circle, Ball State Monograph 6, Muncie Ind 1967 (crit R Axton, MÆ 37.226; N C Schmitt, Theatre Notebook 24.23); The Arena Theatres in Vienna Codices 2535 and 2536, Comparative Drama 2(1968–69).259 (challenges Southern's reconstruction of the theatre in the round; crit M Stevens, CE 32.456 n27).

Schmitt N C, Was There a Medieval Theatre in the Round? A Re-examination of the Evidence, Theatre Notebook 23(1968–69). 130; 24(1969–70).18; rptd in Medieval English Drama, J Taylor and A H Nelson, edd, Chicago and London 1972, p 292 (challenges Southern's reconstruction; crit R Hosley, Theatre Survey 12.29n).

Nelson A H, Early Pictorial Analogues of Medieval Theatre-in-the-Round, Research Opportunities in Renaissance Drama 12 (1969).93.

Hosley R, Three Kinds of Outdoor Theatre before Shakespeare, Theatre Survey 12 (1971).1.

Pentzell R J, The Medieval Theatre in the Streets, Theatre Survey 14(1973).1 (crit M del Villar, p 76; reply Pentzell, p 82).

Bibliographies. CHEL, 5.435.

Farmer J S, A Hand List to the Tudor Facsimile Texts, [London] 1914.

Harbage A, Annals of English Drama 975–1700, Phila and London 1940; rvsd S Schoenbaum, Phila 1964, with two supplements.

CBEL, 1.513; 5.246.

Henshaw, PMRS, 21.22.

Stratman, p 166; 2nd edn N Y 1972, 1.523; Dramatic Play Lists: 1591–1963, BNYPL 70.71, 169.

Houle P J, The English Morality and Related Drama: A Bibliographical Survey, n p 1972.

[24] THE PATER NOSTER PLAY.

MSS. No MS extant.

General Treatments and Records. Davies R, ed, Extracts from the Municipal Records of the City of York, London 1843, p 265.

[Raine J], ed, Testamenta Eboracensia, Pt 2, Surtees Soc 30, Durham 1855, p 268.

Smith T, ed, English Gilds, EETS 40, London 1870, p 137 (York).

Smith L T, York Plays, Oxford 1885, p xxviii.

Leach A F, Historical Manuscripts Commission: Report on the Manuscripts of the Corporation of Beverley, London 1900, pp 128, 142, 143 (edn); Some English Plays and Players, An English Miscellany Presented to Dr. Furnivall, Oxford 1901, pp 220, 223 (Beverley, Lincoln).

Chambers, 2.120, 154, 341, 378, 403; Chambers OHEL, p 51.

CHEL, 5.57.

Thompson E N S, The English Moral Plays, Trans Connecticut Acad of Arts and Sciences 14.334.

Young K, The Records of the York Play of the Pater Noster, Spec 7.540.

Raine A, York Civic Records, Yorkshire Archaeological Soc Record Series 115.vi, and see subject index to vols 103, 106, 108, 110, 115; Medieval York, London 1955, p 91.

Gardiner H C, Mysteries' End, YSE 103, New Haven and London 1946, p 75 (York).

Wilson R M, The Lost Literature of Medieval England, London 1952; 2nd edn 1970, pp 217, 220, 223.

Craig ERD, pp 337, 360.

Wickham G, Early English Stages 1300–1660,

Vol One 1300–1576, London 1959, pp 115n, 144, 230, 231, 233, 301.

Potter R A, The Form and Concept of the English Morality Play, diss Claremont 1965 microfilm, pp 156, 173.

Wilson F P, The English Drama 1485–1585, ed G K Hunter, N Y and Oxford 1969, p 4.

Kahrl S J, ed, Records of Plays and Players in Lincolnshire 1300–1585, Malone Soc Collections 8, 1974.

Nelson A H, The Medieval English Stage, Chicago and London 1974, pp 97 (Beverley), 105, 113 (Lincoln), 51, 55, 63, 67, 78 (York).

Johnston A F, The Plays of the Religious Guilds of York: the Creed Play and the Pater Noster Play, Spec 50.55.

Sources and Genre. Ramsay R L, Magnyfycence, EETSES 98, London 1906, p cli.

Creizenach, 1.468.

Craig H, The Pater Noster Play, The Nation 104(1917).563 (argues for cycle of saints' plays); challenged by Allison, PMLA 39.791; returns to argument Shakespeare Quart 1 (1950).65.

Craig ERD, p 337.

Allison T E, The Paternoster Play and the Origin of the Vices, PMLA 39.789 (Hugo of St Victor).

Owst G R, Literature and Pulpit in Medieval England, Cambridge 1933; 2nd edn N Y 1961, p 537.

Bloomfield SDS, pp 83, 364 n135, 365 n145.

Doyle A I, A Survey of the Origins and Circulation of Theological Writings in English in the 14th, 15th, and Early 16th Centuries, diss Cambridge 1953, p 87.

Pantin W A, The English Church in the Fourteenth Century, Cambridge 1955, p 243 n3 and passim.

Hussey M, The Petitions of the Paternoster in Mediaeval English Literature, MÆ 27.11.

Anderson M D, Drama and Imagery in English Medieval Churches, Cambridge 1963, pp 60, 84.

Aarts F G A M, The Pater Noster in Medieval English Literature, Papers on Lang and Lit 5(1969).12.

Bibliography. Stratman, p 154; 2nd edn N Y 1972, 1.618.

[25] THE CREED PLAY.

MSS. No MS extant.

General Treatments and Records. Davies, Extracts from the Municipal Records of the City of York, pp 171, 257, 266.

[Raine J], Surtees Soc 30.117.

[Scaife R H], ed, The Register of the Guild of Corpus Christi in the City of York, Surtees Soc 57, Durham 1872, pp 293, 307.

Smith, York Plays, p xxx.

Chambers, 2.120, 130, 404; Chambers OHEL, p 33; CHEL, 5.57.

Thompson, Trans Connecticut Acad of Arts and Sciences 14.334.

Westlake H F, The Parish Gilds of Mediaeval England, London 1919, p 57.

Raine A, Yorkshire Archaeological Soc Record Series, see subject index to vols 98, 103, 106, 108, 112.

Gardiner, YSE 103.73.

Wilson, Lost Literature of Medieval England, 2nd edn 1970, p 224.

Craig ERD, p 334.

Wickham, Early English Stages, 1.114, 230, 231, 233, 301, 372 n2.

Nelson, The Medieval English Stage, pp 51, 57, 60, 65, 67, 78.

Johnston, Spec 50.55.

Sources and Genre. Creizenach, 1.468.

Owst, Literature and Pulpit in Medieval England, p 537.

Craig ERD, p 334 (argues for cyclic play on lives of the apostles).

Anderson, Drama and Imagery in Eng Medieval Churches, p 37 (scheme for a Creed Play based on the Arundel Psalter).

Woolf R, The English Mystery Plays, London 1972, pp 60, 72, 358 n24 and n25.

[26] THE PRIDE OF LIFE.

MS. Dublin Public Record Office (Christ Church Collection 235), back of Account Roll 2 (1400–50; imperfect; destroyed by fire in 1922).

Brown-Robbins, Robbins-Cutler, no 2741.

Mills, edn, pp ix, xxv, 185.

Brandl, edn, p viii.

Waterhouse, edn, p lxiv.

Seymour St J D, Anglo-Irish Literature 1200–1582, Cambridge 1929, p 120.

Davis N-CP, pp lxxxv, xcvi.

Editions. Mills J, Account Roll of the Priory of the Holy Trinity, Dublin, 1337–1346, with the Middle English Moral Play The Pride of Life, from the Original in the Christ Church Collection in the Public Record Office, Royal Soc of Antiquaries of Ireland, Dublin 1891, p 1[26].

Brandl A, Quellen des weltlichen Dramas in

England vor Shakespeare, QF 80, Strassburg 1898, p 1 (based on Mills edn, with collation of MS by Skeat and new collation by Mills, and German trans on opposite pages to fill in gaps; crit J M Manly, JEGP 2.419, 423).

Holthausen F, The Pride of Life, Arch 108.32 (based on Brandl edn, with emendations from Manly and Kaluza); Der König des Lebens, in Probleme der englischen Sprache und Kultur, Festschrift Johannes Hoops, ed W Keller, Heidelberg 1925, p 152 (metrical German trans).

Waterhouse O, The Non-Cycle Mystery Plays, together with . . . The Pride of Life, EETSES 104, London 1909, p 88 (MS collated with Mills edn and compared with Brandl and Holthausen edns).

Davis N-CP, p 90 (based on the earlier printed edns; emendations in ftnts; crit D Bevington, Spec 46.733; A C Cawley, N&Q 216.71; R Axton, MÆ 41.157; D C Baker, Eng Lang Notes 9[1971–72].293; G Wickham, Yearbook of Eng Stud 2[1972] .235; G H V Bunt, ESts 54.60).

Happé P, The Tudor Interlude, Harmondsworth 1972, p 41 (text, with glosses in ftnts), p 380 (notes).

Textual Matters and Notes. Mills, edn, p 186.

Brandl, edn, p 650.

Manly J M, JEGP 2.419 (emendations to Brandl edn).

Kaluza M, DLz 20.1714 (emendations to Brandl edn).

Holthausen, Arch 108.48; Festschrift Johannes Hoops, p 167.

Brown C, The Pride of Life and the Twelve Abuses, Arch 128.76.

Mackenzie W R, The Debate over the Soul in The Pride of Life, Washington Univ Stud Humanistic Series 9²(1922).265 (prologue line 100[=98], dispyte).

Davis N-CP, p lxxxvi (includes reading of geyl, line 333).

Hengstebeck I, The Pride of Life, Vers 444, NM 72.739; Wer träumt in The Pride of Life, Arch 208.120 (prologue line 81, dremit/dremith).

Language. Mills, edn, p xxvi.

Brandl, edn, p ix.

Kild Ged, p 66.

Waterhouse, edn, pp lxv, 107 (discussion, glossary).

Hogan J J, The English Language in Ireland, Dublin 1927, p 21.

McIntosh A and M L Samuels, Prolegomena to a Study of Mediaeval Anglo-Irish, MÆ 37.1.

Davis N-CP, pp xc, 134 (discussion, glossary).

Versification. Brandl, edn, p xix.

Holthausen, Arch 108.56 (alliteration).

Ramsay R L, Magnyfycence, EETSES 98, London 1906, p cxxxvi.

Waterhouse, edn, p lxxiii.

Eckhardt E, Die metrische Unterscheidung von Ernst und Komik in den englischen Moralitäten, EStn 62.153.

Davis N-CP, p lxxxix.

Date and Authorship. Brandl, edn, pp xi, xix.

Waterhouse, edn, p lxvii.

Davis N-CP, p xcix.

Sources and Literary Relations. Brandl, edn, p xiv (relation to Everyman, Dance of Death, etc).

Manly, JEGP 2.423 (challenges origin of Pride of Life in Dance of Death).

Waterhouse, edn, p lxx (links with Dance of Death).

Thompson E N S, The English Moral Plays, Trans Connecticut Acad of Arts and Sciences 14.353, 358.

Brown, Arch 128.72 (lines 327–54 based on Twelve Abuses).

Owst G R, Literature and Pulpit in Medieval England, Cambridge 1933; 2nd edn N Y 1961, pp 527, 531.

Farnham W, The Medieval Heritage of Elizabethan Tragedy, Berkeley 1936, p 181 (relation to Dance of Death and De Casibus themes).

Whiting B J, Proverbs in the Earlier English Drama, HSCL 14.67.

De Vocht H, Everyman: A Comparative Study of Texts and Sources, Materials for the Study of the Old Eng Drama 20.179 (Pride of Life as model for Everyman).

Clark J M, The Dance of Death in the Middle Ages and the Renaissance, Glasgow Univ Publ 86.92.

Rossiter A P, English Drama from Early Times to the Elizabethans, London 1950, pp 96, 168 n30 (relation to debat).

Craig ERD, p 346 (origin in Dance of Death).

Peter J, Complaint and Satire in Early English Literature, Oxford 1956, p 191.

Potter R A, The Form and Concept of the English Morality Play, diss Claremont 1965 microfilm, p 151 (possible relation to the mummers' play).

Davis N-CP, p xcvii (relation to Kildare poems).

Axton R, Popular Modes in the Earliest Plays, in Medieval Drama, ed N Denny, Stratford-upon-Avon Stud 16, London and N Y 1973, p 35; European Drama of the Early Middle Ages, London 1966, p 166 (relation to earlier popular drama).

Rôles and Themes. Mackenzie W R, The English Moralities from the Point of View of Allegory, Harvard Stud Eng 2.203 (Summons of Death); Washington Univ Stud Humanistic Series 9².263 (reviews opinions on ending and suggests Intercession of the Virgin as motif).

Zandvoort R W, The Messenger in the Early English Drama, ESts 3.104; rptd Collected Papers, Groningen 1954, p 26.

Tomlinson W E, Der Herodes-Charakter im englischen Drama, Palaes 195.49.

Boughner D C, Retribution in English Medieval Drama, N&Q 198.506; Vice, Braggart, and Falstaff, Angl 72.36; The Braggart in Renaissance Comedy, Minneapolis 1954, p 148.

Davis N-CP, p lxxxviii (certainty of death).

Literary Criticism. Waterhouse, edn, p lxxii.

Haller J, Die Technik des Dialogs im mittelalterlichen Drama Englands, Worms a Rh 1916, p 102.

Staging. Brandl, edn, p xix (challenged by F I Carpenter, MLN 14.135[270]).

Waterhouse, edn, p lxxiii.

Fifield M, The Castle in the Circle, Ball State Monograph 6.19.

General References. Morley, 7.173; Chambers, 2.155, 436; Chambers OHEL, pp 53, 217.

CHEL, 5.58; Creizenach, 1.471.

Brooke C F Tucker, The Tudor Drama, Boston 1911, p 50.

Baugh LHE, p 284.

Clark W S, The Early Irish Stage, Oxford 1955, p 9.

Craig ERD, pp 343, 347.

Williams A, The Drama of Medieval England, East Lansing Mich 1961, p 143.

Bibliography. CBEL, 1.514; Stratman, p 224; 2nd edn N Y 1972, 1.625.

THE MACRO PLAYS (THE CASTLE OF PERSEVERANCE, WISDOM, MANKIND).

[27] THE CASTLE OF PERSEVERANCE.

MS. Folger Shakespeare Libr V.a.354 (formerly Macro), ff 154ª–191ª [ff 38ª–75ª] (ca 1440).

Brown-Robbins, Robbins-Cutler, no 917.

Macray W D, The Manuscripts of the Late John Henry Gurney, Esq of Keswick Hall, Norfolk, Historical Manuscripts Commission: 12th Report, Appendix, Pt 9, London 1891, p 164 (the Macro Plays).

Furnivall and Pollard, edn, pp ix, xxviii (the Macro Plays), xxxi (The Castle of Perseverance).

Farmer, edn, p v; A Hand List to the Tudor Facsimile Texts, [London] 1914, p 11.

de Ricci Census, 2.2272, no 5031 (the Macro Plays).

Eccles MP, pp vii, viii (the Macro Plays, The Castle of Perseverance).

Bevington, edn, pp viii, xvii (the Macro Plays), xviii, xx (The Castle of Perseverance).

Editions. Furnivall F J and A W Pollard, The Macro Plays, EETSES 91, London 1904, p 75; reissued 1924 (based on the MS).

Farmer J S, The Castle of Perseverance, London and Edinburgh 1908 (Tudor Facsimile Texts, Macro Plays 3; Students' Facsimile Edn, Amersham 1914).

Adams CPSD, p 265 (based on Furnivall and Pollard edn; abridged).

Pollard EMP, p 64 (based on Furnivall-Marx transcript of MS; selections).

Eccles MP, p 1 (based on the MS; collated with Furnivall and Pollard edn; crit T Turville-Petre, SN 42.496; A C Cawley, N&Q 216.70; W Habicht, Angl 89.137; S J Kahrl, Spec 46.144).

Bevington D, The Macro Plays . . . A Facsimile Edition with Facing Transcripts, N Y 1972, p 1 (emendations of Furnivall and Eccles, marginalia in ftnts).

Modernizations. Langentels I, The Castle of Perseverance: A Free Adaptation from the Macro Play, London 1948.

Hopper V A and G B Lahey, Medieval Mystery Plays, Morality Plays, and Interludes, Great Neck N Y 1962, p 147 (abridged).

Schell E T and J D Shuchter, English Morality Plays and Moral Interludes, N Y etc 1969, p 1 (based on Furnivall and Pollard edn).

Textual Matters and Notes. Kölbing E, Kleine Beiträge zur Erklärung und Textkritik vor-Shakespeare'scher Dramen, EStn 21.167.

Furnivall and Pollard, edn, p 187 (notes).

Smart W K, The Castle of Perseverance: Place, Date and a Source, Manly Anniv Stud in Lang and Lit, Chicago 1923, pp

43, 47.

Pollard EMP, pp 197, 224d (notes).

Withington R, The Castle of Perseverance, Line 695, PQ 14.270.

Zandvoort R W, The Castell of Perseverance, Line 26, ESts 24.178; rptd Collected Papers, Groningen 1954, p 32 (suggests spyll for per[yll]).

Willis J, Stage Directions in The Castell of Perseverance, MLR 51.404.

Southern R, The Medieval Theatre in the Round, London 1957, pp 34, 188, and chap 12 (stage directions); p 81 (definition of styteler).

Cauthen I B, The Foule Flibbertigibbet, N&Q 203.98.

Bennett J, À Linguistic Study of The Castle of Perseverance, diss Boston Univ 1960 microfilm; DA 21.872; The Castle of Perseverance: Redactions, Place, and Date, MS 24.141 (crit Eccles MP, p xvi).

Henry A K, The Castle of Perseverance: The Stage Direction at Line 1767, N&Q 210.448.

Eccles MP, pp xvii, 185 (redactions, notes).

Language. Furnivall and Pollard, edn, pp xxxv, xli (discussion); 189 (glossary).

Patch H R, The Ludus Coventriae and the Digby Massacre, PMLA 35.337 n36.

Smart, Manly Anniv Stud, p 42.

Bennett, A Linguistic Study of The Castle of Perseverance, pp 1, 44, 138; MS 24.141, 148, 151.

Eccles MP, pp xi, 229 (discussion, glossary).

Eccles M. Ludus Coventriae: Lincoln or Norfolk?, MÆ 40.138 (brief).

Versification. Furnivall and Pollard, edn, p xxvi.

Ramsay R L, Magnyfycence, EETSES 98, London 1906, p cxxxvii.

Patch, PMLA 35.337 (relation to metre of prologue of Ludus Coventriae).

Eckhardt E, Die metrische Unterscheidung von Ernst und Komik in den englischen Moralitäten, EStn 62.161, 164.

Bennett, A Linguistic Study of The Castle of Perseverance, p 9; MS 24.142.

Eccles MP, p xv.

Date. Furnivall and Pollard, edn, p xxiii.

Smart, Manly Anniv Stud, p 46.

Bennett, A Linguistic Study of The Castle of Perseverance, pp 1, 141; MS 24.141, 150.

Eccles MP, p x.

Sources and Literary Relations. Furnivall and Pollard, edn, p xxxix (Piers Plowman, Chasteau d'Amour).

Traver H, The Four Daughters of God,

BrynMawrMon 6.125, 135, 138 (relation of Castle of Perseverance version to Charter of the Abbey and to Ludus Coventriae Salutation), 150 (relation to Piers Plowman).

Thompson E N S, The English Moral Plays, Trans Connecticut Acad of Arts and Sciences 14.312, 354, 358.

Mackenzie W R, The Origin of the English Morality, Washington Univ Stud 4s 2² (1915).156 (dramatized version of the allegory of The Castle of Love).

Ramsay R L, Morality Themes in Milton's Poetry, SP 15.123.

Loomis R S, The Allegorical Siege in the Art of the Middle Ages, AJA 2s 23.266; Lincoln as a Dramatic Centre, Mélanges . . . offerts à Gustave Cohen, Paris 1950, p 241 (relation to Ludus Coventriae).

Wharey J B, Bunyan's Holy War and the Conflict-Type of Morality Play, MLN 34.66.

Block K S, Ludus Coventriae, EETSES 120, London 1922, p liv.

Smart, Manly Anniv Stud, p 49 (common source with Friar Daw and Piers Plowman in Lollard Antichrist lit).

Allison T E, On the Body and Soul Legend, MLN 42.102.

Cornelius R D, The Figurative Castle, Bryn Mawr Pa 1930, p 62 (relation to Piers Plowman, Chasteau d'Amour).

Bühler C F, The Sources of the Court of Sapience, Beiträge zur englischen Philologie 23, Leipzig 1932, p 18.

Owst G R, Literature and Pulpit in Medieval England, N Y 1933; 2nd edn 1961, pp 85, 92, 535.

Brunner K, Der Streit der vier Himmelstöchter, EStn 68.188 (a ME version of the allegory).

Farnham W, The Medieval Heritage of Elizabethan Tragedy, Berkeley 1936, p 188 (relation to Dance of Death and De Casibus themes).

Hammerle K, The Castle of Perseverance und Pearl, Angl 60.401 (parallels in phrasing).

Whiting B J, Proverbs in the Earlier English Drama, HSCL 14.68.

Reddoch Sister M C, Non-Dramatic Sources and Analogues in a Typical English Morality The Castell of Perseverance, MA diss Catholic Univ of America 1944.

Chew S C, The Virtues Reconciled: An Iconographic Study, Toronto 1947, pp 44, 68.

De Vocht H, Everyman: A Comparative

Study of Texts and Sources, Materials for the Study of the Old Eng Drama 20.182.

Towne F, Roister Doister's Assault on the Castle of Perseverance, Research Stud of the State Coll of Washington 18(1950).175.

Klinefelter R A, The Four Daughters of God: A New Version, JEGP 52.90.

Craig ERD, pp 266, 279 (relation to Hegge plays).

Schell E T, On the Imitation of Life's Pilgrimage in The Castle of Perseverance, JEGP 67.235; rptd in Medieval English Drama, J Taylor and A H Nelson, edd, Chicago and London 1972, p 279 (compares the play to poems such as Le Pèlerinage de la vie humaine; crit S Wenzel, MS 35.382).

Eccles MP, p xix.

Nelson A H, Of the Seuen Ages: An Unknown Analogue of The Castle of Perseverance, Comparative Drama 8(1974–75).125.

Rôles and Themes. Cushman L W, The Devil and the Vice in the English Dramatic Literature before Shakespeare, SEP 6.40, 45 (Devil), 55 and passim (Vice).

Loomis, AJA 2s 23.266.

Mackenzie W R, The Debate over the Soul in The Pride of Life, Washington Univ Stud Humanistic Series 9²(1922).263.

Allison, MLN 42.102.

Tomlinson W E, Der Herodes-Charakter im englischen Drama, Palaes 195.52.

Farnham, The Medieval Heritage of Elizabethan Tragedy, p 188.

Koldewey E, Über die Willensfreiheit im älteren englischen Drama, Würzburg 1937, p 24.

McCutchan J W, Covetousness in The Castle of Perseverance, Eng Stud in Honor of James Southall Wilson, Univ of Virginia Stud 4[5], Charlottesville 1951, p 175.

Boughner D C, Vice, Braggart, and Falstaff, Angl 72.36; The Braggart in Renaissance Comedy, Minneapolis 1954, pp 146, 149, 155.

Bennett, A Linguistic Study of The Castle of Perseverance, p 29; MS 24.145 (suggests Intercession of the Virgin as subject of original ending).

Literary Criticism. Gayley C M, Representative English Comedies, N Y 1903, l.lviii.

Furnivall and Pollard, edn, p xxiii.

Crowley T J, Character-Treatment in the Mediaeval Drama, Notre Dame Ind 1907, p 128.

Mackenzie W R, The English Moralities from the Point of View of Allegory, Harvard Stud Eng 2.58.

Haller J, Die Technik des Dialogs im mittelalterlichen Drama Englands, Worms a Rh 1916, p 87.

Weiner K, Die Verwendung des Parallelismus als Kunstmittel im englischen Drama vor Shakespeare, Hamburg 1916, p 13.

Rossiter A P, English Drama from Early Times to the Elizabethans, London 1950, pp 96, 99.

Lombardo A, Morality Play: The Castle of Perseverance, Everyman, Rivista di letterature moderne 4[14](1953).268; Il dramma pre-shakespeariano, Venezia 1957, p 73.

Bennett, A Linguistic Study of The Castle of Perseverance, pp 20, 30, 140; MS 24.141, 144, 146, 150.

Bevington D M, From Mankind to Marlowe, Cambridge Mass 1962, p 117.

Schell, JEGP 67.235; Medieval English Drama, p 279.

Eccles MP, pp xviii, xxiv.

Kelley M R, Fifteenth-Century Flamboyant Style and The Castle of Perseverance, Comparative Drama 6(1972–73).14.

Staging. Hone W, Ancient Mysteries Described, London 1823, p 227.

Sharp T, A Dissertation on the Pageants . . . Anciently Performed at Coventry, Coventry 1825, facing p 23 (Castle of Perseverance staging plan).

Furnivall and Pollard, edn, pp xxvii, xxxiii.

Thompson, Trans Connecticut Acad of Arts and Sciences 14.389.

Brooke C F Tucker, The Tudor Drama, Boston 1911, p 54.

Smart, Manly Anniv Stud, p 43 (locale of performance).

Stoddard H C, The Presentation of The Castle of Perseverance, MA diss Univ of Chicago 1929.

Nicoll A, Masks, Mimes, and Miracles: Studies in the Popular Theatre, London and N Y 1931, pp 202, 204 (plan); The Development of the Theatre, 5th edn rvsd London etc 1966, pp 58 (plan), 62, 64.

Fischel O, Art and the Theatre, Burlington Magazine 66(1935).14.

Craig ERD, pp 119, 348.

Southern, The Medieval Theatre in the Round (includes a detailed analysis of the presentation in chap 12; crit above, under GENERAL TREATMENTS, *Records and*

Staging).

Craik T W, The Tudor Interlude, Leicester 1958, pp 9, 50, 56, 64, 82.

Arnott P D, The Origins of the Medieval Theatre in the Round, Theatre Notebook 15(1960–61).84 (affinities with the tournament; crit J F Arnott, Theatre Notebook 16[1961–62].32).

Freeman A, A Round outside Cornwall, Theatre Notebook 16.10 (crit N C Schmitt, Theatre Notebook 24.22).

Robinson J W, Three Notes on the Medieval Theatre, Theatre Notebook 16.60 (opening procession of actors; use of prompters).

Bevington, From Mankind to Marlowe, pp 48, 117 and passim; edn, p ix.

Fifield M, The Castle in the Circle, Ball State Monograph 6.1 (crit R Axton, MÆ 37.226; N C Schmitt, Theatre Notebook 24.23); The Arena Theatres in Vienna Codices 2535 and 2536, Comparative Drama 2(1968–69).259 (challenges Southern's reconstruction of the theatre in the round; crit M Stevens, CE 32.456 n27).

Schmitt N C, Was There a Medieval Theatre in the Round?: A Re-examination of the Evidence, Theatre Notebook 23(1968–69) .130; 24(1969–70).18; rptd in Medieval English Drama, J Taylor and A H Nelson, edd, Chicago and London 1972, p 292 (challenges Southern's reconstruction; evidence includes other allegories of the castle; crit R Hosley, Theatre Survey 12.29n).

Eccles MP, p xxi.

Forstater A and J L Baird, Walking and Wending: Mankind's Opening Speech, Theatre Notebook 26(1971–72).60.

Hosley R, Three Kinds of Outdoor Theatre before Shakespeare, Theatre Survey 12 (1971).1.

Pentzell R J, The Medieval Theatre in the Streets, Theatre Survey 14(1973).1 (crit M del Villar, p 76; reply by Pentzell, p 82).

General References. Collier J P, The History of English Dramatic Poetry, London 1831, 2.279.

Klein, 2.8; Brandl, § 121; Chambers, 2.155, 437; Chambers OHEL, pp 55, 217; Creizenach, 1.468.

Brooke, The Tudor Drama, p 51.

Pollard EMP, pp xlv, 197; Baugh LHE, p 285.

Craig ERD, pp 119, 266, 279, 343, 348.

Williams A, The Drama of Medieval England, East Lansing Mich 1961, p 148.

Bibliography. CBEL, 1.514; Stratman, p 176; 2nd edn N Y 1972, 1.545.

[28] WISDOM.

MSS. 1, Bodl 1734 (Digby 133), ff 158ᵃ–169ᵇ (ca 1490–1500; lines 1–752); 2, Folger Shakespeare Libr V.a.354 (formerly Macro), ff 98ᵃ–121ᵃ [14ᵃ–37ᵃ] (ca 1475).

Brown-Robbins, no 1440.

Macray W D, Catalogi Codicum Manuscriptorum Bibliothecae Bodleianae, Pt 9, Oxford 1883, no 133.9 (MS 1 only).

Furnivall, EETSES 70.xv (MS 1 only).

Furnivall and Pollard, EETSES 91.ix, xxviii, xxx.

Farmer, edn, p v; A Hand List to the Tudor Facsimile Texts, [London] 1914, p 30.

de Ricci Census, 2.2272, no 5031.

Baker D C and J L Murphy, The Late Medieval Plays of MS Digby 133: Scribes, Dates, and Early History, Research Opportunities in Renaissance Drama 10(1967).156, 162, 163.

Eccles MP, pp viii, xxvii, xxx.

Bevington, edn, pp viii, xvii, xix.

Editions. Sharp T, Ancient Mysteries from the Digby Manuscripts, Abbotsford Club, Edinburgh 1835, p 16[5] (MS 1).

Turnbull W B D D, Mind, Will, and Understanding: A Morality from the Macro MS, Abbotsford Club, Edinburgh 1837 (from J P Collier transcript of MS 2).

Furnivall F J, The Digby Plays, EETSES 70, London 1896, p 137; rptd from New Shakespere Soc edn 1882; EETS edn reissued 1930, 1967 (MS 1).

Furnivall F J and A W Pollard, The Macro Plays, EETSES 91, London 1904, p 35; reissued 1924 (based on MS 2, compared with Furnivall edn of MS 1).

Farmer J S, Wisdom or Mind, Will, and Understanding, London and Edinburgh 1907 (Tudor Facsimile Texts, Macro Plays 2; Students' Facsimile Edn, Amersham 1914; MS 2).

Eccles MP, p 113 (based on MS 2; collated with MS 1 and Furnivall-Pollard edn).

Bevington D, The Macro Plays . . . A Facsimile Edition with Facing Transcripts, N Y 1972, p 155 (MS 2; variants, emendations by earlier editors, and marginalia in ftnts).

Modernizations. Tickner EED, p 213 (MS 1); Baldwin EED, p 267.

Brock A J and D G Byrd, The Digby Plays,

Dallas 1973, p 99 (prose).
Textual Matters and Notes. Furnivall and Pollard, EETSES 91.187 (note).
Eccles MP, pp xxx, 203 (relation of the two MSS, notes).
Bevington, edn, p xix (relation of the two MSS).
Language. Schmidt K, Die Digby-Spiele, Angl 8.391.
Furnivall, EETSES 70.229 (glossary).
Furnivall and Pollard, EETSES 91.xix, xxxv, xli (discussion), 189 (glossary).
Eccles MP, pp xxx, 229 (discussion, glossary).
Versification. Schmidt, Angl 8.392.
Furnivall and Pollard, EETSES 91.xxii.
Ramsay R L, Magnyfycence, EETSES 98, London 1906, p cxxxviii.
Eckhardt E, Die metrische Unterscheidung von Ernst und Komik in den englischen Moralitäten, EStn 62.155 and passim.
Eccles MP, p xxxii.
Date and Authorship. Furnivall and Pollard, EETSES 91.xix.
Smart W K, Some English and Latin Sources and Parallels for the Morality of Wisdom, Menasha Wisc 1912, pp 82 (authorship), 87 (date).
Eccles MP, p xxx.
Sources and Literary Relations. Horstman C, Orologium Sapientiae or The Seven Poyntes of Trewe Wisdom, aus MS Douce 114, Angl 10.323.
Smart, Some English and Latin Sources and Parallels for the Morality of Wisdom.
Schleich G, Auf den Spuren Susos in England, Arch 156.184.
Smith Sister M F, Wisdom and Personification of Wisdom Occurring in Middle English Literature before 1500, Washington D C 1935, p 151 (relation of the morality Wisdom to Orologium Sapientiae).
Green J C, The Medieval Morality of Wisdom Who is Christ: A Study in Origins, Nashville Tenn 1938 (interpretation against philosophical, theological, psychological background).
Whiting B J, Proverbs in the Earlier English Drama, HSCL 14.75.
Molloy, A Theological Interpretation of Wisdom (see below, under *Rôles and Themes*), pp xii n9 and passim.
Doyle A I, A Survey of the Origins and Circulation of Theological Writings in the 14th, 15th, and Early 16th Centuries, diss Cambridge (Downing) 1953 (section on Orologium Sapientiae).

Eccles MP, p xxxiii.
Rôles and Themes. Cushman L W, The Devil and the Vice in the English Dramatic Literature before Shakespeare, SEP 6.55.
Thompson E N S, The English Moral Plays, Trans Connecticut Acad of Arts and Sciences 14.338 (combination of doctrinal theology and practical ethics).
Russell H K, Tudor and Stuart Dramatizations of the Doctrines of Natural and Moral Philosophy, SP 31.3.
Koldewey E, Über die Willensfreiheit im älteren englischen Drama, Würzburg 1937, p 51.
Green, The Medieval Morality of Wisdom, pp 1, 40 (concept of Wisdom, psychological concepts).
Molloy J J, A Theological Interpretation of the Moral Play, Wisdom, Who is Christ, Washington D C 1952 (crit T A Kirby, MLN 69.150; H Koziol, Angl 73.218).
Boughner D C, Vice, Braggart, and Falstaff, Angl 72.37; The Braggart in Renaissance Comedy, Minneapolis 1954, p 149.
Bevington D, Political Satire in the Morality Wisdom Who is Christ, Renaissance Papers 1963[1964].41; included with minor revisions in Tudor Drama and Politics, Cambridge Mass 1968, p 28 (the evil of maintenance); edn, p xii.
Literary Criticism. Mackenzie W R, The English Moralities from the Point of View of Allegory, Harvard Stud Eng 2.149.
Haller J, Die Technik des Dialogs im mittelalterlichen Drama Englands, Worms a Rh 1916, p 96.
Green, The Medieval Morality of Wisdom, p 114.
Bevington D M, From Mankind to Marlowe, Cambridge Mass 1962, p 124.
Eccles MP, p xxxv.
Koontz C, The Duality of Styles in the Morality Play Wisdom Who is Christ: A Classical-Rhetorical Analysis, Style 7(1973).251.
Staging, Audience, Locale. Furnivall, EETSES 70.xiii, 168 (evidence for London performance).
Furnivall and Pollard, EETSES 91.xxiii.
Thompson, Trans Connecticut Acad of Arts and Sciences 14.394, 396.
Smart, Some English and Latin Sources and Parallels for the Morality of Wisdom, pp 78 (argues for a monastic audience), 85 (Bury as locale).
Molloy, A Theological Interpretation of Wisdom, pp 84, 192, 198 (argues for London

locale and lay audience).

Craik T W, The Tudor Interlude, Leicester 1958, pp 51, 56, 75, 88.

Bevington, From Mankind to Marlowe, pp 50, 124 and passim; edn, p xi.

Fifield M, The Use of Doubling and Extras in Wisdom, Who is Christ, Ball State Univ Forum 6³(1965).65; The Castle in the Circle, Ball State Monograph 6.23.

Eccles MP, p xxxiv.

General References. Collier J P, The History of English Dramatic Poetry, London 1831, 2.287.

Klein, 2.11; Brandl, § 131; Chambers, 2.155, 438; Chambers OHEL, pp 59, 217; Creizenach, 1.470.

Brooke C F Tucker, The Tudor Drama, Boston 1911, p 61.

Baugh LHE, p 285; Craig ERD, pp 344, 349.

Williams A, The Drama of Medieval England, East Lansing Mich 1961, p 157.

Bibliography. CBEL, 1.514.

Molloy, A Theological Interpretation of Wisdom, p 217.

Stratman, p 237; 2nd edn N Y 1972, 1.653.

[29] MANKIND.

MS. Folger Shakespeare Libr V.a.354 (formerly Macro), ff 122ᵃ–134ᵃ [1ᵃ–13ᵃ] (ca 1475).

Brown-Robbins, Robbins-Cutler, no 3495.

Brandl, edn, p xxi.

Furnivall and Pollard, edn, pp ix, xxviii.

Farmer, edn, p v; A Hand List to the Tudor Facsimile Texts, [London] 1914, p 29.

de Ricci Census, 2.2272, no 5031.

Eccles MP, pp viii, xxxvii.

Bevington, edn, pp viii, xvii, xx.

Editions. Manly Spec, p 315 (based on Furnivall-Marx transcript of MS).

Brandl A, Quellen des weltlichen Dramas vor Shakespeare, QF 80, Strassburg 1898, p 37 (based on Furnivall-Marx transcript).

Furnivall F J and A W Pollard, The Macro Plays, EETSES 91, London 1904, p 1; reissued 1924 (based on the MS with emendations from Manly Spec and Brandl edns).

Farmer J S, Mankind, London and Edinburgh 1907 (Tudor Facsimile Texts, Macro Plays 1; Students' Facsimile Edn, Amersham 1914).

Adams CPSD, p 304 (based on Furnivall and Pollard edn, with emendations from Manly Spec edn).

Eccles MP, p 153 (based on the MS; collated with earlier printed edns).

Bevington D, The Macro Plays . . . A Facsimile Edition with Facing Transcripts, N Y 1972, p 253 (emendations by earlier editors, marginalia in ftnts).

Modernizations. Farmer J S, Recently Recovered Lost Tudor Plays, London 1907, p 1.

Somerset J A B, Four Tudor Interludes, London 1974, p 26.

Textual Matters and Notes. Brandl, edn, p 651 (notes).

Manly J M, JEGP 2.421 (emendations to Brandl edn).

Carpenter F I, MLN 14,138(275) (emendations to Brandl edn).

Furnivall and Pollard, edn, pp 19, 74, 187 (notes).

Farmer, Lost Tudor Plays, pp 371, 430 (notebook and word-list).

Smart W K, Some Notes on Mankind, MP 14.48, 56, 293; Mankind and the Mumming Plays, MLN 32.21 (lines 426–68).

Jones C, Walsyngham Wystell, JEGP 35.139.

Coogan Sister M P, An Interpretation of the Moral Play, Mankind, Washington D C 1947, pp 7 n18, 106, 118.

Eccles MP, p 216 (notes).

Somerset, Four Tudor Interludes, p 165 (notes).

Language. Brandl, edn, pp xxii, xxx (Latinized words).

Furnivall and Pollard, edn, pp xi, xviii, xxxv, xli (discussion), 189 (glossary).

Eccles MP, pp xxxviii, 229 (discussion, glossary).

Versification. Brandl, edn, p xxiv.

Furnivall and Pollard, edn, p xviii.

Ramsay R L, Magnyfycence, EETSES 98, London 1906, p cxxxix.

Eckhardt E, Die metrische Unterscheidung von Ernst und Komik in den englischen Moralitäten, EStn 62.154 and passim.

Eccles MP, p xl.

Date. Brandl, edn, p xxvi.

Furnivall and Pollard, edn, p xi.

Smart, MP 14.45.

Coogan, An Interpretation of the Moral Play, Mankind, pp 104, 113.

Baker D C, The Date of Mankind, PQ 42.90.

Eccles MP, p xxxviii.

Authorship. Brandl, edn, p xxx.

Smart, MP 14.308.

Coogan, An Interpretation of the Moral Play, Mankind, p 116.

Sources and Literary Relations. Brandl, edn, p xxviii (Wisdom, Lydgate's Assembly of Gods, etc).

Keiller M M, The Influence of Piers Plowman on the Macro Play of Mankind, PMLA 26.339.

Mackenzie W R, A New Source for Mankind, PMLA 27.98 (challenges Keiller; suggests Merci Passith Ri3twisnes).

Smart, MP 14.312 (minimizes importance of both Keiller's and Mackenzie's sources); MLN 32.21 (link with mumming plays).

Patch H R, The Ludus Coventriae and the Digby Massacre, PMLA 35.341 (relation of Mankind to Ludus Coventriae).

Whiting B J, Proverbs in the Earlier English Drama, HSCL 14.73.

Coogan, An Interpretation of the Moral Play, Mankind, pp 1, 22, 38 (parallels with a sermon in Jacob's Well).

Brown A, Folklore Elements in the Medieval Drama, Folklore 63(1952).69.

Eccles MP, p xli.

Axton R, European Drama of the Early Middle Ages, London 1974, p 199 (relation to mummers' plays).

Rôles. Bolte J, Der Teufel in der Kirche, ZfVL 11.264 (Titivillus).

Cushman L W, The Devil and the Vice in the English Dramatic Literature before Shakespeare, SEP 6.45, 51 (Devil), 55 and passim (Vice).

Coogan, An Interpretation of the Moral Play, Mankind, p 58 (Titivillus).

Boughner D C, Vice, Braggart, and Falstaff, Angl 72.38; The Braggart in Renaissance Comedy, Minneapolis 1954, p 150.

Spivack B, Shakespeare and the Allegory of Evil, N Y 1958, p 123 (Titivillus).

Anderson M D, Drama and Imagery in English Medieval Churches, Cambridge 1963, pp 173, 176 (stage demon).

Happé P, The Vice and the Folk-Drama, Folklore 75(1964).167.

Weimann R, Rede-Konventionen des Vice von Mankind bis Hamlet, Zeitschr f Anglistik und Amerikanistik 15(1967).117; slight revisions in Shakespeare und die Tradition des Volkstheaters, Berlin 1967, p 176.

Themes. Koldewey E, Über die Willensfreiheit im älteren englischen Drama, Würzburg 1937, p 44.

Coogan, An Interpretation of the Moral Play, Mankind (argument for Shrovetide play; crit G D Willcock, YWES 28.104; A W Reed, RES 24.246).

Wenzel S, The Sin of Sloth, Chapel Hill N C 1967, p 150.

Bevington D, Tudor Drama and Politics, Cambridge Mass 1968, p 39 (social unrest).

Literary Criticism. Gayley C M, Representative English Comedies, N Y 1903, l.lviii.

Furnivall and Pollard, edn, p xvii.

Thompson E N S, The English Moral Plays, Trans Connecticut Acad of Arts and Sciences 14.387.

Mackenzie W R, The English Moralities from the Point of View of Allegory, Harvard Stud Eng 2.65.

Haller J, Die Technik des Dialogs im mittelalterlichen Drama Englands, Worms a Rh 1916, p 99.

Smart, MP 14.309.

Coogan, An Interpretation of the Moral Play, Mankind, pp 57, 92.

Rossiter A P, English Drama from Early Times to the Elizabethans, London 1950, p 100.

Lombardo A, Morality e interlude, English Miscellany 5(1954).10; Il dramma pre-shakespeariano, Venezia 1957, p 120.

Bevington D M, From Mankind to Marlowe, Cambridge Mass 1962, pp 15, 137.

Righter A, Shakespeare and the Idea of the Play, London 1962, p 29.

Eccles MP, p xliii.

Neuss P, Active and Idle Language: Dramatic Images in Mankind, in Medieval Drama, ed N Denny, Stratford-upon-Avon Stud 16, London and N Y 1973, p 41.

Somerset, Four Tudor Interludes, p 6.

Staging, Locale, Season. Brandl, edn, p xxxii.

Furnivall and Pollard, edn, p xi.

Thompson, Trans Connecticut Acad of Arts and Sciences 14.391.

Brooke C F Tucker, The Tudor Drama, Boston 1911, p 63.

Smart, MP 14.45 (season), 48, 306 (locale).

Pollard EMP, p lv.

Coogan, An Interpretation of the Moral Play, Mankind, p 7 (season).

Craik T W, The Tudor Interlude, Leicester 1958, pp 20, 55, 83, 128 n40.

Bevington, From Mankind to Marlowe, p 15 and passim; edn, p xi; Popular and Courtly Traditions on the Early Tudor Stage, in Medieval Drama, ed N Denny, Stratford-upon-Avon Stud 16, London and N Y 1973, p 96 (modifies earlier view).

Fifield M, The Castle in the Circle, Ball State Monograph 6.27.

Eccles MP, p xlii.

Southern R, The Staging of Plays before Shakespeare, London 1973, pp 21, 143, 330.

Clopper L M, Mankind and Its Audience, Comparative Drama 8(1974–75).347 (suggests private auspices).
General References. Collier J P, The History of English Dramatic Poetry, London 1831, 2.293.
Klein, 2.14; Brandl, § 121; Chambers, 2.155, 438; Chambers OHEL, pp 61, 85, 218; Creizenach, 1.470.
Brooke, The Tudor Drama, p 63.
Baugh LHE, p 285; Craig ERD, pp 343, 350.
Williams A, The Drama of Medieval England, East Lansing Mich 1961, p 154; opinions rvsd in The English Moral Play before 1500, Annuale Mediaevale 4(1963).15.
Kahrl S J, Traditions of Medieval English Drama, London 1974, p 114.
Bibliography. CBEL, 1.514.
Coogan, An Interpretation of the Moral Play, Mankind, p 121.
Stratman, p 209; 2nd edn N Y 1972, 1.606.

[30] EVERYMAN.

MSS. No MS extant. PRINTS: 1, Bodl (Douce fragment f.10), four defective leaves (C only), R Pynson ca 1510–25 (STC, no 10604); 2, BM (C21.c17), 10 leaves (wants A), R Pynson ca 1525–30 (STC, no 10603); 3, BM (Huth 32), 16 leaves, J Skot ca 1530–35 (STC, no 10605); 4, Huntington 14195 (formerly Lincoln Cathedral; Britwell Court), 16 leaves, J Skot ca 1528–29 (STC, no 10606).
Robbins-Cutler, no 1341.8.
Halliwell J O, A Handlist of the Early English Literature Preserved in the Douce Collection in the Bodleian Library, London 1860, p 45 (PRINT 1 only).
Hazlitt W C, Handbook to the Popular, Poetical and Dramatic Literature of Great Britain from the Invention of Printing to the Restoration, London 1867, p 463.
[Ellis F S and W C Hazlitt], A Catalogue of the Printed Books, Manuscripts, Autograph Letters, and Engravings, Collected by Henry Huth, London 1880, 4.1417 (PRINT 3 only).
Logeman, edn, pp v, 98.
Greg, edn, Materialien zur Kunde des älteren englischen Dramas, 4.vii; 24.vii; 28.v, vi, 33; A Bibliography of the English Printed Drama to the Restoration, Bibliographical Soc Illust Monographs 24, London 1939, 1.3, no 4.
[Pollard A W], Catalogue of the Fifty Manu-

scripts and Printed Books Bequeathed to the British Museum by Alfred H Huth, London 1912, p 53 (PRINT 3 only).
Farmer J S, A Hand List to the Tudor Facsimile Texts, [London] 1914, p 15.
Hodnett E, English Woodcuts 1480–1585, Bibliographical Soc Illust Monographs 22, London 1935, pp 61, 106, 446 no 2370 (PRINTS 3, 4 only).
De Vocht H, Professor Willy Bang and His Work in English Philology, Materials for the Study of the Old English Drama 25, Louvain 1958, p 111.
Cawley, edn, pp ix, 39 (prints, woodcuts).
Editions. Hawkins T, The Origin of the English Drama, Oxford 1773, 1.27 (based on PRINT 4).
An Unknown Edition of the Interlude of Every Man Printed by Pynson, The Shakespeare Society's Papers 3, London 1847, p 147 (PRINT 1).
Goedeke K, Every-man, Homulus und Hekastus: ein Beitrag zur internationalen Litteraturgeschichte, Hannover 1865 (based on Hawkins edn, with parallel German trans).
Logeman H, Elckerlijk, a Fifteenth Century Dutch Morality (presumably by Petrus Dorlandus), and Everyman, a Nearly Contemporary Translation, Univ de Gand, Recueil de travaux publiés par la Faculté de Philosophie et Lettres 5, Gand 1892 (parallel Dutch and English texts; Everyman based on PRINT 3, with variants in ftnts; crit J Bolte, Arch 88.413; G Kalff, Taal en Letteren 4.112; F Holthausen, Arch 92.411).
Moses M J, Everyman, A Morality Play, N Y 1903, 1908.
Greg W W, Everyman, Materialien zur Kunde des älteren englischen Dramas 4, Louvain 1904 (PRINT 4); Materialien zur Kunde des älteren englischen Dramas 24, Louvain 1909 (PRINT 3); Materialien zur Kunde des älteren englischen Dramas 28, Louvain 1910 (PRINTS 1, 2).
Farmer J S, Everyman, London and Edinburgh 1912 (Tudor Facsimile Texts: Students' Facsimile Edn Amersham 1912; PRINTS 3, 2).
Adams CPSD, p 288 (based on Greg edn of PRINT 4, compared with the other early prints).
Pollard EMP, p 77 (selections; based on transcript of PRINT 4; 1890 edn crit E Kölbing, EStn 21.170).

Cawley A C, Everyman, Manchester 1961 (based on PRINT 4; variants in ftnts; glossary, p 41; crit R W Zandvoort, ESts 42.316; D Gray, Journ Australasian Univ Lang and Lit Assoc 17(1962).100; P Bacquet, EA 19.281).

Modernizations. Hazlitt W C, A Select Collection of Old English Plays Originally Published by Robert Dodsley in the Year 1744, London 1874, 1.93.

Sidgwick F, Everyman, A Morality Play with an Introduction and Notes, London 1902; edn de luxe 1911, with plates after J H Amschewitz (based on PRINT 3).

Pollard A W, Fifteenth Century Prose and Verse, Arber's English Garner, London 1903, 1.277 (based on PRINTS 3, 4).

Everyman, A Moral Play, N Y 1903 (Fox, Duffield and Company; based on Hazlitt).

Farmer J S, Six Anonymous Plays ls, London 1905, p 89 (Early English Dramatists; based on Hazlitt); The Summoning of Everyman, London 1906 (Museum Dramatists; based on Hazlitt).

Everyman, A Moral Play, London [1906] (Broadway Booklets).

Everyman, A Morality, with Designs by Ambrose Dudley, London 1906.

Everyman . . . Reprinted in Modern English from the First Edition, London and Glasgow 1906 (Gowan's International Libr).

Brooke C F Tucker, Everyman, A Morality Play, with an Introduction by A T Quiller-Couch, Oxford [1908] (Select English Classics; based on PRINT 4, collated with PRINT 3).

R[hys] E, Everyman with Other Interludes, London 1909 and many rpts (Everyman's Libr).

Child C G, The Second Shepherds' Play, Everyman, and Other Early Plays, Boston N Y and Chicago 1910, p 65 (free trans).

Tatlock J S P and R G Martin, Representative English Plays, N Y 1917, p 31 (based on Greg edn of PRINT 4).

Everyman and Other Plays, Decorated by John Austen, [London] 1925.

Tickner EED, p 227; Baldwin EED, p 280.

Hubbell J B and J O Beaty, An Introduction to Drama, N Y 1927, p 107.

Rubinstein H F, Great English Plays, London and N Y 1928, p 26.

Schweikert H C, Early English Plays, N Y 1928, p 139.

Lieder P R, R M Lovett and R K Root, British Drama, Boston 1929, p 27 (based on Child).

Everyman, London Toronto and N Y 1930 (text arranged and illust by Thomas Derrick; based on Everyman's Libr edn).

Clark B H, World Drama, N Y and London 1933, 1.351.

Mantle B and J Gassner, A Treasury of the Theatre, N Y 1935, p 1339 (modernization by Gassner); rvsd edn Gassner, N Y 1951, 1.204; rptd in Gassner, Medieval and Tudor Drama, N Y 1963, p 207.

Parks E W and R C Beatty, The English Drama: An Anthology 900–1642, N Y 1935, p 57.

Kreymborg A, Poetic Drama, N Y 1941, p 208.

Everyman, A Morality, London 1941 (Zodiac Books 25; rptd from Everyman's Libr edn).

Loomis R S and H W Wells, Representative Medieval and Tudor Plays, N Y 1942, p 208.

Brooks C and R B Heilman, Understanding Drama, N Y etc 1945, p 86.

Heilman R B, An Anthology of English Drama before Shakespeare, N Y 1952, p 73.

Bentley G E, The Development of English Drama, N Y 1950, p 35.

Crump G H, Selections from English Dramatists, 2nd edn London 1950, p 41 (abridged).

Allen J, Three Medieval Plays, London 1953 (The Drama Libr); rptd N Y 1968 (Theatre Arts Books).

Cawley A C, Everyman and Medieval Miracle Plays, London and N Y 1956, p 205; 2nd edn 1958 (based on PRINT 4).

Schell E T and J D Shuchter, English Morality Plays and Moral Interludes, N Y etc 1969, p 111 (based on Heilman 1955 edn, compared with early prints).

For other modernizations, see Stratman, p 242; 2nd edn N Y 1972, 1.554; and J M and B M Connor, Ottemiller's Index to Plays in Collections, 5th edn Metuchen N J 1971, p 9.

Textual Matters and Notes. Logeman, edn, p 96 (notes on Everyman); Elckerlyc-Everyman: De vraag naar de prioriteit opnieuw onderzocht, Univ de Gand, Recueil de travaux publiés par la Faculté de Philosophie et Lettres 28, Gand 1902 (crit W Bang, EStn 35.116).

Holthausen F, Arch 92.411 (emendations of Logeman's text); AnglB 32.212.

Kölbing E, EStn 21.170 (crit of Pollard EMP 1890); reply by Holthausen, EStn 21.449; counter-reply by Kölbing, EStn 21.449.

Sidgwick F, Everyman, Line 407, N&Q 9s

11.106.
Greg, edn, Materialien zur Kunde des älteren engl Dramas 28.36, 40 (corrigenda, collations of four early prints).
Wood F A, Elckerlijc-Everyman: The Question of Priority, MP 8.279.
Pollard EMP, pp 202, 224d (notes).
Eliason N E, I take my cap in my lappe . . , PQ 14.271.
Zandvoort R W, Elckerlijc-Everyman, ESts 23.1.
De Vocht H, Everyman: A Comparative Study of Texts and Sources, Materials for the Study of the Old English Drama 20, Louvain 1947, p 219 (comparative list of variants in Everyman and Elckerlijc) and passim (crit H J E Endepols, Roeping 25 [1948].150; R W Zandvoort, RES 25.66).
Van Mierlo J, De prioriteit van Elckerlijc tegenover Everyman gehandhaafd, Koninklijke Vlaamse Academie voor Taal- en Letterkunde 3s 27, Antwerpen 1948, p 5 (crit H J E Endepols, Leuvensche Bijdragen 38, nos 3–4[1948].50; A Van Elslander, Revue Belge de Philologie et d'Histoire 30[1952].250); Elckerlijc. Nieuwe bijdragen met geëmendeerde uitgave, Kon Vlaamse Acad voor Taal- en Letterk 3s 29, Turnhout 1949, pp 7, 34.
Cawley, edn, pp x, 29 (relationship of Everyman prints, notes).
Kossman H, Felawship His Fer: A Note on Everyman's False Friend, ESts 45, Suppl, p 157 (legal parlance in line 253).
Vos R, Elckerlijc-Everyman-Homulus-Der Sünden Loin ist der Toid, TNTL 82.129.
Conley J, The Reference to Judas Maccabeus in Everyman, N&Q 212.50 (allusions to the Nine Worthies in ME verse).
Wasson J M, Interpolation in the Text of Everyman, Theatre Notebook 27(1972–73) .14.
And see Everyman-Elckerlijc Priority below.
The Rodde-Roeyken Controversy. Kalff G, Taal en Letteren 4(1894).122.
De Raaf K H, Den Spyeghel der Salicheyt van Elckerlijc (see below, under Sources and Literary Relations), p 13.
CHEL, 5.59n; Creizenach, 1.473n.
Maximilianus P, Het roeyken in Elckerlyc (v 749), TTL 14.1; reply by H van de Wijnpersse, Elckerlijc's roeyken, Nieuwe Taalgids 20(1926).258.
De Vocht, Materials for the Study of the Old Eng Drama 20.158.
Van Mierlo, Kon Vlaamse Acad voor Taal-

en Letterk 3s 27.73, 105.
Peeters L, Elckerlijc's roeyken, TNTL 76.228.
And see Everyman-Elckerlijc Priority below.
Versification. Ramsay R L, Magnyfycence, EETSES 98, London 1906, p cxliii.
Greg, edn, Materialien zur Kunde des älteren engl Dramas 28.56 (list of imperfect rimes).
Manly J M, Elckerlijk-Everyman: The Question of Priority, MP 8.269.
Eckhardt E, Die metrische Unterscheidung von Ernst und Komik in den englischen Moralitäten, EStn 62.153, 159, 162, 165, 166.
De Vocht, Materials for the Study of the Old English Drama 20.102.
Cawley, edn, p xxvii.
And see Everyman-Elckerlijc Priority below.
Date. Logeman, edn, p xvii.
Van Mierlo, Kon Vlaamse Acad voor Taal- en Letterk 3s 29.30.
Cawley, edn, p xiii.
Ausems T, Elckerlijc's première, Ons Geestelijk Erf 38(1964).393.
Vos R, De datering van de Elckerlijc, Spiegel der Letteren 9(1965–66).101.
Authorship. Logeman, edn, p xvii (suggests Petrus Dorlandus as author of Elckerlijc).
Muller J W and H Logeman, Die Hystorie van Reynaert die Vos, Zwolle 1892, p xlii nl (suggests Caxton translated Everyman; supporting evidence reviewed by Vos, TNTL 82.141).
Willems L, Is Pieter Doorlant de auteur van den Elckerlyc? Elckerlyc-Studiën, The Hague 1934, p 1.
Van Mierlo J, Antonis de Roovere, de dichter van Elckerlijc? VMKVA 1943, p 251 (argues for Petrus Dorlandus).
Cawley, edn, p xiii (evidence for Laurence Andrewe as trans of Everyman).
Ausems T, Elckerlijc's auteur, Dr L Reypens-Album, ed A Ampe, Antwerpen 1964, p 37 (argues for Petrus Dorlandus).
Vos R, Is Petrus Dorlandus de auteur van de Elckerlijc? Ons Geestelijk Erf 39(1965) .408; reply by Ausems, p 426.
And see Everyman-Elckerlijc Priority below.
Sources and Literary Relations. Goedeke, edn, p 33 (testing of friends parable).
Herford C H, Studies in the Literary Relations of England and Germany in the Sixteenth Century, Cambridge 1886, pp 120n, 381.
Bolte J, De düdesche Schlömer, ein niederdeutsches Drama, von Johannes Stricker (1584), Norden und Leipzig 1889, p *45 (table of relationships of Everyman theme);

Drei Schauspiele vom sterbenden Menschen, Bibliothek des Literarischen Vereins 269–70, Leipzig 1927, pp viii, x, xviii.

Logeman, edn, p xxv.

De Raaf K H, Den Spyeghel der Salicheyt van Elckerlijc, Critisch uitgegeven en van een inleidung en aanteekeningen voorzien, Groningen 1897.

Roersch A, Chr Ischyrius Homulus, Ghent 1903 (Latin text with introd and notes); Elckerlijc-Everyman-Homulus-Hekastus, Arch 113.13 (relation to Sunamitis Querimonia).

van Bart J W, Een Comedia ofte Spel van Homulus, herdrukt naar de uitgave van Harmen van Borculo, met inleiding, Utrecht 1904, pp xi (sources of Everyman), xiii (common source of Everyman-Elckerlijc in Latin original Quilibet).

Bang W, Zu Everyman, EStn 35.444 (relation to third of The Thrie Tailis of the Thrie Priests of Peblis).

Creizenach, 2.137.

Bates E P, Everyman and the Talmud, Athen Nov 29 1913, p 624.

Landa M J, Everyman in the Midrash, Athen Dec 6 1913, p 660 (reply to Bates).

Vos R, De Elckerlijc en een Joodse parabel, Nieuwe Taalgids 59(1966).363 (qualifies Landa's argument).

Brecht W, Die Vorläufer von Hofmannsthals Jedermann, Osterreichische Rundschau 20 (1924).281.

Lindner H, Hugo von Hofmannsthals Jedermann und seine Vorgänger, Leipzig 1928, p 9.

Scholte J H, Duitsche moraliteiten uit de zestiende eeuw, Neophil 13.196.

Eckhardt E, Deutsche Bearbeitungen älterer englischer Dramen, EStn 68.195.

Owst G R, Literature and Pulpit in Medieval England, Cambridge 1933; 2nd edn N Y 1961, pp 527, 531.

Whiting B J, Proverbs in the Earlier English Drama, HSCL 14.92.

Taylor A, Problems in German Literary History of the Fifteenth and Sixteenth Centuries, N Y and London 1939, p 105.

Ross W O, Middle English Sermons, EETS 209, London 1940, p 345 (ME versions of testing of friends tale).

O'Connor Sister M C, The Art of Dying Well, N Y 1942.

De Vocht, Materials for the Study of the Old Eng Drama 20.97, 164.

Feldman A B, Dutch Humanism and the Tudor Dramatic Tradition, N&Q 197.357.

Takahashi G, A Study of Everyman with Special Reference to the Source of Its Plot, [Tokyo 1953] (Buddhist parables; crit A Williams, Spec 28.616; R Vos, Nieuwe Taalgids 56[1963].165).

Adolf H, From Everyman and Elckerlijc to Hofmannsthal and Kafka, CL 9.204.

Van Stockum T C, Das Jedermann-motiv und das Motiv des verlorenen Sohnes im niederländischen und im niederdeutschen Drama, MKAW ns 21.199.

Kornbluth M L, A Twentieth-Century Everyman, CE 21.26 (Murder in the Cathedral).

Kaula D, Time and the Timeless in Everyman and Dr Faustus, CE 22.9.

Cawley, edn, p xiii.

Thomas H S, Some Analogues of Everyman, Mississippi Quart 16(1962–63).97 (relation to the ars moriendi tradition).

Anderson M D, Drama and Imagery in English Medieval Churches, Cambridge 1963, p 72.

Potter R A, The Form and Concept of the English Morality Play, diss Claremont 1965 microfilm, p 61 (Poel's revival; relation of Everyman to modern morality plays).

Wiemken H, Vom Sterben des reichen Mannes: Die Dramen von Everyman, Homulus Hecastus und dem Kauffmann Nach Drucken des 16 Jahrhunderts übersetzt, herausgegeben und eingeleitet, Bremen [1965], p ix.

Vos, TNTL 82.129.

Knust H, Moderne Variationen des Jedermann-Spiels, in Helen Adolf Festschrift, ed S Z Buehne et al, N Y 1968, p 309.

Hertel G, Die Allegorie von Reichtum und Armut, Erlanger Beiträge zur Sprach- und Kunstwissenschaft 33, Nürnberg 1969, p 143.

Kolve V A, Everyman and the Parable of the Talents, in The Medieval Drama, ed S Sticca, Albany 1972, p 69; rptd in Medieval English Drama, J Taylor and A H Nelson, edd, Chicago and London 1972, p 316.

The Dance of Death. Seelmann W, Die Totentänze des Mittelalters, Jahrbuch des Vereins für niederdeutsche Sprachforschung 17 (1891).1.

Thompson E N S, The English Moral Plays, Trans Connecticut Acad of Arts and Sciences 14.352.

Butterworth W, The Dance of Death, Manchester Quart 165.33.

Kurtz L P, The Dance of Death and the Macabre Spirit in European Literature,

N Y 1934.

Stammler W, Der Totentanz, Entstehung und Deutung, München 1948.

Clark J M, The Dance of Death in the Middle Ages and the Renaissance, Glasgow Univ Publ 86.92 (bibl p 121 and in ftnts).

Craig ERD, pp 345, 348.

Cosacchi S, Makabertanz: Der Totentanz in Kunst, Poesie und Brauchtum des Mittelalters, Meisenheim am Glan 1965.

Rosenfeld H, Der mittelalterliche Totentanz, Köln 1968 (revision of Münster 1954 edn; comprehensive survey with bibl, p 337).

Recent Editions of Elckerlijc. Van Mierlo, Kon Vlaamse Acad voor Taal- en Letterk 3s 29.

Endepols H J E, Den Spyeghel der Salicheyt van Elckerlijc, 6th edn Groningen 1955 (comprehensive introd).

Vos R, Den Spieghel der Salicheit van Elckerlijc, Groningen 1967 (with introd and appendices incorporating earlier articles, bibl).

Van Elslander A, Den Spyeghel der Salicheyt van Elckerlijc, 4th edn Antwerpen 1968 (comprehensive introd and full bibl).

Everyman-Elckerlijc Priority. Kalff G, Elckerlijc, Homulus, Hekastus, Everyman, TNTL 9.12.

Logeman, edn, p xxv; Elckerlyc-Everyman: De vraag naar de prioriteit (see above, under *Textual Matters*).

De Raaf, Den Spyeghel der Salicheyt van Elckerlijc, p 1; Nogmaals een en ander over de verhouding van Den Spyeghel der Salicheyt van Elckerlijc tot The Somonyng of Everyman, TNTL 22.241.

Brandl A, QF 80.xiv.

CHEL, 5.59n; Creizenach, 1.473n.

Manly, MP 8.269; Wood, MP 8.279.

Maximilianus, TTL 14.1; reply by Wijnpersse, Nieuwe Taalgids 20.258.

Michels L C, Elckerlijc, Handelingen van het veertiende Nederlandsche Philologen-Congres, Groningen 1931, p 47; rptd Filologische Opstellen 1, Zwolse Reeks van Taal- en Letterkundige Studies 2, Zwolle 1957, p 119 (catholic doctrine in relation to priority).

Willems L, Elckerlye-Studiën, VMKVA 1933, p 1010; rptd The Hague 1934, p 159 (1934 vol contains edn of 16 cent MS of Elckerlijc, p 120).

Muller J W, Over Elckerlijc: Tekstcritische en exegetische aanteekeningen, VMKVA 1935, p 289n.

Tigg E R, Is Elckerlijc Prior to Everyman?, JEGP 38.568 (rime evidence for priority of Elckerlijc); Neophil 26.121 (previous item with minor variations).

Kazemier G, Elckerlijc, het Dal sonder Wederkeeren en de mystiek, Nieuwe Taalgids 34.87, 116 (affinity with other Dutch works argues priority of Elckerlijc).

Zandvoort, ESts 23.1; RES 25.66; Everyman-Elckerlijc, EA 6.8 (rptd Collected Papers, Groningen 1954, p 41).

De Vocht, Materials for the Study of the Old Eng Drama 20 (detailed argument for priority of Everyman); 25.116.

Van Mierlo, Kon Vlaamse Acad voor Taal-en Letterk 3s 27.5 and 29.7 (challenge to De Vocht).

Mak J J, Elckerlyc en Everyman, TNTL 67.24 (review of controversy).

Cawley, edn, p x.

Vos, TNTL 82.129.

And see *Textual Matters* above.

Themes. Mackenzie W R, The English Moralities from the Point of View of Allegory, Harvard Stud Eng 2.206 (Summons of Death).

Vanderheijden J, Het thema en de uitbeelding van den dood in de poëzie der late middeleeuwen en der vroege renaissance in de Nederlanden, Koninklijke Vlaamse Academie voor Taal- en Letterkunde 6s Bekroonde Werken 47.191.

Farnham W, The Medieval Heritage of Elizabethan Tragedy, Berkeley 1936, p 201 (death as retribution).

Koldewey E, Über die Willensfreiheit im älteren englischen Drama, Würzburg 1937, p 47.

De Vocht, Materials for the Study of the Old Eng Drama 20.168 (repentance and pilgrimage).

Ryan L V, Doctrine and Dramatic Structure in Everyman, Spec 32.722; rptd in Middle English Survey, ed E Vasta, Notre Dame and London 1965, p 283.

Van Stockum, MKAW ns 21.199.

Thomas H S, The Meaning of the Character Knowledge in Everyman, Mississippi Quart 14(1960–61).3 (includes review of scholarship on the meaning of Knowledge).

Cawley, edn, p xix (doctrine of Holy Dying).

Bevington D, Tudor Drama and Politics, Cambridge Mass 1968, p 35 (doctrines in Everyman compared with those of Thomas à Kempis).

Conley J, The Doctrine of Friendship in Everyman, Spec 44.374.

Hertel, Erlanger Beiträge zur Sprach- und Kunstwissenschaft 33.143.

Kolve, The Medieval Drama, p 69; Medieval English Drama, p 316 (summons to an accounting as the play's central concern; includes discussion of Knowledge).

Literary Criticism. Percy T, Reliques of Ancient English Poetry, London 1765, 1.120.

Crowley T J, Character-Treatment in the Mediaeval Drama, Notre Dame Ind 1907, p 138.

Wood, MP 8.302 (artistic inferiority of Everyman to Elckerlijc).

Haller J, Die Technik des Dialogs im mittelalterlichen Drama Englands, Worms a Rh 1916, p 112.

Zandvoort, ESts 23.2; EA 6.1 (rptd Collected Papers, p 33).

Brooks and Heilman, Understanding Drama, p 100.

De Vocht, Materials for the Study of the Old Eng Drama 20.64, 99.

Van Mierlo, Kon Vlaamse Acad voor Taal- en Letterk 3s 29.95.

Rossiter A P, English Drama from Early Times to the Elizabethans, London 1950, p 98.

Lombardo A, Morality Play: The Castle of Perseverance, Everyman, Rivista di letterature moderne 4[14](1953).273; Il dramma pre-shakespeariano, Venezia 1957, p 91.

Cormican L A, Morality Tradition and the Interludes, The Age of Chaucer, ed B Ford, London 1954, p 189.

Ryan, Spec 32.722; Middle English Survey, p 283.

Cawley, edn, pp xiii, xix, xxiv.

Corder J, Everyman: The Way to Life, Drama Critique 6(1963).136; reply C J Stratman, Everyman: The Way to Death, Drama Critique 7(1964).61.

Van Laan T F, Everyman: A Structural Analysis, PMLA 78.465.

Johnson W H, The Double Desertion of Everyman, AN&Q(New Haven) 6(1967–68).85 (playwright combined two versions of his source).

Kolve, The Medieval Drama, p 69; Medieval English Drama, p 316.

Moran D V, The Life of Everyman, Neophil 56.324.

Staging. Speaight R, William Poel and the Elizabethan Revival, London 1954, p 161 (Poel's productions in and after 1901).

Williams R, Drama in Performance, London

1954; new edn N Y 1969, p 43.

Craik T W, The Tudor Interlude, Leicester 1958, pp 31, 50, 55, 78.

Cawley, edn, p xxix.

Fifield M, The Castle in the Circle, Ball State Monograph 6.37.

Wasson, Theatre Notebook 27.16 (casting pattern).

General References. Collier J P, The History of English Dramatic Poetry, London 1831, 2.310.

Klein, 2.36; Ten Brink, 2.302; Brandl, § 121; Ward Hist, 1.119; Chambers, 2.155, 217, 439; Chambers OHEL, pp 62, 218; Gayley, p 296; CHEL, 5.59, 436; Creizenach, 1.472.

Brooke C F Tucker, The Tudor Drama, Boston 1911, p 66.

Baugh LHE, p 286; Craig ERD, pp 344, 346, 378.

Williams A, The Drama of Medieval England, East Lansing Mich 1961, p 161; slightly rvsd in The English Moral Play before 1500, Annuale Mediaevale 4(1963).18.

Bibliography. CBEL, 1.515; 5.247; Henshaw, PMRS 21.22.

Stratman, p 241; 2nd edn N Y 1972, 1.554.

Vos, Den Spieghel der Salicheit van Elckerlijc, p 29 (bibl of Elckerlijc studies).

Van Elslander, Den Spyeghel der Salicheyt van Elckerlijc, p xvii (Elckerlijc studies).

[31] NATURE.

MSS. No MS extant. PRINTS: 1, Camb Univ Syn 4.53.11, 36 leaves a-i[4], ?W Rastell 1530–34; 2, BM (C34.e31; formerly C34.e54), with duplicate sheet c.1.4 at end; 3, Bodl (Rawlinson 4° 598.12), a[4] only; 4, State Libr of Victoria, Melbourne (Sticht Collection no 38; formerly Fenn Collection), g[4] only, def; 5, Huntington 131401, h[1-3] only (STC, no 17779).

Robbins-Cutler, no 3302.3.

Brandl, edn, p xxxiii (PRINT 2 only).

[Sayle C E], Early English Printed Books in the University Library Cambridge, vol 1, Cambridge 1900, no 351 (corr= no 535) (PRINT 1 only).

Farmer, edn, p v (PRINTS 2, 3, 4 only); A Hand List to the Tudor Facsimile Texts, [London] 1914, p 31 (PRINTS 2, 3, 4 only).

de Ricci S, Fulgens and Lucres, N Y 1920, p 11 (Henry E Huntington Facsimile Reprints 1; PRINTS 1, 2, 3, 4 only).

Reed, Early Tudor Drama (see below, under *Author*), p 77 (William Rastell as printer).

Foxcroft A B, A Catalogue of English Books and Fragments from 1477 to 1535 in the Public Library of Victoria, Melbourne 1933, p 45 (PRINT 4 only).

Greg W W, A Bibliography of the English Printed Drama to the Restoration, Bibliographical Soc Illust Monographs 24, London 1939, 1.93, nos 17–18.

Moeslein, edn, p 164 (includes discussion of Joseph Ritson MS copy of PRINT 1, ca 1783).

Editions. Brandl A, Nature, A goodly interlude of Nature compylyd by mayster Henry Medwall chapleyn to the ryght reuerent father in god Johan Morton somtyme Cardynall and arche byshop of Canterbury, Quellen des weltlichen Dramas in England vor Shakespeare, QF 80, Strassburg 1898, p 73 (based on transcript of PRINT 2).

Bang W and R B McKerrow, The Enterlude of Youth, nebst Fragmenten des Playe of Lucres und von Nature, Materialien zur Kunde des älteren englischen Dramas 12, Louvain 1905, p 105 (from PRINT 4; supplies facsimiles of lines from clipped f xxviii of PRINT 2).

Farmer J S, Nature, by Henry Medwall, London and Edinburgh 1908 (Tudor Facsimile Texts; Students' Facsimile Edn, Amersham 1914).

Moeslein M E, A Critical Edition of the Plays of Henry Medwall, diss Univ of North Carolina, Chapel Hill 1968; DA 29.2270A; microfilm, p 193 (based on PRINT 1; collated with earlier printed edns).

Modernization. Farmer J S, Recently Recovered Lost Tudor Plays, London 1907, p 41.

Textual Matters and Notes. Brandl, edn, p 654.

Manly J M, JEGP 2.391, 410 (emendations to Brandl edn).

Carpenter F I, MLN 14.138(275) (emendations to Brandl edn).

Farmer, Lost Tudor Plays, pp 371, 442 (notebook and word-list).

Zandvoort R W, Privy Council in Brandl's Edition of the Interlude of Nature, Collected Papers, Groningen 1954, p 30.

Moeslein, edn, pp 171 (discussion), 331 (notes), 363 (press-variants).

Southern R, The Staging of Plays before Shakespeare, London 1973, p 70.

Language. Brandl, edn, p xxxiii.

Versification. Brandl, edn, p xxxvii.

Ramsay R L, Magnyfycence, EETSES 98, London 1906, p cxl.

Eckhardt E, Die metrische Unterscheidung von Ernst und Komik in den englischen Moralitäten, EStn 62.156 and passim.

Bernard J E, The Prosody of the Tudor Interlude, YSE 90, New Haven and London 1939, p 18.

Date. Farmer, edn, p vi.

Author. Bale J, Scriptorum illustrium maioris Bryttanie . . . catalogus, Basel 1557–59, 2.71.

Pitseus J, Relationum historicarum de rebus anglicis, tomus primus, Paris 1619, p 678.

DNB, 37.207.

Brandl, edn, p xliv.

Reed A W, The Beginnings of the English Secular and Romantic Drama, Shakespeare Assoc Papers 7, London 1922, p 11; Early Tudor Drama: Medwall, the Rastells, Heywood and the More Circle, London 1926, p 101 (crit J M Manly, RES 3.350); Fulgens and Lucres, Oxford 1926, p xv (with F S Boas).

Sterry W, London Times Apr 15 1936, p 11; The Eton College Register 1441–1698, Eton 1943, p 229.

Hogrefe P, The Sir Thomas More Circle, Urbana 1959, pp 65, 253, 257 (crit below, under *Rôles and Themes*).

Emden A B, A Biographical Register of the University of Cambridge to 1500, Cambridge 1963, p 399.

Bevington D, Tudor Drama and Politics, Cambridge Mass 1968, pp 42, 51 (Medwall's career and political milieu).

Sources and Literary Relations. Brandl, edn, p xl (relation to Castle of Perseverance, Interlude of the Four Elements, etc).

Manly J M, JEGP 2.425 (relation to Interlude of the Four Elements).

Carpenter F I, MLN 14.136(271) (relation to Interlude of the Four Elements).

Fischer J, MSEP 5.5 (relation to Interlude of the Four Elements).

Thompson E N S, The English Moral Plays, Trans Connecticut Acad of Arts and Sciences 14.332 (relation to the Psychomachia); 378 (Interlude of the Four Elements).

Mackenzie W R, A Source for Medwall's Nature, PMLA 29.189 (Lydgate's Reson and Sensuallyte).

Macauley E R, Notes on the Sources for Medwall's Nature, MLN 32.184.

Wharey J B, Bunyan's Holy War and the Conflict-Type of Morality Play, MLN 34.72.

Whiting B J, Proverbs in the Earlier English Drama, HSCL 14.77.

De Vocht H, Everyman: A Comparative Study of Texts and Sources, Materials for the Study of the Old English Drama 20.185 (relation of Nature to Castle of Perseverance).

McCutchan J W, Similarities between Falstaff and Gluttony in Medwall's Nature, Shakespeare Assoc Bull 24(1949).214.

Spivack B, Falstaff and the Psychomachia, Shakespeare Quart 8(1957).454; slightly rvsd in Shakespeare and the Allegory of Evil, N Y 1958, p 86 (Falstaff and the vices in Nature).

Hogrefe, The Sir Thomas More Circle, pp 259, 264, 318, 326.

Rôles and Themes. Cushman L W, The Devil and the Vice in the English Dramatic Literature before Shakespeare, SEP 6.55 and passim.

Knowlton E C, Nature in Middle English, JEGP 20.186 (diagram of rôle of Nature in ME), 194.

Russell H K, Tudor and Stuart Dramatizations of the Doctrines of Natural and Moral Philosophy, SP 31.4.

Farnham W, The Medieval Heritage of Elizabethan Tragedy, Berkeley 1936, p 199 (law of retribution).

Koldewey E, Über die Willensfreiheit im älteren englischen Drama, Würzburg 1937, p 35.

Boughner D C, Vice, Braggart, and Falstaff, Angl 72.40; The Braggart in Renaissance Comedy, Minneapolis 1954, p 153.

Hogrefe, The Sir Thomas More Circle, p 257 (crit L Bradner, MLN 75.707; R J Schoeck, RN 13.175; E Surtz, JEGP 59.732; J L Barroll, MLR 56.99).

Bevington, Tudor Drama and Politics, p 51.

Literary Criticism. Gayley C M, Representative English Comedies, N Y 1903, 1.lix.

Mackenzie W R, The English Moralities from the Point of View of Allegory, Harvard Stud Eng 2.70.

Haller J, Die Technik des Dialogs im mittelalterlichen Drama Englands, Worms a Rh 1916, p 105.

Reed, Shakespeare Assoc Papers 7.10; Early Tudor Drama, p 100.

Hecht H, Henry Medwalls Fulgens and Lucres, Palaes 148.83.

Rossiter A P, English Drama from Early Times to the Elizabethans, London 1950, p 103.

Greenfield T N, The Clothing Motif in King Lear, Shakespeare Quart 5(1954).281 (treats symbolic use of clothing in Nature).

Wierum A, Actors and Play Acting in the Morality Tradition, Renaissance Drama ns 3(1970).195.

Bawcutt N W, Policy, Machiavellianism, and the Earlier Tudor Drama, Eng Literary Renaissance 1(1971).197.

Staging. Brandl, edn, p xlv.

Nicoll A, The Development of the Theatre, 3rd edn N Y 1946, London 1948, p 72.

Craik T W, The Tudor Interlude, Leicester 1958, pp 22, 31, 56, 58, 83 96.

Southern, The Staging of Plays before Shakespeare, pp 45, 55, 330.

General References. Collier J P, The History of English Dramatic Poetry, London 1831, 2.298.

Klein, 2.22; Brandl, § 121; Ten Brink, 3.124; Ward Hist, 1.117; Chambers, 2.200, 443; Creizenach, 1.472.

Brooke C F Tucker, The Tudor Drama, Boston 1911, pp 71, 98.

Baugh LHE, p 359; Craig ERD, pp 344, 378, 382.

Wilson F P, The English Drama 1485–1585, ed G K Hunter, N Y and Oxford 1969, pp 1, 2, 6, 10, 24, 222.

Bibliography. CBEL, 1.514; Stratman, p 215; 2nd edn N Y 1972, 1.612.

[32] A SPEECH OF DELIGHT (REYNES EXTRACT).

MS. Bodl 10234 (Tanner 407), ff 43ᵇ–44ᵃ (late 15 cent).

Brown-Robbins, Robbins-Cutler, no 1927.

Hackman A, Catalogi Codicum Manuscriptorum Bibliothecae Bodleianae, Pt 4, Oxford 1860; rptd 1966, no 407.21 (included within partial list of items in Reynes's commonplace book).

Calderhead, edn, p 1.

Davis N-CP, p cxx.

Editions. Calderhead I G, Morality Fragments from Norfolk, MP 14.6.

Davis N-CP, p 121.

Language. Calderhead, edn, p 8.

Davis N-CP, pp cxxii, cxxiv.

Versification. Davis N-CP, p cxxi.

Date. Davis N-CP, p cxx.

For EPILOGUE (Brown-Robbins, no 2380), see [21] above.

[33] PROCESSUS SATANAE.

MS. Welbeck Abbey fragment, strips 1ᵃ, 2ᵃ,

3[a,b] (ca 1570–80).

British Museum, MS Facs *305 (photograph of MS).

Greg, edn, p 239.

Edition. Greg W W, Processus Satanae, Malone Soc Collections 2³(1931).243 (actor's part for God).

Date. Greg, edn, p 240.

Sources and Literary Relations. Heinzel R, Excurs über den Mythus von den vier Töchtern Gottes, ZfDA 17.45 (der Process Belial).

Traver H, The Four Daughters of God, Bryn-MawrMon 6.49; The Four Daughters of God: A Mirror of Changing Doctrine, PMLA 40.44.

Chew S C, The Virtues Reconciled: An Iconographic Study, Toronto 1947, pp 41, 67 (the Processus Belial).

Wilson F P, The English Drama 1485–1585, ed G K Hunter, N Y and Oxford 1969, p 5.

Bawcutt N W, Policy, Machiavellianism, and the Earlier Tudor Drama, Eng Literary Renaissance 1(1971).203.

General References. Chambers OHEL, p 64.

Wilson R M, The Lost Literature of Medieval England, 2nd edn London 1970, p 215.

Bibliography. Stratman, p 154; 2nd edn N Y 1972, 1.452.

3. THE FOLK DRAMA

by

Francis Lee Utley and Barry Ward

(Note: This is a selected bibliography, with stress only on the medieval pieces and on a number of basic books and articles which may encourage comparison of the medieval and modern English and Continental phases. Because of their importance in the new views of the folk play and medieval drama, a few unpublished dissertations are included.)

I. The Medieval Texts

[34] ROBIN HOOD AND THE SHERIFF OF NOTTINGHAM.

MSS. 1, Trinity Camb (formerly W Aldis Wright; formerly La Neve, Norroy King-at-Arms), separate half leaf (ca 1475); la, transcript by Stukeley; lb, transcript by Bradshaw.
Robbins-Cutler, no 3118.4 (21 short couplets).
Editions. J M G, Dr Stukeley's Manuscripts Drawings and Books, N&Q 12(1853).131 (MS la).
Child F J, English and Scottish Ballads, Boston 1857–58, 5.429 (MS lb); The English and Scottish Ballads, Boston 1882–98, 3.90 (MS lb).
Manly Spec, p 279 (also contains [37] below, Robin Hood and the Potter, The Oxford and Lutterworth St George Plays, and the Revesby Sword Play); Specimens of Early English Drama, Boston 1897–1904, 1.297 (MS lb).
Greg W, Malone Soc Collections, Oxford 1908, 2.117 (MS 1 with facsimile; an insert on p 123 attempts to complete Manly's reconstruction).
Adams CPSD, p 345 (MS 1).
Early References. Gairdner J, ed, The Paston Letters 1422–1509 A D, 4 vols, Edinburgh 1910 (the classic reference to St George and Robin Hood plays is on p 89 of vol 3).
Davis N, Paston Letters and Papers of the Fifteenth Century, pt 1, Oxford 1971 (ar-

ranged by writers; lacks Sir John Paston on the plays—he will appear in pt 2).

[35] ST. GEORGE CAROL.

MS. Egerton 3307 (formerly Windsor Chapel Royal?), f 63[b] (post-Agincourt, temp Henry VI?).
Robbins-Cutler, no 4229.5.
Editions. Schofield B, A Newly Discovered 15th-Century Manuscript of the English Chapel Royal—Pt I, Musical Quart 32 (1946).13 (dates MS after Agincourt and assumes allusions to Henry V).
Stevens J [E], Medieval Carols, Musica Britannica IV, London 1958 (modernization with 2-pt musical arrangement).
Copley J, A Second Carol of Agincourt, N&Q 203(1958).23.
Davies R R T, Medieval English Lyrics, Evanston 1964 (London 1963), p 185.
Greene R L, A Selection of English Carols, Oxford 1967, p 124.
Discussions. Schofield, p 509 (MS from Chapel Royal, Windsor).
Bukofzer M F, A Newly Discovered 15th-Century Manuscript of the English Chapel Royal—Pt II, Musical Quarterly 33(1947).38 (adds to Schofield); Holy-Week Music and Carols at Meaux Abbey, in Studies in Medieval and Renaissance Music, N Y 1950, p 113.
McPeek G S, Dating the Windsor MS, Journ

of the American Musicological Soc 3(1950)
.156 (MS to be dated nearer 1435 than
1415, possibly between 1425 and 1435 or
1440).
Greene R L, Two Medieval Musical Manuscripts: Egerton 3307 and Some Univ of
Chicago Fragments, Journ of the American
Musicological Soc 7(1954).1 (other Agincourt and St George Carols always with
"our Lady's Knight" formula; St George's
Day honored after 1416 and not after 1552;
folk plays; skeptical about either St George
Chapel or Chapel Royal Windsor connec-
tions or relationship to Henry V or VI;
possibly monastic in origin; dialect would
fit Meaux Abbey and Beverley as suggested
by Bukofzer).

[36] ST. GEORGE CHARM.

MSS. 1, Bodl 15353 (Rawlinson C.506), f 297[a]
(early 15 cent; prose, 1 triplet, 3 couplets).
PRINTS: 2, Blundeville T, The fower
chiefest offices belonging to Horsemanship,
London 1565–66, Pt 4, chap 23, f 17[b] (in
4 pts: Breeding, Riding, Dieting, and Dis-
eases; STC, no 3152); 3, Scot R, The dis-
couerie of witchecraft, London: William
Brome, 1584, bk 4, chap 11, pp 86–88 (from
copy in Univ of Virginia Libr; STC, no
21864).
Brown-Robbins, Robbins-Cutler, no 2903 (erroneously gives chap 12 in PRINT 2).
Note: PRINT 2 several times rptd: STC, no
3153 (1570?), f xiiij[b]; STC, no 3154 (1580),
f 11[b]; STC, no 3155 (1593), f 11[b]; STC, no
3156 (1597), f 11[b]; see Univ Microfilms STC
project reels, nos 523, 283, 175. PRINT 3
often rptd in modern edns: Univ Microfilms 1116; London 1651; London 1665;
London 1886 (ed B Nicholson); London
1930 (ed M Summers), p 49; Amsterdam
and N Y: Da Capo Press (The English Experience, facsimile) 1971; N Y 1972 (Dover).
Editions. E B, An Old Charm, N&Q 61(1880)
.54 (from PRINT 2).
Kittredge G L, Witchcraft in Old and New
England, Cambridge Mass 1929, p 220
(from E B).
Robbins SL (1952 edn), no 66, pp 61, 246
(from MS 1).
Greene R L, A Selection of English Carols,
Oxford 1967, p 228.

[37] ROBIN HOOD AND THE FRIAR:
ROBIN HOOD AND THE POTTER.

MSS. No MS extant. PRINT: A Merye Geste
of Robyn Hood and of hys lyfe, wyth a
newe pleye for to be pleyed in Maye games
very pleasante and full of pastyme, London: W Copland at the Crane Wharf, n d
(1560?), f J 1[a] (101 lines; the play follows
the ballad Geste; STC, no 13691).
Editions. Manly Spec, p 281.
Greg W, Malone Soc Collections, Oxford
1911, 2.125.
Discussions. Greg W, A Bibl of the English
Printed Drama to the Restoration, Bibliographical Soc 1939–59, 1.108 (no 32, identifies with the Stationers' Register entry
of ?1560 Nov 30—the address of Copland
limits to 1559–62).
For other 16 and 17 cent Robin Hood plays
see Greg, 1.288 (no 179, The Downfall of
Robert Earl of Huntington [1601]); Greg,
1.289 (no 180, The Death of Robert Earl
of Huntington [1601]); Greg, 2.746 (no 618,
The Sad Shepherd [1641]); Greg, Lost
Plays, p 986 (no [-]13, Robin Hood and
Little John [14 May 1594], perhaps related
to the present item); Greg, Lost Plays, p
999 (nos [-]147, [-]148, Robin Hood, may
be either nos 179–80 or no 32 ["the may-
games"]).

II. Bibliographies: General

Frazer J G, The Golden Bough a Study in
Magic and Religion, 12 vols, London 1911–
15; rvsd The New Golden Bough, ed T H
Gaster, N Y 1959.
PMLA, Annual Bibliography 1922—. See
separate Folklore section, vol 44(1929) for
previous year 1928; separate section on
Folkdrama under Folklore, vol 72(1957) for
1956; sections on Dramatic Folklore and
Folk Drama in the separate fascicules of
PMLA beginning in 1970 (vol 1, English
etc).
James E O, Christian Myth and Ritual a
Historical Study, London 1933.

Southern Folklore Quart 2(1938—) (selective bibl begins in this vol and covers 1937 and some items from previous years; annual in first no of each year; special section on Folk Drama beginning in vol 4[1940] for the year 1939).

Haywood C, A Bibliography of North American Folklore and Folksong, N Y 1951 (see index under Drama).

Geiger P and R Wildhaber, Bibliographie internationale des arts et traditions populaires; International Folklore Bibliography; Volkskundliche Bibliographie (founded in 1917 by J Meier and E Hoffmann-Krayer; recently under subsidy of UNESCO). On drama see, for instance, XIX, Volkschaus-

piel, in the 1957–58 vol (Bonn: Rudolf Habelt Verlag, 1963), pp 479–86.

James E O, Seasonal Feasts and Festivals, London 1961.

Evans-Pritchard E E, Essays in Social Anthropology, N Y 1963.

Lessa W A and E Z Vogt, Reader in Comparative Religion an Anthropological Approach, 2nd edn, N Y 1965.

Cawte E C, A Helm and N Peacock, English Ritual Drama a Geographical Index, London 1967 (basic bibl of obscure references to plays).

Stratmann C J, Bibliography of Medieval Drama, 2nd edn, 2 vols, N Y 1972, pp 660–70 (much expanded bibl of folk drama).

III. Modern References, Medieval to Modern Folk Drama

1. British and American

Jackson J, The History of the Scottish Stage, Edinburgh 1793.

Johnson R, The Renowned History of the Seven Champions of Christendom, London 1824.

Hone W, The Every-Day Book, 2 vols, London 1826–27.

Brand J, Observations on Popular Antiquities, rvsd and ed H Ellis, 2 vols, London 1841.

Ashton J, A Righte Merrie Christmasse, London and N Y n d (a 19th cent account).

Bede C, Modern Mumming, N&Q 2s 11(1861).271.

Burne S, Guizer's Play Songs and Rhymes from Staffordshire, Folklore Journ 4(1866).350.

Addis J, St George and the Dragon, N&Q 5s 1(1874).227.

Lee F G, Oxfordshire Christmas Miracle Play, N&Q 5s 2(1874).503.

Arnott S, The Christmas Play of the Seven Champions, N&Q 5s 10(1878).489.

Child F J, ed, The English and Scottish Popular Ballads, 5 vols in 10, Boston 1882–96. See the convenient reprints, 5 vols in 3, N Y 1956 and 5 vols in 5, N Y 1965. (For the general treatment of Robin Hood, which refers again and again to the folk drama, and its continuity, see vol 3, pp 39–

233 and the chapter on the Ballad yet to be published in the present series. The play is most closely related to Child ballad 118, Robin Hood and Guy of Gisbourne, from the Percy Folio MS of the 17th cent; valuable bibl in vol 5).

A[mery] P S F, The Christmas Play of St George, Western Antiquary 3(1883).168.

Lack-Szyrma W S, Christmas Play of St George, Western Antiquary 3(1884).198.

Chambers R, The Book of Days, 2 vols, London and Edinburgh 1886.

Ordish T F, Collection, Univ of London, Folklore Soc Libr; Folk Drama, Folklore 2(1891).314; English Folk-Drama, Folklore 4(1893).149.

Christmas Customs in Newfoundland, Journ of American Folklore 6(1893).63.

Buchanan W, The Christmas Boys or Mummers, Wiltshire Archaeological and Natural History Magazine 27(1894).311.

Manly Spec.

Andre J L, St George the Martyr in Legend, Ceremonial, Art, The Archaeological Journ 57(1900).204.

Cushman L W, The Devil and the Vice in the English Dramatic Literature before Shakespeare, Halle a S 1900.

Boger J T C, The Play Acted by the Tipteers at West Wittering Chichester, Sussex Archaeological Collection 44(1901).14.

Ditchfield P H, Old English Customs, London 1901 (contains some texts; not trustworthy; mostly secondhand information).

Matzke J E, Contributions to the History of the Legend of St George, PMLA 17.464; 18.99.

Chambers.

Cherry M G, The Plough Monday Play in Rutland, Rutland Magazine and County Historical Record 1(1903–04).195.

Beatty A, The St George or Mummers' Play: a Study in the Protology of the Drama, Trans Wisconsin Acad of Science 15²(1907). 273 (important early article).

Crowther-Beynon V B, Morris Dancers Play —Edith Weston, Rutland, Rutland Magazine and County Historical Record 2(1905–06).177.

Dawkins R M, The Modern Carnival in Thrace and the Cult of Dionysus, Journ of the Hellenic Soc 26(1906).191 (important for Life-Cycle theory; Dawkins' findings have been used to fill in for "missing" elements in English plays).

Addy S O, Guising and Mumming in Derbyshire, Journ of the Derbyshire Archaeological and Natural History Soc 29(1907).31.

Balch E E, In a Wiltshire Village: Some Old Songs and Customs, The Antiquary 45 (1908).379.

Kille C, The Old Minehead Christmas Mummers Play, Minehead 1908.

Cocks A H, The Wooburn Version of the Mummers' Play, in Records of Buckinghamshire, The Architectural and Archaeological Soc for the County of Buckingham, Aylesbury 1909, p 222.

Burne S, Reminiscences of Lancashire and Cheshire When George IV Was King, Folklore 20(1909).207.

Sharp C, The Sword Dance of Northern England, 3 vols, London 1912; Field Notebooks, Clare College Cambridge (microfilm copies in the Vaughan Williams Libr, Cecil Sharp House, London).

Jones B, Christmas Mumming in Ireland, Folklore 27(1916).301.

Chalk S, The Silverton Mummers' Play, Devon and Cornwall Notes and Queries 9(1916–17).228.

Baskerville C R, Dramatic Aspects of Medieval Folk Festivals in England, SP 17.19.

Weston J, From Ritual to Romance, Cambridge 1920 (connects ancient ritual plays with Arthurian Grail story; highly controversial).

John G, The Derbyshire Mumming Play of St George and the Dragon or as it is sometimes called The Pace Egg, Folklore 32 (1921).181.

Withington R, Additional Notes on Modern Folk-Pageantry, PMLA 37.347.

Baskerville C R, Mummers' Wooing Plays in England, MP 21.225.

Adams CPSD (earliest texts).

Dowson F W, Notes on the Goathland Folk Play, Trans of the Yorkshire Dialect Soc 28(1926).36.

Boyd A W, The Comberback (Cheshire) Version of the Soul-Caking Play, Trans of the Lancashire and Cheshire Antiquarian Soc 44(1927).50.

Mill A J, Mediaeval Plays in Scotland, Edinburgh 1927 (St Andrews Univ Publ no 24).

Pollard EMP.

Hannam-Clark T, Drama in Gloucestershire (the Cotswold Country), London 1928.

Karpeles M, Some Fragments of Sword Dance Plays, Journ of the English Folk Dance Soc 2s 2(1928).35.

Kirke J, The Seven Champions of Christendom, ed G E Dawson, Western Reserve Univ Bull ns 32, Cleveland 1929.

Baskerville C R, The Elizabethan Jig and Related Song Drama, Chicago 1929.

Kennedy D, Observations on the Sword Dance and Mummers Play, Journ of the English Folk Dance Soc 2s 3(1930).36.

Jenkinson A J, Ploughboys Play, The Cornhill Magazine ns 68(1930).96.

Boyd A W, The Tichborne Mummers' Play, Cheshire Notes & Queries (1931), p 93.

Chambers E K, The English Folk Play, Oxford 1933 (traces relationships to literary sources; texts and geographical distribution).

Cook T D, A Northumbrian Sword Dance, Journ of the English Folk Dance and Song Soc 1(1933).112.

Gallop R, The Origins of the Morris Dance, Journ of the English Folk Dance and Song Soc 1(1934).122.

Welsford E, The Fool: His Social and Literary History, London 1935.

Needham J, The Geographical Distribution of English Ceremonial Dance Traditions, Journ of the English Folk Dance and Song Soc 3(1936).1.

Campbell M, Survivals of Old Folk Drama in the Kentucky Mountains, Journ of American Folklore 51(1938).10.

Alford V, Some Hobby Horses of Great Britain, Journ of the English Folk Dance and Song Soc 3(1939).221.

Mill A J, The Hull Noah Play, MLR 35.489 (related to Plough Monday).

Honigman J J, An Interpretation of the Social-Psychological Functions of the Ritual Clown, Character and Personality 10 (1942).220.

Charles L H, The Clown's Function, Journ of American Folklore 58(1945).25.

Green E R R, Christmas Rhymers and Mummers, Ulster Journ of Archaeology 3s 9 (1946).3.

Cathcart-Smith, Two Variations of the Folk Play and a Further Account of the Old Hoss, Journ of the English Folk Dance and Song Soc 5(1947).81.

Gatty I, The Eden Collection of Mummary Plays, Folklore 59(1948).16.

Henshaw M, The Attitude of the Church Toward the Stage to the End of the Middle Ages, Medievalia et Humanistica 5–8(1948–54).3.

Kennedy D, Dramatic Elements in the Folk Dance, Journ of the English Folk Dance and Song Soc 6(1949).1.

Helm A, The Cheshire Soul Caking Play, Journ of the English Folk Dance and Song Soc 6(1950).45.

Foster J C, Ulster Folklore, Belfast 1951.

Brown A, Folklore Elements in the Medieval Drama, Folklore 63(1952).65.

Brown T, The Mummers Play in Devon and Newfoundland, Folklore 63(1952).30.

Cross T P, Motif-Index of Early Irish Literature, Indiana Univ Publ, Folklore Series, no 7, Bloomington Ind 1952.

Haworth D and W M Comber, edd, Cheshire Village Memories, Cheshire 1952.

Holmes J G, Plough Monday Plays, The Nottinghamshire Countryside 13(1952).7.

Kennedy P, The Symondsbury Mumming Play, Journ of the English Folk Dance and Song Soc 7¹(Dec 1952).1.

Barley M W, Plough Plays in the East Midlands, Journ of the English Folk Dance and Song Soc 7²(Dec 1953).68.

Hudleston N A, The Ebberston Mummers Play, Journ of the English Folk Dance and Song Soc 7²(Dec 1953).130.

Dean-Smith M, Folk Play Origins of the English Masque, Folklore 65(1954).74.

Morse J M, The Unity of the Revesby Sword Play, PQ 33.81.

Cawte E C, Rapper at Winlaton in 1955, Ibstock Leicester n d.

H[ole] C, The North Newington Mumming Play, Oxfordshire and District Folklore Soc Annual Record 8(1956).14.

Nance R M, The Cledry Plays: Drolls of Old Cornwall for Village Acting and Home Reading, Marazion and Penzance (The Federation of Old Cornwall Societies), 1956 (folk-derived, but interesting for the area illustrated).

Aram C H, Ipsey Pipsy Palsy Gout, The Nottinghamshire Countryside 17(1956–57).25.

Montgomerie W, Folk Play and Ritual in Hamlet, Folklore 67–68(1956–57).214.

Lowe B, Early Records of the Morris in England, Journ of the English Folk Dance and Song Soc 8(1957).61.

Dean-Smith M, The Life Cycle or Folk Play, Folklore 69(1958).237 (seminal work advancing life-cycle theory).

Cline H, Belsnickles and Shanghais, Journ of American Folklore 71(1958).164.

Wickham G, Early English Stages 1300 to 1660, London and N Y 1959, 1.191 (chap 6, Mummings and Disguisings).

Cawte E C, A Helm, R J Marriott and N Peacock, A Geographical Index of the Ceremonial Dance in Great Britain, Journ of the English Folk Dance and Song Soc 9(1960).1.

Utley F L, Folklore Myth and Ritual, in Critical Approaches to Medieval Literature, ed D Bethurum, N Y 1960, p 83.

MacNeill F M, The Silver Bough, vol 3 (A Calendar of Scottish National Festivals, Hallowe'en to Yule), Glasgow 1961.

Southern R, The Seven Ages of the Theatre, N Y 1961.

Alford V, Sword Dance and Drama, London 1962.

Dean-Smith M, Mummers' Plays, N&Q 207 (ns 9).428 (see also p 311); Disguise in English Folk-Drama, Folk Life 1–3(1963–65).97.

Welch C D Jr, Common Nuisances: The Evolution of the Phila Mummers Parade, Keystone Folklore Quarterly 8(1963).95.

Abrahams R D, The Cowboys in the British West Indies, in A Good Tale and a Bonnie Tune, edd M C Boatright, M Hudson and A Maxwell, Dallas 1964, p 168.

Kennedy D, English Folk Dancing Today and Yesterday, London 1964.

Happe P, The Vice and the Folk-Drama, Folklore 75–76(1964–65).161.

Helm A, Five Mumming Plays for Schools, London 1965; In Comes I St George, Folklore 76(1965).11.

Dean-Smith M, An Unromantic View of the Mummers Play, Theatre Research (International Federation for Theatre Research) 8(1966).89.

Welch C D Jr, Oh Dem Golden Slippers: The Phila Mummers' Parade, Journ of American Folklore 79(1966).523.

Gailey A, The Folk Play in Ireland, Studia Hibernica 6(1966).133; The Rhymers of South-East Antrim, Ulster Folklife 13(1967). 18.

Helm A and E C Cawte, Six Mummers' Acts, Ibstock Leicester 1967.

Abrahams R D, Pull Out Your Purse and Pay: a St George Mumming from the British West Indies, Folklore 79(1968).176.

Gailey A, Christmas Rhymers and Mummers in Ireland, Ibstock Leicester 1968; Irish Folk Drama, Cork 1968; Straw Costume in Irish Folk Customs, Folk Life 6(1968).83.

Green R J, Some Notes on the St George Play, Theatre Survey 9(1968).21.

Helm A, Cheshire Folk Drama, Ibstock Leicester 1968.

Malin S D, Character Origins in the English Folk Play, unpubl diss Univ of Florida 1968; DA 30(1969).637A.

Rossiter A P, English Drama from Early Times to the Elizabethans: Its Background * Origins and Development, London 1969.

Helm A, The Chapbook Mummers' Plays: a Study of the Printed Versions of the North-West of England, Ibstock Leicester 1969 (important pamphlet establishing relationship between contemp versions and 19th cent chapbook versions).

Helm, MS Collection, 35 vols (held by E C Cawte, Ibstock Leicestershire).

Christmas Mumming in Newfoundland: Essays in Anthropology Folklore and History, ed Halpert and G Story, Toronto 1969 (adopts functional approach; model study).

Abrahams R D, British West Indian Folk Drama and the Life Cycle Problem, Folklore 81(1970).241 (advances thesis that clowning is most important aspect of folk drama; discounts idea that "folk" think in terms of life-cycle).

Brody A, The English Mummers and Their Plays, Phila 1970 (especially valuable for development of ties between English plays and classical analogues).

Kirby E T, The Origin of the Mummers' Play, Journ of American Folklore 84(1971) .275.

Davis N, ed, Paston Letters and Papers of the Fifteenth Century, pt 1, Oxford 1971 (arranged by writers; lacks Sir John Paston, who will appear in pt 2).

Preston M J, The British Folk Play: an Elaborate Luck-Visit? Western Folklore 30 (1971).45; The Revesby Sword Play, Journ of American Folklore 85(1972).51.

Tiddy R J E, The Mummers' Play, Oxford 1923; rptd Chicheley 1972 (remains one of the most sensible works on the play; fine collection of texts).

Ward B J, A Functional Approach to English Folk Drama, unpubl diss Ohio State Univ 1972.

Preston M J, The Oldest British Folkplay, Folklore Forum 6(1973).168 (Islip Mummers' Play of 1780).

2. Continental

Mannhardt W, Wald- und Feldkulte, 2nd edn, 2 vols, Berlin 1904–05.

Binney E H, The Alcestis as Folk Drama, Classical Rev 19(1905).18.

Wace A J B, North Greek Festivals, Annual of the British School at Athens 16(1909–10) .232; Mumming Plays in the Southern Balkans, Annual of the British School at Athens 19(1912–13).248.

Ridgeway W, The Origin of Tragedy, Cambridge 1910; The Dramas and Dramatic Rituals of Non-European Races, Cambridge 1915.

Durkheim E, The Elementary Forms of Religious Life, trans J W Swain, N Y 1915.

Harrison J E, Themis, Cambridge 1927.

Stumpfl R, Kultspiele der Germanen als Ursprung des mittelalterlichen Dramas, Berlin 1936 (one of the major modern exponents of folk origin for medieval drama in general).

Schmidt L, Volksschauspiel Deutsche Philologie im Aufriss, ed W Stammler, Berlin 1952–57.

Gaster T H, Thespis: Ritual Myth and Drama in the Ancient Near East, N Y 1961.

Schmidt L, Das Deutsche Volksschauspiel: ein Handbuch, Berlin 1962 (full bibl and geographical index); ed, Le théâtre populaire Européen, Paris 1965 (texts).

Ujvary Z, Tarsadalmi Konfliktust megjelenito harom nepi szinjatek [Social Conflict in Three Folk Plays], Muveltseg Es Hagyomany, Debrecen Hungary 1968 (for summary see no 561 in Abstracts of Folklore Studies, vol 8, no 3, Fall 1970).

Dömötör T, Nepi szinjatektipusok [Types of

Folk Plays], Muveltseg Es Hagyomany, Debrecen Hungary 1968, p 161 (for summary see no 560 in Abstracts of Folklore Studies, vol 8, no 3, Fall 1970).

Warner L, The Russian Folk Play Tsar Maximillian, Folklore 82(1971).177 (ties Russian play into Mummers' Play tradition; some discussion of English play).

3. Spanish and Latin American (with the special help of Frances Gillmor)

Santoscoy A, La fiesta de Los Tastoanes: estudio etnológico-histórico, in Apuntamientos historicos y bibliograficos Jaliscienses, ed J G Montenegro, Jalisco 1889, p 71.

Bourke J G, The Miracle Play of the Rio Grande, Journ of American Folklore 6 (1893).89.

Starr F, The Tastoanes, Journ of American Folklore 15(1902).73.

Loubat F -F, Letra de la Danza de Pluma de Moctezuma y Hernando Cortés con los capitanes y reyes que intervinieron en la conquista de México, Proc of the 12th Congress of Americanists 1900, Paris 1902.

Cole M R, ed and trans, Los Pastores: A Mexican Play of the Nativity, Boston 1907 (Memoirs of Am Folklore Soc 9).

Ricard R, Les fêtes de Moros y cristianos au Mexique, Journ de la Société des Americanistes ns 24(1932).51, 287; 29(1937).220.

Istituto General Franco para la Investigación Hispano-Arabe, Madrid 1933—(studies by Bejarama Robles, Garcia Figueras, Touceda Fontenla, etc on fiestas y drama).

Anuario de la Sociedad Folklorica de Mexico, 1938–57 (a folk drama in each issue).

Boggs R S, Bibliografia del folklore mexicano, Boletin bibliografico de antropologia americana, Mexico 1939; Bibliography of Latin American Folklore, N Y 1940; Una bibliografia completa clasificada y comentada de los articulos de Mexican Folkways con indice, Boletin bibliografico de antropologia americana, Mexico 1942, p 221.

Englekirk J E, Notes on the Repertoire of the New Mexican Spanish Folk Theater, Southern Folklore Quart 4(1940).227.

Gillmor F, Spanish Texts of Three Dance Dramas of Mexican Villages, Humanities Bull. 4 (Univ of Arizona 1942); The Dance

Dramas of Mexican Villages, Humanities Bull 5 (Univ of Arizona 1943).

Arco y Garay R de, Notas de folk-lore altoaragones, Madrid 1943.

Cornejo Franco J, La danza de la conquista, Anuario de la Sociedad Folklórica de México 4(1944).155 (Guadalajara text).

Boggs R S and V T Mendoza, Representación del drama de la Pasión in Ixtapalala, D F México, Anuario de la Sociedad Folklórica de México 6(1945).139.

Pearce T M, Los Moros y Los Christianos: Early American Play, New Mexico Folklore Record 2(1947–48).58.

Horvasitas Pimentel F, Piezas teatrales en lengua Nahuatl: bibliografia descriptiva, Boletin bibliografico de antropologia americana 11(1949).154.

Tully M F and J B Rael, An Annotated Bibliography of Spanish Folklore in New Mexico and Southern Colorado, Albuquerque 1950.

Larrea Palacín A de, El dance aragones y las representaciónes de Moros y Christianos: contribution al estudio del teatro popular, Tetuán 1952.

Lea A L-W, Literary Folklore of the Hispanic Southwest, San Antonio Tex 1953.

Barker C, ed and trans. The Shepherd's Play of the Prodigal Son (Coloquio de pastores del hijo prodigo): A Folk Drama of Old Mexico, Folklore Studies 2, Berkeley 1953 (texts and bibl).

Robe S L, ed, Coloquios de pastores from Jalisco Mexico, Folklore Studies 4 (texts and bibl).

Espejo A, La Danza de Los Tecuanes en Acatlán Puebla, Anuario de la Sociedad Folklórica de México 9(1955).117.

Englekirk J E, El teatro folklórico Hispanoamericano, Folklore Américas 17(1957).1; The Source and Dating of New Mexican Folk Spanish Folk Plays, Western Folklore 16(1957).232.

Robe S L, The Relationship of Los Pastores to other Spanish-American Folk Drama, Western Folklore 16(1957).281.

Robb J D, The Music of Los Pastores, Western Folklore 16(1957).363 (see other articles in this vol, especially devoted to folk drama).

Ricard R, Otra contribusion al estudio de las fiestas de moros y cristianos, in Miscellanea Paul Rivet Octogenario dicata, Publicaciones del Instituto de Historia, 1s, no 50, Universidad Nacional Autónoma de México 1958, 2.871.

Hoyos Sancho N de, Una diesta peninsular Arraigada en America: los Moros y Christianos, Miscellanea Paul Rivet 2.717.

Salva i Ballester A, Bosqueig historic i bibliografic de les festes de Moros i Christians, Alicante 1958.

Andrade M de, Dancas dramaticas do Brasil, Sao Paulo 1959, 3 vols.

Painter M T, Easter at Pascua Village, Tucson 1960 (Yoqui Indians, on which extensive work has been done by F Gillmor's seminar at Univ of Arizona).

Correa G, C Cannon, W A Hunter and B Bode, The Native Theater in Middle America, Middle American Research Institute, Tulane Univ Publ 27.

Coloma R, Libro de la fiesta de Moros y Christianos de Alcoy, Alcoy 1962.

Carrasco Urgioti M S, Aspectos Folcloricos y literarios de la fiesta de moros y christianos en Espana, PMLA 78.476.

Rael J B, The Sources and Diffusion of the Mexican Shepherd's Plays, Guadalajara 1965 (dates ultimate Spanish sources as early as the late 12th or early 13th cent).

Amades J, Las danzas de Moros y Christianos, Valencia 1966.

Pino Saavedra T, La Historia de Carlomagno y Los Doce Pares de Francia en Chile, Folklore Americas 26(1966).1.

Englekirk J E, The Passion Play in New Mexico, Western Folklore 25(1966).17, 105.

Gillmor F, Diferentes conceitos de Los Tastoanes un drama tradicional de Jalisco, Revista Brasilerira de folclor, Año 10, no 28(1970), p 215.

Major M and T M Pearce, Southwest Heritage: a Literary History with Bibliographies, 3rd edn, Albuquerque 1972, pp 31, 258, 267 (Spanish-American folk drama).

XIII. POEMS DEALING WITH CONTEMPORARY CONDITIONS

by

Rossell Hope Robbins

BACKGROUND BOOKS: The following important, frequently listed entries, here given full statement, are referred to in abbreviated form in the pages that follow. For abbreviations not appearing in this list, consult the general Table of Abbreviations.

Kingsford EHL   Kingsford C L, English Historical Literature in the Fifteenth Century, Oxford 1913.

New CBEL   Watson G, The New Cambridge Bibliography of English Literature, vol 1, Cambridge 1974.

Scattergood PP   Scattergood V J, Politics and Poetry in the Fifteenth Century, London 1971 (crit J R Lander, AHR 78.419; R H Robbins, Clio 4.247).

Sisam Oxf Book MEV   Sisam C and K Sisam, The Oxford Book of Medieval English Verse, Oxford 1970.

Wilson Lost Lit   Wilson R M, The Lost Literature of Medieval England, London 1952; 2nd edn London 1970.

[1] LIST OF POEMS.

List of poems in Brown-Robbins, Robbins-Cutler with Conversion Table to items entered in this chapter.

0.3	[169]	28.5	[170]	52	[278] (b)
5	[209]	33.3	[278] (a)	86.5	[237]
23.5	[304] (a)	33.5	[157]	143.8	[163]

3923.5	[16] (a)	4034	[76]	4144	[37]
3924	[63]	4036	[303]	4154.3	[304] (t)
3929	[183]	4038.5	[304] (s)	4165	[82]
3945	[275]	4044.6	[134]	4189.5	[18] (e)
3951.5	[277]	4050	[295]	4235	[15]
3955.5	[21] (b)	4056.8	[76]	4236	[90]
3989	[288]	4062	[211]	4254.5	[161]
3993	[284]	4070	[64]	4255	[161]
4005.5	[286]	4071	[214]	4257	[242]
4008	[285]	4085	[96]	4261	[195]
4014.8	[304] (r)	4088	[288]	4263.3	[234]
4018	[299]	4093	[136]	*4267.5	[210]
4018.5	[299]	4098.3	[114]	4268	[85]
4028.6	[167] (d)	4105.5	[280]	4280	[40]
4029	[281]	4128.8	[263]	4284.8	[10] (a)
4030.5	[281]				

[2] GENERAL WORKS.

Editions. Wright PS.
Wright PPS.
Robbins-HP (crit B Lindheim, Angl 80.335;
T V Tuleja, CHR 45.519; A M Kinghorn,
Dalhousie Rev 40.108; A A Prins, ESts 45.53;
M Fifield, JEGP 59.273; M. Schlauch, Kwartalnik Neofilologiczny 7.236; K B McFarlane, MÆ 30.57; R L Greene, MLN 75.606;
R M Wilson, MLR 55.419; E T Donaldson,
MP 60.56; E Seaton, RES ns 13.400; L
Glanville, SN 32.188).
Versification. Oakden J P, Alliterative Poetry
in ME, 2 vols, Manchester 1930, 1935.
Other Scholarly Problems. Taylor R, The Political Prophecy in England, N Y 1911.
Owst G R, Literature and Pulpit in Medieval
England, Cambridge 1933.
Starke, F J, Populäre engl Chroniken des 15
Jahrhunderts, Berlin 1935.
Wilson Lost Lit, p 192; 2nd edn, p 187.
Robbins R H, ME Poems of Protest, Angl
78.194.
Richert W G, Anonymous Vernacular Protest
of the Middle Ages 1216–1485, diss. Colorado 1967; DA 28.1057A.
Literary Criticism. Kingsford EHL.
Kingsford C L, English History in Contemporary Poetry, no 2, London 1913.

Bruce H, English History in Contemporary
Poetry, no 3, London 1914.
Frazer N L, English History in Contemporary
Poetry, no 3, London 1914.
Oliver R, Poems without Names, Berkeley
1970, p 11 (crit R H Robbins, Style 7.376).
Kinney T L, The Temper of Fourteenth-Century English Verse of Complaint, Annuale
Medievale 7.74.
Scattergood PP.
General References. Wright T, Essays on the
Literature, Popular Superstitions, and History of England in the Middle Ages, London 1846, 2.256.
Wright PPS, 1.ix; 2.vii; Ten Brink, 1.314;
Courthope, 1.185; Schofield, pp 363, 368;
CHEL, 1.411.
Corson L, A Finding List of Political Poems,
1910; rptd N Y 1970.
Chambers OHEL, p 41.
Bagley J J, Historical Interpretation, London
1965, p 227.
Bibliography. CBEL, 1.195, 270; Robbins-HP,
p 242; Scattergood PP, p 395; New CBEL,
1.473, 545, 686.

[3] GENERAL WORKS: LATIN AND
FRENCH POEMS.

Editions. Wright PS.

Wright T, The Latin Poems Commonly Ascribed to Walter Mapes, Camden Soc 16.
Wright PPS; Wright SLP.
Wright T, The Anglo-Latin Satirical Poets, Rolls Series 59.
Aspin I S T, Anglo-Norman Political Songs, Oxford 1953.

[4] CORPUS OF MANUSCRIPTS.

Bodl 815 [249] (1440–50).
Bodl 1045 [99] (15 cent).
Bodl 1063 [6] (before 1200).
Bodl 1117 [99] (15 cent).
Bodl 1414 [296] (1400–25).
Bodl 1486 [208] (14 cent).
Bodl 1595 [8] (1300).
Bodl 1642 [114, 115], (1400–20).
Bodl 1690 [279] (14 cent).
Bodl 1703 [56–65] (1400–25).
Bodl 1771 [13] (14 cent).
Bodl 1787 [13] (1300–50); [100, 279] (1450–1500).
Bodl 1797 [124, 257] (ca 1400); [104] (1450–1500).
Bodl 1885 [82] (ca 1425).
Bodl 1986 [137] (ca 1490).
Bodl 2090 [99] (15 cent).
Bodl 2157 [279] (1465).
Bodl 2293 [170] (ca 1420).
Bodl 2305 [99] (15 cent).
Bodl 2712 [140] (early 15 cent).
Bodl 2752 [256] (1388).
Bodl 3041 [17, 279] (1375–1400).
Bodl 3338 [279] (1550).
Bodl 3354 [129] (ca 1486).
Bodl 3562 [74] (1425–50).
Bodl 3712 [97] (late 14 cent).
Bodl 3888 [228, 248] (1489).
Bodl 3904 [23] (1300–25).
Bodl 3938 [85, 209] (ca 1385).
Bodl 4062 [273, 278, 279, 290, 293, 304] (1450).
Bodl 4192 [224] (1630).
Bodl 4197 [213] (1650).
Bodl 6683 [290] (16 cent).
Bodl 6922 [97] (14 cent).
Bodl 6933 [68, 134] (ca 1560).
Bodl 6943 [138, 184] (1447–56).
Bodl 8241 [279] (ca 1600).
Bodl 8258 [290] (16 cent).
Bodl 8915 [228, 248] (ca 1675).
Bodl 9914 [278] (17 cent).
Bodl 10234 [131] (1480–1500).
Bodl 11224 [130] (early 16 cent).
Bodl 11566 [17] (15 cent).
Bodl 11951 [72, 86] (1480–1500).
Bodl 12514 [99] (15 cent).
Bodl 12653 [236, 278, 291] (1530–40).

Bodl 13679 [23] (1375–1400).
Bodl 13814 [290, 297, 304] (16 cent).
Bodl 14526 [249] (1450–1500).
Bodl 14637 [221] (1600–50).
Bodl 15165 [274] (1450–1500).
Bodl 15444 [255] (1425–45).
Bodl 21626 [156] (mid 15 cent).
Bodl 21652 [210] (1450–75).
Bodl 21669 [247] (ca 1450).
Bodl 21678 [142] (1475–1500).
Bodl 21831 [132] (15 cent).
Bodl 25174 [279] (1400).
Bodl 29734 [90, 125, 126, 127, 155] (1460–80).
Bodl 29746 [260] (1430–50).
Bodl 40359 [290] (17 cent).
Bodl Astor 2 [160] (1450–1500).
Bodl Eng poet B.4 [93] (1450–1500).
Bodl Lat misc E.85 [185] (early 16 cent).
Bodl Lyell 34 [197] (1450–60).
Bodl Lyell 35 [281, 185] (ca 1482).
All Souls Oxf 39 [23] (1325–75).
All Souls Oxf 103 [249] (ca 1450).
Balliol Oxf 320 [169] (late 13 cent).
Balliol Oxf 354 [74, 233–235, 241, 255] (1518–36).
Corp Christi Oxf 237 [89] (1475–1500).
Corp Christi Oxf 274 [137, 141] (early 15 cent).
Jesus Oxf 29 [96] (after 1256).
Magdalen Oxf Charter Misc 36 [261] (mid 15 cent).
St John's Oxf 57 [207] (late 15 cent).
St John's Oxf 209 [253] (ca 1465).
Univ Oxf 154 [161] (15 cent).
Camb Univ Dd.1.1 [240] (1400–25).
Camb Univ Dd.2.5 [13] (1350).
Camb Univ Dd.13.27 [206] (early 16 cent).
Camb Univ Dd.14.2 [253] (1432).
Camb Univ Ee.1.12 [186] (1492).
Camb Univ Ff.1.6 [205] (ca 1500).
Camb Univ Ff.1.27 [9] (12 cent).
Camb Univ Ff.5.31 [106] (16 cent).
Camb Univ Ff.5.48 [290] (15 cent).
Camb Univ Ff.6.2 [103] (early 16 cent).
Camb Univ Gg.1.1 [15, 23] (1300–25).
Camb Univ Gg.4.12 [20] (ca 1450).
Camb Univ Hh.2.6 [89] (early 16 cent).
Camb Univ Hh.4.12 [233] (1490–1510).
Camb Univ Hh.6.9 [74] (1434).
Camb Univ Ii.3.8 [143] (1400–50).
Camb Univ Ii.6.11 [297. 299] (15 cent).
Camb Univ Kk.1.5, IV [285, 293] (1480–1500).
Camb Univ Kk.1.5, V [281] (late 15 cent).
Camb Univ Kk.6.16 [278–279, 304] (1490–1510).
Camb Univ Ll.1.18 [282] (late 15 cent).
Camb Univ Ll.4.14 [246] (1450–75).
Camb Univ Ll.5.10 [159, 286] (ca 1622).
Camb Univ Mm.4.42 [251] (1470–1500).
Camb Univ Add 4407 [29, 81] (end 14 cent).

Caius Camb 71 [99] (15 cent).
Caius Camb 174, IV [154] (1480–1500).
Caius Camb 221 [12] (13 cent).
Caius Camb 249 [279, 281] (1464).
Caius Camb 261 [156] (14 cent).
Caius Camb 267 [279] (15 cent).
Caius Camb 364 [99] (15 cent).
Caius Camb 408 [136] (13 cent).
Corp Christi Camb 7 [256] (early 15 cent).
Corp Christi Camb 167 [20] (ca 1500).
Corp Christi Camb 329 [279] (15 cent).
Corp Christi Camb 354 [18] (16 cent).
Corp Christi Camb 369 [257] (1385–1400).
Pembroke Camb 281 [7] (12 cent).
Pepys 1236 [277] (ca 1460).
Pepys 1461 [249] (1450–75).
Pepys 2253 [16, 159, 248, 286] (1570–90).
Peterhouse Camb 104 [82] (1350).
St John's Camb 112 [80] (1300–25).
St John's Camb 195 [102–103] (1425).
St John's Camb 204 [18] (ca 1400).
St John's Camb 234 [206] (early 16 cent).
Sidney Sussex Camb 39 [304] (1500–25).
Trinity Camb 35 [279] (15 cent).
Trinity Camb 323 [99] (1255–60).
Trinity Camb 594 [112] (late 14 cent).
Trinity Camb 595 [109] (1600–25).
Trinity Camb 599 [172] (1500–25).
Trinity Camb 601 [166, 202] (1470–80).
Trinity Camb 1105 [8] (1175–1200).
Trinity Camb 1144 [105] (ca 1490).
Trinity Camb 1157 [161, 297–298] (1460–80).
Trinity Camb 1413 [74] (1425–75).
Fitzwilliam Mus Deposit Bradfer-Lawrence 8 [203] (15 cent).
Arundel 57 [289] (ca 1350).
Arundel 66 [279] (1450–1500).
Arundel 292 [168, 171] (1375–90).
Cotton Calig A.ii [230] (1425–50).
Cotton Claud E.iii [256] (15 cent).
Cotton Cleop B.ii [100–101] (1382).
Cotton Cleop C.iv [71] (ca 1443); [279, 297–298] (1475–1500); [67, 285] (ca 1550).
Cotton Cleop C.viii [253] (ca 1400).
Cotton Domit A.9 [279] (1350–1400).
Cotton Faust B.ix [256] (early 15 cent).
Cotton Galba E.viii [74] (1425–40).
Cotton Galba E.ix [43–54, 75, 154, 258, 273] (1440–50); [284, 304] (16 cent).
Cotton Julius A.v [23, 292] (1325–50).
Cotton Nero A.vi [183] (1450–1500).
Cotton Nero D.xi [16] (1450–75).
Cotton Tib B.i [6] (before 1200).
Cotton Tib B.iv [6] (before 1200).
Cotton Tib C.vii [256] (15 cent).
Cotton Tib D.vii [18] (ca 1400).
Cotton Titus A.xx [17] (15 cent).
Cotton Titus A.xxv [304] (late 15 cent).

Cotton Titus A.xxvi [148] (ca 1470).
Cotton Titus D.xii [279] (14 cent).
Cotton Vesp A.xii [302] (late 15 cent).
Cotton Vesp B.xvi [120] (1450–60); [183, 193] (1475–1500).
Cotton Vesp D.ix [119] (early 15 cent).
Cotton Vesp E.vii [279] (1460–80).
Cotton Vesp E.viii [285] (16 cent).
Cotton Vesp E.ix [22] (15 cent).
Cotton Vitell A.xii [279]
Cotton Vitell D.xii [148] (1475–1500).
Cotton Vitell D.xii, II [72] (ca 1410).
Cotton Vitell D.xx [9] (early 13 cent).
Cotton Vitell E.x [249, 290] (1450–75).
Cotton Vitell F.xiii [304] (15 cent).
Cotton Rolls ii.23 [174, 189–190, 192, 194–195, 281, 283, 297, 299, 304] (1450–52).
Egerton 1995 [74] (1470–80).
Egerton 2257 [74] (19 cent).
Egerton 2810 [95] (mid 15 cent).
Egerton 3309 [22] (1440–70).
Harley 78 [109] (1460–70); [249] (ca 1500).
Harley 114 [23] (1350).
Harley 116 [230] (1475–1500).
Harley 226 [74] (1475–1500).
Harley 245 [225] (late 16 cent).
Harley 247 [259] (16 cent).
Harley 271 [249] (ca 1500).
Harley 293 [67, 220] (ca 1550).
Harley 367 [158, 218] (1600–25).
Harley 372 [161] (1440–60).
Harley 533 [9] (19 cent).
Harley 536 [86] (1450–1500).
Harley 541 [221] (16 cent).
Harley 542 [158] (ca 1600).
Harley 543 [191] (ca 1450).
Harley 545 [261] (ca 1550).
Harley 559 [281, 285, 290, 297–299] (1540–50).
Harley 565 [72] (1440–50).
Harley 753 [74] (1475–1500).
Harley 913 [33–39] (ca 1330).
Harley 941 [86] (1450–1500).
Harley 1002 [167] (1475–1500).
Harley 1717 [281] (15 cent).
Harley 1735 [150] (1456–83).
Harley 1900 [18] (ca 1425).
Harley 2251 [229] (1460–70).
Harley 2252 [106, 123, 220, 223] (1510–30).
Harley 2253 [24–32, 288] (ca 1340).
Harley 2256 [74] (1450–75).
Harley 2259 [237] (15 cent).
Harley 2316 [127, 238] (1350–1400).
Harley 2338 [275] (1536).
Harley 2382 [278] (1470–1500).
Harley 3362 [104, 255] (1475–1500).
Harley 3606 [232] (17 cent).
Harley 3634 [256] (ca 1388).
Harley 3908 [279] (15 cent).

Harley 3952 [212] (ca 1485).
Harley 4011 [249] (1450–75).
Harley 4690 [66] (1475–1500).
Harley 5396 [91–92] (1450–60).
Harley 6148 [279] (mid 17 cent).
Harley 6641 [113] (15 cent).
Harley 6909 [16] (late 17 cent).
Harley 7332 [278, 297] (17 cent).
Harley 7371 [173] (1500).
Lansdowne 122 [279].
Lansdowne 197 [16] (after 1500).
Lansdowne 205 [214] (1587).
Lansdowne 207 [14] (1638).
Lansdowne 210 [18] (mid 16 cent).
Lansdowne 239 [13] (1375–1425).
Lansdowne 285 [178] (ca 1470).
Lansdowne 418 [38, 40] (early 17 cent).
Lansdowne 762 [111, 122, 128, 162, 275–276, 278, 281, 290–291, 297–298, 301, 304] (1500–40).
Lansdowne 796 [250] (1480–1500).
Royal 7.A.ix [279, 285] (16 cent).
Royal 8.C.xvii [279] (1375–1400).
Royal 12.C.xiv [226] (1325–50).
Royal 13.E.ix [256] (ca 1400).
Royal 17.D.xv [204] (1470–80).
Royal 17.D.xx [16] (1440–50).
Royal 18.B.xvii [109] (ca 1520).
Royal 18.D.ii [224] (1516–23).
Royal 20.A.ii [23] (1300–50).
Royal 20.A.xi [23] (1325–75).
Royal App 58 [116] (1500–10).
Stowe 65 [18] (ca 1425).
Stowe 393 [258] (16 cent).
Sloane 252 [77] (1500).
Sloane 1584 [166] (1500–20).
Sloane 1802 [279, 281, 285] (1600).
Sloane 1825 [234] (16 cent).
Sloane 2232 [156] (17 cent).
Sloane 2578 [281, 285, 290, 297] (1547).
Sloane 4031 [242, 281] (early 16 cent).
BM Addit 6702 [290] (early 17 cent).
BM Addit 14997 [165] (1500).
BM Addit 20059 [239] (15 cent).
BM Addit 20091 [35, 38] (19 cent).
BM Addit 22283 [85, 209] (1380–1400).
BM Addit 24194 [18] (ca 1410).
BM Addit 24663 [281] (late 16 cent).
BM Addit 24848 [279] (16 cent).
BM Addit 27223 [227] (15 cent).
BM Addit 27879 [55, 69, 74, 216–220, 245] (ca 1650).
BM Addit 31042 [94, 243–244] (ca 1450).
BM Addit 33994 [244] (1475–1500).
BM Addit 34360 [229] (1460–70).
BM Addit 40673 [249] (1450–75).
BM Addit 41666 [246] (1430–60).

BM Addit 45102 [222] (early 16 cent).
BM Addit 45896 [118] (1349).
Aberdeen Univ 21 [18] (ca 1400).
Advocates 1.1.6 [129, 159] (ca 1568).
Advocates 19.2.1 [80, 82] (1330–40).
Advocates 19.2.3 [16] (1480).
Advocates 19.2.4 [16] (1500–25).
Advocates 19.3.1 [179] (1480–1500).
Advocates 651 [16] (late 15 cent).
Armagh [137] (1418–39).
Belfast Queen's Univ [249] (15 cent).
Chetham Libr 11379 [18] (ca 1415).
Coll of Arms Arundel 7 [256] (15 cent).
Coll of Arms Arundel 14 [23] (1300–50).
Coll of Arms Arundel 58 [66] (1450–1500).
Coll of Arms Arundel 61 [23] (1325–50).
Coventry Corp Leet Book [264, 266–267] (ca 1500).
Dublin State Paper Office [42] (ca 1600).
Durham Univ Cosin V.iii.9 [124] (16 cent).
Durham Univ Cosin V.iii.10 [167] (15 cent).
Edinburgh Univ 82 [99] (15 cent).
Edinburgh Univ 181 [279].
Edinburgh Univ 186 [16] (ca 1450).
Ely Cath [8] (13 cent).
Eton Coll 34 [99] (15 cent).
Fountains Abbey [187] (1339).
Hunterian Mus 83 [18] (15 cent).
Hunterian Mus 230 [127] (early 16 cent).
Hunterian Mus 367 [18] (late 14 cent).
Inner Temple Petyt 511, VII [23] (ca 1400).
Ipswich County Hall [144] (1450–1500).
Lambeth 6 [76] (1450–75).
Lambeth 78, V [99] (15 cent).
Lambeth 131 [23] (1425–50).
Lambeth 306 [175, 199–200] (1460–70); [261] (1490–1520); [193] (1560–1600).
Lambeth 331 (74] (1475–1500).
Lambeth Carew 617 [41] (ca 1350).
Lincoln Cath 44 [99] (15 cent).
Lincoln Cath 91 [107, 290] (1430–40).
Lincoln Cath 132 [164] (1475–1500).
Liverpool Pub Libr [18].
London Guildhall [269] (1225–50).
Nat Libr Scot Gaelic 37 (formerly Lismore) [133] (early 16 cent).
Nat Libr Wales Addit 441C [285] (16 cent).
Nat Libr Wales Peniarth 26 [281, 285, 299, 304] (1450–75).
Nat Libr Wales Peniarth 50 [278, 281, 285, 300, 304] (1425–50).
Nat Libr Wales Peniarth 53 [151, 278] (1485–1500).
Nat Libr Wales Peniarth 58 [281].
Nat Libr Wales Peniarth 94 [285] (ca 1595).
Nat Libr Wales Peniarth 395 [85] (early 15 cent).

Nat Libr Wales Llanstephen 119 [285] (1600–50).
Nat Libr Wales Deposit Porkington 10 [147, 281] (1450–75).
Norwich City Book of Pleas [263] (15 cent).
Public Record Office, Ancient Indictments K.B.9, no 144, m 31 [258] (end 14 cent).
Public Record Office, Chancery Miscellanea, Bundle 34 [88] (ca 1400).
Public Record Office, Coram Rege Rolls 5.28 [258] (end 14 cent).
Public Record Office, State Papers Henry VIII [285] (early 16 cent).
Rylands Libr Eng 113 [211] (1483–85).
Rylands Libr Eng 955 [249] (mid 16 cent).
Rylands Libr Latin 228 [304] (15 cent).
Rylands Libr Latin 394 [156] (mid 15 cent).
St Andrew's Univ T.T.66 [16] (1500–50).
St Paul's Cath [303] (15 cent).
Soc of Antiquaries 47 [279] (15 cent).
Soc of Antiquaries 101 [200, 249, 279, 283, 304] (ca 1450).
Stanbrook Abbey 3 [270] (1410–40).
Trinity Dublin 172 [279] (14 cent).
Trinity Dublin 214 [254] (15 cent).
Trinity Dublin 432 [176, 196, 198–199] (1460).
Trinity Dublin 516 [86, 177, 180–182, 193, 262, 279, 281, 297, 304] (1450–75).
Ushaw St Cuthbert's Coll 10 [188] (1475–1500).
Victoria and Albert Mus Dyce 45 [304] (ca 1550–70).
Wellcome Hist Med Libr 673 [83] (1430–50).
Westminster Abbey 27 [279, 281, 285] (15 cent).
Worcester Cath F.19 [99] (late 14 cent).
Worcester Cath Q.3 [99] (15 cent).
Worcester Cath 174 [79] (ca 1180).
York Cath A.xvi.I.12 [14] (1350).
Bateman [218] (ca 1660).

Buccleugh [74] (1450–75).
Charlemont [74] (15 cent).
Cole [219, 259].
Colville [16] (after 1500).
Cox [21, 253] (mid 15 cent).
Deritend House [87] (ca 1400).
Ferguson [16].
Harmsworth [74] (15 cent).
Holkham Hall 670 [74] (1475–1500).
Kilkenny Castle, Ormond [88] (1450–1500).
Littledale [187] (mid 15 cent).
Lyme [217] (ca 1580–1600).
Marchmont A.C.15 [228, 248] (ca 1500).
Mostyn 133 [285] (1600–23).
Nuton [74] (1425–75).
Perrins 33 [304] (15 cent).
Stockdale Hardy Leicester Psalter [145] (15 cent).
Wemyss [16] (1500–50).
Brussels Bibliothèque royale 4628 [228] (ca 1500).
Naples Royal Libr 13.B.29 [140] (1450–75).
Paris Bibl Nat fr 12154 [23] (14 cent).
Rome Venerable Eng Coll 1306 [75, 77, 160] (1450–1500).
Tours 520 [279].
Boston Public Libr 92 [249] (before 1471).
Chicago Univ 697 [279] (late 14 cent).
Huntington Libr EL 26.C.3 [215] (1450–80).
Huntington Libr HM 140 [249] (1450–80).
Huntington Libr 28561 [18].
Morgan Libr 775 [178] (ca 1486).
Pennsylvania State Univ Prophecies of Merlin [278] (e) (late 15 cent).
Princeton Univ Garrett 151 [18] (15 cent).
Texas Univ 8 [110] (early 16 cent).
Yale Univ Beinecke Libr [280] (ca 1440).
Penrose 12 [18] (ca 1400).

1. VERSES INSERTED INTO CHRONICLES

I. Miscellaneous Scraps

[5] MISCELLANEOUS SCRAPS

General References. Förster M, Kleinere me Texte, Angl 42.145.
Starke F J, Populäre engl Chroniken des 15 Jahrhunderts, Berlin 1935, passim (for extensive use of political verses in Brut).
Wilson R M, More Lost Literature in Old and ME, Leeds SE 5.46.

Wilson EMEL, p 268.
Wilson Lost Lit, p 192; 2nd edn, p 188.

[6] THE OLD ENGLISH CHRONICLE FRAGMENTS

MSS. 1, Bodl 1063 (Laud Misc 636) (to 1154); 2, Cotton Tib B.i (to 1066); 3, Cotton Tib B.iv (to 1079).

Not listed Brown-Robbins, Robbins-Cutler.
Editions. Thorpe B, The Anglo-Saxon Chronicle, Rolls Series 23, 1.238, 332, 340, 348, 355.
Earle J, Two of the Saxon Chronicles Parallel, Oxford 1865; rvsd C Plummer, Oxford 1892; rvsd D Whitelock, Oxford 1952, pp 187, 192, 201, 210, 220, 239.
Classen E and F E Harmer, An Anglo-Saxon Chronicle, Manchester 1926, pp 81, 84, 88, 93 (fragments a, b, c, d).
Rositzke H A, The C-Text of the Old English Chronicles, Beiträge zur engl Philologie 34, Bochum-Langendreer 1940, p 78 (fragment b).
Clark C, The Peterborough Chronicle 1070–1154, Oxford 1958; 2nd edn 1970, pp 6, 13, 32 (fragments d, e, f).

[7] PEMBROKE CAMBRIDGE SCRAPS.

a. Ynguar and Vbbe.
MS. Pembroke Camb 281, f 1ᵃ (12 cent).
Robbins-Cutler, no 1267.5.
Editions. Förster M, Kleinere me Texte, Angl 42.147.
James M R, A Descriptive Catalogue, Cambridge 1905, p 71.
Wells Manual, p 1052.
Wilson Lost Lit, p 43; 2nd edn, p 38.
Literary Relations. Förster, Angl 42.147 (additional tags).
b. In clenche.
MS. Pembroke Camb 281, f 1ᵃ (12 cent).
Robbins-Cutler, no 1477.5.
Editions. James, Cat, p 71.
Wells, p 1053.

[8] LIBER ELIENSIS.

MSS. 1, Bodl 1595 (Laud Misc 647), f 45ᵇ (1300); 2, Trinity Camb 1105, f 87ᵇ (1175–1200); 3, Ely Cath (13 cent).
Brown-Robbins, Robbins-Cutler, no 2164.
Editions. Gale T, Historiae Britannicae Saxonicae, Anglo-Danicae Scriptores XV, Historia Ecclesiae Eliensis, Oxford 1691, 1.505, 593.
Todd H J, Illustrations of the Lives and Writings of Gower and Chaucer, London 1810, p 289 (MS 2; as for all following edns).
Stewart D S, Liber Eliensis, London 1848, p 202.
Morley, 1.468.
Kluge F, Me Lesebuch, Halle 1904, p 139.
CHEL, 2.397; Wells, p 490.
Sampson G, Cambridge Book of Prose and Verse, Cambridge 1924, p 172.
Zupitza J, Alt- und me Uebungsbuch, Vienna

1928, p 68.
Greene E E Carols, p xxxiv.
Williams C, New Book of English Verse, N Y 1936, p 27.
Brook G L, The Harley Lyrics, 3rd edn, Manchester 1964, p 4.
Wilson EMEL, p 253.
Wilson R M, More Lost Literature in Old and ME, Leeds SE 5.34.
Wilson Lost Lit, p 171; 2nd edn, p 159.
Chambers OHEL, p 73.
Kaiser R, Alt- und me Anthologie, Berlin 1954, p 363.
Ker N R, Catalogue of Manuscripts Containing Anglo-Saxon, Oxford 1957, p 137.
Kaiser R, Medieval English, Berlin 1958, p 160.
Davies R T, Medieval English Lyrics, London 1963, p 30.
Stevick R D, One Hundred ME Lyrics, Indianapolis 1964, p 3.
Sisam Oxf Book MEV, p 549.
Versification. Saintsbury G E B, History of English Prosody, London 1906, 1.30 (with text).
Sources and Literary Relations. Chambers OHEL, p 177.
Pound L, King Cnut's Song and Ballad Origins, MLN 34.162 (with text).
Wilson EMEL, p 254.
Literary Criticism. Peck R A, Public Dreams and Private Myths Perspective in Middle English Literature, PMLA 90.464.
General References. DNB, 56.173.
Gummere F B, The Popular Ballad, Boston 1888, pp 58, 249.
Todd, edn, p 288; Morley, 3.239; CHEL, 2.451; Ten Brink, 1.148; Paul Grundriss, 2nd edn, 2¹.1084; Wilson EMEL, p 258; Chambers OHEL, p 73.
Blake E O, The Historia Eliensis as a Source for Twelfth-Century History, JRLB 41.304.
Bibliography. Gross C, Sources and Literature of English History, 2nd edn, London 1915, no 1372.

[9] DESCRIPTION OF DURHAM.

MSS. 1, Cotton Vitell D.xx (early 13 cent; MS burned in 1731); 2, Camb Univ Ff.1.27, p 202 (12 cent); 2a, Harley 533 (19 cent transcript).
Robbins-Cutler, no 1608.5.
Editions. Hickes G, Thesaurus, Oxford 1705, 1.178 (MS 1).
Twysden R, Historiae Anglicanae Scriptores Decem, London 1652 (Simeon Monachus Dunelmensis) (MS 2 and all following edns).

Oelrichs J, Angelsächsische Chrestomathie, Hamburg 1798.

Rel Ant 1.159.

Arnold T, Symeonis Monachi Opera, Rolls Series 75, 1.221.

Wülcker R, Kleinere angelsächsische Dichtungen, Halle 1879, p 76; Bibliothek der angelsächsischen Poesie, Hamburg 1921, 1.391.

Schlauch M, An Old English Encomium Urbe, JEGP 40.14.

Craigie W A, Specimens of Anglo-Saxon Poetry, Edinburgh 1923, 3.42.

Krapp G P and E V L Dobie, Anglo-Saxon Poetic Records, London 1942, 6.27.

Kaiser R, Medieval English, Berlin 1958, p 144.

Language. Oakden J P, Alliterative Poetry in ME, Manchester 1930, 1935, 1.40; 2.235.

Versification. Oakden, 1.136.

Literary Criticism. Wülcker, pp 345, 351, 516.

Schlauch, JEGP 40.14.

General References. Brandl, pp 52, 59.

Schlauch M, English Medieval Literature and its Social Foundation, Warsaw 1956, p 91.

Bibliography. CBEL, 1.84.

[10] TAGS IN MATTHEW OF PARIS.

MSS. No MS extant. PRINT: Matthaei Paris Angli Historia Major, 1571 (STC, no 19209).

    a. Battle of the Standard.

Robbins-Cutler, no 4284.8.

Editions. Madden F, Matthaei Parisiensis Historia Anglorum, Rolls Series 44, 1.260.

Royster J F, English Tags in Matthew of Paris, MLR, 4.509.

    b. Dream of Bartholomew.

Brown-Robbins, no 2830.

Editions. Madden, Rolls Series 44, 1.312.

Royster, MLR 4.510.

    c. Song of the Flemish Soldiers.

Brown-Robbins, Robbins-Cutler, no 1252.

Editions. Lambarde W, Dictionarium Angliae, London 1730, p 36.

Madden, Rolls Series 44, 1.381.

Percy T, Reliques of Ancient English Poetry, London 1859, Essay on Ancient Minstrels, note U 3.

Wright T, Essays on the Literature, Popular Superstitions, and History of England, London 1846, 2.260.

Ritson AS, p xxxv.

Royster, MLR 4.509.

Greene E E Carols, p xxxiv.

Wilson R M, More Lost Literature in Old and ME, Leeds SE 5.45.

Wilson EMEL, p 270.

Wilson Lost Lit, p 207; 2nd edn, p 201.

    d. Song of Geoffrey's Soldiers.

Brown-Robbins, Robbins-Cutler, no 1335.

Editions. Round J H, Geoffrey de Mandeville, London 1892, p 213.

Royster MLR 4.509.

Wilson, Leeds SE 5.42.

Wilson EMEL, p 269.

Wilson Lost Lit, p 206; 2nd edn, p 201.

Scattergood PP, p 23.

Literary Criticism. Friedman A B, Medieval Popular Satire in Matthew Paris, MLN 74.673.

[11] HUGH BIGOD'S DEFIANCE OF KING HENRY.

MSS. No MS extant. PRINTS: 1, Harrison W, Description of England, in R Holinshed, The First Volume of the Chronicles of England, 1577 (STC, no 15368); 1587 (STC, no 13569); 2, Camden W, Britannia, 2nd edn 1587 (STC, no 4504), Art Suffolk.

Robbins-Cutler, no 1417.3.

Editions. Percy T, Reliques of Ancient English Poetry, London 1859, Essay on Ancient Minstrels, note U 3.

Furnivall F J, Holinshed's Chronicles, New Shakespere Soc, London 1877–1908, 2.xiv.

General References. Wright PS, p 67; DNB, 5.22.

OED, Cockney, 2 c.

[12] A WELL-ORDERED KINGDOM.

MS. Caius Camb 221, f 47[b] (13 cent).

Brown-Robbins, no 1824.

Editions. James M R, A Descriptive Catalogue, Cambridge 1908, 1.259.

Brown Reg, 1.205.

[13] WALTER OF GUISBOROUGH'S FRAGMENT.

MSS. 1, Bodl 1771 (Digby 170) (14 cent); 2, Bodl 1787 (Digby 186) (1300–50); 3, Camb Univ Dd.2.5 (1350); 4, Lansdowne 239 (1375–1425).

Robbins-Cutler, no 1844.5.

Rothwell, edn, p xii (MSS described).

Editions. Hamilton H C, Chronicon Domini Walteri de Hemingburgh, London 1849, 2.7.

Wilson EMEL, p 269.

Wilson Lost Lit, p 196; 2nd edn, p 190.

Rothwell H, The Chronicle of Walter of Guisborough, Camden Soc 3s, 89.216n.

Robbins R H, A Highly Critical Approach to the ME Lyric, CE 30.75.

[14] A LAMENT AFTER THE DEATH OF ROBERT DE NEVILLE.

MSS. 1, Lansdowne 207, f 434ᵃ (1638 transcript from lost original in Durham Cath); 2, York Cath A.xvi.I.12, f 219ᵇ (1350).

Robbins-Cutler, no 3857.5 (delete Brown-Robbins, no 3894).

Editions. Ellis H and F Douce, A Catalogue of the Lansdowne MSS, London 1819, 2.76 (MS 1).

Sharp C, Bishopric Garland, Durham 1834 (MS 1 type).

Dibdin T F, Bibliographical Antiquarian Tour in the Northern Counties of England and in Scotland, London 1838, 1.283 (MS 1 type).

Raine J, Historiae Dunelmensis Scriptores Tres, Surtees Soc 9.112 (MS 2).

Dodds M H, Northern Minstrels and Folk Drama, Archaeologia Aeliana 4s 1.33 (MS 2).

Wilson R M, More Lost Literature in Old and ME, Leeds SE 5.49 (MS 2).

Wilson Lost Lit, p 187; 2nd edn, p 181 (MS 2).

Dickins and Wilson, p 118 (MS 2).

Stevick R D, One Hundred ME Lyrics, Indianapolis 1964, p 35 (MS 2).

Reiss E, A Critical Approach to the ME Lyric, CE 27.377 (MS 2).

Robbins R H, A Highly Critical Approach to the ME Lyric, CE 30.74 (MSS 1, 2).

Hughes A and G Abraham, New Oxford History of Music, London 1960, 3.144 (MS 2).

Cottle B, [review,] JEGP 63.764 (MS 2).

Reiss E, The Art of the ME Lyric, Athens Ga 1972, p 94 (MS 2 erroneously cited as MS 1).

Sisam Oxf Book MEV, p 552 (MS 2).

Sources and Literary Relations. Robbins, CE 30.75.

Literary Criticism. Reiss, CE 27.378; Robbins, CE 30.75; Reiss, Reply, CE 30.78.

Peck R A, Public Dreams and Private Myths Perspective in Middle English Literature, PMLA 90.461.

General References. Wilson EMEL, p 272.

Wilson Lost Lit, p 186; 2nd edn, p 180.

[15] EVIL TIMES OF EDWARD II.

MS. Camb Univ Gg.1.1, f 489ᵇ (1300–25).

Brown-Robbins, Robbins-Cutler, no 4235.

Meyer, edn, p 283 (MS described).

Editions. Sternberg R, Ueber eine versificirte

me Chronik, EStn 18.11.

Meyer P, Manuscrits français de Cambridge, Rom 15.338.

Zettl E, An Anonymous Short English Metrical Chronicle, EETS 196, London 1934, p 107.

Robbins R H, ME Poems of Protest, Angl 78.193.

Literary Relations. Wright PS, p 241.

General Reference. Robbins, Angl 78.193.

[16] WYNTOUN'S CHRONICLE FRAGMENTS.

MSS. 1, Cotton Nero D.xi (1450–75); 2, Lansdowne 197 (after 1500); 3, Royal 17.D.xx (1440–50); 4, Advocates 19.2.3 (1480); 5, Advocates 19.2.4 (1500–25); 6, Advocates 651 (late 15 cent); 7, St Andrew's Univ T.T.66 (1500–50); 8, Colville (after 1500); 9, Ferguson, Duns, Berwickshire (present location not known); 10, Wemyss (1500–50); 10a, Harley 6909 (late 17 cent transcription; abridged).

Brown-Robbins, Robbins-Cutler, no 399.

Amours, edn, PSTS 50.v; PSTS 63.lxvi (descriptions of MSS 1, 10).

Craigie W A, The St Andrews MS of Wyntoun's Chronicle, Angl 20.363 (description of MS 7).

        a. Times following death of Alexander III.

Robbins-Cutler, no 3923.5.

Editions. Macpherson D, The Orygynale Cronykill of Scotland, London 1795.

Laing D, The Orygynale Cronykil, Edinburgh 1872, 2.266 (MS 3).

Ellis EEP, 1.233.

Eyre-Todd G, Early Scottish Poetry, Glasgow 1891, p 162; Scottish Ballad Poetry, Glasgow 1893, p 17.

Brandl, p 649; CHEL, 2.116.

Murray J A H, The Dialects of the Southern Counties of Scotland, London 1873, p 28.

Amours F J, The Original Chronicle of Andrew of Wyntoun, PSTS 56.145 (MSS 1, 10).

Mackie R L, A Book of Scottish Verse, London 1934; 2nd edn 1967, p 1.

Wilson R M, More Lost Literature in Old and ME, Leeds SE 5.44 (MS 1).

Wilson EMEL, p 271 (MS 1).

Wilson Lost Lit, p 205; 2nd edn, p 200.

MacQueen J and T Scott, Oxford Book of Scottish Verse, Oxford 1966, p 8.

Textual Matters. Amours, PSTS 63.92.

        b. Song Against Black Agnes.

Brown-Robbins, Robbins-Cutler, no 1377.

Editions. Macpherson, Orygynale Cronykill

(MS 3).
Laing, Orygynale Cronykil, 2.436 (MS 3).
Amours, PSTS 57.91 (MSS 1, 10).
Wilson, Leeds SE 5.44 (MS 1).
Wilson Lost Lit, p 213; 2nd edn, p 207 (MS 1).
Textual Matters. Amours, PSTS 63.117.

    c. Marriage of Robert II to Elizabeth Moor.

MSS. 1, Royal 17.D.xx (1440–50); 2, Edinburgh Univ 186 (ca 1450).
Robbins-Cutler, no 3168.6.
Editions. Hearne T, Joannis de Fordun Scotichronicon, Edinburgh 1759, vol 2, Appendix, p 15 (MS 2).
Laing, Orygynale Cronykil, 3.8 (MS 1).

    d. Duke of Orleans' Defense of the Scots.

MSS. 1, Cotton Nero D.xi, f 207^a (1450–75); 2, Royal 17.D.xx, f 276^b (1440–50); 3, Magdalene Camb Pepys 2253, p 105 (1570–90) (64 lines).
Brown-Robbins, Robbins-Cutler, no 2697.
Editions. Laing, Orygynale Cronykil, 3.56 (MS 2).
Amours, PSTS 57.368 (MS 1).
Laing D, Select Remains of the Ancient Popular and Romance Poetry of Scotland, rvsd J Small, Edinburgh 1885, p 196 (MS 3); Early Popular Poetry of Scotland, rvsd W C Hazlitt, London 1895, 1.305 (MS 3).
Craigie W A, The Maitland Folio Manuscript, PSTS ns 7.125 (MS 3).
Textual Matters. Amours, PSTS 63.136.
Craigie, PSTS ns 20.92.

[17] NEVILLE'S CROSS FRAGMENT.

MSS. 1, Bodl 3041 (Bodley 851), f 116^a (1375–1400); 2, Bodl 11566 (Rawl B.214), f 124^b (15 cent); 3, Cotton Titus A.xx, f 82^b (15 cent).
Robbins-Cutler, no 1445.6.
Editions. Wright PPS, 1.48 (MS 3).
Wilson Lost Lit, p 190; 2nd edn, p 180 (MS 3).

[18] TREVISA'S POLYCHRONICON FRAGMENTS.

MSS. 1, Corp Christi Camb 354, ff 1^a-200^b (16 cent); 2, St John's Camb 294, ff 19^a-280^a (ca 1400); 3, Cotton Tib D. vii (ca 1400) (MLA Rotograph no 185); 4, Harley 1900, ff 44^a-310^b (ca 1425); 5, Stowe 65, ff 1^a-201^b (ca 1425); 6, BM Addit 24194, ff 21^a-262^b (ca 1410); 7, Aberdeen Univ 21, ff 1^a-171^b (ca 1400); 8, Chetham Libr 11379, ff 35^a-178^b (ca 1415); 9, Hunterian Mus 83, ff 1^a-148^b (15 cent); 10, Hunterian Mus 367, ff 3^a-209^b (late 14 cent); 11, Liverpool Pub Libr ; 12, Penrose 12, ff 1^a-212^b (ca 1400, present location not known); 13, Huntington Libr 28561 ; 14, Princeton Univ Garrett 151, ff 1^a-212^b (15 cent). PRINTS: 15, Trevisa Discripcion of Britayne, Caxton, 1480 (STC, no 13440a); 16, de Worde, 1498 (STC, no 13440b); 17, Trevisa Prolicronycon, Caxton, 1482 (STC, no 13438); 18, de Worde, 1495 (STC, no 13439); 19, Treveris, 1527 (STC, no 13440).
Edwards A S G, A Sixteenth Century Version of Trevisa's Polychronicon, ELN 11.34n (MSS noted).
Edition. Babington C and J R Lumby, Polychronicon Ranulphi Higden with Trevisa's Translation, Rolls Series 41 (MS 2).
Date. Galbraith V H, Thomas Walsingham and the S Albans Chronicle, EHR 48.18.
Authorship. DNB, 57.212; CHEL, 2.73.
Wilkins H J, Was J Wycliffe a Negligent Pluralist? also J de Trevisa His Life and Work, Westbury and Bristol Records 4, 1915.
Fowler D C, More About John Trevisa, MLQ 32.243.
Literary Criticism. Kingsford EHL, pp 8, 136, 262.
Krapp G P, Rise of English Literary Prose, NY 1916, p 20.
Berdan J M, Early Tudor Poetry, N Y 1920, p 118.
Perry A J, John Trevisa Fourteenth-Century Translator, Manitoba Essays, Toronto 1937.
Bennett OHEL, p 120.
General References: Schofield, p 45; Wells, p 204.
Snell F J, The Age of Chaucer, London 1912, p 53.
Sisam K, Fourteenth-Century Verse and Prose, Oxford 1921, p 145.
Patterson R F, Six Centuries of English Literature, London 1933, 1.60.
Kinkade B L, The English Translation of Higden's Polychronicon, Urbana 1934.
Mackie J D, The Early Tudors, Oxford 1952, p 26.
Fowler D C, New Light on John Trevisa, Trad 18.316.
Bibliography. Wells Manual, pp 797, 1008.
Bennett OHEL, p 299.

    a. In Praise of Rome.

Robbins-Cutler, no 2831.4.
Editions. Babington and Lumby, Roll Series 41, 1.213.
Mätzner E, Ae Sprachproben, Berlin 1867, 2.359.

b. Epitaph for the Giant Pallas.
Robbins-Cutler, no 2736.2.
Editions. Babington and Lumby, Rolls Series 41, 1.225.
Mätzner, Ae Sprachproben, 2.363.
    c. A Riddling Couplet Inscribed on a Pillar.
Robbins-Cutler, no 1426.6.
Editions. Babington and Lumby, Rolls Series 41, 1.237.
Mätzner, Ae Sprachproben, 2.364.
    d. Verses on a Table of Brass.
Robbins-Cutler, no 746.5.
Editions. Babington and Lumby, Rolls Series 41, 1.237.
Mätzner, Ae Sprachproben, 2.367.
    e. Couplet from Ovid.
Robbins-Cutler, no 4189.5.
Editions. Babington and Lumby, Rolls Series 41, 1.239.
Mätzner, Ae Sprachproben, 2.368.
    f. Of the Land of Wales.
Robbins-Cutler, no 2361.5; Ringler BEV, no 52.
Editions. Babington and Lumby, Rolls Series 41, 1.395.
Berdan, Early Tudor Poetry, p 169 (extracts).
    g. Peaceful England.
Robbins-Cutler, no 3218.3.
Edition. Babington and Lumby, Rolls Series 41, 2.39.
Selection. Coulton G G, Social Life in Britain, Cambridge 1918, p 3.
    h. Translation of Lines in Virgil.
Robbins-Cutler, no 399.5.
Edition. Babington and Lumby, Rolls Series 41, 2.39.
    i. Verses on Chester Castle.
Robbins-Cutler, no 1637.6.
Edition. Babington and Lumby, Rolls Series 41, 2.81.
    j. The Chair of a Judge.
MS. Also occurs separately in Lansdowne 210, f 70ᵃ (mid 16 cent).
Brown-Robbins, Robbins-Cutler, no 1811 (correct first line to Sittynge on this see).
Edwards A S G, A Sixteenth-Century Version of Trevisa's Polychronicon, ELN 11.35 (MS described).
Edition. Babington and Lumby, Rolls Series 41, 3.175.
General Reference. Edwards A S G, Trevisa's Polychronicon and The Index of ME Verse A Correction, PBSA 67.442.
    k. The Virtues of the Book.
Robbins-Cutler, no 3917.3; (delete Brown-Robbins, no 3252); Ringler BEV, no 81.

Edition. Dibdin T F, Typographical Antiquities, London 1810, 2.50.

[19] SCOTICHRONICON FRAGMENTS.

MSS. Described by Murray D, The Black Book of Paisley, Paisley 1885.
Edition. Goodall W, Joannis de Fordun Scotichronicon, Edinburgh 1759.
    a. Against Young Men's Counsel.
Robbins-Cutler, no 1824.4.
Edition. Goodall, Scotichronicon, 2.344.
    b. Against Fashionable Ladies.
Robbins-Cutler, no 299.8.
Edition. Goodall, Scotichronicon, 2.374.
    c. "Indisciplinata mulier."
Robbins-Cutler, no 3492.5.
Edition. Goodall, Scotichronicon, 2.376.
Sources and Literary Relations. Brennan M M, Babco and Twelfth-Century Profane Comedy, diss South Carolina 1967, DA 28.4593A.
    d. Don't Trust Women.
Robbins-Cutler, no 3742.5.
Edition. Goodall, Scotichronicon, 2.377.
    e. Four Macaronic Lines.
Brown-Robbins, Robbins-Cutler, no 2787.
Edition. Goodall, Scotichronicon, 2.474.
    f. Warning to Lord Montague.
Not listed Brown-Robbins, Robbins-Cutler.
Edition. Goodall, Scotichronicon, 2.325.
    g. "Now row we merely."
Not listed Brown-Robbins, Robbins-Cutler.
Edition. Goodall, Scotichronicon, 2.362.
Literary Relations. Robbins-Cutler, no 2832.5 (a similar secular tag in several early chronicles, sung by the watermen of the Thames to John Norman, Mayor of London, in 1453: Rowe the bote Norman / Rowe to thy lemman—see Ellis H, The New Chronicles, London 1811, p 628; Kingsford C L, Chronicles of London, Oxford 1905, p 164; Wilson Lost Lit, p 204; 2nd edn, p 199).
    h. "Scotia sit guerra pedibus."
Robbins-Cutler, no 2685.8.
Editions. Goodall, Scotichronicon, 2.232.
Pinkerton J, Ancient Scottish Poems, London 1786, 1.lxxxiv.
Literary Relations. Goodall, edn, 2.427 (Henry IV's prose challenge).
Brown-Robbins, Robbins-Cutler, nos 1181, 2667, 4247 (Ane Ballet of the Nine Nobles).

[20] JOHN CAPGRAVE'S VERSE FRAGMENTS.

MSS. 1, Camb Univ Gg.4.12, ff 1ᵃ–204ᵇ (ca 1450); 2, Corp Christi Camb 167, ff 1ᵃ–196ᵇ

(ca 1500).
Not listed Brown-Robbins, Robbins-Cutler.
Edition. Hingeston F C, The Chronicle of
England by John Capgrave, Rolls Series 1.
  a. "What gile in women is."
Edition. Hingeston, Rolls Series 1.56.
  b. Simon of Norwich.
Editions. Hingeston, Rolls Series 1.158.
Corson L, A Finding List of Political Poems,
1910; rptd NY 1970, p 8.
  c. On Pope Benedict.
Edition. Hingeston, Rolls Series 1.173.
  d. The Great Hurricane.
Editions. Hingeston, Rolls Series 1.221.
Corson, Finding List, p 36.
  e. Bridlington's Prophecy.
Edition. Hingeston, Rolls Series 1.290.
  f. The Emperor's Farewell to Eng-
land.
Editions. Hingeston, Rolls Series 1.290.
Scattergood PP, p 59.

[21] THE FABYAN CHRONICLE VERSES.

MSS. No MS extant. PRINTS: 1, The Chronicles of England, Caxton, 1480 (STC, no
9991); 2, Fabyan R, The New Chronicles of
England and France, Pynson, 1516 (STC, no
10659).
Edition. Ellis H, The New Chronicles, Lon-
don 1811.
Literary Relations and General Criticism.
Kingsford EHL, pp 71, 103, 105, 262, 273,
and passim.
Ker N R, Medieval MSS in British Libraries,
Oxford 1969, 1.86 (for Great Chronicle).
  a. Verses.
Note: Verses are found at the following pages
in Ellis, New Chronicles; such verses not
enumerated in Robbins-Cutler are presumed to be too late for inclusion here.
Items b, c, d below also fall into this class.
Edition. Ellis, New Chronicles, pp 2 (Robbins-
Cutler, no 3955.5), 9, 19, 33, 40, 54, 74, 93,
126, 127, 146, 178, 185, 199, 200, 227, 238,
239, 256, 259, 260 (Robbins-Cutler, no
1820.8), 264, 272, 275, 277, 281, 290, 293,
302, 314, 322 (Robbins-Cutler, no 2541.5),
335, 369, 388, 394, 398 (Robbins-Cutler, no
3918.5), 398 (Robbins-Cutler, no 3558.5 B),
405, 406, 420 (Robbins-Cutler, no 2039.3),
430, 431, 440 (Brown-Robbins, Robbins-
Cutler, no 1934), 488, 489, 569, 574, 590, 600
(Brown-Robbins, Robbins-Cutler, no 1929),
603 (Robbins-Cutler, no 227.5), 603 (Robbins-Cutler, no 3866.3), 604 (Robbins-Cutler,
no 3206.8), 604 (Robbins-Cutler, no 1929.3),

605 (Robbins-Cutler, no 728.5), 606 (Robbins-Cutler, no 578.5), 606 (Robbins-Cutler,
no 3785.8), 620, 628 (Robbins-Cutler, no
2832.5; see [19] (g)), 672 (Robbins-Cutler,
no 3318.7), 674, 682.
  b. Prologue.
Robbins-Cutler, no 3955.5.
Edition. Ellis, New Chronicles, p 2.
  c. King John.
Robbins-Cutler, no 2541.5.
Edition. Ellis, New Chronicles, p 322.
General Reference. Wilson Lost Lit, p 194;
2nd edn, p 189.
  d. Death of Henry III.
Robbins-Cutler, no 1820.8.
Edition. Ellis, New Chronicles, p 260.
  e. Song of the Scots at Berwick.
Robbins-Cutler, no 3918.5.
Editions. Ellis, New Chronicles, p 398.
Wright T, Essays on the Literature, Popular
Superstitions, and History of England, Lon-
don 1846, 2.261.
Wilson R M, More Lost Literature in Old
and ME, Leeds SE 5.43.
Literary Relations. Caxton, Chronicles
(PRINT 1).
Ellis H, John Rastell Pastime of People or
Chronicles [London 1533], London 1811, p
196.
Stevenson J, Chronicon de Lanercost, Edin-
burgh 1839, p 66.
Riley H T, W Rishanger Annales Angliae et
Scotiae, Rolls Series 28, 2.373.
Corson L, A Finding List of Political Poems,
1910, rptd N Y 1970, p 21.
Brie F, The Brut, EETS 131, London 1906,
p 191.
Wilson, Leeds SE 5.43; Wilson Lost Lit, p
208; 2nd edn, p 202.
Legge M D, AN Literature, Oxford 1963, p
252.
Sisam Oxf Book MEV, p 58.
Literary Criticism. Legge, AN Lit, p 353.
General References. Baskerville C R, The
Elizabethan Jig and Related Song Drama,
Chicago 1929, p 40.
  f. Song of the English.
Robbins-Cutler, no 3558.5 B; Ringler BEV,
no 73a.
Editions. Ellis, New Chronicles, p 398.
Ellis, Rastell Chronicles, p 197.
Wright, Essays, 2.261.
Wilson, Leeds SE 5.44.
Scattergood V J, Revision in some ME Politi-
cal Verses, Archiv 211.288.
Literary Relations. Brie, EETS 131.191.
Greene E E Carols, p liii.

General Reference. Weever J, Ancient Funerall Monuments, London 1631, p 458.
    g. Song of the Scots at Bannockburn.
MS. Also appears separately in J Stevens Cox (Beaminster, Dorset) (mid 15 cent).
Robbins-Cutler, no 2039.3; Ringler BEV, no 45a.
Editions. Caxton, Chronicles (PRINT 1).
Ellis, New Chronicles, p 420.
Ellis, Rastell Chronicles, p 204.
Woods M L, Ballads, TRSL ns 6.28.
Literary Repository, no 4 (Sept 1957), p 1 (Cox MS).
Literary Relations and Analogues. Pinkerton J, Ancient Scottish Poems, London 1786, p 494.
Aytoun W E, The Ballads of Scotland, 2nd edn Edinburgh 1859.
Eyre-Todd G, Scottish Ballad Poetry, Glasgow 1893, p 17.
Furnivall F J, Captain Cox, Ballad Soc 7.clvi.
Corson, Finding List, p 28.
Schofield, p 364.
Brie, EETS 131.208.
Baskerville, Elizabethan Jig, p 41.
Greene E E Carols, p liii.
Wilson, Leeds SE 5.44; Wilson Lost Lit, p 213; 2nd edn, p 206.
Literary Repository, no 4, p 1.
Robbins-HP, p 262.
Kendall P M, The Yorkist Age, N Y 1966, p 258 (for Bristol scrap).
Sisam Oxf Book MEV, p 554.
Other Scholarly Problems. Mackenzie W M, The Battle of Bannockburn, Glasgow 1913 (study of medieval warfare).
Mackie J D, The Battle of Bannockburn, SHR 29.207 (military aspects).
General References. Brandl, p 653.
Schofield W H, The Sea-Battle in Chaucer's Legend of Cleopatra, in Anniv Papers by Colleagues and Pupils of George Lyman Kittredge, 1913; rptd N Y 1967, p 149, n 1 (sailors' refrain).
Johnstone H, Letters of Edward Prince of Wales, Roxb Club 194.xxxviii; Edward of Carnarvon, Manchester 1946, pp 130, 131.
Carus-Wilson E M, Medieval Merchant Adventurers, London 1954, p 12.
Wilson Lost Lit, p 213; 2nd edn, pp 178, 207.
    h. Song of the Scots in Derision of the Marriage.
Brown-Robbins, Robbins-Cutler, no 1934; Ringler BEV, no 45.
Edition. Ellis, New Chronicles, p 440.
Literary Relations. Camden W, Remaines of a Greater Worke Concerning Britaine, London 1636, p 194.

Strutt J, Horda Angel-Cynnan, London 1775, 2.83.
Furnivall F J, Thynne's Animadversions, ChS 2s 13.xlvi; EETSES 9, London 1869, p xlvi.
Wright, Essays, 2.261; Wright PPS, 2.251.
Fairholt E W, Satirical Songs and Poems on Costume, PPS 27.55.
Thompson E M, Chronicon Galfridi le Baker de Swynebroke, Oxford 1889, p 212.
Henderson T F, Scottish Vernacular Literature, 3rd edn Edinburgh 1910, p 18.
Corson, Finding List, p 32.
Brie, EETS 131.249.
Wilson, Leeds SE 5.46; Wilson Lost Lit, p 197; 2nd edn, p 191.
Taylor J, The French Brut and the Reign of Edward II, EHR 72.433.
Literary Criticism. Owst G R, Literature and Pulpit in Medieval England, Cambridge 1933, p 407.
Baskerville, Elizabethan Jig, p 41.
Robbins R H, A ME Diatribe against Philip of Burgundy, Neophil 39.141.
Jones G F, Sartorial Symbols in Mediæval Literature, MÆ 25.68.
Robbins-HP, p xxxviii.
    i. The Sotelties at the Coronation Banquet.
Brown-Robbins, Robbins-Cutler, no 1929 (see complete entry under Lydgate).
Edition. Ellis, New Chronicles, p 600.
    j. Pageant Verses: Confound the King's Enemies (=Lydgate, stanza 13).
Robbins-Cutler, no 277.5.
Editions. Ellis, New Chronicles, p 603.
Gattinger E, Die Lyrik Lydgates, Wiener Beitrage 4.24.
Literary Relations. Kingsford C L, Chronicles of London, Oxford 1905, p 97 (Lydgate's Coronation poem on the King's Triumphal Entry into London; Brown-Robbins, Robbins-Cutler, no 3799; edition from MS Cotton Julius B.ii; prose paraphrases occur in MSS Cotton Vitell A.xvi, Egerton 1995, College of Arms Arundel 19).
Rigg A G, A Glastonbury Miscellany of the Fifteenth Century, Oxford 1968, p 49 (other related prose paraphrases for French pageants of 1431).
Scattergood PP, p 82.
General References. Kingsford EHL, pp 87, 88, 92, 105, 232.
    k. Pageant Verses: Nature, Grace, and Fortune (=Lydgate, stanzas 20–22).
Robbins-Cutler, no 3866.3.
Editions. Ellis, New Chronicles, p 603.

Gattinger, Wiener Beitrage 4.25.
    l. Pageant Verses: Roundel (=Lyd-
    gate, stanza 31).
Robbins-Cutler, no 3206.8.
Editions. Ellis, New Chronicles, p 604.
Gattinger, Wiener Beitrage 4.26.
Literary Relations. Robbins, Neophil 39.132
(Rome English Coll MS).
    m. Pageant Verses: Dame Sapience
    (=Lydgate, stanza 38).
Robbins-Cutler, no 1929.3.
Editions. Ellis, New Chronicles, p 604.
Gattinger, Wiener Beitrage 4.26.
    n. Pageant Verses: Cleanness (=Lyd-
    gate, stanzas 42–43).
Robbins-Cutler, no 1924.4.
Editions. Ellis, New Chronicles, p 605.
Gattinger, Wiener Beitrage 4.27.
    o. Pageant Verses: Enok and Eli
    (=Lydgate, stanzas 54–55).
Robbins-Cutler, no 728.5.
Editions. Ellis, New Chronicles, p 605.
Gattinger, Wiener Beitrage 4.28.
    p. Pageant Verses: The Tree of Jesse
    (=Lydgate, stanzas 58–59).
Robbins-Cutler, no 578.5.
Editions. Ellis, New Chronicles, p 606.
Gattinger, Wiener Beitrage 4.28.
    q. Pageant Verses. At the Conduit at
    Paul's Gate (=Lydgate, stanzas 63–
    64).
Robbins-Cutler, no 3785.8.
Editions. Ellis, New Chronicles, p 606.
Gattinger, Wiener Beitrage 4.29.
    r. Against Advisers of Richard III.
Robbins-Cutler, no 3318.7.
Editions. Ellis, New Chronicles, p 672.
Wilson Lost Lit, p 197; 2nd edn, p 194.
Robbins-HP, p xxxviii.
Scattergood PP, p 211.
Literary Relations. Ellis H. Holinshed's
Chronicles, London 1807, 3.422.
Ellis H, Hall's Chronicle, London 1809, p 398.
DNB, 9.284.
Flügel NL, p 269.
Davies J S, English Chronicle, Camden Soc
64.91.
Sheppard J B, Christchurch Letters, Camden
Soc ns 19.96.
Roskell J S, William Catesby Counsellor to
Richard III, JRLB, 42.168.
Sisam Oxf Book MEV, p 567.
Robbins-Cutler, no 4174.5 (Pepys Chronicle).
General References. Ramsay J H, Lancaster
and York 1399–1485, Oxford 1892, 2.528.
Wilson Lost Lit, p 197; 2nd edn, p 194.
Mackie J D, The Earlier Tudors, Oxford
1952, p 53.

Bagley J J, Historical Interpretation, Harmondsworth 1965, p 230.

[22] LATER MISCELLANEOUS INDI-
VIDUAL FRAGMENTS.

    a. Four Lines on Henry Hotspur.
MS. Egerton 3309 (formerly Castle Howard),
p 204 (1440–70).
Brown-Robbins, Robbins-Cutler, no 1185.
Editions. Fowler J T, The Life of St Cuthbert,
Surtees Soc 87.245.
Wilson Lost Lit, p 203; 2nd edn, p 198.
Literary Relations. Robbins-Cutler, no 631.8
(Praise of Percy Family).
    b. Approach of Earl of March on
London.
MS. Egerton 1995, f 206ᵇ (1470–80).
Robbins-Cutler, no 1147.9.
Editions. Gairdner J, Historical Collection of
a Citizen of London in the Fifteenth Cen-
tury, Camden Soc ns 17.215.
Thompson E, The Wars of York and Lan-
caster 1450–1485, London 1892, p 80.
Thorney I D, England under the Yorkists,
London 1920, p 12.
Kingsford C L, Prejudice and Promise in
Fifteenth Century England, Oxford 1925,
p 117.
Wilson Lost Lit, p 204; 2nd edn, p 197.
Scattergood PP, p 189.
    c. Scripture for a London Pageant.
MS. Egerton 1995, f 180ᵃ (1470–80).
Robbins-Cutler, no 1240.5.
Edition. Gairdner, Camden Soc ns 17.174.
    d. Profits from Fishing for Bristol
    Merchants.
MS. Cotton Vesp E.ix, f 100ᵇ (The Noumbre
of Weyghtes) (15 cent).
Not listed Brown-Robbins, Robbins-Cutler.
Editions. Carus-Wilson E M, Medieval Mer-
chant Adventurers, London 1954, p 21.
Scattergood PP, p 331.
    e. The Hawleys of Dartmouth.
MSS. No MS extant. See Historical MSS Com-
mission V, 601–04.
Not listed Brown-Robbins, Robbins-Cutler.
Editions. Green A S, Town Life in the Fif-
teenth Century, London 1894, 2.73.
Scattergood PP, p 331.
General Reference. Kingsford C L, Prejudice
and Promise in Fifteenth Century Eng-
land, Oxford 1925, p 82.
    f. John Barton the Wool Merchant.
MSS. No MS extant. Inscription in window
of Barton's house in Holme juxta Newark.
Not listed Brown-Robbins, Robbins-Cutler.
Editions. Raine J, Testamenta Eboracensia,

Surtees Soc 4.61.
Power E and M M Postan, Studies in English Trade in the Fifteenth Century, London 1933, p 41.
Kendall P M, The Yorkist Age, N Y 1962, p 267.
Scattergood PP p 331.
  g. Warning to John Howard.

MSS. MS not identified.
Robbins-Cutler, no 1654.5.
Editions. Weever J, Ancient Funerall Monuments, London 1631, p 830.
Holinshed's Chronicles, London 1808, 3.444.
Hall's Chronicle, London 1809, p 413.
Wilkinson B, The Later Middle Ages in England 1216–1485, London 1969, p 304.

II. Tags in Langtoft and Mannyng

[23] TAGS IN LANGTOFT AND MANNYNG.

MSS of Langtoft. 1, Bodl 3904 (Fairfax 24) (fragmentary; 1300–25); 2, All Souls Oxf 39 (1325–75); 3, Camb Univ Gg.1.1 (1300–25); 4, Cotton Julius A.v (1325–50); 5, Harley 114 (1350); 6, Royal 20.A.ii (1300–50); 7, Royal 20.A.xi (1325–75); 8, Coll of Arms Arundel 14 (1300–50); 9, Coll of Arms Arundel 61 (1325–50); 10 and 11, Paris Bibl nat fr 12154, ff 1ª–38ᵇ, ff 39ª–108ᵇ (two MSS bound as one; 14 cent).
MSS of Mannyng. 12, Bodl 13679 (Rawl D.913), f 4ª (fragment; lines 13018–13193, lacks tags; 1375–1400); 13, Inner Temple Petyt 511, VII, ff 1ª–195ᵇ (ca 1400); 14, Lambeth 131, ff 1ª–71ᵇ (begins at line 199; ends imperfectly before death of Richard I; some other passages missing; 1425–50).
Brown-Robbins, Robbins-Cutler, no 1995.
Liebermann F, Monumenta Germaniae Historica Scriptorum XXVIII, Hannover 1884, p 649 (MSS described).
Vising J, AN Language and Literature, London 1923, p 74 (MSS described).
Legge M D, A List of Langtoft MSS with Notes on MS Laud Misc 637, MÆ 4.20 (lists 15 MSS, but there are no tags in MSS Laud Misc 637, Douce 120, Cotton Vitell A.x; MS Phillipps 25970 is incomplete; the location of Savile Sale, 1802, Item 28, is not known).
Stepsis R, The MSS of Robert Mannyng of Brunne's Chronicle of England, Manuscripta 13.131 (unaware of Robbins-Cutler; erroneous identification of MS 12).
Editions. Wright PS (MS 3).
Wright T, The Chronicle of Pierre de Langtoft, Rolls Series 47 (MS 4).
Hearne T, Mannyng's Chronicle, Oxford 1725, 1810 (MS 13).
Furnivall F J, The Story of England, Rolls Series 87 (MSS 13, 14).
Zetsche A, Chronik des Robert von Brunne, Angl 9.43 (MS 14).

Kölbing E, Ein Fragment von Robert Mannyng's Chronicle, EStn 17.168 (MS 12, erroneously identified as Bodl 14099, Rawl Misc 1370).
Language. Moore S, S B Meech, H Whitehall, ME Dialect Characteristics and Dialect Boundaries, Michigan Essays and Studies in Comp Lit 13.55.
Authorship. Crosby R, Robert Mannyng of Brunne: A New Biography, PMLA 57.15.
Seaton E, Robert Mannyng of Brunne in Lincoln, MÆ 12.77 (crit G D Willcock, YWES 24.59).
Sources and Literary Relations. A [French] prose account of Edward I's invasion of Scotland occurs in MSS Ashmole 865, Cotton Domit XVIII, Harley 1309, and BM Addit 5758, printed in Nicolas N H, A Narrative of the Progress of King Edward the First in his Invasion of Scotland, Archaeol 21.478, 493 (Harley MS).
Behrenroth W, Das Verhältnis des ersten Teiles der Reimchronik Pierre de Langtofts zu seinen Quellen, diss Göttingen 1912.
Tischbein W H A L, Ueber Verfasser und Quellen des zweiten Teiles der altfranzösischen Reimchronik Peter Langtofts, Göttingen 1913.
B[randl] A, Schottische politische Lyrik um 1295, Arch 111.408 (comparison to tags in other chronicles).
Legge M D, AN Literature, Oxford 1963, p 353.
Other Scholarly Problems. Goddall W, Joannis de Fordun Scotichronicon, Edinburgh 1759, 2.250 (for Baston).
Howlett R, Chronicles of Stephen, Rolls Series 82.iii (for Fantosme).
Thummig M, Über die ae Ubersetzung der Reimchronik Peter Langtofts durch Robert Manning von Brunne, Angl 14.14 (comparison of verses in Langtoft and Mannyng).
Legge M D, A List of Langtoft Manuscripts, MÆ 4.20.

Literary Criticism. Schofield, p 363.
Wilson Lost Lit, p 207; 2nd edn, p 201.
Stepsis R, Pierre de Langtoft's Chronicle, Medievalia et Humanistica 3.51.
General References. Brandl, pp 647, 667.
CHEL, 1.250.
Corson L, A Finding List of Political Poems, 1910; rptd N Y 1970, p 20.
Wells, p 199.
Wilson Lost Lit, p 34; 2nd edn, p 30.

        a. The Battle of Ellendune, A D 825.
Robbins-Cutler, no 718.5.
Editions. Wright, Chronicle, 1.298.
Hearne, Chronicle, 1.14.
Wilson Lost Lit, p 34; 2nd edn, p 30.
Literary Relations. Arnold T, Henrici Archdiaconi Huntendunensis Historia Anglorum, Rolls Series 74.132.

        b. Against Balliol.
Not listed Brown-Robbins, Robbins-Cutler.
Editions. Wright PS, p 275.
Wright, Chronicle, 2.222.
Legge M D, AN Literature, Oxford 1963, p 353.

        c. Against the Scots I.
Robbins-Cutler, no 3799.3.
Editions. Wright PS, p 391.
Wilson Lost Lit, p 207; 2nd edn, p 202.
Corson, Finding List, p 20.

        d. Jeering of the Scots at Edward's Earthworks.
Brown-Robbins, Robbins-Cutler, no 2754.
Editions. Hearne, Chronicle, p 273.
Wright PS, pp 286, 392.
Wright, Chronicle, 2.xi, 234.
Corson, Finding List, p 21.
Flügel NL, p 506.
Wilson Lost Lit, p 208; 2nd edn, p 202.
Legge, AN Lit, p 352.
Sisam Oxf Book MEV, p 58.
Literary Relations. Ellis H, New Chronicles of England and France by Robert Fabyan, London 1811, p 398.
Stevenson J, Chronicon de Lanercost, Edinburgh 1839, p 166.
Hamilton H C, Chronicon Domini Walteri de Hemingburgh, London 1848, 2.99.
Riley H T, Willelmi Rishanger Chronica et Annales, Rolls Series 28, 2.373.
B[randl], Arch 111.408.
Brie T, The Brut, EETS 131, London 1906, p 189.
Legge, AN Lit, p 353.
General References. Brandl, p 649.
Neilson G, Peel Its Meaning and Derivation, Glasgow 1893, p 10.

        e. The Messenger's Speech to Balliol.
Brown-Robbins, Robbins-Cutler, no 2686.

Editions. Hearne, Chronicle, p 276.
Wright PS, pp 292, 393.
Wright, Chronicle, 2.244.
Wilson Lost Lit, p 209; 2nd edn, p 203.
Literary Criticism. Wilson Lost Lit, p 212.

        f. Diatribe at Defeat of Scots at Dunbar.
Brown-Robbins, Robbins-Cutler, no 3352.
Editions. Hearne, Chronicle, p 277.
Wright PS, pp 295, 394.
Wright, Chronicle, 2.248.
Corson Finding List, p 21.
Wilson Lost Lit, p 209; 2nd edn, p 203.
Sisam Oxf Book MEV, p 58.

        g. Against the Scots II.
Brown-Robbins, Robbins-Cutler, no 841.
Editions. Hearne, Chronicle, p 278.
Wright PS, pp 298, 395.
Wright, Chronicle, 2.252.
Corson, Finding List, p 21.
Wilson Lost Lit, p 210; 2nd edn, p 203.
Scattergood V J, Revision in some ME Political Verses, Archiv 211.288.

        h. Admonition to Edward for Vengeance against Balliol.
Brown-Robbins, Robbins-Cutler, no 814.
Editions. Hearne, Chronicle, p 280.
Wright PS, p 300.
Wright, Chronicle, 2.254.
Wilson Lost Lit, p 210; 2nd edn, p 204.

        i. Against the Scots III.
Brown-Robbins, Robbins-Cutler, no 310.
Editions. Hearne, Chronicle, p 281.
Wright PS, pp 305, 396.
Wright, Chronicle, 2.260.
Wilson Lost Lit, p 211; 2nd edn, p 205.

        j. Merlin's Prophecies Fulfilled in Edward.
Robbins-Cutler, no 3291.5.
Editions. Hearne, Chronicle, p 282.
Wright PS, p 308.
Wright, Chronicle, 2.266.

        k. Against the Scots after Dunbar.
Brown-Robbins, Robbins-Cutler, no 848.
Editions. Wright PS, p 318.
Wright, Chronicle, 2.x.
Meyer P, Manuscrits français de Cambridge, Rom 15.314 (lines 4–9 only).
Corson, Finding List, p 22 (lines 1–3 only).
Wilson Lost Lit, p 211; 2nd edn, p 205.

        l. Exultation over the Execution of Wallace.
Brown-Robbins, Robbins-Cutler, no 313.
Editions. Hearne, Chronicle, p 330.
Wright PS, pp 323, 398.
Wright, Chronicle, 2.364.
Corson, Finding List, p 23.
Wilson Lost Lit, p 211; 2nd edn, p 205.

2. POLITICAL POEMS IN MS HARLEY 2253

[24] MS HARLEY 2253: POLITICAL POEMS.

MS. Harley 2253 (ca 1340).
Brook G L, The Harley Lyrics, Manchester 1956, p 1 (MS described).
Robbins-HP, p xxxiii.
Facsimile Edition. Ker N R, Facsimile of British Museum MS Harley 2253, EETS 255, London 1964.
Editions. Wright PS.
Böddeker AED (crit E Kölbing, EStn 2.499; J Schipper, Angl 2.507; T Wissman, LfGRP 1.214).
Brook G L, Collation of the Text of the English Lyrics of MS Harley 2253, Leeds SE 1.28 (corrects errors in Böddeker).
Gibson J A, The Lyrical Poems of the Harley MS 2253, diss London Univ 1914.
Robbins-HP, p 7.
Language. Wright T, Specimens of Lyric Poetry, PPS 4.vi (Leominster).
Onions C T, RES 3.62n (Wright's arguments inconclusive).
Oakden J P, Alliterative Poetry in ME, Manchester 1930, 1.122.
Brook G L, The Original Dialect of the Harley Lyrics, Leeds SE 2.38.
Versification. Schipper 1.215, 217.
Brown A C L, Origin of Stanza-Linking in English Alliterative Verse, RomR 7.274.
Schoeck R J, Alliterative Assonance in Harley MS 2253, ESts 32.68.
Stemmler T, Die engl Liebesgedichte des MS Harley 2253, Bonn 1962, pp 64, 99 (crit R H Robbins, Angl 82.505).
Date. Gibson, edn.
Aspin I S T, AN Political Songs, Anglo-Norman Text Soc 11, Oxford 1953, no 10.
Stemmler T, Zur Datierung des MS Harley 2253, Angl 80.111.
Ker, EETS 255.xxi.
Literary Relations. Aust J, Beiträge zur Geschichte der me Lyrik, Arch 71.253.
Dronke P, Medieval Latin and the Rise of European Love-Lyric, 2nd edn, Oxford 1968, 1.112.
Literary Criticism. Robbins, Angl 82.505.
Hogan M T C, A Critical Study of the ME Lyrics of British Museum MS Harley 2253, diss Notre Dame 1962; DA 23.1350.
General References. Wright T, Essays on the Literature, Popular Superstitions, and History of England, London 1846, 2.262.

Courthope, 1.187.
Legge M D, AN Literature, Oxford 1963, p 354.
Kane G, An Essay on the Middle English Secular Lyric, NM 73.113.
Bestull T H, Satire and Allegory in Wynnere and Wastoure, Lincoln Neb 1974, p 86.
Stanley E G, Richard Hyrd (?) Rote of Resoun Ryht in MS Harley 2253, N&Q ns 22.155.
For further references, see the chapter on Lyrics.

[25] A SONG OF LEWES.

MS. Harley 2253, ff 58ᵇ–59ᵃ (1340).
Brown-Robbins, Robbins-Cutler, no 3155.
Facsimile Edition. Ker N R, Facsimile of British Museum MS Harley 2253, EETS 255, London 1964.
Editions. Percy T. Reliques of Ancient English Poetry, London 1765, 3.3.
Ritson AS, p 11.
Warton T, History of English Poetry, London 1824, 1.47.
Gutch J M, A Lytyll Geste of Robin Hode, London 1847, 1.373.
Wright PS, p 69.
Mätzner E, Ae Sprachproben, Berlin 1867, 1.152.
Böddeker AED, p 98.
Brandl A and O Zippel, Me Sprach- und Literaturproben, Berlin 1917, p 129.
Williams C, New Book of English Verse, N Y 1936, p 24.
Brown ELxiiiC, p 131.
Dickins and Wilson, p 10.
Kaiser R, Alt- und me Anthologie, Berlin 1954, p 364; Medieval English, Berlin 1958, p 349.
Davies R T, Medieval English Lyrics, London 1963, p 55.
Sisam Oxf Book MEV, p 103.
Selection. Sampson G, Cambridge Book of Prose and Verse, Cambridge 1924, p 395.
Modernizations. Benham A R, English Literature from Widsith to Death of Chaucer, New Haven 1918, p 472.
Stone B, Medieval English Verse, Harmondsworth Middlesex 1964, p 112.
Textual Matters. Brown ELxiiiC, p 222.
Versification. Schipper 1.388.
Previté-Orton C W, Political Satire in English Poetry, Cambridge 1910, p 12.

Literary Relations and Analogues. Wright PS, pp 72 (Latin poem on battle), 125 (French poem on Simon), 139 (Latin poem on Simon).

Kingsford C L, Song of Lewes, Oxford 1890 (Latin poem on battle).

Previté-Orton, Political Satire, p 13 (Latin poem).

Aspin I S T, AN Political Songs, Anglo-Norman Text Soc 11, Oxford 1953, p 24.

Beamish T, Battle Royal, London 1965, p 159 (English trans of Latin poem by J Hodlin).

Wilson Lost Lit, p 192; 2nd edn, p 187.

Shields H, The Lament for Simon de Montfort An Unnoticed Text of the French Poem, MÆ 41.202.

Other Scholarly Problems. Lee A, The Bataille of Lewes, Lewes 1847.

Powicke M et al, The Battle of Lewes 1264, Lewes 1964.

General References. Percy, edn, 3.3.

Warton T, History of English Poetry, ed W C Hazlitt, London 1871, 2.46.

Koch H, Richard von Cornwall, Strassburg 1887.

Ten Brink, 1.314; Brandl, p 626; Schofield, p 364; CHEL, 1.368.

Ker W P, English Literature Medieval, London 1912, p 149.

Denholm-Young N, Richard of Cornwall, N Y 1947, p 127.

Wilson EMEL, p 271.

Davies, edn, p 311.

Kinney T L, The Temper of Fourteenth-Century English Verse of Complaint, Annuale Mediaevale 7.85.

Bibliography. Beamish, Battle Royal, p 265 (includes minor military references).

[26] SONG OF THE HUSBANDMAN.

MS. Harley 2253, f 64ᵃ (1340).

Brown-Robbins, no 696; Robbins-Cutler, no 1320.5.

Editions. Wright PS, p 149 (with trans).

Wülcker R P, Ae Lesebuch, Halle 1874, 1.71.

Böddeker AED, p 102.

Brandl A and O Zippel, Me Sprach- und Literaturproben, Berlin 1917, p 134.

Sampson G, Cambridge Book of Prose and Verse, Cambridge 1924, p 396.

Kaiser R, Alt- und me Anthologie, Berlin 1954, p 171; Medieval English, Berlin 1958, p 171.

Robbins-HP, p 7.

Sisam Oxf Book MEV, p 111.

Modernization. Shackford M H, Legends and

Satires from Medieval Literature, Boston 1913, p 131.

Textual Matters. Kölbing E, Kleine Beiträge zur Erklärung und Textkritik me Dichtungen, EStn 17.297 (lines 4, 14, 24, 46).

Holthausen F, Zur Textkritik me Dichtungen, Arch 90.144 (line 46).

Robbins-HP, p 249.

Language. Kölbing E, EStn 2.502.

Oakden J P, Alliterative Poetry in ME, Manchester 1930, 1.105.

Versification. Robson J, Three ME Metrical Romances, Camden Soc 18.xxi.

Schipper, 1.422.

Medary M P, Stanza-Linking in ME Verse, RomR 7.259.

Tatlock J S P, Dante's Terza Rima, PMLA 51.900 (stanza-linking).

Oakden, Alliterative Poetry, 1.206.

Matonis A T E, An Investigation of Celtic Influences on MS Harley 2253, MP 70.91.

Date. Brandl, p 628.

Stemmler T, Die engl Liebesgedichte des MS Harley 2253, Bonn 1962, p 33.

Other Scholarly Problems. Salter E, Piers Plowman and The Simonie, Arch 203.253 (influence on Piers Plowman).

Mann J, Chaucer and Medieval Estates Satire, Cambridge 1973, pp 164, 242.

Literary Criticism. CHEL, 1.370.

Oakden, Alliterative Poetry, 2.10, 13.

Moore A K, The Secular Lyric in ME, Lexington Kentucky 1951, p 85.

Kinney T L, The Temper of Fourteenth-Century English Verse of Complaint, Annuale Mediaevale 7.78.

General References. Wright PS, p 148; Courthope, 1.188; Schofield, p 369.

Tucker S M, Verse Satire in England before the Renaissance, N Y 1908, p 60.

Robbins R H, ME Poems of Protest, Angl 78.194.

Keller J R, The Triumph of Vice, Annuale Mediaevale 10.122.

Scattergood PP, p 351.

White B, Poet and Peasant, in The Reign of Richard II, Essays in Honour of May McKisack, ed F R H Du Boulay and C M Barron, London 1971, p 69.

Elliott T J, ME Complaints Against the Times To Contemn the World or to Reform It, Annuale Mediaevale 14.26.

[27] THE FLEMISH INSURRECTION.

MS. Harley 2253, ff 73ᵇ–74ᵇ (ca 1340).

Brown-Robbins, Robbins-Cutler, no 1894.

Editions. Ritson AS, p 44.
Wright PS, p 187.
Böddeker AED, p 116.
Robbins-HP, p 9.
Selection. Sampson G, Cambridge Book of Prose and Verse, Cambridge 1924, p 399.
Textual Matters. Robbins-HP, p 250.
Versification. Schipper, 1.361.
Sources and Literary Relations. Jahn J, Die me Spielmannsballade von Simon Fraser, BSEP 13.45 (crit W Fischer, AnglB 33.32; H M Flasdieck, EStn 59.295; W Keller, ShJ 58.141; F Liebermann, Arch 144.278; J H Schutt, Museum 30.21).
General References. Warton T, History of English Poetry, ed W C Hazlitt, London 1871, 2.71.
Böddeker AED, p 112; Ten Brink, 1.315; Brandl, p 634; Schofield, p 364.

[28] THE EXECUTION OF SIR SIMON FRASER.

MS. Harley 2253, ff 59ᵇ–61ᵇ (ca 1340).
Brown-Robbins, Robbins-Cutler, no 1889.
Facsimile Edition. Ker N R, Facsimile of British Museum MS Harley 2253, EETS 255, London 1964.
Editions. Pinkerton J, Ancient Scottish Poems, London 1786, p 488.
Ritson AS, p 25.
Wright PS, p 212.
Böddeker AED, p 126.
Brandl A and O Zippel, Me Sprach- und Literaturproben, Berlin 1917, p 129.
Kaiser R, Medieval English, Berlin 1958, p 355.
Robbins-HP, p 14.
Textual Matters. Böddeker AED, p 121.
Robbins-HP, p 252.
Versification. Schipper, 1.219, 389.
Turville-Petre T, Summer Sunday De Tribus Regibus Mortuis and the Awyntyrs off Arthure Three Poems in the Thirteen-Line Stanza, RES ns 25.1.
Authorship. Jahn J, Die me Spielmannsballade von Simon Fraser, BSEP 13 (crit W Fischer, AnglB 33.32; H M Flasdieck, EStn 59.295; W Keller, ShJ 58.141; F Liebermann, Arch 144.278; J H Schutt, Museum 30.21).
Sources and Literary Relations. Wright PS, p 381 (Tprot Scot).
Baskerville C R, Dramatic Aspects of Medieval Folk Festivals in England, SP 17.54, 55 (folk festival matter).

Hinton J, Notes on Walter Map's De Nugis Curialium, SP 20.463 (Tprot Scot).
General References. Ten Brink, 1.315; Brandl, p 634; Schofield, p 364.
Tucker S M, Verse Satire in England before the Renaissance, N Y 1908, p 61.
Ker W P, English Literature Medieval, London 1912, p 150.
Kinney T L, The Temper of Fourteenth-Century English Verse of Complaint, Annuale Mediaevale 7.85.

[29] THE DEATH OF EDWARD I.

MSS. 1, Camb Univ Add 4407, Art 19, fragments a, b, c (lines 6–12, 20–29, 83–88 with 4 new lines; end 14 cent); 2, Harley 2253, ff 73ᵃ–73ᵇ (ca 1340).
Brown-Robbins, Robbins-Cutler, no 205.
Facsimile Edition. Ker N R, Facsimile of British Museum MS Harley 2253, EETS 255, London 1964.
Editions. Percy T, Reliques of Ancient English Poetry, London 1765, 2.7.
Warton T, History of English Poetry, London 1824, 1.106.
Wright PS, p 246.
Böddeker AED, p 140.
Zupitza J, Alt- und me Uebungsbuch, Vienna 1928, p 158.
Segar M G and E Paxton, Some Minor Poems of the Middle Ages, London 1917, p 15.
Aspin I S T, Anglo-Norman Political Songs, Oxford 1953, p 90.
Kaiser R, Alt- und me Anthologie, Berlin 1954, p 367; Medieval English, Berlin 1958, p 357.
Robbins-HP, p 21.
Davies R T, Medieval English Lyrics, London 1963, p 91.
Skeat W W, Elegy on the Death of King Edward I from a New MS, MLR 7.149 (MS 1).
Modernization. Weston J L, The Chief ME Poets, Boston 1914, p 32.
Textual Matters. Holthausen F, Zur alt- und me Denkmälern, Angl 15.189 (lines 141, 146, 177, 181).
Robbins-HP, p 256.
Versification. Schipper, 1.312, 419.
Sources and Literary Relations. Wright PS, p 241 (French original in Camb Univ Gg.1.1, f 489ᵃ).
Böddeker AED, p 453 (French original).
Aspin, edn, p 83 (French original).

Legge M D, AN Literature, Oxford 1963, p 354.
General References. Percy, edn, 2.6.
Warton T, History of English Poetry, ed W C Hazlitt, London 1871, 2.104.
Ten Brink, 1.321; Brandl, p 641; CHEL, 1.370.
Davies, edn, p 318.

[30] SATIRE ON THE CONSISTORY COURTS.

MS. Harley 2253, ff 70ᵇ–71ª (ca 1340).
Brown-Robbins, Robbins-Cutler, no 2287.
Facsimile Edition. Ker N R, Facsimile of British Museum MS Harley 2253, EETS 255, London 1964.
Editions. Wright PS, p 155.
Böddeker AED, p 107.
Robbins-HP, p 24.
Selection. Sampson G, Cambridge Book of Prose and Verse, Cambridge 1924, p 393.
Textual Matters. Kölbing E, Kleine Beiträge zur Erklärung und Textkritik engl Dichter, EStn 3.102 (line 64).
Cook A S, A Problem in ME, MLN 2.70 (line 37).
Robbins-HP, p 258.
Language. Oakden J P, Alliterative Poetry in ME, Manchester 1930, 1.111.
Versification. Schipper, 1.411.
Oakden, Alliterative Poetry, 1.219, 224, 227, 229.
Other Scholarly Problems. Revard C, The Lecher The Legal Eagle and the Papelard Priest ME Confessional Satires in MS Harley 2253 and Elsewhere, His Firm Estate Essays in Honor of Franklin James Eikenberry, ed D E Hayden, Tulsa 1967, p 54.
Literary Criticism. Oakden, Alliterative Poetry, 2.11.
General References. Warton T, History of English Poetry, ed W C Hazlitt, London 1871, 2.45.
Brandl, p 648; Schofield, p 369.
Tucker S M, Verse Satire in England before the Renaissance, N Y 1908, p 56.
Sampson, Cambridge Book, p 393.
Kinney T L, The Temper of Fourteenth-Century English Verse of Complaint, Annuale Mediaevale 7.86.
Mann J, Chaucer and Medieval Estates Satire, Cambridge 1973, p 139.
Elliott T J, ME Complaints Against the Times to Contemn the World or to Reform It, Annuale Mediaevale 14.27.

[31] SATIRE ON THE RETINUES OF THE GREAT.

MS. Harley 2253, ff 124ª–125ᵇ (ca 1340).
Brown-Robbins, Robbins-Cutler, no 2649.
Facsimile Edition. Ker N R, Facsimile of British Museum MS Harley 2253, EETS 255, London 1964.
Editions. Wright PS, p 237.
Wülcker R P, Ae Lesebuch, Halle 1874, 1.73.
Böddeker AED, p 135.
Sampson G, Cambridge Book of Prose and Verse, Cambridge 1924, p 404.
Robbins-HP, p 27.
Textual Matters. Robbins-HP, p 259.
Language. Oakden J P, Alliterative Poetry in ME, Manchester 1930, 1.123.
Versification. Schipper, 1.222, 371.
Oakden, Alliterative Poetry, 1.238.
Literary Criticism. Tucker S M, Verse Satire in England before the Renaissance, N Y 1908, p 62.
Eberhard O, Der Bauernaufstand vom Jahr 1381 in der engl Poesie, AF 51.9.
General References. Brandl, p 628; Schofield, p 369; CHEL, 1.370.
Oakden, Alliterative Poetry, 2.10.
Kinney T L, The Temper of Fourteenth-Century English Verse of Complaint, Annuale Mediaevale 7.85.
Mann J, Chaucer and Medieval Estates Satire, Cambridge 1973, p 138.

[32] THE FOLLIES OF FASHION.

MS. Harley 2253, f 61ᵇ (ca 1340).
Brown-Robbins, Robbins-Cutler, no 1974.
Facsimile Edition. Ker N R, Facsimile of British Museum MS Harley 2253, EETS 255, London 1964.
Editions. Fairholt F W, Satirical Songs and Poems on Costume, PPS 27.40.
Wright PS, p 153.
Böddeker AED, p 106.
Brown ELxiiiC, p 133.
Dickins and Wilson, p 124.
Kaiser R, Medieval English, Berlin 1958, p 480.
Textual Notes. Brown ELxiiiC, p 224.
Dickins and Wilson, p 234.
Language. Oakden J P, Alliterative Poetry in ME, Manchester 1930, 1.110.
Brook G L, MÆ 2.80 (line 29).
Menner R J, Notes on ME Lyrics, MLN 55.244 (lines 29–30).
Malone K, Notes on ME Lyrics, ELH 2.63

(line 29).
Meroney H, Line Notes on the Early English
Lyrics, MLN 62.186 (line 2).
Dickins and Wilson, p 233.
Versification. Schipper, 1.390.
Oakden, Alliterative Poetry, 1.218, 228.
Turville-Petre T, Summer Sunday De Tribus

Regibus Mortuis and the Awntyrs off
Arthure Three Poems in the Thirteen-
Line Stanza, RES ns 25.2.
General References. Oakden, Alliterative Po-
etry, 2.11.
Utley CR, pp 50, 54, 182.
Wilson EMEL, p 271.

3. Political Poems in the Kildare MS

[33] THE KILDARE MS.

MS. Harley 913 (ca 1330).
Pinkerton W, Early Anglo-Irish Poetry, Ul-
ster Journ of Archaeology 8.268 (MS de-
scribed).
Seymour, p 5 (see below under *Literary Crit-
icism*; MS described).
Edition. Kild Ged.
Textual Matters. Holthausen F, Das me
Spottgedicht auf die Bewohner von? Angl
40.358; AnglB 28.254.
Language. Kild Ged, p 20.
Holthausen, Angl 40.358.
Richardson F E, A ME Fragment from the
First Book of Kilkenny, N&Q 207.47 (Liber
Primus Kilkenniensis).
Date. Hardy A, Nicholas Bozon and a ME
Complaint, N&Q 210.90.
Garbáty T J, Studies in the Franciscan The
Land of Cokaygne in the Kildare MS,
Franziskanische Studien 45.193.
Literary Criticism. Seymour St J D, Anglo-
Irish Literature 1200–1582, Cambridge 1929,
p 103 (crit F Delatte, Rev Belge de Phi-
lologie et d'Histoire 9.608; R Flower, RES
8.244; F P Magoun, MLN 46.422; R. Steele,
MLR 25.243).
General References. Croker T C, Popular
Songs of Ireland, ed H Morley, London
1886, p 262.
Fitzmaurice E B and A G Little, Materials
for the History of the Franciscan Province
of Ireland, British Soc of Franciscan Studies 9.121.

[34] THE LAND OF COKAYGNE.

MS. Harley 913, ff 3ᵃ–6ᵇ (ca 1330).
Brown-Robbins, Robbins-Cutler, no 762.
Editions. Hickes G, Thesaurus, Oxford 1705,
1.231.
Ellis EEP, 1.82.
Furnivall EEP, p 156.
Haupt M and A H Hoffman, Altdeutsche

Blätter, Leipzig 1836, 1.396.
Mätzner E, Ae Sprachproben, Berlin 1867,
1.147.
Morley H, Shorter English Poems, N Y 1876,
p 18.
Kild Ged, p 145.
Kuriyagawa F, The Land of Cokaygne, Eigo
Seinen 101, nos 5–8 (with Japanese trans).
Robbins-HP, p 121.
Bennett J A W and G V Smithers, Early ME
Verse and Prose, Oxford 1966, p 136.
Haskell A S, A ME Anthology, N Y 1969, p
375.
Sisam Oxf Book MEV, p 159.
Dunn C W and E T Byrnes, ME Literature,
NY 1973, p 188.
Selections. Warton T, History of English Po-
etry, ed W C Hazlitt, London 1871, 2.54.
Cook A S, A Literary ME Reader, Boston
1915, p 367.
Sampson G, Cambridge Book of Prose and
Verse, Cambridge 1924, p 428.
Kaiser R, Medieval English, Berlin 1958, p
473.
Modernizations. Shackford H M, Legends and
Satires from Medieval Literature, Boston
1913, p 128.
Weston J L, The Chief ME Poets, Boston
1914, p 279.
Seymour St J D, Anglo-Irish Literature 1200–
1582, Cambridge 1929, p 104 (selections).
Adamson M R, A Treasury of ME Verse, N Y
1930, p 21.
Loomis R S and R Willard, Medieval Eng-
lish Verse and Prose, N Y 1948, p 91 (selec-
tions).
Oxford Anthology of English Literature Vol-
ume 1, N Y 1973, p 487.
Textual Matters. Haupt and Hoffman, edn,
1.400.
Holthausen F, Das me Spottgedicht auf die
Bewohner von? Angl 40.358.
Robbins-HP, p 317.
Bennett and Smithers, edn, p 336.
Language. Gröber, 2¹.905.

Authorship. Robbins R H, The Authors of the ME Religious Lyrics, JEGP 39.235.

Garbáty T J, Studies in the Franciscan The Land of Cokaygne in the Kildare MS, Franziskanische Studien 45.146, 149.

Sources and Literary Relations. Histoire littéraire de la France, Paris 1733–1895, 23.149.

Warton T, History of English Poetry, ed W C Hazlitt, London 1871, 2.46.

Barbazan E, Fabliaux et Contes, Paris 1808, 4.175.

Haupt and Hoffman, edn, 1.163, 396 (German and Dutch analogues).

Wright T, St Patrick's Purgatory, London 1844, p 56.

Wright PS, p 137 (French poem in MS Harley 2253).

Meyer K, The Vision of MacConglinne, London 1892, p 86.

Poeschel J, Das Märchen von Schlaraffenlande, BGDSL 5.389, 413.

Cross T P and C H Slover, Ancient Irish Tales, N Y 1936, pp 562, 572 (Irish analogues).

Patch H R, The Other World, Cambridge Mass 1950, pp 7, 134.

Aspin I S T, AN Political Songs, Anglo-Norman Text Soc 11, Oxford 1953, p 130.

Väänänen V, Le fabliau de Cocagne, NM 48.3 (French and Dutch analogues).

Henry P L, The Land of Cokaygne Cultures in Contact in Medieval Ireland, English Studies Today 5.175.

Other Scholarly Problems. Byrne Sister M, The Tradition of the Nun in Medieval England, Washington D C 1932, p 167.

Morton A L, The English Utopia, London 1952, p 1 (folk background).

Howard I, The Folk Origins of The Land of Cokaygne, Humanities Assoc Bull (Canada) 18, pt 2, p 72.

Davidson C, The Sins of the Flesh in the Fourteenth Century ME Land of Cokaygne, Ball State Univ Forum 11, pt 4, p 21.

Hill T D, Parody and Theme in the ME Land of Cokaygne, N&Q ns 22.55.

Literary Criticism. Tucker S M, Verse Satire in England, N Y 1908, p 58.

Kild Ged, p 141; CHEL, 1.365, 477.

Graf A, Miti Leggende e Superstizioni del Medo Evo, Torino 1925, p 169.

Mann J, Chaucer and Medieval Estates Satire, Cambridge 1973, passim.

General References. Strutt J, Horda Angel-Cynnan, London 1775, 3.173.

Wright, St Patrick's Purgatory, p 53.

Morley, 3.354.

Croker T C, Popular Songs of Ireland, London 1839, p 285; ed H Morley, London 1886, p 269.

Ten Brink, 1.259; Brandl, p 629; Schofield, pp 325, 369, 461.

Seymour, Anglo-Irish Lit, p 103.

Kinney T L, The Temper of Fourteenth-Century English Verse of Complaint, Annuale Mediaevale 7.86.

Scattergood PP, p 353.

Mann, Chaucer and Medieval Estates Satire, p 19.

Bibliography. Körting, p 157.

[35] SATIRE ON THE PEOPLE OF KILDARE.

MSS. 1, Harley 913, ff 7ᵃ–8ᵇ (ca 1330); 1a, BM Addit 20091, ff 65ᵃ–73ᵃ (19 cent transcript).

Brown-Robbins, Robbins-Cutler, no 1078.

Editions. Rel Ant, 2.174.

Furnivall EEP, p 152.

Pinkerton W, Early Anglo-Irish Poetry, Ulster Journ of Archaeology 8.270 (with facsimile of f 7ᵃ).

Kild Ged, p 154.

Sisam Oxf Book MEV, p 156.

Selection. Kaiser R, Medieval English, Berlin 1958, p 474.

Modernization. Seymour St J D, Anglo-Irish Literature 1200–1582, Cambridge 1929, p 110.

Textual Matters. Kild Ged, p 150.

Holthausen F, Das me Spottgedicht auf die Bewohner von? Angl 40.362.

Language. Pinkerton, edn, p 270.

Seymour, Anglo-Irish Lit, p 109.

Versification. Schipper, 1.314, 331, 381.

Authorship. Garbáty T J, Studies in the Franciscan The Land of Cokaygne in the Kildare MS, Franziskanische Studien 45.150.

Sources and Literary Relations. Madden F, Ancient Norman-French Poem on the Erection of the Walls of New Ross in Ireland A D 1265, Archaeol 22.307 (commentary), 315 (text).

Croker T C, Popular Songs of Ireland, London 1839, p 291; ed H Morley, London 1886, p 175 (text and English trans).

Seymour, Anglo-Irish Lit, p 22 (Entrenchment of Ross).

General References. Strutt J, Horda Angel-Cynnan, London 1775, 3.48, 59.

Croker, Popular Songs, 1886, p 271.

Brandl, p 627; CHEL, 2.502.

Tucker S M, Verse Satire in England, N Y 1908, p 59.

Schofield, p 373.
Seymour, Anglo-Irish Lit, p 113.
Byrne Sister M, The Tradition of the Nun in Medieval England, Washington D C 1932, p 168.

[36] HOMILY BY FRIAR MICHAEL KILDARE.

MS. Harley 913, ff 9ᵃ–9ᵇ (ca 1330).
Brown-Robbins, no 3234.
Editions. Rel Ant, 2.190.
Kild Ged, p 79.
Modernization. Seymour St J D, Anglo-Irish Literature 1200–1682, Cambridge 1929, p 52.
Textual Matters. Kild Ged, p 79.
General References. Croker T C, Popular Songs of Ireland, London 1839, p 282; ed H Morley, London 1886, p 267.
Brandl, p 640; CHEL, 2.425.
Seymour, Anglo-Irish Lit, p 57.

[37] SONG ON THE TIMES OF EDWARD II.

MS. Harley 913, ff 44ᵇ–47ᵇ, 52ᵃ, 52ᵇ (ca 1330).
Brown-Robbins, Robbins-Cutler, no 4144.
Editions. Wright PS, p 195 (with modern Eng trans).
Kild Ged, p 133.
Brandl A and O Zippel, Me Sprach- und Literaturproben, Berlin 1917, p 182.
Selections. Sampson G, Cambridge Book of Prose and Verse, Cambridge 1924, p 400.
Kaiser R, Medieval English, Berlin 1958, p 374.
Modernization. Seymour St J D, Anglo-Irish Literature 1200–1582, Cambridge 1929, p 77 (selections).
Textual Matters. Kild Ged, p 131.
Literary Relations. Seymour, Anglo-Irish Lit, p 77 (Latin song in Red Book of Ossory).
Greene R L, The Lyrics of The Red Book of Ossory, Oxford 1974, pp 55, 84 (Latin songs).
Colledge E, The Latin Poems of Richard Ledrede O F M, Toronto 1974, pp 90, 142 (Latin songs).
Other Scholarly Problems. Hardy A, Nicholas Bozon and a ME Complaint. N&Q 210.90 (Bozon).
Kinney T L, The Temper of Fourteenth-Century English Verse of Complaint, Annuale Mediaevale 7.87.
General References. Courthope, p 188; Brandl, p 628.
Yunck J A, The Lineage of Lady Meed,

Notre Dame 1963, pp 227, 242.

[38] SIR PERS OF BIRMINGHAM.

MSS. 1, Harley 913, ff 50ᵃ–51ᵇ (ca 1330); 1a, Lansdowne 418, f 88ᵃ (early 17 cent transcript); 1b, BM Addit 20091, ff 50ᵇ–57ᵇ (19 cent transcript).
Brown-Robbins, Robbins-Cutler, no 3126.
Kild Ged, p 7 (description of MS 1a).
Editions. Ritson AS, p 60.
Kild Ged, p 161.
Modernization. Seymour St J D, Anglo-Irish Literature 1200–1582, Cambridge 1929, p 82.
Textual Matters. Kild Ged, p 158.
Date. Croker T C, Popular Songs of Ireland, London 1839, p 283; ed H Morley, London 1886, p 167.
Seymour, Anglo-Irish Lit, p 88.
Other Scholarly Problems. Seymour, Anglo-Irish Lit, p 86 (historical elucidation).
General References. Brandl, p 641.
Seymour, Anglo-Irish Lit, p 81.
Garbáty T J, Studies in the Franciscan The Land of Cokaygne in the Kildare MS, Franziskanische Studien 45.147.

[39] SONG OF NEGO.

MS. Harley 913, f 58ᵇ (ca 1330).
Brown-Robbins, Robbins-Cutler, no 1638.
Editions. Wright PS, p 210.
Kild Ged, p 139.
Textual Matters. Kild Ged, p 139.
General References. Brandl, p 628; Schofield, p 370.
Seymour St J D, Anglo-Irish Literature 1200–1582, Cambridge 1929, p 116.

[40] WARNING TO THE YOUNG MEN OF WATERFORD.

MS. Lansdowne 418, f 94ᵃ (early 17 cent copy of MS Harley 913).
Brown-Robbins, Robbins-Cutler, no 4280.
Kild Ged, p 7 (MS described).
Editions. Kild Ged, p 11.
Seymour St J D, Anglo-Irish Literature 1200–1582, Cambridge 1929, p 88.
Wilson R M, More Lost Literature in Old and ME, Leeds SE 5.46.
Wilson Lost Lit, p 205; 2nd edn, p 199.
General References. Croker T C, Popular Songs of Ireland, London 1839, p 286; ed H Morley, London 1886, p 270.

Seymour, edn, pp 7, 88.

[41] ON THE DECAY OF THE ENGLISH
LANGUAGE IN IRELAND.

MS. Lambeth Carew 617, p 35 (ca 1350).
Brown-Robbins, no 573.
Seymour, edn, p 142 (MS described).
Editions. Calendar of the Carew Manuscripts,
5.421 (Albus Liber).
Davys J, A Discovery of the True Causes Why
Ireland Was Never Entirely Subjugated,
1612; ed H Morley, Carisbrook Libr 1,
London 1890, p 213.
Seymour St J D, Anglo-Irish Literature 1200–
1582, Cambridge 1929, p 99.
General Reference. Seymour, edn, p 99.

[42] THE MAYOR OF WATERFORD'S
METRICAL EPISTLE.

MS. Dublin State Paper Office (MS not fur-
ther identified; ca 1600).
Robbins-Cutler, no 2571.5.
Croker, edn, 1886, p 293 (MS described).
Edition. Croker T C, Popular Songs of Ire-
land, London 1839, p 318; ed H Morley,
London 1886, p 310.
Literary Relations. Croker, edn, 1839, p 312;
1886, p 294.
General References. Croker, edn, 1839, p 310;
1886, p 294.
Seymour St J D, Anglo-Irish Literature 1200–
1582, Cambridge 1929, p 88.

4. War Poems by Laurence Minot

[43] LAURENCE MINOT.

Biography. Moore S, Lawrence Minot, MLN
35.78.
Hall, edn, p x.
MS. Cotton Galba E.ix (1440–50).
Hall, edn, p vii (MS described).
Hulme W H, The Harrowing of Hell, EETSES
100, London 1967, p xxiv (MS described).
Editions. Ritson J, Poems of Minot, London
1795, 1825.
Wright PPS, 1.58.
Scholle W, Laurence Minots Lieder, QF 52
(crit A Brandl, AfDA 11.35; E Einenkel,
Angl 7.111; F Rosenthal, EStn 8.162; G
Sarrazin, LfGRP 6.108).
Hall J, The Poems of Laurence Minot, 3rd
edn, Oxford 1914.
Stedman D C, The War Ballads of Laurence
Minot, Dublin 1917 (crit J D J, MLR
13.511).
Textual Matters. Bierbaum F J, Ueber
Laurence Minot und seine Lieder, Halle
1876.
Language. Bierbaum, Ueber Laurence Minot.
Scholle, QF 52.x.
Hall, edn, p xiv.
Oakden J P, Alliterative Poetry in ME, Man-
chester 1930, 1.106.
Versification. Schipper, 1.218, 264, 385.
Körting, p 164.
Hall, edn, p xviii.
Medary M P, Stanza-Linking in ME Verse,
RomR 7.261.

Tatlock J S P, Dante's Terza Rima, PMLA
51.900 n (for stanza linking).
Oakden, Alliterative Poetry, 1.107, 239; 2.343.
Authorship. Hall, edn, p x.
Ker W P, English Literature Medieval, Lon-
don 1912, p 151.
Literary Criticism. Marsh G P, Origin and
History of the English Language, N Y 1866,
pp 277, 283.
Dangel M, Laurence Minots Gedichte (Pro-
gramm des städtischen Realgymnasiums),
Königsberg 1888.
CHEL, 2.398; 3.274.
Reed E B, English Lyrical Poetry, New Ha-
ven 1912, p 68.
Snell F J, The Age of Chaucer, London 1912,
p 6.
Baldwin C S, An Introduction to English
Medieval Literature, N Y 1914, p 152.
Moore A K, Secular Lyrics in ME, Lexington
Ky 1951, p 94.
General References. Ritson, edn, p v.
Wright PPS, 1.xxii; Ten Brink, 1.403; Brandl,
p 648; Morley, 4.258; Courthope, p 196;
Schofield, p 365; CHEL, 1.290, 335, 352,
356, 476; 2.422.
Ker, English Lit Medieval, London 1912, p
151.
Bibliography. Körting, p 163; CBEL, 1.270.
New CBEL, 1.710.

[44] THE BATTLE OF HALIDON HILL I.

MS. Cotton Galba E.ix, f 52ᵃ (1440–50).
Brown-Robbins, Robbins-Cutler, no 3801.

Editions. Ritson J, Poems of Minot, London 1795, 1825, p 1.

Wright PPS, 1.58.

Mätzner E, Ae Sprachproben, Berlin 1867, 1.321.

Scholle W, Laurence Minots Lieder, QF 52.1 (crit A Brandl, AfDA 11.35; E Einenkel, Angl 7.111; F Rosenthal, EStn 8.162; G Sarrazin, LfGRP 6.108).

Kluge F, Me Lesebuch, Halle 1904, p 109.

Hall J, The Poems of Laurence Minot, 3rd edn, Oxford 1914, p 1.

Emerson O F, A ME Reader, N Y 1915, p 157.

Stedman D C, The War Ballads of Laurence Minot, Dublin 1917, p 1 (crit J D J, MLR 13.511).

Kaiser R, Alt- und me Anthologie, Berlin 1954, p 369; Medieval English, Berlin 1958, p 380.

Dunn C W and E T Byrnes, ME Literature, N Y 1973, p 231.

Modernization. Pancoast H S, English Prose and Verse, N Y 1915, p 36.

Textual Matters. Ritson, edn, p 55.

Scholle, QF 52.41.

Hall, edn, p 37.

Emerson, edn, p 291.

Stedman, edn, p 40.

Other Scholarly Problems. Snyder E D, The Wild Irish, MP 17.712 (lines 59–60).

[45] BANNOCKBURN AVENGED.

MS. Cotton Galba E.ix, f 52[b] (1440–50).

Brown-Robbins, Robbins-Cutler, no 3080.

Editions. Ritson J, Poems of Minot, London 1795, 1825, p 6.

Warton T, History of English Poetry, ed W C Hazlitt, London 1871, 3.122.

Wright PPS, 1.61.

Mätzner E, Ae Sprachproben, Berlin 1867, 1.323.

Wülcker R P, Ae Lesebuch, Halle 1874, 1.77.

Flügel NL, p 96.

Scholle W, Laurence Minots Lieder, QF 52.5 (crit A Brandl, AfDA 11.35; E Einenkel, Angl 7.111; F Rosenthal, EStn 8.162; G Sarrazin, LfGRP 6.108).

Kluge F, Me Lesebuch, Halle 1904, p 110.

Zupitza J, Alt- und me Uebungsbuch, Vienna 1928, p 164.

Hall J, The Poems of Laurence Minot, 3rd edn, Oxford 1914, p 4.

Emerson O F, A ME Reader, N Y 1915, p 160.

Stedman D C, The War Ballads of Laurence Minot, Dublin 1917, p 5 (crit J D J, MLR 13.511).

Sisam K, Fourteenth Century Verse and Prose, Oxford 1921, p 152.

Kaiser R, Alt- und me Anthologie, Berlin 1953, p 369; Medieval English, Berlin 1958, p 381.

Robbins-HP, p 30.

Sisam Oxf Book MEV, p 170.

Modernization. Stone B, Medieval English Verse, Harmondsworth Middlesex 1964, p 113.

Textual Matters. Ritson, edn, p 67.

Scholle, QF 52.42.

Hall, edn, p 45.

Emerson, edn, p 292.

Robbins-HP, p 261.

Versification. Schipper, 1.375.

Other Scholarly Problems. Snyder E D, The Wild Irish, MP 17.712 (line 6).

Literary Criticism. Robbins-HP, p xvii.

General Reference. Benham A R, English Literature from Widsith to the Death of Chaucer, New Haven 1916, p 179.

[46] THE EXPEDITION TO BRABANT.

MS. Cotton Galba E.ix, ff 52[b]–53[a] (1440–50).

Brown-Robbins, Robbins-Cutler, no 987.

Editions. Ritson J, Poems of Minot, London 1795, 1825, p 8.

Evans T, Old Ballads, ed R H Evans, London 1810, 2.296.

Wright PPS, 1.63.

Marsh G P, Origin and History of the English Language, N Y 1866, p 278.

Mätzner E, Ae Sprachproben, Berlin 1867, 1.324.

Scholle W, Laurence Minots Lieder, QF 52.7 (crit A Brandl, AfDA 11.35; E Einenkel, Angl 7.111; F Rosenthal, EStn 8.162; G Sarrazin, LfGRP 6.108).

Morris Spec, 2.315.

Hall J, The Poems of Laurence Minot, 3rd edn, Oxford 1914, p 6.

Emerson O F, A ME Reader, N Y 1915, p 161.

Stedman D C, The War Ballads of Laurence Minot, Dublin 1917, p 7 (crit J D J, MLR 13.511).

Textual Matters. Ritson, edn, p 68.

Scholle, QF 52.42.

Morris Spec, 2.315

Hall, edn, p 50.

Emerson, edn, p 293.

General Reference. Snell F J, Age of Chaucer, London 1912, p 7 (corrected by Emerson, edn, p 293).

[47] THE FIRST INVASION OF FRANCE.

MS. Cotton Galba E.ix, ff 53ᵃ–53ᵇ (1440–50).
Brown-Robbins, Robbins-Cutler, no 709.
Editions. Warton T, History of English Poetry, ed W C Hazlitt, London 1871, 3.10.
Ritson J, Poems of Minot, London 1795, 1825, p 13.
Wright PPS, 1.66.
Mätzner E, Ae Sprachproben, Berlin 1867, 1.326.
FitzGibbon H M, Early English Poetry, London 1887, p 9.
Morris Spec, 2.131.
Hall J, The Poems of Laurence Minot, 3rd edn, Oxford 1914, p 10.
Cook A S, ·A Literary ME Reader, Boston 1915, p 422.
Stedman D C, The War Ballads of Laurence Minot, Dublin 1917, p 12 (crit J D J, MLR 13.511).
Sampson G, The Cambridge Book of Prose and Verse, Cambridge 1924, p 363.
Mossé F, A Handbook of ME, Baltimore 1952, p 234.
Textual Matters. Ritson, edn, p 77.
Scholle, QF 52.43.
Morris Spec, 2.316.
Hall, edn, p 55.
Mossé, edn, p 378.

[48] THE SEA FIGHT AT SLUYS.

MS. Cotton Galba E.ix, ff 53ᵇ–54ᵃ (1440–50).
Brown-Robbins, Robbins-Cutler, no 2189.
Editions. Ritson J, Poems of Minot, London 1795, 1825, p 18.
Wright PPS, 1.70.
Scholle W, Laurence Minots Lieder, QF 52.16 (crit A Brandl, AfDA 11.35; E Einenkel, Angl 7.111; F Rosenthal, EStn 8.162; G Sarrazin, LfGRP 6.108).
Hall J, The Poems of Laurence Minot, 3rd edn, Oxford 1914, p 14.
Stedman D C, The War Ballads of Laurence Minot, Dublin 1917, p 16 (crit J D J, MLR 13.511).
Textual Matters. Ritson, edn, p 87.
Scholle, QF 52.43.
Hall, edn, p 60.
Stedman, edn, p 43.
Other Scholarly Problems. Parker R E, Laurence Minot's Tribute to John Badding, PMLA 37.360 (identification of John Badding, line 59).
General Reference. Morley, 4.260.

[49] THE SIEGE OF TOURNAY.

MS. Cotton Galba E.ix, ff 54ᵃ–54ᵇ (1440–50).
Brown-Robbins, no 3796.
Editions. Ritson J, Poems of Minot, London 1795, 1825, p 22.
Wright PPS, 1.72.
Scholle W, Laurence Minots Lieder, QF 52.20 (crit A Brandl, AfDA 11.35; E Einenkel, Angl 7.111; F Rosenthal, EStn 8.162; G Sarrazin, LfGRP 6.108).
Hall J, The Poems of Laurence Minot, 3rd edn, Oxford 1914, p 17.
Stedman D C, The War Ballads of Laurence Minot, Dublin 1917, p 20 (crit J D J, MLR 13.511).
Textual Matters. Ritson, edn, p 99.
Scholle, QF 52.44.
Hall, edn, p 67.
Stedman, edn, p 45.
Versification. Schipper, 1.348, 386.

[50] THE BATTLE OF CRECY.

MS. Cotton Galba E.ix, ff 54ᵇ–55ᵇ (1440–50).
Brown-Robbins, Robbins-Cutler, no 2149.
Editions. Ritson J, Poems of Minot, London 1795, 1825, p 26.
Wright PPS, 1.75.
Scholle W, Laurence Minots Lieder, QF 52.23 (crit A Brandl, AfDA 11.35; E Einenkel, Angl 7.111; F Rosenthal, EStn 8.162; G Sarrazin, LfGRP 6.108).
Morris Spec, 2.134.
Hall J, The Poems of Laurence Minot, 3rd edn, Oxford 1914, p 21.
Stedman D C, The War Ballads of Laurence Minot, Dublin 1917, p 23 (crit J D J, MLR 13.511).
Brandl A and O Zippel, Me Sprach- und Literaturproben, Berlin 1917, p 135.
Kaiser R, Medieval English, Berlin 1958, p 381.
Selection. Warton T, History of English Poetry, ed W C Hazlitt, London 1871, 3.12.
Textual Matters, Ritson, edn, p 100.
Scholle, QF 52.44.
Morris Spec, 2.317.
Hall, edn, p 74.
Stedman, edn, p 46.

[51] THE SIEGE OF CALAIS.

MS. Cotton Galba E.ix, ff 55ᵇ–56ᵃ (1440–50).
Brown-Robbins, Robbins-Cutler, no 585.
Editions. Ritson J, Poems of Minot, London 1795, 1825, p 34.

Wright PPS, 1.80.
Marsh G P, Origin and History of the English Language, N Y 1866, p 281.
Scholle W, Laurence Minots Lieder, QF 52.30 (crit A Brandl, AfDA 11.35; E Einenkel, Angl 7.111; F Rosenthal, EStn 8.162; G Sarrazin, LfGRP 6.108).
Hall J, The Poems of Laurence Minot, 3rd edn, Oxford 1914, p 27.
Morley H, Shorter English Poems, N Y 1876, p 30.
Stedman D C, The War Ballads of Laurence Minot, Dublin 1917, p 29 (crit J D J, MLR 13.511).
Sisam K, Fourteenth Century Verse and Prose, Oxford 1921, p 153.
Robbins-HP, p 34.
Selection. Kaiser R, Medieval English, Berlin 1958, p 382.
Textual Matters. Ritson, edn, p 127.
Scholle, QF 52.45.
Hall, edn, p 83.
Stedman, edn, p 46.
Robbins-HP, p 266.
General References. Morley, 4.259.
Baldwin C S, Three Medieval Centuries of Literature in England, Boston 1932, p 150.

[52] THE BATTLE OF NEVILLE'S CROSS.

MS. Cotton Galba E.ix, ff 56ᵃ–56ᵇ (1440–50).
Brown-Robbins, Robbins-Cutler, no 3117.
Editions. Ritson J, Poems of Minot, London 1795, 1825, p 39.
Wright PPS, 1.83.
Wülcker R P, Ae Lesebuch, Halle 1874, 1.78.
Scholle W, Laurence Minots Lieder, QF 52.34 (crit A Brandl, AfDA 11.35; E Einenkel, Angl 7.111; F Rosenthal, EStn 8.162; G Sarrazin, LfGRP 6.108).
Hall J, The Poems of Laurence Minot, 3rd edn, Oxford 1914, p 30.
Morley H, Shorter English Poems, N Y 1876, p 32.
Stedman D C, The War Ballads of Laurence Minot, Dublin 1917, p 33 (crit J D J, MLR 13.511).
Kaiser R, Medieval English, Berlin 1958, p 383.
Robbins-HP, p 31.
Selections. Warton T, History of English Poetry, ed W C Hazlitt, London 1871, 2.14.
Ashwell W J, Edward III and His Wars, London 1887, p 112.
Textual Matters. Ritson, edn, p 145.
Scholle, QF 52.45.

Hall, edn, p 87.
Robbins-HP, p 263.
Sources and Literary Relations. Wright PPS, 1.40, 52, 83 (Latin poems).
White R, The Battle of Neville's Cross, Archaeologia Aeliana ns 1.271 (comparison with chronicles), 297 (Latin poems from MS Cotton Titus A.xx, ff 82ᵇ–86ᵃ).
PFMS, 2.191 (Durham Field).
Hall, edn, p 112 (French and Latin poems).
Sidgwick F, Ballads and Poems Illustrating English History, Cambridge 1907, p 22 (Durham Field).
Other Scholarly Problems. Longstaffe W H D, The Banner and Cross of Saint Cuthbert, Archaeologia Aeliana ns 2.51.
Burne A H, The Battle of Neville's Cross, DUJ 41.100 (site of battle).
General Reference. Morley, 4.259.

[53] THE DEFEAT OF THE SPANIARDS.

MS. Cotton Galba E.ix, ff 56ᵇ–57ᵃ (1440–50).
Brown-Robbins, Robbins-Cutler, no 1401.
Editions. Ritson J, Poems of Minot, London 1795, 1825, p 45.
Wright PPS, 1.87.
Scholle W, Laurence Minots Lieder, QF 52.37 (crit A Brandl, AfDA 11.35; E Einenkel, Angl 7.111; F Rosenthal, EStn 8.162; G Sarrazin, LfGRP 6.108).
Hall J, The Poems of Laurence Minot, 3rd edn, Oxford 1914, p 33.
Morley H, Shorter English Poems, N Y 1876, p 35.
Stedman D C, The War Ballads of Laurence Minot, Dublin 1917, p 36 (crit J D J, MLR 13.511).
Williams C, New Book of English Verse, N Y 1936, p 28.
Textual Matters. Ritson, edn, p 157.
Scholle, QF 52.45.
Hall, edn, p 92.
Stedman, edn, p 48.
General Reference. Warton T, History of English Poetry, ed W C Hazlitt, London 1824, 3.14.

[54] THE TAKING OF GUINES.

MS. Cotton Galba E.ix, ff 57ᵃ–57ᵇ (1440–50).
Brown-Robbins, Robbins-Cutler, no 3899.
Editions. Ritson J, Poems of Minot, London 1795, 1825, p 48.
Wright PPS, 1.89.
Scholle W, Laurence Minots Lieder, QF 52.39 (crit A Brandl, AfDA 11.35; E Einenkel,

Angl 7.111; F Rosenthal, EStn 8.162; G
Sarrazin, LfGRP 6.108).
Hall J, The Poems of Laurence Minot, 3rd
edn, Oxford 1914, p 34.
Morley H, Shorter English Poems, N Y 1876,
p 36.
Stedman D C, The War Ballads of Laurence
Minot, Dublin 1917, p 39 (crit J D J, MLR
13.511).
Robbins-HP, p 37.
Textual Matters. Ritson, edn p 159.
Scholle, QF 52.45.
Hall, edn, p 96.
Robbins-HP, p 267.
General Reference. Morley, 4.261.

[55] DURHAM FIELD.

MS. BM Addit 27879, pp 245–249 (ca 1650).

Robbins-Cutler, no 1992.5.
Editions. PFMS, 2.191.
Child F J, The English and Scottish Popular
Ballads, Boston 1889, 3.284 (no 159).
Modernization. Sidgwick F, Ballads and
Poems Illustrating English History, Cam-
bridge 1907, p 22.
Literary Relations. Bellum Dunelmense
(Latin poem in Harley 4843).
Other Scholarly Problems. McMillan D J,
Folk Projection and Historic Truth, AN&Q
2.190.
Literary Criticism. McMillan D J, Some Pop-
ular Views of Four Medieval Ballads,
Southern Folklore Quart 30.179.
General References. PFMS, 2.190.
Child, edn, 3.282.
Chambers OHEL, pp 156, 163.

5. POLITICAL POEMS IN MS DIGBY 102

[56] MS DIGBY 102.

MS. Bodl 1703 (Digby 102) (1400–25).
Kail, edn, p vii (MS described).
Edition. Kail J, Twenty-six Political and
Other Poems, EETS 124, London 1904
(complete edn).
Selections. Robbins-HP, pp 39, 45, 50 ([58],
[62], [65]).
Language. Kail, EETS 124.ix.
Date. Kail, EETS 124.x.
Authorship. Kail, EETS 124.vii.
Literary Relations. Mohl R, The Three Es-
tates in Medieval and Renaissance Litera-
ture, N Y 1933, p 109.
General References. Kingsford EHL, p 233.
Mohl, Three Estates, p 108.
Chambers OHEL, p 117.
Pecheux M C, Aspects of the Treatment of
Death in ME Poetry, Washington D C
1951, pp 38, 42.
Scattergood PP, pp 116, 122, 128, 225, 229,
232, 312, 356.

[57] LOVE GOD AND REDRESS ABUSES.

MS. Bodl 1703 (Digby 102), ff 98ª–98ᵇ (1400–
25).
Brown-Robbins, no 697.
Edition. Kail J, Twenty-six Political and
Other Poems, EETS 124, London 1904, p 1.
General Reference. Kail, EETS 124.x.

[58] WHAT PROFITS A KINGDOM.

MS. Bodl 1703 (Digby 102), ff 100ª–101ᵇ
(1400–25).
Brown-Robbins, Robbins-Cutler, no 817.
Editions. Kail J, Twenty-six Political and
Other Poems, EETS 124, London 1904, p 9.
Robbins-HP, p 39.
Textual Matters. Robbins-HP, p 268.
Date. Kail, EETS 124.xii.
Literary Relations. Robbins-HP, p 268.

[59] DO EVIL AND BE FEARED—A
SATIRE.

MS. Bodl 1703 (Digby 102), ff 104ª–104ᵇ
(1400–25).
Brown-Robbins, no 1845.
Edition. Kail J, Twenty-six Political and
Other Poems, EETS 124, London 1904, p
25.

[60] EVILS IN THE CHURCH.

MS. Bodl 1703 (Digby 102), ff 105ᵇ–106ª
(1400–25).
Brown-Robbins, no 2054.
Edition. Kail J, Twenty-six Political and
Other Poems, EETS 124, London 1904, p
31.
Date. Kail, EETS 124.xiv.

[61] EVILS IN THE STATE.

MS. Bodl 1703 (Digby 102), ff 106ᵇ–108ᵃ (1400–25).
Brown-Robbins, no 3608.
Other Poems, EETS 124, London 1904, p
Edition. Kail J, Twenty-six Political and Other Poems, EETS 124, London 1904, p 34.
Date. Kail, EETS 124.xiv.
Robbins-HP, p xxiv.

[62] GOD SAVE KING HENRY V.

MS. Bodl 1703 (Digby 102), ff 110ᵇ–111ᵇ (1400–25).
Brown-Robbins, Robbins-Cutler, no 910.
Editions. Kail J, Twenty-six Political and 50.
Robbins-HP, p 45.
Textual Matters. Robbins-HP, p 270.
Date. Kail, EETS 124.xvi.
General Reference. Rowse A L, Bosworth Field, Garden City N Y 1966, p 63.

[63] MAINTAIN LAW AND HENRY'S FOREIGN POLICY.

MS. Bodl 1703 (Digby 102), ff 111ᵇ–113ᵃ (1400–25).
Brown-Robbins, Robbins-Cutler, no 3924.
Edition. Kail J, Twenty-six Political and Other Poems, EETS 124, London 1904, p

55.
Date. Kail, EETS 124.xvii.
General Reference. Kail, EETS 124.xviii.

[64] THE STATE COMPARED TO MAN'S BODY.

MS. Bodl 1703 (Digby 102), ff 114ᵃ–115ᵃ (1400–25).
Brown-Robbins, no 4070.
Edition. Kail J, Twenty-six Political and Other Poems, EETS 124, London 1904, p 64.
General References. Yunck J A, The Lineage of Lady Meed, Notre Dame 1963, p 272.
Scattergood PP, p 268.

[65] THE FOLLIES OF THE DUKE OF BURGUNDY.

MS. Bodl 1703 (Digby 102), ff 115ᵃ–116ᵃ (1400–25).
Brown-Robbins, Robbins-Cutler, no 1939.
Editions. Furnivall F J, Three ME Poems, EStn, 23.438.
Kail J, Twenty-six Political and Other Poems, EETS 124, London 1904, p 69.
Robbins-HP, p 50.
Textual Matters. Robbins-HP, p 272.
Date. Kail, EETS 124.xxi.
Literary Relations. Robbins-HP, p 272.
General Reference. Scattergood PP, p 69.

6. HISTORICAL BALLADS AND POEMS IN CHRONICLES

[66] THE BATTLE OF HALIDON HILL II.

MSS. 1, Harley 4690, ff 82ᵇ–83ᵃ (1475–1500); 2, Coll of Arms Arundel 58, f 334ᵇ (1450–1500).
Brown-Robbins, Robbins-Cutler, no 3539.
Editions. Hearne T, Robert of Gloucester's Chronicle, Oxford 1724; London 1810, l.lxxxiii (MS 1).
Ritson J, Poems of Minot, London 1795, 1825, p 62 (MS 1).
Hall J, The Poems of Laurence Minot, 3rd edn, Oxford 1914, p 101 (MS 1).
Brie F, The Brut, EETS 131, London 1906, p 287 (MSS 1, 2).
Modernization. Adamson M R, A Treasury of ME Verse, N Y 1930, p 43.
Literary Relations. Starke F J, Populäre engl Chroniken des 15 Jahrhunderts, Berlin

1915, p 10.
General References. Brie F W D, Geschichte und Quellen der me Prosachronik, Marburg 1905, pp 74, 75.
Schofield, p 367.

[67] THE BATTLE OF OTTERBURN.

MSS. 1, Cotton Cleop c.iv, ff 64ᵃ–68ᵇ (added ca 1550); 2, Harley 293, ff 52ᵃ–54ᵇ (ca 1550; 57 stanzas only).
Kingsford C L, Chronicles of London, Oxford 1905, p ix (description of MS 1).
Editions. Percy T, Reliques of Ancient English Poetry, London 1765, 1.21 (MS 2); London 1775, 1.22 (MS 1); London 1847, p 5 (MS 1).
Ritson AS, p 83 (MS 1).
Ritson J, Northern Garlands (Pt 3: Northumberland Garland), London 1810, p 3 (MS 1).

Gummere F B, Old English Ballads, Boston 1888, p 94 (MS 1).

Child F J, The English and Scottish Popular Ballads, Boston 1889, 3.295 (no 161; MS 1).

Flügel NL, p 191 (MS 1).

Arber E, The Dunbar Anthology, London 1901, p 50 (MS 1).

Sargent H C and G L Kittredge, English and Scottish Popular Ballads, Boston 1904, p 387 (MS 1).

Sidgwick F, Ballads, London 1925, p 192 (MS 1).

Mackie R L, A Book of Scottish Verse, London 1934; 2nd edn 1971, p 119 (MS 1).

Leach MacE, Ballad Book, N Y 1955, p 436 (MS 1).

Robbins-HP, p 64 (MS 1).

Selection. MacQueen J and T Scott, Oxford Book of Scottish Verse, Oxford 1966, p 264.

Textual Matters. Robbins-HP, p 282.

Versification. Schipper, 1.350; 2.166, 176, 520.

Sources and Literary Relations. Child, edn, 3.289.

Bland D S, The Evolution of Chevy Chase and the Battle of Otterburn, N&Q 196.160.

Robbins-HP, p 260.

Herd D, Ancient and Modern Scottish Songs, Edinburgh 1776, 1.153; rptd Minstrelsy of the Scottish Border, Kelso 1802, 1.34; rptd Child, edn, 3.299 (later version).

Scott W, Minstrelsy of the Scottish Border, 1833; rvsd T F Henderson, Edinburgh 1932, 1.345; rptd Child, edn, 3.299 (later version).

Other Scholarly Problems. McMillan D J, Folk Projections and Historic Truth, AN&Q 2.149.

Literary Criticism. CHEL, 2.398, 415.

Chambers OHEL, p 159.

Fowler D C, The Hunting of the Cheviot and the Battle of Otterburn, Western Folklore 25.165.

McMillan D J, Some Popular Views of Four Medieval Ballads, Southern Folklore Quart 30.179.

General References. Percy, edn, 1765, 1.1, 18, 231.

Child, edn, 3.289.

Brandl, p 708.

Courthope, p 446.

Gerould G H, The Ballad of Tradition, Oxford 1932, p 56.

[68] THE HUNTING OF THE CHEVIOT.

MS. Bodl 6333 (Ashmole 48), ff 15ᵇ–18ᵃ (ca 1560).

Robbins-Cutler, no 3445.5.

Brydges [S] E and J Haslewood, Author of Chevy Chase, The British Bibliographer, London 1814, 4.97 (MS described).

Editions. Hearne T, Guilielmi Neubrigiensis Historia, Oxford 1719, 1.lxxxii.

Percy T, Reliques of Ancient English Poetry, London 1765, 1.4.

Wright T, Songs and Ballads, Roxb Club 78, London 1860, p 24.

Skeat Spec, p 67.

Ritson AS, p 92.

Gummere F B, Old English Ballads, Boston 1888, p 105.

Child F J, The English and Scottish Popular Ballads, Boston 1889, 3.307 (no 162).

Flügel NL, p 198.

Sargent H C and G L Kittredge, English and Scottish Popular Ballads, Boston 1904, p 393.

Bronson W C, English Poems, Chicago 1910, 1.216.

Sidgwick F, Ballads, London 1925, p 177.

Hodgart M, The Faber Book of Ballads, London 1965, p 96.

Modernization. Pancoast H S, English Prose and Verse, N Y 1915, p 90.

Textual Matters. Hamer D, Towards Restoring The Hunting of the Cheviot, RES ns 20.1 (includes restored version).

Versification. Schipper, 2.176, 520.

Authorship. Brydges [S] E and J Haslewood, Richard Sheale, The British Bibliographer, 4.99 (includes The Chaunt of Richard Sheale).

Wright, edn, p ii.

May S W, Sheale and the Ballad of Chevy Chase, AN&Q 9.115.

Literary Relations. Child, edn, 3.304.

Other Scholarly Problems. McMillan D J, Folk Projection and Historic Truth, AN&Q 2.148.

Literary Criticism. CHEL, 2.398, 415.

Chambers OHEL, p 161.

Fowler D C, The Hunting of the Cheviot and the Battle of Otterburn, Western Folklore 25.165.

McMillan D J, Some Popular Views of Four Medieval Ballads, Southern Folklore Quart 30.179.

General References. Percy, edn, 1765, 1.1, 18, 231.

PFMS, 2.1.

Child, edn, 3.303.

Courthope, p 447.

Robbins-HP, p 280.

Bibliography. New CBEL, 1.1120.

[69] CHEVY CHASE.

MS. BM Addit 27879, pp 188–191 (ca 1650).
Robbins-Cutler, no 960.1.
Editions. Collection of Old Ballads, Glasgow 1747, 1.108.
Percy T, Reliques of Ancient English Poetry, London 1765, 1.235.
PFMS, 2.7.
Child F J, The English and Scottish Popular Ballads, Boston 1889, 3.311 (no 162B).
Modernizations. Sidgwick F, Ballads and Poems Illustrating English History, Cambridge 1907, p 31.
Gerould G H, Old English and Medieval Literature, London 1929; rptd N Y 1969, p 333.
Authorship. May S W, Richard Sheale and the Ballad of Chevy Chase, AN&Q 9.115.
Literary Relations. Child, edn, 3.304.
Gerould G H, The Ballad of Tradition, Oxford 1932, p 122.
Other Scholarly Problems. Nessler K, Geschichte der Chevy Chase, Palaes 112.
Literary Criticism. Hales J W, Chevy Chase, Gentleman's Magazine 266.396; rptd Folia Literaria, N Y 1893, p 128.
Chambers OHEL, pp 143, 162.
General References. Percy, edn, 1765, 1.1, 18, 231.
Heywood T, The Earls of Derby and the Verse Writers and Poets of the Sixteenth and Seventeenth Centuries [Stanley Papers, pt 1], Chetham Soc 29.15.
PFMS, 2.1.
CHEL, 2.415.
Robbins-HP, p 280.
Bibliography. Child, edn, 3.303 (for later broadsides).
Chambers OHEL, p 229.

[70] THE BATTLE OF HARLAW.

MSS. No MS extant. PRINT: Ramsay A, The Ever Green, Glasgow 1724; rptd Glasgow 1875, 1.78; rptd R Foulis, Two Old Historical Scots Poems, Glasgow 1748.
Not listed Brown-Robbins, Robbins-Cutler.
Editions. Sibbald J, Chronicle of Scottish Poetry, Edinburgh 1802, 3.288.
Finlay J, Scottish Historical Romances and Ballads, Edinburgh 1808, 1.163.
Ritson J, Caledonian Muse, London 1821, p 177.
[Laing D,] Early Metrical Tales, Edinburgh 1826, p 227.

Irving D, History of Scottish Poetry, ed J A Carlyle, Edinburgh 1861, p 161.
Laing D, Early Popular Poetry of Scotland, rvsd W C Hazlitt, London 1895, 1.116.
Modernization. Sidgwick F, Ballads and Poems Illustrating English History, Cambridge 1907, p 41.
Date. Chambers OHEL, p 155.
Sources and Literary Relations. Clyne N, Ballads from Scottish History, Edinburgh 1863, p 244.
Child F J, The English and Scottish Popular Ballads, Boston 1889, 3.316 (for later versions.)
Other Scholarly Problems. McMillan D J, Folk Projections and Historic Truth, AN&Q 2.148.
Literary Criticism. Chambers OHEL, p 168.
McMillan D J, Some Popular Views of Four Medieval Ballads, Southern Folklore Quart 30.179.
General References. Laing, edn, p xlv.
Morley, 6.165.
Snell F J, The Age of Transition, London 1905, 1.71.
Courthope, p 446.

[71] THE BATTLE OF AGINCOURT I.

MS. Cotton Cleop C.iv, ff 25^b–26^a (ca 1443).
Brown-Robbins, Robbins-Cutler, no 3213.
Kingsford, edn, p ix (MS described).
Editions. Nicolas N H, History of the Battle of Agincourt, London 1833, p 281.
Wright PPS, 2.125.
Kingsford C L, Chronicles of London, Oxford 1905, p 120.
Robbins-HP, p 74.
Textual Matters. Kingsford, edn, p 305.
Robbins-HP, p 286.
Language. Oakden J P, Alliterative Poetry in ME, Manchester 1930, 1.129.
Literary Relations. Robbins-HP, p 285.
General References. Brandl, p 700.
Hammond E P, English Verse between Chaucer and Surrey, Durham N C 1927, p 233.
Kingsford EHL, p 240.
Robbins-HP, p xxiii.
Perroy E, The Hundred Years War, London 1951, p 238.
Scattergood PP, p 144.
Bibliography. Hammond, English Verse, p 233.
Chambers OHEL, p 223.

[72] THE BATTLE OF AGINCOURT II.

MSS. 1, Bodl 11951 (Rawl C.86), ff 178ª–186ª (1480–1500); 2, Cotton Vitell D.xii, II, f 214ª (ca 1410; MS burned in 1731); 3, Harley 565, ff 102ª–114ª (1440–50).
Brown-Robbins Robbins-Cutler, no 969.
Kingsford C L, Chronicles of London, Oxford 1905, p x (description of MS 3).
Editions. Hearne T, Thomas de Elmham Vita et Gestae Henrici Quinti, Oxford 1727, p 359 (MS 2).
Evans T, Old Ballads, ed R H Evans, London 1810, 2.334.
Nicolas N H and E Tyrrell, Chronicle of London, London 1827, p 216 (MS 3).
Nicholas N H, History of the Battle of Agincourt, London 1833, pp 301 (MS 3), 303 (MS 2).
Authorship. Wylie J H, The Agincourt Chaplain, Athen 120(1902).254.
Hazlitt Rem, 2.93 (accepts Lydgate).
Emmerig O, The Bataile of Agyncourt im Lichte geschichtlicher Quellenwerke, Munich 1906 (accepts Lydgate; crit F Brie, EStn 38.82; J T, EHR 23.197).
Kingsford EHL, pp 232, 238 (rejects Lydgate).
Kingsford C L, English History in Contemporary Poetry No 2, London 1913, p 9.
MacCracken H N, Lydgate's Minor Poems, EETSES 107, London 1910, p xlvii (rejects Lydgate).
Sources. Kingsford, Eng Hist in Contemp Poetry, p 11.
General References. Warton T, History of English Poetry, London 1824, 2.345.
Hazlitt Rem, 2.93.
Chambers OHEL, p 123.
Robbins-HP, p 285.
Scattergood PP, pp 53, 143, 158.
Bibliography. PFMS, 2.159.
Hammond E P, English Verse between Chaucer and Surrey, Durham N C, p 233.
Chambers OHEL, p 223.

[73] THE BATAYLL OF EGYNGS-COURTE.

MSS. No MS extant. PRINT: The Batayll of Egyngscourte, J Skot, London [ca 1530] (STC, no 198).
Not listed Brown-Robbins, Robbins-Cutler.
Editions. Nicolas N H, History of the Battle of Agincourt, London 1833, Appendix, p 69.
PFMS, 2.158.

Hazlitt Rem, 2.88.
Modernizations. Arber E, The Dunbar Anthology, London 1901, no 8.
Pollard A W, Fifteenth Century Prose and Verse, Westminster 1903, p 1.
Date. Hazlitt Rem, 4.364.
Authorship. Wylie J H, The Agincourt Chaplain, Athen 120(1902).254.
Literary Relations. PFMS, 2.159.
Kingsford C L, English History in Contemporary Poetry No 2, London 1913, p 12.
See also Agincourte Battell (BM Addit 27879, pp 241–243), PFMS, 2.166; and for two other Agincourt ballads, PFMS, 2.595, 597.

[74] THE SIEGE OF ROUEN.

MSS. 1, Bodl 3652 (e Museo 124), ff 28ª–42ᵇ (1425–50; lines 1–946, ends imperfectly); 2, Balliol Oxf 354, ff 128ª–138ᵇ (1518–36); 3, Camb Univ Hh.6.9, ff 258ᵇ–261ª (1434; cap 247 only); 4, Trinity Camb 1413, ff 195ᵇ–197ª (1425–75); 5, Cotton Galba E.viii, ff 140ª–143ᵇ (1425–40; 669 lines); 6, Egerton 1995, ff 87ª–109ᵇ (1470–80); 7, Harley 226, ff 136ᵇ–142ᵇ (1475–1500); 8, Harley 753, ff 177ª–182ᵇ (1475–1500); 8a, Egerton 2257, ff 17ª–19ª (19 cent transcript; 82 lines only); 9, Harley 2256, ff 189ª–193ᵇ (1450–75; lines 1–1312); 10, BM Addit 27879, pp 523–525 (ca 1650; MS badly damaged; lines 1–119, 176–202, 226–285, 349–376 of MS 6); 11, Lambeth 331, ff 107ᵇ–112ª (1475–1500); 12, formerly Buccleugh (Quaritch Sale Cats, 1916, nos 303, 344) (1450–75); 13, formerly Charlemont, f 23 (sold Sotheby 1865) (15 cent); 14, Holkham Hall 670 (formerly Coke), ff 125ª–125ᵇ (1475–1500; lines 637–773); 15, formerly Sir R L Harmsworth (Sotheby Sale Cat, 15 Oct 1945, Lot 1951) (15 cent); 16, formerly Nuton (Quaritch Sale Cat, 1916, no 344) (1450–1500).
Brown-Robbins, Robbins-Cutler, no 979.
Huscher, edn, p 1 (MSS described).
Editions. Conybeare J J, Poem Entitled The Siege of Rouen, Archaeol 21.48 (MS 1; described as Bodley 124, but actually e Museo 124).
Madden F, Old English Poem on the Siege of Rouen, Archaeol 22.361 (MS 9, collated with MS 8).
Gairdner J, Historical Collection of a Citizen of London in the Fifteenth Century, Camden Soc ns 17.1 (MS 6).
PFMS, 3.533 (MS 10).
Brie F, The Brut, EETS 136, London 1908,

p 404 (MS 5).
Huscher H, John Page's Siege of Rouen, Kölner Anglistische Arbeiten 1.138 (critical text based on MS 6; crit A Brandl, Arch 153.121; M Day, RES 3.492; E von Erhardt-Siebold, EStn 63.261; W van der Graf, ESts 10.18; F Holthausen, AnglB 39.68; F Wild, LfGRP 49.350).
Selection. Kaiser R, Medieval English, Berlin 1958, p 540.
Textual Matters. Madden, Archaeol 22.385.
Huscher, edn, p 203.
Language. Huscher, edn, p 99.
Versification. Huscher, edn, p 75.
Date. Huscher, edn, p 108.
Authorship. Huscher, edn, p 120.
Literary Relations. Starke F J, Populäre engl Chroniken des 15 Jahrhunderts, Berlin 1935, p 136 (parallels in Brut).
Literary Criticism. Gairdner, Camden Soc ns 17.xi.
Kingsford EHL, pp 116, 118, 237.
Huscher, edn, p 111.
General References. Conybeare, Archaeol 21.43.
Brandl, p 710.
Brie F W D, Geschichte und Quellen der me Prosachronik, Marburg 1905, pp 89, 90, 92.
Oman C, Political History of England, London 1906, 4.501 (minimizes value).
Kingsford C L, English History in Contemporary Poetry No 2, London 1913, p 13.
Bagley J J, Historical Interpretation, Harmondsworth Middlesex 1965, p 228.
Scattergood PP, p 61.
Bibliography. Kingsford EHL, p 116.
Huscher, edn, p 111.

[75] THE SIEGE OF CALAIS.

MSS. 1, Cotton Galba E.ix, ff 113ᵇ–114ᵇ (1440–50); 1a, Egerton 2257 ff 2ᵃ–4ᵇ (19 cent transcript); 2, Rome Venerable Eng Coll 1306, ff 85ᵃ–87ᵃ (1450–1500).
Brown-Robbins, Robbins-Cutler, no 1497.
Klinefelter R A, A Newly Discovered Fifteenth-Century English Manuscript, MLQ 14.3 (description of MS 2).
Robbins R H, A ME Diatribe against Philip of Burgundy, Neophil 39.131 (description of MS 2).
Editions. Wright PPS, 2.151 (MS 1).
Rel Ant, 2.21 (MS 1).
Klinefelter R A, The Siege of Calais A New Text, PMLA 67.890 (MS 2).

Robbins-HP, pp 78 (MS 2), 290 (MS 1 variant).
Textual Matters. Robbins-HP, p 289.
Language. Lindheim B von, Studien zur Sprache des Manuskriptes Cotton Galba E.ix, WBEP 59 (crit K Brunner, EStn 73.252; F Holthausen, ALb 60.178; K Wittig, AnglB 49.306).
Date. Kingsford EHL, p 241.
Literary Relations. Robbins, Neophil 39.136.
Robbins-HP, p xxii.
General References. Browne M (pseud W B Rands), Chaucer's England, London 1869, 2.262.
Brandl, p 710.
CHEL, 2.423.
Kingsford C L, English History in Contemporary Poetry No 2, London 1913, p 22.
Scattergood PP, p 88.

[76] MOCKERY OF THE FLEMINGS.

MS. Lambeth 6, ff 256ᵃ–257ᵃ (1450–75).
Robbins-Cutler, no 4056.8 (delete Brown-Robbins, no 4034).
Millar E G, Bulletin de la Société française de Reproductions de Manuscrits à Peintures, Paris 1925 (MS described).
James and Jenkins, edn, p 15 (MS described).
Editions. Williams B, Satirical Rhymes of the Defeat of the Flemings, Archaeol 33.130.
Brie F, The Brut, EETS 136, London 1908, p 582.
James M R and C Jenkins, A Descriptive Catalogue, Cambridge 1930, p 16.
Robbins-HP, p 83.
Textual Matters. Robbins-HP, p 292.
Authorship. MacCracken H N, Lydgate's Minor Poems, EETSES 107, London 1910, p xvii.
Literary Relations. Starke F J, Populäre engl Chroniken des 15 Jahrhunderts, Berlin 1935, p 136.
Robbins-HP, p xiii.
Other Scholarly Problems. Aston M, The Fifteenth Century The Prospect of Europe, London 1968, p 41 (nationalism).
General References. Tucker S M, Verse Satire in England before the Renaissance, N Y 1908, p 125.
Kingsford EHL, p 241.
Wilson R M, More Lost Literature in Old and ME, Leeds SE 5.44.
Wilson Lost Lit, p 214; 2nd edn, p 208.
Holmes G A, Libelle of Englysche Polycye,

EHR 76.212.
Scattergood PP, pp 86, 89 (Cotton tag).

[77] SCORN OF THE DUKE OF BUR-
GUNDY.

MSS. 1, Sloane 252, f 169ᵃ (1500; 43 lines
only); 2, Rome Venerable Eng Coll 1306, ff
83ᵇ–84ᵇ (1450–1500).
Brown-Robbins, Robbins-Cutler, no 3682.
Editions. Wright PPS, 2.148 (MS 1).
Robbins R H, A ME Diatribe against Philip
of Burgundy, Neophil 38.138 (MS 2).
Robbins-HP, p 86 (MS 2).
Date. Kingsford EHL, p 241.
Literary Relations. Robbins, Neophil 39.142

(resemblance to other poems and chroni-
cles).
Scattergood PP, p 85 (reference to Brown-
Robbins, no 2657).
General References. Kingsford C L, English
History in Contemporary Poetry No 2,
London 1913, p 21.
Weiss R, Humphrey Duke of Gloucester and
Tito Livio Frulovisi, in Fritz Saxl 1890–
1948 A Volume of Memorial Essays, ed D J
Gordon, London 1957, p 222.
Holmes G A, Libelle of Englysche Polycye,
EHR 76.212.
Klinefelter R A, The Siege of Calais, A New
Text, PMLA 67.889.
Scattergood PP, pp 84, 151.

7. Politics in Song

See appropriate section of the Commentary in the present chapter.

8. The Wicked Age: Satires and Complaints

I. General Evils: Summaries

See appropriate section of the Commentary in the present chapter.

II. General Evils: Expansions of the Abuses of the Age

[78] SATIRES AND COMPLAINTS.

Editions. Wright PS.
Wright T, The Latin Poems Commonly
Ascribed to Walter Mapes, Camden Soc 16.
Fairholt F W, Satirical Songs and Poems on
Costume, PPS 27.
Wright PPS.
Wright T, The Anglo-Latin Satirical Poets,
Rolls Series 59.
Robbins-HP.
General References. Alden R M, The Rise
of Formal Satire in England under Classi-
cal Influence, Phila 1899.
Haessner M, Die Goliardendichtung und die
Satire im 13 Jarhundert in England,
Leipzig 1905.
Manitius M, Die Engl Satire des 12 Jahrhun-

derts, Allgem Zeitung, Beilage, Munich
1906, p 193.
Tucker S M, Verse Satire in England before
the Renaissance, N Y 1908 (crit A Andrae,
AnglB 21.2; F Brie, LfGRP 31.318; M
Lederer, LZ 61.24).
Previté-Orton C W, Political Satire in Eng-
lish Poetry, Cambridge 1910, p 7 (crit
[anon] N&Q 11s 2.38; C Bastide, RCHL
71.33; W Fischer, DLz 33.480; M Lederer,
LZ 62.99).
Wolfe H, Notes on English Verse Satire, Lon-
don 1929 (crit W van Doorn, ESts 14.229;
H E A Northcutt, RES 7.114).
Byrne Sister M, The Tradition of the Nun
in Medieval England, Washington D C
1932, p 161.
Owst G R, Preaching in Medieval England,

Cambridge 1926, p 295; Literature and Pulpit in Medieval England, Cambridge 1933, pp 210, 247.
Utley CR (crit TLS, Apr 14 1945, p 176; H Braddy, MLN 60.421; H A Kahin, MLQ 7.357; E Seaton and E Gibson, YWES 25.11, 208; J W Spargo, Spec 20.365 [with further bibliographies]; E J Sweeting, MLR 40.316; W D Taylor, RES 22.63).
Davidson C E, ME Verse Satire, diss Yale 1953.
Peter J D, Complaint and Satire in Early English Literature, Oxford 1956.
Kinney T L, English Verse of Complaint, diss Michigan 1959.
Kernan A, The Cankered Muse Satire of the English Renaissance, New Haven 1959, p 43.
Kinney T L, The Temper of Fourteenth-Century English Verse of Complaint, Annuale Mediaevale 7.74.
Keller J R, The Triumph of Vice A Formal Approach to the Medieval Complaint against the Time, Annuale Mediaevale 10.120.
Elliott T J, Complaint as a ME Genre, diss Michigan 1970.
Scattergood PP.
Elliott T J, ME Complaints Against the Times To Contemn the World or to Reform It, Annuale Mediaevale 14.22.

[79] WORCESTER CATHEDRAL FRAGMENT.

MS. Worcester Cath 174, f 63ª (ca 1180).
Robbins-Cutler, no 3074.3.
Editions. Phillips T, Fragment of Aelfric's Grammar, London 1838, p 5.
Varnhagen H, Zu me Gedichten IX, Angl 3.423.
Wright T, Biographia Britannica Literaria, London 1842, 1.59.
Hall Selections, 1.1; 2.223.
Dickins and Wilson, p 2.
Schnith K, Von Symeon von Durham zu Wilhelm von Newburgh Speculum Historale, Freiburg 1965, p 244.
Textual Matters. Holthausen F, Zum Fragment von Worcester, Arch 106.347.
Language. Schlemilch W, Beiträge zur Sprache und Orthographie spätaltenglische Sprachdenkmäler der Übergangzeit, SEP 34.
Oakden J P, Alliterative Poetry in ME, Manchester 1930, 1.42, 138 (Worcester dialect).
Versification. Oakden, Alliterative Poetry, 1.42, 138; 2.236.

General References. Brandl, p 615.
Paul Grundriss, 2nd edn, 2¹.1133.
Brüll H, Die ae latein Grammatik des Aelfric, Berlin 1900, p 3.
Keller W, Die literarischen Bestrebungen von Worcester in angelsächsischen Zeit, QF 84.64.

[80] THE SAYINGS OF THE FOUR PHILOSOPHERS.

MSS. 1, St John's Camb 112, f 400ª (1300–25); 2, Advocates 19.2.1, f 105ª (1330–40).
Brown-Robbins, Robbins-Cutler, no 1857.
Laing D, A Penni Worth of Witte, Abbotsford Club 29, Edinburgh 1857, p xiii (MS 2 described).
Carr M B, Notes on a ME Scribe's Methods, Univ of Wisconsin Studies 2.153 (MS 2 described).
Loomis L H, The Auchinleck MS and a Possible London Bookshop, PMLA 57.626 (MS 2 described); Chaucer and the Auchinleck MS, E&S Brown, p 111 (MS 2 described).
Bliss A J, Notes on the Auchinleck MS, Spec 26.652 (MS 2 described).
Smithers G V, Another Fragment of the Auchinleck MS, in Medieval Literature and Civilization Studies in Memory of G N Garmonsway, ed D A Pearsall and R A Waldron, London 1969, p 192 (MS 2 described).
Weiss J, The Auchinleck MS and the Edwardes MSS, N&Q ns 26.44 (MS 2 described).
Editions. Marsh G P, Origin and History of the English Language, N Y 1806, p 244 (MS 2).
Laing D, Owain Miles, Edinburgh 1837, no 3 (MS 2).
Wright PS, p 253 (MS 2).
Ellis A J, Early English Pronunciation, EETSES 7, London 1869, p 499 and ChS 2s 4.499 (MS 2).
Wülcker R P, Ae Lesebuch, Halle 1874, 1.74 (MS 2).
Vatke T, Lied auf den Bruch der Magna Charta durch Edward II, Arch 72.467 (with German trans; MS 2).
Herrtage S J H, The Early Versions of the Gesta Romanorum, EETSES 33, London 1879, p 498 (MS 2).
James M R, A Descriptive Catalogue, Cambridge 1913, p 146 (MS 1).
Holmstedt G, Speculum Christiana, EETS 182, London 1933, p clxxxv (MS 2).

Aspin I S T, AN Political Songs, Oxford 1953, p 62 (MSS 1, 2).
Robbins-HP, pp 140 (MS 2), 325 (MS 1).
Sisam Oxf Book MEV, p 74 (MS 2).
Versification. Schipper, 1.398.
Wehrle W O, The Macaronic Hymn Tradition in Medieval English Literature, Washington D C 1933, p 41.
Date. Scattergood V J, Political Context Date and Composition of The Sayings of the Four Philosophers, MÆ 37.157.
Sources and Literary Relations. Holmstedt, EETS 182.xvi.
Brown C, The Pride of Life and the Twelve Abuses, Arch. 128.72.
Robbins-HP, p 325.
General References. Ten Brink, 1.318.
Courthope, p 190.
Schofield, pp 365, 370.
Previté-Orton C W, Political Satire in English Poetry, Cambridge 1910, p 17.
Robbins-HP, p 324.
Robbins R H, ME Poems of Protest, Angl 78.199.
Scattergood PP, p 300.
Mann J, Chaucer and Medieval Estates Satire, Cambridge 1973, p 164.
Elliott T J, ME Complaints Against the Times, Annuale Mediaevale 14.24.
Scattergood V J, Revision in some ME Political Verse, Archiv 211.294.

[81] THE WICKEDNESS OF THE TIMES.

MS. Camb Univ Add 4407, Art 19.g (end 14 cent).
Robbins-Cutler, no 2685.5 (delete Brown-Robbins, no 1580).
Edition. Skeat W W, Elegy on the Death of King Edward I, MLR 7.150 (one stanza only).

[82] A SATIRE OF EDWARD II'S ENGLAND.

MSS. 1, Bodl 1885 (Bodley 48), ff 325ᵇ–330ᵇ (two leaves cut out between f 325 and f 326; ca 1425); 2, Peterhouse Camb 104, ff 210ᵃ–212ᵃ (1350); 3, Advocates 19.2.1, ff 328ᵃ–334ᵇ (1330–40).
Brown-Robbins, Robbins-Cutler, no 4165.
Ross, edn, p 10 (MSS described).
For MS 3 see under [80] above.
Editions. Wright PS, p 323 (MS 3).
Hardwick C, A Poem on the Times of Edward II, PPS 28.1 (MS 1).
Brandl A and O Zippel, Me Sprach- und Lit-

eraturproben, Berlin 1917, p 184 (MS 3).
Ross T W, On the Evil Times of Edward II A New Version from MS Bodley 48, Angl 75.177 (MS 1); A Satire of Edward II's England, Colorado College Studies 8, Colorado Springs 1966, p 17 (comparative text).
Selections. James M R, A Descriptive Catalogue, Cambridge 1899, p 122 (MS 2).
Kaiser R, Medieval English, Berlin 1958, p 184 (MS 3).
Textual Matters. Ross, Angl 75.177.
Ross, Satire, pp 9, 14, 36.
Language. Carr M B, Notes on an English Scribe's Methods, Wisconsin Studies in Lang and Lit no 2, p 153.
Versification. Schipper, 1.384, 389.
Date. Wright T, A History of Caricature and Grotesque, London 1875, p 185.
Ross, Satire, p 15.
Sources and Literary Relations. Mohl R, The Three Estates in Medieval and Renaissance Literature, London 1933, p 98.
Mann J, Chaucer and Medieval Estates Satire, Cambridge 1973, pp 205, 238.
Scholarly Problems. Salter E, Piers Plowman and The Simonie, Arch 203.241 (influence on Piers Plowman).
Literary Criticism. Ten Brink, 1.318.
Kinney T L, The Temper of Fourteenth-Century English Verse of Complaint, Annuale Mediaevale 7.80.
General References. Wright T, Womankind in All Ages of Western Europe, London 1869, pp 176, 203.
Brandl, p 628.
Schofield, p 370.
Tucker S M, Verse Satire in England before the Renaissance, N Y 1908, p 64.
Ross, Angl 75.173.
Yunck J A, The Lineage of Lady Meed, Notre Dame 1963, p 228.
Elliott T J, ME Complaints Against the Times to Contemn the World or to Reform It, Annuale Mediaevale 14.27.

[83] DE VERITATE ET CONSCIENCIA.

MS. Wellcome Hist Med Libr 673 (formerly Phillipps 18134), ff 8ᵃ–8ᵇ (1430–50).
Robbins-Cutler, no 3173.5.
Edition, Kane G, ME Verse, LMS 2¹.61.
General Reference. Kane, LMS 2¹.54.

[84] ON HAMDEN OF HAMDEN.

MSS. MS not established.
Not listed Brown-Robbins, Robbins-Cutler.

Editions. Halliwell-Phillipps J O, Popular Rhymes and Nursery Tales, London 1849, p 194.

Corson L, A Finding List of Political Poems, 1910; rptd N Y 1970, p 36.

[85] THE INSURRECTION AND EARTHQUAKE OF 1382.

MSS. 1, Bodl 3938 (Vernon), f 411ª (ca 1385); 2, BM Addit 22283, f 132ᵇ (1380–1400); 3, Nat Libr of Wales Peniarth 395, pp 346–347 (12 stanzas; early 15 cent).

Summary Cat, vol 2, pt 2, p 789 (MS 1 described).

Serjeantson M S, The Index of the Vernon Manuscript, MLR 32.222 (MS 1 described).

Sajavaara K, The Relationship of the Vernon and Simeon MSS, NM 68.428; ME Translations of Robert Grosseteste's Chateau d'Amour, Helsinki 1967, p 103 (MS 1 described).

Catalogue of Additions to the Manuscripts in the British Museum in the Years 1854–60, London 1875, p 623 (MSS 1 and 2 described).

Doyle A I, The Shaping of the Vernon and Simeon Manuscripts, in Chaucer and Middle English Essays in Honour of Rossell Hope Robbins, ed B Rowland, London 1974, p 328 (MS 1 described).

Editions. Conybeare J J, Two English Poems, Archaeol 18.26 (MS 1).

Wright PPS, 1.250 (MS 2).

Furnivall F J, The Minor Poems of the Vernon MS, EETS 117. 719 (MS 1).

Brown RLxivC, p 186 (MS 1).

Robbins-HP, p 57 (MS 1).

Selections. Kaiser R, Medieval English, Berlin 1958, p 387 (MS 1).

Dobson R B, The Peasants' Revolt of 1381, London 1970, p 358 (MS 1).

Sisam Oxf Book MEV, p 347 (MS 1).

Textual Matters. Brown RLxivC, p 281.

Malone K, Further Notes on ME Lyrics, ELH 23.12 (line 53).

Robbins-HP, p 276.

Literary Criticism. Tucker S M, Verse Satire in England before the Renaissance, N Y 1908, p 93.

General References. Eberhard O, Der Bauernaufstand vom Jahr 1381 in der engl Poesie, AF 51.35.

Robbins-HP, p xli.

Yunck J A, The Lineage of Lady Meed, Notre Dame 1963, p 270.

Scattergood PP, p 356.

[86] ON THE TIMES OF RICHARD II.

MSS. 1, Bodl 11951 (Rawl C.86), f 59ª (lines 1–4 only; 1480–1500); 2, Harley 536, ff 34ª–35ᵇ (1450–1500); 3, Harley 941, ff 21ᵇ–22ª (1450–1500); 4, Trinity Dublin 516, ff 108ª–110ª (140 lines; 1450–75).

Brown-Robbins, Robbins-Cutler, no 3113.

Editions. Fairholt F W, Satirical Songs and Poems on Costume, PPS 27.44 (MS 2).

Wright PPS, 1.270 (MS 4).

Date. Matthew G, The Court of Richard II, London 1968, p 26.

Mann J, Chaucer and Medieval Estates Satire, Cambridge 1973, p 311.

General References. Brandl, p 667.

Schofield, p 372.

Tucker S M, Verse Satire in England before the Renaissance, N Y 1908, p 93.

Wehrle W O, The Macaronic Hymn Tradition in Medieval English Literature, Washington D C 1933, p 47.

Yunck J A, The Lineage of Lady Meed, Notre Dame 1963, p 270.

Mann, Chaucer and Medieval Estates Satire, p 116.

[87] ON KING RICHARD'S MINISTERS.

MS. Deritend House (present ownership and location not established; ca 1400).

Brown-Robbins, no 3529.

Editions. Wright PPS, 1.363.

Hamper W, Sarcastic Verses, Archaeol 21.89.

Textual Matters. Hamper, Archaeol 21.89.

General References. Brandl, p 657.

Tucker S M, Verse Satire in England before the Renaissance, N Y 1908, p 97.

Previté-Orton C W, Political Satire in English Poetry, Cambridge 1910, p 27.

Kinney T L, The Temper of Fourteenth-Century Verse of Complaint, Annuale Mediaevale 7.85.

Scattergood PP, p 110.

[88] THE DANGERS OF PRIDE.

MSS. 1, Public Record Office, Chancery Miscellanea, Bundle 34, File 1, No 12 (ca 1400); 2, Kilkenny Castle, Ormond, a strip of vellum (ca 1450–1500).

Brown-Robbins, no 2774.

Greene E E Carols, p 335 (MS 1 described).

Edition. Seymour St J D, Three Medieval Poems from Kilkenny, Proc Royal Irish Acad 41.207.

General Reference. Wilson Lost Lit, p 183;

2nd edn, p 176.

[89] NOW IS ENGLAND PERISHED.

MSS. 1, Corp Christi Oxf 237, f 243ᵇ (16 lines; 1475–1500); 2, Camb Univ Hh.2.6, f 58ᵃ (28 lines; early 16 cent).
Brown-Robbins, Robbins-Cutler, no 2335.
Editions. Wright PPS, 2.252 (MS 1).
Robbins-HP, p 149 (MS 2).
Sisam Oxf Book MEV, p 450 (MS 1).
Sources and Literary Relations. Wright PPS, 2.253 (Latin epigram from MS Bodley 832, f 177ᵃ).
General References. Robbins-HP, p 330.
Scattergood PP, pp 99, 305.

[90] THIS WORLD IS VARIABLE.

MS. Bodl 29734 (Eng Poet e.l), ff 16ᵃ–16ᵇ (1460–80).
Brown-Robbins, Robbins-Cutler, no 4236.
Editions. Wright T, Songs and Carols of the Fifteenth Century, PPS 23.9.
Ch&Sidg, p 178.
Robbins-HP, p 148.
Textual Matters. Robbins-HP, p 329.
Literary Criticism. Curtius E R, trans W Trask, European Literature and the Latin Middle Ages, N Y 1953, p 94.
General Reference. Robbins R H, ME Poems of Protest, Angl 78.199.

[91] ALAS THAT KYNDEMAN WANTYS GODE.

MS. Harley 5396, ff 310ᵇ–311ᵃ (1450–60).
Brown-Robbins, Robbins-Cutler, no 1319.
Edition. Rel Ant, 1.77.

[92] THE BISSON LEADS THE BLIND.

MS. Harley 5396, ff 295ᵃ–296ᵇ (1450–60).
Brown-Robbins, Robbins-Cutler, no 884.
Editions. Rel Ant, 2.238.
Wright PPS, 2.235.
Robbins-HP, p 127.
Textual Matters. Robbins-HP, p 319.
Date. Robbins R H, On Dating a ME Moral Poem, MLN 70.474.
Robbins-HP, p xxiv.
Sources and Literary Relations. Gairdner J, Historical Collections of a Citizen of London, Camden Soc ns 17.199.
Rollins H E, The Pack of Autolycus, Cambridge Mass 1927, p 3 (Tudor ballad on abuses).
Robbins, MLN 70.473.
Grandsen K W, Tudor Verse Satire, London 1970, p 78 (Tudor ballad).
General References. Tucker S M, Verse Satire in England before the Renaissance, N Y 1908, p 132.
Kingsford EHL, p 245.
Robbins R H, ME Poems of Protest, Angl 78.196, 198.
Scattergood PP, pp 175, 305.

[93] THE WORLD UPSIDE DOWN I.

MS. Bodl Eng poet B.48, f 1ᵇ (fragment; 1450–1500).
Brown-Robbins, Robbins-Cutler, no 2805.
Editions. Robbins R H, The World Upside Down A ME Amphibole, Angl 72.386.
Robbins-HP, p 150.
Selection. L[obel] E, Notes and News, BQR 3.220 (1st stanza only).
Textual Matters. Robbins-HP, p 330.
Date. Lobel, BQR 3.220.
Literary Relations. Brown-Robbins, nos 199, 3655.
Cheyney E P, Social Change in England in the Sixteenth Century as Reflected in Contemporary Literature, Phila 1895.
Frazer N L, English History in Contemporary Poetry, London 1914, p 39.
Scattergood PP, p 303.
Literary Criticism. Robbins, Angl 72.386.
General Reference. Scattergood PP, p 302.

[94] THE WORLD UPSIDE DOWN II.

MS. BM Addit 31042, f 97ᵇ (ca 1450).
Brown-Robbins, no 3778.
Editions. Catalogue of Additions to the Manuscripts 1876–1881, London 1882, p 149.
Brunner K, HS Brit Mus Additional 31042, Arch 132.318.

[95] THE KINDS OF USURY.

MS. Egerton 2810, ff 180ᵇ–181ᵃ (inserted leaves in mid 15 cent hand).
Brown-Robbins, Robbins-Cutler, no 2671.
Edition. Bowers R H, A ME Mnemonic Poem on Usury, MS 17.230.
Literary Relations. Brandeis A, Jacob's Well, EETS 115, London 1900, p 122.
Bowers, MS 17.228.
General Reference. Bowers, MS 17.226.

III. The Clergy

[96] AGAINST SIMONY.

MS. Jesus Oxf 29, f 254[b] (after 1256).
Brown-Robbins, Robbins-Cutler, no 4085.
Hill B, The History of Jesus College Oxford
MS 29, MÆ 32.204 (MS described).
Editions. Morris A, An Old English Miscellany, EETS 49, London 1871, p 89.
Kaiser R, Medieval English, Berlin 1958, p 321.
Modernization. Adamson M R, A Treasury of ME Verse, N Y 1930, p 17.
Date. Wells J E, The Owl and the Nightingale, Boston 1909, p xix.
Literary Criticism. Ten Brink, 1.316.
Schofield, p 370.
CHEL, 1.251.
Tucker S M, Verse Satire in England before the Renaissance, N Y 1908, p 53.
Kinney T L, The Temper of Fourteenth-Century English Verse of Complaint, Annuale Mediaevale 7.80, 87.
General References. Brandl, p 619.
Child G C, The Natural History of Dragons, in In Honor of the Ninetieth Birthday of Charles Frederick Johnson Professor of English in Trinity College 1883–1906 Papers Essays and Stories by his Former Students, ed O Shepard and A Adams, Hartford Conn 1928, p 101.
Yunck J A, The Lineage of Lady Meed, Notre Dame 1963, p 228.

[97] AGAINST WORLDLY CLERICS.

MSS. 1, Bodl 3712 (e Museo 198), ff 172[a]–172[b] (late 14 cent); 2, Bodl 6922 (Ashmole 60), ff 1[a]–7[b], 97[a]–97[b] (14 cent).
Brown-Robbins, Robbins-Cutler, no 1425.
Edition. Furnivall F J, Ballads from MSS, Ballad Soc, London 1868, 1.63 (MS 2).
Selections. Halliwell J O, The Thornton Romances, Camden Soc 30.259 (latter portion only).
Allen WAR, p 391.

[98] ABC POEM AGAINST PRIDE OF CLERGY.

MS. MS not identified. PRINT: Foxe J, Actes and Monuments, J Day, 1563 (STC, no 11222).
Robbins-Cutler, no 455.8.
Edition. Townsend G, Actes and Monuments

of John Foxe, London 1843, 4.259.
General Reference. Bennett OHEL, p 182.

[99] AGAINST LAZY CLERICS.

MSS. (In Fasciculus Morum:) 1, Bodl 1045 (Laud Misc 213), f 80[b] (15 cent); 2, Bodl 1117 (Laud Misc 568), f 63[a] (15 cent); 3, Bodl 2090 (Bodley 187), f 172[a] (15 cent); 4, Bodl 2305 (Bodley 410), f 51[a] (15 cent); 5, Bodl 12514 (Rawl C.670), f 90[a] (15 cent); 6, Caius Camb 71, f 58[b] (15 cent); 7, Caius Camb 364, f 84[b] (15 cent); 8, Canterbury Cath D.14, f 116[b] (15 cent); 9, Edinburgh Univ 82, f 110[b] (15 cent); 10, Eton Coll 34, f 50[b] (15 cent); 11, Lincoln Cath 44, f 197[b] (15 cent); 12, Worcester Cath F.19, f 198[b] (late 14 cent); 13, Worcester Cath Q.3, f 99[a] (15 cent). (Appearing separately:) 14, Trinity Camb 323, f 28[a] (1255–60); 15, Lambeth 78, V, f 277[a] (15 cent).
Brown-Robbins, Robbins-Cutler, no 1935.
Editions. Little A G, Studies in English Franciscan History, Manchester 1917, p 153 (MS 10).
Foster F A, Some English Words from the Fasciculus Morum, E&S Brown, p 153 (MS 5).
Silverstein T, Medieval English Lyrics, London 1971, p 81 (MS 5).
Reichl K, Religiöse Dichtung im engl Hochmittelalter, Munich 1973, p 33 (all texts, MSS 1–15).
Wenzel S, The English Verses in the Fasciculus Morum, in Chaucer and Middle English Studies in Honour of Rossell Hope Robbins, ed B Rowland, London 1974, p 240 (MS 5).
Sources. Foster F A, A Note on the Fasciculus Morum, Franciscan Studies ns 8.202.
Literary Relations. Rel Ant, 1.90 (for comparable Latin lines).
Reichl, edn, p 325.
General Reference. Wenzel, edn, p 246.

[100] AGAINST THE FRIARS I.

MS. Cotton Cleop B.ii, ff 62[b]–64[a] (1382).
Brown-Robbins, Robbins-Cutler, no 2777.
Editions. Brewer J S, Monumenta Franciscana, Rolls Series 4, 1.601.
Wright PPS, 1.263.
Robbins-HP, p 157.
Selections. Cook A S, A Literary ME Reader,

Boston 1915, p 361 (lines 1–84).
Bennett H S, England from Chaucer to Caxton, London 1928, p 203 (10 stanzas).
Kaiser R, Medieval English, Berlin 1958, p 322 (10 stanzas).
Sisam Oxf Book MEV, p 365 (omits lines 73–96, 121–56).
Modernizations. Benham A R, English Literature from Widsith to the Death of Chaucer, New Haven 1916, p 297.
Rickert E, Chaucer's World, N Y 1948, p 374.
Textual Matters. Robbins-HP, p 333.
Sources and Literary Relations. Wright PPS, 1.253 (Latin O and I poem).
Brewer, Rolls Series 4, 1.592 (Latin O and I poem).
Heuser W, With an O and an I, Angl 27.315 (Latin O and I poem).
Rigg A G, A Glastonbury Miscellany of the Fifteenth Century, Oxford 1968, p 76 (Latin O and I poem).
Mann J, Chaucer and Medieval Estates Satire, Cambridge 1973, pp 225, 228.
Other Scholarly Problems. Schneider R, Der Mönch in der engl Dichtung, Palaes 155 (on monks).
Szittya P R, Caimes Kynde The Friars and the Exegetical Origins of Medieval Antifraternalism, diss Cornell 1971; DAI 33.287.
Literary Criticism. Tucker S M, Verse Satire in England Before the Renaissance, N Y 1908, p 88.
General References. Brandl, p 667.
Browne M (pseud W B Rands), Chaucer's England, London 1869, 2.205.
Little A G, Studies in English Franciscan History, Manchester 1917, p 117.
Jusserand J J, trans L T Smith, English Wayfaring Life, rvsd London 1929, p 305.
Eberhard O, Der Bauernaufstand vom Jahr 1381 in der engl Poesie, AF 51.37.
Baugh LHE, p 267.
Moorman J, A History of the Franciscan Order, Oxford 1968, p 138.

[101] AGAINST THE FRIARS II.

MS. Cotton Cleop B.ii, f 64^b (1382).
Brown-Robbins, Robbins-Cutler, no 2663.
Editions. Rel Ant, 1.322.
Brewer J S, Monumenta Franciscana, Rolls Series 4, 1.606.
Wright PPS, 1.268.
Heuser W, With an O and an I, Angl 27.302.
Cook A S, A Literary ME Reader, Boston 1915, p 364.

Robbins-HP, p 163.
Selection. Davies R T, Medieval English Lyrics, London 1963, p 141.
Textual Matters. Robbins-HP, p 337.
Versification. Schipper, 1.375.
Other Scholarly Problems. (O and I refrains). Schipper, 1.374.
Brandl, p 700.
Heuser, Angl 27.283.
Brunner K and K Hammerle, With an O and an I, Angl 54.288, 292.
Hammerle K, Verstreute me und frühne Lyrik, Arch 166.195.
Spanke H, Klangspielereien im mittelalterlichen Liede, Studien zur lateinischen Dichtung des Mittelalters Ehrengabe für Karl Strecker, ed W Stach and H Walther, Dresden 1931, p 171.
Raby F J E, A History of Secular Latin Poetry in the Middle Ages, Oxford 1934, 2.330.
Greene E E Carols, pp 53, 95, 135.
Mustanoja T, ME With an O and an I, NM 56.161.
Robbins-HP, p 335.
Greene R L, A ME Love Poem, MÆ 30.170.
(Pageants or wall paintings) Wright PPS, 1.lxix.
Robbins-HP, p 335.
Brian B, Franciscan Scenes in a Fourteenth-Century Satire, MÆ 41.27.
General References. Heuser, Angl 27.301.
Schneider R, Der Mönch in der engl Dichtung, Palaes 155.
Jusserand J J, trans L T Smith, English Wayfaring Life, rvsd London 1929, p 307.
Seymour St J D, Anglo-Irish Literature 1200–1582, Cambridge 1929, p 114.
Davies, Medieval English Lyrics, p 331.
Williams A, Chaucer and the Friars, Spec 28.504, 512.
Mann J, Chaucer and Medieval Estates Satire, Cambridge 1973, p 48.

[102] THE LAYMAN'S COMPLAINT AGAINST THE FRIARS.

MS. St John's Camb 195, f 1^b (1425).
Brown-Robbins, Robbins-Cutler, no 3697.
Editions. Utley F L, The Layman's Complaint and the Friar's Answer, Harvard Theological Rev 38.144.
Person H A, Cambridge Lyrics, Seattle 1952, p 41.
Kaiser R, Medieval English, Berlin 1958, p 323.
Robbins-HP, p 166.

Sisam Oxf Book MEV, p 410.
Selection. James M R, A Descriptive Catalogue, Cambridge 1913, p 230 (stanza 1 only).
Textual Matters. Utley, edn, p 141.
Robbins-HP, p 338.
Scattergood PP, p 247.

[103] THE FRIARS' ANSWER.

MS. St John's Camb 195, ff 1ᵇ–2ᵇ (1425).
Brown-Robbins, Robbins-Cutler, no 161.
Editions. Utley F L, The Layman's Complaint and the Friar's Answer, Harvard Theological Rev 38.145.
Person H A, Cambridge Lyrics, Seattle 1952, p 42.
Kaiser R, Medieval English, Berlin 1958, p 323.
Robbins-HP, p 166.
Davies R T, Medieval English Lyrics, London 1963, p 265.
Sisam Oxf Book MEV, p 411.
Textual Matters. Utley, edn, p 141.
Robbins-HP, p 338.
Davies, edn, p 362.
Scattergood PP, p 247.

[104] CARMINA IOCOSA.

MSS. 1, Bodl 1797 (Digby 196), f 196ᵃ (lines 1–4 on flyleaf; 1450–1500); 2, Harley 3362, f 24ᵃ (1475–1500).
Brown-Robbins, Robbins-Cutler, no 808.
Edition. Rel Ant, 1.91 (MS 2).
General Reference. Rel Ant, 1.91.

[105] FRIARS, MINISTRI MALORUM.

MS. Trinity Camb 1144, f 58ᵇ (ca 1490).
Brown-Robbins, Robbins-Cutler, no 871.
Editions. Rel Ant, 2.247.
Wright PPS, 2.249.
Robbins-HP, p 164.
Textual Matters. Robbins-HP, p 337.
Versification. Schipper, 1.350.
General References. CHEL, 2.422.
Scattergood PP, p 245.

[106] LAMPOONS ON THE FRIARS.

a. Couplets.
MS. Harley 2252, f 1ᵇ (1510–30).
Brown-Robbins, Robbins-Cutler, no 1148.
Besserman L L, G Gilman and V Weinblatt, Three Unpublished ME Poems from the Commonplace-book of John Colyns (BM MS Harley 2252), NM 71.212 (omits this poem and other items; MS described).
Edition. Bowers R H, A ME Anti-Mendicant Squib, ELN 1.163.
Bibliography. New CBEL, 1.515.
    b. Flyleaf.
MS. Camb Univ Ff.5.31, f iv (16 cent).
Brown-Robbins, no 2531.
Edition. Raymo R R, Quod the Devill to the Frier, ELN 4.180.
Literary Relations. Rigg A G, Two Latin Poems against the Friars, MS 30.106 (friars enslaving Oxford).
Raymo R R, A ME Version of the Epistola Luciferi ad Cleros, in Medieval Literature and Civilization Studies in Memory of G N Garmonsway, ed D A Pearsall and R A Waldron, London 1969, p 233.

[107] LYARDE.

MS. Lincoln Cath 91, ff 148ᵃ–148ᵇ (1430–40).
Brown-Robbins, Robbins-Cutler, no 2026.
Edition. Rel Ant, 2.280.
Selection. Sisam Oxf Book MEV, p 403 (lines 1–12).
General Reference. Scattergood PP, p 245.

[108] ALLITERATIVE PIECES.

General References. PFMS, 3.xi.
Rosenthal F, Die alliterierende engl Langzeile im 14 Jahrhundert, Angl 1.414.
Schipper, p 32.
Schroeder A, A Comedy Concernynge Thre Lawes von Johan Bale, Angl 5.240.
Menthel E, Zur Geschichte des Otfridischen Verses im Engl, AnglA 8.49; Angl 10.105.
Luick K, Die engl Stabreimzeile im XIV, XV und XVI Jahrhundert, Angl 11.392, 553; Zur Metrik der me reimend-allitierenden Dichtung, Angl 12.437.
Teichmann E, Zur Stabreimzeile in William Langland's Buch von Peter dem Pflüger, Angl 13.140.
Amours F J, Scottish Alliterative Poems, PSTS 27.
Kaluza M, Strophische Gliederung in der me alliterierenden Dichtung, EStn 16.169.
Teichmann E, Zum Texte von William Langland's Vision, Angl 15.229, 244.
Lawrence W W, Chapters on Alliterative Verse, London 1893.
Kaluza M, Studien zur germanischen Alliterationsvers, Berlin 1894.

Trautmann M, Zur Kenntnis des altgermanischen Verses vornehmlich des Ae, AnglB 5.87; Zur Kenntniss und Geschichte der me Stabzeile, Angl 18.83.

Förster M, Das stabreimende ABC des Aristoteles, Arch 105.296.

Paul Grundriss, 2nd edn, 2¹.160.

Steffens H, Versbau und Sprache des me stabreimenden Gedichtes The Wars of Alexander, BBA 11 (crit O Ritter, Arch 113.183).

Deutschbein M, Zur Entwicklung des engl Alliterationsverses, Halle 1902.

Schneider A, Die Me Stabzeile im 15 und 16 Jahrhundert, BBA 12.103 (crit G H Gerould, EStn 34.99).

Pilch L, Umwandlung des ae verses in dem me alliterations-Reimvers, Königsberg 1904.

CHEL, 2.1, 35.

Thomas J, Die alliteriendende Langzeile des Gawayndichters, diss Jena 1908.

Schumacher K, Studien über den Stabreim in der me Alliterationsdichtung, BSEP 11.1, 139.

Menner R J, Purity, A ME Poem, YSE 61.xix.

Rankin J W, Rhythm and Rime before the Norman Conquest, PMLA 36.401.

Hulbert J R, The West Midland of the Romances, MP 19.1.

Serjeantson M S, Dialects of the West Midlands in ME, RES 3.54, 186, 319 (crit D Everett, YWES 8.128).

Hulbert J R, An Hypothesis Concerning the Alliterative Revival, MP 24.405 (crit D Everett, YWES 12.98).

Day M, Strophic Division in ME Alliterative Verse, EStn 66.245 (crit D Everett, YWES 12.99).

Andrew S O, Huchoun's Works, RES 5.12.

Andrew S O, Preterite in North West Dialects, RES 5.431.

Scripture E W, Die Grundgesetze des ac Stabreimverses, Angl 52.69.

Oakden J P, Alliterative Poetry in ME, vol 1, Manchester 1930 (crit [anon,] TLS Sept 17 1931, p 703; A Brandl, Arch 159.293; K Brunner, AnglB 42.334; E E Erickson, SP 29.128; D Everett, YWES 11.92; 13.111; 14.129; W van der Graf, ESts 13.142; W W Greg, Libr 13.188; [answered by J P Oakden, Libr 14.353]; W W Greg, The Continuity of Alliterative Tradition, MLR 27.453 [answered by J P Oakden, MLR 28.233]; J R Hulbert, MP 28.483; K Luick, LfGRP 52.233; C T Onions, RES 9.89; A H Smith, MLR 27.72; F Wild, EStn 66.406).

Oakden J P, Alliterative Poetry in ME, vol 2, Manchester 1935 (crit [anon,] TLS Jan 25 1936, p 67; K Brunner, AnglB 47.231; J R Hulbert, MP 34.198; R Kaiser, Arch 170.113; E C Knowlton, JEGP 36.120; F Mossé, Revue Anglo-Américaine 13.501; E S Olszewka, Leeds SE 5.50; H L Savage, MLN 52.430; M S Serjeantson, YWES 16.121; G V Smithers, RES 13.217).

Andrew S O, The OE Alliterative Measure, Croydon 1931 (crit K Brunner, AnglB 44.71; J R H, MP 29.376; K Malone, JEGP 31.639; S Potter, RES 9.85).

Koziol H, Zur Frage der Verfasserschaft einiger me Stabreimdichtungen, EStn 67.175 (crit D Everett, YWES 13.110).

Koziol H, Grundzüge der Syntax der me Stabreimdichtungen, WBEP 58 (crit M Callaway, Lang 10.212; A Dekker, Neophil 20.56; W Franz, DLz 54.1606; H Heuer, LfGRP 56.17; K Jost, AnglB 46.363; J Koch, EStn 68.249; H Marcus, Arch 165.254; H C Matthes, GRM 22.409; C S Northup, JEGP 34.440; C L W[renn], RES 12.246).

Oslzewska E S, Norse Formulas, Norse Alliterative Tradition in ME, Leeds SE 2.76; 6.50.

Oakden J P, The Survival of a Stylistic Feature of Indo-European Poetry in Germanic, Especially in ME, RES 9.50.

Stobie M R R, The Influence of Morphology on ME Alliterative Poetry, JEGP 39.319.

Leonard W E, Scansion of ME Alliterative Verse, Wisconsin Stud in Lang and Lit 11.58 (crit T S Graves, SAQ 20.371).

Hulbert J R, Quatrains in ME Alliterative Poems, MP 48.73.

Everett D, Essays in ME Literature, Oxford 1955, pp 23, 26, 37, 47, 139.

Hussey S S, Langland's Reading of Alliterative Poetry, MLR 60.163.

Salter E, The Alliterative Revival, MP 64.146, 233.

Suzuki E, Poetic Synonyms for Man in ME Alliterative Poems, Essays and Stud in Eng Lang and Lit, nos 49–50, p 209.

Salter E, Piers Plowman and The Simonie, Arch 203.241.

Moorman C, The Origins of the Alliterative Revival, The Southern Quart 7.345.

Shepherd G, The Nature of Alliterative Poetry in Late Medieval England, Proc Brit Acad 56.57.

Burrow J A, Ricardian Poetry, London 1971, p 33.

[109] PIERCE THE PLOUGHMAN'S CREDE.

MSS. 1, Trinity Camb 595, ff 305ᵃ–317ᵇ (1600–25); 2, Harley 78, f 3ᵃ (lines 172–207; 1460–70); 3, Royal 18.B.xvii, ff 1ᵃ–13ᵇ (ca 1520). PRINTS: 4, Wolfe R, Pierce the Ploughmans Crede, London 1553 (STC, no 19904; omits lines 822–23, 828–30; inserts 5 spurious lines as 817–21); 5, Rogers O, Pierce the Ploughmans Crede, London 1561 (STC, no 19908).

Brown-Robbins, Robbins-Cutler, no 663.

James M R, A Descriptive Catalogue, Cambridge 1901, 2.65 (MS 1 described).

Manly & Rickert, 1.527 (MS 1 described).

Doyle, Spec 34.428 (MS 2 described).

Warner G F and J P Gilson, Catalogue of the Western Manuscripts, London 1921, 2.293 (MS 3 described).

Whitaker T D, Wolfe's Pierce the Ploughmans Crede (London 1553), London 1814 (PRINT 4 rptd).

Editions. Wright T, The Vision and Creed of Piers Ploughman, 1st edn, London 1842; 2nd edn, London 1856 (MS 1).

Skeat W W, Pierce the Ploughman's Crede, EETS 30, London 1867; rvsd 1895, p 1 (MS 1 collated).

Skeat W W, Pierce the Ploughman's Crede, Oxford 1906 (reissue of EETS 30; crit R W C, MLR 2.190).

Doyle A I, An Unrecognized Piece of Piers the Ploughman's Creed and Other Works by Its Scribe, Spec 34.435 (MS 2).

Selections. Warton T, History of English Poetry, London 1824, 2.123.

Marsh G P, Origin and History of the English Language, N Y 1866, p 328.

Skeat Spec, p 1.

Cook A S, A Literary ME Reader, Boston 1915, p 352.

Textual Matters. Skeat, edn, EETS 30.33.

Skeat W W, Putting a Man under a Pot, N&Q 3s 11.277.

Sala G A, Putting a Man under a Pot, N&Q 3s 12.211.

Skeat W W, Christ-Cross, N&Q 3s 11.352 (line 1).

Skeat Spec, p 357.

Skeat, edn, Oxford 1906, p 35.

R W C, MLR 2.190 (line 2).

Williams W H, Pierce the Plowman's Crede 372, MLR 4.235 (line 372).

Haberly L, Mediaeval English Pavingtiles, Oxford 1937, p 18 (line 193).

Fleming J, Gestes of Rome (Pierce the Ploughman's Crede 45), N&Q ns 11.210.

Language. Skeat, edn, Oxford 1906, p xxviii.

Oakden J P, Alliterative Poetry in ME, Manchester 1930, 1.89, 153.

Versification. Rosenthal F, Die alliteriende engl Langzeile im 14 Jahrhundert, Angl 1.419.

Schipper, pp 197, 206.

Oakden, Alliterative Poetry, 1.193.

Date. Skeat W W, The Vision of Piers Plowman, EETS 54, London 1873, p xii; Skeat, edn, Oxford 1906, p xxvii.

Authorship. Skeat, edn, EETS 30.xi.

Lounsbury T R, Studies in Chaucer, N Y 1892, 1.460.

Oxf Ch, 7.xxxi.

Skeat W W, The Chaucer Canon, Oxford 1900, p 99.

Skeat, edn, Oxford 1906, p xx.

Bradley H, The Plowman's Tale, Athen 120 (1902).62.

CHEL, 2.39.

Sources and Literary Relations. Skeat, edn, Oxford 1906, p xxiii.

Oakden, Alliterative Poetry, 2.58.

Other Scholarly Problems. Skeat, edn, Oxford 1906, p vii (printed and MS texts).

Jones G F, Twey Mitenes As Mete, MLN 67.512 (mittens indicative of social class).

Mann J, Chaucer and Medieval Estates Satire, Cambridge 1973, p 133.

Literary Criticism. Skeat, edn, EETS 30.xvi.

Ten Brink, 2.201.

CHEL, 2.44, 493.

Skeat, edn, Oxford 1906, p xxviii.

Tucker S M, Verse Satire in England before the Renaissance, N Y 1908, p 80.

Oakden, Alliterative Poetry, 2.59.

Kinney T L, The Temper of Fourteenth-Century English Verse of Complaint, Annuale Mediaevale 7.86.

General References. Warton, Hist of Eng Poetry, 2.123.

Strutt J, Horda Angel-Cynnan, London 1775, 3.173.

Morley, 6.92.

Brandl, pp 657, 701.

Jusserand J J, trans L T Smith, English Wayfaring Life, rvsd London 1929, p 301.

Bennett H S, English Books and Readers 1475–1557, Cambridge 1952, p 208.

Schlauch M, English Medieval Literature and Its Social Foundations, Warsaw 1956, p 287.

White B, Poet and Peasant in the Reign of Richard II Essays in Honour of May McKisack, ed F R H Du Boulay and C M Barron, London 1971, p 70.

Utley F L, Manual, 3.707.
Mann, Chaucer and Medieval Estates Satire, p 49.
Elliott T J, ME Complaints Against the Times To Contemn the World or to Reform It, Annuale Mediaevale 14.31.
Bibliography. Körting, p 173; New CBEL, 1.5440.

[110] THE COMPLAINT OF THE PLOWMAN or THE PLOWMAN'S TALE.

MSS. 1, Texas Univ 8 (formerly Ashburnham), ff 1ª–8ᵇ (early 16 cent). PRINTS: 2, The Workes of Geffray Chaucer, Thomas Godfray, ca 1532 (STC, no 5068); 3, Thynne W, London 1542 (STC, no 5069); 4, Hyll W, The Plowmans Tale, London ca 1548 (STC, no 5100); 5, The Ploughmans Tale, London 1606 (STC, no 5101).
Brown-Robbins, Robbins-Cutler, no 3448.
de Ricci Census, 3.2157 (MS 1 described).
Irvine A S, A MS Copy of the Plowman's Tale, Texas SE 12.27 (crit D Everett, YWES 13.93; MS 1 described).
Editions. Stow J, The Woorkes of Geffrey Chaucer, London 1561 (STC, no 5075).
Speght T, The Workes of Geffrey Chaucer, London 1598 (STC, no 5077).
Urry J, The Works of Geoffrey Chaucer, London 1721, p 178.
Anderson R, The Works of the British Poets, London 1795, 1.218.
Chalmers A, The Works of the English Poets, London 1810, 1.623.
Wright PPS, 1.304.
Oxf Ch, 7.147.
Wawn A N, The Plowman's Tale, diss Birmingham 1969.
Textual Matters. Oxf Ch, 7.484.
Date. Skeat W W, Pierce the Ploughmans Crede, EETS 30, London 1867, p xv.
Skeat W W, The Vision of Piers Plowman, EETS 54, London 1873, p xii.
Oxf Ch, 7.xxxiv.
Bradley H, The Plowman's Tale, Athen 120 (1902).62 (14 cent Lollard piece expanded to present form during 16 cent).
Wawn A N, The Genesis of The Plowman's Tale, Yearbook of English Studies 2.21 (basically early 15 cent).
Authorship. Skeat, EETS 30.xi.
Oxf Ch, 7.xxxi.
Bradley, Athen 120(1902).62.
Skeat W W, The Chaucer Canon, Oxford 1900, p 99.
Lounsbury T R, Studies in Chaucer, N Y

1902, 1.460.
CHEL, 2.39.
Sources and Literary Relations. Marx K, Das Nachleben Piers Plowman bis zu Bunyan's The Pilgrim's Progress, Königsberg 1931.
Other Scholarly Problems. Work J A, Echoes of The Plowman's Tale in Chaucer, PMLA 47.426.
Williams F B, Unnoted Chaucer Allusions 1550–1650, PQ 16.70 (PRINT 5 used as Protestant propaganda).
Literary Criticism. Ten Brink, 2.204.
CHEL, 2.44, 491, 494.
Tucker S M, Verse Satire in England before the Renaissance, N Y 1908, p 89.
General References. Hearne T, Robert of Gloucester's Chronicle, Oxford 1724; London 1810, 2.605.
Todd H J, Illustrations of the Lives and Writings of Gower and Chaucer, London 1810, p xxxix.
Morley, 6.97.
Brandl, p 657.
Berdan J M, Early Tudor Poetry, N Y 1908, p 117.
Yunck J A, The Lineage of Lady Meed, Notre Dame 1963, p 270.
Kinney T L, The Temper of Fourteenth-Century English Verse of Complaint, Annuale Mediaevale 7.85.
Elliott T J, ME Complaints Against the Times To Contemn the World or to Reform It, Annuale Mediaevale 14.32.
Bibliography. Hammond, pp 444, 540.
New CBEL, 1.545.

[111] GOD SPEED THE PLOW I.

MS. Lansdowne 762, ff 5ª–6ᵇ (1500–40).
Brown-Robbins, no 363.
Edition. Skeat W W, Pierce the Ploughmans Crede, EETS 30, London 1867, p 69.
Textual Matters. Skeat, EETS 30.73.
General References. Brandl, p 701.
Frazer N L, English History in Contemporary Poetry, London 1914, p 36.
Schlauch M, Medieval English Literature and Its Social Foundations, Warsaw 1956, p 289.
Bibliography. Körting, p 174.

[112] GOD SPEED THE PLOW II.

MS. Trinity Camb 594, f iiiᵇ (late 14 cent).
Robbins-Cutler, no 964.5.
Edition. James M R, The Western Manuscripts in the Library of Trinity College Cambridge, Cambridge 1901, 2.64.

[113] JACK UPLAND.

MSS. 1, Camb Univ Ff.6.2, ff 71ᵃ–80ᵃ (early 16 cent); 2, Harley 6641, ff 1ᵃ–25ᵇ (15 cent). PRINTS: 3, Gough J, Jack vp Lande, London ca 1536 (STC, no 5098); 4, Speght T, The Workes of Geffrey Chaucer, London 1602, ff 348ᵃ–350ᵇ (STC, no 5080), and London 1687.

Robbins-Cutler, no 3782.5.

Heyworth, edn, pp 1 (MSS described), 5 (PRINTS described).

Heyworth P L, The Earliest Black-letter Editions of Jack Upland, HLQ 30.307 PRINTS described).

Editions. Urry J, The Works of Geoffrey Chaucer, London 1721, p 590.

Townsend G, Actes and Monuments of John Foxe, London 1843, 2.357.

Wright PPS, 2.16 (PRINT 4).

Oxf Ch, 7.191 (PRINT 3).

Heyworth P L, Jack Upland Friar Daw's Reply and Upland's Rejoinder, Oxford 1968, p 54 (critical text; crit R H Robbins, N&Q 215.266).

Selection. Sibbald J, Chronicle of Scottish Poetry, Edinburgh 1802, 2.31.

Textual Matters. Oxf Ch, 7.492.

Heyworth, edn, p 114.

Raymo R R, A ME Version of the Epistle Luciferi ad Cleros, in Medieval Literature and Civilization Studies in Memory of G N Garmonsway, ed D A Pearsall and R A Waldron, London 1969, p 234 (lines 398–99).

Language. Oakden J P, Alliterative Poetry in ME, Manchester 1930, 1.94.

Heyworth, edn, p 19.

Versification. Schipper, 1.198.

Luick K, Die engl Stabreimzeile, Angl 11.601.

Oakden, Alliterative Poetry, 1.180; 2.60.

Heyworth, edn, p 28.

Date. Kingsford EHL, p 233.

Heyworth, edn, p 9.

Authorship. Heyworth, edn, p 6.

Other Scholarly Problems. Utley F L, How Judicare Came into the Creed, MS 8.303.

Heyworth P L, Notes on Two Uncollected ME Proverbs, N&Q ns 17.86.

Literary Criticism. Tucker S M, Verse Satire in England before the Renaissance, N Y 1908, p 90.

CHEL, 2.45, 494.

Oakden, Alliterative Poetry, 2.60.

General References. Morley, 6.234.

Brandl, p 700.

Oxf Ch, 7.xxxv.

Skeat W W, The Chaucer Canon, Oxford

1900, p 141.

Bennett OHEL, p 155.

Elliott T J, ME Complaints Against the Times To Contemn the World or to Reform It, Annuale Mediaevale 14.31.

Bibliography. Oxf Ch, 7.xxxv.

Hammond, p 430.

Heyworth, edn, p 174.

Scattergood PP, p 239.

New CBEL 1.546, 687.

[114] FRIAR DAW'S REPLY.

MS. Bodl 1642 (Digby 41), ff 2ᵃ–16ᵇ (1400–20).

Robbins-Cutler, no 4098.3.

Heyworth, edn, p 2 (MS described).

Editions. Wright PPS, 2.39.

Heyworth P L, Jack Upland Friar Daw's Reply and Upland's Rejoinder, Oxford 1968, p 73 (crit R H Robbins, N&Q 215.266).

Selection. Cook A S, A Literary ME Reader, Boston 1915, p 336.

Textual Matters. Heyworth P L, ME alumere and snowcrie Two Ghosts, Eng Philological Stud 10.57 (line 900).

Heyworth, edn, p 137.

Language. Oakden J P, Alliterative Poetry in ME, Manchester 1930, 1.94.

Heyworth, edn, p 19.

Versification. Schipper, 1.198.

Luick K, Die engl Stabreimzeile, Angl 11.599.

Schneider A, Die Me Stabzeile im 15 und 16 Jahrhundert, BBA 12.107, 125.

Bennett OHEL, p 155.

Heyworth, edn, p 28.

Date. Kingsford EHL, p 233.

Heyworth, edn, p 9.

Robbins, [review,] N&Q 215.266.

Scattergood PP, p 241.

Authorship. Heyworth, edn, p 7.

Literary Relations. Rigg A G, A Glastonbury Miscellany, Oxford 1968, p 76.

Raymo R R, A ME Version of the Epistola Luciferi ad Cleros, in Medieval Literature and Civilization Studies in Memory of G N Garmonsway, ed D A Pearsall and R A Waldron, London 1969, p 234.

Literary Criticism. Oakden, Alliterative Poetry, 2.60.

General References. Morley, 6.235.

Brandl, p 700.

CHEL, 2.45, 494.

Bloomfield M W, The Seven Deadly Sins, East Lansing 1952, p 213.

Scattergood PP, pp 241, 252.

Wawn A N, The Genesis of The Plowman's Tale, Yearbook of English Studies 2.27.

Bibliography. Heyworth, edn, p 174.

[115] JACK UPLAND'S REJOINDER.

MS. Bodl 1642 (Digby 41), ff 2ª–16ᵇ (added
on margins; 1400–20).
Robbins-Cutler, no 1653.5.
Heyworth P L, Jack Upland's Rejoinder A
  Lollard Interpolator and Piers Plowman
  B.x.249.f, MÆ 36.242.
Editions. Wright PPS, 2.39.
Heyworth P L, Jack Upland Friar Daw's
  Reply and Upland's Rejoinder, Oxford
  1968, p 102 (crit R H Robbins, N&Q
  215.266).
Textual Matters. Heyworth, MÆ 36.242; edn,
  p 163.
Language. Oakden J P, Alliterative Poetry
  in ME, Manchester 1930, 1.94.
Heyworth, edn, p 19.
Versification. Heyworth, edn, p 28.
Date. Heyworth, edn, p 9.
Robbins, N&Q 215.266.
Authorship. Heyworth, edn, p 6.
Literary Criticism. Oakden, Alliterative Po-
  etry, 2.60.
Heyworth, MÆ 36.245.
General References. Morley, 6.235.
Scattergood PP, p 244.
Bibliography. Heyworth, edn, p 174.
New CBEL, 1.546.

[116] FRERE GASTKYN WO YE BE.

MS. Royal App 58, f 22ᵇ (1500–10).
Robbins-Cutler, no 870.5.
Editions. Flügel E, Liedersammlungen, Angl
  12.268.
Rimbault F E, A Little Book of Songs and
  Ballads, London 1851, p 35.

[117] THE EPISTILL OF THE HERMEIT
OF ALAREIT TO THE GRAY FREIRS.

MSS. MS not identified.
Not listed Brown-Robbins, Robbins-Cutler.
Editions. Knox J, History of the Reformation
  in Scotland, London 1644, p 26.
Knox J, History of the Reformation, London
  1732, p 25.
[Laing D,] Early Metrical Tales, Edinburgh
  1826, p 257.
Hazlitt W C, Early Popular Poetry of Scot-
  land, London 1895, 1.175.
Dickinson W C, John Knox's History, N Y
  1950, 2.333.
General Reference. [Laing,] edn, p liii.

[118] THE PAPELARD PRIEST.

MS. BM Addit 45896, Art 1 (1349).
Robbins-Cutler, no 2614.5.
Edition. Smith A H, ME Lyrics, LMS 2¹.42.
Textual Matters. Smith, LMS 2¹.48.
Language. Smith, LMS 2¹.40.
Scholarly Problems. Revard C, The Lecher
  The Legal Eagle and the Paplard Priest
  ME Confessional Satires in MS Harley 2253
  and Elsewhere, in His Firm Estate Essays
  in Honor of Franklin James Eikenberry, ed
  D E Hayden, Tulsa 1967, p 67.
General Reference. Smith, LMS 2¹.37.

[119] WHY I CAN'T BE A NUN.

MS. Cotton Vesp D.ix, ff 177ª–182ᵇ, 190ª–190ᵇ
  (begins and ends imperfectly; early 15
  cent).
Brown-Robbins, no *17; Robbins-Cutler, no
  *316.3.
Edition. Furnivall EEP, p 138.
General References. Schofield, p 373.
Power E, Medieval English Nunneries, Cam-
  bridge 1922, p 545.
Byrne Sister M, Tradition of the Nun in
  Medieval England, Washington D C 1932,
  p 174.
Utley CR, p 111.
Bloomfield M W, The Seven Deadly Sins,
  East Lansing 1952, p 205.
Scattergood PP, p 235.

[120] DEFEND US FROM ALL
LOLLARDRY.

MS. Cotton Vesp B.xvi, ff 2ᵇ–3ª (1450–60).
Brown-Robbins, Robbins-Cutler, no 1926.
Editions. Turner S, History of England, Lon-
  don 1814, 3.227.
Wright PPS, 2.243.
Ritson AS, p 105.
Robbins-HP, p 152.
Textual Matters. Robbins-HP, p 331.
Date. Kingsford EHL, p 234.
Literary Relations. Wright PPS, 1.231.
Scattergood PP, p 129.
General References. Brandl, p 700.
Kingsford C L, English Literature in Con-
  temporary Poetry, No 2, London 1913, p 8.
Eberhard O, Der Bauernaufstand vom Jahr
  1381 in der engl Poesie, AF 51.52.
Rowse A L, Bosworth Field, Garden City
  N Y 1966, p 43.
Scattergood PP, pp 132, 255.

IV. Women

[121] ATTACKS ON WOMEN.

General References. Wright T, Womankind in All Ages of Western Europe, London 1869, pp 251, 257.

Tucker S M, Verse Satire in England before the Renaissance, N Y 1908.

Allinson A, The Sword and Womankind, London 1921.

Utley CR.

Rogers K M, The Troublesome Helpmate, Seattle 1966, p 73.

[122] ADVICE ON MARRIAGE I.

MS. Lansdowne 762, f 91ᵇ (1500–40).

Brown-Robbins, Robbins-Cutler, no 2633.

Editions. Rel Ant, 1.288.

Herrtage S J H, The Early English Versions of the Gesta Romanorum, EETSES 33, London 1879, p 510.

Literary Relations. Ritchie W T, The Bannatyne Manuscript, PSTS 26.36 (for text of Bannatyne poem).

Ault W, Elizabethan Lyrics, London 1925, p 35 (for text of Tom Tyler carol).

Utley CR, p 145 (for Tom Tyler carol).

General Reference. Utley CR, p 218.

[123] ADVICE ON MARRIAGE II.

MS. Harley 2252, f 84ᵇ (1510–30).

Brown-Robbins, Robbins-Cutler, no 3172.

Editions. Rel Ant, 1.259.

Flügel NL, p 140.

General Reference. Utley CR, p 235.

[124] ADVICE ON MARRIAGE III.

MSS. 1, Bodl 1797 (Digby 196), f 20ᵃ (ca 1400); 2, Durham Univ Cosin V.iii.9, ff 16ᵇ, 37ᵇ, 85ᵇ (later additions; 16 cent).

Brown-Robbins, Robbins-Cutler, no 1829.

Macray G D, Catalogi Codicum MSS Bibliothecae Bodleianae, Codices Digby, Oxford 1883, p 212 (MS 1 described).

Editions. Furnivall F J, Hoccleve's Minor Poems, EETSES 61, London 1892, pp 124, 156, 228 (MS 2).

Robbins SL, p 37 (MS 1).

Textual Matters. Robbins SL, p 239.

Literary Relations. Utley CR, p 155 (for dispraise of women).

General Reference. Utley CR, p 171.

[125] ADVICE ON MARRIAGE IV.

MS. Bodl 27934 (Eng poet e.1), f 26ᵃ (1460–80).

Brown-Robbins, Robbins-Cutler, no 2049.

Editions. Wright T, Songs and Carols of the Fifteenth Century, PPS 23.35.

[Masters J E,] Rymes of the Minstrels, Shaftesbury Dorset 1927, p 17.

General Reference. Utley CR, p 187.

[126] ADVICE ON MARRIAGE V.

MS. Bodl 29734 (Eng poet e.1), f 26ᵃ (1460–80).

Brown-Robbins, Robbins-Cutler, no 3919.

Editions. Wright T, Songs and Carols of the Fifteenth Century, PPS 23.35.

[Masters J E,] Rymes of the Minstrels, Shaftesbury Dorset 1927, p 17.

Robbins SL, p 37.

Textual Matters. Robbins SL, p 239.

General Reference. Utley CR, p 187.

[127] ADVICE ON MARRIAGE VI.

MSS. 1, Bodl 29734 (Eng poet e.1), f 26ᵃ (1460–80); 2, Harley 2316, f 56ᵇ (1350–1400); 3, Hunterian Mus 230, f 248ᵇ (early 16 cent; included in Robbins-Cutler, no 1628.8).

Brown-Robbins, Robbins-Cutler, no 2056.

Editions. Wright T, Songs and Carols of the Fifteenth Century, PPS 23.35 (MS 1).

Wright T, Latin Stories, PPS 8.83 (MS 2).

Ward, 2.307 (MS 2).

[Masters J E,] Rymes of the Minstrels, Shaftesbury Dorset 1927, p 17 (MS 1).

General Reference. Utley CR, p 187.

[128] ADVICE ON MARRIAGE VII.

MS. Lansdowne 762, f 92ᵃ (1500–40).

Brown-Robbins, Robbins-Cutler, no 1392.

Editions. Rel Ant, 1.289.

Robbins SL, p 239.

Literary Relations. Utley CR, p 237, 130 (for Spektakle of Luf).

General Reference. Utley CR, p 156.

[129] VIRTUOUS MAIDENS BUT WICKED WIVES.

MSS. 1, Bodl 3354 (Arch Selden B.24), ff 119ᵇ–120ᵃ (ca 1486); 2, Advocates 1.1.6, ff

262ᵇ–263ᵃ (ca 1568). PRINT: 3, Chepman and Myllar, London ca 1508.
Brown-Robbins, Robbins-Cutler, no 679.
Brown J T T, The Authorship of the Kingis Quair A New Criticism, Glasgow 1896, p 5 (MS 1 described).
Hammond, p 342 (MS 1 described).
Root R K, The Manuscripts of Chaucer's Troilus, ChS 1s 98 (MS 1 described).
Craigie W A, The Language of The Kingis Quair, E&S 25.22 (MS 1 described).
Parkes M, English Cursive Book Hands 1250–1500, Oxford 1969, p 13 (MS 1 described).
Norton-Smith J, James I of Scotland The Kingis Quair, Oxford 1971, p xxxi (MS 1 described).
McDiarmid M, The Kingis Quair of James Stewart, London 1973, p 2 (MS 1 described).
Stevenson G, Pieces from the Makculloch and the Gray MSS Together with the Chepman and Myllar Prints, PSTS 65.217 (PRINT 3 rptd).
Beattie W, The Chepman and Myllar Prints, Edinburgh Biblio Soc, Oxford 1950, p 145 (facsimile of PRINT 3).
Editions. Murdoch J B, The Bannatyne Manuscript, Hunterian Club, 4 vols, Glasgow 1873, 4.766 (MS 2).
Ritchie W T, The Bannatyne Manuscript, PSTS ns 26.34 (MS 2).
Date. McDiarmid, Kingis Quair, p 2.
Authorship. Hammond, p 341.
Utley CR, p 124.
Literary Relations. Rel Ant, 1.29 (for Peter Idley, MS Laud 416).
D'Evelyn C, Peter Idley's Instructions to His Son, MLA Monograph 6, p 143.
General Reference. Utley CR, p 124.

[130] **THE SNARES OF WOMEN.**

MS. Bodl 11224 (Rawlinson A.338), ff 111ᵇ–112ᵃ (early 16 cent).
Robbins-Cutler, no 1166.5.

[131] **THE TRIALS OF MARRYING A YOUNG WIFE I.**

MS. Bodl 10234 (Tanner 407), f 38ᵇ (1480–1500).
Brown-Robbins, Robbins-Cutler, no 1278.
Edition. Robbins SL, p 164.
Textual Matters. Robbins SL, p 280.

[132] **THE TRIALS OF MARRYING A YOUNG WIFE II.**

MS. Bodl 21831 (Douce 257), f 99ᵇ (added on flyleaf; 15 cent).

Brown-Robbins, no *63; Robbins-Cutler, no *3533.5.
Editions. Rel Ant, 2.113 (2nd stanza only). Robbins SL, p 38.
Textual Matters. Robbins SL, p 240.
Literary Relations. Utley CR, pp 101, 108 (for Folye of ane Auld Man).
General Reference. Utley CR, p 259.

[133] **SORROWS OF MARRIAGE.**

MS. Nat Libr Scot Gaelic 37 (formerly Lismore), p 48 (early 16 cent).
Not listed Brown-Robbins, Robbins-Cutler.
MacLaughan T, The Dean of Lismore's Book, Edinburgh 1862 (MS described).
Cameron A, Reliquiae Celticae, 1.2 (MS described).
Watson W J, Scottish Verse from the Book of the Dean of Lismore, Edinburgh 1937, p xi (MS described).
Ross N, Heroic Poetry from the Book of the Dean of Lismore, Edinburgh 1939, p xiii (MS described); Treasures from Scottish Libraries, Edinburgh 1964, p 29 (MS described).
Edition. Stemmler T, Medieval English Love-Lyrics, Tübingen 1970, p 36.

[134] **IRONIC PRAISE OF WOMEN.**

MS. Bodl 6933 (Ashmole 48), ff 88ᵃ–90ᵇ (ca 1560).
Robbins-Cutler, no 4044.6.
Edition. Wright T, Songs and Ballads, Roxb Club 78.145.
Date. Rollins H, Concerning Bodleian MS Ashmole 48, MLN 34.349.
Seaton E, Sir Richard Roos, London 1961, p 190.
Literary Relations. Utley CR, p 165 (destroying burden).
Rogers K M, The Troublesome Helpmate, Seattle 1966, p 62.
Brown-Robbins, Robbins-Cutler, nos 212, 1593, 3174.5, 3909.6 (punctuation poems).
MS Cotton Titus A.xxiv, ff 79ᵃ, 85ᵃ (mid to late 16 cent; satirical verses in dispraise of women).
General References. Utley CR, p 299.
Seaton, Sir Richard Roos, p 190.

[135] **LATER POEMS ATTACKING WOMEN.**

General References. Utley CR, pp 210 (Women Will Have Their Will), 249 (Discontented Husband), 125 (Doctrina et Consilium Galiensis), 175 (Curste Wyfe), 280 (God Gif I Were Wedow Now), 164 (Wo Worth Maryage), 131 (To Soone Maryed), 104 (To Late Maryed), 141, 148, 301 (Forester carols), 114 (Gyl of Braintford's Testament), 305 (Seuen Sorowes), 239 (XV Joyes of Maryage).

Rogers K M, The Troublesome Helpmate, Seattle 1966, p 61.

See also [139] below.

[136] AGAINST WOMEN'S HORNS I.

MS. Caius Camb 408, f 258ᵃ (13 cent).
Brown-Robbins, Robbins-Cutler, no 4093.
Editions. James M R, A Descriptive Catalogue, Cambridge 1908, 2.476.
Robbins-HP, p 324.
General Reference. Utley CR, pp 50, 54, 303.

[137] AGAINST WOMEN'S HORNS II.

MSS. 1, Bodl 1986 (Bodley 123), f 6ᵇ (ca 1490); 2, Corp Christi Oxf 274, f 155ᵃ (early 15 cent); 3, Armagh, Bishop John Swayne's Register (1418–39).
Brown-Robbins, Robbins-Cutler, no 811.
Editions. Coxe H O, Catalogus Codicum MSS Qui in Collegiis Aulisque Oxoniensibus Hodie Adservantur, Oxford 1852, p 117 (MS 2).
Wright PPS, 2.252 (MS 2).
Cotton H, Fasti Ecclesiae Hiberniae, Dublin 1845, 3.vi (MS 3).
Seymour St J D, Three Medieval Poems from Kilkenny, Proc Royal Irish Acad 41.209 (MS 3).
Robbins-HP, p 323 (MS 3, stanza 2 only).
Wilson Lost Lit, 2nd edn, p 200.
General References. Utley CR, p 130.
Scattergood PP, p 345.
Wenzel S, Unrecorded Middle-English Verse, Angl 94.61.

[138] AGAINST WOMEN'S HORNS III.

MS. Bodl 6943 (Ashmole 59), f 73ᵃ (1447–56).
Brown-Robbins, Robbins-Cutler, no 3698.
Edition. Robbins-HP, p 139.
Literary Relations. Robbins-HP, p 323 (15 cent poems).
General References. Utley CR, p 265.
Scattergood PP, p 342.

[139] FURTHER LATER POEMS ATTACKING WOMEN.

General References. Utley CR, pp 233 (In Contemptioun of Syde Taillis), 235 (Satire on the Town Ladies), 258 (Of Nyce Wyues), 172 (To an Olde Gentlewoman), 116 (Treatyse).
Rogers K M, The Troublesome Helpmate, Seattle 1966, pp 73, 86, 90, 94.

[140] EPIGRAM ON EXTRAVAGANCE I.

MSS. 1, Bodl 2712 (Bodley 315), f 268ᵃ (20 lines; early 15 cent); 2, Naples Royal Libr 13.B.29, p 113 (lines 1–4 only; 1450–75).
Robbins-Cutler, no 4135.5; Brown-Robbins, no 1156 (lines 1–4 only).
Editions. Rel Ant, 2.67 (MS 2).
Rose-Troup F, Verses in the Hall at Launceston, Devon and Cornwall Notes and Queries 19.154 (MS 1).
Robbins R H, Wall Verses at Launceston Priory, Arch 200.342 (MSS 1, 2).
Literary Relations. Robbins, Arch 200.338.

[141] EPIGRAM ON EXTRAVAGANCE II.

MS. Corp Christi Oxf 274, f 155ᵃ (flyleaf; early 15 cent).
Brown-Robbins, Robbins-Cutler, no 2010.
Edition. Coxe H O, Catalogus Codicum MSS Qui in Collegiis Aulisque Oxoniensibus Hodie Adservantur, Oxford 1852, p 117.
Wright PPS, 2.252.

[142] TUTIVILLUS: AGAINST GOSSIPING WOMEN.

MS. Bodl 21678 (Douce 104), f 112ᵇ (flyleaf; 1475–1500).
Brown-Robbins, Robbins-Cutler, no 3812.
Editions. Rel Ant, 1.257.
Kild Ged, p 223.
Brown RLxvC, p 277.
Davies R T, Medieval English Lyrics, London 1963, p 198.
Sisam Oxf Book MEV, p 484.
Textual Matters. Brown RLxvC, p 348.
Davies, edn, p 346.
Literary Relations. Robbins-Cutler, nos 707.5, 1214.9, 1655.5 (for macaronic songs).
Smart W K, Mankind and the Mumming Plays, MLN 32.21 (Tutivillus and Mankind).

Wells, p 235 (Tutivillus, Narratio Sancti Augustini, and Towneley Judgment).
Brown RLxvC, p 348 (Tutivillus and Mankind).
Utley CR, pp 55, 202, 279 (Tutivillus and Vitaspatrum).
General Reference. Cushman L W, The Devil and the Vice in English Dramatic Literature, 1900; rptd N Y 1970, pp 31, 35, 46.
Bibliography. Cushman, p 35.

[143] AGAINST INDISCREET WOMEN.

MS. Camb Univ Ii.3.8, f 68ᵇ (1400–50).
Brown-Robbins, Robbins-Cutler, no 514.
Erb, MS 33.63 (MS described).
Edition. Erb P C, Vernacular Material for Preaching in MS Cambridge University Library Ii.III.8, MS 33.72.
General Reference. Utley CR, p 115.

[144] THE HART LOVETH THE WOOD.

MS. Ipswich County Hall Deposit, Hillwood (formerly Brome), f 1ᵃ (1450–1500).
Robbins-Cutler, no 3372.6.
Greene R L, The Book of Brome Appearance and Disappearance, Yale Univ Libr Gazette, Oct 1967, p 107.
Edition. Smith L T, A Commonplace Book of the Fifteenth Century, Norwich 1886, p 11.
Literary Relations. Rel Ant, 2.40.
Utley CR, p 257.
Opie I and P Opie, Oxford Dictionary of Nursery Rhymes, Oxford 1951, p 200.
General Reference. Utley CR, p 248.

[145] ADVICE ON CONDUCT.

MS. Stockdale Hardy Leicester Psalter (15 cent; present location not known).
Brown-Robbins, Robbins-Cutler, no 2033.
Edition. Rel Ant, 2.117.
General References. Wells, p 235.
Utley CR, pp 51, 54, 186.

[146] THE ALE-WIFE GROUP.

General References. Browne M, Chaucer's England, London 1869, p 190.
Wright T, Womankind in All Ages of Western Europe, London 1869, p 269.
Utley CR, pp 158 (If I Be Wanton), 241 (Take IIJ Clateras), 99 (A Harlatt), 103

(IIJ Propretes), 163 (John Wallys' Lampoon).
Robbins R H, Good Gossips Reunited, BMQ 27.12.

[147] THE GOSSIPS' MEETING.

MS. Nat Libr Wales Deposit, Porkington 10, ff 56ᵇ–59ᵇ (1450–75).
Brown-Robbins, Robbins-Cutler, no 1852.
Kurvinen A, MS Porkington 10 Description with Extracts, NM 54.33 (MS described).
Edition. Furnivall F J, Jyl of Breyntford's Testament and Other Poems, London 1871, p 29.
Literary Relations. Furnivall, edn, p 6.
General Reference. Utley CR, p 183.

[148] GOOD GOSSIPS.

MSS. 1, Cotton Titus A.xxvi, ff 161ᵃ–162ᵃ (ca 1470); 2, Cotton Vitell D.xii, f 43ᵃ (stanzas 1–3 only; 1475–1500).
Brown-Robbins, no *32; Robbins-Cutler, no 2358.5.
Editions. Ritson AS, 1790, 1.77; 1829, 1.136; 1877, 2.117 (MS 1).
Wright T, Songs and Carols of the Fifteenth Century, PPS 23.104 (MS 1).
Arber E, The Dunbar Anthology, London 1901, p 108 (MS 1).
Dyboski R, Songs Carols and Other Miscellaneous Poems, EETSES 101, London 1907, p 187 (MS 1).
Flügel E, Liedersammlungen des XVI Jahrhunderts, Angl 26.213 (MS 1).
Masters J E, The Gossips, Shaftesbury Dorset 1926 (MS 1).
Greene E E Carols, p 283 (MS 1).
Greene R L, Selection of English Carols, Oxford 1962, p 148 (MS 1).
Robbins R H, Good Gossips Reunited, BMQ 27.12 (MS 2).
Literary Relations. Greene E E Carols, p 280.
Deemling H, The Chester Plays, EETSES 62, London 1892, p 57.
Rollins H E, The Pepys Ballads, Cambridge Mass 1929, 2.175 (Foure Wittie Gossips).
Utley CR, pp 139, 152, 183, 197, 198, 241, 282.
Bibliography. Robbins, BMQ 27.14.

[149] THE GOSSIPS' ROYAL FEAST.

MSS. No MS extant. PRINT: Cryste Crosse me Spede, de Worde, n d.

Robbins-Cutler, no 603.5.
General Reference. Dibdin T F, Typographical Antiquities, London 1810, 2.368.

[150] JOHN CROPHILL'S ALE POTS.

MS. Harley 1735, f 48ᵃ (1456–83).
Robbins-Cutler, no 870.8.
Edition. Robbins R H, John Crophill's Ale-Pots, RES ns 20.185.
Textual Matters. Robbins, RES ns 20.188.
Authorship. DNB, 13.208.
Talbert E W, The Notebook of a Fifteenth-Century Practicing Physician, Texas SE 21.5.
Robbins, RES ns 20.182.
Literary Criticism. Robbins R H, The Fraternity of Drinkers, SP 47.36 (tail-rime stanzas).
General References. Scattergood V J, Correspondence, RES ns 21.337.
Talbot C H and E A Hammond, The Medical Practitioners in Medieval England, London 1965, p 138.
Talbot C H, Medicine in Medieval England, London 1967, p 190.

[151] THE FRATERNITY OF DRINKERS.

MS. Nat Libr Wales Peniarth 53, pp 103–111

(1485–1500).
Brown-Robbins, Robbins-Cutler, no 1726.
Historical MSS Commission: Report on MSS in the Welsh Language, London 1899, 1.403 (MS described).
Editions. Baugh A C, A Fraternity of Drinkers, in Philologica The Malone Anniv Stud, ed T A Kirby, Baltimore 1949, p 202.
Robbins R H, The Fraternity of Drinkers, SP 47.36.
Literary Relations. Wright PS, p 137 (Order of Fair Ease).
Literary Criticism. Baugh, edn, p 200.

[152] PROSE PIECES AGAINST WOMEN.

General References and Bibliographies. Utley CR, pp 139 (Gospelles of Dystaues), 221 (Proude Wyues Pater Noster).

[153] LATER POEMS AGAINST WOMEN WITH DOUBLE ENTENDRE.

General References and Bibliographies. Utley CR, pp 290 (To a Fickle and Unconstaunt Dame), 237 (Sore This Dere Strykyn Ys), 148 (I Haiff a Littill Fleming Berge), 209 (Now Gossop I Must Neidis Begon), 205 (My Mistress Is In Musik), 216 (Off Cullouris Cleir).

V. Contemporary Life: Vignettes

[154] NARRACIO DE DOMINO DENARII.

MSS. 1, Caius Camb 174, IV, pp 484–86 (1480–1500); 2, Cotton Galba E.ix, ff 50ᵇ–51ᵃ (1440–50).
Brown-Robbins, Robbins-Cutler, no 1480.
Editions. Ellis EEP, 1.269 (MS 2).
Ritson APP, p 103 (MS 2).
Rel Ant, 2.108 (MS 1).
Wright T, Latin Poems Commonly Attributed to Walter Mapes, Camden Soc 16.359 (MS 2).
Hazlitt Rem, 1.161 (MS 1).
FitzGibbon H M, Early English Poetry, London 1887, p 13 (MS 2).
Hall J, Short Pieces from MS Cotton Galba E.ix, EStn 21.204 (MS 2).
Coulton G G, Social Life in Britain, Cambridge 1918, p 367 (MS 1).
Robbins SL, p 51 (MS 2).
Selection. Segar M G and E Paxton, Some Minor Poems of the Middle Ages, London

1917, p 34.
Modernization. Shackford H M, Legends and Satires from Medieval Literature, Boston 1913, p 134.
Textual Matters. Robbins SL, p 244.
Other Scholarly Problems. Yunck J A, Dan Denarius the Almighty Penny and the Fifteenth Century Poets, American Journ of Economics and Society 20.207.
Literary Relations. Wright, Camden Soc 16.355, 361, 362 (French, Latin and Scottish versions).
Lehmann P, Parodistische Texte, Munich 1923, pp 7, 15 (Latin satires).
Yunck J A, Medieval French Money Satire, MLQ 16.73.
Scattergood PP, p 334.
Elliott T J, ME Complaints Against the Times To Contemn the World or to Reform It, Annuale Mediaevale 14.28.
General References. Warton T, History of English Poetry, London 1824, 3.379.

Brandl, p 710.
Schofield, p 372.
Mohl R, The Three Estates in Medieval and Renaissance Literature, N Y 1933, p 108.
Yunck J A, The Lineage of Lady Meed, Notre Dame Ind 1963, p 309.
Lindsay J, Nine Day's Hero Wat Tyler, London 1964, p 35.
Scattergood PP, p 338.
Bibliography. Yunck, American Journ of Economics and Society 20.221.

[155] THE POWER OF THE PURSE.

MS. Bodl 29734 (Eng poet e.1), ff 26ᵇ–27ᵃ (1460–80).
Brown-Robbins, Robbins-Cutler, no 2082.
Editions. Wright T, Songs and Carols of the Fifteenth Century, PPS 23.35.
Arber E, The Dunbar Anthology, London 1901, p 179.
[Masters J E,] Rymes of the Minstrels, Shaftesbury Dorset 1927, p 10.
Robbins SL, p 55.
Davies R T, Medieval English Lyrics, London 1963, p 224.
General References. Davies, edn, p 353.
Scattergood PP, p 338.

[156] ON PENNY.

MSS. 1, Bodl 21626 (Douce 52), f 15ᵇ (first couplet only; mid 15 cent); 2, Caius Camb 261, f 234ᵃ (14 cent); 3, Sloane 2232, f 9ᵇ (17 cent; variant); 4, Rylands Libr Latin 394, f 7ᵃ (mid 15 cent).
Brown-Robbins, Robbins-Cutler, no 3209.
Editions. Förster M, Die me Sprichwörtersammlung in Douce 52, in Festschrift zum XII Allgemeinen Deutschen Neuphilologentage in München 1906, ed E Strollreither, Erlangen 1906, p 45 (MS 1).
James M R, A Descriptive Catalogue, Cambridge 1907, 1.317 (MS 2).
Greene E E Carols, p 429 (MS 2).
Robbins SL, p 57 (MS 2).
Pantin W A, A Medieval Collection of Latin and English Proverbs, JRLB 14.96 (MS 4).
Kaiser R, Medieval English, Berlin 1958, p 550 (MS 2).
Silverstein T, Medieval English Lyrics, London 1971, p 96 (MS 2).
Scattergood PP, p 336 (MS 2).
General Reference. Scattergood PP, p 336.

[157] GRAMERCY MYN OWN PURSE.

MSS. No MS extant. PRINT: Berners J, Boke

of Hawkynge and Huntynge, de Worde 1496, sig e vi 6 (STC, no 3309).
Robbins-Cutler, no 33.5.
Hands R, Juliana Berners and the Boke of St Albans, RES ns 18.24.
Editions. Ritson AS, 1790, p 89; 1829, 2.6; 1877, p 151.
Haslewood J, London 1810 (facs).
Dibdin T F, Typographical Antiquities, London 1812, 2.60.
Bethune G W, British Female Poets, Phila 1848, p 14.
Ellis Spec, p 363.
Blades W, London 1881 (facs).
Arber E, Dunbar Anthology, London 1901, p 182.

[158] LONDON LICKPENNY.

MSS. 1, Harley 367, ff 127ᵃ, 126ᵃ–126ᵇ (1600–25); 2, Harley 542, ff 102ᵃ–104ᵃ (ca 1600).
Brown-Robbins, Robbins-Cutler, no 3759.
Hammond, edn, Angl 20.404 (MSS described).
Editions. Strutt J, Horda Angel-Cynnan, London 1775, 3.59 (MS 1).
Hughson D, London Being an Accurate History, London 1805, 2.124 (MS 1).
Nicolas N H and E Tyrrell, Chronicle of London, London 1827, p 260 (MSS 1, 2).
Halliwell J O, Lydgate's Minor Poems, PPS 2.103 (MS 1).
Gilfillan G, Specimens of the Less Known British Poets, Edinburgh 1860, 1.49 (MS 1).
Morley H, Shorter English Poems, N Y 1876, p 53 (MS 1).
FitzGibbon H M, Early English Poetry, London 1887, p 68 (MS 1).
Skeat Spec, p 24 (MS 1).
Hammond E P, London Lickpenny, Angl 20.410 (MSS 1, 2).
Bronson W C, English Poems, Chicago 1910, 1.166 (MS 1).
Benham A R, English Literature from Widsith to the Death of Chaucer, New Haven 1916, p 351 (MS 1).
Holthausen F, London Lickpenny, Angl 43.62 (composite text).
Bridge F, Old Cryes of London, London 1921, p 11 (MS 2).
Hammond E P, English Verse between Chaucer and Surrey, Durham N C 1927, pp 237, 476 (MSS 1, 2).
Robbins-HP, p 130 (MS 1).
Tydeman W, English Poetry 1400–1580, N Y 1970, p 43 (MS 2).
Selection. Sisam Oxf Book MEV, p 446 (MS 1, omits lines 15–21, 29–34, 57–63).
Modernizations. Furlong N, English Satire,

London 1946, p 35.
Loomis R S, and R Willard, Medieval English Verse and Prose, N Y 1948, p 395.
Textual Matters. Skeat Spec, p 373.
Holthausen, Angl 43.67.
Robbins-HP, p 300.
Tydeman, edn, p 175.
Authorship. MacCracken H N, Lydgate's Minor Poems, EETSES 107, London 1910, p xlvii.
Kingsford EHL, p 232.
Bennett OHEL, p 141.
Literary Relations. Craigie W A, The Maitland Folio Manuscript, PSTS ns 7.399 (for Sir Penny).
Literary Criticism. Snell F J, The Age of Transition, London 1905, 1.45.
General References. Stow J, Survey of London, London 1598, p 219; rptd Kingsford C L, Stow's Survey of London, Oxford 1908, 1.217; 2.313, 288.
Hammond, Angl 20.407.
Tucker S M, Verse Satire in England before the Renaissance, N Y 1908, p 121.
Schlauch M, English Medieval Literature and Its Social Foundations, Warsaw 1958, p 293.
Lindsay J, Nine Day's Hero Wat Tyler, London 1964, pp 86, 122.
Rowse A L, Bosworth Field, Garden City N Y 1966, p 57.

[159] SIR PENNY.

MSS. 1, Pepys 2553, p 330 (1570–90); 1a, Camb Univ Ll.5.10, f 40ᵃ (transcription, ca 1622); 2, Advocates 1.1.6, f 144ᵃ (ca 1568).
Robbins-Cutler, no 2821.5.
Editions. Ramsay A, The Evergreen, Glasgow 1724; rptd 1785, 1.27 (MS 2).
Dalyrmple D [Lord Hailes], Ancient Scottish Poems, Edinburgh 1770, p 193 (MS 2).
Caledonian Muse, 1785, p 164 (MS 2).
Sibbald J, Chronicle of Scottish Poetry, 4 vols, Edinburgh 1802, 3.227 (MS 2).
Wright T, The Latin Poems Commonly Ascribed to Walter Mapes, Camden Soc 16.362 (MS 2).
Murdoch J B, The Bannatyne Manuscript, Hunterian Club, 4 vols, Glasgow 1873, 3.409 (MS 2).
Craigie W A, The Maitland Folio Manuscript, PSTS ns 7.399 (MS 1).
Ritchie W T, The Bannatyne Manuscript, PSTS ns 23.35 (MS 1).
Other Scholarly Problems. Yunck J A, Dan Denarius the Almyghty Penny and the

Fifteenth Century Poets, American Journ of Economics and Sociology 20(1961).207.
General Reference. Yunck J A, The Lineage of Lady Meed, Notre Dame 1963, pp 76, 206, 211.

[160] A SONG OF GALAUNT.

MSS. 1, Trinity Camb 601, ff 247ᵃ–248ᵇ (1470–80); 2, Bodl Astor 2, ff 210ᵃ–213ᵇ (1450–1500); 3, Rome Venerable Eng Coll 1306, ff 78ᵃ–81ᵃ (1450–1500). PRINT: 4, A Treatyse of a Galaunt, de Worde 1520 (STC, no 24241).
Brown-Robbins, Robbins-Cutler, no 1874.
Davis N, [review,] RES ns 18.445 (MS 2 described).
Klinefelter R A, A Newly Discovered Fifteenth-Century English Manuscript, MLQ 14.3 (MS 3 described).
Robbins R H, A ME Diatribe against Philip of Burgundy, Neophil 39.131 (MS 3 described).
Editions. Brydges S E, Censura Literaria ns 5, London 1805, p 37; 2nd edn 1815, 1.62 (PRINT 4).
Halliwell J C, A Treatyse of a Galaunt, Roxb Club 77, London 1860 (PRINT 4).
Furnivall F J, Ballads from Manuscripts, London 1868, 1.445 (MS 1).
Hazlitt Rem, 3.151 (PRINT 4).
Date. Lee S, Acad 43.104.
MacCracken H N, Minor Poems of John Lydgate, EETSES 107, London 1910, p xxxii.
Robbins, Neophil 39.132.
Authorship. Bühler C F, Libri Impressi cum Notis Manuscriptis Part I, MLN 53.246 (Bishop Alcock's sermon reference to Lydgate).
General References. MacCracken, EETSES 107.xxxiii.
Bloomfield M J, The Seven Deadly Sins, East Lansing 1952, p 206.
Scattergood PP, p 343.

[161] AGAINST PROUD GALAUNTS.

MSS. 1, Univ Coll Oxf 154, flyleaf f iiᵃ (15 cent); 2, Trinity Camb 1157, f 27ᵃ (1460–80); 3, Harley 372, f 113ᵃ (1440–50).
Brown-Robbins, Robbins-Cutler, no 4255; Robbins-Cutler, no 4254.5.
Editions. Strutt J, Horda Angel-Cynnan, London 1775, 3.78 (MS 3).
Wright PPS, 2.251 (MS 3).
Fairholt E W, Satirical Songs and Poems on Costume, PPS 27.56 (MS 3).

General References. Tucker S M, Verse Satire in England before the Renaissance, N Y 1908, p 132.

Kingsford EHL, p 245.

MacCracken H N, Minor Poems of John Lydgate, EETSES 107, London 1910, p xxxii.

Schlauch M, The Revolt of 1381 in England, SciS 4.417.

Scattergood PP, pp 227, 343.

[162] A MACARONIC COUPLET ON GALAUNT.

MS. Lansdowne 762, f 92ᵃ (1500–40).
Robbins-Cutler, no 892.5.
Edition. Rel Ant, 1.268.

[163] AN EPITAPH WITH WARNING TO GALAUNTS.

MSS. No MS extant. Painting with text in Hungerford Chapel, Salisbury Cathedral.
Robbins-Cutler, no 143.8.
Editions. Gough R, Sepulchral Monuments of Great Britain, London 1786, 2.187 (with illust).
Pettigrew T J, Chronicles of the Tombs, London 1875, p 170.
Woolf R, The English Religious Lyric in the Middle Ages, Oxford 1968, p 348.
Gray D, Themes and Images in the Medieval English Religious Lyric, London 1972, p 207.
Literary Relations. Brown-Robbins, Robbins-Cutler, no 892 (Huff a Galaunt); no 36 (Jack Hare).
Robbins-Cutler, no *1585.8 (acephalous attack); no 2832.2 (Jolly Rutterkin); no 4256.8 (Drunkard).
Gough, edn, 2.274 (Latin dialogue).
Hazlitt Rem, 3.148.
Furnivall F J, The Digby Plays, EETSES 70, London 1896, p 73 (Play of Mary Magdalene, lines 491–506).
England G, The Towneley Plays, EETSES 71, London 1897, p 374.
Literary Criticism. Woolf, edn, p 348.

[164] THE SCHOOLBOY'S WISH.

MS. Lincoln Cath 132, f 100ᵃ (1475–1500).
Brown-Robbins, Robbins-Cutler, no 3895.
Editions. Woolley R M, Catalogue of the Manuscripts, London 1927, p 93.
Robbins SL, p 105.
Sisam Oxf Book MEV, p 485.
Textual Matters. Bowers R H, Notes on the ME Schoolboy Verses in Lincoln Cath Chapter Lib MS 132, PQ 16.82.

[165] FULGENS SCOLA DISCOLUS EST MERCATOR PESSIMUS.

MS. BM Addit 14997, f 44ᵇ (1500).
Brown-Robbins, no 2683.
Edition. Hammerle K, Verstreute me und frühne Lyrik, Arch 166.203.
General Reference. Hammerle, Arch 166.202.

[166] THE SCHOOLBOY'S PLEA.

MS. Sloane 1584, f 33ᵃ (1500–20).
Robbins-Cutler, no 320.5.
Editions. Rel Ant, 1.116.
Furnivall F J, The Babees Book, EETS 32, London 1868, p 405; rvsd edn, p 387.
Literary Relations. Halliwell J O, The Moral Play of Wit and Science, Shakespeare Soc, London 1848, p 62 (We poore sylye boyes abyde much woe).

[167] SCHOOLBOY EXERCISES.

a. Names of birds.
MS. Harley 1002, f 72ᵃ (1475–1500).
Not listed Brown-Robbins, Robbins-Cutler.
Edition. Wright C E, Late ME Parerga in a School Collection, RES ns 2.116.
b. Animal noises.
MS. Harley 1002, f 72ᵃ (1475–1500).
Robbins-Cutler, no 430.8.
Editions. Herrtage S J, Catholicon Anglicum, EETS 75, London 1881, p 82.
Wright, RES ns 2.117.
c. Aphorisms.
MS. Harley 1002, f 72ᵇ (1475–1500).
Robbins-Cutler, no 1632.5.
Edition. Wright, RES ns 2.118.
d. In the spring.
MS. Harley 1002, f 72ᵇ (1475–1500).
Robbins-Cutler, no 4028.6.
Editions. Wright, RES ns 2.119.
Robbins R H, Mirth in Manuscripts, E&S 21.26.
e. An aphorism.
MS. Harley 1002, f 72ᵇ (1475–1500).
Not listed Brown-Robbins, Robbins-Cutler.
Edition. Wright, RES ns 2.119.

See also MS Durham Univ Cosin V.iii.10, f 72ᵇ (15 cent) for a similar exercise in translation.
Robbins-Cutler, no 378.5.

Literary Relations. Wright, RES ns 2.114; Robbins, E&S 21.26.

[168] THE CHORISTERS' LAMENT.

MS. Arundel 292, ff 71ᵇ–72ᵃ (1375–90).
Brown-Robbins, Robbins-Cutler, no 3819.
Ward, 2.452 (MS described).
Editions. Haupt M and A M Hoffman, Altdeutsche Blätter, Leipzig 1840, 2.145.
Rel Ant, 1.291.
Utley F L, The Choristers' Lament, Spec 21.196.
Hollander J, Untuning of the Sky, Princeton 1961, p 425.
Sisam Oxf Book MEV, p 184.
Modernization. Rickert E, Chaucer's World, N Y 1948, p 126.
Textual Matters. Utley, Spec 21.198.
Versification. Oakden J P Alliterative Poetry in ME, Manchester 1930, 1.208.
Language. Oakden, Alliterative Poetry, 1.108.
General References. Brandl, p 648.
Utley, Spec 21.195.

[169] HOW MANY MILES TO BEVERLEY.

MS. Balliol Oxf 320, f 153ᵇ (late 13 cent).
Robbins-Cutler, no 0.3.
Editions. Mynors R A B, Catalogue of the Manuscripts of Balliol College Oxford, Oxford 1963, p 242.
Robbins-Cutler, no 0.3.
Literary Relations. Opie I and P Opie, The Oxford Dictionary of Nursery Rhymes, Oxford 1951, p 63.
Mynors, edn, p 242 (for Bodl 8617 [Wood donat 4], p 384).

[170] BLINDMAN'S BUFF.

MS. Bodl 2293 (Bodley 649), f 82ᵃ (ca 1420).
Robbins-Cutler, no 28.5.
Edition. Owst G R, Literature and Pulpit in Medieval England, Cambridge 1933, p 510.
Literary Relations. Owst, edn, p 510.

[171] THE BLACKSMITHS.

MS. Arundel 292, f 72ᵇ (1375–90).
Brown-Robbins, Robbins-Cutler, no 3227.
Ward, 2.452 (MS described).
Editions. Haupt M and A H Hoffman, Altdeutsche Blätter, Leipzig 1840, 2.146.
Rel Ant, 1.240.

Lindberg H, Satire on the Blacksmiths, Arch 101.395.
Sisam K, Fourteenth Century Verse and Prose, Oxford 1921, p 169.
Sampson G, Cambridge Book of Prose and Verse, Cambridge 1924, p 432.
Robbins SL, p 106.
Speirs J, Medieval English Poetry, London 1957, p 94.
Kaiser R, Medieval English, Berlin 1958, p 475.
Davies R T, Medieval English Lyrics, London 1963, p 213.
Haskell A S, A ME Anthology, N Y 1969, p 342.
Silverstein T, Medieval English Lyrics, London 1971, p 143.
Sisam Oxf Book MEV, p 372.
Reiss E, The Art of the ME Lyric, Athens Georgia 1972, p 166.
Dunn C and T E Byrne, ME Literature, N Y 1973, p 521.
Spearing A C and J E, Poetry of the Age of Chaucer, London 1974, p 220.
Modernizations. Coulton G G, Life in the Middle Ages, 2nd edn Cambridge 1929, 3.99.
Rickert E, Chaucer's World, N Y 1948, p 16.
Stone B, Medieval English Verse, Harmondsworth Middlesex 1964, p 106.
Textual Matters. Sisam, Fourteenth Century Verse, p 257.
Robbins SL, p 266.
Language. Oakden J P, Alliterative Poetry in ME, Manchester 1930, 1.45.
Versification. Luick K, Die engl Stabreimzeile, Angl 11.601.
Oakden, Alliterative Poetry, 1.149.
Other Scholarly Problems. Potter S, On the Etymology of Dream, ALg 4.148.
Literary Criticism. Davies, edn, p 350.
Reiss, edn, p 167.
General Reference. Brandl, p 639.

[172] PILGRIMS' SONG.

MS. Trinity Camb 599, ff 208ᵃ–208ᵇ (1500–25).
Brown-Robbins, Robbins-Cutler, no 2148.
Editions. Halliwell J O, Early Naval Ballads, PPS 2.1.
Rel Ant, 1.2.
Furnivall F J, The Stacions of Rome, EETS 25, London 1867, p 37.
FitzGibbon H M, Early English Poetry, London 1887, p 235.
Cook A S, A Literary ME Reader, Boston

1915, p 261.
Kaiser R, Medieval English, Berlin 1958, p 496.
Sisam Oxf Book MEV, p 500.
Selection. Bennett OHEL, p 162.
Modernizations. Bennett H S, England from Chaucer to Caxton, London 1928, p 224.
Adamson M R, A Treasury of ME Verse, N Y 1930, p 111.
Rickert E, Chaucer's World, N Y 1948, p 265.
Versification. Schipper, 1.363.
Literary Relations. Information for Pylgrymes vnto the Holy Londe, de Worde ca 1498 (STC, no 14081); rptd Roxb Club 38, London 1824; rptd E G Duff, London 1893.
Williams C, The Itineraries of William Wey, Roxb Club 76, London 1857.

Dunlap A R, A Pilgrimage to the Holy Land, MLN 63.57.
General References. James M R, A Descriptive Catalogue, Cambridge 1900, 2.73.
Jusserand J J, trans L T Smith, English Wayfaring Life, rvsd edn London 1929, p 379.
Manly & Rickert, 2.73.

[173] THE SHIRES.

MS. Harley 7371, f 80ᵇ (1500).
Brown-Robbins, Robbins-Cutler, no 3449.
Editions. Rel Ant, 1.269.
Sisam Oxf Book MEV, p 499.
Literary Relations. Rel Ant, 1.269 (another unidentified text).

9. THE WARS OF THE ROSES

[174] COTTON ROLLS ii.23 (1450–52).

Descriptions of MS. Wright PPS, 2.lv.
Kingsford EHL, p 358.
Robbins-HP, p xxix.

[175] LAMBETH 306 (1460–70).

Descriptions of MS. Halliwell J O, Observations upon the History of Certain Events in England, Archaeol 29.130.
Gairdner J, Three Fifteenth-Century Chronicles, Camden Soc ns 28.i.
Kingsford C L, Chronicles of London, Oxford 1905, p xi.
Kingsford EHL, p 247.
Robbins-HP, p xxx.

[176] TRINITY DUBLIN 432 (1460).

Descriptions of MS. Abbott T K, Catalogue of the Manuscripts, Dublin 1900, p 67.
Brotanek R, Me Dichtungen, Halle 1940, pp 6, 192, 198 (crit H Marcus, DLz 61.668; F Schubel, EStn 75.88).
Robbins-HP, p xxxi.

[177] TRINITY DUBLIN 516 (1450–75).

Descriptions of MS. Abbott T K, Catalogue of the Manuscripts, Dublin 1900, p 78.
Robbins-HP, p xxxi.
Robbins R H, Victory at Whitby A D 1451, SP 67.495.
Harriss G L and M A Harriss, John Benet's Chronicle for the years 1400 to 1462, Camden Miscellany XXIV, Camden Soc 4s 9, London 1972, p 153.

I. The Lancastrians

[178] THE CORONATION ◇ HENRY VI.

MSS. 1, Lansdowne 285, ff 5ᵇ–6ᵇ (ca 1470); 2, Morgan Libr 775, ff 14ᵃ–15ᵇ, 24ᵃ (ca 1486).
Brown-Robbins, Robbins-Cutler, no 1224.
Arthur, edn, Archaeol 57.27 (MS 2 described).
de Ricci Census, 2.1501 (MS 2 described).
Editions. Wright PPS, 2.146 (MS 1).
Arthur H [Viscount Dillon], On a MS Collection of Ordinances of Chivalry, Archaeol

57.55 (MS 2).
Sources and Literary Relations. Way A, Illustrations of Medieval Manners and Costume, Archaeological Journ 4.226.
Rowe B J H, King Henry's Claim to France, Libr 4s 13.77.
McKenna J W, Henry VI of England and the Dual Monarchy, Journ Warburg and Courtauld Institute 28.145.
Scattergood PP, p 80.

General References. Wright PPS, 2.xxxiv.
Brandl, p 710.
Scattergood PP, p 148.

[179] THAT PEACE MAY STAND.

MS. Advocates 19.3.1, ff 66ª–67ᵇ (1480–1500).
Brown-Robbins, Robbins-Cutler, no 1772.
Editions. Turnbull W D B B, Visions of Tundale, Edinburgh 1843, p 153.
Robbins-HP, p 239.
Textual Matters. Robbins-HP, p 391.
Date. Robbins-HP, p 390.
General References. Scattergood PP, p 101.

[180] VICTORY AT WHITBY.

MS. Trinity Dublin 516, ff 194ᵇ–195ᵇ (1450–75).
Robbins-Cutler, no 3143.5.
Edition. Robbins R H, Victory at Whitby A D 1451, SP 77.499.
Authorship. Robbins, SP 77.502.
Harriss G L and M A Harriss, John Benet's Chronicle for the Years 1400 to 1462, Camden Miscellany XXIV, Camden Soc 4s 9.157.

[181] THE FIVE DOGS OF LONDON.

MS. Trinity Dublin 516, ff 22ᵇ–23ª (1450–75).
Robbins-Cutler, no 2262.3.
Editions. Robbins R H, The Five Dogs of London, PMLA 71.267.
Robbins-HP, p 189.
Textual Matters. Robbins-HP, p 355.
Date and Authorship. Robbins, PMLA 71.264.
Sources and Literary Relations. Flenley R, Six Town Chronicles of England, Oxford 1911, p 144.
Robbins-HP, p xxxii.
General Reference. Scattergood PP, p 178.

[182] THE SHIP OF STATE.

MS. Trinity Dublin 516, ff 32ª–33ª (1450–75).
Brown-Robbins, Robbins-Cutler, no 2727.
Editions. Madden F, Historical Poems, Archaeol 29.326.
Robbins-HP, p 191.
Modernization. Thompson E, The Wars of York and Lancaster 1450–1500, London 1892, p 56.
Textual Matters. Robbins-HP, p 356.
General References. Madden, Archaeol 29.326.
Wright PPS, 2.lxiv.
Kingsford EHL, p 245.

Owst G R, Literature and Pulpit in Medieval England, Cambridge 1933, p 76.
Scattergood PP, p 180.

[183] RECONCILIATION OF HENRY VI AND THE YORKISTS.

MSS. 1, Cotton Nero A.vi, ff 196ª–198ᵇ (added, 1450–1500); 2, Cotton Vesp B.xvi, ff 4ª–4ᵇ (added, 1475–1500).
Brown-Robbins, Robbins-Cutler, no 3929.
Editions. Turner S, History of England, London 1823, 3.269 (MS 2).
Nicholas N H and E Tyrrell, Chronicle of London, London 1827, pp 251 (MS 1), 254 (MS 2).
Ritson AS, 1829, 1.lxix (MS 2).
Wright PPS, 2.254 (MS 2).
Robbins-HP, p 194 (MS 2).
Textual Matters. Robbins-HP, p 357.
Literary Relations. Robbins-HP, p xxi.
General References. Turner, edn, 3.268.
Wright PPS, 2.lxiii.
Ritson AS, p lix.
Brandl, p 701.
Kingsford EHL, p 245.
Kingsford C L, English History in Contemporary Poetry, London 1913, p 37.
Rowse A L, Bosworth Field, Garden City N Y 1966, p 138.
Scattergood PP, p 179.

[184] A PRAYER FOR VICTORY.

MS. Bodl 6943 (Ashmole 59), f 134ª (1447–56).
Brown-Robbins, Robbins-Cutler, no 936.
Editions. Robbins R H, Popular Prayers in ME Verse, MP 36.341.
Robbins-HP, p 196.
Literary Relations. Gilson J P, A Defence of the Proscription of the Yorkists in 1459, EHR 26.512 (from MS Royal 17.D.xv, ca 1460).
Robbins-Cutler, no 1955.5 (a prayer tag for England).

[185] GOD AMEND WICKED COUNSEL.

MS. Bodl Lat misc E.85, ff 83ª–83ᵇ (early 16 cent).
Brown-Robbins, Robbins-Cutler, no 372.
Editions. Robbins R H, God Amende Wykkyd Cownscell, NM 56.97.
Robbins-HP, p 196.
Textual Matters. Robbins-HP, p 359.
Date. Robbins, NM 56.95.

Robbins-HP, p xxv.
Literary Relations. Riley H T, Registrum Abbatis Johannis Whethamstede, Rolls Series 28, 1.414 (for Latin elegy).
Robbins-HP, pp xxv, 360.
Gill P E, Politics and Propaganda in Fifteenth-Century England The Polemical Writings of Sir John Fortescue, Spec 46.332.
Literary Criticism. Robbins, NM 56.100.
General References. Rowse A L, Bosworth Field, Garden City N Y 1966, p 157.
Scattergood PP, p 196.

[186] A REMEMBRANCE OF HENRY VI.

MS. Camb Univ Ee.1.12, ff 72ᵇ–73ᵃ (1492).
Brown-Robbins, Robbins-Cutler, no 2454.
Editions. Zupitza J, Die Gedichte des franziskaners Jakob Ryman, Arch 89.268.
Robbins-HP, p 199.
Textual Matters. Robbins-HP, p 362.
Date. Chambers OHEL, p 97.
Literary Relations. Willis R and J W Clark, Architectural History of the Univ of Cambridge, Cambridge 1886, 1.321 (On King Henry's laying foundation stone at King's College in 1441, poem beginning: Seint Nicholas on whose day was born / Henry the sext our soverein lord the kyng; not listed Brown-Robbins, Robbins-Cutler).
General Reference. Rowse A L, Bosworth Field, Garden City N Y 1966, pp 165, 171.

[187] A PRAYER TO HENRY THE SIXTH I.

MS. Littledale (formerly Pudsey; mid 15 cent).
Robbins-Cutler, no 333.5.
Collier, edn, Camden Soc 67.58 n (MS described).
Edition. Collier J P, Trevelyan Papers, Camden Soc 67.59.
Literary Relations. Other prayers to Henry VI occur in 3 MSS: Bodl 8954 (Jones 46), ff 108ᵃ–117ᵇ; Bodl 18340 (Gough Liturg 7), f 18ᵇ; Victoria and Albert Mus Reid, an English service book with rimed prayers (MS includes Robbins-Cutler, no 3580, MS 7).
Brown-Robbins, Robbins-Cutler, no 2393 ([188]).
Fairfax-Blakeborough J, Fountains Abbey Parchments, N&Q 12s 10.128 (prose prayer for a King Henry; date 1339).

[188] A PRAYER TO HENRY THE SIXTH II.

MS. Ushaw St Cuthbert's Coll 10, flyleaf (1475–1500).
Brown-Robbins, Robbins-Cutler, no 2393.
Editions. Ushaw College Magazine 1902; rptd M R James, Henry the Sixth A Reprint of John Blacman's Memoir, Cambridge 1919, p 50.
Special Problems. McKenna J W, Piety and Propaganda The Cult of King Henry VI, in Chaucer and Middle English Studies in Honour of Rossell Hope Robbins, ed B Rowland, London 1974, p 72.
Literary Relations. Hingeston[-Randolph] F C, The Books of the Illustrious Henries by John Capgrave, Rolls Series 7 (trans from Latin).
For Latin miracles of Henry VI see Royal 13.C.viii (ca 1500), ed R Knox and S Leslie, The Miracles of King Henry VI Taken from the MS in the British Museum, Cambridge 1923.

II. The Yorkists

[189] PRELUDE TO THE WARS.

MS. Cotton Rolls ii.23 (1450–52).
Brown-Robbins, Robbins-Cutler, no 3455.
Editions. Bentley S, Excerpta Historica, London 1831, p 161.
Privy Council Books, 6.xxiv.
Wright PPS, 2.221.
Collier J P, Trevelyan Papers, Camden Soc 67.65.
Gairdner J, Paston Letters, London 1904, 1.66.
Robbins-HP, p 201.
Textual Matters. Collier, Camden Soc 67.65.
Robbins-HP, p 363.
General References. Bentley, edn, p 159.
Wright PPS, 2.lv.
Collier, Camden Soc 67.65.
Vickers K H, Humphrey Duke of Gloucester, London 1907, p 453.
Tucker S M, Verse Satire in England, N Y 1908, p 127.

Kingsford EHL, p 243.
Kingsford C L, English History in Contemporary Poetry, London 1913, p 33; Prejudice and Promise in Fifteenth Century England, Oxford 1925, p 104.
Bagley J J, Historical Interpretation, Harmondsworth Middlesex 1965, p 229.
Rowse A L, Bosworth Field, Garden City N Y 1966, p 129.
Scattergood PP, pp 97 (quotes lines 1–10), 160.

[190] ON BISHOP BOOTH.

MS. Cotton Rolls ii.23 (1450–52).
Brown-Robbins, Robbins-Cutler, no 544.
Editions. Bentley S, Excerpta Historica, London 1831, p 357.
Wright PPS, 2.225.
Collier J P, Trevelyan Papers, Camden Soc 57.68.
Date. Kingsford EHL, p 243.
Scattergood PP, p 168.
General References. Wright PPS, 2.lvi.
Tucker S M, Verse Satire in England, N Y 1908, p 128.
Kingsford EHL, p 242.
Kingsford C L, English History in Contemporary Poetry, London 1913, p 34.
Scattergood PP, pp 160, 168.

[191] BILL AGAINST THE DUKE OF SUFFOLK.

MS. Harley 543, f 144ᵃ (ca 1450).
Robbins-Cutler, no 556.5.
Kingsford EHL, p 368 (MS described).
Editions. Kingsford EHL, p 370.
Wilson Lost Lit, p 199; 2nd edn, p 193.
Robbins-HP, p xxxviii.
Kendall P M, The Yorkist Age, N Y 1962, p 445.
Scattergood PP, p 167.

[192] THE ARREST OF THE DUKE OF SUFFOLK.

MS. Cotton Rolls ii.23 (1450–52).
Brown-Robbins, Robbins-Cutler, no 2338.
Editions. Bentley S, Excerpta Historica, London 1831, p 279.
Wright PPS, 2.224.
Robbins-HP, p 186.
Date. Kingsford C L, English History in Contemporary Poetry, London 1913, p 34.
Robbins-HP, p 349.
General References. Wright PPS, 2.lvi.

Vickers K H, Humphrey Duke of Gloucester, London 1907, p 298.
Tucker S M, Verse Satire in England, N Y 1908, p 128.
Kingsford EHL, p 244.
Scattergood PP, pp 158, 162.

[193] THE DEATH OF THE DUKE OF SUFFOLK.

MSS. 1, Cotton Vesp B.xvi, ff 1ᵇ–2ᵃ (added, 1475–1500); 2, Lambeth 306, ff 51ᵃ–51ᵇ (added, 1560–1600); 3, Trinity Dublin 516, ff 116ᵃ–116ᵇ (1450–75).
Brown-Robbins, Robbins-Cutler, no 1555.
Editions. Turner S, History of England, London 1823, 3.169 (MS 1).
Madden F, Political Poems, Archaeol 29.320 (MS 1).
Wright PPS, 2.232 (MS 1).
Collier J P, Trevelyan Papers, Camden Soc 67.72 (MS 1).
Furnivall F J, Political Religious and Love Poems, EETS 15, London 1866, p 6 (MS 2).
Ritson AS, p 101 (MS 1).
Gairdner J, Three Fifteenth-Century Chronicles, Camden Soc ns 28.99 (MS 2).
Robbins-HP, p 187 (MS 1).
Textual Matters. Madden F, Letter Containing Intelligence 1454, Archaeol 29.314.
Robbins-HP, p 351.
Versification. Schipper, 1.419.
Literary Criticism. Robbins-HP, p xxi.
Other Scholarly Problems. Kingsford C L, Prejudice and Promise in Fifteenth Century England, Oxford 1922, p 146.
General References. Madden, Archaeol 29.319.
Wright PPS, 2.lix.
Brandl, p 701.
CHEL, 2.424.
Vickers K H, Humphrey Duke of Gloucester, London 1907, pp 297, 451.
Tucker S M, Verse Satire in England, N Y 1908, p 129.
Kingsford EHL, p 244.
Kingsford C L, English History in Contemporary Poetry, London 1913, p 35.
Bagley J J, Historical Interpretation, Harmondsworth Middlesex 1965, p 230.
Scattergood PP, pp 158, 165, 167.
Scattergood V J, Revision in some ME Political Verses, Archiv 211.293.

[194] ADVICE TO THE COURT I.

MS. Cotton Rolls ii.23 (1450–52).
Brown-Robbins, Robbins-Cutler, no 818.
Editions. Hearne T, Hemingi Chartularium

Ecclesiae Wigorniensis, Oxford 1723, 2.663.
Madden F, Political Poems, Archaeol 29.325.
Rel Ant, 2.255.
Wright PPS, 2.231.
Robbins-HP, p 203.
General References. Warton T, History of
English Poetry, London 1824, 1.62.
Wright PPS, 2.lix.
Ritson AS, p lx.
Kingsford EHL, p 243.
Robbins-HP, p 365.
Bagley J J, Historical Interpretation, Har-
mondsworth Middlesex 1965, p 229.
Scattergood PP, p 163.

[195] ADVICE TO THE COURT II.

MS. Cotton Rolls ii.23 (1450–52).
Brown-Robbins, Robbins-Cutler, no 4261.
Editions. Bentley S, Excerpta Historica, Lon-
don 1831, p 360.
Wright PPS, 2.229.
Ritson AS, p 63.
Robbins-HP, p 203.
Textual Matters. Robbins-HP, p 365.
General References. Turner S, History of
England, London 1823, 3.155.
Wright PPS, 2.lviii.
Brandl, p 701.
Tucker S M, Verse Satire in England, N Y
1908, p 127.
Kingsford EHL, p 243.
Kingsford C L, English History in Contempo-
rary Poetry, London 1913, p 36.
Scattergood PP, p 160.

[196] TAKE GOOD HEED.

MS. Trinity Dublin 432, ff 69ᵇ–70ᵃ (1460).
Brown-Robbins, Robbins-Cutler, no 455.
Editions. Madden F, Political Poems, Ar-
chaeol 29.340.
Brotanek R, Me Dichtungen, Halle 1940, p
128.
Robbins-HP, p 206.
Textual Matters. Brotanek, edn, p 129.
Robbins-HP, p 367.
Date. Madden, Archaeol 29.340.
Brotanek, edn, p 130.
Kingsford C L, English History in Contempo-
rary Poetry, London 1913, p 40.
Robbins-HP, p 367.
General References. Tucker S M, Verse Satire
in England, N Y 1908, p 130.
Kingsford EHL, p 247.
Scattergood PP, p 181.

[197] BALLADE SET ON THE GATES
OF CANTERBURY.

MS. Bodl Lyell 34 (formerly John Speed
Davies), ff 203ᵃ–204ᵃ (1450–60).
Brown-Robbins, Robbins-Cutler, no 1544.
Editions. Davies J S, English Chronicle, Cam-
den Soc 64.91.
Brotanek R, Me Dichtungen, Halle 1940, p
199.
Robbins-HP, p 207.
Modernization. Thompson E, The Wars of
York and Lancaster 1450–1500, London
1892, p 61.
Textual Matters. Brotanek, edn, p 202.
Robbins-HP, p 369.
Authorship. Davies, Camden Soc 64.201.
Brotanek, edn, p 204.
Sources and Literary Relations. Robbins-HP,
p xxxvii.
Other Scholarly Problems. Kingsford EHL,
p 370.
Wilson Lost Lit, p 199; 2nd edn, p 193.
Robbins-HP, p xxxvii (public bills).
Scattergood PP, p 25.
General References. Madden F, Political
Poems, Archaeol 29.330.
Oman C W, Warwick, London 1891, p 89.
Kingsford EHL, p 246.
Kingsford C L, English History in Contem-
porary Poetry, London 1913, p 38.
Rowse A L, Bosworth Field, Garden City N Y
1966, p 141.
Scattergood PP, p 183.

[198] THE BATTLE OF NORTHAMP-
TON.

MS. Trinity Dublin 432, ff 67ᵃ–69ᵇ (1460).
Brown-Robbins, Robbins-Cutler, no 2609.
Editions. Madden F, Political Poems, Ar-
chaeol 29.334.
Brotanek R, Me Dichtungen, Halle 1940, p
116.
Robbins-HP, p 210.
Textual Matters. Brotanek, edn, p 121.
Robbins-HP, p 371.
Date. Kingsford C L, English History in Con-
temporary Poetry, London 1913, p 39.
Literary Relations. MS Royal 6.B.v, f 186ᵇ
(Latin poem).
Wright PPS, 2.256 (French poem).
General References. Wright PPS, 2.lxv.
Kingsford EHL, p 246.
Jack R I, A Quincentenary The Battle of
Northampton July 10th 1460, Northamp-
tonshire Past and Present 3.24.
Scattergood PP, p 184.

[199] TWELVE LETTERS SAVE ENG-
LAND.

MSS. 1, Lambeth 306, ff 134ᵃ–134ᵇ (1460–70);
2, Trinity Dublin 432, ff 71ᵃ–71ᵇ, 75ᵃ–75ᵇ
(1460).
Brown-Robbins, Robbins-Cutler, no 700.
Editions. Madden F, Political Poems, Ar-
chaeol 29.330 (MS 2).
Furnivall F J, Political Religious and Love
Poems, EETS 15, London 1868, p 1 (MS 1).
Brotanek R, Me Dichtungen, Halle 1940, p
152 (MSS 1, 2).
Robbins-HP, p 218 (MS 2).
Selections. Kingsford EHL, p 246.
Kingsford C L, English History in Contempo-
rary Poetry, London 1913, p 29.
Textual Matters. Brotanek, edn, p 158.
Robbins-HP, p 379.
Versification. Schipper, 1.338, 340.
Date. Scattergood PP, p 191.
Other Scholarly Problems. Furnivall, EETS
15.xi.
General References. Brandl, p 701.
Scattergood PP, p 190.

[200] THE VIRTUES OF THE EARL OF
WARWICK.

MS. Trinity Dublin 432, f 70ᵇ (1460).
Robbins-Cutler, no 3856.5.
Editions. Madden F, Political Poems, Ar-
chaeol 29.332.
Brotanek R, Me Dichtungen, Halle 1940, p
136.
Robbins-HP, p 380.

[201] A POLITICAL RETROSPECT.

MS. Soc of Antiquaries 101, ff 98ᵃ–98ᵇ (ca
1450).
Brown-Robbins, Robbins-Cutler, no 3756.
Editions. Wright PPS, 2.267.
Robbins-HP, p 222.
Textual Matters. Robbins-HP, p 382.
Literary Relations. Halliwell J O, Observa-
tions upon the History of Certain Events,
Archaeol 29.133 (Marriage, Lansdowne 210,
f 50ᵇ), 134 (Affray, Lambeth 448, f 146ᵃ).
Bruce J, Historie of the Arrival, Camden
Soc 1.
Other Scholarly Problems. McKenna J W,
Henry VI of England and the Dual Mon-
archy Aspects of Royal Political Propa-
ganda, Journ Warburg and Courtauld In-
stitute 28.145, n 1; Popular Canonization
as Political Propaganda The Cult of Archbishop Scrope, Spec 45.617.

Scattergood PP, pp 121, 193, 198.
General References. Wright PPS, 2.lxvi.
Vickers K H, Humphrey Duke of Gloucester,
London 1907, pp 298, 306.
Tucker S M, Verse Satire in England, N Y
1908, p 131.
Kingsford EHL, p 248.
Kingsford C L, English History in Contem-
porary Poetry, London 1913, p 41.
Bagley J J, Historical Interpretation, Har-
mondsworth Middlesex 1965, p 230.

[202] THE BATTLE OF BARNET.

MS. Trinity Camb 601, f 244ᵇ (1470–80).
Brown-Robbins, Robbins-Cutler, no 899.
Editions. MacCracken H N, Lydgatiana, Arch
130.309.
Robbins-HP, p 226.
Textual Matters. Robbins-HP, p 383.
Sources and Literary Relations. Wright PPS,
2.271 (The Arrival).
Brown-Robbins, no 2808 ([204] below).
General References. MacCracken, Arch 130.
286.
Kingsford EHL, p 248.
Scattergood PP, p 205.

[203] CONDITIONS IN ENGLAND 1460–
1480.

MS. Camb Fitzwilliam Mus Deposit Bradfer-
Lawrence 8 (formerly Greg, formerly Huth
153), f 16ᵇ (15 cent).
Robbins-Cutler, no 3412.5.

[204] THE RECOVERY OF THE
THRONE BY EDWARD IV.

MS. Royal 17.D.xv, ff 327ᵃ–332ᵇ (1470–80).
Brown-Robbins, no 2808.
Manly & Rickert, 1.476 (MS described).
Edition. Wright PPS, 2.271.
Selection. Thornley I D, England under the
Yorkists, London 1920, p 75.
Sources and Literary Relations. Bruce J, His-
torie of the Arrival, Camden Soc 1.
Nichols J G, The Boke of Noblesse, Roxb
Club 77, London 1860.
Thomson J A F, The Arrival of Edward IV
the Development of the Text, Spec 46.84.
General References. Wright PPS, 2.lxvii
(synopsis).
Morley, 6.235.
Kingsford EHL, p 248.
Kingsford C L, English History in Contem-

porary Poetry, London 1913, p 43.
Kendall P M, The Yorkist Age, N Y 1962, p 458.
Scattergood PP, p 201.

[205] A PRAYER FOR ENGLAND.

MS. Camb Univ Ff.1.6, ff 150ᵇ–159ᵇ (ca 1500).
Brown-Robbins, Robbins-Cutler, no 2317.
Robbins R H, The Findern Anthology, PMLA 69.610 (MS described).
Edition. Wright PPS, 2.238.
Sources and Literary Relations. Adams R P, Pre-Renaissance Courtly Propaganda for Peace in English Literature, Papers of the Michigan Acad of Sciences Arts and Letters 32.431.
General References. Wright PPS, 2.lx.
Tucker S M, Verse Satire in England, N Y 1908, p 132.
Kingsford EHL, p 245.

[206] ANTHEM FOR MARRIAGE OF HENRY VII AND ELIZABETH.

MSS. 1, Camb Univ Dd.13.27, f 31ᵃ (early 16 cent; contra tenor part only); 2, St John's Camb 234, f 28ᵇ (early 16 cent; bass part only).
Robbins-Cutler, no 960.5.
James M R, A Descriptive Catalogue, Cambridge 1913, p 273 (MS 2 described).
Editions. Strickland A, Lives of the Queens of England, Phila 1853, 4.40 (MS not identified).
Flood W H G, Early Tudor Composers, Oxford 1925, p 58.
Authorship. Flood, edn, p 55.
Literary Relations. Flügel NL, p 162 (Harley 2252, f 156ᵃ, political song against Cardinal Wolsey).
Harrison F L, Music in Medieval Britain, London 1958, p 158 (mass by Nicholas Hoker, 1518).
Other Scholarly Problems. Flood, edn, p 57 (reconstructed music).

[207] ON THE UNION OF THE LANCASTRIANS AND YORKISTS.

MS. St John's Oxf 57, cover (late 15 cent).
Robbins-Cutler, no 3452.6.
Edition. Robbins-HP, p 300.

10. THE ESTATES

I. The Rulers

1. Commemoration of Rulers

[208] SUMMER SUNDAY.

MS. Bodl 1486 (Laud Misc 180), ff 237ᵃ–237ᵇ (14 cent).
Brown-Robbins, Robbins-Cutler, no 3838.
Editions. Rel Ant, 2.7.
Brown C, Somer Soneday, in Studies in English Philology in Honor of Frederick Klaeber, ed K Malone and M B Rund, Minneapolis 1929, p 362.
Robbins-HP, p 98.
Modernization. Gardner J, The Alliterative Morte Arthure The Owl and the Nightingale and Five Other ME Poems, Carbondale 1971, p 155.
Textual Matters. Robbins-HP, p 301.

Gardner, Alliterative Morte Arthure, p 295.
Language. Brown, edn, p 369.
Oakden J P, Alliterative Poetry in ME, Manchester 1930, 1935, 1.116; 2.13.
Versification. Oakden, Alliterative Poetry, 1.217.
Turville-Petre T, Summer Sunday De Tribus Regibus Mortuis and the Awntyrs off Arthure Three Poems in the Thirteen-Line Stanza, RES ns 25.1.
Date. Brown, edn, pp 368, 372.
Robbins-HP, p 301.
Gardner, Alliterative Morte Arthure, p 264.
Robbins R H, [review,] Angl 92.231.
Petre, RES ns 25.5.
Literary Relations. Ellis H, New Chronicles of England and France by Robert Fabyan, London 1811, p 430 (trans of Latin lament ascribed to Edward II).

Studer P, An AN Poem by King Edward II King of England, MLR 16.40.

Tout T F, The Captivity and Death of Edward of Carnarvon, Manchester 1920, Appendix 2 (commentary on AN poem).

Brown, edn, p 371 (AN poem).

Aspin I S T, AN Political Songs, Anglo-Norman Text Soc 11, Oxford 1953, p 93 (AN poem).

Miskimin A, Susannah, New Haven 1969, p 57.

Smallwood T M, The Lament of Edward II, MLR 68.521 (AN poem).

Other Scholarly Problems. Bradley H, The Theories as to Huchown, Athen 117(1901) .52 (Fortune's wheel suggested by Morte Arthure).

Patch H R, The Goddess Fortuna in Medieval Literature, Cambridge Mass 1927, p 147.

Literary Criticism. Robbins-HP, p xix.

Gardner, Alliterative Morte Arthure, p 263.

General References. Amours F J, Scottish Alliterative Poems, PSTS 38.lxxxvi.

Gollancz I, Parlement of the Thre Ages, London 1915, p iv note.

[209]   THE DEATH OF EDWARD III.

MSS. 1, Bodl 3938 (Vernon), ff 410[b] 411[a] (ca 1385); 2, BM Addit 22283, ff 132[a]–132[b] (1380–1400).

Brown-Robbins, Robbins-Cutler, no 5.

MSS described under [85] above.

Editions. Conybeare J J, Two English Poems, Archaeol 18.22 (MS 1).

Wright PPS, 1.215 (MS 2).

Marsh G P, Origin and History of the English Language, N Y 1866, p 288 (MS 1).

Furnivall F J, Minor Poems of the Vernon MS, EETS 117, London 1901, p 715 (MS 1).

Sisam K, Fourteenth Century Verse and Prose, Oxford 1921, p 157 (MS 1).

Kaiser R, Medieval English, Berlin 1958, p 384 (MS 1).

Robbins-HP, p 102 (MS 1).

Dobson R B, The Peasants' Revolt of 1381, London 1970, p 88 (MS 1).

Sisam Oxf Book MEV, p 342 (MS 1).

Modernization. Stone B, Medieval English Verse, Harmondsworth Middlesex 1964, p 114.

Textual Matters. Sisam, edn, p 255.

Robbins-HP, p 303.

Literary Relations. Amyot T, Transcript of a Chronicle, Archaeol 22.212 (prose chronicle in MS Harley 6217, f 19, with one leaf from MS Harley 247).

Other Scholarly Problems. Owst G R, Literature and Pulpit in Medieval England, Cambridge 1933, p 75 (for ship imagery).

General References. Wright PPS, 1.liv.

Brandl, p 672.

Liebau G, König Edward III von England, AF 6 (crit A L Jellinek, Arch 109.413).

[210]   THE FALL OF RICHARD II.

MS. Bodl 21652 (Douce 78), ff 1[a]–1[b] (1450–75).

Brown-Robbins, no *78; Robbins-Cutler, no *4267.5.

Edition. Bowers R H, A ME Wheel of Fortune Poem, ESts 41.197.

Literary Relations. Matthews W, Manual, 3.753 (VIII [25]).

General Reference. Bowers, ESts 41.196.

[211]   THE DEATH OF EDWARD IV.

MS. Rylands Libr Eng 113, ff 3[a]–3[b] (1483–85).

Brown-Robbins, Robbins-Cutler, no 4062.

Manly & Rickert, 1.349 (MS described).

Editions. Furnivall F J, Political Religious and Love Poems, EETS 15, London 1903, p xlvi (rvsd edn).

Robbins-HP, p 111.

General References. Robbins-HP, p 306.

Scattergood PP, p 207.

[212]   THE LAMENTATION OF LADIES FOR EDWARD IV.

MS. Harley 3952, f 105[b] (left hand side of page torn; ca 1485).

Brown-Robbins, no 1505.

Edition. Sandison H E, The Chanson d'Aventure in ME, Bryn Mawr 1913, p 128.

General Reference. Richmond V B, Laments for the Dead in Medieval Narrative, Pittsburgh 1966, p 26.

[213]   THE HOUSE OF STAFFORD.

MS. Bodl 4197 (Dodsworth 55), ff 102[a]–103[b] (1650).

Brown-Robbins, no 193.

Edition. Dugdale W, Monasticon Anglicanus, ed J Caley, H Ellis and B Bandinel, London 1817, 6.230.

[214]   THE FOUNDING OF WORKSOP ABBEY.

MS. Lansdowne 205, ff 167[b]–168[b] (1587).

Brown-Robbins, Robbins-Cutler, no 4071.

General Reference. Kingsford EHL, pp 166, 369.

[215] THE HOUSE OF VERE.

MS. Huntington Libr EL 26.C.3, ff ii^b–iv^a (1450–80).
Brown-Robbins, Robbins-Cutler, no 1087.
Manly & Rickert, 1.148 (MS described).
Editions. Todd H J, Illustrations of the Lives and Writings of Gower and Chaucer, London 1810, p 295.
Piper E F, The Royal Boar and the Ellesmere Chaucer, PQ 5.331.
Date. Manly & Rickert, 1.156.
Seaton E, Sir Richard Roos, London 1961, p 422.
Authorship. Todd, edn, p 295.
Furnivall F J, Temporary Prefaces, ChS 2s 3.45.
Lounsbury T R, Studies in Chaucer, N Y 1892, 1.189, 454.
Oxf Ch, 4.xiii.
Piper, PQ 5.330.
Manly & Rickert, 1.155.
Literary Relations. The House of Clare = Dialogue Between a Secular and a Friar (see VII [38] in Manual, vol 3); Brown-Robbins, Robbins-Cutler, no 3910; Viscount Clive, The Lyvys of Seyntys, Roxb Club 50, London 1835, p xvi (suggests Bokenham as author).
Other Scholarly Problems. Seaton, Sir Richard Roos, p 425 (interpretation of political allegory).
Literary Criticism. Seaton, Sir Richard Roos, pp 423, 424.
Bibliography. Hammond, p 446.

[216] THE ROSE OF ENGLAND.

MS. BM Addit 27879, pp 423–424 (ca 1650).
Robbins-Cutler, no 3719.8.
Editions. PFMS, 3.189.
Child F J, The English and Scottish Popular Ballads, Boston 1889, 6.332.
Modernization. Sidgwick F, Ballads and Poems Illustrating English History, Cambridge 1907, p 53.
General References. PFMS, 3.187.
Child, edn, 6.331.
Kingsford C L, English History in Contemporary Poetry, London 1913, p 45.
Kingsford EHL, p 249.
Firth C H, The Ballad History of the Reigns of Henry VII and Henry VIII, Trans Royal Hist Soc 3s 2.23.

Rowse A L, Bosworth Field, Garden City N Y 1966, p 253.

[217] SCOTTISH FEILDE.

MSS. 1, BM Addit 27879, pp 79–90 (ca 1650); 2, Lyme (ca 1580–1600; present location not known; formerly owned by Richard Legh, Lyme Park, Disley); 2a, Bodl Deposit c.130 (photographic facsimile).
Robbins-Cutler, no 1011.5.
Editions. Robson J, The Scottish Field, Chetham Soc 37 (MS 2).
PFMS, 1.212 (MS 1).
Oakden J P, Scotish Feilde, Chetham Soc ns 94 (MS 1).
Child F J, The English and Scottish Popular Ballads, Boston 1889, 6.355 (MS 1).
Selection. Flügel NL, p 156 (MS 1, lines 314–422).
Language. Oakden J P, Alliterative Poetry in ME, Manchester 1930, 1.100.
Versification. Luick K, Die engl Stabreimzeile, Angl 11.608.
Schneider A, Die Me Stabzeile im 15 und 16 Jahrhundert, BBA 12.110, 128.
Oakden, Alliterative Poetry, 1.200.
Stobie M M R, The Influence of Morphology on ME Alliterative Poetry, JEGP 39.319.
Date. PFMS, 1.199, 207.
Oakden, Alliterative Poetry, 1.100.
Authorship. PFMS, 1.199, 207.
Scamman E, The Alliterative Poem Death and Liffe, RadMon 15, Boston 1910.
Oakden, Alliterative Poetry, 1.56 (refutes common authorship with Death and Liffe).
Other Scholarly Problems. PFMS, 1.202 (historical background).
General References. Percy T, Reliques of Ancient English Poetry, London 1812, 2.192; 3.109.
Warton T, History of English Poetry, ed W C Hazlitt, London 1871, 2.283.
PFMS, 1.199.
Firth C H, The Ballad History of the Reigns of Henry VII and Henry VIII, Trans Royal Hist Soc 3s 2.27.
CHEL, 2.46, 494.
Mackenzie W M, Secret of Flodden, Edinburgh 1931, p 19.
Oakden, Alliterative Poetry, 2.82.
Bibliography. New CBEL, 1.546.

[218] THE MOST PLEASANT SONG OF LADY BESSY.

MSS. 1, Harley 367, ff 89^a–100^b (1600–25); 2, BM Addit 27879, pp 464–479 (ca 1650); 3,

Bateman (ca 1600; present location not known).

Robbins-Cutler, no 981.3.

Editions. Heywood T, The Most Pleasant Song of Lady Bessy, London 1829 (MS 3).

Halliwell J O, The Most Pleasant Song of Lady Bessy, PPS 20.1, 43 (MSS 3, 1); Palentine Anthology, London 1850, pp 6, 60 (MSS 3, 1).

Jewitt L, Ballads and Songs of Derbyshire, Derby 1867, p 12 (MS 3).

PFMS, 3.321 (MS 2).

Authorship. Firth C H, The Ballad History of the Reigns of Henry VII and Henry VIII, Trans Royal Hist Soc 3s 2.25.

General References. Heywood T, The Earls of Derby and the Verse Writers and Poets of the Sixteenth and Seventeenth Centuries [The Stanley Papers, part 1], Chetham Soc 29.1.

PFMS, 3.319.

Gairdner J, Life and Reign of Richard III, London 1879, p 401.

Brandl, p 701.

Firth, Trans Royal Hist Soc 3s 2.26.

Kingsford EHL, p 250.

Kingsford C L, English History in Contemporary Poetry, London 1913, p 46.

Chambers OHEL, p 163.

[219] BOSWORTH FIELD.

MSS. 1, BM Addit 27879, pp 434–443 (ca 1650); 2, Cole (present ownership and location not known).

Robbins-Cutler, no 986.5.

Edition. PFMS, 3.235 (MS 1).

Literary Relations. MS Harley 542, ff 31ª–33ᵇ (ca 1600; for prose account, sometimes breaking into verse).

Other Scholarly Problems. Hutton W, The Battle of Bosworth Field, London 1813 (military aspects).

General References. Heywood T, The Earls of Derby and the Verse Writers of the Fifteenth and Sixteenth Centuries [The Stanley Papers, part 1], Chetham Soc 29.19 (includes Cole MS).

PFMS, 3.235.

Kingsford C L, English History in Contemporary Poetry, London 1913, p 46.

Kingsford EHL, p 250.

Rowse A L, Bosworth Field, Garden City N Y 1966, passim.

[220] FLODDEN FIELD.

MSS. 1, Harley 293, ff 55ª–61ᵇ (ca 1550); 2, Harley 367, ff 120ª–125ᵇ (1600–25); 3, Harley 2252, ff 45ᵇ–48ᵇ (1510–30); 4, BM Addit 27879, pp 117–124 (1650).

Robbins-Cutler, no 2574.3.

Editions. The Mirror for Magistrates, J Higgins, London 1587 (STC, no 13445); ed J Haslewood, London 1815, 2.449; ed L B Campbell, Cambridge 1939, p 489 (collated with MS 3).

Weber H W, Flodden Field, London 1808 (MSS 1, 2).

Evans T, Old Ballads, ed R H Evans, London 1810, 3.58 (MS 1).

Dolman A, Ancient Ballads on the Battle of Flodden Field, Gentleman's Magazine 221 (1866).16 (MS 3).

Ritson AS, p 210.

PFMS, 1.318 (MS 4).

Selection. Flügel NL, p 158 (MS 2).

Textual Matters. Weber, edn, p 121.

Flügel NL, p 440.

Literary Relations. Ritson AS 1790, p 115.

Evans, edn, 3.55.

Heywood T, The Earls of Derby and the Verse Writers and Poets of the Sixteenth and Seventeenth Centuries [The Stanley Papers, part 1], Chetham Soc 29.7 (La Rotta del Scocesi).

Child F J, The English and Scottish Popular Ballads, Boston 1889, 6.351.

Sievers R, Thomas Deloney, Berlin 1904, pp 76, 182.

Other Scholarly Problems. McMillan D J, Folk Projection and Historic Truth, AN&Q 2.149.

General References. Heywood, Chetham Soc 29.6.

PFMS, 1.199, 313.

Chambers OHEL, p 157.

Child, Popular Ballads, 6.353.

Firth C H, The Ballad History of the Reigns of Henry VII and Henry VIII, Trans Royal Hist Soc 3s 2.27.

Mackie J D, The Earlier Tudors, Oxford 1952, p 280.

[221] THE CHRONICLE OF STANLEY.

MSS. 1, Bodl 14637 (Rawl Poet 143), B, ff 13ª–26ᵇ (1600–50); 2, Harley 541, ff 183ª–206ᵇ (16 cent).

Not listed Brown-Robbins, Robbins-Cutler.

Edition. Halliwell J O, Palentine Anthology, London 1850, p 208.
Authorship. DNB, 54.50.
General References. Seacome J, Memoirs of the Ancient and Honourable House of Stanley, Liverpool 1739; rvsd edn, Manchester 1840.
Heywood T, The Earls of Derby and the Verse Writers and Poets of the Sixteenth and Seventeenth Centuries [The Stanley Papers, part 1], Chetham Soc 29.16.

[222] LAMENT ON MISFORTUNES FOLLOWING FLODDEN.

MS. BM Addit 45102, u (early 16 cent).
Robbins-Cutler, no 2549.5.
Edition. Wright C E, An Unrecorded Scottish Poem, BMQ 12.14.
Language. Dickins B, Textual Notes on a Newly-Discovered Flodden Poem, Leeds SE 6.74.
General Reference. Wright, BMQ 12.13.

[223] LAMENTATION OF KING OF SCOTS.

MS. Harley 2252, ff 43b–45b (1510–30).
Robbins-Cutler, no 366.8.
Editions. The Mirror for Magistrates, J Higgins, London 1587 (STC, no 13445); ed J Haslewood, London 1815, 2.442; ed L B Campbell, Cambridge 1939, p 483 (collated with MS).
Weber H W, Flodden Field, London 1808.
Halliwell J O, Palentine Anthology, London 1850, p 208.
Dolman A, Ancient Ballads on the Battle of Flodden Field, Gentleman's Magazine 221 (1886).13 (with heraldic interpretations).
Literary Relations. Robbins-Cutler, no 1822.5 (attributed to Skelton).

[224] THE HOUSE OF PERCY.

MSS. 1, Bodl 4192 (Dodsworth 50), ff 119a–140b (lacking 19 stanzas following stanza 35 at f 123a, and the last 2 stanzas; transcript, 1630); 2, Royal 18.D.ii, ff 186a–195a (1516–23).
Robbins-Cutler, no 631.8.
Edition. B[esly] J, Chronicle of Family of Percy, Reprints of Rare Tracts Illustrative of the History of Northern Counties, Newcastle 1845, 1.9 (MS 1).
Literary Relations. MS Bodl 2986 (Bodley

Rolls 5), prose chronicle (to 1454, descent to 1485) by Thomas Pickering.
General References. Flügel E, Kleinere Mitteilungen aus Handschriften, Angl 14.472.
Kingsford EHL, p 252.

[225] THE HOUSE OF WILLOUGBY.

MS. Harley 245, f 107b (late 16 cent).
Robbins-Cutler, no 2462.5.
General Reference. DNB, 45.244.

[226] SIR ROGER BELERS.

MS. Royal 12.C.xiv, f ib (1325–50).
Brown-Robbins, Robbins-Cutler, no 2172.
Edition. Bowers R H, Versus Compositi de Roger Belers, JEGP 56.441.
General Reference. Bowers, JEGP 56.440.

[227] MEMORIAL VERSES FOR THE TOMB OF THE EARL OF DUNBAR.

MS. BM Addit 27223, f 212b (15 cent).
Brown-Robbins, Robbins-Cutler, no 1206.
Editions. Catalogue of Additions to the Manuscripts 1900–1905, London 1907, p 377.
Robbins SL, p 119.

[228] THE LAMENTATION OF THE DAUPHIN FOR HIS WIFE.

MSS. 1, Bodl 3888 (Fairfax 8), ff 188a–189b (1489); 1a, Bodl 8915 (Jones 8), f 555a (transcript, ca 1675); 2, Marchmont A.C.15 (transcript; ca 1500; present location not known); 3, Brussels Bibliothèque royale 4628 (ca 1500).
Brown-Robbins, Robbins-Cutler, no 3430.
Editions. Stevenson J, The Life and Death of King James I of Scotland, Maitland Club 42, Edinburgh 1837, p 17 (MS 1).
Skene F J H, Liber Pluscardensis, Historians of Scotland 10, ed W F Skene, Edinburgh 1877, 7.328 (MS 1a).
General Reference. Lawson A, The Kingis Quair, London 1910, p lix.

[229] EPITAPH FOR THE DUKE OF GLOUCESTER.

MSS. 1, Harley 2251, ff 7a–8b (1460–70); 2, BM Addit 34360, ff 65b–67b (1460–70).
Brown-Robbins, Robbins-Cutler, no 3206.
Hammond E P, Two British Museum Manuscripts, Angl 28.1 (MSS described).

Brusendorff A, The Chaucer Tradition, Copenhagen 1925, pp 181, 222 (MSS described).
Editions. Robbins R H, An Epitaph for Duke Humphrey, NM 66.243 (MS 1).
Robbins-HP, p 180 (MS 1).
Textual Matters. Robbins-HP, p 346.
Authorship. Schick J, Lydgate's Temple of Glass, EETSES 60, London 1891, p xcvi.
MacCracken H N, Lydgate's Minor Poems, EETSES 107, London 1910, p xi.
Vickers K H, Humphrey Duke of Gloucester, London 1907, p 390.
Scattergood PP, p 157.
Literary Relations. Seven stanzas on death of Gloucester occurring separately (Brown-Robbins, Robbins-Cutler, no 711) are actually lines 372–420 of the Fall of Princes (Brown-Robbins, Robbins-Cutler, no 1168).
Haslewood J, ed, The Mirror for Magistrates, London 1815, 2².128.
Other Scholarly Problems. Robbins, NM 66.248 (handbill verse).
General Reference. Robbins, NM 66.241, 247.

[230] ELEGY FOR THE TOMB OF LORD CROMWELL.

MSS. 1, Cotton Calig A.ii, ff 55ᵇ–56ᵃ (1425–50; omits stanza 7); 2, Harley 116, ff 152ᵇ–153ᵇ (1475–1500).
Brown-Robbins, no 2411.
Editions. Varnhagen H, Ein me Gedicht seltener Form, AnglA 7.85 (MS 1).
MacCracken H N, A Meditation upon Death, MLN 26.243 (MS 2).
Brown RLxvC, p 243 (MS 2).
Date. Brown RLxvC, p 340.
General Reference. Brown RLxvC, p 339.

[231] COMMEMORATION OF GEOFFREY BARBER.

MSS. MS to be established (see note in DNB, 33.16). PRINT: Leland J, Itinerary, Oxford 1745, 7.74.
Robbins-Cutler, no 2619.2.
Editions Hearne T, Itinerary of John Leland, Oxford 1769, 7.79.
Smith L T, Leland's Itinerary, London 1910, 5.116.
General References. Ritson J, Bibliographia Poetica, London 1802, p 55.
Smith, edn, 5.113.

[232] OTHER EPITAPHS.

General References. MS Harley 3606 (Le Neve MS; collection of tombstone inscriptions).
Weever J, Ancient Funerall Monuments, London 1631.
Ravenshaw T F, Ancient Epitaphs A D 1250 to A D 1800, London 1878.
Gray D, Themes and Images in the Medieval English Religious Lyric, London 1972, p 197.

[233] THE LAMENT OF THE DUCHESS OF GLOUCESTER.

MSS. 1, Balliol Oxf 354, ff 169ᵇ–170ᵇ (1518–36); 2, Camb Univ Hh.4.12, ff 89ᵃ–91ᵃ (1490–1510).
Brown-Robbins, Robbins-Cutler, no 3720.
Editions. Wright PPS, 2.205 (MS 1).
Flügel E, Liedersammlungen des XVI Jahrhunderts, Angl 26.177 (MS 1).
Hardwick C, Lament of Eleanor Cobham, Cambridge Antiquarian Soc Communications 1.186 (MS 2).
Dyboski R, Songs Carols and Other Miscellaneous Poems, EETSES 101, London 1907, p 95 (MS 1).
Robbins-HP, p 176 (MS 2).
Textual Matters. Hardwick, edn, 1.177 (with historical references).
Robbins-HP, p 344.
Scattergood PP, p 154.
Versification. Schipper, 1.416.
Date. Kingsford EHL, p 242.
Literary Relations. Evans T, Old Ballads, London 1784, 1.317; ed R H Evans, London 1810, 3.1 (a later ballad in quatrains).
Haslewood J, The Mirror for Magistrates, London 1815, 2².112.
Campbell L B, The Mirror for Magistrates, Cambridge 1938, pp 432, 455; Humphrey Duke of Gloucester and Elianor Cobham His Wife, HLQ 5.119 (for version in Mirror for Magistrates).
Robbins-Cutler, no 3193.5 (see XI [22] in Manual, vol 4), a Virelai on his Execution by Anthony Widvill, A.D. 1483.
Robbins-Cutler, no 158.9, a Farewell on his Execution by Edward Stafford, A.D. 1521.
General References. Wright PPS, 2.li.
Brandl, p 700.
Vickers K H, Humphrey Duke of Gloucester, London 1907, pp 271, 277.
Scattergood PP, p 153.

Scattergood V J, Revision in some ME Political Verses, Archiv 211.296.

[234] THE LAMYTACION OF QUENE
ELIZABETH.

MSS. 1, Balliol Oxf 354, ff 175ᵃ–176ᵃ (1518–
36); 2, Sloane 1825, ff 88ᵇ–89ᵇ (added on
flyleaf; 16 cent).
Robbins-Cutler, no 4263.3.
Editions. More T, Works in the Englische
Tonge, Tottell 1557 (STC, no 18076).
Campbell W E, English Works of Sir Thomas
More, London 1931, 1.335 (facsimile of
More edn).
Flügel E, Liedersammlungen des XVI Jahr-
hunderts, Angl 26.184 (MS 1).
Dyboski R, Songs Carols and Other Miscel-
laneous Poems, EETSES 101, London 1907,
pp 97, 185 (MS 1, collated with More edn).
Chambers E K, Oxford Book of Sixteenth
Century Verse, Oxford 1932, p 15.

[235] EPITAPH ON QUEEN ELISABETH.

MS. Balliol Oxf 354, f 176ᵃ (1518–36).
Robbins-Cutler, no 1206.9.
Editions. Flügel E, Liedersammlungen des
XVI Jahrhunderts, Angl 26.188.
Dyboski R, Songs Carols and Other Miscel-
laneous Poems, EETSES 101, London 1907,
p 99 (Latin epitaph on p 98).
Campbell W E, English Works of Sir Thomas
More, London 1931, 1.312.
Literary Relations. Weever J, Ancient Fu-
nerall Monuments, London 1631 (STC, no
25223), p 476 (for Latin epitaph).

[236] EXAMPLES OF MUTABILITY.

MS. Bodl 12653 (Rawl C.813), ff 11ᵃ–12ᵇ
(1530–40).
Brown-Robbins, Robbins-Cutler, no 2228.
Editions. Padelford F M, The Songs of Rawl-
inson MS C 813, Angl 31.325.
Kingsford EHL, p 395.
Robbins-HP, p 184.
Textual Matters. Bolle W, Zur Lyrik der
Rawlinson-HS C.813, Angl 34.301.
Date. Vickers K H, Humphrey Duke of
Gloucester, London 1907, p 277.
General References. Vickers, Humphrey Duke
of Gloucester, pp 295, 306.
Kingsford EHL, p 242.
Robbins-HP, p 348.
Woolf R, The English Religious Lyric in

the Middle Ages, Oxford 1968, p 325.
Scattergood PP, p 153.

2. Advice to Rulers

[237] RULERS' TITLES.

MS. Harley 2259, f 144ᵇ (15 cent).
Robbins-Cutler, no 86.5.

[238] A CHARGE TO JUDGES.

MS. Harley 2316, f 25ᵇ (1350–1400).
Brown-Robbins, Robbins-Cutler, no 3621.
Editions. Rel Ant, 2.120.
Kittredge G L, Earth Upon Earth, MLN
9.271.

[239] ON GOOD RULE.

MS. BM Addit 20059, f 2ᵃ (15 cent).
Brown-Robbins, Robbins-Cutler, no 3364.

[240] ADMONITION ON LOVEDAYS.

MS. Camb Univ Dd.1.1, ff 300ᵇ–302ᵇ (1400–
25).
Brown-Robbins, Robbins-Cutler, no 312.
Selection. Bowers R H, A ME Poem on Love-
days, MLR 47.374 (lines 1–24 only).
Other Scholarly Problems. Bennett J W, The
Mediaeval Loveday, Spec 33.365.

[241] ADVICE TO PRELATES.

MS. Balliol Oxf 354, f 156ᵃ (1518–36).
Brown-Robbins, no 350.
Editions. Flügel E, Liedersammlungen des
XVI Jahrhunderts, Angl 26.169.
Dyboski R, Songs Carols and Other Miscel-
laneous Poems, EETSES 101, London 1907,
p 81.

[242] ADVICE TO THE ESTATES.

MS. Sloane 4031, ff 2ᵃ–2ᵇ (early 16 cent).
Brown-Robbins, Robbins-Cutler, no 4257.
Editions. Bowers R H, The ME Obey Your
King and Lord, Southern Folklore Quart
16.223.
Robbins-HP, p 233.
Selection. Bergen H, Lydgate's Fall of Princes,
EETSES 124, London 1919, p 59.
Literary Relations. Barclay A, The Lyfe of

St George, R Pynson 1515; ed W Nelson, The Life of St George by Alexander Barclay, EETS 230, London 1948, p 57 (text of original).

Edwards A S G, A Manuscript Portion of Barclay's Life of St George, SSL 7.66.

Nichols J G, The Book of Noblesse, Roxb Club 77, London 1860 (prose address to Edward IV on his wars in France).

Bühler C F, A ME Stanza on The Commonwealth and the Need for Wisdom, Eng Lang Notes 2.4 (for Brown-Robbins, no 2820, and Robbins-Cutler, no 856.5).

General References. Robbins-HP, p 388.

Scattergood PP, p 274.

3. Longer Discussions on National Policy

[243] WYNNERE AND WASTOURE.

MS. BM Addit 31042, ff 176ᵇ–183ᵇ (ends imperfectly; ca 1450).

Brown-Robbins, Robbins-Cutler, no 3137.

Editions. Gollancz I, Parlement of the Thre Ages, Roxb Club 132, London 1897, p 88 (crit F Holthausen, AnglB 34.14; E Kölbing, EStn 25.273; G N[eilson], Huchown, Athen 118[1901].559).

Gollancz I, Select Early English Poems 3, London 1920 (crit A Brandl, Arch 149.287; J R Hulbert, MP 18.499; M M Lee, YWES 1.39; J M Steadman, MLN 36.103); 2nd edn rvsd M Day, London 1930 (crit D Everett, RES 9.213; F Holthausen, AnglB 44.173).

Ford B, The Age of Chaucer, London 1954, p 315.

Haskell A S, A ME Anthology, Garden City 1969, p 382.

Selection. Kaiser R, Medieval English, Berlin 1958, p 447.

Modernization. Gardner J, The Alliterative Morte Arthure, Carbondale 1971, p 117.

Textual Matters. Neilson G, Wynnere and Wastoure, Athen 121(1903).626.

Bradley H, Wynnere and Wastoure, Athen 121(1903).657.

Neilson G, Wynnere and Wastoure and the Awntyrs, Athen 121(1903).754.

Bradley H, Wynnere and Wastoure, Athen 121(1903).816.

Neilson G, Wynnere and Wastoure, Athen 122(1903).221.

Steadman J M, Notes on Wynnere and Wastoure, MLN 38.308.

Hanford J H, Dame Nature and Lady Liffe, MP 15.316 (line 206).

Heather P J, Seven Planets, Folklore 54.358 (lines 165–66).

Gardner, Alliterative Morte Arthure, p 291.

Language. Oakden J P, Alliterative Poetry in ME, Manchester 1930, 1.54, 249; A Note on the Unity of Authorship, RES 10.200.

Serjeantson M S, The Dialects of the West Midlands in ME, RES 3.54, 186, 319.

Rainbow R S, A Linguistic Study of Wynnere and Wastoure and the Parlement of the Thre Ages, diss Chicago 1960.

Versification. Oakden, Alliterative Poetry, 1.183.

Everett D, Essays in ME Literature, Oxford 1955, p 49.

Moorman C, The Origins of the Alliterative Revival, Southern Quarterly 7.369.

Bestul T H, Satire and Allegory in Wynnere and Wastoure, Lincoln Nebraska 1974, p 82.

Date. N[eilson] G, A Note on Wynnere and Wastoure, Athen 118(1901).157 (ca 1357–58).

Gollancz I, A Note on Wynnere and Wastoure, Athen 118(1901).254.

N[eilson] G, A Note on Wynnere and Wastoure, Athen 118(1901).319 (also relation as Garter poem to Déduits de la Chasse).

Gollancz I, A Note on Wynnere and Wastoure, Athen 118(1901).350.

N[eilson] G, Huchown, Athen 118(1901).560.

Bradley H, Wynnere and Wastoure, Athen 121(1903).498.

Hulbert J R, The Problems of Authorship and Date of Wynnere and Wastoure, MP 18.31.

Steadman J M, The Date of Wynnere and Wastoure, MP 19.211; [review,] MLN 36.103.

Anderson J M, A Note on the Date of Wynnere and Wastoure, MLN 43.47 (line 317 suggests not before 1453).

McKisack M, The Fourteenth Century, Oxford 1959, p 428.

Moran D V, Wynnere and Wastoure An Extended Footnote, NM 73.683.

Authorship. Oakden, Alliterative Poetry, 1.249.

Hulbert, MP 18.31.

Steadman J M, The Authorship of Wynnere and Wastoure, MP 21.7.

Literary Relations. Neilson G, Huchown of the Awle Ryale The Alliterative Poet,

Glasgow 1902, p 89.
Hanford J H and J M Steadman, Death and Liffe An Alliterative Poem, SP 15.313.
Oakden, Alliterative Poetry, 2.51.
Hussey S S, Langland's Reading of Alliterative Poetry, MLR 60.163.
Brewer D S, An Unpublished Late Alliterative Poem, Eng Philological Stud 9.84.
Other Scholarly Problems. Stillwell G, Wynnere and Wastoure and The Hundred Years War, ELH 8.241 (includes date; crit G D Willcock, YWES 22.75).
Morton A L, A People's History of England, London 1952, pp 1, 24 (social satire).
Hieatt C, Winner and Waster and the Parliament of the Three Ages, AN&Q 4.100 (as dream vision); The Realism of Dream Visions, The Hague 1967, p 100 (as Garter poem).
Banta M W, Dream-Vision and Debate in the Allegorical Mode A Study of Wynnere and Wastoure Parlement of the Thre Ages and Death and Liffe, diss Buffalo 1966; DA 27.741A.
Oiji T, An Essay on Wynnere and Wastoure with Special Reference to the Political Economic and Religious Attitudes of the Poet, Studies in English Literature 43.1.
Elliott R W V, The Topography of Wynnere and Wastoure, ESts 49.134.
Bestul, Satire and Allegory, pp 24, 46.
Literary Criticism. Speirs J, Wynnere and Wastoure and Parlement of the Thre Ages, Scrut 17.221; Medieval English Poetry, London 1957, p 263.
Ford, edn, p 34.
Everett, Essays in ME Lit, p 49.
James J D, The Undercutting of Conventions in Wynnere and Wastoure, MLQ 25.243.
Banta, Dream Vision, passim.
Moran D V, Wynnere and Wastoure and the Parlement of the Thre Ages An Essay in the Alliterative Revival, diss Stanford 1968; DA 29.3978A.
Gardner, Alliterative Morte Arthure, p 256.
Pearsall D and E Salter, Landscapes and Seasons of the Medieval World, Toronto 1973, p 178.
Mann J, Chaucer and Medieval Estates Satire, Cambridge 1973, p 232.
Bestul, Satire and Allegory, p 1.
General References. Schofield, pp 372, 403.
CHEL, 1.372; 2.42.
Peter J D, Complaint and Satire in Early English Literature, Oxford 1956, p 96.
Yunck J A, The Lineage of Lady Meed, Notre Dame Ind 1963, p 269.

Utley F L, Manual, 3.707.
Robbins R H, ME Poems of Protest, Angl 78.193.
Elliott T J, ME Complaints Against the Times To Contemn the World or to Reform It, Annuale Mediaevale 14.30.
Bibliography. Bestul, Satire and Allegory, p 109.
New CBEL, 1.548.

[244] THE PARLEMENT OF THE THRE AGES.

MSS. 1, BM Addit 31042, ff 169ᵃ–176ᵇ (ca 1450); 2, BM Addit 33994 (formerly Ware), ff 19ᵃ–26ᵇ (fragmentary; begins imperfectly at line 226; 1475–1500).
Brown-Robbins, Robbins-Cutler, no 1556.
Catalogue of Additions to the Manuscripts 1876–1881, London 1882, p 148 (MSS described).
Offord, edn, EETS 246.xi (MSS described).
Editions. Gollancz I, The Parlement of the Thre Ages, Roxb Club 132, London 1897 (MSS 1, 2; crit F Holthausen, AnglB 34.14; E Kölbing, EStn 25.273; O N[eilson], Huchown, Athen 118(1901).559).
Gollancz I, Select Early English Poems 2, London 1915 (MS 1; crit [anon,] MLN 31.127).
Offord M Y, The Parlement of the Thre Ages, EETS 246, London 1959 (MSS 1, 2; crit G Mathew, RES ns 12.69).
Dunn C W and E T Byrnes, ME Literature, N Y 1973, p 238 (MS 1).
Haskell A S, A ME Anthology, N Y 1969, p 408 (MS 1).
Selections. Ford B, The Age of Chaucer, London 1954, p 302 (MS 1).
Kaiser R, Medieval English, Berlin 1958, p 446.
Modernizations. Bennett H S, England from Chaucer to Caxton, London 1928, p 92 (lines 1–101 only).
Gardner J, The Alliterative Morte Arthure, Carbondale 1971, p 133.
Textual Matters. Savage H L, A Note on the Parlement of the Thre Ages 38, MLN 43.177 (line 38); A Note on the Parlement of the Thre Ages 220, MLN 45.169 (line 220); Notes on the Prologue of the Parlement of the Thre Ages, JEGP 29.74.
Coffman G R, Old Age in Chaucer's Day, MLN 52.25 (lines 133–35, 150–51, 164–65).
Offord, EETS 246.35.
Gardner, Alliterative Morte Arthure, p 292.
Language. Hulbert J R, The Problems of

Authorship and Date of Wynnere and Wastoure, MP 18.32.

Serjeantson M S, The Dialects of the West Midlands in ME, RES 3.331.

Oakden J P, Alliterative Poetry in ME, Manchester 1930, 1.52, 249 (original, North West Midland; scribe, South East Midland); A Note on the Unity of Authorship, RES 10.200.

Rainbow R S, A Linguistic Study of Wynnere and Wastoure and The Parlement of the Thre Ages, diss Chicago 1960.

Versification. Schumacher K, Studien über den Stabreim in der me Alliterationsdichtung, BSEP 11.170.

Oakden, Alliterative Poetry, 1.182.

Offord, EETS 246.xxix.

Moorman C, The Origins of the Alliterative Revival, The Southern Quart 7.369.

Date. N[eilson], Athen 118(1901).560.

Neilson G, Huchown of the Awle Ryale The Alliterative Poet, Glasgow 1902, p 92.

Hulbert, MP 18.34.

Hussey S S, Langland's Reading of Alliterative Poetry, MLR 60.165.

Lewis R E, The Date of the Parlement of the Thre Ages, NM 69.380.

Authorship. Kölbing E, The Parlement of the Thre Ages, EStn 25.273 (common authorship with Wynnere and Wastoure).

Neilson, Huchown, p 67.

Bradley H, Wynnere and Wastoure, Athen 121(1903).658 (rejects common authorship).

Hulbert, MP 18.31 (rejects common authorship).

Steadman J M, The Authorship of Wynnere and Wastoure and The Parlement of the Thre Ages, MP 21.7 (supports Hulbert).

Oakden, Alliterative Poetry, 1.51, 249.

Savage, JEGP 29.74.

Oakden, RES 10.200.

Offord, EETS 246.xxxiv (common authorship possible but not proved; author of Parlement probably imitator).

Mishikin A, Susannah, New Haven 1969, p 21.

Bestul T H, Satire and Allegory in Wynnere and Wastoure, Lincoln Nebraska 1974, p 82.

Sources. Neilson, Huchown, p 81.

Lascelles M, Alexander and the Earthly Paradise in Mediaeval English Writings, MÆ 5.100.

Offord, EETS 246.xxxix.

Literary Relations. Hussey, MLR 60.163.

Oakden, Alliterative Poetry, 2.53.

Other Scholarly Problems. Loomis R S,

Verses on the Nine Worthies, MP 15.211.

Roberts J H, The Nine Worthies, MP 19.297.

G S C, The Nine Worthies, N&Q 160.191.

Sparke A, The Nine Worthies, N&Q 160.287.

Höltgen K J, Die Nine Worthies, Angl 77.279.

Savage, JEGP 29.75 (autobiographical nature of deerstalking episodes).

Coffman, MLN 52.26.

Philip C, A Further Note on Old Age in Chaucer's Day, MLN 53.181.

Pecheux M C, Aspects of the Treatment of Death in ME Poetry, Washington D C 1951, p 38.

Cary G, The Medieval Alexander, Cambridge 1956, pp 246, 343 (for Nine Worthies).

Offord, EETS 246.xxxiii (relation to other alliterative poems).

Hieatt C, Winner and Waster and The Parliament of the Three Ages, AN&Q 4.100 (as dream vision).

Banta M W, Dream-Vision and Debate in the Allegorical Mode A Study of Wynnere and Wastoure Parlement of the Thre Ages and Death and Liffe, diss Buffalo 1966; DA 27.741A.

Dickins B, The Nine Unworthies, Medieval Literature and Civilization Stud in Memory of G N Garmonsway, ed D A Pearsall and R A Waldron, London 1969, p 228.

Lampe D E, The ME Debate Poems A Genre Study, diss Nebraska 1969; DA 30.3910A (as debate genre).

Ritchie R L G, The Buik of Alexander, pt 4, PSTS 2s 25.402. (lines 9897–10012).

Schroeder H, Der Topos der Nine Worthies in Literatur und bildender Kunst, Göttingen 1971.

Waldron R A, The Prologue to the Parlement of the Thre Ages, NM 73.786 (as dream poem and complaint).

Literary Criticism. Bradley, Athen 121(1903).658.

Speirs J, Wynnere and Wastoure and Parlement of the Three Ages, Scrut 17.221.

Ford, Age of Chaucer, p 34.

Everett D, Essays in ME Literature, Oxford 1955, p 50.

Speirs J, Mediaeval English Poetry, London 1957, pp 266, 289.

Offord, EETS 246.xlii.

Lehman A K, Thematic Patterning and Narrative Continuity in Four ME Alliterative Poems, diss Cornell 1970; DAI 31.6558A.

Gardner, Alliterative Morte Arthure, p 262.

Peck R, The Careful Hunter in The Parlement of the Three Ages, ELH 39.333.

Lampe D E, The Poetic Strategy of The Parlement of the Thre Ages, Chaucer Rev 7.173.

Kernan E, Theme and Structure in The Parlement of the Thre Ages, NM 75.253.

Pearsall D and E Salter, Landscapes and Seasons of the Medieval World, Toronto 1973, p 178.

General References. Brandl, p 665.

Schofield, p 316.

CHEL, 2.42.

Utley F L, Manual, 3.707.

Elliott T J, ME Complaints Against the Times To Contemn the World or to Reform It, Annuale Mediaevale 14.30.

Bibliography. Offord, EETS 246.xliv.

New CBEL, 1.547.

[245] DEATH AND LIFFE.

MS. BM Addit 27879, pp 384–390 (ca 1650).

Brown-Robbins, no 603.

Editions. PFMS, 3.56.

Hanford J H and J M Steadman, Death and Liffe An Alliterative Poem, SP 15.261 (crit C B, MLN 34.63).

Gollancz I, rvsd M Day, Select Early English Poems 3, London 1930 (crit [anon,] N&Q 160.251; D Everett, RES 9.213; D Everett, YWES 11.99; F Holthausen, AnglB 44.173; A W Reed and R W Chambers, MLR 27.326; J M Steadman, MLN 47.261).

Henderson J D, Death and Liffe A Diplomatic Text with Introduction Notes and an Index of Words, diss Southern Illinois 1971; DA 32.3953.

Modernization. Arber E, The Dunbar Anthology, London 1901, p 126 (crit R Brotanek, AnglB 13.176).

Textual Matters. PFMS, 3.49.

Powell Y, Notes on Death and Life, EStn 7.97.

Holthausen F, Zu Death and Liffe, AnglB 23.157; 32.83.

Hanford and Steadman, SP 15.277.

Gollancz and Day, edn, p 17.

Marx K, Das Nachlcbcn Piers Plowman bis zu Bunyan's The Pilgrim's Progress, Königsberg 1931, passim.

Language. Steadman J M, Definitions Wanted, MLN 33.499.

Hanford and Steadman, SP 15.225.

Oakden J P, Alliterative Poetry in ME, Manchester 1930, 1.99.

Gollancz and Day, edn, p xi.

Versification. Hanford and Steadman, SP 15.255.

Oakden, Alliterative Poetry, 1.153.

Schneider A, Die me Stabzeile im 15 und 16 Jahrhundert, BBA 12.108, 126.

Date. Luick K, Die engl Stabreimzeile im XIV, XV und XVI Jahrhundert, Angl 11.612.

Schneider, BBA 12.108.

Hanford and Steadman, SP 15.229.

Gollancz and Day, edn, p ix.

Authorship. Oakden, Alliterative Poetry, 1.256.

Gollancz and Day, edn, p x.

Bestul T H, Satire and Allegory in Wynnere and Wastoure, Lincoln Nebraska 1974, p 84.

Sources and Literary Relations. PFMS, 3.49.

Scamman E, The Alliterative Poem Death and Liffe, RadMon 15.

Hanford J H, Dame Nature and Lady Liffe, MP 15.313.

Hanford and Steadman, SP 15.235, 246.

Other Scholarly Problems. Knowlton E C, Nature in ME, JEGP 20.198 (for allegorical figure of Dame Nature).

Blau E, Death and Liffe Ein Beitrag zur Streitgedichtsforschung, diss Kiel 1922.

Gollancz and Day, edn, pp xii (Dame Nature), 29 (Nine Worthies).

Tuve R, Spring in Chaucer and before Him, MLN 52.13 (Dame Nature).

Literary Criticism. Hanford and Steadman, SP 15.223, 232 (debate form), 237.

Oakden, Alliterative Poetry, 2.63.

Everett D, Essays in ME Literature, Oxford 1955, p 52.

Harrington D V, The Personifications in Death and Liffe A ME Poem, NM 68.35.

General References. CHEL, 2.46, 494.

Elliott T J, ME Complaints Against the Times To Contemn the World or to Reform It, Annuale Mediaevale 14.33.

Utley F L, Manual, 3.707.

Bibliography. New CBEL, 1.546.

[246] MUM AND THE SOTHSEGGER.

MSS. 1, Camb Univ Ll.4.14, ff 107ᵇ–119ᵇ (857 lines, ends imperfectly; 1450–75); 2, BM Addit 41666, ff 1ᵃ–19ᵇ (1751 different lines, begins and ends imperfectly; 1430–60).

Brown-Robbins, no *6; Robbins-Cutler, no *296.3.

Steele R, A New Fragment of Mum and the Sothsegger, TLS Dec 6 1928, p 965 (MS 2 described).

Hodgson and Co, London, Sales Cat no 7 (1928–29), item 385 (MS 2 described; includes facsimile of 1 page).

R F, Mum and Sothsegger: A Lost English Poem Recovered, Brit Mus Quart 3.100 (MS 2 described).

Editions. Wright T, Alliterative Poem on the Deposition of King Richard II, Camden Soc 3.1 (MS 1).

Wright PPS, 1.368 (MS 1).

Skeat W W, The Vision of Piers Plowman, EETS 54, London 1873, p 469 (MS 1).

Skeat W W, Piers Plowman, Oxford 1886, 1.603 (MS 1).

Day M and R Steele, Mum and the Sothsegger, EETS 199, London 1934 (MSS 1, 2; crit TLS Dec 26 1936, p 1064; A Brandl, Arch 170.281; K Brunner, AnglB 48.70; J P Oakden, MLR 32.85).

Selection. Sisam Oxf Book MEV, p 369.

Modernization. Benham A R, English Literature from Widsith to the Death of Chaucer, New Haven 1916, p 185 (selections).

Textual Matters. Bradley H, Richard the Redeless, III 105–6, MLR 12.202.

Snyder E D, The Wild Irish, MP 17.713 (MS 1, Prologue, line 10).

Day and Steele, EETS 199.84.

Language. Oakden J P, Alliterative Poetry in ME, Manchester 1930, 1.91, 251.

Day and Steele, EETS 199.xxx.

Scattergood PP, p 108.

Versification. Schipper, 1.197, 207.

Rosenthal F, Die alliteriende engl Langzeile im 14 Jahrhundert, Angl 1.420.

Luick K, Die engl Stabreimzeile, Angl 11.438.

Oakden, Alliterative Poetry, 1.195.

Day and Steele, EETS 199.xlii.

Date. Skeat, edn, EETS 54.cvi.

Day and Steele, EETS 199.xix.

Cam H M, Liberties and Communities in Medieval England, Cambridge 1944, p 229.

Scattergood PP, p 107.

Authorship. Skeat, edn, Piers Plowman, 1.107 (common authorship with Piers Plowman).

CHEL, 2.41.

Görnemann G, Zur Verfassershaft und Entstehungsgeschichte von Piers the Plowman, AF 48.68 (rejects common authorship; crit E Björkman, AnglB 27.275).

Oakden, Alliterative Poetry, 1.251.

Koziol H, Zur Frage der Verfasserschaft einiger me Stabreimdichtungen, EStn 67.168 (accepts common authorship).

Day and Steele, EETS 199.xv.

Embree D, Richard the Redeless and Mum and the Sothsegger A Case of Mistaken Identity, N&Q ns 22.4 (two distinct and unrelated fragments).

Sources and Literary Relations. Mohl R, The Three Estates in Medieval and Renaissance Literature, N Y 1933, p 105.

Day and Steele, EETS 199.xiv (Piers Plowman), xxiv.

Other Scholarly Problems. Bradley H, A Misplaced Leaf of Piers the Plowman, Athen 127(1906).481.

Mohl R, Theories of Monarchy in Mum and the Sothsegger, PMLA 59.16; rptd Studies in Spenser Milton and the Theory of the Monarchy, N Y 1949, p 42.

Cam, Liberties and Communities, p 223 (detailed political analysis).

Ferguson A B, The Problem of Counsel in Mum and the Sothsegger, Studies in the Renaissance 2.67.

Mann J, Chaucer and Medieval Estates Satire, Cambridge 1973, passim.

Literary Criticism. Ziepel C, The Reign of Richard II and Comments Upon an Alliterative Poem, Berlin 1874 (crit [anon,] Acad 1[1874].660; answered by Ziepel, Acad 2 [1874].322; R W, LZ 1874, p 1051).

Previté-Orton C W, Political Satire in English Poetry, Cambridge 1910, p 22.

Owst G R, Literature and Pulpit in Medieval England, Cambridge 1933, p 76 (ship imagery).

Kinney T L, The Temper of Fourteenth-Century English Verse of Complaint, Annuale Mediaevale 7.83.

General References. Warton T, History of English Poetry, ed W C Hazlitt, London 1871, 2.247.

Ten Brink, 2.202, 210.

Morley, 6.85.

Brandl, p 656.

Holton S H D, Richard the Redeles, Trans Royal Hist Soc ns 10.135.

CHEL, 2.41, 493.

Tucker S M, Verse Satire in England before the Renaissance, N Y 1908, p 95.

Eberhard O, Der Bauernaufstand von Jahre 1381 in der engl Poesie, AF 51.48.

Oakden, Alliterative Poetry, 2.60, 61.

Kleineke W, Engl Fürstenspiegel, SEP 90.152 (crit H Heuer, EStn 75.84).

Schlauch M, English Medieval Literature and Its Social Foundations, Warsaw 1956, p 288.

Yunck J A, The Lineage of Lady Meed, Notre Dame 1963, p 271.

Scattergood PP, pp 108, 112, 124, 228, 231, 237, 293.

Utley F L, Manual, 3.707.

Elliott T J, ME Complaints Against the

Times To Contemn the World or to Reform It, Annuale Mediaevale 14.32.
Bibliography. Körting, p 140.

[247] THE CROWNED KING: ON THE ART OF GOVERNING.

MS. Bodl 21669 (Douce 95), ff 4ᵃ–6ᵃ (ca 1450).
Brown-Robbins, Robbins-Cutler, no 605.
Editions. Skeat W W, The Vision of Piers Plowman, EETS 54, London 1873, p 524.
Robbins-HP, p 227.
Selection. Percy T, Reliques of Ancient English Poetry, London 1794, 2.285 (lines 1–27 only).
Textual Matters. Robbins-HP, p 385.
Language. Oakden J P, Alliterative Poetry in ME, Manchester 1930, 1.97.
Versification. Schipper, 1.197, 206.
Rosenthal F, Die alliterierende engl Langzeile im 14 Jahrhundert, Angl 1.421.
Oakden, Alliterative Poetry, 1.153.
Date. Skeat, EETS 54.cxxiv.
Literary Criticism. Oakden, Alliterative Poetry, 2.63.
General References. Brandl, p 700.
Scattergood PP, p 295.
Elliott T J, ME Complaints Against the Times to Contemn the World or to Reform It, Annuale Mediaevale 14.33.
Bibliography. Körting, p 141.

[248] THE SCOTTISH KINGDOM LIKE A HARP.

MSS. 1, Bodl 3888 (Fairfax 8), ff 190ᵃ–191ᵇ (1489; 291 lines); 1a, Bodl 8915 (Jones 8), ff 562ᵇ–567ᵃ (transcript, ca 1675); 1b, Marchmont A.C.15 (transcript; ca 1500; present location not known); 2, Pepys 2253, p 96 (1570–90; 308 lines). PRINT: 3, Buke of Gude Counsale to the Kyng, Chepman and Myllar, 1508 (224 lines; STC, no 3307).
Robbins-Cutler, no 2818.8.
Beattie W, The Chepman and Myllar Prints, Edinburgh Biblio Soc 1950, p 101 (facsimile of PRINT 3).
Editions. Laing D, Knightly Tale of Golagros, Edinburgh 1827 (PRINT 3).
Stevenson J, The Life and Death of King James I of Scotland, Maitland Club 42, Edinburgh 1837, p 32 (MS 1).
Skene F J H, Liber Pluscardiensis, Historians of Scotland 10, ed W F Skene, Edinburgh 1877, 7.392 (MS 1b).
Stevenson G, Pieces from the Makculloch and the Gray MSS, PSTS 65.171 (PRINT 3).

Craigie W A, The Maitland Folio Manuscript, PSTS ns 7.115 (MS 2).
Craigie W A, The Maitland Folio Manuscript, PSTS ns 20.74 (MS 1b), 75 (MS 1).
Literary Relations. Vogel B, Secular Politics and the Date of Lancelot of the Laik, SP 40.1.

[249] THE LIBEL OF ENGLISH POLICY.

MSS. A Text. 1, Bodl 815 (Laud 704), ff 1ᵃ–20ᵇ (1440–50); 2, All Souls Oxf 103, ff 1ᵃ–12ᵇ (ends imperfectly at line 731; ca 1450); 3, Pepys 1461, ff 1ᵃ–23ᵇ (1450–75); 4, Harley 78, ff 54ᵃ–69ᵃ (begins imperfectly at line 75; ca 1500); 5, Harley 4011, ff 120ᵃ–137ᵇ (lacks line 626–79; ends imperfectly at line 1091; 1450–75); 6, Soc of Antiquaries 101, ff 50ᵃ–67ᵇ (ca 1450); 7, Belfast Queen's Univ, a single leaf (15 cent).
MSS. B Text (1). 8, Bodl 14526 (Rawl F.32), ff 173ᵃ–193ᵇ (1450–1500); 9, Cotton Vitell E.x, ff 192ᵃ–207ᵇ (damaged by fire; 1450–75); 10, BM Addit 40673 (formerly Wrest Park), ff 1ᵃ–16ᵇ (1450–75); 11, Huntington Libr HM 140 (formerly Phillipps 8299), ff 125ᵃ–140ᵇ (1450–80).
MSS. B Text (2). 12, Harley 78, ff 35ᵃ–52ᵇ (damaged; ca 1500); 13, Harley 78, ff 53ᵃ–53ᵇ (one leaf only; lines 968–1042; ca 1500); 14, Harley 271, ff 1ᵃ–25ᵇ (ca 1500); 15, Rylands Libr Eng 955, ff 1ᵃ–2ᵇ, 4ᵃ–5ᵇ, 8ᵃ–27ᵃ (mid 16 cent); 15a, Rylands Libr Eng 955, ff 3ᵃ–3ᵇ (a missing portion of MS 15 added in 16 cent hand); 15b, Rylands Libr Eng 955, ff 6ᵃ–7ᵇ (a missing portion of MS 15 added in 16 cent hand); 16, Boston Public Libr 92 (formerly Gurney 146; formerly Macro 68), ff 167ᵃ–184ᵇ (before 1471); 16a, Boston Public Libr 92 (17 cent transcript inserted at end).
PRINTS. 17, Hakluyt R, Principal Navigations, Voyages, London 1598, 1.187 (A text; STC, no 12626); rptd Glasgow 1903, 2.114; rptd E Rhys, ed, London 1907, 1.174; rptd A R Benham, ed, Seattle 1922; 18, Selden J, Mare Clausum, London 1635, p 261 (including 34 lines from MS 9; STC, no 22175).
Brown-Robbins, Robbins-Cutler, no 3491.
Taylor F, Some Manuscripts of the Libelle of Englysche Polycye, JRLB 24.378 (MSS described).
Warner, edn, p lii (MSS described).
Manly & Rickert, 1.433 (MSS described).
Manwaring G E (letter), TLS June 29 1922, p 428; and A J C Grenville (reply), TLS

July 13 1922, p 460 (MS 10 described).
Editions. Wright PPS, 2.157 (MS 1).
Hertzberg W and R Pauli, Libell of Englishe Policye 1436, Leipzig 1878 (MS 1 with German translation; crit K Böddeker, LfGRP 2.55; F Lindner, EStn 2.488; G F Warner, Acad 14[1879].491).
Benham A R, The Processe of the Libel of English Policye, 2nd edn rvsd Seattle 1926.
Warner G [F], The Libelle of Englysche Polycye, Oxford 1926 (MS 1; crit [anon,] Arch 152.293; C Brinkmann, EHR 43.425; E Curtis, MLR 22.458; R Newhall, AHR 33.179).
Selections. Cook A S, A Literary ME Reader, Boston 1915, p 382.
Hammond E P, English Verse between Chaucer and Surrey, Durham N C 1927, p 244 (MS 5, lines 1–563).
Kaiser R, Medieval English, Berlin 1958 (MS 1, lines 1–125, etc).
Sisam Oxf Book MEV, p 413 (MS 1, lines 1064–75, 1092–1107).
Modernization. Dunham W H and S Pargellis, Complaint and Reform in England 1436–1714, N Y 1938, p 3.
Textual Matters. Degenhert M, Lydgate's Horse Goose and Sheep, MBREP 19.23 n.
Warner, edn, p 21.
Language. Hertzberg, edn, p 21.
Versification. Hertzberg, edn, p 19.
Warner, edn, p xlviii.
Date. Hertzberg, edn, p 16.
Warner, edn, p xiii.
Taylor, JRLB 24.396.
Authorship. Warner, edn, pp xvii, xxxviii (Adam Moleyns).
Taylor, JRLB 24.414, 418 (disputes Warner).
Other Scholarly Problems. Snyder E D, The Wild Irish, MP 17.713 (habitual phrases).
Holmes G A, Libelle of Englysche Polycye, EHR 76.193 (detailed economic analysis).
Baker D C, Gold Coins in Mediaeval English Literature, Spec 36.285.
General References. Strutt J, Horda Angel-Cynnan, London 1775, 3.52.
Macpherson D, Annals of Commerce, London 1805, 1.661.
Craik G L, The History of British Commerce, London 1844, 1.167.
Nicolas H N, History of the Royal Navy, London 1847, 2.421.
Wright PPS, 2.157.
Marsh G P, Origin and History of the English Language, N Y 1866, p 468.
Browne M, Chaucer's England, London 1869, 2.263.

Cunningham D, The Growth of English Industry and Commerce, Cambridge 1890, pp 382, 404; 5th edn Cambridge 1929, p 469.
DNB, 38.131.
Stubbs W, Constitutional History, Oxford 1896, 3.275.
Clowes W L, The Royal Navy, Boston 1897, 1.350.
CHEL, 2.423.
Körting, p 141.
Vickers K H, Humphrey Duke of Gloucester, London 1907, p 319.
Kingsford EHL, p 234.
Kingsford C L, English History in Contemporary Poetry, London 1913, p 24.
Mowat R B, The Wars of the Roses 1377–1471, London 1914, p 257.
Schofield W H, The Sea-Battle in Chaucer's Legend of Cleopatra, in Anniv Papers by Colleagues and Pupils of George Lyman Kittredge, 1913, rptd N Y 1967, p 140, n2.
Holzknecht K J, Literary Patronage in the Middle Ages, Phila 1923, p 142.
Hammond, English Verse, p 240.
Kleinecke W, Engl Fürstenspiegel, Halle 1937, p 179.
Power E E, The Wool Trade in the Fifteenth Century, in Studies in English Trade in the Fifteenth Century, ed E Power and M M Postan, London 1939, p 39 and passim.
Power E, The Wool Trade, Oxford 1941, p 14.
Bennett OHEL, p 160.
Kendall P M, The Yorkist Age, N Y 1962, pp 266, 285.
Bagley J J, Historical Interpretation, Harmondsworth Middlesex 1965, passim.
Carus-Wilson E M, Medieval Merchant Venturers, London 1967, p 52.
Scattergood PP, pp 37, 45, 91, 101, 327, 334.
Postan M M, Medieval Trade and Finance, Cambridge 1973, pp 181, 241, 244, 274.
Scattergood V J, Revision in some ME Political Verses, Archiv 211.291.
Bibliography. Hammond, English Verse, p 244.

[250] ENGLAND'S TRADE POLICY.

MS. Lansdowne 796, ff 1ᵇ–4ᵃ (1480–1500).
Brown-Robbins, Robbins-Cutler, no 921.
Editions. Wright PPS, 2.282.
Robbins-HP, p 168.
Selection. Thornley I D, England under the Yorkists, London 1920, p 198.
Textual Matters. Robbins-HP, p 339.

Date. Robbins R H, A Political Action Poem,
MLN 71.245.
Robbins-HP, p xli.
General References. Morley, 6.236.
Kingsford EHL, p 236.
Kingsford C L, English History in Contempo-
rary Poetry, London 1913, p 44.
Thornley, England under the Yorkists, p 199.
Power E E, The Wool Trade in the Fifteenth
Century, in Studies in English Trade in the
Fifteenth Century, ed E Power and M M
Postan, London 1933, p 39.
Scattergood PP, pp 335, 370.
Postan M M, Medieval Trade and Finance,
Cambridge 1973, p 245.

[251] ACTIVE POLICY OF A PRINCE.

MS. Camb Univ Mm.4.42, ff 2[b]–18[b] (1470–
1500).

Brown-Robbins, no 2130.
Edition. Bateson M, George Ashby's Poems,
EETSES 76, London 1899, p 13.
Selection. Thornley I D, England under the
Yorkists, London 1920, p 55.
Textual Matters. Holthausen F, Active Policy
of a Prince, Angl 45.92.
Date. Scattergood PP, p 282.
Literary Relations. Scattergood PP, p 286.
Other Scholarly Problems. Holzknecht K J,
Literary Patronage in the Middle Ages,
Phila 1923, p 80 (patronage).
General References. Morley, 6.161.
CHEL, 2.239.
Kingsford EHL, p 232.
Scattergood PP, pp 103, 212, 283.
Bibliography. CBEL, 1.253.
Baugh LHE, p 298.

II. The Ruled

[252] MEDIEVAL LIBERTY POEMS.

General References. Mackay C, Songs and
Ballads, PPS 1.
Maurice E C, Lives of English Popular Lead-
ers, London 1872, 2.157.
Powell E, The Rising in East Anglia in 1381,
Cambridge 1896.
Powell E and G M Trevelyan, The Peasants'
Rising and the Lollards, London 1899 (crit
[anon,] Edinburgh Rev 191.76).
Trevelyan G M, England in the Age of Wy-
cliffe, London 1900, p 203.
Oman C, The Great Revolt of 1381, Oxford
1906.
Brie F W D, Wat Tyler and Jack Straw, EHR
21.106.
Wood M M, The Spirit of Protest in Old
French Literature, N Y 1917.
Koht H, Medieval Liberty Poems, AHR
48.281 (European).
Brotanek K, Zu den ältesten engl Hexama-
tern, Arch 133.90.
Eberhard O, Der Bauernaufstand vom Jahre
1381 in der engl Poesie, AF 51.17 (crit
[anon,] Arch 137.128; J Koch, EStn 53.432).
Wilkinson B, Peasants' Revolt of 1381, Spec
15.30.
Schlauch M, Revolt of 1381 in England, SciS
4.414.
Hilton R H and H Fagan, The English
Rising of 1381, London 1950.

Robbins R H, ME Poems of Protest, Angl
78.193.
Dobson R B, The Peasants' Revolt of 1381,
London 1970, p 379.
Roush G J, The Political Plowman The
Expression of Political Ideals in Piers Plow-
man and Its Successors, diss Berkeley 1966;
DA 27.752.
Richert W G, Anonymous Vernacular Verse
Protest of the Middle Ages 1216–1485, diss
Colorado 1966; DA 28.1057A.
Galbraith V H, Thoughts about the Peasants'
Revolt, in The Reign of Richard II Essays
in Honour of May McKisack, ed F R H
DuBoulay and C M Barron, London 1971,
p 46.

[253] THE EVIL STATE OF ENGLAND.

MSS. 1, St John's Oxf 209, f 38[b] (ca 1465);
2, Camb Univ Dd.14.2, f 312[a] (1432); 3,
Cotton Cleop C.viii, f 134[a] (ca 1400); 4,
J Stevens Cox (Beaumont Dorset) (mid 15
cent).
Brown-Robbins, Robbins-Cutler, no 3306.
Editions. Coxe H O, Catalogus Codicum MSS
Qui in Collegiis Aulisque Oxoniensibus
Hodie Adservantur, Oxford 1852, p 74 (MS
1).
Arnold T, Annals and Memorials of St Ed-
munds Abbey, Rolls Series 96, 3.295 (MS 1).

Wright PPS, 1.278 (MS 1).
Corson L, A Finding List of Political Poems, 1910; rptd N Y 1970, p 38 (MS 1).
Sisam K, Fourteenth Century Verse and Prose, Oxford 1921, p 161 (MS 1).
Wilson Lost Lit, p 192; 2nd edn, p 187 (MS 1).
Robbins-HP, pp 54 (MS 2), 273 (MS 1).
Literary Repository, no 4 (Sept 1957), p 1 (MS 4).
Kinney T L, The Temper of Fourteenth-Century English Verse of Complaint, Annuale Mediaevale 7.74 (MS 1).
Dobson R B, The Peasants' Revolt of 1381, London 1970, p 305 (MSS 1, 2).
Wenzel S, Unrecorded ME Verses, Angl 92.70 (MS 3).
General References. Robbins-HP, p 273.
Rowse A L, Bosworth Field, Garden City N Y 1966, p 13.

[254] THE GREAT REBELLION.

MS. Trinity Dublin 214, flyleaf (15 cent).
Robbins-Cutler, no 1498.5.

[255] JOHN BALL'S PROVERBIAL COUPLET.

MSS. 1, Bodl 15444 (Rawl D.328), f 142[b] (1425–45); 2, Balliol Oxf 354, f 200[b] (1518–36); 3, Harley 3362, f 5[a] (1475–1500); and others.
Brown-Robbins, Robbins-Cutler, no 3922.
Editions. Only typical printings can be listed here.
Stow J, Annales, ed E Howes, London 1615, p 293.
Mackay C, Songs and Ballads, PPS 1.1.
Riley H T, Thomas Walsingham Historia Anglicana, Rolls Series 28, 2.32.
Thompson E M, Chronicon Angliae, Rolls Series 64, p 321.
Wright T, Carols, Warton Club 4.103.
Flügel E, Liedersammlungen des XVI Jahrhunderts, Angl 26.203.
Réville A, Le Soulèvement des Travailleurs d'Angleterre en 1381, Paris 1898, p lxi.
Dyboski R, Songs Carols and Other Miscellaneous Poems, EETSES 101, London 1907, p 131.
Sisam K, Fourteenth Century Verse and Prose, Oxford 1921, p 152.
Owst G R, Literature and Pulpit in Medieval England, Cambridge 1933, p 291.
Oxford Dictionary of English Proverbs, Oxford 1935, p 571; 2nd edn Oxford 1948, p 2; 3rd edn Oxford 1970, p 3.
Meech S B, A Collection of Proverbs in Rawlinson MS D.328, MP 38.121.
Eberhard O, Der Bauernaufstand vom Jahr 1381 in der engl Poesie, AF 51.24.
Robbins R H, ME Poems of Protest, Angl 78.202.
Sisam Oxf Book MEV, p 558.
Scattergood PP, p 354.
General References. Steel A, Richard II, Cambridge 1941, p 71.
Lindsay J, Nine Day's Hero Wat Tyler, London 1964, p 63.
Kesteven G R, The Peasant's Revolt, London 1965, p 47.
Rowse A L, Bosworth Field, Garden City N Y 1966, p 11.
Dobson R B, The Peasants' Revolt of 1381, London 1970, p 372.
Scattergood PP, p 354.
Bibliography. Dobson, Peasants' Revolt, p 405.

[256] LETTERS OF THE REBELS.

MSS. 1a, Bodl 2752 (Bodley 316), ff 151[a]–175[b]; 1b, Harley 3634, ff 125[a]–195[b] (ca 1388; Chronicon); 2, Corp Christi Camb 7 (early 15 cent; Walsingham); 3, Cotton Claud E.iii, ff 167[a]–305[a] (15 cent; Knighton); 4, Cotton Faust B.ix, ff 146[a]–241[b] (early 15 cent; Chronicon); 5, Cotton Tib C.vii, ff 1[a]–240[b] (15 ent; damaged by fire; Knighton); 6, Royal 13.E.ix, ff 177[a]–326[b] (ca 1400; Walsingham); 7, Coll of Arms Arundel 7 (15 cent; Walsingham).
Basic References. Stow J, Annales, ed E Howes, London 1615.
Holinshed's Chronicles, London 1807.
Mackay C, Songs and Ballads, PPS 1.
Riley H T, Thomas Walsingham Historia Anglicana, Rolls Series 28.
Thompson E M, Chronicon Angliae, Rolls Series 64.
Lumby J R, Chronicon Henrici Knighton, Rolls Series 92.
Trevelyan G M, England in the Age of Wycliffe, London 1900.
Eberhard O, Der Bauernaufstand vom Jahr 1381 in der engl Poesie, AF 51.
Hilton R H and H Fagan, The English Rising of 1381, London 1950.
Lindsay P and R Groves, The Peasants' Revolt 1381, London [1950].
Lindsay J, Nine Day's Hero Wat Tyler, London 1964.
Dobson R B, Peasants' Revolt of 1381, Lon-

don 1970.
  a. John Ball Saint Mary Priest.
Brown-Robbins, Robbins-Cutler, no 1791.
Editions. Stow, Annales, p 294.
Mackay, PPS 1.2.
Lumby, Rolls Series 92, 2.140.
Eberhard, AF 51.22.
Hilton and Fagan, English Rising, p 102.
Wilson Lost Lit, p 202; 2nd edn, p 197.
Robbins-HP, p 54.
Dobson, Peasants' Revolt, p 381.
Elliott T J, ME Complaints Against the
  Times, Annuale Mediaevale 14.23.
Textual Matters. Robbins-HP, p 273.
Literary Relations. Brown-Robbins, Robbins-
  Cutler, no 2356 (Degeneracy of Age, found
  separately).
Other Scholarly Problems. Lawson J H, The
  Hidden Heritage, N Y 1950, p 51 (use of
  Piers Plowman among rebels).
General References. Schlauch M, Revolt of
  1381 in England, SciS 4.414.
Lindsay and Groves, Peasants' Revolt, pp 74,
  86, 88.
Schlauch M, Medieval English Literature and
  Its Social Foundations, Warsaw 1956, p 207.
Robbins-HP, p xlii.
Lindsay, Nine Day's Hero, p 71.
Scattergood PP, p 354.
  b. John the Miller Hath Ground
    Small.
Brown-Robbins, Robbins-Cutler, no 1796.
Editions. Stow, Annales, p 294.
Holinshed's Chronicles, 2.749.
Mackay, PPS 1.2.
Wright T, Essays on the Literature Popular
  Superstitions and History of England, Lon-
  don 1846, 2.260.
Riley, Rolls Series 28, 2.34.
Thompson, Rolls Series 64, p 322.
Skeat W W, Piers Plowman, Oxford 1886,
  2.lv.
Trevelyan, England in the Age of Wycliffe,
  p 203.
Sisam K, Fourteenth Century Verse and Prose,
  Oxford 1921, p 161.
Eberhard, AF 51.23.
Owst G R, Literature and Pulpit in Medieval
  England, Cambridge 1933, p 221.
Greene E E Carols, p cxliv.
Rickert E, Chaucer's World, N Y 1948, p 362.
Lindsay and Groves, Peasants' Revolt, p 86.
Kaiser R, Medieval English, Berlin 1958, p
  387.
Robbins-HP, p 55.
Dobson, Peasants' Revolt, p 381.
Sisam Oxf Book MEV, p 558.
Textual Matters. Robbins-HP, p 274.

Literary Relations. Wright PPS, 1.227 (for
  Latin poem on Sudbury with nicknames
  of leaders).
Brotanek R, Zu den ältesten engl Hexametern,
  Arch 133.90.
General Reference. Robbins R H, ME Poems
  of Protest, Angl 78.201.
  c. John Ball Greeteth You Well.
Robbins-Cutler, no 1790.8.
Editions. Stow, Annales, p 294.
Lumby, Rolls Series 92, 2.139.
Hilton and Fagan, English Rising, p 100.
Dobson, Peasants' Revolt, p 381.
General Reference. Lindsay, Nine Day's Hero,
  p 70.
  d. Jack Miller.
Brown-Robbins, Robbins-Cutler, no 1654.
Editions. Stow, Annales, p 294.
Mackay, PPS 1.3.
Wright T, Essays on the Literature Popular
  Superstitions and History of England, Lon-
  don 1846, 2.260.
Lumby, Rolls Series 92, 2.138.
Trevelyan, England in the Age of Wycliffe,
  p 204.
Eberhard, AF 51.21.
Lindsay and Groves, Peasants' Revolt, p 87.
Hilton and Fagan, English Rising, p 103.
Dobson, Peasants' Revolt, p 381.
General Reference. Lindsay, Nine Day's Hero,
  p 73.
  e. Jack Trueman.
Brown-Robbins, Robbins-Cutler, no 1655.
Editions. Stow, Annales, p 294.
Mackay, PPS 1.4.
Lumby, Rolls Series 92, 2.139.
Eberhard, AF 51.20.
Lindsay and Groves, Peasants' Revolt, p 87.
Hilton and Fagan, English Rising, p 102.
Dobson, Peasants' Revolt, p 382.
Literary Relations. Rel Ant, 2.6.
General References. Lindsay, Nine Day's Hero,
  p 74.
Keller J R, The Triumph of Vice A Formal
  Approach to the Medieval Complaint
  Against the Times, Annuale Mediaevale
  10.135.
  f. Jack Carter.
Not listed Brown-Robbins, Robbins-Cutler.
Editions. Lumby, Rolls Series 92, 2.139.
Hilton and Fagan, English Rising, p 102.
Dobson, Peasants' Revolt, p 382.
General Reference. Lindsay, Nine Day's Hero,
  p 73.
  g. John Sheep.
Not listed Brown-Robbins, Robbins-Cutler.
Editions. Stow, Annales, p 294.

Holinshed's Chronicle, 2.749.
Mackay, PPS 1.1.
Riley, Rolls Series 28, 2.134.
Thompson, Rolls Series 64, p 322.
Trevelyan, England in the Age of Wycliffe, p 203.
Eberhard, AF 51.23.
Lindsay and Groves, Peasants' Revolt, p 86.
Hilton and Fagan, English Rising, p 101.
Dobson, Peasants' Revolt, p 381.
General Reference. Lindsay, Nine Day's Hero, p 71.

[257] THE COURSE OF REVOLT.

MSS. 1, Bodl 1797 (Digby 196), ff 20ᵇ–21ᵃ (7 stanzas; ca 1400); 2, Corp Christi Camb 369, f 46ᵇ (6 stanzas including 3 variants; 1385–1400).
Brown-Robbins, Robbins-Cutler, no 3260.
Editions. Wright T, Essays on the Literature, Popular Superstitions and History of England, London 1846, 2.266 (MS 2).
Rel Ant, 2.283 (MS 2).
Wright PPS, 1.224 (MS 2).
Kaiser R, Alt- und me Anthologie, Berlin 1954, p 373 (MS 2).
Kaiser R, Medieval English, Berlin 1958, p 386 (MS 2).
Robbins-HP, p 55 (MS 1).
Dobson R B, The Peasants' Revolt of 1381, London 1970, p 358 (MS 1).
Selection. Sisam Oxf Book MEV, p 558 (lines 1–4 only).
Textual Matters. Robbins-HP, p 274.
Literary Relations. Farnham W, The Medieval Heritage of Elizabethan Tragedy, 1936; rptd Oxford 1963, p 380 (drama).
General References. Previté-Orton C W, Political Satire in English Poetry, Cambridge 1910, p 26.
Eberhard O, Der Bauernaufstand vom Jahre 1381 in der engl Poesie, AF 51.25.
Wehrle W O, The Macaronic Hymn Tradition in Medieval English Literature, Washington D C 1933, p 45.
Robbins R H, ME Poems of Protest, Angl 78.196.
Scattergood PP, p 355.

[258] THE YORKSHIRE PARTISANS.

MSS. 1, Stowe 393, f 99ᵇ (16 cent); 2, Public Record Office, Ancient Indictments K.B.9, no 144, m 31 (end 14 cent); 3, Public Record Office, Coram Rege Roll 525 (16 Rich II) Rex, mm.57.d (end 14 cent).

Brown-Robbins, Robbins-Cutler, no 1543.
Editions. Hewlett M H, Two Political Songs of the Middle Ages, Antiquary 2(1880).202 (MS 3).
Powell E and G M Trevelyan, The Peasants' Rising and the Lollards, London 1899, p 19 (MS 3).
Robbins-HP, p 60 (MS 1).
General References. Powell and Trevelyan, edn, p ix.
Eberhard O, Der Bauernaufstand vom Jahr 1381 in der engl Poesie, AF 51.51.
Richardson H G, Year Books and Plea Rolls as Sources of Historical Information, Trans Royal Hist Soc 4s 5.46.
Chambers R W and M Daunt, Book of London English, Oxford 1931, p 276.
Robbins-HP, p 277.
Robbins R H, ME Poems of Protest, Angl 78.202.
Scattergood PP, p 356.

[259] STUDENT ABUSE OF THE MAYOR OF CAMBRIDGE.

MSS. 1, Harley 247, ff 129ᵃ–129ᵇ (Stowe's transcript; 16 cent); 2, Cole (present ownership and location not known).
Robbins-Cutler, no 1941.8.
Editions. Hartshorne C H, Ancient Metrical Tales, London 1829, p 225 (MS 2).
Wright T, Essays on the Literature, Popular Superstitions, and History of England, London 1846, 2.266 (MS 2).
Cooper C H, Annals of Cambridge, Cambridge 1842, 1.160 (MS 2).
Coulton G G, Social Life in Britain, Cambridge 1918, p 66 (MS 2).
Wilson Lost Lit, p 200; 2nd edn, p 194 (MS 2).
Authorship. Scattergood PP, p 368.
Literary Relations. Hingeston F C, The Chronicle of London by John Capgrave, Rolls Series 1, p 314.
Wright PS, p 231.
General References. Wilson Lost Lit, p 200.
Scattergood PP, p 367.

[260] A SONG OF FREEDOM.

MS. Bodl 29746 (Lat theol d.1), f 174ᵃ (1430–50).
Brown-Robbins, Robbins-Cutler, no 849.
Editions. Pfander H G, Popular Sermon, N Y 1937, p 49.
Robbins-HP, p 62.

Date. Robbins-HP, p xxv.
General References. Robbins-HP, p 278.
Robbins R H, ME Poems of Protest, Angl 78.199.
Wilson Lost Lit, 2nd edn, p 197.
Scattergood PP, p 358.

[261] THE KENTISH INSURRECTION.

MSS. 1, Magdalen Oxf Charter Misc 36, art 14 (mid 15 cent); 2, Harley 545, f 166ᵇ (ca 1550).
Brown-Robbins, Robbins-Cutler, no 941.
Editions. Historical MSS Commission Eighth Report, Appendix 1, p 267 (MS 1).
Halliwell J O, Observations Upon Certain Events, Archaeol 29.138 (MS 2).
Wilson Lost Lit, p 204; 2nd edn, p 197.
Robbins-HP, p 63 (MS 1).
Scattergood PP, p 369 (MS 1).
Sources and Literary Relations. Gairdner J, Three Fifteenth-Century Chronicles, Camden Soc ns 28.94 (prose proclamation from MS Lambeth 306, f 49ᵃ).
General References. Stow J, Annales, ed H Howe, London 1615, p 388.
Orridge B B, Illustrations of Jack Cade's Rebellion, London 1869, p 24.
Robbins-HP, p 278.
Rowse A L, Bosworth Field, Garden City N Y 1966, p 124.
Scattergood PP, p 369.

[262] ROBIN OF REDESDALE.

MS. Trinity Dublin 516, f 113ᵇ (1450–75).
Robbins-Cutler, no 1409.8.
Editions. Halliwell J O, A Chronicle . . . of King Edward the Fourth, Camden Soc 10.6.
Thornley I D, England under the Yorkists, London 1920, p 41.

[263] ON JUSTICE IN NORWICH.

MS. Norwich City Book of Pleas, f 72ᵃ (15 cent).
Robbins-Cutler, no 4128.8.
Editions. Hudson W, Records of the City of Norwich, Norwich 1906, 1.334.
Liebermann F, Politische Reimerie, 1433, Arch 126.185.

[264] INJUSTICES AT COVENTRY I.

MS. Coventry Corp Leet Book, f 275ᵇ (ca 1500).

Brown-Robbins, Robbins-Cutler, no 466.
Editions. Harris M D, Laurence Saunders Citizen of Coventry, EHR 9.647.
Harris M D, The Coventry Leet Book, EETS 135, London 1907, p 567.
Wilson Lost Lit, p 198; 2nd edn, p 192.
Kendall P M, The Yorkist Age, N Y 1962, p 107.
Scattergood PP, p 373.

[265] LADY GODIVA.

MSS. No MS extant. Inscription in stained glass window in Trinity Church, Coventry.
Robbins-Cutler, no 1330.3.
Dugdale T, Antiquities of Warwickshire, London 1656, p 86.

[266] INJUSTICES AT COVENTRY II.

MS. Coventry Corp Leet Book, f 277ᵇ (ca 1500).
Brown-Robbins, no 1665.
Editions. Harris M D, The Coventry Leet Book, EETS 135, London 1907, p 577.
Kendall P M, The Yorkist Age, N Y 1962, p 110 (omits first three lines).
Scattergood PP, p 374.
General Reference. Harris M D, Laurence Saunders Citizen of Coventry, EHR 9.649.

[267] INJUSTICES AT COVENTRY III.

MS. Coventry Corp Leet Book, f 278ᵃ (ca 1500).
Brown-Robbins, Robbins-Cutler, no 3322.
Editions. Sharp T, Illustrative Papers on the History and Antiquities of the City of Coventry, Coventry 1871, p 235.
Harris M D, The Coventry Leet Book, EETS 135, London 1907, p 577.
Robbins-HP, p 63.
Kendall P M, The Yorkist Age, N Y 1962, p 110.
General References. Harris M D, Laurence Saunders Citizen of Coventry, EHR 9.650 (includes lines 1–8, 15–24).
Robbins-HP, p 279.
Scattergood PP, p 375.

[268] SEVEN NAMES OF A PRISON.

MSS. MS to be established (not Harley 7256), f 35ᵃ (15 cent).
Brown-Robbins, Robbins-Cutler, no 2778.
Edition. Rel Ant, 1.270.

[269] THE PRISONER'S PRAYER.

MS. London Guildhall, Record Room, De Antiquis Legibus Liber, f 160ᵇ (1225–50).
Brown-Robbins, Robbins-Cutler, no 322.
Editions. Rel Ant, 1.274.
Ellis A J, Contemporary Songs, TPSL 1868, p 104.
Ellis A J, Early English Pronunciation, EETSES 7, London 1869, p 434, and ChS 2s 4.434 (with French and music).
Wülcker R P, Ae Lesebuch, Halle 1874, 1.105.
Brown ELxiiiC, p 10.
Gennrich F, Internationale mittelalterliche Melodien, Zeitschrifte für Musikwissenschaft 11.346.
Ekwall E, An Early London Text, Studien i Modern Sprakvetenskap 17.42.
Aspin I S T, AN Political Songs, Oxford 1953, p 6.
Kaiser R, Medieval English, Berlin 1958, p 216.

Modernization. Adamson M R, A Treasury of ME Verse, N Y 1930, p 31.
Textual Matters. Brown ELxiiiC, p 167.
Menner R J, Notes on ME Lyrics, MLN 55.243.
Ekwall, edn, p 39.
Language. Ekwall, edn, p 43.
Versification. Schipper, 1.399.
Literary Criticism. Brown ELxiiiC, p xvi.
General References. Wager W, English Monody, in G Reese, Music in the Middle Ages, N Y 1940, p 240.
Ekwall E, Studies on the Population of Medieval London, Stockholm 1956, p xvii.

[270] JOHN MY LORD'S HYNE.

MS. Stanbrook Abbey 3 (1410–40).
Robbins-Cutler, no 1793.6.
Edition. Ker N R, ME Verses and a Latin Letter in a Manuscript at Stanbrook Abbey, MÆ 34.231.

11. POLITICAL PROPHECIES

[271] POLITICAL PROPHECIES.

Major Reference. Taylor R, The Political Prophecy in England, N Y 1911 (crit R W Bond, MLR 11.346; G H Gerould, EStn 46.137; H T Price, AnglB 25.49).
Literary Relations. Rel Ant, 2.12, 25, 245 (for Latin and later prophecies).
Dodds M H, Political Prophecies in the Reign of Henry VIII, MLR 11.276.
Scattergood V J, Adam Davy's Dreams and Edward II, Arch 206.223.
Other Scholarly Problems. Taylor, Political

Prophecy, p 45 (animal symbolism).
Griffiths M E, Early Vaticination in Welsh with English Parallels, Cardiff 1937, p 83 (animal symbolism).
Literary Criticism. Kingsford EHL, p 236.
General References. Scattergood PP, p 22.
Mackie J H, The Earlier Tudors, Oxford 1952, p 52.
Bibliography. Taylor, Political Prophecy, p 1.
CBEL, 1.167.
See below under [272], [279], [287], [288].

I. The Merlin Prophecies

[272] MERLIN PROPHECIES.

Sources and Literary Relations. A Lytel Treatyse of the Byrth and Prophecyes of Marlyn, de Worde, London 1510 (STC, no 17841).
Heywood J, The Life of Merlin, London 1641; rptd London 1813.
Brandl, p 710 (French).
Ward, 1.203, 279 (Geoffrey) and (Merlin prophecies) 292, 295, 296, 297, 298, 299, 301, 302, 303, 304, 307, 309, 310, 311, 312, 313, 314, 315, 316, 317, 318, 320.

Radcliffe J, Merlin, N&Q 9s 8.234, 287.
Roberts W, Merlin, N&Q 9s 8.386.
Brie F W D, Geschichte und Quellen der me Prosachronik, Marburg 1905, p 7 (key).
Leach H G, De Libello Merlini, MP 8.607 (Icelandic parallels); Angevin Britain and Scandinavia, HSCL 6.137 (Scandinavian parallels).
Kingsford EHL, p 236.
Parry J J, Vita Merlini, Urbana 1925.
Paton L A, Prophécies de Merlin, N Y 1926 (French parallels; crit E G Gardner, MLR 23.85; A Hilka, ZfRP 56.728; G Lavergne,

Moyen Age 38.349; W A Nitze, MP 27.107;
H Sweet, AHR 33.177; J S P Tatlock, Spec
3.416, answered by Paton, Spec 4.105).

Griscom A, The Historia Regum Britanniae
of Geoffrey of Monmouth, York 1929, pp
67, 134 (Latin parallels).

Faral E, La Légende Arthurienne, Paris 1929,
2.28, 341; 3.307 (Vita Merlini).

Millican C B, The First English Translation
of the Prophecies of Merlin, SP 28.720 (for
Elias Ashmole, 17 cent).

Hammer J, A Commentary on the Propheta
Merlini, Spec 10.3; 15.409.

Griffiths M E, Early Vaticination in Welsh
with English Parallels, Cardiff 1937, p 83
(Welsh parallels).

Manly J M, The Penrose MS of La Resurrection, MP 37.3 (French parallels).

Tatlock J S P, Geoffrey of Monmouth's Vita
Merlini, Spec 18.265.

Patch H R, The Other World, Cambridge
Mass 1950, p 284.

Gerould G H, A Text of Merlin's Prophecies,
Spec 23.102 (for Princeton Univ Libr roll).

General References. Brandl, p 709.

Marston R B, Merlin, N&Q 9s 8.103.

Dean P, The Prophecies of Merlin, N&Q
177.174.

Jaggard W, The Prophecies of Merlin, N&Q
177.251.

Holzknecht K J, Literary Patronage in the
Middle Ages, Phila 1923, pp 91, 137, 215.

Keeler L, Geoffrey of Monmouth and the
Late Latin Chronicles 1300–1500, Berkeley
1946, p 70.

Jones W G, Welsh Nationalism and Henry
Tudor, p 32.

Bibliography. New CBEL, 1.477.

[273] THE PROPHECY OF THE SIX KINGS TO FOLLOW KING JOHN.

MSS. 1, Bodl 4062 (Hatton 56), ff 43ᵃ–45ᵃ
(1450; related variant text, 136 lines); 2,
Cotton Galba E.ix, ff 49ᵃ–50ᵃ (1440–50); 3,
Harley 559, ff 45ᵃ–47ᵇ (1540–50; variant, 141
lines). PRINTS: 4, Whole Prophesie of
Scotland, Waldegrave, Edinburgh 1603 (cf
STC, no W 1060); 5, Andro Hart, Edinburgh 1617 (STC, no 17842); rptd Edinburgh 1714, 1718; Edinburgh and London
1745; Falkirk 1782.

Brown-Robbins, Robbins-Cutler, no 1112.

Laing D, Collection of Ancient Scottish
Prophecies, Bannatyne Club 44, Edinburgh
1833 (PRINT 5 rptd).

Edition. Hall J, The Poems of Laurence
Minot, Oxford 1914, p 103 (MS 2).

Sources and Literary Relations. Wylie H J,
History of England Under Henry the
Fourth, London 1844, 2.375.

Halliwell [-Phillipps] C O, Works of William
Shakespeare, London 1853, 9.401 (Brut version).

Ward, 1.299, 309, 322 (abbreviated Latin versions in: e g, MSS Cotton Julius A.v; Cotton Vesp E.vii, f 89ᵃ).

Meyer P, Manuscrits français de Cambridge,
Rom 15.283 (French text in MS Camb Univ
Gg.1.1, f 120ᵇ).

MS Cotton Julius A.v, ff 177ᵇ–179ᵇ (another
French text).

Taylor R, The Political Prophecy in England, N Y 1911, p 157 (Anglo-French text
in MS Harley 746, abbreviated Latin text
in MS Harley 6148).

Brie F, The Brut, EETS 131, London 1906,
p 72.

Scattergood V J, Adam Davy's Dreams and
Edward II, Arch 206.256.

General References. Webb J, A French Metrical History of the Deposition of King
Richard II, Archaeol 20.250.

Wylie, History of England, 2.375.

Halliwell, Shakespeare, 9.401.

Brandl, p 710.

Kingsford EHL, p 236.

Taylor, Political Prophecy, pp 4, 48, 99, 157,
160, 164.

Dodds M H, Political Prophecies in the
Reign of Henry VIII, MLR 11.279.

Brie, EETS 131.73.

Scattergood PP, p 118.

[274] GEOFFREY OF MONMOUTH'S PROPHECY.

MS. Bodl 15165 (Rawl K.42), pp 104, 103
(1450–1500).

Brown-Robbins, Robbins-Cutler, no 1552.

Editions. Robbins R H, Geoffrey of Monmouth: An English Fragment, ESts 38.261.

Robbins-HP, p 113.

Textual Matters. Robbins-HP, p 308.

Sources. Griscom A, The Historia Regum
Britanniae of Geoffrey of Monmouth, N Y
1929, p 388.

Robbins, ESts 38.260.

Robbins-HP, p 307.

[275] A PROPHECY OF THE CONQUEST OF FRANCE.

MSS. 1, Harley 2338, f 28ᵇ (18 lines, ending
incomplete; 1536); 2, Lansdowne 762, ff
52ᵃ–53ᵇ (52 lines), f 52ᵃ (Declaracio, 18

lines; 1500–40).
Brown-Robbins, Robbins-Cutler, no 3945 (Prophecy); Robbins-Cutler, no 3412.3 (Declaracio).
Edition. Scattergood PP, pp 383, 385.
Textual Matters. Scattergood PP, p 385.
General Reference. Scattergood PP, p 77.

[276] THE STREETS OF LONDON.

MS. Lansdowne 762, ff 63^b–65^a (1500–40).
Brown-Robbins, Robbins-Cutler, no 3510.
Edition. Scattergood PP, p 386.
Textual Matters. Scattergood PP, p 390.
General Reference. Scattergood PP, p 211.

[277] A MERLIN STANZA.

MS. Pepys 1236, f 91^a (ca 1460).
Robbins-Cutler, no 3851.5.
Edition. Robbins-HP, p 316.

[278] UNPUBLISHED MERLIN PROPHECIES.

a. A dragoun with a rede ros that ys of grete fame.
MS. Nat Libr of Wales Peniarth 53, pp 131–136 (1485–1500).
Robbins-Cutler, no 33.3.
b. A king out of the North shull come.
MSS. 1, Bodl 9914 (Tanner 88), f 252^b, repeated at f 253^a (added in 17 cent hand); 2, Harley 7332, f 28^a (17 cent).
Brown-Robbins, Robbins-Cutler, no 52.
c. An Egyll shall ryse with a bore bold.
MS. Lansdowne 762, ff 53^b–54^a (1500–40).

Robbins-Cutler, no 285.5.
d. He that is ded and buried in syght.
MS. Nat Libr of Wales Peniarth 50, p 3 (1425–50).
Robbins-Cutler, no *1153.5.
Scattergood PP, p 392 (MS described).
e. How a lyon shall be banished and to Berwyke gone.
MS. Bodl 12653 (Rawl C.813), Art 53 (1530–40).
Robbins-Cutler, no 1253.5.
Literary Relations. A [prose] prophesye of Marleon occurs at ff 94^b–95^a of this MS, followed by a key (e g, The lylle is the kynge of ffrance, the lyon is fflanders). Another similar key occurs in MS Bodl 13814 (Rawl D.1062), ff 96^b–97^a. See also under [275] above. Another prose prophecy occurs in MS Pennsylvania State Univ Prophecies of Merlin, ff 1^a–5^b (late 15 cent), unpublished.
General Reference. Kingsford EHL, p 236.
f. O myghty mars that marrith many a wight.
MS. Camb Univ Kk.6.16, ff 8^b–10^a (1490–1510).
Brown-Robbins, Robbins-Cutler, no 2515.
g. Of al the merueile of merlyn how he makys his mone.
MS. Harley 2382, f 127^b (1470–1500).
Robbins-Cutler, no 2613.5.
Manly & Rickert, 1.245 (MS described).
h. Thare is a boke men calles merlyns Bulbrane.
MS. Bodl 4062 (Hatton 56), f 34^b (1450).
Robbins-Cutler, no 3528.5.
General References. Kingsford EHL, p 237.
Mackie J D, The Earlier Tudors, Oxford 1952, p 151.

II. The John of Bridlington Prophecies

[279] JOHN OF BRIDLINGTON'S LATIN PROPHECY.

MSS. 1, Bodl 1690 (Digby 89), ff 1^a–55^a (14 cent); 2, Bodl 1787 (Digby 186), f 5^a (1450–1500); 3, Bodl 2157 (Bodley 623), ff 77^a, 91^b (1465); 4, Bodl 3041 (Bodley 851), f 90^a (1375–1400); 5, Bodl 3338 (Arch Selden B.8), f 266^a (1550); 6, Bodl 4062 (Hatton 56), ff 11^a–20^b (1450); 7, Bodl 8241 (Ashmole 337), no 4 (ca 1600); 8, Bodl 25174 (Ashmole 1804), ff 42^b–46^b (1400); 9, Camb Univ Kk. 6.16, ff 170^a–176^b (1490–1510); 10, Caius Camb 249, ff 177^b–180^b (1464); 11, Caius Camb 267, ff 120^a–120^b (15 cent); 12, Corp Christi Camb 329, f 103^b (15 cent); 13, Trinity Camb 35, ff 106^a–116^a (15 cent); 14, Arundel 66, ff 288^a–290^a (1450–1500); 15, Cotton Cleop C.iv, ff 97^a–109^b (ca 1550); 16, Cotton Domit A.9, ff 17^a–82^b (1350–1400); 17, Cotton Titus D.xii, f 81^a (14 cent); 18, Cotton Vesp E.vii, ff 117^b–126^b (1460–80); 19, Cotton Vitell A.xii, ff 132^b–133^b; 20, Harley 3908, ff 106^a–117^b (15 cent); 21, Harley 6148, ff 92, 94^a–94^b (mid 17 cent); 22, Lansdowne 122; 23, Royal

7.A.ix, ff 2ª–2ᵇ (16 cent; 18 lines); 24, Royal 8.C.xvii, ff 1ª–22ᵇ (1375–1400); 25, Sloane 1802, ff 17ᵇ–22ᵇ (1600); 26, BM Addit 24848, ff 1ª–12ᵇ (16 cent); 27, Edinburgh Univ 181, III, ff 33ª–46ᵇ; 28, Soc of Antiquaries 47, f 206ᵇ (15 cent; 11 lines); 29, Soc of Antiquaries 101, f 68ª (ca 1450); 30, Trinity Dublin 172 (14 cent); 31, Trinity Dublin 516, ff 3ª–14ª (1450–75); 32, Westminster Abbey 27 (15 cent); 33, Tours 520; 34, Chicago Univ 697, ff 91ᵇ–98ᵇ (late 14 cent). Not listed Brown-Robbins, Robbins-Cutler. *Edition.* Wright PPS, 1.123, 128. *Date and Authorship.* James M R, Catalogue of Library of Augustinian Friars at York, Fasciculus Ioanni Willis Clark Dicatus, Cambridge 1901, p 11. Warner G F and J P Gilson, Catalogue of the Western Manuscripts in the Old Royal and King's Collections, London 1921, 1.239. Peck Sister H M, The Prophecy of John of Bridlington, Chicago 1931, pp 4, 16. Gwynn A, The English Austin Friars in the Time of Wyclif, Oxford 1940, pp 134, 220. Knowles D, The Religious Orders in England, Cambridge 1955, 2.150. Emden A B, A Biographical Register of the University of Oxford to A D 1500, Oxford 1957, 1.644. Taylor J, Mediaeval Historical Writings in Yorkshire, York 1961, p 23. Meyvaert P, John Erghome and the Vaticinium Roberti Bridlington, Spec 41.656. *Literary Relations.* Taylor R, The Political Prophecy in England, N Y 1911, p 57. Gieraths G, The Bridlington Dialogue, Zeitschrift für Kirchengeschichte 71(1961).172. Finlayson J, Two Minor Sources for the Alliterative Morte Arthur, N&Q ns 9.132. *Other Scholarly Problems.* Taylor, Political Prophecy, p 54 (animal symbolism). *Literary Criticism.* Taylor, Political Prophecy, p 53. *General References.* Taylor, Political Prophecy, p 51. Eberhard O, Der Bauernaufstand vom Jahr 1381 in der engl Poesie, AF 51.18. Griffiths M E, Early Vaticination in Welsh with English Parallels, Cardiff 1937, p 208. Bloomfield M L, A Preliminary List of Incipits of Latin Works on the Virtues and Vices, Traditio 11.300.

[280] A EULOGY OF JOHN THWENGE.

MS. Yale Univ Beinecke Libr, ff 168ª–174ª (ca 1440).

Robbins-Cutler, no 4105.5. *Edition.* Amassian M, A Verse Life of John of Bridlington, NM 71.140. *Textual Matters.* Sleeth C R, Textual Observations on a Verse Life of John of Bridlington, NM 74.128. *Literary Relations.* Brown-Robbins, no *59; Robbins-Cutler, no *3458.5; Brown Reg, 1.286. *Scholarly Problems.* DNB, 10.888 (life). Grosjean P, De S Iohanne Bridlingtoniensi Collectanea, Analecta Bollandiana 53.101 (life). Knowles D, The Religious Orders in England, Cambridge 1955, 2.117 (life). *General References.* Amassian, NM 71.136. Bloomfield M L, A Preliminary List of Incipits of Latin Works on the Virtues and Vices, Traditio 11.300.

[281] THE COCK IN THE NORTH.

MSS. 1, Bodl Lyell 35, ff 26ª–27ª (ca 1482); 2, Camb Univ Kk.1.5, IV, ff 25ª–26ª (139 lines; late 15 cent); 3, Caius Camb 249, ff 227ᵇ–228ᵇ (1464); 4, Cotton Rolls ii.23, Art 9 (75 lines; cf [283] below; 1450–52); 5, Harley 559, f 43ᵇ (76 lines; 1540–50); 6, Harley 1717, f 249ᵇ (73 lines; 15 cent); 7, Lansdowne 762, f 62ª (81 lines headed Brydlyngton, part of [290] below; 1500–40); 8, Sloane 1802, f 7ª (1600); 9, Sloane 2578, ff 15ᵇ–17ª, 100ᵇ–102ª (part of [290] below; 1547); 10, Sloane 4031, f 189ᵇ (80 lines; 16 cent addition); 11, BM Addit 24663, f 13ᵇ (late 16 cent); 12, Nat Libr Wales Peniarth 26, pp 39–41 (1450–75); 13, Nat Libr Wales Peniarth 50, pp 1–3 (1425–50); 14, Nat Libr Wales Peniarth 58, p 18; 15, Nat Libr Wales Deposit Porkington 10, ff 191ª–193ᵇ (1450–75); 16, Trinity Dublin 516, f 114ª (80 lines; preceded by Robbins-Cutler, no 4030.5; 1450–75); 17, Westminster Abbey 27, f 82ª (15 cent). PRINT: 18, Merling saies, Whole Prophesie of Scotland, Waldegrave, Edinburgh 1603. Brown-Robbins, Robbins-Cutler, no 4029. Robbins-Cutler, no 4030.5 (couplet preceding text in MS 16). Laing D, Collection of Ancient Scottish Prophecies, Bannatyne Club 44, Edinburgh 1833, p 6 (PRINT 18 rptd). Haferkorn, edn, p 22 (MSS described). Evans G, Report on MSS in Welsh Language, 1, pt 2, pp 336, 351, 389, 576 (MSS 12–16 described). Jackson W A Robert Waldegrave and the

Books He Printed or Published in 1603, Library 5s 13.231 (PRINT 18 described).

Kurvinen A, MS Porkington 10 Description with Extracts, NM 54.33 (MS 15 described).

Editions. Lumby J R, Bernardus de Cura Rei Famuliaris, EETS 42, London 1870, p 18 (MS 2).

Hermentrude, Notes on Fly Leaves, N&Q 3s 8.326 (MS 6).

Brandl A, The Cock in the North, Sitzungs-berichte der königliche preussischen Akademie der Wissenschaften, Berlin 1909, p 1166 (composite text from 13 MSS).

Haferkorn R, Eine politische Prophezeiung des 14 Jahrhunderts, Beiträge zur engl Philologie 19.109 (composite text from 3 MSS; crit A C Baugh, MLN 48.128; A Brandl, Arch 161.301; D Everett, RES 10.215; YWES 13.109; H Koziol, LfGRP 55.228; F Krog, AnglB 44.227; H Marcus, EStn 68.251; M S Serjeantson, ESts 16.61).

Robbins-HP, p 115 (MS 4).

Textual Matters. Haferkorn, edn, p 117.

Robbins-HP, p 309.

Language. Oakden J P, Alliterative Poetry in ME, Manchester 1930, 1.98, 153.

Versification. Luick K, Die engl Stabreimzeile im XIV, XV und XVI Jahrhundert, Angl 11.601.

Schipper, 1.198.

Oakden, Alliterative Poetry, 1.197.

Date. Brandl, p 710.

Ward, 1.325.

Murray J A H, The Romances and Prophecies of Thomas of Erceldoune, EETS 61, London 1875, p xxix.

Taylor R, The Political Prophecy in England, N Y 1911, p 75.

Robbins-HP, p 310.

Literary Relations. MS Cotton Vesp E.viii, f 132ª (Latin poem).

Rel Ant, 2.12 (early 16 cent prophecy in Camb Univ Kk.1.6).

Taylor, Political Prophecy, p 57.

Other Scholarly Problems. Dalrymple D [Lord Hailes], Remarks on the History of Scotland, Edinburgh 1773, chap 3.

J B, Notes on Fly-Leaves, N&Q 3s 8.521 (prophecies in Stuart uprisings).

General References. Pinkerton J, Notes on Fly Leaves, N&Q 3s 8.401.

Griffiths M E, Early Vaticination in Welsh with English Parallels, Cardiff 1937, p 209.

[282] AN ALLITERATIVE POLITICAL PROPHECY.

MS. Camb Univ Ll.1.18, ff 128ª–128ᵇ (a single leaf; late 15 cent).

Brown-Robbins, no *9; Robbins-Cutler, no *308.5.

Edition. Day M, Fragment from an Alliterative Political Prophecy, RES 15.61.

Textual Matters. Day, RES 15.64.

[283] A SECOND ALLITERATIVE POLITICAL PROPHECY.

MSS. 1, Cotton Rolls ii.23, Art 9 (1450–52; 36 lines; cf [281] above); 2, Soc of Antiquaries 101, f 72ᵇ (82 lines; ca 1450).

Robbins-Cutler, no 2834.3.

General Reference. Ward, 1.325.

[284] A PROPHECY FOR 1560.

MS. Cotton Galba E.ix, f 66ᵇ (added in 16 cent hand).

Robbins-Cutler, no 3912.5.

Edition. Hulme W H, The Harrowing of Hell, EETSES 100, London 1907, p xxiv.

[285] WHEN ROME IS REMOVED.

MSS. A Text. 1, Bodl Lyell 35, ff 24ª–25ᵇ (ca 1482); 2, Camb Univ Kk.1.5, IV, ff 33ª–34ª (71 lines; 1480–1500); 3, Nat Libr Wales Peniarth 26, pp 129–131 (1450–75); 4, Nat Libr Wales Peniarth 50, pp 4–7 (90 lines; 1425–50); 5, Nat Libr Wales Peniarth 94, pp 174, 262, 167 (beginning 35 lines, 33 lines, and last 13 lines; ca 1595); 6, Nat Libr Wales Addit 441C, pp 49–51 (86 lines; 16 cent); 7, Nat Libr Wales Llanstephen 119 (95 lines; 1600–50); 8, Public Record Office, State Papers Henry VIII (early 16 cent); 9, Westminster Abbey 27, f 31ᵇ (15 cent); 10, Mostyn 133, pp 331–341 (96 lines; 1606–23).

MSS. A Text Fragments. 11, Harley 559, f 10ª (7 lines; 1540–50); 12, Sloane 2578, ff 44ᵇ–45ª (medley of single lines written as prose; 1547); 13, Sloane 2578, f 67ª (lines 1–40; mid 16 cent); 14, Nat Libr Wales Peniarth 26, p 127 (7 lines; 1450–75).

MSS. B Text (begins at line 16 of A Text). 15, Cotton Vesp E.viii, ff 21ª–22ᵇ (87 lines; 16 cent); 16, Sloane 1802, ff 10ᵇ–14ᵇ (90 lines; 1600).

MSS. C Text. 17, Cotton Cleop C.iv, f 86ᵇ (14 lines; added ca 1550); 18, Royal 7.A.ix, ff 4ª–4ᵇ (14 lines; 16 cent); 19, Nat Libr Wales Peniarth 26, p 122 (14 lines; 1450–75); 20, Nat Libr Wales Peniarth 94, p 257 (ca 1595); 21, Nat Libr Wales Llanstephen 119, p 177 (1600–50).

PRINT. 22, Prophecie of St Beid, Whole Prophesie of Scotland, Waldegrave, Edinburgh 1603 (B Text, 90 lines).

Brown-Robbins, Robbins-Cutler, no 4008 (delete Brown-Robbins, nos 4007, 4009, 4010, 4011, and subsume under no 4008).

Laing D, Collection of Ancient Scottish Prophecies, Bannatyne Club 44, Edinburgh 1833, p 9 (PRINT 22 rptd).

Ward, 1.310, 326, 333, 334, 336, 337 (MSS described).

Haferkorn, edn, p 22 (MSS described).

Editions. Stevenson J, The Scottish Metrical Romance of Lancelot du Lak, Maitland Club 48, Edinburgh 1839, p 157 (MS 2).

Wright PPS, 2.249 (MS 17).

Lumby J R, Bernardus de Cura Rei Familiaris, EETS 42, London 1870, p 32 (MS 2).

Furnivall F J, Ballads from Manuscripts, Ballad Soc, London 1868, p 317 (MS 8).

Haferkorn R, Eine politische Prophezeiung des 14 Jahrhunderts, Beiträge zur engl Philologie 19.92, 104, 112, 114 (composite text).

Robbins-HP, pp 118 (MS 2), 313 (MS 18).

Textual Matters. Haferkorn, edn, p 117.

Robbins-HP, p 312.

Language. Oakden J P, Alliterative Poetry in ME, Manchester 1930, 1935, 1.99, 153; 2.83, 263.

Haferkorn, edn, p 40.

Versification. Haferkorn edn, p 48.

Date. Haferkorn, edn, p 129.

Robbins-HP, p 314.

Literary Relations. Haferkorn, edn, pp 21, 155 and 144 (Welsh parallels).

Other Scholarly Problems. Haferkorn, edn, pp 59 (Galfridian symbols), 64 (weather prognostications), 77 (Evils of the Age).

[286] SCOTLAND'S FUTURE PROSPERITY.

MSS. 1, Camb Univ Ll.5.10, f 57ᵃ (ca 1622); 2, Pepys 2253, p 293 (1570–90).

Robbins-Cutler, no 4005.5.

Edition. Craigie W A, The Maitland Folio Manuscript, PSTS ns 7.342.

III. The Thomas of Erceldoune Prophecies

[287] THOMAS RYMOUR OF ERCELDOUNE.

Collected Editions. Whole Prophesie of Scotland, Waldegrave, Edinburgh 1603; rptd D Laing, Collection of Ancient Scottish Prophecies, Bannatyne Club 44, Edinburgh 1833, p 18.

Stevenson J, The Scottish Metrical Romance of Lancelot du Lak, Maitland Club 48, Edinburgh 1839.

Sources and Literary Relations. Schmidt W, Die Volksballaden von Tom dem Reimer, Angl 61.193.

Murray J A H, The Romances and Prophecies of Thomas of Erceldoune, EETS 61, London 1875, pp 52 (Rymour, Reid, and Marlyng in MSS Lansdowne 762 and Rawl C.813), 62 (Gladsmoor, Sandisford, and Seyton, and the Seye in MS Sloane 2578).

Child F J, The English and Scottish Popular Ballads, Boston 1889, 1.317.

Saalbach A, Entstehungsgeschichte der schottischen Volksballade Thomas Rymer, diss Halle 1913 (ballad antedates romance; crit F Gschwind, AnglB 24.366; H Lötschert, EStn 47.256).

Flasdieck H M, Tom der Reimer, Wort und Brauch 23 (romance antedates ballad).

Schmidt W, Die Volksballaden von Tom dem Reimer, Anglia 61.193 (romance antedates ballad).

Nelson C E, The Origin and Tradition of the Ballad of Thomas Rhymer A Survey, in New Voices in American Studies, ed R B Browne, Purdue 1966, p 138.

Lyle E B, The Turk and Gawain as a Source of Thomas of Erceldoune, Forum Mod Lang Stud 6.98.

General References. Scott W, Minstrelsy of the Scottish Border, 1833; rvsd T F Henderson, Edinburgh 1932, 4.79, 98, 103, 125.

Murray, EETS 61.ix.

Veitch J, The Feeling for Nature in Scottish Poetry, Edinburgh 1887, 1.119.

Morley, 3.280.

Ward, 1.328.

Eyre-Todd G, Early Scottish Poetry, Glasgow 1891, p 11 (Thomas as author of Sir Tristram).

Brandl, pp 643, 649, 667.

Schofield, pp 208, 368.

Körting, p 124.

Burnham J M, A Study of Thomas of Erceldoune, PMLA 23.375.

Taylor R, The Political Prophecy in England, N Y 1911, p 62.

Geddie W, Thomas the Rymour and his

Rhymes, Edinburgh 1920.
MacCulloch J A, Medieval Faith and Fable, London 1932, p 49.
Bibliography. New CBEL, 1.475.

[288] THOMAS OF ERCELDOUNE'S PROPHECY.

MS. Harley 2253, f 127[a] (ca 1340).
Brown-Robbins, Robbins-Cutler, no 3989.
For MS see under [24] above.
Editions. Pinkerton J, Ancient Scottish Poems, London 1786, 1.lxxviii.
Scott W, Minstrelsy of the Scottish Border, 1833; rvsd T F Henderson, Edinburgh 1932, 4.99.
Murray J A H, The Romances and Prophecies of Thomas of Erceldoune, EETS 61, London 1875, p xviii.
Laing D, Select Remains of the Ancient Popular and Romance Poetry of Scotland, rvsd J Small, Edinburgh 1885, p 401.
Laing D, Early Popular Poetry of Scotland, rvsd W C Hazlitt, London 1895, 1.88.
Brandl A and O Zippel, Me Sprach- und Literaturproben, Berlin 1917, p 133.
Robbins-HP, p 29.
Modernization. Taylor R, The Political Prophecy in England, N Y 1911, p 65.
Textual Matters. Murray, EETS 61.xviii.
Robbins-HP, p 260.
Date. Murray, EETS 61.xix.
Brook G L, The Harley Lyrics, 3rd edn, Manchester 1964, p 3.
Sources and Literary Relations. Anderson M O, The Scottish Materials in a Paris Manuscript, SHR 28.33 (Latin prophecy ca 1307).
Fowler D C, A Literary History of the Popular Ballad, Durham N C 1968, p 139.
Other Scholarly Problems. Scott, edn; rvsd Henderson, 4.100 (historical background and dating).
Salter E, Piers Plowman and The Simonie, Arch 203.253 (influence on Piers Plowman).
General References. Warton T, History of English Poetry, London 1824, 1.80; rvsd W C Hazlitt, London 1871, 2.87.
Laing, edn, Early Popular Poetry, 1.81.
Ward, 1.329.

[289] TONIGHT IS BORN A BAIRN.

MS. Arundel 57, f 8[b] (ca 1350).
Brown-Robbins, no 3762.
Editions. Rel Ant, 1.30.
Morris R, Don Michel's Ayenbite of Inwyt,

EETS 23, London 1866, pref (not paginated).
Corson L, A Finding List of Political Poems, 1910; rptd N Y 1970, p 32.
Brandl A and O Zippel, Me Sprach- und Literaturproben, Berlin 1917, p 134.

[290] TOMAS OF ERSSELDOUNE.

MSS. 1, Bodl 13814 (Rawl D.1062), ff 92[a]–93*[a] (16 cent; lines 1–132, 181–201); 2, Camb Univ Ff.5.48, ff 119[a]–128[b] (15 cent; 492 lines); 3, Cotton Vitell E.x, ff 255[b]–258[a] (1450–75; imperfect, 564 lines); 4, Lansdowne 762, ff 24[a]–31[a] (1500–40; 491 lines, including [281] above); 5, Sloane 2578, ff 6[a]–11[b] (1547; imperfect, 321 lines; lacks fit 1); 6, Lincoln Cath 91, ff 149[b]–153[b] (1430–40; imperfect, 636 lines and prologue of 24 lines).
MSS. Fragments. 7, Bodl 4062 (Hatton 56), ff 39[a]–40[b] (ca 1450); 8, Bodl 6683 (Ashmole 337, IV) (16 cent); 9, Bodl 8258 (Ashmole 1386, III) (16 cent); 9a, Bodl 40359 (Ashmole 1835), f 1[a] (17 cent transcript); 10, Harley 559 (ca 1540–50); 11, BM Addit 6702 (early 17 cent).
PRINT. 12, Whole Prophesie of Scotland, Waldegrave, Edinburgh 1603.
Brown-Robbins, Robbins-Cutler, no 365.
Laing D, Collection of Ancient Scottish Prophecies, Bannatyne Club 44, Edinburgh 1833, p 18 (PRINT 12 rptd).
Editions. Jamieson R, Popular Ballads and Songs, Edinburgh 1802, 2.11 (MS 2).
Halliwell [-Phillipps] J O, Illustrations of the Fairy Mythology of Midsummer Night's Dream, Shakespeare Soc 26, London 1845, p 58 (MS 2).
Murray J A H, The Romances and Prophecies of Thomas of Erceldoune, EETS 61, London 1875 (critical edn excluding MS 2).
Brandl A, Thomas of Erceldoune, Sammlung engl Denkmäler 2, Berlin 1880, p 75 (MS 5).
Laing D, Select Remains of the Ancient Popular and Romance Poetry of Scotland, rvsd J Small, Edinburgh 1885, p 142 (MS 6).
Laing D, Early Popular Poetry of Scotland, rvsd W C Hazlitt, London 1895, 1.81 (MS 6).
Hazlitt W C, Early Popular Poetry of Scotland, London 1895, 1.81 (MS 6).
Flasdieck H M, Tom der Reimer von keltischen Feen und politischen Propheten, Wort und Brauch 23, Breslau 1934 (crit H Audoin, Rev Anglo-Américaine 12.240; D Everett, YWES 15.122; F Krog, AnglB

48.166).

Scott W, Minstrelsy of the Scottish Border, 1833; rvsd T F Henderson, Edinburgh 1932, 4.92 (MS 3).

Nixon I, Thomas of Erceldoune, diss Edinburgh 1947.

Downing J Y, A Critical Edition of Cambridge University MS Ff.5.48, diss Univ of Washington 1969; DA 30.2480A (MS 2).

Selections. Child F J, The English and Scottish Popular Ballads, Boston 1889, 1.326 (MS 6, fit 1).

Cook A S, A Literary ME Reader, Boston 1915, p 72 (MS 6).

Sampson G, Cambridge Book of Prose and Verse, Cambridge 1924, p 304 (MS 6, fit 1).

Kaiser R, Medieval English, Berlin 1958, p 445 (MS 6).

Dunn C W and E T Byrnes, ME Literature, N Y 1973, p 496 (MS 6).

Textual Matters. Holthausen F, Zu ae und me Dichtungen, Angl 14.310 (line 639).

Laing, Select Remains, p 398.

Murray, EETS 61.lxix.

Brandl, edn, p 131.

Language. Brandl, edn, p 49.

Brandl, p 643.

Lyle E B, A Reconsideration of the Place Names in Thomas the Rhymer, Scottish Studies 13.68.

Versification. Brandl, edn, p 44.

Paul Grundriss, 2^1.1010 (including stanza linking).

Medary M P, Stanza Linking in ME Verse, RomR 7.258.

Lyle E B, Comment on the Rhyme-Scheme of Two Stanzas in Thomas of Erceldoune, N&Q ns 16.48.

Date. Flügel E, Zur Chronologie der engl Balladen, Angl 21.318.

Scott, edn; rvsd Henderson, 4.97.

Sources and Literary Relations. Sibbald J, Chronicle of Scottish Poetry, Edinburgh 1802, 3.128.

Brandl, edn, pp 1, 12.

Saalback A, Entstehungsgeschichte der schottischen Volksballade Thomas Rymer, diss Halle 1913, p 32.

Chaytor H J, The Troubadours and Their England, Cambridge 1923, p 129.

Nixon I ,Thomas of Erceldoune, diss Edinburgh 1947.

Fowler D C, A Literary History of the Popular Ballad, Durham N C 1968, p 184.

Lyle E B, The Turk and Gawain as a Source of Thomas of Erceldoune, Forum for Mod Lang Studies (St Andrews Univ) 6.98.

Lyle E B, The Relationship between Thomas the Rhymer and Thomas of Erceldoune, Leeds SE ns 4.23.

Other Scholarly Problems. Brandl, p 667.

Loomis R S, The Spoils of Annwn, PMLA 56.894, n 58 (parallel for fairy castle on a hill).

Patch H R, The Other World, Cambridge Mass 1950, p 262.

Miller H C, A Study of Thomas of Erceldoune, diss Lehigh 1965; DA 26.7299.

Nelson C E, The Origin and Tradition of the Ballad of Thomas Rhymer A Survey, in New Voices in American Studies, ed R B Browne et al, Purdue 1966, p 138.

Lyle E B, The Celtic Affinities of Thomas of Erceldoune, Eng Lang Notes 8.161.

Lyle E B, The Visions in St Patrick's Purgatory Thomas of Erceldoune Thomas the Rhymer and the Daemon Lover, NM 72.716.

General References. Scott, edn; rvsd Henderson, 4.86.

Halliwell[-Phillipps], edn, p 55.

Ward, 1.331.

Murray, EETS 61.ix.

Morley, 3.280.

Brandl, pp 667, 841.

Taylor R, The Political Prophecy in England, N Y 1911, p 67.

Kane G, Middle English Literature, London 1951, p 15.

Bibliography. Körting, p 140.

[291] **THE PROPHISIES OF RYMOUR, REED, AND MARLYNG.**

MSS. 1, Bodl 12653 (Rawl C.813), f 72^b (1530–40); 2, Lansdowne 762, ff 75^a–88^a (1500–40).

Robbins-Cutler, no 3889.5.

Editions. Sibbald J, Chronicle of Scottish Poetry, Edinburgh 1802, 3.129 (complete text).

Murray J A H, The Romances and Prophecies of Thomas of Erceldoune, EETS 61, London 1875, p 52 (MS 2).

Literary Relations. The Whole Prophesie of Scotland, Waldegrave, Edinburgh 1603; ed Murray, EETS 61.48; cf Robbins-Cutler, no 3889.5.

Prophesie of Sir Thomas of Astledowne, Sundry Strange Prophecies, 1652; ed W P Albrecht, The Loathly Lady in Thomas of Erceldoune with a Text of the Poem Printed in 1652, Univ of New Mexico Publ in Lang & Lit no 11, Albuquerque N M 1954.

General Reference. Albrecht W P, A Seventeenth Century Text of Thomas of Erceldoune, MÆ 23.88; cf Robbins-Cutler, no 3889.5.

[292] A BALLAD ON THE SCOTTISH WARS.

MS. Cotton Julius A.v, f 180ᵃ (1325–50).
Brown-Robbins, Robbins-Cutler, no 379.
Editions. Ritson AS, p 35.
Finlay J, Scottish Historical Romances and Ballads, Edinburgh 1808, 2.168.
Wright T, The Chronicle of Pierre de Langtoft, Rolls Series 47, 2.452.
Child F J, English and Scottish Popular Ballads, Boston 1889, 1.333 (prophecies omitted).
Brandl A and O Zippel, Me Sprach- und Literaturproben, Berlin 1917, p 137.
Versification. Medary M P, Stanza Linking in ME Verse, RomR 7.260.
Date. Flügel E, Zur Chronologie der engl Balladen, Angl 21.318.
Literary Relations. Dibdin T F, Typographical Antiquities, London 1812, 2.254.
Child, edn, 1.329.
Hall J, The Poems of Laurence Minot, 3rd edn, Oxford 1914, p 76.
Taylor R, The Political Prophecy in England, N Y 1911, p 65.
Literary Criticism. Sandison H, Chanson d'Aventure in ME, Bryn Mawr 1913, p 144.
General References. Finlay, edn, 2.163.
Brandl, p 667.
Ward, 1. 299.

IV. The Thomas à Becket Prophecies

[293] MIRACLES AND PROPHECIES OF ST THOMAS OF CANTERBURY.

MSS. 1, Bodl 4062 (Hatton 56), ff 45ᵃ–46ᵇ (100 lines, ends imperfectly; 1450); 2, Camb Univ Kk.1.5, ff 27ᵇ–32ᵇ (256 lines, lacks lines 1–28; 1480–1500).
Brown-Robbins, Robbins-Cutler, no 3665 (delete Brown-Robbins, no *66).
Editions. Stevenson J, The Scottish Metrical Romance of Lancelot du Lak, Maitland Club 48, Edinburgh 1839, p 135 (MS 2).
Lumby J R, Bernardus de Cura Rei Familiaris, EETS 42, London 1870, p 23 (MS 2).
Brandl A, Thomas Beckets Weissagung über Edward III und Heinrich V, Arch 102.354 (MS 1).
Selection. Taylor R, The Political Prophecy in England, London 1911, p 165 (MS 1, lines 1–30).
Language. Oakden J P, Alliterative Poetry in ME, Manchester 1930, 1.98 (Scottish, Midland alliteration).
Versification. Oakden, Alliterative Poetry, 1.197; 2.83.
Date. Oakden, Alliterative Poetry, 1.98.
Sources and Literary Relations. Todd J H, The Last Age of the Church, Dublin 1840, p lxxxiii (Latin text in MS Cotton Cleop D.iii).
Ward, 1.318 (MS Cotton Cleop).
Scattergood V J, Adam Davy's Dreams and Edward II, Arch 206.256.
General References. AELeg 1881, p 527 (erroneously identifies MS as Hatton 37).
Brandl, p 661.
Hall J, The Poems of Laurence Minot, Oxford 1914, p 76.
Taylor, Political Prophecy, pp 58, 61.

V. Other Prophecies

[294] ALDRED'S CURSE ON URSE.

MSS. MS not identified.
Robbins-Cutler, no 1119.8.
Editions. William of Malmesbury, Gesta Pontificum Anglorum, chap 115.
Hamilton N E S A, De Gestis Pontificum Anglorum, Rolls Series 52, p 253.
DNB, 1.250.
Morley, 3.241.
Paul Grundriss, 2nd edn, 2¹.1096.
Förster M, Yorkshire-Dialekt um 1200, Arch 119.433.
Wells, p 221.
Zupitza J, Alt- und me Uebungsbuch, Vienna 1928, p 86.

[295] THE HERE PROPHECY.

MSS. MS to be established.
Brown-Robbins, Robbins-Cutler, no 4050.
Editions. Stubbs W, The Chronicle of Ben-

edict of Peterborough, Rolls Series 49, 2.139.

Riley H T, Roger of Hoveden, London 1853, 2.170.

Morley H, English Writers, London 1864, 1.658.

Hales J W, The Here Prophecy, Acad 30 (1886).380; rptd Folia Literaria, N Y 1893, p 56.

Saintsbury G, History of English Prosody, London 1908, 1.28.

Taylor R, The Political Prophecy in England, N Y 1911, p 22.

Shumacher K, Studien über den Stabreim in der me Alliterationsdichtung, BSEP 11.4.

Sources and Literary Relations. Taylor, edn, p 22n.

General References. Morley, edn, 1.657 (London 1864 edn only).

Hales, edn, Folia Literaria, p 55.

Brandl, p 622.

CHEL, 1.242.

Schofield, p 368.

[296] ADAM DAVY'S FIVE DREAMS ABOUT EDWARD II.

MS. Bodl 1414 (Laud Misc 622), ff 26ᵇ–27ᵇ (1400–25).

Brown-Robbins, no 3763.

Editions. Furnivall F J, Adam Davy's Five Dreams about Edward II, EETS 69, London 1878, p 11.

Emerson O F, A ME Reader, London 1932, p 227.

Selections. Kluge F, Me Lesebuch, Halle 1904, p 92.

Brandl A and O Zippel, Me Sprach- und Literaturproben, Berlin 1917, p 180.

Textual Matters. Emerson, edn, p 314.

Heather P J, Seven Planets, Folklore 54.356 (lines 23–24).

Language. Dölle E, Zur Sprache Londons vor Chaucer, Studien zur englischen Philologie, Halle 1913, 32.3.

Date. Emerson O F, The Date of Adam Davy's Dreams, MLR 21.187.

Taylor R, The Political Prophecy in England, N Y 1911, p 94.

Authorship. DNB, 14.183.

Taylor, Political Prophecy, p 96.

Sources and Literary Relations. Scattergood V J, Adam Davy's Dreams and Edward II, Arch 206.253.

General References. Warton T, History of English Poetry, London 1824, 2.47; ed W C Hazlitt, London 1871, 2.205.

Brandl, p 637.

Ten Brink, 1.321.

CHEL, 1.244.

Schofield, p 367.

Taylor, Political Prophecy, p 92.

Sampson G, Cambridge Book of Prose and Verse, Cambridge 1924, p 359.

[297] A PROPHECY BY THE DICE.

MSS. 1, Bodl 13814 (Rawl D.1062), f 93ᵇ (14 lines; 16 cent); 2, Camb Univ Ii.6.11, flyleaf (14 lines; preceded by [299] below; 15 cent); 3, Trinity Camb 1157, f 41ᵃ (11 lines; followed by [298] below; 1460–80); 4, Cotton Cleop C.iv, f 123ᵇ (12 lines; preceded by [298] below; 1475–1500); 5, Cotton Rolls ii.23, Art 22 (20 lines; 1450–52); 6, Harley 559, f 34ᵃ (23 lines; preceded by [299] below; 1540–50); 7, Harley 559, f 39ᵃ (10 lines; followed by [298] below; 1540–50); 8, Harley 7332, f 28ᵇ (10 lines; 17 cent transcript of text dated 1453); 9, Lansdowne 762, f 96ᵃ (10 lines; followed by [298] below; followed by [304](i) below; 1500–40); 10, Sloane 2578, ff 45ᵇ, 67ᵃ, and variants at 45ᵇ, 64ᵇ, 67ᵃ (ca 1550); 11, Trinity Dublin 516, f 118ᵃ (10 lines; 1450–75).

Robbins-Cutler, no 734.8; incorporates parts of texts listed in Brown-Robbins, Robbins-Cutler, no 4018.

Editions. Furnivall F J, Ballads from Manuscripts, Ballad Soc 1.319 (MS 2).

Furnivall F J, Thynne's Animadversions, ChS 2s 13.xlv (MS 11).

Viles E and F J Furnivall, Awdelay's Fraternitye of Vacabondes, EETSES 9, London 1869, p xiv (MS 11).

Robbins-HP, p 120 (MS 11).

Textual Matters. Robbins-HP, p 316.

Scattergood PP, p 360.

Literary Relations. Utley CR, p 201.

General Reference. Scattergood PP, p 359.

[298] A PROPHECY BY THE STARS.

MSS. 1, Trinity Camb 1157, f 42ᵃ (7 lines; 1460–80); 2, Cotton Cleop C.iv, f 123ᵇ (7 lines; followed by [297] above; 1475–1500); 3, Harley 559, f 39ᵃ (1540–50); 4, Lansdowne 762, f 96ᵃ (12 lines; followed by [304](i) below; 1500–40).

Robbins-Cutler, no 3308.5.

[299] A PROPHECY BY THE DOMINICAL LETTERS.

MSS. 1, Camb Univ Ii.6.11, flyleaf (14 lines; 15 cent); 2, Cotton Rolls ii.23, Art 22 (20 lines; 1450–52); 3, Harley 559, f 34ᵃ (23

lines; 1540–50); 4, Nat Libr Wales Peniarth 26, p 59 (4 lines; 1425–50).
Robbins-Cutler, no 4018.5 (text comprises the introd only of Brown-Robbins, Robbins-Cutler, no 4018).
Literary Relations. Robbins-Cutler, nos 2183.5 (More's Book of Fortune); 3694.3 (Divination by dice); 752.5 ([302] below).

[300] A PROPHECY ON THE STATES OF EUROPE.

MS. Nat Libr Wales Peniarth 50, pp 251–252 (1425–50).
Brown-Robbins, Robbins-Cutler, no 1564.
Edition. Scattergood PP, p 391.
General Reference. Scattergood PP, pp 221, 392.

[301] AN ANIMAL PROPHECY.

MS. Lansdowne 762, ff 59ª–61ª (1500–40).
Brown-Robbins, Robbins-Cutler, no 3375.
Edition. Bowers R H, When Cuckow Time Cometh Oft So Soon A Middle English Animal Prophecy, Angl 73.292.
Textual Matters. Bowers, Angl 73.297.

[302] ROSS OF WARWICK'S PROPHECY.

MS. Cotton Vesp A.xii, f 116ª (late 15 cent).
Robbins-Cutler, no 3862.5.
Edition. Hearne T, Rossi Warwicensis Historia Regum Angliae, Oxford 1716, p 130.

[303] A PROPHECY OF THE END OF THE WORLD.

MS. St Paul's Cath 8, f 47ª (15 cent).
Brown-Robbins, no 4036.
Ker N R, Medieval Manuscripts in British Libraries, Oxford 1969, 1.248, n 1 (Ker writes of these verses: "I have been unable to find them.").
Editions. Rel Ant, 1.166 (numbers MS 9.D.xix).
Wenzel S, Unrecorded ME Verses, Anglia 92.76.

[304] MISCELLANEOUS UNPUBLISHED PROPHECIES.

a. A Bastar schall come owt of the west.
MS. Nat Libr Wales Peniarth 26, p 117 (1450–75).
Robbins-Cutler, no 23.5.
b. As I mused in my dys mekyll towart.

MS. Nat Libr Wales Peniarth 26, pp 112–116 (1450–75).
Robbins-Cutler, no 366.5.
c. Burnys ne battelles brytten ut schall be.
MS. Nat Libr Wales Peniarth 26, pp 60–61 (1450–75).
Robbins-Cutler, no 552.3.
d. Criste hathe made hys complainte.
MS. Victoria and Albert Mus Dyce 45, f 18ª (ca 1550–70).
Robbins-Cutler, no 607.3.
e. Fals love when VI setteth ayenst VIIJ.
MS. Camb Univ Kk.6.16, f 153ᵇ (1490–1510).
Brown-Robbins, Robbins-Cutler, no 757.
f. France and Flaunders than shall ryse.
MS. Lansdowne 762, f 53ᵇ (1500–40).
Robbins-Cutler, no 864.5.
g. In may when myrth moves vpon lofte.
MS. Cotton Titus A.xxv, f 105ᵇ (added in late 15 cent hand).
Robbins-Cutler, no 1507.5.
h. O Albeon of all landes to behold.
MS. Bodl 13814 (Rawl D.1062), f 119ª (16 cent).
Robbins-Cutler, no 2384.3.
i. R shall rech and the p shall prech.
MS. Lansdowne 762, f 97ª (inserted; 15 cent), copied ff 96ª–96ᵇ (1500–40).
Robbins-Cutler, no 2793.5.
j. Schall come trewly as y ow say.
MS. Nat Libr Wales Peniarth 50, pp 263–264 (1425–50).
Robbins-Cutler, no *3091.5.
k. The beme schall bynde that berys the assise.
MS. Nat Libr Wales Peniarth 26, p 62 (1450–75).
Robbins-Cutler, no 3306.5.
l. The prophecy professed and j-pight.
MS. Cotton Rolls ii.23, Art 18 (1450–52).
Robbins-Cutler, no 3451.5.
General Reference. Ward, 1.325.
m. The sone shall the fadre slo.
MS. Cotton Vitell F.xiii, f 76ᵇ–81ª (15 cent).
Robbins-Cutler, no 3473.5.
n. Then a ded mon shall aryse and agrement make.
MS. Lansdowne 762, f 54ᵇ (1500–40).
Robbins-Cutler, no 3513.5.
o. Then all bestis and fowles shall maike thaym gaie.
MS. Sidney Sussex Camb 39, ff 1ª–69ᵇ (1500–

25).

Brown-Robbins, Robbins-Cutler, no 3514.

      p. This is the propheci that thai have in wales.

MS. Trinity Dublin 516, f 16ᵃ ̄ (1450–75). Robbins-Cutler, no 3618.5.

      q. Thre flourys in a nyght can spryng.

MS. [Dyson] Perrins 33 (15 cent; present ownership and location not established). Brown-Robbins, no *68; Robbins-Cutler, no *3708.5.

General Reference. Ward, 1.100.

      r. Quhen sharpe and fair field are maried in fere.

MS. Rylands Libr Latin 228, f 49ᵇ (15 cent). Robbins-Cutler, no 4014.8.

      s. When the pellican begynnyth to fle.

MS. Nat Libr Wales Peniarth 50, pp 269–270 (1425–50). Robbins-Cutler, no 4038.5.

      t. Who so wyll the cronycles grathely loke.

MS. Bodl 4062 (Hatton 56), ff 41ᵇ–52ᵃ (1450). Robbins-Cutler, no 4154.3.

INDEX

A bold-face number indicates the main reference in the Commentary; a number preceded by B indicates the reference in the Bibliography. Titles are indexed under the first word following an article. Indexed are all literary works and their authors, names of early printers, and main subdivisions. No attempt has been made to index the names of characters and places in the literary works nor the names of scholars.